A Guide to Fiction Set in Vermont for Children & Young Adults

A Guide to Fiction Set in Vermont for Children & Young Adults

Ann McKinstry Micou

VERMONT
Humanities
COUNCIL

Montpelier, Vermont

2008

Vermont Humanities Council
11 Loomis Street, Montpelier, Vermont 05602-3021
802.262.2626
info@vermonthumanities.org
www.vermonthumanities.org

....

The Vermont Humanities Council thanks the Vermont Department of Libraries for assistance in the publication of this book.

The Vermont Humanities Council, Montpelier, VT 05602

Published March 2008

Cover and book design by The Laughing Bear Associates, Montpelier, Vermont

Artwork by Joy Huckins-Noss, Adamant, Vermont

Printed in Canada

ISBN: 978-0-9768355-1-6

For my friend, Grace Worcester Greene,
with gratitude and affection

Contents

Preface

The Vermont Humanities Council is pleased to present *A Guide to Fiction Set in Vermont for Children & Young Adults*. It is a companion volume to VHC's first publication, *A Guide to Fiction Set in Vermont* (2005), also by the indefatigable Ann McKinstry Micou. After reading her way through the state's literary incarnations in 484 novels and short stories set in the Green Mountain State between 1835 to 2005, she has completed the equally daunting task of reading and setting forth here all the known fiction for children and young adults that is set in Vermont. The result is this charming and valuable Guide.

The Guide includes 441 titles; of these titles, 49 are set only partially in Vermont. They are the work of 255 different authors; 136 (fifty-three percent) live—or have lived—in Vermont, full-time or part-time.

The titles are presented in two sections: Easy Readers and Picture Books and Children's and Young Adult Fiction. Easy Readers and Picture Books (E) has 69 such titles in this Guide. Children's Fiction (CF) includes books for those between seven and twelve years of age; 208 such titles are included here. Young Adult Fiction (YA) embraces work for the group that is twelve-to-eighteen years of age—pre-teens and teenagers who are in either middle school or high school; here there are 164 such titles.

Books written for children and young adults are not, of course, only for the young. Like the circus, they can be "for children of all ages." And, I might add, it has been said that genius is the ability to recall childhood at will. And so adults will enjoy surveying the variety of fiction for young readers that has been set in Vermont and discovering what stories have been set in their favorite Vermont towns.

The Guide's variety of indexes and appendixes makes the Guide valuable and enjoyable to explore. Like its predecessor volume, this Guide includes, in addition to a bibliography, five appendixes listing: authors and titles by age group, by publication date, and by genre (38 percent realistic fiction, 25 percent historical fiction, 14 percent humor, 10 percent fantasy/science fiction, 7 percent mystery, and 3 percent each for romance and short stories); the towns where Vermont authors live or have lived; and the authors and titles of Dorothy Canfield Fisher Children's Book Award winners and nominees and Red Clover Award nominees that are included in this collection.

In addition, there are four indexes: a subject index directs readers to books having to do with any of myriad of topics or themes. Another directs readers to references to real Vermont places in the fiction—whether it be, for example, their hometown or a mountain; and two other indexes guide readers to individual titles and book illustrators.

Some hearty souls may read this guide from cover to cover, but it is meant essentially as an encyclopedia, a reference tool that one will reach for again and again. The audience for this Guide is primarily librarians, teachers, home-schooling parents, parents, and grandparents. It will also be of interest to children's literature collectors, scholars, historians, and lay people interested in Vermont generally and in children's literature.

As inclusive as this guide is, it is surely not wholly complete. Please let us know if there are titles that have been inadvertently missed.

The Vermont Humanities Council is pleased and honored to publish this volume because it, like its companion volume, furthers the Council's mission, which is to create a state in which every individual reads, participates in public affairs, and continues to learn throughout life. Both books encourage reading and life-long learning, and, by encouraging pride and connectedness with one's community and state, they also promote civic engagement.

The Vermont Humanities Council is enormously grateful to Ann McKinstry Micou for her remarkable work and her desire to share this resource with the public. Heartfelt thanks also to State Librarian Sybil Brigham McShane for the Vermont Department of Libraries' financial support, which made this project possible; to Grace Worcester Greene, Children's Services Consultant at the Vermont Department of Libraries, for her invaluable counsel, expertise, and help; to Amy Howlett, Southeast Regional Consultant at the Vermont Department of Libraries, for her interest, advice, and support; to Larissa Vigue Picard and Sylvia Plumb at the Vermont Humanities Council for their editorial and project supervision; and to Mason Singer of The Laughing Bear Associates for design and production.

Peter A. Gilbert
Executive Director
Vermont Humanities Council

VERMONT
Humanities
COUNCIL

Vermont Humanities Council

Sharing Our Past — Shaping Our Future

A statewide nonprofit organization and affiliate of the National Endowment for the Humanities, VHC believes that engagement with the world of ideas, in interaction with others, contributes uniquely to richer lives, stronger communities, a more humane society, and a better world. Because the humanities and the world of ideas belong to everyone, the VHC has developed a broad range of programs that serve Vermonters of all ages and backgrounds. They include book discussions, speaker events, conferences, a statewide one-book community reading program, and a grants program that supports humanities projects of other nonprofit organizations. These programs and events strengthen Vermont's communities not only by their character and design, but also by happening in the facilities of key town organizations, such as libraries, museums, community centers, and schools. Moreover, humanities-based literacy programs are targeted at childcare providers, middle school students, teen parents, incarcerated adults, and adult basic education students.

The humanities are those subjects that help us understand the human experience. They are the tools of self-reflection. The humanities include history, literature, ethics, philosophy, archaeology, linguistics, comparative religion, jurisprudence, and the history, criticism, and theory of the arts.

Foreword

I met Ann McKinstry Micou at the Vermont Library Conference in May 2006. I knew of her by reputation because of her wonderful first book, *A Guide to Fiction Set in Vermont*. It is definitely my kind of book: it is a list; it is about my favorite state; it is superbly well researched and documented; and it gives me many suggestions of good books to read that I probably would not have found otherwise. I had asked for and received it the previous Christmas and had spent many hours reading away at it. Nevertheless, being one who does not mince words, I told Ann that it had a major flaw. She was a bit startled but gamely asked me what I meant. I explained that, although the book is indeed useful and important, it had overlooked the most vital part of literature: that written for children and young adults. Ann had, of course, thought of this, and, before the conference was over, we were planning her next major project, the result of which is this book that you are holding in your hands.

As the children's literature specialist at the Vermont Department of Libraries, I try to keep abreast of books about Vermont or set in Vermont. When I came to this job in 1986 I inherited a long annotated bibliography, "The Green Mountain Sampler," a list of books owned by DOL that are set in Vermont. Over the years I have updated it every few years, and it is now in the sixth edition. However, once Ann started doing real research, I discovered what a pitiful thing it was! Ann's meticulous searching has filled in great gaps: not only has she added many books published prior to 1950, but she has found newer ones that I had overlooked or not known about. This, then, is a huge gift to the libraries, schools, and people of Vermont: an historical record the likes of which has never been seen before, the only comprehensive record that any state (as far as we know) has of its literature for the young.

In addition to its use as an historical record, this volume has many immediate pragmatic uses, too. Teachers looking for books set in Vermont during a particular historical period; librarians wanting to expand their collection of Vermont books; artists looking for Vermont picture books to inspire them; children looking for a good book to read for a report; researchers wondering about the correlation of author residence and their settings; writers wanting to know more about their particular towns or area will all find answers in this volume.

It may take a village to raise a child, but it takes a whole library system to keep up with Ann McKinstry Micou! I would like to thank Linda Willis-Pendo at the Midstate Regional Library in Berlin, Vermont, and Greg McCandless at the Northeast Regional Library in St. Johnsbury, Vermont, for their quick and helpful responses each time I requested a book for Ann. My former assistant, Jenn Weed, cheerfully packaged up and mailed out hundreds of books to Ann, and Meg Page, interlibrary loan librarian extraordinaire, searched out and requested books from all over the country for this project.

Grace Worcester Greene
Children's Services Consultant,
Vermont Department of Libraries

Introduction

While the themes and topics in adult fiction set in Vermont are diverse, Vermont-based fiction for children and young adults tends to center around three common aspects: youthful protagonists, country life, and family structures. Reading the stories in this volume was for me a joyful, often poignant, process of discovery. From among the impressions received and lessons learned, I offer four insights to users of this reference work.

The first insight is the extent to which reading has a nourishing effect on the imaginations of the protagonists in these stories. Their favorite books offer them solace, instruction, and a frame of reference. The second insight is the extent to which reconciliation is central to the process of growing up. The characters initially meet challenges with uncertainty, resentment, or indifference but overcome them with acceptance, understanding, or forgiveness. The third insight is the extent to which family dynamics and school experiences have an impact on the development and enlightenment of the young characters. They learn about coping with events like death or divorce from a range of different relatives at home and about attributes like discipline or courage from compassionate teachers and librarians at school. The fourth insight is the extent to which the protagonists feel an attraction to Vermont. They may be native-born or come reluctantly to the state, but they become engaged in, and eventually part of, the landscape.

First, what is the effect of childhood reading on the sensibilities and the choices of the characters in these books? In Jessie Haas's *Working Trot*, James MacLeish, who is concerned about his future, relaxes by rereading *Wuthering Heights*, as does Drusie, in

Nancy Means Wright's *Down the Strings*, who is examining her next steps in life. Lily, in Natalie Kinsey-Warnock's *If Wishes Were Horses*, broods upon an injustice by rereading *Black Beauty*, while in Mildred Walker's *A Piece of the World*, Calder consoles herself with *The Wind in the Willows*. Katherine Paterson's title character, Lyddie, a child mill worker, slakes her parched existence with *Oliver Twist*; in Elizabeth Winthrop's *Counting on Grace*, Grace and Arthur, also mill workers, sustain themselves with *The Red Badge of Courage*. In Marion Doren's *Nell of Blue Harbor*, Nell struggles to cope with an adult emergency and wonders how her idol, Laura Ingalls Wilder in *The Little House in the Big Woods*, would handle it.

Finally, in Mary Stolz's novel, *By the Highway Home*, Catty mourns her brother, killed in Vietnam. She looks with affection at her books, filled with characters that make her weep—the Little Mermaid, Oliver, Little Nell, Charlotte, Beth, and Bambi. She searches for and copies comforting quotations into her commonplace book. In a Simone Weil essay, she finds the following advice: "Do not grieve, or keep me always in your thoughts, but think of me as you would remember a book you loved in childhood."

Second, what role does reconciliation play as the protagonists attempt to resolve problems and face reality? In Jacqueline Jackson's *A Taste of Spruce Gum*, Libby's young heart feels betrayed by her mother's remarriage, wounded by her stepfather's behavior, and offended by her harsh new environment. Circumstances force her into a context in which she not only takes charge but also recognizes with "a sob of pain and joy" how much she loves her new "Papa." In Laura Stevenson's *Happily After All*, Becca is forced to come to Vermont to live with a mother who, she thinks, abandoned her. At first, she cannot adjust to Vermont, which is pretty, though in a "different way," but she finally makes peace with her mother, who turns out to have been her loving Book Fairy all along. In Nancy Price Graff's *A Long Way Home*, Riley sulks when his mother brings him to Vermont and cannot understand why her childhood friend, Sam, refused to fight in Vietnam. A poignant revelation about the Civil War enables him to grasp the meaning of courage and, in a moving resolution, to respect his friend.

Keeping secrets plays a critical role before the process of reconciliation begins. In Amy Ehrlich's *Where It Stops, Nobody Knows*, Nina begins to realize that her mother has not been telling her the truth; in Julia Alvarez's *Finding Miracles*, Milly initially keeps her adoption and her native country a secret. Sonny in Joseph Bruchac's *Hidden Roots* knows that his parents are concealing something about Uncle Louis's identity. Eleanor Hodgson Porter's eponymous heroine, Pollyanna, senses that Aunt Polly is harboring a secret about her past. Paterson's title character, Jip, comes to grips with and affirms his parentage. Only when secrets are laid bare can differences and misunderstandings be resolved.

Third, what sort of influence does the particular ambiance of family and school have on the growth of the characters? Dorothy Canfield Fisher's eponymous heroine in *Understood Betsy* has not been asked to take responsibility or make a decision until she comes to live with her off-hand, eccentric relatives in Vermont; she then remodels her life through their mature, serene, and loving examples. Facing disasters like floods or fires, family members unite in new ways. Frances Frost's *Maple Sugar for Windy Foot* pits the Clark family against a terrible flood. Toby Clark is waist-deep in water helping to get the horses out of the barn as another family's house whirls by. Afterward, with his father, he views the barn "with its dead cattle, its destroyed hay and grain" and the "river-battered acres of what had once been a beautiful farm." Having come through this crisis together, Toby feels he is "deep-down friends" with his father. In Natalie Kinsey-Warnock's *As Long as There Are Mountains*, a fire devastates the Andersons' dairy farm. Almost overcome by smoke and flames, family members manage to save the horse and a few of the cows; Iris's brother, Lucien, has to shoot through the barn windows to kill the rest of the cows before the fire reaches them. After the smoke clears, neighbors arrive to raise a new barn, women with food, men with tools and lumber—one of scores of vignettes in these stories in which bone-weary women and burdened men come to the aid of their less fortunate neighbors.

Often, the protagonists have life-changing experiences over a summer vacation. For Gus in Graff's *Taking Wing* and Martin in Newlin Wildes's *The Best Summer*, it was the hardest—and the best—summer of their lives. Gus knows that he and his parents have changed irretrievably during their separation, but he has met Louise, whose struggling father finally gives up and takes the family back to Canada. Gus looks at the ruins of Louise's family's failed farm: "She was the sun that had warmed the grass and turned it into hay and brightened this rundown place..." During his summer job, Martin suffers indignities under Jud, a hard taskmaster, but when he discovers the tragic circumstances of the hired man's life, Martin tries to take the blame for a serious mistake Jud makes. Martin has learned to empathize.

Complementing the importance of family relationships and the discipline of farm life is the influence of teachers and librarians. In Gail Gauthier's *Hero of Ticonderoga* and *Saving the Planet & Stuff*, which are comic in tone but serious at the core, the two protagonists, both uninterested students, become engaged in and fascinated by research. In Eugenie Doyle's *Stray Voltage*, "The only person in his world who makes Ian feel valuable is Mrs. Worth, his sixth-grade teacher." In Winthrop's *Counting on Grace*, when Grace and Arthur must give up school to work in the mill, Miss Lesley tutors them on weekends in her spare time. In Paterson's *Jip, His Story*, Lyddie, now a teacher, lends books to Jip and assures him of her protection.

Fourth, to what extent do the characters have a close, beneficial, and devoted relationship to Vermont? The historical novels in this guide emphasize the statement that Cornelia Meigs, in *The Covered Bridge*, attributes to folk hero Ethan Allen: "No person has come to live here who did not love the land." The Vermont scene is rich and vibrant with pride in heritage, family roots in the land that go back generations, the tradition of neighbor helping neighbor, and challenges and hard work. As Harry observes in Jessie Haas's *Unbroken*, "everything was work here. Everything was food and firewood and racing the summer to get both put away in time."

The experiences of ancestors' hewing out a life in the wilderness produce the qualities that the young protagonists find in their households of aunts, uncles, grandmothers, or grandfathers—wisdom, endurance, strength, humor, diligence, and optimism. Robert Davis's title character, Gid Granger, exchanges only a glance with his mother after backbreaking sugaring that enables them to pay their taxes: "They were Vermonters, and they didn't show their feelings before a stranger." The sense of wilderness is expressed in David Budbill's *Snowshoe Trek to Otter River* and *Bones on Black Spruce Mountain*, quintessential expressions of boys' coping on their own, independent and self-reliant. In the outdoors the lake was "a wild and secret place;" they love the smell of the concoction they use to fend off bugs: "It meant adventure. It meant wilderness." In Mildred Walker's *A Piece of the World*, the young heroine, Calder, becomes devoted to the erratic boulder that she found in the woods. When a developer moves it to the town square, Calder's wise friend, Mr. Cooley, says that the rock "has brought the wilderness to the village."

At the end of Jessie Haas's *Working Trot*, James understands his calling. He "sees himself rooted in the Vermont hills, making the native conditions his tools as he schooled Vermont horses to perfection..." In Hildreth T. Wriston's *Hill Farm*, Dave, who thinks at first he does not want to be a farmer, learns to love the land—"the smell of the cows and the smell of the sun on the ferns along the edge of the woods"—and has never felt so much a part of it.

Connie in Meigs's *The Covered Bridge* loves the way of life in Vermont: "You could always think about coming back to a farm. That was the last beautiful thing to think about, that the valley and the mountains and the long slope of the hill would always be there, would always be the same." Her words foreshadow those of Kinsey-Warnock's Iris in *As Long as There Are Mountains*: "As long as I live and even after, as long as there are mountains, and rivers, and stars in the sky, I'll miss this farm with all my heart." Eddie, in Flavia Canfield's *The Kidnapped Campers*, exclaims: "There's no place in the world like our dear old Vermont!" For Bill Littlefield's heroine in *The Circus in the Woods*, "The stars always seemed closer and brighter in Vermont."

The imagery in these stories evokes an appealing sense of place. In *The Horse That Had Everything*, Newlin B. Wildes compares the weather in April to "a good apple pie, warm in the middle and crisp around the edges," while for David Budbill in *Snowshoe Trek to Otter River*, fall is "crisp and cool as a carrot." Frances Frost notes in *Sleigh Bells for Windy Foot* that the sky turns the "cold apple green of a winter sunset." In *Taking Wing*, Nancy Price Graff likens the woods that encircle the pond and farmhouse to "a Christmas wreath." In *The Language of Loons*, Natalie Kinsey-Warnock finds that an old barn has "weathered to the color of twilight." For Mary Stolz in *Cat Walk*, the hills were "spice-colored" in the late afternoon. In spring in Katherine Paterson's *Lyddie*, "the cheek of the hill wore a three-day growth of green." Paul Fleischman in *Coming-and-Going-Men* sees in a village "a church sharp-spired and white as a bride." In Roberta Piper's *Little Red*, Nan's playing with shy Rebecca is "like picking violets." In Phoebe Stone's *All the Blue Moons at the Wallace Hotel*, when the girls' mother emerges from mourning she has a look about her "like a freshly swept room."

The picture books, outstanding for their illustrations, also create word pictures. Nathaniel Tripp, in *Snow Comes to the Farm*, describes an owl as "silent as the smoke from their fire." In Nan Parson Rossiter's *Sugar on Snow*, when the children finally taste their sugary treat, "all the sweetness of the day melted on their tongues." In Nancy Dingman Watson's story of the same name, when Peter drills a hole in the maple tree, "snowy chips and silver slivers sifted" over his boots. In *Silent Night*, Will Moses describes the way the snow starts, "like a sheetful of cotton thrown to the wind." In *A Christmas Like Helen's*, Kinsey-Warnock writes that "overhead the stars will be thick enough to pick up with a spoon."

We all—librarians, teachers, and parents—remember with affection "the books we loved in childhood" and the incalculable effect they have had upon our lives. The stories in this collection are the stuff of future memories for the young readers we esteem, serve, support, and love.

Ann McKinstry Micou

About the Author

Ann McKinstry Micou has a bachelor's degree in English, Phi Beta Kappa, from Mills College in Oakland and a master's degree from The New School in Manhattan. She taught high school English at Concord Academy in Concord, Massachusetts, the Sarah Dix Hamlin School in San Francisco, and the National Cathedral School in Washington, D.C. She and her family lived in the Middle East for five years. In Ankara, Turkey, she edited *The Turkish Journal of Pediatrics* at Hacettepe University; in Tehran, Iran, she taught American literature at Pars College and wrote *Handbook for Iran* and *You Already Know Persian*, both published by the American Women's Club. At the Institute of International Education in New York, she directed the Southern African Information Exchange, producing dozens of directories on resources for anti-apartheid groups. She wrote *Listening to the Stakeholders: The Impact of U.S. Private Funding in Southern Africa*, published under a grant from the Aspen Institute, and *U.S Independent Sector Involvement in Southern Africa*, published by the Southern Africa Grantmakers' Affinity Group. Her hobby is reading fiction by common theme, such as capital punishment, unplanned pregnancy, utopias, and island or campus settings. The author of *A Guide to Fiction Set in Vermont* (Vermont Humanities Council, November 2005), she lives in South Newfane, Vermont, with her husband of fifty-one years, Paul Micou, a retired United Nations officer.

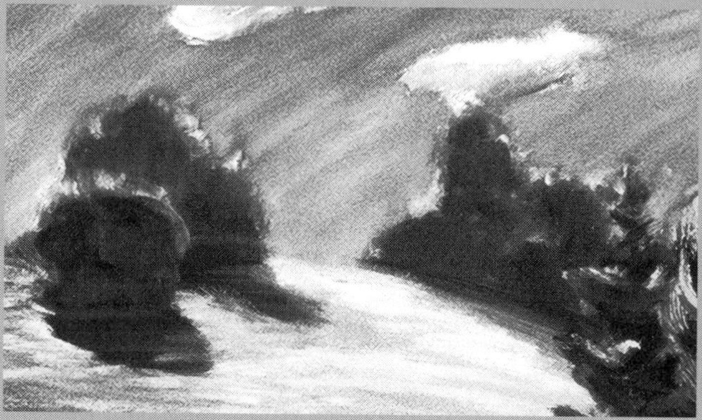

Summary Descriptions

Picture Books and Easy Readers

Children's and Young Adult Fiction

These descriptions are presented alphabetically by author, with titles by publication date in ascending order, except when sequels are grouped together.

Picture Books and Easy Readers

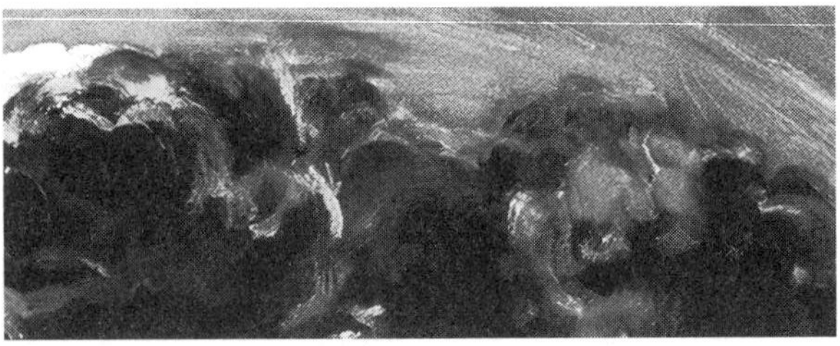

A

Jim Arnosky

The first story in ***Nathaniel*** (1978), called "Gathering Wood," contains pictures and no words. A bear, coming upon Nathaniel chopping wood, carries him and the wood to his lair and makes them into a nest. "The Bat" is in the form of a letter to a hat company ordering a new hat because, as Nathaniel explains at length, he was using his hat to chase a bat out of his house when the bat flew off in his hat. In "Diary," Nathaniel's efforts at recording his experiences are thwarted by the letters' flying off the page and escaping no matter what action he takes by way of glue or nails. In "The Lucky Pipe," Nathaniel's diary records a hornet's biting him while he is looking for his lucky pipe. In "The Orphan," Nathaniel feels sorry for a motherless duckling and lovingly raises the duck until it takes over his house, and he has to remove it to a lake.

The stories in ***Mud Time and More*** (1979) are entirely wordless. In "Mud Time," a cow tries to pull Nathaniel's little car out of the mud. When the car sinks, the cow carries Nathaniel and his groceries up to the house. In "The Weathervane," Nathaniel carves several birds and a fish out of wood to adorn the top of his house, but they escape. He settles for making a replica of the house. In "Gathering Eggs," he ignores a giant ram, which tries to seize his attention by battering him and breaking his eggs. The woodchuck in "Picking Apples" can eat the fruit faster than Nathaniel can pick it. In exasperation, Nathaniel pours the entire sack of apples down the woodchuck's hole.

Kay Avery

In ***Wee Willow Whistle*** (1947), Ellen, four, lives in the country. Her grandfather, a courtly farmer and former army officer, lives next door and takes her for a daily walk. One day by the riverbank he cuts a short willow branch. Carving a notch at one end, he peels off the bark, hollows out the soft insides, and creates a whistle. The creatures they pass in the woods hear Ellen when she tries out her whistle. She blows it again for the animals on the farm. After their walk, her grandfather says goodbye politely. When it is time for Ellen to go to sleep, her grandfather comes over to say goodnight.

Mary Azarian

A Farmer's Alphabet (1981) presents the alphabet set in both upper and lower case. The letters appear in woodcuts with rural themes. For example, one woodcut shows a couple picking **a**pples, another a **b**arn in the snow; others, a woman milking a **c**ow, a **d**og asleep in an armchair, and a **f**arm and its surroundings. Still more depict two **h**orses standing in the door of a barn, two **l**ambs with their mother, a **m**aple sugar shack and trees ready for tapping, a handmade **q**uilt, and an old-fashioned Sterling **s**tove.

B

Robert Bright

In ***Miss Pattie*** (1954), Miss Sarah Williams, a former schoolteacher, is no longer surprised by anything; her neighbor, Farmer Pope, is often surprised, particularly when his barn cat moves into Miss Williams's house. When he brings over the milk, the cat introduces herself as Miss Pattie. She can read as well as talk, a feat that astonishes Farmer Pope even more, although her clever cat does not surprise Miss Williams at all. Miss Pattie plays dominoes and crochets soft articles of clothing. During the winter, Miss Pattie helps out by feeding the canary, tending the houseplants, and shoveling snow. In spring, she feeds the chickens and attends to the small washing. One day, she moves back to the barn where Farmer Pope finds her with four kittens. She does not speak any more—only purrs, which does not surprise Miss Williams at all.

Winifred Bromhall

For Mrs. Polly, the heroine of ***Mrs. Polly's Party*** (1949), every party is a fine event. In fact, whenever the children come to visit, it is a party. Even the animals in the neighboring woods enjoy gatherings at Mrs. Polly's: she is happy to share her cabbages with the rabbits and her new green peas with the deer. Perhaps the best amusement, of all the lovely parties in the changing seasons, is the sugar-on-snow activity. She never forgets anything at her entertainments. "It was a beautiful party," the children always call out to her as they leave.

Marc Brown

Buster Baxter is a white bunny who travels around the country with his father, sending postcards to his friends describing his adventures. In ***Buster's Sugartime*** (2006), he and his father travel to Vermont, the Green Mountain State, where they learn about mud season and the way to drill the trunk of a maple tree for sap. Their visit ends with a big bonfire, where they and their new friends say goodbye to winter. (An introductory page provides basic facts about the state.)

Joseph Bruchac

Jamie Bowman, six, lies in bed in ***Fox Song*** (1993) and thinks about her great-grandmother, "Grama" Bowman, who was ninety when she came to live with them on the Winooski River. Jamie's grandmother's people were Abenaki; Jamie's father's ancestors were from France. Jamie appreciates the way her grandmother prepared Jamie for her grandmother's death. She and her grandmother walked up Fox Hill to eat wild blackberries. Her grandmother taught Jamie to take birch bark without harming the tree. She showed Jamie the way to make a basket sewn together with spruce roots. She took Jamie up to the sugar bush, where they saw animal tracks. She told Jamie that when she is alone in the woods she should look for a fox and remember her grandmother. They tasted the sap to discern whether it was good. She strolled with Jamie in the autumn, saying, "those who are gone are no further away from us than the leaves that have fallen." She taught Jamie a song to welcome the new day. After savoring these memories, Jamie jumps from bed, runs up the slope, and sings the song. A fox comes out of the bushes and sits down to listen. When she looks again, the fox is gone, but "she knew she would never be alone."

David Budbill

In ***Christmas Tree Farm*** (1974), Marcel and his Christmas tree farmers pull tiny evergreens from the moss and plant and fertilize them, mow or cut between the rows, prune and tag the ones they want to cut, and drag them to large piles. After a machine wraps the trees in netting, they are hauled away to be sorted by size. When a truck is loaded, it heads for the city. Marcel takes a tree home to his family. Future Christmas trees stand waiting silently in the snow.

C

Carol Carrick

In ***The Highest Balloon on the Common*** (1977), Paul's father buys him a balloon at Old Home Day, but it flies away. With a second balloon tied to his wrist by an extra-long string, Paul wanders off to watch the pony-pulling contest. When he starts back to his mother's table, everything at the fair looks unfamiliar. He is lost and does not know what to do. Suddenly, he hears his father calling. His father finds Paul because his balloon is the highest one on the common.

Donald Carrick

The lonely deer in ***The Deer in the Pasture*** (1976) is an orphan, which begins grazing with Mr. Wakeman's herd of cows and is soon following them into the barn every night. When deer-hunting season comes, Mr. Wakeman and the game warden are worried because the deer is so tame. They put him in the truck, take him far away, and set him free, but he will not leave them. Finally, with a shot into the sky, the game warden frightens him off. That year, Mr. Wakeman does not choose to go deer hunting.

Eileen Christelow

Ezra, an elderly bachelor, lives with five dogs on a windy hilltop in ***The Five-Dog Night*** (1993). Betty, his neighbor and contemporary, regularly checks on his welfare. She bakes him cookies and warns that he will need an extra blanket now that the weather is changing. That night, Betty puts another blanket on her bed; Ezra needs just one dog. Betty worries about his being cold; he sleeps with a second dog. Betty takes out her winter quilt; Ezra puts another dog on the bed. One night, when the temperature drops below zero, Betty does not glimpse any smoke from his chimney. She hurries to his house to wake him. He tells her she is a "nosy old busybody"; she drives away in a huff. When spring comes and she still stays away, Ezra realizes he misses her. He bakes some cookies and walks down the hill to Betty's, where her five new dogs greet him. Ezra and Betty make up and happily start arguing again.

The Great Pig Escape (1994) introduces Bert and Ethel, growers of wonderful vegetables in Putney, who decide to raise pigs as well. The six piglets grow, wallow, and snuffle until they are ready for market. Bert and Ethel load the frisky pigs into the truck. At each stop along the way—the gas station, the food co-op, the railroad track—two of the six pigs escape. When Bert and Ethel reach the auction yard, all the pigs are gone from the truck. No one has seen them, but many items have disappeared from clotheslines and scarecrows. The disguised pigs take a bus to Florida and send back the missing clothes neatly washed and pressed.

The Great Pig Search (2001) follows Bert and Ethel to Florida where they are determined to retrieve their pigs. They seek them everywhere but do not recognize them, although the pigs are in plain view on every page, generally in sunglasses and big hats—in the police station, the nightclub, the taxicab. When Bert and Ethel go fishing, Bert falls overboard and is rescued by a fisherman. It is only when they see the picture in the local paper that they recognize who—or what—the fisherman is.

Linda Cunningham

Ethan Piper founds Piper's Mill in 1820 in ***The Copper Angel of Piper's Mill*** (1989) when he builds a barrel factory and a fine house there. He marries; his wife's sister and her preacher husband, Ephraim Trueheart, follow him to Piper's Mill, where the minister erects a church and desires a weathervane for the steeple like the fine one down in Brattleboro. The town grows to thirty-seven residents. On a trip to Boston, the Pipers buy a copper angel for the church. Time passes; the population expands. The textile mills in Massachusetts and Connecticut close, putting an end to the spindle mill in Piper's Falls. The men fight in World War I and, instead of coming back to the village, move to the city. The barrel factory closes, as does the post office. A descendant of the founders realizes the church roof is in bad shape. His assessment reveals that the foundation, too, needs shoring up, and the windows require caulking. No money exists for renovations. At a town meeting, the town votes to part with the copper angel. Peter Trueheart sells it in Boston for thirty-eight thousand dollars. This money would enable the town to endow a college scholarship fund were any children remaining in the village. Peter decides to move back to Piper's Mill to buy the Kimball farm. More and more families follow his example. Jeff Benedict starts a forge and creates a bronze bell, adorned with the image of the copper angel, for the church steeple.

E

Amy Ehrlich

When little Millie leaves the pasture gate open in ***Parents in the Pigpen*** (1993), the animals look in the window of the farmhouse to observe the way humans live. The first animal to invite herself to move in with them is Bossy the cow. Next, the chickens follow their mother in from the yard and sit down at the breakfast table, demanding Cornflakes. Four sheep arrive, climb the stairs, and take over the hired man's room, which comes as a surprise to the hired man when he returns from work. It is fairly noisy in the house now, and the humans are exhausted. When the barnyard pond dries up, the animals insist upon using the bathtub. Two horses enter and settle in front of the TV. A dozen ducks walk in. After the animals leave the water running upstairs, the ceiling collapses. Finally, the humans retreat to the big old barn, carrying their possessions. With no animals to care for, they play all the time. Soon the humans are bored; the animals, lonely. They decide to switch back to the previous arrangement. It turns out the animals were not good housekeepers.

F

Rachi Farrow

In ***Charlie's Dream*** (1978), Charlie the ram is the head of a large sheep family on a farm in Vermont. Life is full and happy. Robin, who has been away all winter in Florida, asks what Charlie's family does in the winter. He replies that they do their work, like shoveling snow, but they also ski, skate, and throw snowballs. In spring, they shear their fleece, and the ewes have their lambs. In summer, they weed the garden and cut, dry, and bale the hay. In autumn, they chop wood for their winter fire and pick and store vegetables. Robin says it sounds as though all they do is prepare for winter; in Florida, he lies on the beach, swims, and fishes. Charlie broods about what Robin says and feels old and sad. Finally, he decides to take the family to Florida. Robin will lead the way. The sheep pile in the truck and drive to Florida, but, once there, they sit perspiring on the beach, thinking about what fun they have in Vermont in the winter.

Sid Fleischman

The Hey Hey Man (1979) of the title is a tree spirit living in the Hey Hey Tree, a chestnut in the Vermont farmlands. A passing thief hiding in a haystack fills his clothes with straw to keep warm. While there, the thief sees Farmer Anton bury a boot filled with gold under the tree, admonishing the Hey Hey Man, if he exists, to watch his loot. The thief digs up the boot and makes off with it. When he stops by a wall to catch his breath, he sees a "banty little man" in leather breeches, knee socks, and an Alpine hat. The thief, scorning the Hey Hey Man, strides into the woods until he is lost. The Hey Hey Man materializes, advises the thief to follow his nose, and transforms it into a long, lumpy appendage. The thief hurries on and bumps into the Hey Hey Man once more, who tells him the farmer and his dogs are in pursuit. When the thief refuses to believe this news, the Hey Hey Man turns his ears into cabbage leaves. The farmer follows the trail of gold falling from a hole in the boot. The thief rushes on and runs into the Hey Hey Man, who offers to turn the old boot into a sack to carry the gold. The thief declares he is in need of a horse. The Hey Hey Man uses the straw stuffing to make a horse, and away gallops the horse with the thief clinging to him. Before long they are back in the farmer's stack of hay, where the chase began. The Hey Hey Man turns the gold into fleas. When the farmer returns, the fleas jump on his dogs; the thief escapes. The farmer is surprised and delighted as the fleas turn back into the gold coins, his life savings.

G

Patricia Lee Gauch

In ***Aaron and the Green Mountain Boys*** (1972), nine-year-old Aaron Robinson lives near Bennington in 1777 with his tavern-keeper grandfather, his mother, and his father, one of the Green Mountain Boys. Many Americans, including the Robinsons, do not believe the king rules fairly. When word comes that the redcoats are on the way after recapturing Fort Ticonderoga, the Green Mountain Boys send to New Hampshire for help; General John Stark answers the call with his band of farmer-soldiers. Aaron wants to go to the battle but must stay home to chop wood and mix batter to help his grandfather bake three hundred loaves of bread. The next day, the Green Mountain Boys have not yet arrived; the redcoats are only one town away. Since the regular bread wagon is broken, Aaron and his grandfather deliver the bread to Stark's camp. General Stark regrets having to attack without the Green Mountain Boys. When Aaron and his grandfather reach home, his father and some Green Mountain Boys are there, exhausted, soaking wet, and hungry. His mother brings them plates of warm bread and pails of milk. Aaron keeps the fires hot all night. When the sun is up, Aaron directs the men to the river camp and stays with the horses. The Battle of Bennington has already begun when the Green Mountain Boys and the New Hampshire farmers surge against the enemy. The Americans win. No one will forget that night. (Aaron Robinson was a real boy. The bread and the fires the villagers made enabled the Green Mountain Boys to reach the battle scene with full stomachs and dry rifles. Ten of Aaron's uncles fought in the battle.)

Gail Gibbons

Mr. and Mrs. Mapleworth and their horse, Max, are sugaring in ***The Missing Maple Sugar Sap Mystery*** (1979), as they do every year. Mr. Mapleworth taps a spout into each hole; Mrs. Mapleworth hangs a bucket beneath each. When they emerge in the morning, the buckets are empty. After this event recurs, they try to stay up to spy on the thieves, but they fall asleep. Next morning, the buckets are empty again. The following night they awake to find Max with a sap bucket on his head: he is the culprit. That night they close him in the pasture. The next day they pour the contents of the full buckets into the gathering tank, and Max pulls the dray to the sugarhouse. Mr. Mapleworth starts a big fire under the evaporator, and Mrs. Mapleworth lets the sap flow in. After boiling, the sap turns into maple syrup. They eat the syrup on pancakes and pour it on snow, where it becomes thick and stringy.

H

Jessie Haas

Mowing (1994) is the first in a quartet of stories (the others are *No Foal Yet*, *Sugaring*, and *Hurry!*) about Nora and her grandparents on a farm. They cut the grass, which will dry in the sun and turn into hay. Nora's special job is to watch out for small animals that might be hurt by the cutter bar. She worries about the woodchucks, but they dive into their holes. Then she cries for her grandfather to look out—a spotted fawn is curled up "behind a curtain of grass stems." His mother told him to stay there and not move. Nora keeps her eyes open as they move on, leaving "an island" of grass with the deer hidden in it. When the horses stop, Nora runs up to see what is wrong. A killdeer (plover) sits unmoving on the ground. Her grandfather leaves another "tall island" of grass around the bird. Nora climbs up in her grandfather's lap for the ride home.

In ***No Foal Yet*** (1995), Nora and her grandfather are waiting for Bonnie, the workhorse, to foal. Every night they check on her. Her sides are "big and round." In the mornings, there is no foal yet. At school, Nora's schoolmates ask when the foal will be born. Soon, says Nora. Every day Nora leads Bonnie out for a little exercise. Her grandfather goes to the barn many times during the night. One night he falls asleep before supper. Nora visits the barn one more time; in the straw is a little brown foal. Bonnie did not need any help after all. When her grandmother exclaims that the foal has finally arrived, Nora decides that is what they are going to call him — "Finally."

In ***Sugaring*** (1996), Nora's grandfather says, "Cold nights and sunny days—that's sugaring weather." They gather sap, pouring it from buckets into pails. Bonnie and Stella, the workhorses, pull the big tank. Her grandfather drains the sap into a holding tank; the sap flows into a long pan set over the fire in the sugarhouse and begins to boil. When the bubbles rise too high, Nora flicks a drop of cream on them. After the syrup is ready, it runs through a faucet into a kettle. She tries unsuccessfully to cup some syrup in her hands for the horses; her grandmother makes maple sugar, which the horses eat easily. Nora heads back to the woods with her grandfather to collect more sap.

Hurry! (2000) focuses on the crucial moment when Nora's grandfather must bring in the hay before the rain. "Nothing's more important on this farm than hay," he says. They have to wait until the hay dries and then rake it into long windrows and hitch the hayloader to the wagon. Nora drives the two workhorses, while the hayloader pours the hay into the wagon, and her grandfather and grandmother move the hay around with pitchforks. It starts to rain just as they finish carrying most of the hay into the barn. (This book is dedicated to Lenore Blegvad, whose novel, *Kitty and Mr. Kipling*, is included in this collection.)

Kathleen McKinley Harris

The Wonderful Hay Tumble (1988) is about a young farmer so poor he can afford only a hillside farm on the highest mountain in the town of Mansfield before 1848 (in 1848, the town of Mansfield was divided into Stowe and Underhill). His few cows grow pointy noses from grazing between the rocks and shorter hind legs from standing on the hill. It hurts and embarrasses the young man when his wife has to hitch one of the milk cows to the wagon to drive the milk cans to the creamery. He is so overcome by his undone chores that he weeps. Then he has an idea: why not roll the hay down the mountain instead of carrying it into the barn? The hay tumble gathers momentum and grows too big to fit through the loft door. As the large hay stack turns over and over, it arranges the sap buckets in compact rows, rolls away the weeds in the garden, fells and limbs bare the trees in its path, cleans the trout in the brook, and assembles the stones in the pasture into a neat wall. The hay tumble heads for the cow and the cart carrying his wife and baby. Just in time, the land levels out, and the hay tumble stops. This fortunate event signals the beginning of good luck for the farmer.

Stephen Huneck

In ***Sally's Snow Adventure*** (2006), the fifth book about Sally, a big black Labrador, she goes on a ski trip to a dog-friendly lodge. The Vermont Snow Angels, wearing red skiers' bibs with white crosses, warn the visiting dogs to stay on the trails. After Sally skis and toboggans, she takes a shortcut through the woods to the lodge and is soon lost. Realizing Sally is missing, her friends summon the rescue dogs. Sally is reunited with her friends.

I

Anne Isaacs

Pancakes for Supper! (2006) is a tall tale about Toby, who is heading with her mother and father to Whisker Creek. Their wagon hits a bump: Toby flies high into the sky and tumbles into a pile of snow. When a ferocious wolf threatens to eat her, she offers him her blue coat with the purple lining; the wolf struts off grandly. Running through the woods, she confronts a fierce cougar, which she placates with her beautiful yellow sweater. Shivering, she hurries into the path of a skunk but, before he can spray her, she presents him with her leather boots. To pacify a porcupine, Toby gives him her brown dress, leaving her in red long johns and an orange hat and mittens. Before a huge bear can eat her, she hands him her mittens to wear on his ears. Hearing an uproar, she hides in a tree to peer down at the dressed-up animals arguing over which is the grandest. They angrily chase each other around a huge maple tree until they melt into a golden puddle. Toby retrieves her clothes and runs to greet her worried parents. Her mother makes pancakes while Toby collects syrup from a woodpecker's hole in the tree. After eating many pancakes, she is allowed, because she is so brave, to drive the horses to Whisker Creek. (The author wrote to me that the setting for this story, based on Helen Bannerman's *The Story of Little Black Sambo*, 1899, is western Vermont, an unsettled wilderness territory in the early 1800s where the animals featured were not yet extinct.)

J

Woody Jackson

With a cow or two (or more) in each illustration, ***A Cow's Alfalfa-Bet*** (2003) depicts country scenes from **a**lfalfa to **z**ucchini, with images in between for words like **b**arn, **h**ay, **j**erseys, **p**umpkins, **t**ractor, and **v**illage.

William Jaspersohn

The Two Brothers (2000), set in the 1880s, is the story of Heinrich and Friedrich Eurich, poor brothers born in Prussia. After Heinrich earns sufficient money, he emigrates to America; he will send for his mother and brother when he can earn their passage. The immigration official calls him "Henry" and assigns him to work in Vermont for Farmer Tucker at Tucker Hill Farm, in "a landscape of snow-covered fields and wooded mountains." Henry loves the life. He gathers maple sap, plows and plants, helps deliver baby lambs, cuts firewood, mows hay, and milks the cows. He learns English and attends town meetings. His only worry is that he does not have enough money to transport his mother and brother. Meanwhile, his mother dies; Friedrich sells his possessions and travels to America. The immigration official calls him "Fred" and assigns him to work in Vermont for Farmer Kew. For fifteen months, Fred lives on the farm next to his brother without knowing Henry is there. One day the two brothers meet, laughing and crying. They know they are in the right place. In the coming years, they buy the Tucker farm. Henry marries and raises a family. Every so often, one of the children asks him to tell about how the two brothers came to America.

K

Vivian Kill

Vivian lives with her parents and brother on a dairy farm on Sharon Hill in ***Crazy Jane*** (2004). She and her mother take the milk to town daily in a wagon pulled by the mare, Jane. They reach the Prims' place where Jane stops, sits down on the road, and rolls over and over, scratching her back in the dirt. When she is ready, she starts off again. Next day she repeats her performance in the same place. No one in the family can make Jane behave. Out in the pasture, something frightens Jane—a snake. Vivian's mother ties a large knot in one end of a piece of rope. The next time Vivian stops, Vivian's mother waves the rope snake in the air, and Jane takes off. They have no more trouble with Crazy Jane, as she is now known.

Natalie Kinsey-Warnock

In ***Wilderness Cat*** (1992), Serena and Hannah live with their mother, father, and brother, Luke, in Craftsbury in the 1700s. Serena's favorite companion is her black cat, Moses. When her father decides to move the family into the Canadian wilderness, he informs Serena that Moses cannot come. Sick at heart, she leaves the cat with the Andersons. Loading everything into a cart, Serena's family spends four days on the road before arriving at a shanty in a clearing. Serena hears the wolves at night and misses Moses. Sometimes St. Francis Indians come to trade game for potatoes. Her father is so worried about feeding his family that three times during the winter he returns to Craftsbury fifty miles away to earn a bushel of oatmeal. One day, while he and Luke are hunting, the mother and two little girls have nothing to eat. That night,

Serena hears something crying outside. It is Moses; he has brought them a snowshoe hare. Their father and Luke come home to a glorious feast. They will never part with Moses again.

It is winter at the beginning of ***When Spring Comes*** (1993). The narrator is thinking about spring. When spring comes, the Canada geese will fly north; the members of the family will gather sap from the sugar bush and eat candy; and they will put away winter clothes. They will go fishing and take a wildflower walk in the woods; the apple trees will blossom; and the birds will come home. They will plow and sow crops and pick wild berries. Now, in winter, she enjoys activities like packing the roads with the snow roller and sleigh riding with her father. She wonders if, when spring comes, it will be as wonderful as it currently is in winter.

Since Emma's parents must work in Boston over the summer in ***A Farm of Her Own*** (2001), they send her, aged ten, to Sunnyside Farm to stay with Great-aunt Ada and Great-uncle Will. At first, Emma does not want to go, but, at the end of the summer, she does not want to leave. She loves the sounds and smells of the farm. Work is plentiful, but so is time for playing with her cousins, climbing apple trees, and swimming in the pond. She helps care for the animals. At haying time, Emma and her cousins trample down the dry hay in the wagon. In the evenings, Will spins tales about his ancestors' coming from Scotland. Emma decides she wants to be a farmer like Ada, who gardens, churns butter, cooks, preserves berries, and hugs five children all at once. Emma goes back to Boston, dreaming of Sunnyside Farm. When Ada and Will die, someone purchases the farm but does not take care of it. One day the house is again for sale. Emma buys it and lives there with her family. She thinks continually of Ada and hears "her sweet laughter ring like birdsong."

In ***From Dawn to Dusk*** (2002), the narrator's brothers and sisters grow up in the Northeast Kingdom on a farm where work keeps them busy from dawn to dusk. Why, they wonder, did their Scottish ancestors come *here*? They discuss moving away one day but then remember what they would miss. They would miss warming up in the sugarhouse after the cold work of sugaring; farmers with horses pulling them out without charge when cars and trucks become stuck in mud season; and fishing in the evenings after building fences all day. They would miss enjoying the birds "skittering" across the fields after the backbreaking task of picking up stones the frost has pushed to the surface; and swimming in the pond after the sweaty, itchy job of haying. They would miss playing baseball by the light of the fireflies after picking gallons of berries; looking for kittens in the haymow after milking and shoveling manure; and eating fresh vegetables after weeding and hoeing.

In ***A Christmas Like Helen's*** (2004), Helen is the youngest of seven children living with their parents on a hill farm in Vermont before the coming of electricity, cars, or telephones. In the evenings, Helen's father tells stories about his grandfathers: one came from Scotland; the other fought in the Civil War. The barn is full of cows and workhorses and piles of hay to feed them. Wild animals, such as deer and bear, and domestic animals, like lambs and pigs, abound. Even on severely cold days, Helen walks to the schoolhouse holding the hand of her big sister. The family works hard all year round, sugaring for maple sugar, weeding corn and potatoes for the Christmas feast, and picking apples for Christmas pies. The boys and men hay fields and cut wood for one injured neighbor and raise a new barn for another whose barn burned down. Helen's brothers cut and drag home a Christmas tree. Many relatives come to celebrate. Everyone skates at midnight, including Helen, although she is the littlest. They attend church on Christmas Eve. "Overhead the cold stars will be thick enough to scoop up with a spoon." In the middle of the night her father takes Helen to the barn to admire a new foal. She knows that "everything she ever wanted, or ever will want, is right there on that farm."

Nora's Ark (2005) chronicles the courage and selflessness displayed by a community during the flood of 1927. Horace and Nora, Wren's grandparents, own a little farm by a river. On a hill, Horace is building a new house with all modern conveniences for Nora. On November second, it starts to rain. Nora bakes twenty-seven loaves of bread. The river rises fast. They walk up to the new house, carrying quilts, candles, and a sack of potatoes. Wren puts the bread in her old baby carriage, covers it with oilcloth, and pushes it up the hill. Horace lets all the cows and horses out of the barn. The Guthries, whose barn is flooded, bring up their chickens in burlap bags. Horace goes out to nudge the heifers onto higher ground. Major, the Fergusons' horse, shoves his way through the door, welcomed as a way to heat the house. Mrs. Lafleur and Madeleine, who speak little English, arrive. By nightfall twenty-three people and many animals are safe in the house. The river rises all around; their neighbors' houses are washed away. Nora and Wren are worried about Horace. Bread and dried apples make up the supper, but no one complains. They huddle for warmth. The next morning, Wren and Nora set out in the rowboat to search for Horace. Nothing in the landscape looks the same. They save Sam Burroughs's collie, stranded on a roof. They find Horace wedged with a cow into the crook of a tree. When they have to leave the cow, Horace cries—not for that one animal, but for all the drowned cows, the horse, the house, the barn, all gone. Nora says they will start over. When the neighbors greet Horace at his house, he calls it "Nora's ark." Today, Wren continues to live there. The horse's hoof prints, still imprinted on the floor, remind her of what is important: family, friends, and neighbors helping neighbors. As Nora would say, "Everything else is just gravy."

L

Willem Lange

In *John and Tom* (2001), John is a young logger; Tom is his Morgan horse. They understand each other perfectly; John never uses reins. One day, while John is sawing trees, an accident occurs: a big pine tree jumps sideways off its stump and pins John's foot to the ground. He calls Tom, who, though tied to a tree, chews through his rope. John manages to drape the chain around the tree; Tom, using all his strength, pulls the tree off John's foot. Unable to walk, John drags himself onto the horse, and they head for home. His worried father is looking for John, saying he must never go out in the woods alone. John points out that he was not working alone but with the best friend a man could have.

Julius Lester

It is so hot in the Florida swamp that Adalbert in **"The Incredible Adventure of Adalbert the Alligator"** (2001) decides to move to Vermont for a change of climate. Not knowing where Vermont is, he asks his bird friends for help. They agree to direct him to Vermont if he will not eat any more of their kind. Adalbert, who is sensitive about his appearance because alligators are considered ugly, arrives in Vermont to find a nice lake in which to lie. One day the leaves are no longer green; they begin to fall. When snow comes, Adalbert seeks shelter; he is cold and wishes he were back in his sweaty swamp. He meets Bertrice, a bear, who admires Adalbert's looks. What is more, Bertrice invites Adalbert to hibernate with him. They spend a cozy winter in Bertrice's cave and, when spring comes, decide they make a good team. The moral is, "You are what you think you are and not what others think you aren't."

Reeve Lindbergh

In ***The Visit*** (2005), two sisters, Beth and Jill, visit Aunt Laura and Uncle Ted in the country, where everything is different and wonderful. They enjoy the smells of "haystacks and leather" in the truck, scuffing down dusty lanes, tasting honey from their own bees, exploring barns, stables, and stalls, viewing a variety of trees, and eating blueberry pie.

Sara London

Firehorse Max (1997) is about Grandpa Lev, a peddler in Burlington in 1900. His horse, Bubba, pulls his wagon filled with goods.

Sometimes Simon and Yetta, his grandchildren, go on his rounds with him. One day, old Bubba can no longer pull the cart. Fortunately, the firehouse acquires new engines and auctions off its firehorses. Grandpa Lev bids for a horse called Max. Out on the road, Max hears the fire bells clanging and takes off for the fire. All over town, people pick up Grandpa Lev's possessions and return them to him. Max behaves the same way a few days later. The next time Grandpa Lev hears the fire bells, he grabs his violin, rushes into the barn, and begins to play. Max stops to listen: Grandpa Lev has found the one sound Max prefers to fire alarms.

Elizabeth Low

Summer is just underway in ***Mouse, Mouse, Go Out of My House*** (1958), and Toby is helping Aunt Bee open her little country house. They dust, clean, and chase a flying squirrel out of the chimney. Washing the windows, they find and remove a bat. Sweeping the porch, they scare away a mole. Out from under Toby's bed pops a little brown mouse. Downstairs, Aunt Bee, finding the red felt chewed off the piano hammers, is muttering about mousetraps. Toby captures the mouse and quietly carries him out to the meadow to free him. Now Toby has nothing to play with until he spies in the woodpile a white cat and three kittens. They follow him inside to stay.

Summer is over in ***Snug in the Snow*** (1963), and Jamie has stayed behind with Aunt Kate to help her close up the summer cottage on the lake. All the other cottages are shuttered and dark. If only it would snow, he thinks, they could stay on a little longer. Aunt Kate is worried, though, because they have used up all their provisions, and sends him out to pick the last of the vegetables. He chooses some grapes and spreads them on the ground for the partridges. He leaves the corn for the raccoons. He gives hickory nuts to the red squirrels and the chipmunks. He scatters the last apples for the deer. Now he and Aunt Kate are out of food, but she tells him she would have done the same. During the night, it snows. "The whole world was alight and beautiful." They will stay another day, and neighbor Ralph will bring them some food that night. They go hungry until Jamie remembers the pumpkin he grew, which is wrapped to take home. Aunt Kate makes a spicy, golden pumpkin pie. Later, Ralph brings bread and milk. The trains will be running again the next day. The animals will find the food he left and be "snug, snug, snug in the snow."

M

Michael & Angela Medearis

Jessie ("Daisy") Turner in ***Daisy and the Doll*** (2000) is eight years old, one of thirteen children of Alec and Sally Turner, who live on a farm in Grafton in 1891. Daisy's teacher, Miss Clark, whose students are studying different nations around the world, assigns each child a doll and an appropriate poem to recite. When Miss Clark presents Daisy with a black doll, the little girl is flabbergasted: she has never thought about the color of her skin. When she tells her father, he says she is the prettiest little girl in Grafton. At the program, she feels ashamed of the way she looks. When she climbs onto the stage to recite, a passion and anger overtake her. She changes the words of Miss Clark's poem to express to the audience the way she feels. A shocked silence follows. Then the judge announces that Daisy Turner wins the prize for "originality and honesty." (Daisy's father, Alec Turner, married Sally Early, the daughter of Jubal Early and his slave, Rachel. For the story of Daisy's father's childhood, see Mildred Pitts Walter's *Alec's Primer* in this collection.)

Cornelia L. Meigs

It has been a hard and anxious year for George and Mary Gilbertson in ***Mother Makes Christmas*** (1940), but, when George sells his grain and colts, Mary can "make Christmas," which means in Vermont that she can hold the family feast at their house. Mary invites twenty relatives and friends, and Sally, eleven, welcomes two more whom she sees at the railroad station—Great-uncle Silas and Sally's cousin, Hugh Evans, who is spending the holiday with Great-uncle Silas. Sally loves the "cool touch" of the first snowflake on her face. At supper that evening, with Sally and her younger brother, Billy, present, George delivers bad news: the buyer has reneged on the sale. How will Mary make Christmas? Sally pledges her assistance and her ideas. They trade their two small guinea hens to Mrs. Haskins for two turkeys. They exchange pumpkins and squash at the local store for plum-pudding makings. Sally and Billy share the task of taking care of the colts. When Billy falls ill, Hugh helps Sally fork down the hay in the barn and brings over Josiah, the old white duck that Great-uncle Silas contributes to the dinner. They agree to take care of the duck in his old age rather than eat him. Just as the whole party sits down to dinner, a storm blows open the stable door, allowing the colts to escape. Hugh rides out on Bess; George and the two children run out, too. A tree falls, tangling Sally, Billy, and the two colts under a "tent" of broken branches. Hugh and George free them with axes. No one is hurt during this exciting interlude to a lovely day.

Will Moses

It is Christmas Eve in ***Silent Night*** (1997), and everyone makes preparations. Benjamin Rogers stocks shelves at the general store. Deacon Henry Heinz lights the church lamps. The warmly dressed carolers stroll along the lanes. At the Millers' farm on the headwaters of Black Creek, Tom Henry and Andy skate home dragging a tree. Their father, James, herds the cows into the barn and harnesses the horses so that he and the boys can meet the local from Bellows Falls to pick up Grandma Stokes (known privately as General Grant). "Like a sheetful of cotton thrown to the wind, the snowflakes started..." They go through the covered bridge, stop at the general store, and pass the wagon shop and the gristmill. While they are gone, Mrs. Miller tells Old Paul, the hired man, to ride for Doc Herrick. When James returns to the house, Grandma Stokes takes over, issuing orders left and right. The boys trim the tree. Just after midnight, they hear a cry and are allowed to go upstairs. "Isn't that a holy child?" asks their father. They all give homemade presents to the baby, except Andy, who was not aware of the custom. The news of the baby's birth goes out over "that snowy Vermont valley." The carolers come up Sycamore Lane to sing "Silent Night" outside Mrs. Miller's window. Dr. Herrick regrets missing Christmas Eve with his own family but considers every birth a miracle. Andy, who loves his skates better than anything in the world, sneaks into his mother's room, presents his skates to his baby sister, and falls asleep on the coverlet near her sweet breath. (An Austrian clergyman, Joseph Mohr, wrote the lyrics to the song, "Silent Night," in 1816.)

O

Margaret Otto

Miss Anne Paulie Marvelous, a pastry chef, lives in Westville in ***Syrup*** (1956) with her three dogs, Pumpkin, Ginger, and Spice. When Spice has three puppies, Miss Marvelous decides to give one, Syrup, to Sally and Jimmy Henry, whose parents are summer people; one, Peanuts, to Polly and Jack Bates, who live next door; and one, Taffy, to her friend, Timothy Silver, a carpenter. The Henrys decide to seek permanent residence in Vermont. After Miss Marvelous agrees to marry Timothy, the Henrys buy her house. While wedding preparations take place, the puppies grow. Syrup vanishes several times: once, he falls asleep in a boot and is taken away by the shoemaker; another time, he slumbers under one of Miss Marvelous's big hats. Timothy builds a commodious cage so the puppies can safely attend the festivities. The wedding ceremony and subsequent party are a great success. When the Silvers drive away on their wedding trip, Pumpkin, Ginger, and Spice are sitting up in the back seat.

P

Katherine Paterson

The father of seven-year-old Marvin Gates works on Brock's dairy farm in ***The Smallest Cow in the World*** (1991), the first of a trio of stories about Marvin (the others are *Marvin's Best Christmas Present Ever* and *Marvin One Too Many*). Marvin loves Rosie best of all the cows. When Brock decides to sell out and move to a warmer climate, Marvin's father has to find another job. Marvin, his mother and father, and his elder sister, May, move to a different farm where they all adjust to their new lives except Marvin, who badly misses Rosie and thinks about her every day. After someone covers the trailer with graffiti and destroys the garden plants, Marvin's parents are angry and disappointed. Marvin explains that Rosie joined them and committed these naughty acts because she does not want to move and does not enjoy being little. A witch had turned her into the smallest cow in the world, he explains. The family acquiesces to Marvin's imaginative fancy. His father gives him a small bottle to use as a barn for Rosie. Marvin plays with her all summer and, when school starts, takes her to school with him. All the children make fun of Marvin except May's new friend, Jenny, who admires Marvin's inventiveness. Inspired by Jenny's appreciation, May tells Marvin that Rosie will have to stay home from school because she is expecting a calf. His parents promise Marvin that, even if they move to another farm, Rosie and her calf will always accompany them.

Marvin and his family are living in a trailer on the Smiths' dairy farm in ***Marvin's Best Christmas Present Ever*** (1997). With Christmas coming, Marvin is worried about what to give his parents. May is writing and illustrating a beautiful book. He decides to make a wreath to hang on the end of the trailer. When he has trouble attaching the branches, May offers to help. His parents love the wreath. Long after Christmas, when the wreath is brown and withered, Marvin's parents want to take it down, but he begs them to keep it up a little longer. Marvin is sad the wreath cannot last because it is the best present he ever made. In the spring, a bird makes her nest in the wreath and lays six eggs. May wishes she could make such a lovely present; Marvin offers to help.

Marvin enters a new school in ***Marvin One Too Many*** (2001) to be greeted by his unprepared teacher with, "One more? That is one too many." All the children, except Marvin, have cards with their names on them. Marvin cannot read. The teacher gives Marvin a note for his parents, asking them to read with him every day. He tears up the note: she does not understand how busy his parents are on a dairy farm. The other children make fun of him; he gets into fights. He hates school. Mercifully, it snows, so he can stay home. His elder sister, Mary, prints letters on some cards and tries to teach him to read. "Reading is dumb," says Marvin. When the electricity goes off, Marvin thinks he is responsible because he did not want to go to school. He confides his worry to his father, who reads him a funny poem about a purple cow. Suddenly Marvin catches on: he can sound out the letters all by himself.

Tracey Campbell Pearson

The general store is the hub of activity in a small town like Jericho. In ***The Storekeeper*** (1988), the store's owner rises early to greet the whole town. She tidies her stock, sorts mail, sells a few items, deals with salespeople, and welcomes town workmen. Amid the apparent bedlam and myriad children underfoot, she remains calm and cheerful while she serves the townspeople. She stays open into the evening, works late, and finally closes down with an affectionate "goodnight" to the town.

In ***Where Does Joe Go?*** (1999), everyone in Jericho loves to stop by Joe's Snack Shop for treats in the summer. When fall comes, white-bearded Joe disappears and does not reappear until spring. Where does he go? Everyone tries to guess. To the moon? The beach? The pyramids? On a cruise? An archeological dig? A safari? No matter where they think he might be, they always visualize his snack bar and umbrella right there with him. No one ever guesses that Joe is Santa Claus, who heads for the North Pole every year.

Robert Newton Peck

In ***Little Soup's Birthday*** (1991), Rob Peck hurries through his chores because of the occasion—the ninth birthday of his best friend, Robert Wesley Vinson or "Soup." Rob's mother makes a freezer of fresh ice cream for the party. At Soup's, while his mother makes the cake, the boys plan the games. They wrap up Rob's junk collection for prizes. The time seems to pass slowly. It is snowing so hard they fear no one will come to the party, but Mr. McKell brings the five guests in his sleigh. The party is a huge success, although the boys notice that Mrs. Vinson takes an aspirin after it is over. The boys live in the town of Learning near Rutland.

Aunt Clara gives Soup a bunny for Easter in ***Little Soup's Bunny*** (1993). Bucky, a baby buck, takes turns sleeping inside the boys' shirts. Soup and Rob collect and dye eggs in a bucket of cold water. On Easter, they try to hide them in an empty nest, but it is too high, so they use a basket. Bucky escapes in the night, but they find him in the barn eating carrots. When the boys present the grownups with their surprise, the eggs break. Now they remember why their mothers always boil the water. (Descriptions of the books in the series about Soup and Rob continue in the next section.)

Carol Purdy

The central figure in ***Least of All*** (1987), set in 1900, is Raven Hannah, the youngest of six children and the only girl in the family. They call her "Hannah" because all the boys' names are from the Bible and "Raven" because of the color of her hair and the story of Noah's Ark. The father, mother, grandmother, and the boys have a great deal of work to do, but she is too little to cut and saw firewood or boil the maple sap. "You're too young" or "Better let the boys do it" are all she hears. Finally, she is allowed to churn butter, but she is lonely down in the cellar; she takes the Bible with her and teaches herself to read while she works. She likes the familiar stories; her favorite part is Noah's sending the raven from the ark, "a bird so strong he flew round and round until the floodwaters dried up from the face of the earth." When the first snowstorm comes, the members of the family crowd around the cookstove and notice Hannah with her book. They are amazed that she taught herself to read. The adults wipe away tears; none of them is literate. Raven Hannah is overjoyed that at last she can do something they cannot. During the long, cold Vermont winter, she teaches the whole family to read. (From the King James version, Genesis 8:7, "And he sent forth a raven, which went forth to and fro, until the waters were dried up from off the earth.")

R

Nan Parson Rossiter

In late October in ***The Way Home*** (1997), Samuel, his father, and their dog, Ben, come upon a small Canada goose tangled in a fishing line. While Samuel's father frees and picks up the wounded goose, a gander moves out from a grove of spruce trees. Samuel's father carries the goose into the farmhouse, leaving the door open so the gander can see his mate. All night the lonely gander honks. In the morning, Samuel feeds the goose a bowl of oat mash with milk, which she greedily eats and hobbles slowly outside. She rests all day; the gander watches carefully. Samuel names the goose "Chicory"; the gander he calls "Spruce Goose." During the nights of the following two weeks, Samuel's father shuts the pair in the barn to keep them safe from foxes. They take a practice flight but return to the farm; the next day they fly away. Samuel feels proud but sad: he misses them a great deal. One morning in spring

Samuel hears a faint sound. Spruce Goose and Chicory return with five "fuzzy, noisy" goslings. "The farm felt complete again." (The author wrote to me that the license plate for the pickup truck on the cover, Vermont BN5391, represents the initials of the author and her husband and the date of their wedding; they became engaged in Stowe, Vermont.)

Sugar on Snow (2002) is about Seth and his younger brother, Ethan, who are excited because the sap is running. The day for sugaring off has come. The boys ride with their father on the tractor, which pulls a trailer with the holding tank. Their mother follows with the lunch and their black Labrador, Chloe. Seth steers the tractor for the first time. Ethan helps empty the buckets into the tank. When they head for the sugarhouse, a light snow is falling. Their father starts boiling the sap in the big evaporator pan. The boys are amazed at the amount of sap, though their father tells them it takes forty gallons of sap to make one gallon of maple syrup. The boys pack bowls with snow, which their father drizzles with syrup. "All the sweetness of the day melted on their tongues."

Ken Rush

What About Emma? (1996), dedicated to Vermont farming families, is told from the point of view of Sue, whose father can no longer afford to run a dairy farm because of the high cost of feed and new equipment and the low price of milk. Their mother assures Sue and her brother, Peter, they will continue to have vegetables, chickens, ducks, and goats, even though they must sell the cows. "What about Emma?" asks Sue. Their parents will keep her until she calves. After the other cows are gone, Sue and Pete take care of Emma. Sue trains her like a trail horse. A snowstorm arrives. Emma's calf is overdue. The children see her heading for the woods and follow. Sue jumps on her back and rides her out of the woods, following the light from Pete's flashlight to the barn. Emma has her calf, which they call "Snowy." They all go to bed. The next day, Sue will ask if they can keep Emma and Snowy.

S

Leda Schubert

Here Comes Darrell (2005) is a tribute to Darrell, who is hardworking, loyal, thoughtful, and neighborly. In winter, he is up at four in the morning to plow people's driveways. He takes time to give a little boy a ride in his cab. In spring, Darrell splits logs, loads the wood onto his truck, and delivers it, even though some people cannot pay right away. Periodically, his wife reminds him that their barn roof needs work. In summer, he uses his backhoe to excavate for a homeowner's new room and digs a pond for the owners. In autumn, Darrell and his wife visit the neighbors to list their needs for the ensuing months. Just when it is time for Darrell's animals to stay inside the barn, the roof falls in. The neighbors arrive for a roof raising and bring supper, too.

Martina Selway

Don't Forget to Write (1992) records the trauma of Rosie's leaving her home in Hartford, Connecticut, for the first time to stay with her grandfather and Aunt Mabel on their farm in Manchester. Rosie begins a letter to her mother that reveals her homesickness. She wants to go home. She does not understand her grandfather's sense of humor. She starts to look around the farm and help with chores. She searches her grandfather's treasures and finds pictures of her mother when she was little. She goes fishing with her grandfather and wishes she had a river at home. She attends an auction and wishes she could be there when her grandfather sells his calf. When it is time to leave, she has not yet mailed her letter to her mother. She sends it off, begging to stay in Vermont a little longer.

Esphyr Slobodkina

High up the mountain in a little Vermont town in ***The Clock*** (1956) stands a white church with a tall steeple and a tower clock, which chimes every hour. Townspeople like the milkman, the grocer, the postman, the baker, and the schoolchild know what time it is, and what they have to do. Everything runs like clockwork. One morning the clock does not chime; they all stay in bed. When they discover the time, they are annoyed with the clock and decide to replace it. The preacher calms the townspeople and calls a repairman, who cleans out "the rust and the dust" and oils all the parts. The old clock takes up its work again and faithfully rings out the time every hour. Everyone is back on schedule.

T

Abigail Thomas

In ***Lily*** (1994), the story is told from the perspective of a small, black dog living with Aunt Eliza in her apartment in Boston. Suddenly, Aunt Eliza informs Lily they are moving to Vermont. She has no time for Lily while she packs her boxes. The movers, large and frightening men, arrive. Lily shivers in the car all the way to Vermont. There she finds "soft grass and more grass and trees as far as she can see." Finally Aunt Eliza finishes putting away her possessions. "Everything was in its rightful spot, just the way Lily liked it."

Eliza Thomas

In ***The Red Blanket*** (2004), the narrator lives with her dog, Lily, in a house outside of town where apple trees grow in the front yard and a pond lies on the other side of the road. Sad and lonely because she has no children, she decides to adopt a baby. With her neighbors to see her off, she packs little garments and a red blanket and travels all the way to China to pick up a baby girl named PanPan. At first the baby is distressed and sleepless in the hotel, but her new mother wraps her in the comforting, safe red blanket. As PanPan grows up, she carries the blanket with her everywhere. "It's special," she explains. (While the narrator's residence is not explicitly identified, the author has already written about bringing PanPan to Vermont in her nonfiction account of the adoption, *The Road Home*.)

Nathaniel Tripp

A boy remembers one special snowstorm in ***Snow Comes to the Farm*** (2001). He knows winter has come when "frost feathers" grow on his windowpanes at night. One morning his elder brother announces a snowstorm is due. He takes the boy up to the owl woods to watch the snow arrive. They build a fire and eat their sandwiches. "The biggest storms begin with the smallest flakes." They see small animals bustling about, then an owl, "silent as the smoke from their fire." Piles of snow slide down from the trees. His brother puts out the fire and leads him home. The storm blows harder. The snow keeps falling "like owl down." They are warm and snug inside.

Tasha Tudor

Corgiville Fair (1971) is set "west of New Hampshire and east of Vermont" in a village with a church, an inn, a post office, a general store, and a Civil War statue. Its inhabitants are corgis, cats, rabbits, and boggarts (trolls). Mr. Bixby Brown, First Selectman and Road Agent, raises racing goats. Everyone in the village prepares for the fair. Mert Boggart, who runs a fireworks factory, helps Mr. Brown's son, Caleb, ready Josephine for the Grand Race. Edgar Tomcat's racing goat, Red Pepper, provides Josephine's main competition. Rumor has it that Edgar is placing bets on the race. The tents are raised; the exhibits are set up. Mert warns Caleb to guard Josephine during the fair, but, when Edgar offers him a hotdog, Caleb cannot refuse. Drugged by a powder in the food, Caleb falls sound asleep; Edgar seizes the opportunity to feed greedy Josephine mince pies and cigars. Ten minutes before the race, Caleb wakes to find Josephine incapacitated; he runs to Mert, who gives the goat as many rockets as she can swallow. After she wins the race by five goat-lengths, she and Caleb lead the grand parade. In the evening, dancing is followed by a Boggart fireworks display.

V

Kathryn Mademann Vaughan

Little One—Goodnight (2003) is a lullaby in honor of a Morgan horse named Little One. (The book is accompanied by a compact disk.)

W

Mildred Pitts Walter

In ***Alec's Primer*** (2004), five-year-old Alec Turner lives with his mother, who is a slave on a Virginia plantation in 1850. When he displeases the mistress of the house, the overseer sends him to work under the broiling sun in the fields. When he is eight, the overseer assigns him to the cool milk house. Miss Zephie, the granddaughter of the white owner, wants to run away to Vermont and take Alec with her. First, she offers to teach him to read. He does not know whether to trust her. Every day she gives him a lesson, until her grandmother sees Alec reading his primer and slashes his face with her riding crop. She angrily reminds Zephie that the law forbids teaching a slave to read. Alec is ready to flee to Vermont when he hears from other slaves that Union soldiers are enlisting slaves in the fight for freedom. He joins the Union army. After the Civil War, a freeman, he goes to Vermont. (Alec Turner, 1845-1923, was born a slave and ran away from his plantation to join the First New Jersey Cavalry in 1862. Learning he would be a freeman if he went to Vermont, he found a job in Grafton with the local lumber industry. For a story about Alec's daughter, see Michael and Angela Medearis's *Daisy and the Doll* in this collection.)

Nancy Dingman Watson

In ***Sugar on Snow*** (1964), Cammie plans to have a sugar-on-snow party for her birthday. Her sister, Cait, worries that it might not snow. When it is time for the sap to rise in the maples, Peter and the two horses carry the children in the sled to the sugar bush. Peter makes a hole in the first tree. "Snowy chips and silver slivers sifted" over his boots. They haul the sap to the sugarhouse, where it goes through a pipe into the sugar pan. It boils and jumps over the fire. On Cammie's birthday, snow covers the ground. All her friends come to the party. The hot syrup on the cold snow is waxy and chewy. They eat it with cider, doughnuts, and pickles.

Rosemary Wells

Berty idolizes his elder brother, Luther, in ***Waiting for the Evening Star*** (1993). They live on a farm in Barstowe near Brandon with their parents and grandmother. When Berty is three, ten-year-old Luther takes him to Ellis Lake to watch workmen cut ice. Their mother brings the workmen homemade cider heated with cloves and a vanilla bean. In sugaring season, half the farmers leave their work to go out to tap trees. The boys eat candy made from hot syrup poured on fresh snow. Berty and his grandmother plant seeds in small indoor pots for the summer garden; she teaches him to wish on the evening star. When Berty is seven, Luther starts high school in Brandon. Berty fetches the three milk cows from the pasture in the late afternoons. His grandmother makes cheddar cheese, dying it yellow with carrot water. Their father believes "the rest of the world was just full of war and foreign languages." When Berty asks Luther why he wants to travel, he responds, "to see what's over the mountains," but Berty thinks they have everything they need here in Vermont. In the evenings, the family watches the trains go by. On the Fourth of July in 1917, Luther plays first trumpet in the Barstowe village band. In September, the family sees Luther off on the train to war. His grandmother tells Berty to wait for the evening star: he makes a wish for Luther's safety.

Children's and Young Adult Fiction

A

Jacob Abbott

Marco Paul's Voyages & Travels in Vermont (1852) is one of six adventure-cum-instruction tales in which twelve-year-old Marco Baron, son of a New York merchant, travels with his cousin Forester, nineteen, variously in New York, on the Erie Canal, in Maine, in Vermont, in Boston, and at the Springfield Armory. In Vermont, Marco and Forester head alongside the Connecticut River by stagecoach toward Forester's father's fine house near Montpelier, where they will stay for three months. While Marco is sitting up behind the driver, the coach hits a rut and expels the driver (unhurt) onto the road, carrying the reins along with him. Marco, who attends a gymnasts' class in New York, climbs along the "pole" or wooden shaft that extends from the front axle to the collars of the animals, retrieves the reins, and guides the horses until he can turn them into a farmyard. Before joining his parents, Forester takes Marco to spend a night with a prosperous farmer at his great "grass farm," using the experience to teach Marco about agriculture and animal husbandry in Vermont. The physical situation of the village where the Foresters live gives the young tutor the opportunity to illustrate the entire development of a Vermont village. Commencing with a waterfall, he explains to Marco about waterpower and the role of sawmills and gristmills. They visit a blacksmith's shop, discuss the importance of the general store, and visualize the part played by the carpenter, mason, physician, and lawyer in the community. When Marco wants to go hunting with a gun, Forester gives him a reasoned reply about the risk being too great for the benefit. Forester has carefully devised a system and schedule for their study, which will take place in his father's office. While Marco is doing his lessons, Forester will concentrate on his preparation for the law. Working in the mornings only, they will begin with a short period of instruction, after which Marco will work alone at his arithmetic, writing, and reading (the shelves are filled with reference works). During this study period, Marco is not to ask questions or bother his tutor; rather, if he faces a problem, the "rule" is to act according to his own judgment. This self-directed discipline is based upon complete confidence on the part of the instructor. The plan works well until, one morning, Marco glimpses two boys his age digging worms for bait. Noting his cousin is out of the room, Marco decides it will do no harm for him to chat with the boys for a minute. They urge him to join them. His transgression is natural and understandable; his guilty secret is an acute weight on his conscience. He wants to tell his cousin about his escapade but fears not punishment, but acknowledging his mistake. Suffering all afternoon and evening, he feels exquisite relief in confessing to Forester, who already knew about the incident. Marco learns a serious lesson about betraying a trust bestowed upon him. He acquires another valuable insight when he does an injustice to the gardener by accusing him of something he did not do. The afternoons are reserved for outdoor play, most notably a boating expedition with some local boys. Forester procures for them a fine boat with oars and teaches the boys such exercises as "tossing" and "letting fall" the oars. Forester and Marco's last adventure is to hike for a distance to fetch two horses for Forester's father. Tutor and student are caught in an unanticipated snowstorm and are for a time lost in the woods. Forester calmly sets forth the options before them, settling on the plan to find a stream and follow it down to the river. They come out close to the place where the horses are pastured and ride home safely. Marco enthusiastically reports their adventures to his aunt, concluding that "he would just as lief get lost in the woods as not. It was good fun."

Jane D. Abbott

The inhabitants of the mansion in ***Happy House*** (1920) are distinctly unhappy until Anne ("Nancy") Leavitt, eighteen, arrives on North Hero Island to visit her Aunt Sabrina Leavitt.

In fact, Aunt Sabrina is not Nancy's aunt, but the aunt of one of Nancy's Cornell University roommates, whose name is also Anne Leavitt. The genuine Anne has an opportunity to visit Russia; since her aunt has not seen her for years, Anne sends Nancy to North Hero in her stead. The other roommate, Claire Wallace, had hoped Nancy would come to her house in Long Island to meet her handsome brother, Barry. Once in North Hero, Nancy finds Aunt Sabrina chilly, aristocratic, and obsessed with the heroic history of the Leavitt family, whose members first came to Vermont from Montreal in 1740 and were Ethan Allen's comrades. Undaunted by her reception, Nancy sets about bringing joy to the entire family, including Aunt Milly, who is treated unnecessarily as an invalid after a train wreck, and the "no-good" Hopgood children, neighbors whom Aunt Sabrina and certain other members of North Hero society spurn. Nancy is rather taken aback by the overly friendly manner of the neighbor's hired man, Peter Hyde. She finds him appealing—they spend a lovely day together on Isle La Motte—but she cannot believe she would ever want to marry a farmer. It turns out that both Nancy and Peter are pretending to be someone they are not: Peter is actually Claire's brother, Barry; Nancy discovers that by a twist of fate she is the real Anne Leavitt.

Katharine Adams

The title character in ***Mehitable*** (1920) is Mehitable Webster, sixteen, an orphan in the custody of her Aunt Comfort in Cherryville in 1913. Somewhat cowed by her aunt, Mehitable is well cared for by the housekeeper, Desire, and the hired man, Silas. Mehitable enjoys a crowd of spirited contemporaries with whom she picnics in the woods. She loves to read—*Lorna Doone* is a favorite—and is writing a "winter play" for her friends. Her close friend, Johnnie Gray, is eager to leave Vermont to become an artist; Mehitable has never dreamed of leaving Cherryville, which is "all the dreams in the world come true." She looks out the window: "Far and far away stretched the purple-blue mountains, the blue valleys, and above them a sky of crimson rose." When her mother's friend, Mrs. Lindsay, offers to send Mehitable to school near Paris, Aunt Comfort knows this is an extraordinary opportunity for her niece. Desire knits her a red hood and cape; Silas finds some "dream roses" in the woods. Her friends bid her a fond farewell. After reading Aunt Comfort's farewell note, she digests the fact that she is the only family member remaining to Aunt Comfort. The remainder of the book, describing Mehitable's experiences in France, underscores the idea that no matter what glorious sights she sees nor what glamorous people she meets, she will never forget Cherryville and her roots: Vermont is always with her. She befriends Phillippe, the grandson of the owner of the chateau where her school is housed; soon his mother, the young Madame de Villiers, comes from England and sees in Mehitable the daughter she never had. The "young madame," as she is known, recognizes Mehitable's artistic talent; Mehitable tries to express to her how different life is in Cherryville, where she will earn her living as a schoolteacher. Miss Lindsay sends an emissary to buy Mehitable some new clothes, which Mehitable would dearly love but cannot accept because Aunt Comfort does not approve of luxurious outfits. When Mehitable does well in class, she does so to please Aunt Comfort. At the end of the school year in 1914, Mehitable is invited to Belgium with the de Villiers. When Major de Villiers returns from Algiers, young madame goes to France to greet him, leaving the young people with a chaperone. The Germans invade Belgium. Mehitable and Philippe can hear the cannonading in the distance as they board a train for France. Mehitable thinks of Cherryville and Aunt Comfort. In France, they are reunited with Phillippe's mother and father. The father will go to his regiment; they, to England. Mehitable will be brave like her grandfather, a hero in the American Civil War.

Louisa May Alcott

In "**A Country Christmas**" (1874), Sophie Vaughan, eighteen, who lives in the city and has a millionaire beau, invites her friends, socialite Emily Herrick and popular novelist Leonard

Randall, to spend the holiday with Aunt Plumy Basset in "the wilds of Vermont." The sophisticated city folk arrive, a bit condescending about "primitive pastimes" in the country, to meet Mrs. Basset's handsome son, Saul, a major in the Civil War, and her pretty younger daughter, Ruth. Randall went abroad instead of serving in the army. When asked about his books, he talks in a supercilious way about the glamorous people he features in his stories. Aunt Plumy points out with asperity that they have libraries in the country and access to books. She prefers stories about real human beings, common people, like the characters of Charles Dickens and Harriet Beecher Stowe. Sophie organizes a Christmas dance, for which Aunt Plumy provides antique costumes. Randall tries to flirt with Ruth, only to learn that she is to marry the local minister in the spring. When the guests ready themselves to leave, Sophie announces she is not going back with them: she plans to marry Saul on the same occasion as Ruth's wedding.

Merritt P. Allen

Raiders' Hoard (1936) is set in St. Albans, where an elderly couple, Jerusha and Hebron Otis, are still suffering from the 1864 raid when Confederate officers robbed Hebron's grandfather of twenty thousand dollars in gold. Since then, the Otis men have been unable to clear the heavy mortgage on their farm. Seventeen-year-old Philip Lake, Jerusha's cousin, spends a school vacation helping the young hired hand, Joe Bangs, eighteen, with the chores. A stranger named Terryvale makes his way to the house during a storm. Thinking he has left, Hebron tells Philip and Joe about the gold; finding Terryvale's footprints outside the window, the young men are certain that he overheard. Terryvale announces he is writing a newspaper article about the St. Albans Raid. Their suspicions aroused, they follow him that evening and watch him cutting a hole in the ice below the bridge. Joe believes he is an opium smuggler. When Terryvale proposes renting Hebron's house for two months, the owner refuses: "We farmers don't rent our houses; we live in 'em." The cellar catches fire; soon the whole house is aflame. Sad to lose the family house, Hebron and Jerusha move to the old house on their property, which is tight but in need of repairs. In a matter of minutes, neighbors assemble to scrub, clean, hammer, and install; they bring vegetables and canned goods. The next night, Philip and Joe, after watching Terryvale drop something into the ice hole, wait until he leaves and then pull out a clock part. Terryvale rents a house on the Sheldon road (used by the raiders). The next night, Philip and Joe creep up to Terryvale's house to see him burying a box under a tree. Philip takes a small sample of the contents to send to a scientist friend for analysis. They see Terryvale in hip boots, carrying a shovel and hunting for something near the old road. The next time Terryvale drops by the Otis house, the cellar catches fire shortly thereafter, but Philip and Joe extinguish it. Their surmise is that Terryvale set both fires using oily rags and parts of a clock for a timer, but they cannot prove it. The next night Philip goes to Terryvale's house to find the rest of the clock. When Philip does not return, Joe notifies the sheriff. Together they head for Terryvale's, where the sheriff arrests him for suspicion of selling drugs and rescues Philip, who is tied up in the barn. Terryvale is the great-nephew of Captain Daniel E. Gibson, the one Confederate raider left behind for lack of a horse. Gibson had put Captain Otis's gold in a kettle, deposited it in a creek, and made notes of the exact location. In 1870, he wrote to a St. Albans Bank describing the whereabouts of the money; the letter fell into Terryvale's hands. For Jerusha and Hebron, "The Civil War is over."

The Green Cockade (1942) begins in 1774 with a trial conducted by Ethan Allen in the New Hampshire Grants. Two Yorkers, Hubert Gort (accompanied by his son, Walter) and Ike Javers, a surveyor, claim land that Squire Stonebridge purchased from King George's representative in New Hampshire and "won every inch of the place in a struggle against the wilderness." Stonebridge's son, Hal, sixteen, watches as the Green Mountain Boys whip the two men with green beech strips, a punishment called "the beech seal," because the courts offer no redress. Hal fears Gort will seek revenge but feels sorry for Gort's son. Stonebridge is tired of obeying a king who rules "by chance of birth rather than by consent of the governed." Wearing a sprig of evergreen given to him by Ethan Allen, Hal joins the Green Mountain Boys. When Hal comes upon Walter being attacked by an Indian, he intervenes and helps Walter make his way to the Stonebridge farm. After a month with the Stonebridges, Walter understands their perspective on the New Hampshire Grants dispute, learns what "tyranny" means, and admires those who resist it. Hal gives Walter a small pistol as a parting gift. In Bennington, Hal catches sight of the Yorker Javers and rushes home. He is too late: Javers has burned down his house and killed his father. At the scene is Hal's pistol. Hal becomes the man of the house, taking care of his mother and little sisters, Comfort, ten, and Delight, eight. They start over, salvaging possessions, making a shelter, snaring rabbits, and fashioning snowshoes. The nearest neighbor, Mr. Mead, goes to Bennington to report the Squire's murder to Ethan Allen. Hal, his mother, and the two "pioneer children" are determined to persevere. In spring, with no sugaring equipment save one iron kettle, Hal whittles sap spouts from poplar branches; his mother and sisters make two-gallon birch-bark containers. Colonel Allen lends them money to buy oxen. The British attack the Minutemen at Lexington and Concord. Seth Warner, second in command of the Green Mountain Boys and a cool and cautious balance to the "tempestuous" Allen, arrives in Bennington. The Connecticut Committee of Safety approves the attack on Fort Ticonderoga; Hal, leaving his family, meets the rebels at the staging area in Castleton. Hal believes in the rightness of their cause: preventing a foreign power from threatening American families. The rebels seize Fort Ticonderoga. Several years pass. The effort of taking care of his family pushes Hal almost to the limits of his endurance. At Hubbardton, Hal is wounded, but he survives to fight at Bennington. The New Hampshire Grants are now known as Vermont. At Saratoga, seeing Walter with a group of General Schuyler's Continentals, Hal throws himself savagely at his enemy. When Colonel Dan Morgan pulls him off, Hal exclaims that Walter is the Tory murderer of his father; Hal is detained briefly and released. Shocked by the ferocity and senselessness of the battle, Hal, witnessing the British hero, General Simon Fraser, receive a mortal wound, withdraws sobbing from the field. A dozen Indians and a Royalist officer—Javers—capture Hal. Javers is about to torture Hal when Captain Hubert Gort appears and arrests Javers. Gort explains to Hal that Walter lent his pistol to Javers, who is the killer of Hal's father. Hal, who once hated the Gorts, is now filled with great regret and perplexity over all that has happened. He can see that Tory Hubert Gort is an authentic man. The war for liberty has resulted in bloodshed and murder. When news comes that Walter is dead, Hal is sunk into remorse and depression; Walter returns alive, however, and he and Hal reconcile.

The Flicker's Feather (1953) features Duff Johnson, seventeen, an orphan who sells his parents' New Hampshire farm in 1758 for fifty dollars in gold and stops at a county fair to enter a jumping contest with Davy Mack, a young man about his size. Captain John Stark offers to hold Duff's rifle and, after the contest, shows him around the fair. They speak to a peddler named Comical Smith. Duff knows Stark's reputation as a famous Indian fighter in Roberts's Rangers who was captured and sold by St. Francis Indians. Duff, who does not want to be a British soldier but is eager to help end the conflict with the French and Indians, volunteers to join Stark's company. Stark describes the life of a scout, rarely seeing a town while spying and harassing the enemy. Stark agrees to meet Duff later at the Rangers' camp; Duff lends him his fifty gold pieces for an impending emergency. Supping at the tavern, Davy becomes involved in a barroom brawl. Sheriff Styles arrests and jails Duff for intervening on Davy's behalf. Using a saw, Comical frees Duff and takes him to Albany where Duff sets out to find the Rangers. At the British camp, he is treated arrogantly; most of the British redcoats look down their noses at the

A

"colonials" or "provincials." British General George Howe, kind, intelligent, and revered by his troops, arranges for Duff to sign up with Stark's company. Duff meets John Elwing, General Howe's aide (and son of a lord). Near Fort Ticonderoga, Duff runs into some Rangers, including his old acquaintance, Davy Mack, and meets Major Rogers, the best scout and woods fighter in the world. The Rangers' objective is to reconnoiter Fort Ticonderoga. Duff admires the harmonious collaboration between Stark and Rogers. General Abercrombie heads the large force of British regulars and American militia; General Montcalm is in charge of defending the French-held fort. The French erect defenses of huge pointed timbers. A sniper kills General Howe. When Abercrombie rashly orders his troops to storm the breastworks, many are slaughtered. Duff and Davy, wounded, are evacuated to Lake George. From the heights, Duff looks at the virgin forests of the New Hampshire Grants and imagines living on a farm there one day: that is why he is fighting. The winter of 1758-1759 is long and bitter, with more skirmishes. Duff has grown strong and skillful. General Amherst takes command of the British and American armies. When a Ranger lieutenant, Josh Peech, is ordered to explore Otter Creek in the Grants, Duff volunteers to go. He loves Otter Falls and the surrounding soil. He finds the feather of a flicker (a large North American woodpecker); according to an old saying, "you will go back to the place where you find a flicker's feather." He is manning the watch when fourteen Indians rush him; his companions are all killed and scalped. Taken to Montreal as a prisoner, Duff finds John Elwing there. Months pass, with no parole and no sign of General Amherst. Miraculously, Comical (who is an American spy) helps Duff and John to escape. John and Duff are now comrades, although they cannot understand each other's philosophy of life. Amherst, who retook Fort Ticonderoga in 1759, embarks with his army for Canada and captures Montreal in 1760. Duff, who is recovering from smallpox, does not go on the expedition. Sheriff Styles finally finds Duff, not to arrest him but to introduce him to a lawyer with astonishing news: Duff's father's surname was Blake-Johnson, his grandfather was Sir John Blake-Johnson, and Duff is heir to their estate and title. Duff relinquishes his rights to his cousin—John Elwing. As a reward for lending General Stark fifty gold pieces, Duff receives from Governor Wentworth five hundred acres in the New Hampshire Grants. Duff loves the "rolling green forest and far blue mountains" of his new residence.

Julia Alvarez

In ***How Tía Lola Came to Visit / Stay*** (2001), ten-year-old Miguel and seven-year-old Juanita Guzmán move to Middlebury with their mother, Linda, who is divorcing their father. Because Linda is working as a summer counselor at Middlebury College, she invites her Aunt (*Tía*) Lola to come from the Dominican Republic to help out with the children and do the cooking. Miguel is aghast when Tía Lola arrives, wearing high heels and a turban, and hopes to keep her presence a secret from his friends. Soon everyone knows and loves Tía Lola, who is warm, demonstrative, enthusiastic, and uninhibited. Rudy, the local restaurant owner and Little League coach, comes to her for Spanish lessons on his days off. Tía Lola puts special treats in Miguel's lunchbox to make him strong for the baseball team. It seems as though spring will never arrive. As someone points out, "[Vermont] makes for a long winter...but it keeps the flatlanders away." The children help Tía Lola learn English. When they plant their vegetable garden, Tía Lola swerves up and down in high heels while the children drop seeds in the holes: she has shaped the plot like the Dominican Republic. Finally, the long, sweet, sunny days of summer come, each one "like a piece of fancy candy in a gold-and-blue wrapper." Their landlord, Colonel Charles Charlebois, permits the baseball team to practice in the backyard; Miguel is chosen captain. When Tía Lola paints the house purple, Linda is worried about the colonel's reaction, but Tía Lola is working "the magic of understanding." The colonel is entirely won over when the team appears in purple and white uniforms (designed and sewn by

Tía Lola) with "Charlie's Boys" stitched across their backs. Tía Lola organizes a surprise party for Linda, to which she invites the entire village. Afterward, the four of them drive up the mountain to look out at the valley. The last episode takes place in the Dominican Republic, celebrating Christmas with their extended family. Miguel worries that Tía Lola will stay on the island, but when Santa Claus (a beauty mark adorns Santa's cheek) asks what he wants for Christmas, he answers that the best present would be for Tía Lola to come home with them to Vermont.

In the first part of ***Finding Miracles*** (2004), Millie Kaufman, fifteen, lives near Burlington with her father, George, a secular Jew and a carpenter; her mother, Sylvia, a family therapist; her sister, Kate, fifteen; and her brother, Nate, eight. Millie is troubled by a secret. Fifteen years earlier, when her parents served with the Peace Corps in Latin America, Sylvia gave birth to Kate and then adopted Milly. To celebrate Millie's birthday, Happy, their "rich, impossible" grandmother, arrives with many relatives. Milly is annoyed when visitors complain about the winter weather as though they had made a dangerous trek: "It's only Vermont, not the North Pole, for heaven's sake." Millie feels she is not a genuine member of the family because Happy does not treat her like the other children; in fact, Happy apportions her estate to her other grandchildren, with only a "stipend" for Millie. Her father explains to Millie that Happy is annoyed by his refusal to join the family company. A new boy, Pablo Antonio Bolívar Sanchez, enters Millie's ninth grade. She suspects that he recognizes her country of origin and tries to avoid him, but, after her father hires Pablo's father as a carpenter, and Pablo's mother takes a job next door caring for a crippled woman, Millie and Pablo spend time together after school. Finding him sympathetic, she confides her secret to him. He says her eyes are like those of the people of Los Luceros, a remote place in his country where the revolutionaries hide. Millie looks at her adoption papers: her given name is "Milagros" (miracle). The Bolívars invite the Kaufmans to their modest apartment to hear the election results from the Dominican Republic where, after many years and terrible suffering, the Liberation Party overthrows the CIA-installed dictator. Classmate Jack Cohen asks Millie to run as class senator on his slate for president of the class. In Millie's candidate speech, delivered to the entire student body, she congratulates Pablo on his country's democratic victory and announces that she, too, is a native of his country. The second part of the narrative takes place in the Dominican Republic where Millie accompanies the Bolívars on a trip. She is caught up in the celebration of the victory of the Liberation Party, meetings with family members, and a poignant exchange with a nun who was at the orphanage where she was found. A glorious reunion and a private reconciliation occur when the entire Kaufman family, including an apologetic Happy, flies to the Dominican Republic.

A

Grace Neil Anderson

In the Shadow of Cox Mountain (1993) chronicles the decade between 1773 and 1782 through the experiences of William Cox and his wife, Beulah, a midwife, who bring their large family of girls to Pittsford, where William owns a New Hampshire Grant. Speculators from New York try to sell off lots in Rutland and Pittsford. The oldest daughter, Sarah, is thirteen; Betsey is a few years younger. The rustic cabin William built is a substantial change from their comfortable home in Massachusetts, but they look forward to the day when Pittsford will be as developed as Bennington. Neighbor Ephraim Stevens, a tall, handsome fifteen-year-old, invites them to a cabin raising at his brother Roger's, giving the Cox family a chance to meet neighbors like the Cooleys and the Rowleys. In 1774, they experience their first winter. After sugaring, the Coxes give a party; Sarah is attracted to Ephraim. Ephraim takes part in the capture of Fort Ticonderoga; his brother, Roger, is a Tory. Many Pittsford men whose terms of enlistment have expired return home after the capture of Montreal, but Seth Warner sends for them the following year. With the men away, Sarah kills a deer in the woods, dresses the animal, and drags it home on a makeshift sled. When Ephraim returns, he embraces Sarah warmly. The summer of 1776 is a desperate time for the patriots, who take some strength from the presence of Fort Ticonderoga and Mount Independence. Ephraim assures Sarah that he loves her but does not want to be a farmer. In 1777, as the Indians and redcoats advance, many people leave their homes; the Americans retreat from Fort Ticonderoga to Hubbardton. Ephraim proceeds with Warner toward Bennington, where the patriots defeat the British. After the Pittsford men build a palisade around the Cox cabin, many families move inside the fort, having learned of Indian atrocities (including the scalping of Jane McRae, a young Loyalist woman), and the capture and removal to Canada of many young sons of their friends. Families return to rebuild; the first school in Pittsford opens its doors; the first dance is held. Sarah's parents do not approve of Ephraim, deeming him undependable. Although she resists their advice at first, Sarah eventually realizes that Ephraim is not ready to settle down and agrees to marry Joshua June, a young man who has been courting her since Ephraim's departure. Sarah and Joshua begin to build a cabin on one hundred acres given to them by her father. Indians attack Neshobe, killing two men, burning houses, and taking prisoners; Roger Stevens, Ephraim's Tory brother, is one of the leaders of the Indian raids. After Indians kill a settler in the fort, the settlers rename it Fort Vengeance. In 1781, when Indians threaten again, the settlers make for the fort, where they hear that Cornwallis has surrendered. Indians captured Ephraim, who returns in 1782. When he sees Sarah again, he realizes his mistake; she knows she made the right choice in marrying Joshua. (The author's great-grandmother, Eliza Tarble Barnard, was a great-granddaughter of Sarah Cox.)

M.T. Anderson

In ***The Game of Sunken Places*** (2004), thirteen-year-old best friends, Gregory Buchan and Brian Thatz, travel by train to Gerenford to spend a vacation with Gregory's honorary uncle, Maximilian Grendle, and his twenty-three-year-old daughter, Prudence. Upon arrival, the scene strikes the boys as odd: an ancient, gloomy Victorian mansion; an eccentric gentleman in period dress who speaks in aphorisms; drawing-room comedy servants; and nineteenth-century clothes for the boys to don. They then discover the board game that becomes the centerpiece of their visit, with place names like "The Stony Path," "The Dark Wood," "The Ring," and "The Club of Snarth." Brian, who is intellectual, observant, and polite, and Gregory, who is light-hearted, sarcastic, and bossy, both feel they are in a dream. Have they been brought there for a purpose? Against whom are they playing? A suspicious man, Jack Stimple, whom they saw on the train, warns them that the game is dangerous, and he presents them with a summoning grenade in case of need. Soon they realize they are playing the frightening game in earnest, faced with arbitrary rules and an unknown enemy. Stimple frightens Brian, out exploring alone, who screams for help. "That won't do you any good," says Stimple, "You're in Vermont." The characters they meet—an amusing troll, Snarth, a terrifying ogre, the vastly tall Speculant—offer them clues whose riddles they must solve in order to proceed. They discover hidden staircases, subterranean passages, and a dark river with a small boat. They learn they are pawns in a game featuring two adversarial groups—the People of the Norumbega and the Thussers, who drove the former from their homes. As the game becomes more lethal, the friendship between the boys strengthens: "We're risking our lives together ...that's what friendship is about." They break the Rules by going off the path to meet the elf, Sniggleping. He reveals that all the characters in the game, except Prudence, are machines that he invented. As the boys near the end of the game, they solve the final riddle by venturing into the past. Surrounded with flailing, bestial guardian creatures, Brian judges it is time to forfeit the game; he tosses the summoning grenade into the mob. The boys escape, with Stimple in pursuit. They achieve the final task—borrowing the Emperor of Norumbega's coronet to crown the statue of the faceless king—as Stimple reappears. Suddenly Brian understands: Stimple is not their opponent; they are playing against each other, testing their friendship. Prudence explains that she won the last game, granting her the honor of inventing the new game, based on the Victorian novels she fancies. Brian, winner of this game, assumes the task of developing the next one.

Kenneth Andler

In ***Mission to Fort No. 4*** (1975), David Bradford, fifteen, travels on April 26, 1775, from Lexington, Massachusetts, to the Bedford, New Hampshire, home of Samuel Farnsworth, surveyor and woodsman. British soldiers killed David's parents when the army retreated from Concord. Farnsworth plans to take David on a mission organized by Colonel John Goffe, a French and Indian Wars fighter. The mission is to recruit men for an assignment northwest through the New Hampshire Grants, on the theory that the British will try to extend their control of Lake Champlain. Farnsworth's route is through Fort No. 4 (Charlestown, New Hampshire) to the Crown Point Road and on to Lake Champlain. In 1760, Goffe laid out the Crown Point Road through Springfield, Rutland, and Brandon. Farnsworth's task is to assess whether cannon can be hauled on the road, which families living along the route are Tories, what supplies remain at Charlestown, and which Indians in Hanover are patriots. Goffe chooses Farnsworth because he can travel in the guise of a surveyor. Farnsworth and David camp out on the way while Farnsworth shows David surveying techniques like "running a line." They find Fort No. 4 in disarray—no longer a "fighting fort"—and hear that Ethan Allen and the Green Mountain Boys captured Fort Ticonderoga. Their messenger, Dan Jenkins, is one of the eighty-two men involved in the surprise seizure; he is now on his way to Boston with a list from Ethan Allen of all the materiel—cannon, howitzers, muskets—captured by the patriots. Farnsworth goes to Hanover, using as messenger an Indian student at Dartmouth College, Daniel Simons. David stays with Colonel Hunt and his family in Charlestown, where he plans to make his permanent home. (The epilogue describes the amazing exploit in which all the equipment captured at Fort Ticonderoga was moved to Cambridge, Massachusetts, in December 1775 and January 1776. For two adults novels about this event, both published in 1977, see Robert Newton Peck's *The King's Iron* and F. Van Wyck Mason's *Guns for Rebellion*.)

Jennifer Armstrong

Steal Away (1992) begins in 1896 when Mary Eleanor Emmons, thirteen, travels with her grandmother, Susannah McKnight Emmons, to Toronto to see Susannah's friend, Bethlehem Reid, and Bethlehem's friend, Free, who is Mary's age. There, the two elder women tell Mary and Free the story that Mary recounts in this narrative. In 1842, Susannah is born on a farm in Bennington. After her parents' deaths in 1855, she goes to Virginia to stay with relatives. Having never seen slaves, she is aghast at the idea of slavery and at the sermons her uncle preaches in its defense. She decides to steal away to Vermont, taking with her a thirteen-year-old slave, Bethlehem, whom she has befriended. The two girls travel for two weeks disguised as boys to reach Emmitsburg, Maryland, where, even though it is a free state, notices printed with their names are posted everywhere, and they are almost apprehended. In Pennsylvania, Susannah cuts her hand; the wound becomes infected and causes a high fever. Bethlehem finds a Quaker farmer to help them; members of the local abolition movement plot the girls' trip north. In Vermont, they part: Susannah stays in Bennington, while Bethlehem continues to Canada. This meeting in Toronto is the first since their poignant farewell forty years earlier.

Jim Arnosky

Before moving to California, Gina and Bobby Gennard, seven and ten, in ***Little Champ*** (1995) are visiting their grandparents, Charlie and Adele Gennard, who run a general store on an island in Lake Champlain. Spring comes: the lake is "sparkling blue and calm." One day, the children see a large sea creature rear out of the water.

A

Believing their story, their grandfather takes them out on his boat, *Crayfish*, with their grandmother and a picnic lunch, to look for their big fish. They have no luck that day, or the next; they see a giant turtle and a large log but no glimpse of the monster, which they call "Little Champ." Another day, when young Fred Sinclair is with them, Charlie uses his electronic fish-finder, which picks up all kinds of fish, including a huge "toothy" pike. Suddenly two "smears" appear on the screen. They make out a gigantic creature and her large baby, but Fred is so frightened Adele persuades Charlie to go ashore. Everyone makes fun of Gina and Bobby for claiming they have seen Lake Champlain monsters. Gina and Bobby take the rowboat out fishing. Little Champ, attracted to the fish Gina hooks, lifts the boat with his back. A storm blows up and carries the children quite far out. Bobby starts the little engine, but they run out of gas. While Charlie is trying to rescue them in *Crayfish*, he runs into a shoal. The children use all their might to row toward *Crayfish* and clamber aboard. While they are waiting for help, Champ and Little Champ swim up and nudge them off the shoal. At that moment, Mr. Sinclair pulls up in his boat. The Gennards decide not to tell anyone about their adventure: some people do not believe in "mystery, in the infinite possibilities of life."

Robert Arthur

In **"Obstinate Uncle Otis"** (1963), Aunt Edith Morks summons her nephew, Murchison Morks, to Hillport because his Uncle Otis was struck by lightning. Uncle Otis, who has a reputation for obstinacy, refuses to acknowledge the existence of objects that he dislikes; for example, the statue of his enemy, Ogilby, in the village square; or Willoughby's barn, which mars Uncle Otis's view. Aunt Edith worriedly explains to Murchison that since the accident Uncle Otis seems keyed up by some mysterious energy. Worse, the barn and the statue no longer stand, as though Uncle Otis "disbelieved things right out of existence." Now, he claims the state's dam, which flooded some of his land, does not exist. She fears that, if he refuses to accept the existence of the dam, the village will be wiped out and the inhabitants drowned. When Uncle Otis falls and strikes his head, he awakens thinking he is Eustace Lingham, a farm machinery salesman from Ohio. His wife and nephew assure him he is Otis Morks; he rejects the idea of such a person. That night, his room is empty. He has disbelieved himself out of existence.

Frank Asch

Devin (the author's son) and his friend, Caleb, volunteer in ***Up River*** (1995) to spend the day with the Otter Creek River Cleanup, organized by Andy, with Mike, a retired science teacher, as one of the leaders. The boys cut sharp sticks for spearing garbage and take off in their canoes. As they go, they sort the trash they collect into separate containers. Caleb remembers that Otter Creek was called "Indian road," a main thoroughfare for Abenakis. The boys do not see an otter, but they spy a great blue heron and a beaver and his burrow. At the take-out spot, they haul the garbage up a steep embankment to the road, where cars are waiting. Someone leaves Caleb all the returnable cans for him to redeem in order to buy the bicycle he covets.

Robert Ashley

Rebel Raiders (1956) begins in a Union prison near Chicago in 1864, where Bennett H. Young, twenty, and his cousin, Davie Hunter, fifteen, both veterans of Morgan's Raid (a forty-six day incursion into Northern states in 1863 by Confederate cavalry, led by General John Hunt Morgan), are detained. They and their fellow prisoners, pallid, undernourished, vermin-infested, and desperate, begin digging a tunnel under the washhouse. A former prisoner, who managed to break out, returns disguised as a prison inspector for a charitable organization to offer support and advice. After they escape, Ben and Davie board the Confederate blockade-runner, *The Whippet*, bound for North Carolina. Pursued by a Yankee square-rigger, they run aground and are about to be captured when someone shouts, "Ship's going to blow!" Everyone jumps overboard; the Yankees withdraw. In June Ben and

Davie reach Washington, D.C., where they are briefed on Confederate plans to raid Yankee towns to frighten the North into sending troops to guard the Northern border states. Promoted to lieutenant, Ben, with Davie, reports to Confederate Commissioner Clement Clay for instructions, transport, rations, and clothing. Ben recruits twenty other escaped Confederate prisoners to rendezvous in Chicago; meeting on neutral Canadian soil is against the law. Ben orders his men to travel separately to St. Albans to reconnoiter and plan their raid. They each wear one piece of Confederate equipment to avoid being taken for spies. Ben (whose alias for the raid is Alan Jones) dresses as a divinity student on holiday; another is a butterfly collector; others are fishermen. They consult in Ben's hotel and fan out to learn everything they need to know about the town—hours of banks and guards, logistics of horse hiring, market day schedule, and periods the legislators are in session in Burlington and Montpelier. Two Union soldiers are in town—Captain George Conger, a discharged veteran of the First Vermont Cavalry, and Lieutenant Stuart Stranahan, a cavalryman on leave. As the Confederates carry out their assignments, they identify themselves as soldiers acting in the name of the Confederate States of America, prosecuting a legitimate act of war. Ben is forced to shoot one man—ironically, a Confederate sympathizer. The residents are marched to the village green. The raiders, their mission accomplished, form up to leave town when Conger fires at them. The raiders reach Sheldon with a troop of horsemen in pursuit. Ben torches a wagonload of hay to slow down the pursuers, and the other Confederates press on through Enosburg and Berkshire to cross into Canada. Ben and Davie climb into a hayloft to rest; Captain Conger, Lieutenant Stranahan, and five armed men capture and put them in a wagon under guard. Ben and Davie throw off their guard and drive away but are recaptured and taken to Montreal. The United States demands extradition; a hearing is called to settle this point. Ben has no copy of his commission or his official orders; the defense is given a delay to send secret agents to Richmond to collect them. The raiders become the heroes of the hour. The *St. Albans Messenger* sends them back copies of stories the newspaper ran on the raid. Union troops are rushed to the border, just as the raiders had hoped. At the last minute, a chaplain in the Confederate Army arrives with the necessary papers, and the prisoners are discharged amid cheers from the entire crowd.

Kay Avery

All for a Horse (1955) is the first novel in a trilogy about Tom Hayes (the others are *All for a Friend* and *All for a Ghost*). Tom, thirteen, has one dream—to own a horse. He, his mother and father, and sister, Sally, eleven, inhabit a village nine miles from Larson Junction on the Connecticut River. To earn money, Tom wants a job at Chump Jones's Emporium, but Andy Simpson, bossy and bigger than Tom, is also applying. Mr. Jones, a wise man who runs an outwardly chaotic enterprise, hires both boys. Tom straightens the credit slips (though it is a cash store): the two largest piles are for Judge Simms, who never pays cash because he is rich, and Mrs. Jenkins, who never pays cash because she is poor. On Saturdays, the store is jammed with shoppers. Tom suspects Andy is stealing merchandise. Mr. Smith, who does odd jobs, cannot keep his mare, Polly, because of her swollen, lame legs. Tom offers to care for her in his father's barn, taking the responsibility seriously. Mr. Jones discovers that two local suppliers, the Jason brothers, have sold him watered maple syrup. When Tom and Andy have a fistfight, Mr. Jones fires Tom for being unable to control his temper. That night Polly dies. Sad and angry, Tom cannot find another job; Sally suggests they tap the maples in their own sugar bush. The children work long, hard hours before school gathering the sap and, in the afternoons, boiling it down and carrying it into the house for transformation into syrup and straining into glass jars. Tom is grateful to Sally, who works "as hard as a boy" and is a good sport. Mr. Jones buys five gallons of the syrup and rehires Tom. Tom hears people moving around the store's cellar and calls Judge Simms. The thieves turn out to be the Jason brothers. The climax of the school year is the seventh and eighth grade race to the fire tower on Bald Top. Tom was sick last year but hopes to win this time. Mr. Jones gives him and Andy the day off and pledges a dollar to the winner. The group of runners passes farms, dogs, cows, and a colt. A mother duck and a string of ducklings cross the road: "The whole procession stopped the boys dead as a traffic light." Tom heads the pack, with Andy just behind, accompanied by his dog, Frieda. Spying a rattler, Tom shouts a warning to Andy, who, startled, falls over a cliff. Stricken with guilt, Tom works his way down the cliff to Andy, who is lying on the ground, his leg twisted. Andy commands Frieda to run for help. Andy confides to Tom that Mr. Jones has been giving him food, but Andy does not want people to know he and his mother accept charity. After this incident, the boys become close friends. Mr. Jones gives them full-time jobs and doubles their pay. Tom admires Mr. Jones and wants to protect him from people who take advantage of him. Andy recommends that Tom ride the milk truck to Larson Junction where his Cousin Jim, a veterinarian, is looking for a home for Folly, his piebald mare. Tom happily buys Folly; Jim throws her saddle and bridle into the bargain.

In ***All for a Friend*** (1956), the second in the series, Tom works at the store with Andy and also hays for Max Reuben to raise enough money to enter Folly in the county fair. At the swimming hole, the other boys propose contributing to a fund to buy firecrackers for the Fourth of July. Because Andy has no money, Tom pays Andy's share with his haying money: "A friend is more important than a horse." Tom takes Folly out the evening before the Fourth of July celebration. Suddenly, lightning splinters a pine tree. At the sound of the crash, Folly bolts. Joe, the Indian who lives up the mountain, throws himself at the horse to stop him. They take Folly to Joe's cabin to rest. People in town say Joe is "crazy," but Tom finds him wise, good, and knowledgeable about horses. Sally is helping Mrs. Jenkins run her gas pump this summer. Max Reuben has an Australian Merino lamb whose ewe will not let it nurse; Tom asks Max if Sally could care for it all summer and enter it in the fair. To earn his own money, Tom enlists Andy in a plan to sell lemonade by the gas pump. They do a brisk business. When the sawmill catches fire, everyone rushes to help. Someone circulates the rumor that Joe started the fire; Tom hates the town's prejudice against Joe. Tom and Andy, searching for Andy's dog, Frieda, surprise a large bear in the berry patch. Joe, who finds Frieda caught in a trap, frightens off the bear. When Tom arrives home, Max's lamb is dead. Feeling he failed in his responsibility, he wonders what he will have to pay Max. Max, ever "decent," asks nothing and, moreover, gives Sally a pullet. Tom still needs money to compete at the fair. He and Andy sell hot dogs at the Field Day parade and baseball game. On one of Tom's evening rides, Folly stumbles and injures her knee. Tom consults Joe, who prescribes herbs to cure her sprain. Knowing Folly is not in shape to run, Tom withdraws her from the race. Sally wins first prize for her three-fruit marmalade. With his new .22-caliber rifle, Tom goes hunting with Andy. Tom fires at a bush and finds Joe on the ground, not shot but suffering from malnutrition. Tom, horrified that he might have hurt Joe, is ashamed that he never publicly acknowledged Joe as his friend. Everyone rallies around, donating clothes and food; Tom nurses Joe back to health. In return, Joe gives him his large bow. Tom thanks him for the gift and, more importantly, for his friendship.

In ***All for a Ghost*** (1957), the third and last in the series, everyone is atwitter about a ghost in town. Andy is superstitious and believes in ghosts; Tom believes neither in ghosts nor in luck. Sam Benton, who frequents Jones's store, claims he heard peculiar sounds issuing from the Perkins house, untenanted for years. Other habitués at the store are Judge Simms and Freddie Hopkins, a slow-witted lad. Tom and Andy head for Joe's cabin in the beautiful October weather: "yellow poplars soft as butter. Sugar maples scarlet and unashamed. Giant oaks subdued but brilliant." Tom is proud that Joe, "calm and wise," is his friend. At home, Sally, in the spirit of the occasion, is reading about the headless horseman in *The Legend of Sleepy Hollow*. At Chet Peters's turkey shoot, Tom wins a goose; now he is ready for a deer. Tom rides Folly up to visit Joe and finds him skinning a great buck, which he shot with a bow and arrow. Joe's advice to Tom is, "Take life by the handle and not by the hot end." In the woods with his bow and arrow, Tom sees a doe, which looks him directly in the eyes. Tom feels sick and is afraid to shoot. On Friday the thirteenth everything goes wrong. Sally's dog, Sport, runs off; Folly is sick. At the post office, Mr. Moriarty is trapped in the box stall with his bull, Lucifer, menacing him. Quick of wit, Tom distracts Lucifer with a wooden rake, allowing the postmaster to escape through the window. After Sport makes his way home, porcupine quills worked deep into his face, one eye blinded, Tom's father has to shoot the dog. Tom determines to find the money to buy Sally another dog, but first he must cure Folly. Joe gives him some herbs for his horse. Tom confides to Joe that he failed to draw his bow on his first deer. Joe says, "You will get your deer when it is time." More ghostly signs appear, sounds continue to flow from the Perkins house, items disappear from the store, and painted signs appear on barns. Investigating the house at night, Tom finds a string running from a piano's keys to the outside; someone, unseen, could tug the string to make ghostly sounds. Tom and Andy venture out together to surprise the ghost—Freddie Hopkins. He invented the ghostly tricks because he craves attention and wants to incriminate Tom and Andy. They consult with Chet, who counsels them not to tell anyone but to encourage Freddie to use his talents in a constructive direction. Freddie is not so "dumb" as the town believes. They find Freddie a job at the store; Tom asks his parents to include Freddie at Thanksgiving: "He probably doesn't receive many invitations." Tom collects and sells butternuts to raise money for Sally's beagle. Maybe tomorrow he will bag his buck.

Susan Riley, thirteen, in ***Goodbye Blue Jeans*** (1963) also has a motive for raising money—to buy a typewriter. A tall, lanky tomboy, Susan scorns skirts and girls like that "nincompoop," Dorothy. Susan lives in Linville with her father and mother; her elder brother is stationed in Japan. Her best friend, Joe Grimes, is unaccountably attracted to Dorothy. When summer comes, and the children head to Peters's Pond to swim, they find that Samuel P. Peters has put up a "No Trespassing" sign. Susan expresses her outrage about the "meanest man in town" to her parents, who explain that Mr. Peters's wife died, his beautiful ancestral home burned to the ground, and he has no one left to love but his dog, Shep. Susan, Joe, and Fred Stevens, a bright boy whose father owns the local inn, decide to publish a weekly newspaper to influence public opinion against Mr. Peters. They call it *The Linville News*, with Fred the manager, Susan as editor, and Joe in charge of advertising. They keep the enterprise a secret and set up shop in Susan's cellar. Meanwhile, Susan's father and others meet regularly with the Water Committee to monitor the polluted town-water supply. One cause is the river that runs through Mr. Peters's unfenced cow pasture. For their first issue, Susan writes an editorial about needed improvements in recreational facilities; Fred provides a scoop—the inn is sponsoring a fancy dress ball for charity later in the summer. After she finishes the stencils for the first edition, Susan feels lonely: Fred asks her on a date, but she wishes Joe had. They sell out their print run; receipts roll in. The second week, Susan's editorial about manners being a two-way street between grown-ups and children makes the residents angry and causes some shopkeepers to cancel their advertisements. Her next editorial is an open letter to Mr. Peters about his refusing to let the children use the pond. What she cannot know is that his beloved dog, Shep, died the night before the paper comes out. Her feelings of guilt and sympathy are profound. When she tries to apologize, he will not listen. The following week, she writes an open letter to Shep to serve as his obituary. Still needing a place to swim, the three friends decide to call for volunteers to clean out the river: the editorial is titled, "Children can cooperate." Mr. Peters announces that he owns the land between the road and the river, but a selectman opines that, when Mr. Peters let the town pile rubbish on the bank, he relinquished his rights. The children work hard on the cleanup; the Men's Club donates a truckload of sand. The town doctor posts a "Water Polluted No Bathing" sign, forcing the Water Committee to make decisions about a filter for the town's water. Susan finds a stray dog, which she calls Wags and takes to Mr. Peters. Susan and Mr. Peters have a serious talk: he confesses he is still confused about the night of the fire and how it started. He says he will take down the sign at the pond and recommends that she go home and put on a skirt. Susan wonders if she has been trying too hard to be like a boy. She goes to the dance in a kimono her brother sends her from Japan. She wins the prize for the best costume—and Fred walks her home.

B

Katharine Jay Bacon

The title children in ***Pip and Emma*** (1986), twelve and ten respectively, belong in West Virginia but spend summers with their grandmother, Georgia ("Gee"), at Bell Brook Farm in the village of Doe's Crossing, adjacent to the larger town of Winston. Mount Ascutney is in the near distance. This year they are staying with Gee through the winter to enable their mother, Nell, to paint fulltime in Europe. Gee's farm is always filled with visiting friends and members of her five-daughter family. This summer her daughter, Libba, is to marry; it is also the season that Pip experiences extrasensory perception (ESP). The first time, wasps in the barn attack Emma, their friend, Joey, and Pip, who summons a special inner power to repel the pests. The second time, escaped convicts come to the farm while everyone is away at Mrs. Archer's Fourth of July picnic except Emma, who is baby-sitting with her Aunt Pam's baby. Pip, at the picnic, hears in his head Emma's calling and rushes home with Gee to save her. Pip is aware of the aura of Mamie, his great-grandmother, who became a close friend before she died. Several years earlier, he found Henry Klissen tapping their maples; now he finds evidence that Henry, a candidate for selectman, is stealing the tops of their spruces. Angry about his mother's absence, Pip cultivates the rage toward Henry that is building inside him. On a picnic, Pip tells Emma about his ESP. One afternoon, Gee goes for a long ride on her chestnut, Hal. Pip and Emma are at home when Hal returns, without a rider and covered with bee stings. The children, frantic because Gee is allergic to bee stings and did not take her antihistamine kit, follow her into the forest and become hopelessly lost. Terrified but keeping their heads, they look for water and follow the stream home. Gee, surprised to see them, explains that Hal, frightened by a rifle shot in the woods, threw her; unhurt, she walked home and was cozily having a late supper. On another ride, Pip and Emma find Flanagan clear-cutting on a neighbor's property, with Henry on the crew. Emma is coaxing her pony across a temporary bridge when the legs of the pony slip down between the crossbeams. Possibly unaware of the situation, Henry, driving the skidder, almost runs over the child and her horse; Mr. Flanagan stops him at the last moment. Pip falls ill with meningitis; Dr. Langdon tells Gee that Pip is dying. During the peak of his illness, Pip has an out-of-body experience, seeing and talking to Mamie, who is the source of his power. After Pip recovers, he makes peace with Henry and shakes hands like a man. Nell arrives in time for Libba's wedding, during which Emma and Pip exchange meaningful glances: she understands what he has undergone.

The action in ***Shadow and Light*** (1987), a sequel, takes place six years later. Emma, about to turn sixteen, is spending the summer with Gee in order to enter a statewide competition at the high school junior level for best summer work project and report. Emma, always attuned to Gee's wellbeing, immediately senses something is different: Gee, who looks older and grayer, seems close to her handsome new lawyer, Jim Fothergill. Emma reads a letter from Jim indicating that Gee is dying. Emma confesses to Gee, who, while waiting for more tests, wants Jim to arrange a way to keep the farm in the family. Gee pledges Emma to secrecy. Meanwhile, Emma's horse, Chloe, is pregnant; Emma curries her and readies the foaling stall. As Emma's routine unfolds—feeding, grooming, doctoring, training, cleaning, and exercising—she keeps meticulous notes of her tasks. Their neighbor, John Lunt, and his nephew begin haying: "The landscape [changed] as the tall, lush hay went down and the great south meadow became a geometric tapestry of silver-green windrows." Emma helps load bales in the hayloft. As always, Gee expects company for the Fourth of July. Chloe has her foal. The aunts and their children arrive; they go to Mrs. Archer's picnic. When her brother, Pip, arrives, Emma tells him the news about Gee. A local boy, Joey Perry, invites Emma to the movies and kisses her. She wonders if she wants to have a boyfriend. Returning just as an electric storm occurs, Emma finds Gee has fallen, and the telephone wires are out. Riding bareback to fetch the doctor, Emma returns just as Jim arrives and looks at her with an expression she has never seen. Gee's accident hastens the progress of her illness, but she refuses to tell her family. The loyal hired woman, Bertha, is there daily; family members visit as often as they can. When Emma comments on Gee's bravery, she says, "I am busy. I am paying attention." Gee's funeral occurs, followed by packing and cleaning. Joey continues to ask Emma out and kiss her "lavishly." She decides she does not like this game, intoxicating though it may be. She is simply bored with Joey, but she does not know why. Jim, who is in love with Emma and willing to wait until she grows up, arranges everything for the family: he finds a young couple, a doctor and his wife, as tenants for Bell Brook Farm; he locates homes for the animals; he takes care of the horse problem. Her riding friend, Lettie, buys Chloe and asks Emma to help with her riding school the following summer. Jim leaves on a business trip before Emma's sixteenth birthday, but she looks forward to their next meeting. Her heart is light: he is the one person with whom she wants to be.

The fifteen-year-old title character in ***Finn*** (1998) is sole survivor of an airplane crash that killed his parents and sister. He lives with his grandmother at Riverview Farm. A deep scar on Finn's face, a cast on his broken ankle, and a black glove on his badly burned hand are the outward signs of the accident. Inwardly, Finn is so full of pain from grief and guilt that he is literally unable to speak—a victim of elective mutism. Neighbor Julia Hatch, fourteen, was the best friend of his sister, Penny. Joyful and loving, she wants to comfort Finn; numb and dumb, he rejects her overtures and refuses to share his anguish. When they were children, Finn, Julia, and Penny made a pretend fort out of Gram's springhouse in the pinewoods. A group of drug dealers is using the well for a drop. Also in the dense woods lives a wolf dog, Toq (the reader knows his name because his is one of the points of view), which Finn glimpses one day: the two lonely, wounded creatures look deeply into each other's eyes. Julia reports that narcotics agents are in town. Meanwhile, coyotes are killing livestock; everyone assumes the culprit is the wolf dog. On the eve of Julia's departure for dance camp, she and Finn visit their old fort; on the way, they find Toq caught in a forgotten trap. Finn frees him: dog and boy bond. Before Julia leaves, she and Finn share a tender, palliative kiss. While she is away, Finn finds a dropped packet of cocaine; in a moment of desperation, he considers using some but instead takes it home to hide in his room. Julia, back again, decides to help Finn by returning the drugs to the scene. There, one of the drug dealers drops her in the well—too deep for her to climb out. Then he passes out with a lit cigarette in his hand. When Finn realizes Julia has taken the packet, he climbs with difficulty onto the aging mare, Belle, to ride to the springhouse. Smelling smoke, he is traumatized by memories of trying to rescue his family from the burning plane. When he hears Julia crying out, he shouts aloud that he is coming. Using a broken branch, he manages to lean far into the well to drag her out: Toq plants his feet on the ground and hangs onto Finn's cast with his teeth. After Finn and Julia are home safely, he goes out to the barn to thank Belle for saving them: the extreme effort has cost the loyal mare her life. Finn glances up to see Toq looking at him. The dog approaches a short distance then stops. Finn knows it will take time for Toq to trust him: he can wait.

Arthur Scott Bailey

The Tale of Muley Cow (1921) is set in the Pleasant Valley barnyard of Farmer Green, who gave Muley Cow, his oldest and favorite cow, to his son, Johnnie, eight, when he learned to milk her. The other cows are jealous, even though she is the aunt of some of them, because Farmer Green curries and brushes her in the same way he does his old horse, Ebenezer. Muley Cow jumps the fence to taste the young corn and teases Johnnie by running away at milking time, until he learns to lasso her. Cuffy Bear rises out of the thicket one day: he is more frightened than either Johnnie or Muley Cow. Billy Woodchuck's mother, a gossip, tells Aunt Polly Woodchuck that Muley Cow is wearing a poke bonnet. When they hurry to view her, they find her in the wooden collar designed to keep her from jumping over the fence. Johnnie begs his father to remove the device. Liberated, Muley Cow dances off to the millpond to have a drink: Paddy Muskrat asks her to stop before she drains the pond. Tommy Fox almost lures a young gobbler, Turkey Proudfoot, to his death. The woodchucks sneak into the cows' clover patch. Muley Cow jumps the fence to the orchard one more time, eats many apples, and staggers about making strange sounds. Farmer Green rams the whip stock down her throat to stop her from choking on a whole apple. Mr. Crow is jealous because the cows are fed all year round. Johnnie sets a Jack O'Lantern on the fence post, which frightens all the passers-by, but Muley cow knocks it off and eats up the broken pumpkin pieces. When Farmer Green buys a milking machine, Muley Cow vows never to allow him to use it on her. When he compliments her in front of the other cows, however, she agrees to set an example as always.

In ***The Tale of Nimble Deer*** (1922), the new fawn, Nimble Deer, lives with his mother near Farmer Green's. When Mr. Grouse admires her son and warns her against the foxes, Nimble Deer's mother teaches him a few defensive tricks. He steals away one night but hurries back when he sees a coon, thinking it is a fox. He loves to stand at the edge of Broad Brook nibbling water lilies and dreaming of eating carrots in Farmer Green's garden. He makes the mistake of telling Cuffy Bear, Jimmy Rabbit, and Fatty Coon about a picnic his mother is planning; when they all show up, his mother is annoyed. One night Nimble Deer and his mother are at the edge of the swamp when hunters come in a boat with a lantern (hunting with a jacklight, or deer jacking) and shoot at them, against the game warden's rules. Nimble Deer is delighted when he grows spike horns but frightened when they loosen and drop off. He samples the cabbages and carrots at Farmer's Green's, but Spot, the dog, chases him away. On Blue Mountain, Cuffy Bear shows Nimble Deer his cave. When Cuffy Bear enters the cave and does not emerge, Nimble Deer is worried, until he learns about hibernation. Soon he sprouts two-point antlers, followed each year by more. He and Dodger the Deer stage a mock battle to show off their new antlers. Brownie Beaver asks Nimble Deer to stop by his pond to give him a flag for his chimney. Nimble Deer explains that Mr. Crow was only teasing: Nimble's flag is his tail, which he waves in the air when he is startled. He has a jumping contest with Muley Cow, which he wins—but graciously. When Jimmy Rabbit gives a party, he asks Nimble to help by offering his antlers as a hat rack, though it is far too high for most of the guests.

Carolyn S. Bailey

In **"A Sugar Heart for Bethia"** (1941), March—and sugaring—are approaching. School is closed due to the amount of work on the farms. Bethia's school friend, Timothy Brewster, is on his first trading trip to Boston. When his wagon becomes stuck, she helps him shovel out because other teams are waiting on the road. After his return, he invites her to bring a girlfriend to spend an evening at his parents' maple-sugar grove up Barre Mountain. In the clearing in the center of the grove is a two-foot stone fireplace. Over the hickory-log fire sits a great iron kettle, into which the sap is poured. Bethia and Emily feast on maple sugar, alternating the sweet tastes with bites of tart pickles. Timothy makes Bethia a sugar cake in the form of a heart. She is sensitive enough to know he is taking a risk: some of the children at school will tease him about her. The shape of the cake gives her an idea: that season she and Timothy mold warm maple sugar into many shapes and take them to school in their dinner pails. Soon they are selling them at Timothy's father's store. Timothy's father goes into the business of making them; the children share in the profits. In time, the farms at the foot of Barre Mountain "become lost in the smoke of a factory or the taller chimneys of the mill," but every spring the workers go up the mountain to sugar. The old evenings' fun of sugaring off is over, but the products of a Vermont maple-sugar grove still travel all over the country.

Carin Greenberg Baker

In ***A Time to Love*** (1994), Holly Paige, seventeen, lives in modest circumstances in the small town of Landon near Burlington with her large, supportive family. Before her father, a carpenter, lost his large house when he was unable to pay the taxes, he was the mayor of the town. At that time, he opposed plans by a large tourist development company, financed and operated by the wealthy Franklin family, to build the luxurious Mountain Resort. In her last year of high school, when Holly was diagnosed with lupus (systemic lupus erythematosus, a chronic autoimmune disease that affects skin, joints, and organs), her plans for the future changed. After a year of struggling with her illness, she is in remission and working for her mother in a diner, while trying to finish her high school equivalency. A son of the influential owners of Mountain Resort, Chris Franklin, whom Holly knew in elementary school, returns to Landon from Dover Prep on his way to Yale. He and Holly fall in love, although she cannot bear to tell him her secret. Chris learns of her illness and, defying his parents and their ambitions for him, takes Holly away on a romantic trip. (This journey is the subject of Book II, *Goodbye to Love.*)

In ***Pride of the Green Mountains*** (1996), Rosalie Goodman, ten, is not so advanced in school as her younger sister, Mathilda, seven, perhaps because Rosalie dreams all day of her horse, Major, a ten-year-old bay Morgan with black mane and tail. Rosalie and Mathilda are in Morrisville in 1864 with their mother, Rachel, and their brother, Albert, nine. Their father, with his horse, Captain, Major's younger brother, is away at war with the First Vermont Cavalry. Rosalie finds her mother crying one day because she does not have enough money to meet the mortgage payment. Many of their cows died, making it impossible to keep up with the demand for their Goodman cheddar cheese. She is forced to sell Major and lay off Ed, the hired man; the children will have to stay home from school to do the chores. Heartbroken, Rosalie racks her brains to think of a way to keep the horse. One day, Eve Decker, widowed owner of the general store, starts off to Burlington with a broken-down horse; Rosalie offers to rent Major to her. When neighbor Joseph Green proposes to buy Major to clear his land, Rosalie persuades her mother to rent the horse instead. Major attacks the task of pulling logs and stumps out of deep mud with his usual intelligence and strength, while a huge hired Percheron is stymied by the job and runs away. When Rosalie is taking Major home after a day's work, a boy challenges her to a race. She wins the race and doubles Major's earnings; her mother, shocked by her gambling, makes her give back the fifty cents she won. Soon Major has a number of jobs for hire—logging, sugaring, hauling, and providing stud services. Rachel is able to rehire Ed. One day, Rosalie is riding Major home when he breaks into a gallop. Far up the road Rosalie sees a horse: it is Captain, carrying her dirty, ragged, feverish father back from the war. He is proud of Rosalie: she and Major saved the farm. (An appendix provides a list of facts about the Morgan breed.)

Jeff Barth

Jacob and Rebekah Barton in ***A Thanksgiving Story in Vermont—1852*** (1989) used to live in town with Peter and Molly, but, after Jacob lost his job in a furniture shop, they bought a country farm abandoned by a couple following the gold rush to California. In the winter, Jacob augments his income as a cooper, building barrels, casks, tubs, and pails. His old Belgian draft horse, Jeb, is retired; he uses his younger horse, Prince, for skidding logs and other heavy jobs. The belief in the goodness of God's Providence informs every undertaking of the Barton family. On Thanksgiving, Prince is lame and unable to pull the family sleigh to their grandparents' house thirty miles away in Stowe; Jacob harnesses old Jeb. Overtaken by a blizzard, the family loses its way; Jacob loosens the reins, and Jeb, remembering the trail, takes them directly to the grandparents' house. Perhaps there is a reason why Prince went lame, and they were forced to take Jeb.

Hetty B. Beatty

After his father's death (his mother died years earlier), Ken Baxter, ten, in ***Bryn*** (1965) moves to a city apartment with his Uncle John and Aunt Abbie. Uncle John grew up on a farm in Vermont, where his parents own sheep. He long ago rejected their way of life, though he keeps a camp on a lake in the northwestern part of the state. Ken's aunt and uncle take him to this camp for a month, where he is lonely and misses his father. To keep him company, Uncle John buys Ken a Border collie puppy, Bryn, and makes him promise to give up the dog at the end of their stay. Ken hopes Uncle John will change his mind, although his uncle seems unpleasant and interested only in keeping his new car clean. Ken and Bryn become inseparable and spend a blissful month together. After Uncle John reiterates that he cannot keep the dog in his apartment, Ken is so heartsick that Uncle John relents and pays a neighbor to keep the dog over the winter. They drive to the farm of Ken's grandparents, who affirm they would have been glad to keep Bryn. Meanwhile, Bryn sits by the roadside for four days waiting for Ken to return and then runs off to find him. A radio station airs a story on the runaway dog, but no one responds. A year passes in which Bryn is cold, lonely, afraid, and hungry; for a time, he befriends a hobo, Andy Mathews. During that period, Ken, unable to get along with his uncle, moves to his grandparents' farm, where he is happy. Bryn is slowly heading north. Someone looks at the name on his collar and remembers the radio show. Ken hears the report that Bryn was last seen in northwestern Massachusetts; the station offers a reward. Seventy miles away, Bryn crosses the Vermont border. Shot by a chicken farmer, he finally limps onto Ken's grandfather's property. Ken is ecstatic. At first suspicious of the dog, his grandfather begins to teach Bryn to work the sheep with his old dog, Trigger, and is pleased with Bryn's skill. With the help of two dogs, his grandfather can enlarge his herd. Taking wool to the mill in town, his grandfather meets Andy, who by coincidence is looking for a haying job. When Ken sees how attached Bryn is to his old traveling companion, he bravely concedes that Bryn may choose to go with Andy when he leaves. Bryn follows Andy for a short distance and then runs home to Ken. His aunt and uncle stop by to report that Uncle John has sold Ken's father's house, leaving Ken ample money for boarding school and college. Ken does not want to leave the farm: he loves it here, despite his uncle's scorn of farm life. Ken agrees with his grandfather's suggestion that he attend agricultural school at the University of Vermont. When a wild dog attacks the sheep and seriously wounds Trigger, Bryn saves Trigger and the sheep by killing the large dog.

Jeanne Betancourt

In ***The Rainbow Kid*** (1983), the first of five novels about Aviva Granger's growing up in Burlington (the others are *Turtle Time*, *Puppy Love*, *Crazy Christmas*, and *Valentine Blues*), Aviva, about to turn twelve, comes home from summer camp to learn that her parents have separated. Her mother, Jan, keeps the old house on Elm Street; Roy, a college professor, moves into a small apartment. Aviva, certain her parents will come together and be a family again, is in joint custody—one week with her father and one with her mother. When Aviva goes to her father's one day, she can tell that a girlfriend of her father's has been there; her mother starts seeing George O'Connell, an IBM employee. At school, Josh Greene, the most badly behaved boy in sixth grade, torments Aviva. Her best friend, Sue Crandall, has a real family—a mother, a father, and two brothers. When Roy's apartment manager will not accept Aviva's beloved dog, Mop, Aviva and Mop run away. After Mop becomes infested with ticks, Aviva hurries him home. They have a family conference about where Aviva would be happiest; she chooses to continue alternating weeks at each parent's house. At her Halloween birthday party, her parents humiliate Aviva by fighting in front of her friends. Much to Aviva's dismay, her mother hires Josh to walk Mop while she is away. When Aviva learns that Josh's mother died, his father left him, and his aging grandmother will not let him have a dog of his own, she realizes she is luckier than she thought. She is glad Josh will take care of Mop during the weeks she is away.

In ***Turtle Time*** (1985), Aviva, almost thirteen, is jealous and annoyed that George is moving into their house. Josh lends Aviva a turtle named Myrtle for her father's apartment. The new seventh grade teacher, Mr. Jackson, is a tall, stern African-American who calls the students by their surnames; he is also their gym teacher. Aviva and Josh compete for the top basketball-player slot. While Josh is in charge of Mop, the dog is hit and killed by an automobile. Aviva, heartbroken, blames Josh; Josh, who also loved the dog, is in despair. The grownups in her life beg her to forgive him; she is adamant. After Aviva sees Josh weeping at Mop's grave, she goes to his house to apologize. Together, they put stones on Mop's grave. This year, she gives up costumes for her Halloween birthday party and invites some of the boys from her class, including Josh.

In ***Puppy Love*** (1986), Aviva, now thirteen, sits next to Josh in eighth grade. Josh's elderly grandmother died; he lives in St. Joseph's Home for Boys and works for Angelo's Animal Care after school. Jan, married to George, is pregnant; George's college-aged daughter, Cindy, also lives with them. Aviva's father, Roy, has moved into the apartment of his new girlfriend, Miriam. He now runs a clothing store for men in the mall; Miriam manages Miriam's Magic, a boutique. Jan has her baby, John Edward Linton O'Connell, whom Aviva dubs "Jelo." Sometimes Aviva feels she does not belong anywhere: when Roy and Miriam argue, Aviva wonders if she is to blame; at Jan's house, everyone's attention centers on the baby. Aviva and her group of girlfriends go out together on Saturday nights, hoping to see some of the high school students. They drop in at Miriam's Magic, where Miriam gives Aviva a beautiful sweater, making Aviva suspect that Miriam is trying to buy her affection. Josh's father, who disappeared after Josh's birth twelve years earlier, suddenly returns. Josh, shocked, runs away. George and Aviva search for Josh to tell him that his father returned only to find out if Josh's mother left any money when she died. On her fourteenth birthday, Aviva goes to the high school dance, acting, under Miriam's counsel, "confident and nonchalant." Bob Hanley, whom she greatly admires, dances with her—but just to make his girlfriend jealous. Josh rescues Aviva and takes her to the movies.

In ***Crazy Christmas*** (1988), Aviva continues to struggle with being a "joint-custody kid." The most trying time of year is Christmas, when she divides her time between the two households for the festivities. Even worse, Jan, George, and their family are leaving the comfortable old house where Aviva grew up for a farmhouse about nine miles from Burlington. Aviva hates saying goodbye to her familiar room and finds the farmhouse "grungy." Miriam's pristine and sophisticated condominium is quite a contrast; Aviva's new puppy, Willie, a present from Josh, is not welcome there. Aviva's main present from Roy and Miriam is a trip to New York City. When they suggest she bring "a friend," she invites Josh. Just before Aviva goes on her trip, George tells Aviva that he and Jan want Josh to live with them as part of their family and asks her to think about it. She already knows her answer: "No." The trip to New York City is full of exciting activities, but the most serious for Josh and Aviva is a search for his father, whose address was on file at the orphanage. They find him drunk in a bar, where Josh screams at him. They return to the hotel without telling the grownups. Then Josh disappears, believing his duty is to stay with his father. Roy accompanies

Aviva to find Josh. To persuade Josh to come home with them, Aviva tells him that Jan and George want him to join the family on their farm. When Aviva arrives home, the family has made over her bedroom, with fresh paint, new curtains, and lovely feminine touches. She knows there is plenty of love in the house for everyone—including Josh. The first day Josh stays in his room for hours. Aviva worries that he is unhappy. When he comes downstairs, he presents her with hand-carved bookends—Myrtle on one end, Willie on the other. Aviva loves the fact that bookends are like families: "they hold you up." When it is time to choose his place at the circular dining table, Josh sits next to Aviva, "just like at school."

In ***Valentine Blues*** (1990), Aviva and Josh, both fourteen, now ride the school bus together during the weeks Aviva is not with Roy and Miriam. The other girls in Aviva's grade think Josh is "cute." Roy and Miriam still work at the mall and continue to have extended fights. One night at dinner with them, Aviva feels in the way and procures a ride to her mother's house with Lily, the daytime bus driver. Arriving unexpectedly, Aviva finds that her mother and George are out; Josh is babysitting with Jelo and entertaining his friend, Ronnie Cioffi. Aviva does not reveal her presence, because Josh is breaking a house rule by having company while babysitting. She overhears them opening cans of beer and discussing the relative merits of the girls in their grade. Humiliated, Aviva feels unloved and unwanted in her two homes. Jealous that Jan and George think Josh is perfect, Aviva tattles on Josh, who is punished. Aviva is furious with Josh—with everyone. Her parents ask if she would rather stay full-time at one household or the other. She begs them not to make her choose. Aviva and Josh apologize: people who live in the same house should trust each other.

More than Meets the Eye (1990) raises some issues of racial prejudice in Ethan Allen High School and in the town of Rutland. Elizabeth Gaynor, fifteen, has grown up there. Her mother, Diane, is a nurse's aide; her father, Tom, runs the local shoe store and is president of the Chamber of Commerce. Elizabeth is a superlative student; her parents are ambitious for her to be first in her class, valedictorian, and a student at the University of Vermont. Elizabeth's science-laboratory partner is a Chinese-American, Benjamin Lee, who vies with her for first place in their sophomore class. He is self-possessed, mature, and slightly mysterious: she finds him appealing. Her childhood friend, Brad Mulville, "oversized, loud, dumb," has not kept up with Elizabeth socially or intellectually. When school opens, a Cambodian woman, a two-year resident of Vermont, enters her refugee niece in the school. Elizabeth guides Dary Sing, who speaks no English, through her first weeks of school. At the Valentine's Day party, Ben and Elizabeth dance together and acknowledge their mutual attraction. Brad, jealous and angry, shouts offensive remarks at Ben. Because Ben's parents, who run the local Chinese restaurant, are traditional, he must keep secret his relationship with Elizabeth. Ben and Elizabeth hold hands at the movies: Elizabeth has never been so happy. As she spends time with Dary, inventing ways to increase her English vocabulary, Elizabeth's parents pressure her to study harder. Brad is more and more unpleasant to Ben, using disgusting language. A Korean family moves to Rutland, buys the Italian vegetable-and-fruit market, and affixes an "open twenty-four hours" sign, which outrages the downtown merchants. Brad, pining for Elizabeth and for some self-esteem, starts doing his homework and volunteers to help the two new Korean students. He and Ben have an altercation every time they meet. Elizabeth and Ben's relationship goes awry: she finds him prejudiced toward the new Asian students. Tom fears that cultural differences will divide the residents. Elizabeth and Ben reconcile. He realizes that he, too, has been prejudiced, unwilling, as someone born in America, to be considered part of an immigrant group. He also concedes he should not have responded to Brad's taunts by calling him "stupid." A town meeting confronts the issues of diversity, the young people are friends again, and Ben and Elizabeth are serious about each other.

Cynthia Blair

The seventeen-year-old Pratt twins, Christine and Susan, in ***The Candy Cane Caper*** (1987) are surprised when their parents decide to celebrate a second honeymoon in Mexico and send the girls to Ridgewood near Montpelier to stay with their grandparents over Christmas. They are even more surprised when their grandparents decide to sell their house and move to a retirement village in Florida. The twins meet two young men, Andy Connors, who does odd jobs for their grandfather, and Brian Barker, who is paying for his tuition at the local university by working part-time at Ridgewood Children's Hospital. When Brian tells the girls the hospital may close for lack of funds, they see a double opportunity: to organize a Christmas Bazaar to raise funds for the hospital and to demonstrate to their grandparents that they are vitally needed in Ridgewood. The bazaar is a vast success, and, in the process of engaging the community, the girls learn of suspicions that Mr. Stone, the hospital administrator, is an embezzler. During the Christmas Eve party at the hospital, Christine and Susan switch identities to trick Mr. Stone into thinking both of them are at the party, when one is actually finding the incriminating evidence in his office. They surpass their goals with the arrest of Mr. Stone, the saving of the hospital, and the decision of their grandparents to stay in Ridgewood.

Lenore Blegvad

In ***Kitty and Mr. Kipling*** (2005), Rudyard Kipling, back in England in 1896, sends Mary Sadie ("Kitty") her inscribed copy of *The Jungle Book*. In 1892, Kitty, eight, lives in Dummerston with her mother, logger father, and brother, Silas, ten. The neighborhood feels invaded (reporters are everywhere) when the famous English author, Rudyard Kipling, and his American wife, Caroline, buy property belonging to her brother, Beatty Balestier. Everyone says that Beatty acts wild, drinks, and gets into trouble. At first the Kiplings rent Bliss Cottage in Dummerston. Kitty, calling on them one day with a blueberry pie from her mother, overhears Mrs. Kipling tell her husband that he must hurry and "dress" for dinner. Kitty cannot imagine what she means. She learns that they have a serving maid from Sweden. Mr. Kipling tells Kitty he has a muse (he calls it his "daemon") to help him write and reads her the first words of *The Jungle Book*. The Kiplings have no Vermont friends; her mother tells Kitty it is because he has been "disrespectful" about America. Mr. Kipling is building a big new house with Beatty's assistance, but he needs Kitty's father's help with renovations at Bliss Cottage because Mrs. Kipling is expecting a baby. When snow falls, "thick, silent, and lovely," Kitty teaches Mr. Kipling to snowshoe; he shows her how to play snow-golf. After little Josephine is born, a nanny comes from England. Beatty finishes the house—called "Naulakha," meaning "precious jewel" in Hindi—and the family moves in. Then everything goes wrong. Neighbors think Mrs. Kipling is a snob: she hires a coachman from England. Mrs. Kipling becomes more and more upset with her brother. She plants a garden on land that Beatty wants to keep in meadow to feed his animals. They do not speak to each other. Naulakha's fancy water pump breaks; the Kiplings must use water from Beatty's well. By this time Kitty is eleven; Josephine, three. Kitty no longer feels brave or confident like Mowgli. Kitty and Mr. Kipling continue to meet and talk. When he asks what she wants to do, she says she has no plans. He tells her that whatever she decides to do, she must do it "proudly" and take a great "interest" in it. "To be doing, to be working, to be a person of action, that's what tells us who we are in the universe." She thinks his meaning is like one of her father's sayings: "The world is your cow, but it's you who has to do the milking." The gossips say Beatty is bankrupt; her father says, "Say nothing and saw wood." When Beatty threatens to kill Mr. Kipling, the Kiplings have him arrested. The feud spirals out of control and reaches the pages of *The New York Times*. Kitty thinks Mr. Kipling probably assumed the sheriff would tell Beatty how to behave, and he would obey, like Mowgli and the wolf pack with the Law of the Jungle. Spectators and reporters fill the town of Brattleboro. Kitty offers to go to Naulakha every day after school to cheer up Josephine. When Mr. Kipling leaves town for a few days, he gives Kitty a little notebook to record for him what happens in the nursery. One afternoon, she is with Mr. Kipling at the house. The sky was a "perfect blue." "Beyond the meadow below them a row of dark pines stood as still as soldiers." Mr. Kipling looks off at Mount Monadnock, that "giant thumbnail pointing heavenward," as he calls it. Kitty knows he and his family are leaving forever. When they say goodbye, she quotes her father: "Long hellos and short goodbyes are best." She does not cry until she is outside. She finds one of Kipling's lost golf balls and carries the treasure home. She is going to be a writer about "ordinary things but somehow not so ordinary after all." (For an adult novel about a child's friendship with Rudyard Kipling in Dummerston, see Victoria Vinton's *The Jungle Law*.)

Larry Bograd

In **"Willie and the Christmas Spruces"** (2005), Willie Johnson, twelve, lives on a farm in Saint Johnsbury with his parents and elder sister, Kate, nineteen, the single mother of a baby. Frost and snow come early this year, which is good news for skiers, but not for the Johnsons, who depend for some of their scarce cash on the sugaring they do in the fall. As they deliver their small amount of syrup to the distributor in White River Junction, their old truck shows signs of breaking down; Kate turns toward home off Interstate 91 to follow Route 5 through the small towns along the Connecticut River — East Thetford, Fairlee, Bradford, Wells River. The river is "a frozen gray, like trapped smoke." Their two-hundred-year-old stone house has been in the family for four generations; Willie has never lived anywhere else. He knows his parents are worried about money; the baby has a bad cold and few warm clothes. When he helps his father cut down a spruce for their Christmas, he has an idea: Christmas trees are fetching thirty dollars in town; why not cut down a truckload of spruces to sell in Boston for a great deal more? His parents cannot leave the farmwork, but they permit Kate and Willie to make the run. The drive is exhausting and the day, frustrating: they are ultimately forced to reduce their prices, but they manage to sell all the trees, bringing home almost five hundred much-needed dollars. Willie is sad to see the bare stumps the next morning, but he knows their fresh trees will give people pleasure on Christmas day; better still, the brother and sister have spent a wonderful, productive day together and appreciate each other even more. (The accompanying teaching unit discusses the way the author establishes the setting, which is central to the story.)

Carole Bolton

The Dark Rosaleen (1964) takes place in New York City, where Barbara Leventhal, sixteen, and her sister, Carolyn, thirteen, enjoy comparative comfort with their Irish Catholic mother, Maggie, and Jewish father, Louis. Also staying with them is Maggie's father, Desmond ("Pop") Ryan, a janitor at Gotham House, a residential hotel. Barbara, who has some snobbish ideas, is embarrassed that Pop works where some of her friends live. His kind and ebullient ways banish her unworthy feelings. These prejudices reemerge, however, when Pop buys a car, which he names Rosaleen, and she meets, at the garage where he has the car serviced, a young mechanic, Ben Stone. She is immediately attracted to him, but her classist sensibilities are alerted: what could they possibly have in common? After all, he has not read *A Catcher in the Rye*. She lays plans to remold him into an appropriate suitor. The rest of the novel tests Barbara's love for Ben, who is "straightforward, pure, and unassuming." The Vermont episode occurs when Pop invites Barbara, Ben, and Carolyn to accompany him to test Rosaleen's prowess on the road. Leaving the Merritt Parkway, they head up Route 7, spending a night in Rutland and pressing on to St. Albans, where Pop tells them about the Confederate raid. They head to Mount Mansfield, and then to Smugglers' Notch, and finally to a motel near Stowe. They turn south to Mount Snow and back to New York. It is a glorious trip. When Pop dies later in an automobile accident, Barbara often thinks of how happy he was, singing on the Vermont roads. (The title comes from a nineteenth century Irish ballad by James Clarence Mangan.)

Gary Bowen

The initial letters of the towns in ***The Mare's Nest*** (2001) spell "whitewasher," which is the clue to the mystery. In 1846, an itinerant artist learns from the farmers he visits that their animals are vanishing. A mare disappears from Whitingham, a rabbit from Heartwellville, a cow from Ira, black sheep from Thetford, gray goats from Ewell's Mills, a dog from Wallace Pond, sheep from Albany, cygnets from Swanton, hens from Hinesburg, and calico cats from East Middlebury. In Rutland panic sets in. A widow from Whiteface Farms brings her famous white livestock to auction at the county fair. When torrential rains fall, it becomes clear that the animals are not naturally white—their true identity has been disguised with whitewash. The citizens have been victims of a "mare's nest"—a hoax.

Bianca Bradbury

In ***Laughter in Our House*** (1964), Gilly Lannon, seventeen, is a junior at a private school in New York City; her brother, Emmett, is a junior at Yale. When their mother, Eileen, has a nervous breakdown, a psychiatrist prescribes a summer in the country. Both young people have other plans, but, on the financial advice of Bob Ames, their mother's attorney, they respond to the emergency by buying a house near Lake Champlain. The "old Dennison house," built in 1782, stands on Cobble Hill in Foxton, a crossroads near the town of North Melton. The house is filthy, with no electricity, indoor plumbing, or telephone. Gilly and Emmett hire a local contractor named Shedd, whose elder children, John ("Woody") and Sue, are two attractive, red-haired contemporaries of the Lannons. Once Gilly and Emmett see work begin on the house, their spirits rise. Two-hundred-year-old oak boards gleam beneath layers of old carpets and newspapers. Eileen, once a hard-driving advertising executive, is a different person—lethargic, silent, and bored. The Shedds, who become great friends of the Lannons, give Eileen a large cat, Mose, which seems to please her. Eileen tends to wander off and to act in odd and distracted ways; the neighbors comment upon her behavior. Gilly and Emmett question whether they are equal to the challenge of caring for her. Their only diversion is to see as much as they can of Sue and Woody; two love affairs are brewing. One day, the four take the ferry to Lake Champlain and return to swim on the Vermont shore, leaving Eileen with a neighbor. When they reach home, Eileen has vanished. The police find her in Pittsfield, Massachusetts. The children wonder what they will do with their mother when they are back at school. On a ride with Woody, Gilly's horse throws her to the ground, injuring the hand on one arm and breaking the other. Trying to light a match for the stove, Gilly ignites the gauze wrapping on her hand and screams for help. The experience arouses a passionate protectiveness in Eileen that jars her out of her disturbed state. She weeps profusely over Gilly (who is not hurt) and emerges as her old self. Emmett diagnoses the problem: "not enough tears, not enough laughter" in the house.

B

Ann Brashares

Forever in Blue (2007), the fourth in a series about four teenagers who share a pair of special blue jeans as a token of their friendship, follows the young women's experiences through one summer between freshman and sophomore college years. Tibby is going to New York, Lena to Greece, Bridget to Turkey, and Carmen Lowell to the Village Summer Theater Festival in central Vermont. Carmen, who felt "dull, mute, invisible" at Williams College, compensated by overeating, and was surprised when Julia Riley, witty, gregarious, and stylish, befriended her. It is Julia who persuaded Carmen to work on sets in college theatrical productions and to go to Vermont with her. The Vermont performing arts center is not far from Dartmouth on a hill overlooking a "lush, sweet" valley. Carmen frankly wonders what Julia sees in her, since Julia is frequently condescending and cold. Three simultaneous productions are planned for the Main Stage, the Second Stage, and the Community Stage. A professional director, Andrew Kerr, is directing *The Winter's Tale* on the Main Stage, with professional actors in his cast. Julia continually asks Carmen to hear her lines for the part of Perdita. Urged by the casting director, Carmen tries out for and wins the role of Perdita. Julia, who is given a minor part at the end of the Community Stage production, is cold with fury and jealousy. Carmen, who started out the summer feeling "lost and undeserving," becomes a happy person again and wears pretty clothes and cosmetics. She reads and rereads the play to absorb Perdita's character. Her fellow actors love her. Once Julia sees how successful Carmen is, she sets out to sabotage her. She marks up Carmen's script under the pretext of explaining the meter to her. She confuses her by urging her to read heavy tomes about Elizabethan drama. She almost succeeds in spoiling Carmen's performance. Fortunately, the casting director takes Carmen aside and begs her to "trust herself." Carmen recognizes Julia's purpose and resists her offers of fattening food and poisonous advice; she avoids Julia and the script and slowly becomes the character of Perdita again. Opening night, her three best friends are in the audience; she rediscovers her "simplicity" and her compassion for Perdita, the lost girl who was found. "Carmen's winter ended and she felt the return of her own extravagance."

Alice Brown

When her Aunt Tabitha goes to Europe to study singing in ***The Secret of the Clan*** (1912), Laura Whiteley, thirteen years old, spends a year in Montpelier with her three second cousins, Marcia, Kate, and Ruth Baker, and their step-grandmother, Amelia. Amelia, who is gracious, kind, and beautiful, tries to make Laura, who lacks self-confidence, feel a part of the Clan, as she calls the family. The other member of the Clan is Uncle Terry, who, the children tell Laura, is a widower. Their governess leaves; they await a new one at Christmastime. Amelia's house, close to the capitol, abuts a huge wood called "The Plantation," where stands a Playhouse, which they call the House of the Clan. Laura suggests they pretend to be an Indian tribe and assume appropriate names. Each makes a resolution (Ruth's is to overcome her fear of the dark), and all swear secrecy. In the evenings, they play backgammon and read *Little Women*. Sometimes, during the day, the children walk over to the State House and play in the Senate Chamber. They run down the River Road, scuffing yellow leaves. It is fall, and Laura loves the "soft enchantment of the hour when the mists rolled off the nearby hills and they stood out, all purple-black and soft, and the world smelled of apples and pears and ripened leaves." Ruth disappears one evening to spend the night in the Senate Chamber. The children, knowing her purpose and honoring their oath, refuse to tell Amelia where she is. Amelia, deciding she has failed in her duties as disciplinarian, sends for their other grandmother, Susan, cross and authoritarian, who announces that she will take Ruth home with her. The other children rebel, saying they refuse to be separated. Amelia introduces a beautiful young lady, Maisie Delorme, as their temporary governess. The children are enchanted with Maisie, who looks like a princess. Uncle Terry seems oddly upset by her presence, often stares at her strangely, and leaves the room while she is there. She confesses that she does not know what a governess does but will teach them French, German, Italian, and dancing. She helps them to write and perform a play about Little Red Riding Hood, making the costumes themselves, and sets them to memorizing parts for *The Merchant of Venice*. Uncle Terry receives some marvelous news: Mr. Drayton, a famous producer, wants to start rehearsals for his new play right away. Amelia reveals that Maisie and Uncle Terry are married (he was never a widower), but they quarreled over her acting in one of his plays. Now they have resolved their differences. Word comes from Europe that Aunt Tabitha is to marry Paul Meredith; Laura can stay with her grandmother and her cousins.

Edna A. Brown

In ***At the Butterfly House*** (1918), Charles Dexter, a schoolteacher, grew up in Ridgefield in his Aunt Nancy's "Butterfly House." At her death, she bequeathed the house to a cousin, Anthony

Davenport; Charles received an antique secretary and a rag doll. Now Charles is returning to Vermont as principal of Ridgefield High School with his wife, Anne, and daughters Cary, fifteen, and Christine, five. Cousin Anthony, who has always wanted to make reparation, offers them the use of Butterfly House. Lizzie Phillips takes over the housekeeping duties, as she did for Aunt Nancy. Candace Halliday, sixteen, lives in a cottage with her grandmother on Thorn Mountain; her parents are dead. Each morning before going to school, Candace completes the farm chores, carries the milk down to market, and does housework for a woman in the village. She yearns sometimes for the advantages that the other girls enjoy, but her grandmother reminds her that her ancestors helped settle Ridgefield when the valley was a wilderness. Charles Dexter was a friend of Candace's father. Cary makes friends with Amy Richards, whose father is the minister and whose brothers are serious Cutler and mischievous Van. Cary is jealous of Candace, who is both clever and beautiful. When Cary's French exercise book goes missing, she jumps to the conclusion that Candace took it to achieve a higher grade in French than Cary. When Candace finds the book among her possessions and apologizes, Cary is ungracious. The Hatch Prize is given annually for the best declamation. Cary is annoyed that Candace has chosen the poem Cary wanted to recite. Her gentle and mannerly parents are disappointed that Cary is so competitive, particularly since Candace needs the monetary award. Candace and Van win the two prizes. When Candace's grandmother dies, Dexter offers to act as Candace's guardian; he will hold her property until she is of age and, in the meantime, invites her to stay with them to continue her schooling. Anne, an artist, sells a painting of Candace, using the fee to buy her some pretty clothes. Cary begrudges the attentions Candace lavishes on Cary's mother. Cary, Candace, and two boys are chosen from the sophomore class to speak for three minutes before the whole school on a topic of current interest. Candace's subject is the introduction of the British tank on the battlefield of the Somme. She is aghast when Cary, who is first, speaks on the same topic to try to rattle Candace. Instead of losing her head, Candace speaks extemporaneously about women's war work. After Anne is hurt in a sledding accident, Cary and Candace make up. While they are walking together, a truck, out of control, heads for two children in the street. Quick as lightning, Candace pushes the children out of harm's way. A reporter from a New York weekly witnesses the event; the Carnegie Hero's Fund awards Candace two thousand dollars for heroism, enabling her to attend college. At last Cousin Anthony discovers a transfer deed: Butterfly House belongs to the Dexters.

Joseph Bruchac

In ***Hidden Roots*** (2004), the atmosphere is uneasy in the New York household of Howard ("Sonny") Camp, eleven. Jake, Sonny's father, is angry; Martha, his mother, is keeping a secret from him. The year is 1954: Jake works at the paper mill; Martha seems different from other mothers. Sonny loves his Uncle Louis Lester, but his father objects to Uncle Louis's presence. Sonny wonders why Uncle Louis never had children. Uncle Louis tells Sonny that Jake's greatest disappointment came after he enlisted in the marines in World War II, when he was injured badly in a motorcycle accident, and his unit went overseas without him. Uncle Louis says Sonny is "tall enough to see the mountaintop" and takes him and Martha to Vermont to see some deer, even though Uncle Louis hates the state. To Sonny, "Vermont seemed to be so strange and far away, a place with something about it that was mysterious and maybe even a little threatening." Sonny imagines something bad happened to Uncle Louis in Vermont, maybe something to do with Indians, whom Sonny knows little about. They arrive in Arlington, where the mountains are close to the road, "leaning over us like friendly giants." Uncle Louis drives to a spot where a herd of deer grazes on a hillside. They walk slowly among the deer, holding out their hands and softly saying "hello" to each one. Not a deer runs away. A tourist drives up and shouts out the window; the deer take flight. "They were gone from my sight, but not from my memory." The next day, Sonny's father shows him the river where the plant is dumping toxic waste from making paper. Uncle Louis tells Sonny about his experience as a lumberman and the cruel treatment of the Indians, many of whom were forced to hide their heritage. At the plant, a fire rages; Sonny's father heroically saves lives and loses part of his hand in the process. He cannot hunt; Uncle Louis provides a deer for the family's winter food. Sonny's father repeats that he does not want Uncle Louis hanging around—"people will notice." Jake keeps his head down at school, trying to be invisible, but he likes Mrs. Rosen, the librarian, who is Uncle Louis's friend, too; he explains to Sonny that she lost her family in the Holocaust. Now that Jake cannot work, Martha takes a job at the five-and-dime store; Uncle Louis stays with Sonny after school and cooks supper. Finally, Louis explains to Sonny about his hidden roots. Uncle Louis's wife, Sophia Lester, was from Highgate. In 1932, under a Vermont law, the state sterilized Sophia—not because she was "feeble-minded," but because she was an Indian. The Lesters, Uncle Louis continues, are primarily Abenaki; Jake Camp has some Indian blood, too. In Vermont, Indians were treated like gypsies. Sophie and Louis had one child, Martha. Sophie died after the operation and, because the state was taking Indian people's children away, Louis gave Martha to a kind, loving white couple named Henry. Jake did not want Sonny to know about his roots, but, according to Uncle Louis, "roots are what help a tree stand up against the wind." Finally, Jake and Louis accept each other; the family members embrace.

Marge Bruchac

Malian's Song (2006) recounts the experience of a seven-year-old Abenaki Indian girl and her extended family during the French and Indian War. The story is set in the village of Odanak, on the St. Francis River near the St. Lawrence, north of Montreal, in October 1759. Malian fishes with her father, helps her grandmother pack for winter camp, and carries corn into storage, before falling asleep when her cousin, Maliazonis, goes off to join in a great feast and celebration at the Council House. In the middle of the night, Maliazonis receives an unexpected warning that the village is about to be attacked; the elders take the children to a safe hiding place at the ravine north of the village. Malian is almost forgotten, but her father Simôn rescues her before daybreak when the village is set on fire by the man whom the Abenaki people still call the "White Devil"—English Major Robert Rogers. Young Malian makes a "Lonesome Song" to commemorate the thirty-two people, including her father, who died in the raid, and later, as an old woman, she recounts these events to her grandchildren. (The author wrote to me that "Abenaki people living at Odanak, Missisquoi, Cowass, and other village sites across present-day Vermont were all closely related and moved back and forth between these sites frequently, before the Canadian border or the state of Vermont even existed. The book draws on Abenaki oral traditions, French Jesuit records, and other historical sources to reveal the fact that Rogers inflated the number of dead in his official account and to show how one of his own scouts, a Stockbridge Mohican man named Samadagwis, warned the Abenaki villagers. The historically accurate illustrations and the historical essay that ends the book include substantive details about Abenaki history for sophisticated readers of any age. The uplifting ending stresses the importance of family and memory.")

Bonnie Bryant

In ***Snow Ride*** (1992), Stevie Lake, sixteen, belongs to the Saddle Club, a group of young women riders at the Pine Hollow Stable in Virginia. A former member of Pine Hollow, Dinah Slattery, invites Stevie to spend a week in Vermont. Sugarbush, where Dinah rides, holds a competition each year to identify the trio of young riders collecting the most sap. With their third teammate, Betsy Hale, the three girls insert their spiles (spigots) and hang their buckets. During the sugaring off, members are not allowed to ride the trails, according to rules set by the director, Mr. Daviet. Dinah asks Betsy's sister, Jodi, the person in charge at Sugarbush, for permission to take out two horses. With Stevie on Evergreen and Dinah on Goldie, they head for the Rocky Road Trail. Frightened by the booming of melting ice, Goldie takes off. Loosened rocks roll down the hill in an avalanche. Goldie rears, flinging Dinah into the path of the oncoming rocks. Stevie urges Evergreen into a canter straight at Dinah and hauls her onto her horse's rear end. Dinah, knowing they have broken the rules, refuses to see a doctor, although she is seriously bruised, and swears Stevie to secrecy. They all go to the Sugar Hut that night to watch the sap bubbling in the evaporation area. They enjoy sugar-on-snow. When Dinah hears that her parents plan to ride the Rocky Road Trail, she confesses to Mr. Daviet about their expedition. Now that the secret is out, the Slatterys take Dinah to a doctor, and, as punishment, forbid her to ride for a month. Mr. Daviet fires Jodi, holding her responsible for letting the girls ride that day when she knew that the trail was unsafe. Stevie returns home to tell her friends about sugaring.

Louella Bryant

The Black Bonnet (1996) recounts the exhausting, dangerous escape in 1858 of two slave sisters from Roanoke, Virginia. Bea, sixteen, is a field slave; Charity, twelve, a house slave. The two girls spend a night in Vergennes; the next day they stop with the Robinsons at Rokeby mansion in Ferrisburgh. On the way to Burlington and the church on Pearl Street, Charity is mistaken for a white girl: the knowledge of this confusion becomes her secret weapon. At the church, Reverend Joshua Young welcomes them; Lucius Bigelow, the newspaper owner, carries them to his house in the fake bottom of his wagon. They hide in his attic with an old woman; two male slaves seek refuge in the cellar, connected by a tunnel to the female seminary next door. Both sisters are worn out; Bea seems ill. Because Charity can pass as white, Cecilia Young lends her some clothes, including a large black bonnet, and takes her on a tour of Burlington. At the train station, they spot slave hunters loitering; one is Hendrick, whom Charity knows Bea fears. Charity saves Cecilia from drowning when she breaks through the ice in the lake. Franklin Boggs, an injured fugitive in the cellar, wants to go to Liberia. Bigelow, who knows the head of the local Colonization Society, believes he can help. While Bea tends Franklin, they fall in love. Bea reveals to Charity that her father was Master Pearson; Bea slept with overseer John Morris in exchange for his help in their escape and became pregnant. The fugitives separate: Bea and Franklin head in one direction; Charity goes with Ellen and William Craft to Canada. Once safely there, she receives a package from Cecilia Young containing the old black bonnet and the news that Hendrick recaptured Frederick and Bea—the former, carried off in chains; the latter, dead. Charity writes to her stepsister, Elizabeth Pearson in Roanoke, saying she knows her true identity and hopes they may meet one day. (Reverend Young was an historical character, as was Lucius Bigelow and others in the novel. For Dorothy Canfield Fisher's adult story about Reverend Young, under the name Ellsworth, see "Deep Channel," from the collection, *Raw Material*. The controversial American Colonization Society, with a branch in Vermont, formed in 1819 to raise funds to purchase slaves and return them to Africa.)

Pearl S. Buck

"The Christmas Secret" (1972) is set in the Green Mountains, where David and Mary Alston grew up and went to high school together. They now live in the "rambling white frame house with the green shutters, stretching from the parlor on the south, their living room, to the old barn at the far end, next to the big maple tree." Their family consists of two boys and a little half-Vietnamese girl, Susan, whom they have recently adopted. They had learned, by mistakenly opening a letter addressed to "Mr. Alston," that the little girl was the daughter of David's brother, Richard, fathered when he was in Vietnam. David decided not to tell his single-minded, politically ambitious brother about his daughter; David and Mary are enchanted with Susan, who has the Alston blond hair and bright blue eyes—"so odd in that little Asian face," exclaims Mary dotingly.

Christmas Day, snow, and Richard and his wife, Miranda, arrive. David and Mary are disquieted by the suspense: will Richard somehow recognize and claim Susan, the loveliest child they have ever seen? They need not have worried: the self-absorbed couple barely notices Susan. (Two adult stories in the collection—implicitly, "A Certain Star" and, explicitly, "Christmas Verities"—also take place in Vermont.)

B

David Budbill

The three stories in ***Snowshoe Trek to Otter River*** (1976) are about Daniel and Seth, both eleven, and center on three seasons—winter, spring, and autumn. In winter, Daniel meticulously packs his equipment for an outing, knowing that gear is important, especially if one is caught in a blizzard. His parents are dairy farmers; a French-Canadian neighbor, Bateau, a hunter, fisherman, and trapper, is his mentor. Daniel heads for the Otter River to check on a lean-to that he and Seth built the year before. On snowshoes, he starts to cross the river when the ice opens, and in he falls. He uses his hatchet to hack his way to shore; when his wet clothes meet the cold air they freeze. He coaxes a fire into flame, hangs his clothes on a pole, and climbs into a sleeping bag where he rests for a short while.He wants to be home before dark. Realizing he is lost, he thinks calmly about the way to retrace his steps. He arrives home safely. In spring, Daniel and Seth travel by canoe down the Tamarack into Bear Swamp. To fend off bugs, they use a strong concoction whose smell they love: "It meant adventure. It meant wilderness." They push through alders and beaver dams to reach the lake —"a wild and secret place." They fish for trout and catch a big one for an ideal lunch of bacon, bread and butter, fish, and tea. In autumn, on "one of those perfect October days, crisp and cool as a carrot," Seth and Daniel argue about whether to spend the night in the woods. Seth decides to go alone. In this season, "a time of clarity and stillness," Seth plans to hike to the camp he and Daniel built on Bear Swamp. He looks into Isaiah Morey's sugarhouse, where he finds a dead porcupine. He glimpses a passing hunter carrying two grouse. At the bottom of the falls, Seth finds a deer skull. Their camp is in good shape, supplied with a modest amount of equipment, such as a tea pail. A great blue heron rises out of the cattails. Seth left his food and cook pots somewhere on the trail; he improvises, finding berries, wintergreen for tea, and cattail roots to substitute for potatoes. He catches and eats two trout. He is nervous in the night and feels "loose in his bones," but he has accomplished what he set out to do.

In a sequel, ***Bones on Black Spruce Mountain*** (1978), Daniel and Seth, now thirteen, have been friends for five years, ever since Daniel's parents adopted him. Their fathers' farms adjoin each other in Judevine. Their neighbor, Bateau, taught them everything they know about camping and fishing. He tells them about an orphan who lived in Hardwick seventy-five years earlier, was beaten by his foster father, and ran away to live on Black Spruce Mountain ("which stood above its neighbors like a huge fist thrust against the sky"), where the boy died. According to legend, his skeleton still lies there; Daniel and Seth undertake an expedition to look for the bones. They arrange their supplies and fill their backpacks (a useful list is included of what they take). They begin hiking. "The August sun made jigsaw patterns of light and dark as it danced across the forest floor." Before long, they pass the ruins of Isaiah Morey's sugarhouse. While organizing the campsite, they experience their first fight; it seems to Seth that Daniel is angry about something. Experienced campers, they set up their lean-to, build a fire, fashion implements, dig a toilet, and lay out hemlock boughs for a bed. They fish for high wild mountain trout for their supper. They cook a real meal, including a pot of potatoes, beans, and onions, and make club bread to accompany their trout. The next day, they hike to Eagle Ledge and on to Black Spruce Mountain, where they find a well, lined with stones. They realize someone once lived here. A cave is filled with the items farmers reported missing—an old shovel, the remains of a horse blanket, the blade of a hoe. They know now the story is true, but they find no bones. From the top of the mountain, they can glimpse

Hardwick, the place from which the boy escaped. They can also see Seth's and Daniel's farms and, sixty miles to the west, "the blurred crooked ribbon" of Lake Champlain. As they use their rope to climb down the cliff, Seth is suddenly paralyzed with fear. Daniel calmly coaches him down. They come to a ledge with a cave—and the skeleton of the boy. They are moved and awed. A storm comes up, trapping them for awhile. When the rain stops, they climb back up. As they start running toward their campsite, Seth falls and cuts himself seriously on a rock. Daniel ties on a tourniquet and helps him back to camp. That night, Daniel tells Seth why he feels so close to the dead boy, whom he believes survived for several years and then died of loneliness. Daniel knows what it is like to be an orphan: by the time he was eight, he had moved to twelve different foster families. They return to the cave to bury the boy's skeleton by covering it gently with stones. It is their secret.

Cynthia Butler

Michael Hendee (1976) is an eight-year-old boy in Royalton on the White River in 1780. When word comes that Indians are burning cabins, Michael's father rides to Bethel to seek help. The marauders torch twenty-one homes and sixteen barns and slaughter sheep and cattle. Michael knows the British have paid the Indians to carry out these heinous acts. Mistress Hendee, Michael, and his little sister, Lucy, flee into the woods, where Michael leads them to a hiding place in a hollow log. A tall Indian, whom Michael calls "Goosefeather," seizes Michael and carries him to the other side of the White River, where Lieutenant Horton waits in the British camp. Michael, determined to escape rather than serve the British, patiently weighs his opportunities. Hearing shouts across the river, Michael sees another Indian dragging his friends, Joseph Rix and Dan Downer, screaming and kicking, into camp. An Indian wearing Mistress Parkhurst's cloak arrives with Roswell Parkhurst; still another brings the Durkee twins and Nat Evans. Suddenly, Michael's mother and little Lucy, unaccompanied, appear on the opposite bank. When Michael tries to join them, Goosefeather ties him to a tree. His mother asks Lieutenant Horton to grant Michael's freedom; the British officer refuses. As soon as the Indian scouts return, Michael, without asking permission, simply summons the other captive children and leads them across the river. Before departing, he says goodbye to an old Indian sitting by the river, who calls Michael his "brave friend." Michael understands that "the old Indian is my enemy, but he is not unfriendly." Michael feels the same way about the British officer. (For another Indian captivity narrative, see Marguerite Allis's *Not Without Peril*, an adult novel about the experiences of Vermont settler Jemima Sartwell and her children in the decade before the American Revolution.)

C

Eleanor Cameron

In ***To the Green Mountains*** (1975), Kathryn ("Kath") Vaughan Rule, fifteen, visited her grandmother in Vermont once, when she was four. Now her hopes and desires are focused on returning to the Green Mountains with her mother, Elizabeth, who left Vermont when she was twenty to marry Jason Rule. Jason works a failing farm in southern Ohio; Kath and her mother live in one room in the hotel her mother manages. Jason appears from time to time, never saying a kind word to Kath. Elizabeth tries to help one of her employees, an African-American named Willie Grant, by giving him used law books to spur his interest in becoming a lawyer. The town gossip spreads rumors about Elizabeth's romantic interest in the married Grant. Kath is more and more desperate to leave. Elizabeth summons the courage to tell Jason she is divorcing him and writes her mother that she and Kath are coming to Vermont. Everyone is at the train station to send them off. Kath's dream is coming true. She can visualize the Green

Mountains, "the bosses of rock on either hand, the patterns they make against the sky." She will look up at the "dizzying heights of pines to where their tips pierce the blinding sky."

Flavia Camp Canfield

C

The wealthy parents of Archie Stebbins, eight, in ***The Kidnapped Campers*** (1908) see no alternative but to seek professional help: Archie is sickly, dispirited, and lonely; his weak eyes are not improving. Leaving him in Vermont with his aunt and the hired girl, they depart to consult their doctor. The next day, a young stranger arrives to take Archie on a camping expedition. His name is Williams, he says, but Archie may call him "Uncle Weary." Picking up a nine-year-old orphan named Eddie, they take a train to a country village and set out for Melton. This is indeed an adventure for Archie, who has never slept out on boughs, washed in the river, gone barefoot, handled worms, nor eaten fried foods. It seems odd to him that Uncle Weary does not want him to talk to anyone, but he does not concern himself with that aspect of the expedition. They procure a ride on a butter-and-milk wagon with Scalawag Jenkins, whom Uncle Weary invites to join them any time. When the owner of an old horse drawing the streetcar decides to put down his animal, Uncle Weary, a veterinarian, buys the horse and revives him with food, water, and a good sponge bath. With Staggers, Uncle Weary's name for the horse, carrying some of the load, Uncle Weary leads them to a big cave, with a clean, dry gravel floor. They make improvements to the site and learn to trout-fish. Uncle Weary cuts Archie's long red locks, dyes the new mop dark brown, and outfits him with more manly clothes. He sets the boys to gathering raspberries to sell at the summer hotel. By now, the boys are accustomed to following Uncle Weary's instructions; his goal is to make them men who keep their word and obey orders. Archie has lost his "languid delicate looks." Uncle Weary buys a wagon and lets the boys paint it. The Taggarts, a couple at the hotel, think they recognize Eddie. Uncle Weary brings Emma Moore, the niece of the owner of the hotel, to the cave for supper. On the Fourth of July, he buys firecrackers for a celebration. Scalawag, enlisted to help with the berry picking, tells the boys about the counterfeiters' cave in the area. Along the way, they collect a small menagerie—a wounded dog, a sick kitten, a cracked turtle, and a fawn with a broken leg. Uncle Weary takes them for a climb to survey the lovely view. "There's no place in the world like our dear old Vermont!" exclaims Eddie. They can see the Green Mountains on the opposite side of the valley—"the red and yellow and brown farmhouses," the "rich masses of foliage," and "the young and slender" white birch trees. In a "contribution-to-science" hike, Uncle Weary leads them into an underground cave. He sends a little fire balloon up the chimney, which he measures at one hundred and five feet. Archie feels as though he is in *Alice's Adventures in Wonderland*. When Uncle Weary receives a telegram calling him away, he sends the boys to the Stones' farm. On the way with their dog, Jip, they tumble into a deep hole. They find a lantern (Eddie has matches) and a spring. The cave has been occupied, because someone has left blankets and a few rations. Brave and hopeful, they start a fire (there is an opening in the roof). Eddie figures out a way to make a ladder to reach a rope hanging from the ceiling. Jip, who becomes ill in the night, cannot climb; they pull him up in a blanket. When they reach the Stones' farm, Uncle Weary, already there, is proud of their courage and ingenuity. He calls a powwow: people in the village are saying he kidnapped them. Do they want to go home or move somewhere else? Unanimously, they vote to stay with him and press on to his cousin's farm near Jericho. The weather turns bad, and they take shelter in an abandoned barn. Uncle Weary is hoarse and feverish; soon he is ill, coughing and pale with a red spot on each cheek. When he hemorrhages, Archie runs to a neighboring house to seek help. A kind Finnish couple takes in the three of them. Because the man of the house is sick and his horse lame, Eddie and Archie use Staggers to deliver his milk. Uncle Weary is so sick they call for Em, who, fearing the worst, sends for a minister to marry her and Uncle

Weary (they were to marry in the spring). When Uncle Weary is better, she tells him that even though he stole the children she will stand by him. He explains that Archie's father's doctor devised the plan to give the boy some outdoor experience while his parents were in Europe. Uncle Weary is gratified by the way the boys look and behave. The Taggarts want to adopt Eddie. The Stebbinses are so delighted by the change in Archie that they entreat Uncle Weary to recuperate on their Florida estate and offer a sum of money that Uncle Weary is reluctant to accept: "I guess he's done as much for me as I have for him."

Margaret F. Carty

The first of the three stories in ***Christmas in Vermont*** (1983), "**Meddles, the Christmas Elf**," begins on Christmas Eve when Santa gives Meddles a special assignment to reinvigorate old Sairie Simms's Christmas spirit. Armed with a magic box, the elf, invisible to humans, makes his way to her Green Mountain home where he finds her dispirited and cross. Disguising his voice as Sairie's, he telephones Hiram Hinckley to ask him to come over to fix a leaking faucet. The old people are shy and unfriendly with one other. Meddles removes two red hearts from the box and affixes them to the old people's shirts. Soon they are reminiscing about their school days; they decide to spend Christmas together. As Jason watches his children open their presents in "**A Child Shall Lead Them**," he remembers one Christmas when he was a boy with no money for Christmas. He decided to sell his prize possession—a birthday book from his father—to buy gifts for his family. In a series of mishaps, he took the wrong jacket from the church bazaar, arrived at the store with no money, returned to find the store closed, and came home empty-handed. Suddenly, a man in a Santa Claus outfit drove up to the house with Jason's jacket, the gifts he had hoped to buy, and his book. After the stranger left, Jason hurried outside; neither footprints nor tire tracks could be seen in the snow. In "**All God's Children**," Miss Bess, the teacher, arrives early at school on the day of the Christmas pageant. Before the students arrive, Miss Bess tears down the Christmas decorations and hides the tree in the trunk of her car. The perplexed and disappointed children clean up the mess and wonder what they might do to make the room look festive. They are expecting the principal and the parents for the afternoon program of carols, recitations, and Bible readings. The discarded star gives the children the idea of creating a nativity scene. Using their own imaginations, they spread out to look for props: hay from a farmer, a doll from home, a crib out of a cardboard box, and robes from curtains in the supply room. Each child helps. The program is beautiful, especially the final grouping around the manger. Everyone is moved, pleased, and proud, including Miss Bess, who knows that her work with this particular class is finished.

Jean Caryl

Unwilling to put up with his son's overeating in ***Bones and the Smiling Mackerel*** (1964), Mr. Cluett sends Boniface ("Bones"), twelve, to Camp Crescendo, a coeducational music camp in South Hill. Bones already plays the guitar; his father wants him to study the trombone, his own instrument. The first night, in the "dry, pine-scented Vermont air," Bones meets the head of the camp, Willard Frenzle. Hank Fulweiler, the fair-minded and sympathetic counselor in Bones's cabin, is determined in a good-humored way to help Bones lose weight. His assistant, Chester, is self-absorbed and without empathy. Hank begins to coach Bones to compete in a tennis tournament. All campers are required to report to the coed drama class to try out for parts in *A Midsummer Night's Dream*. The teacher wants Bones to read for Bottom; Bones is sensitive to any reference to his body. Bones enjoys guitar class but cannot blow a single note on the trombone. The teacher offers to give him extra tutoring in a building in the woods, where Bones observes a consultation between Chester and a grim-looking man. In the cabin, most of the boys read forbidden comics. One boy's mother has sent along *A Tale of Two Cities*; another comments, "That's a good book, once you get into it." Chester, an aspiring actor, comports himself well in the faculty play. Hubert Updegraff, a wealthy developer interested in promoting regional repertory, attends the play and unctuously compliments Chester. Bones, who thinks Updegraff looks like a smiling mackerel, suddenly recognizes him: he is the man who was talking to Chester in the woods. Bones and a friend are out on Rainbow Lake when the tiller breaks; the boat's paddle is missing. A counselor rescues and takes them to Mr. Frenzle (Bones fantasizes it will be like going before the Wizard of Oz). Although Bones hates his Bottom costume, he throws himself into the burlesque aspects of the part, and the play is a success. Bones is losing weight because Hank makes him do "the right thing by being interested in you." Bones enters the tennis tournament and, though he loses, puts up a good fight. Bones sees Mr. Updegraff give Chester a heavy white bag, which Chester conceals beneath the main house. Bones investigates and finds rats in a container. Mr. Updegraff is trying to ruin the camp's reputation in order to buy the prime property at a low price. Mr. Updegraff has blackmailed Chester by promising to make him a star. Bones urges Chester to confess to Mr. Frenzle, whose interest is building the boys' characters. Mr. Updegraff leaves angrily. Bones took the honorable course by trusting Chester; they become friends.

Betty Cavanna

After her father is killed in an airplane crash in ***Angel on Skis*** (1957), Angela Dodge, fourteen, her mother, Janet, and her brother, Chip, nine, move from Philadelphia to Peru to run a ski lodge. Angela, a freshman at the high school in Manchester, helps her mother with the housework and yearns to ski, although they have no extra money. Dave Colby, who delivers their milk and is a junior at the high school, fixes up a pair of used skis so she can practice in the back pasture. When she walks to Chip's school to pick him up, she looks at the green salt-box schoolhouse with white trim and the church with the square steeple housing the bell and thinks that she "might have been walking into a painting by...Grandma Moses." She soon loves skiing, although she struggles with her handmade poles. Chip reminds her that Hans Brinker used homemade wooden skates before he had silver ones. Dave brings over his skis and gives her a lesson; he thinks she shows promise. Fresh snow brings many boarders. When Angel fails two courses at school, her mother threatens that, unless she improves her grades, she will not be allowed to ski the following winter. The next year the Bromley Mountain management sends Janet a Swiss ski instructor as a boarder. Jacques Brenner, twenty, pleasant, and engaged to a girl at home, spends his spare time coaching Angela. As her skiing prowess increases, she becomes prettier and more animated. Dave asks her to a dance after a basketball game. Jacques trains her to race. While practicing the slalom, Angela, who is now almost sixteen, meets Gregg Harrison from Dartmouth and is immediately attracted to him. She performs badly in the races. Jacques is disappointed, not in her loss, but in her lack of enthusiasm. Because she is no longer having fun skiing, he thinks she should take some time off. During her third winter, in love with Gregg, her passion for the sport returns. He invites her to the Dartmouth Winter Carnival and comes to Vermont to watch her race. She places second, but the three men who are rooting for her—Jacques, Dave, and Gregg—think she is the best.

Cora Cheney

In ***The Doll of Lilac Valley*** (1959), Laurie Coxe, nine, clutching her precious doll, Kathleen, goes to Vermont under the auspices of the Fresh Air Fund, while her mother trains to be a librarian. Laurie, who has never traveled alone, changes buses in Brattleboro. When she arrives in Townshend, she discovers to her dismay that she has left her doll and her new red purse in the Brattleboro bus station. Hattie and Henry Hardwicke, her hosts, are kindly dairy farmers. Thoughtful Henry buys Laurie a substitute plastic doll, which does not appeal to her. Every day she hopes to receive a package containing Kathleen. Hattie finds a doll-sized stove for Laurie. The Hardwickes look forward to an auction (they enjoy watching the summer people), but Hattie sprains an ankle and suggests Laurie go alone. Laurie has never walked anywhere by herself. Miss Saidie's collection of old-fashioned dolls is up for sale. Laurie, who has only three cents, bids—and fails—on each doll. Finally, the sympathetic auctioneer gives her a bag of scraps for dolls' clothes. Inside is an antique doll. After some strangers express an interest in the doll, Henry takes Laurie to the Newfane Museum; they learn Laurie's acquisition is a Queen Anne doll worth about two hundred and fifty dollars. Laurie must decide whether to play with a museum-quality doll or sell it. Laurie, proud of making her own choice, sells the doll to help her hard-pressed mother. When her original doll is returned, Hattie says, "It's so nice to see everything come out right in the end."

In ***The Mystery of the Disappearing Cars*** (1964), Sam Houston Jones, seventeen, arrives by bus from New York to Johnson's Junction, where, following instructions, he is to make his way, without hitchhiking, to Marble Hill Hotel near Brattleboro. Through a summer's labor, he will try to prove himself worthy of an Ezra Plympton scholarship to Winthrop College. At the bus station, he meets another scholarship nominee, John Wellington ("Windy") Dubois, an artist. Having missed the last bus, they pay a truck driver to take them to the hotel. On the way they see a broken down antique car (a "coupelet"); when the boys get out to assist the owner, the truck driver takes off. Mr. Plympton's hotel is full of rich guests. Sam and Windy approach their many chores with gusto, but, trying to show initiative, they frequently make mistakes and annoy their employer. They befriend Jimmie, a nine-year-old, who reveres them. Word circulates that someone stole an antique car and left the owner tied up in a sugar shack. Mrs. Whittington, the hotel chef, asks the boys to catch some fish for dinner. On their way to the brook, they find an abandoned barn with an old car inside. They decide to fix up the car and sell it to one of the guests. Naively, they ask the local constable the way to procure a clear title to a car in Vermont; state troopers, believing the boys are the thieves, question them about the night of their arrival. Soon more cars disappear on the way to the old-car rally in Brattleboro. Sam and Windy tell Mr. Plympton that they want to clear their names; he puts them on yard detail so they can set their own hours. Sam and Windy figure out that the only place the thieves could take the cars is up the mountain, but how do the thieves cross a stream with no bridge? Sam notices signs of a portable bridge. As they start up the mountain, a masked man with a gun detains them; two other people, one the truck driver, tie them up. Determined to escape, Sam and Windy maneuver their positions until they can untie each other's bonds. Just as the thieves are about to murder the boys, the police arrive, alerted by Jimmie, who followed the boys on their adventure.

Marjorie Chickering

In ***Hayseed Summer*** (1963), fourteen-year-old Andy Adams's widowed, hard-working mother sends him to the farm, in Hillsboro in northwestern Vermont, where his father grew up. There he will stay with his Uncle Art Cheever, his Aunt Milly, and his cousin, Janie. Andy, who often blames others for his own failures, feels deflated and misunderstood. Changing buses, he misses the one to Hillsboro and catches a ride with Mr. Wilson and his son, Roy, who, Andy feels, patronizes him. Furious with his mother, Andy sighs with boredom at the farm. He watches Sim Stevens, the hired man, split kindling. Finally, he condescends to mow the lawn, which seems to please Aunt Milly. Uncle Art takes Andy for a ride in his light tractor "doodlebug," a stripped-down Packard. Driving along the Bayley-Hazen Road, Uncle Art says it was once lined with farms and has now gone back to timber. It was hard for younger settlers to establish themselves in the older settlements, he explains, and this land was cheap; the settlers went out West because of problems with distributing their goods and with the thin, worn-out land. Uncle Art also describes the strategic importance of the road. (Stretching fifty-four miles from Wells River to Hazen's Notch in Westfield, the road was constructed in 1776 and 1779 as a means of facilitating the movement of troops into lower Canada.) From the top of the hill, Uncle Art points out Mount Washington to the east and, to the west, Camel's Hump and Mount Mansfield. Andy learns that his great-great-grandfather owned the mill. As Andy helps Sim around the farm, he unwittingly benefits from the older man's wisdom. When Roy Wilson trades him a cheap harmonica for a good knife, Andy swears revenge: he resents being considered an unsophisticated country fellow. Every day Andy learns something new about farming, from feeding the bull to cutting rhubarb, but he cannot accept his own limitations. When Sim warns Andy that he does not have enough experience to drive the hay into the barn, he forges ahead and drops the whole load. He is defensive and full of self-pity when his uncle asks him to fork the hay back onto the wagon. He is homesick, disgusted with himself, and eager to leave. Then he remembers what his uncle said about Mr. Wilson: "Some people never get grown up enough to profit by their mistakes." Andy trades Roy a worthless watch; in retaliation, Roy takes Andy fishing, leads him far into the woods, and abandons him. Andy is thoroughly lost but keeps his head and finally finds the road. Sim invites Andy to go hiking and fishing with him at Steam Millpond over the weekend. When their canoe capsizes, Andy rescues Sim, who cannot swim, and dives repeatedly to bring up Sim's father's creel. Andy finds an arrowhead, which he gives to Janie, and catches a big fish, which he enters in a contest. Mr. Wilson angrily accuses Andy of stealing the fish from his pond. When Andy wins, he gives the prize, a fine fishing rod, to Roy. In a final act of heroism, when a bull gets loose and threatens Janie, Andy saves her life by grabbing a wheelbarrow and crashing it into the bull. Uncle Art makes up with Mr. Wilson. Andy cannot wait for his mother to come to pick him up. When she asks what has come over him, he will respond: "I just changed my attitude!" (Hillsboro is based on Walden, where the farm in the story was deeded to the author's family in 1795.)

The sixteen-year-old title hero in ***Yankee Trader: Ben Tanner—1799*** (1966) lives in St. Johnsbury with his mother; his father, Reuben; his brother, Will, a scholar who aims to attend Peacham Academy; and his little sister, Goody. Ben's favorite possession is a rifle given him by a dying veteran of Shay's Rebellion. (In western Massachusetts in 1786, Captain Daniel Shays led debt-ridden farmers against the state government. Many of the unsuccessful rebels, including Shays, sought refuge in southern Vermont.) Ben's greatest ambition is to see the world by working for trader Luther Chickering. Unfortunately, Luther already has an assistant, Plin Edwards, whom Ben considers timid and ineffective. On his way to Barnet, Ben meets young Martin Peck, who is boiling sap by himself because his mother is sick. Ben spends the morning chopping wood for him and meets Martin's pretty sister, Jennett. That morning Ben also sees a bear, which he believes to be an outlaw. Surveyor of Highways Horace Cutler, a bad-tempered, authoritarian figure, impresses all the young men into repairing the Danville road. The selectmen vote for a summer-school term to be held at Dr. Lord's inn. The new teacher, Mr. Hammond from Dartmouth, calls on the Tanners. Ben's brother, Will, explains that the town is named for St. John de Crevecoeur, who knew Ethan Allen and Benjamin Franklin. Ben considers his scholarly brother a weakling; he admires Mr. Hammond, however, because he is able to control the big, obstreperous boys at school. At Dartmouth Hammond studied Latin, Greek, calculus—and wrestling. After Plin breaks his leg, Luther hires Ben temporarily, although he knows Ben's reputation for lack of self-control. A substantial portion of the narrative details the trip to Portland, New Hampshire. Ben is a handy camper and hunter, but the trail, with its dips and twists, makes difficult going. They finally reach Portland where, amid a confusing amount of trading activity, Luther maintains his calm, wise, and experienced persona. After many adventures, they head home to St. Johnsbury. Ben is driving Luther's new span of oxen, with Plin lying in the wagon, when Ben sees the same bear, close and threatening. Ben jumps from the wagon to draw a bead on him. Plin, balancing on one leg in the wagon, throws a pitchfork at the bear, hitting him in the throat. Ben kills the animal with one shot. Ben now knows Plin is not a coward. While Ben was away, Plin was accused of stealing some counterfeit money; Ben's brother, Will, testified on Plin's behalf. Ben realizes Will is brave, too. Plin becomes a clerk at the store; Luther hires Ben as a Yankee trader. Ben sees Jennett again and walks her home. He promises to buy the buttons she fancies next time he is in Portsmouth and looks forward to dancing with her at Lettice Barber's wedding. (The author's husband's great-great-great-grandfather was Luther Chickering, the Yankee trader.)

Marilyn C. Childs

As is appropriate in an autobiography, ***Mandate for a Morgan Horse*** (1967) begins with the birth of a Thoroughbred Morgan in Randolph in 1940. Mandate enjoys cavorting with the other colts and begins his education. When he is three, a young girl buys and takes him to Springfield, Massachusetts, for further training and competitions in which they win medals and ribbons. They enter events like the Fifty-Mile Trail Ride in Vermont and begin jumping. When he is five, he sires a stream of colts, all with a "man" or a "date" in their names. Mandate moves to Kentucky with his mistress. She shows him at the Pennsylvania National Horse Show, where no one has ever seen a Morgan. His mistress always returns with him to Vermont for the National Morgan Horse Show. After his mistress marries, they move to Pennsylvania. The horse in the next stall, Sally, is also from Vermont. Mandate and Sally have several sons. After Mandate wins every existing title, his mistress tries him in harness racing at the National; unfortunately, he has not received enough training to succeed. Mandate returns to Chelsea to spend his last years looking back on his happy life as his mistress's favorite mount. Perhaps this was his "mandate in life—to do it all," just like his forebear, Justin Morgan.

Florence Choate & Elizabeth Curtis

The Wheeler children, recent orphans in ***Linda Takes Over*** (1949), are now living on the hill farm near Hillsboro where generations of Wheelers, including their father, were born. Their cousins, Albert, quiet and distracted, and his sister, Cora, stern and sensible, are unaccustomed to children. Linda, fifteen, feels deeply responsible for her four siblings—Olive, thirteen; Bob, twelve; and the little ones, Lois and Jerry—and their beloved dog, Reilly. Everyone but Jerry rides the bus to school in Fairmont. The first day, Linda has a mild altercation with Alan Walcott, a leading scholar and athlete, which makes her feel cross and resentful. Linda soon learns why Cousin Albert is worried: the government has plans to "condemn the valley" by building a dam and turning the entire area into a lake. Linda and the children climb Skunk Hill to look out on the rich farmland that will be flooded. On their way, they find a fawn savaged by a wild animal. Linda carries him to the shack of the hermit, Old Jake, to beg him to care for the wounded animal. Cousin Albert is an organizer of the opposition to the dam, which has hired engineers to develop a substitute proposal to stem floods. A meeting with Mr. Rollins, the lead engineer for the government, is unproductive. Cousin Albert circulates a petition to send to the governor. Bob begins sneaking out of his window at night; when challenged by Linda, he refuses to say where he has been. At the Decoration Day (later called Memorial Day) Ceremony, Linda sees Alan playing in the band; his brother, John, was wounded in France and may never walk again. For high school commencement, the local chapter of the Daughters of the American Revolution offers a prize for the best composition on Vermont history. Linda weaves into her essay excerpts from a diary written by a "hilltop Wheeler," a Civil War veteran, and wins the prize. Alan, the popular captain of the baseball team, avoids her; she knows she has been haughty and unfriendly. At the Fairmont Town Hall, an attractive boy named Kenneth dances with Linda. When Cousin Albert learns he is the son of Mr. Rollins, the government engineer, he forbids Linda to have anything to do with him. After the governor refuses the opposition's petition, Cousin Albert faces the fact that they will lose their farm; the three elder children will have to go to boarding school. Linda

C

pledges not to allow her siblings to be separated. She learns that Bob is involved with the gang of boys vandalizing the Rollins property. When a terrible storm arises and the two little children do not return home, Linda and Olive set out to find them. Spraining her ankle and forced to turn back, Olive runs into Alan and sends him to help. Alan and Linda find the children and resolve their quarrel, whatever it was. Rollins disappears. Because Rollins received threatening letters, the police take in Bob for questioning. Linda and her dog, Reilly, find Rollins still alive. Old Jake shot him in the leg and subsequently died of a heart attack. Later, Rollins summons Linda to his hospital room to thank her. He offers her a college education, but she asks only that he meet again with the opposition engineers. He accepts the substitute plan involving smaller dams and no destruction of the valley. Alan and Linda dance at her sixteenth birthday party. They will be students together at the University of Vermont the following year and are already talking of marrying one day.

C

Barbara Clayton

In ***Halfway Hannah*** (1964), Hannah-Jo Hansen, seventeen and motherless, is surrounded by many loving friends in a town in the South. When her father decides to move to Alpine College to chair the history department, Hannah can tell from the name of the town—Alps Junction—that she is going to hate living there. Worse still, because the inn where they planned to stay has burned down, they have to board at Adams Acres, a farm just out of town. (The environs remind Hannah, an artist, of a Grandma Moses painting.) Jonathan and Martha Adams have an eighteen-year-old son, Kimball, who is at Alpine College, and a daughter, Abby, in her late twenties, who teaches at Alps Junction High School. Hannah can barely disguise her scorn for these "Vermont farmers," although she is taken aback to find that the high school is more advanced in many ways than her former school in the city. Hannah's father, outspoken and interested in local affairs, immediately becomes embroiled in the controversy over enforced double sessions at the high school; Hannah holds back, makes no friends, and spends lonely hours sketching on Copper Mine Hill. When the Adams family gives a party to introduce the Hansens to their friends, Hannah is impressed that Tregar Smoklokoff, a famous artist, and Marianne Muldoon, a well-known poet, live not far away. Closely connected to the education problem is the closing of the woolen mill: unemployed workers are not in a position to vote for spending on schools. Hannah sulks in ski school with Kim as instructor and hates it when he calls her "Halfway Hannah." She starts training by herself on Copper Mine Hill, where she sees a suspicious stranger wandering around. Neighbor Herb Wendell, who has been laid off, receives a huge offer for his parcel on Copper Mine Hill (which used to belong to the Adams farm). When Dr. Hansen investigates ways to bring new industry to Alps Junction, he receives unexpected opposition from Orrin Rogers, head of the largest local bank and of the Chamber of Commerce. The Hansens spend a wonderful Christmas with the Adams family; Hannah cannot help noticing that her father and Abby seem to be enjoying each other's company. After Martha Adams receives an overly generous offer for Adams Acres, Hannah's suspicions are confirmed. Someone is trying to buy up the property: can the lure be uranium? Hannah and Kim, who become friends, climb the mountain and find notched poles to measure snowfall. Kim learns that a syndicate wants to build a ski resort on their property; he believes the family and the town residents could run the project themselves. The land developers threaten other farmers with foreclosure. A town meeting considers the question: should the syndicate take over Copper Mine Hill or should the town try to develop the mountain as a local effort? Hannah takes the initiative to alert a magazine to the conflict; a reporter arrives, asking Hannah to translate "Vermontese" for him. The residents vote overwhelmingly to support local development; the magazine article brings a great deal of favorable publicity. Everything works out well: Alps Junction administers its mountain development; Dr. Hansen marries Abby; and Hannah and Kim are sweethearts.

Jessica Clerk

After the death of her parents in New York City in ***Sukey Johnson Builds a House*** (2001), Sukey, a nine-year-old African-American, comes to Rutland to live with her Uncle Wilson, Aunt Nora, and their two daughters, Jas and Leteshsa. Everyone welcomes the little girl, although Letesha is disappointed because she has to share a room with her younger sister. A bat hanging on the curtain frightens Sukey, but her cousins, whose father is a veterinarian, reassure her that bats are gentle; they are also beneficial because they eat bugs. The girls explain to Sukey that bats use echolocation—bat radar—when they fly. Their father opens the window and frees the bat. The next day it rains, and Uncle Wilson suggests they build a bat house; bats have lost much of their habitat and need a place to keep themselves and their babies safe from predators. Sukey asks Letesha why she is unhappy; the latter responds that she had hoped for a room to herself. Sukey wants to share a room because she is so lonely; Jas happily invites her to bunk with her. Sukey looks out the window at the bat flying to his new home; she has found hers, too.

Catherine Cate Coblentz

When a blue kitten is born in 1835 in ***The Blue Cat of Castle Town*** (1949), his mother is anxious because he listens to the river and learns the river's song. The river speaks to the blue kitten about Castle Town, where a greedy and ambitious man, Arunah Hyde, is weaving a spell over the "beauty, peace, [and] contentment" created by settlers who came up from Connecticut, cleared the land, and planted corn. The blue kitten, like a small knight sent on a quest armed only with a song, must find a mortal who will listen to his song. If the blue kitten is welcomed at this person's hearthside, he will live forever. First, the blue kitten visits the house of Ebenezer Southmayd, a pewterer. "Sing your own song," the kitten purrs to Ebenezer, "all that is worth doing is worth doing well." Southmayd realizes that he hates the cheap and ugly work he is doing for Arunah Hyde, starts over, and creates his best teapot. "It is fit for a king," he rejoices; the next minute he is dead. The blue kitten visits the house of John Gilroy, the weaver, and sings the river's song. The weaver removes the woolen cloth destined to become a suit for Arunah Hyde and begins to weave a fine tablecloth with a picture of Remington Tavern on it. When impatient Arunah arrives, the weaver puts aside "his own song" and returns to the wool. The kitten has failed. Rich, powerful Arunah takes the kitten to live at pretentious Mansion House. "Quick! Quick!" he says to some of his servants; "Late! Late!" to others. He will make Vermont the center of the universe. He owns mills, runs quarries, and plans to bring the railroad to town. "Speed and gain and power" are overtaking Castle Town. The blue cat (no longer a kitten) escapes and meets a friendly barn cat belonging to Sylvanus Guernsey, a spinning-wheel maker, and his daughter, Zeruah. As the blue cat walks around the village, he can hear the effects of Arunah's spell. Everyone is talking about "gold and power and possession." The blue cat fails in his quest and forgets the river's song. He meets Thomas Royal Dake, a carpenter, who consults with the church building committee about a new pulpit. The members want him to skimp on materials: Thomas doubts that "God counted the cost in fashioning that hill." Thomas sings the song that the blue cat has lost and spends his own money creating the pulpit, which has "an everlasting radiance about it." The cat returns to Zeruah, who is lonely and sad because she is ugly and slovenly. "Sing your own song," purrs the cat, "with you life fashions beauty." After the girl views the pulpit and the teapot, she asks her father to make her a frame. She embroiders a carpet with the likenesses of many animals, including one of the blue cat. Zeruah cleans her house and becomes beautiful. The cat's image will live forever in the rug (now hanging in the Metropolitan Museum of the City of New York).

Carroll B. Colby

The Weirdest People in the World (1973) is a collection of more than one hundred brief legends and ghost stories, five of which are set in Vermont. **"The Little Egyptian Prince"**

C

tells how a stolen Egyptian mummy finds its way to the Sheldon Museum in Middlebury. When it inevitably deteriorates, the chairman of the board, George Walcott Mead, has the mummy cremated and buried in his family plot, where he joins it a few years later. A Vermont settler lives on the edge of the woods in **"Escape from Wolves,"** where he often sets traps to collect wolf pelts. One night he is walking to a neighbor's with his daughter when they are set upon by a wolf pack. Carrying his daughter and racing for their lives, he outwits the wolves by sheltering her inside one of the traps before climbing a tree. The following week, on his way to Montpelier, the wolves devour him. **"Plague of Worms"** describes an invasion of caterpillars in Thetford in the early 1770s. Farmer Jacob Burton is the first to see them eating everything in sight. They grow longer and move more rapidly. The farmers try every possible method to rid themselves of the pest; suddenly, the worms vanish, leaving not a trace. **"Skeleton in the Pasture"** is set in northern Vermont close to the Canadian line. Fascinated as a boy by Indian lore, a farmer finds later in life an old iron tomahawk, which becomes his prized possession. He whittles a handle for it. One night he has a vivid dream about killing an Indian with his weapon and burying his victim in the pasture. In the daytime, he cannot find his tomahawk. He digs where he buried the body in his dream—and there lies an ancient Indian skeleton, with the tomahawk (and the farmer's new handle) in its skull. **"The Deacon and the Lynx,"** set in 1725, concerns Deacon Isaac Jones, a homesteader in the Green Mountains, whose wife asks him to borrow, from a neighbor five miles away, a cauldron for making soft soap. The cauldron is so heavy he inverts it and puts it over his head, with the legs pointing upward and the rim resting on his shoulders. Suddenly, he is knocked to the ground. He throws off the kettle and desperately looks around for a weapon. He does not need one because, impaled on one of the legs of the cauldron, is a huge lynx—dead.

Jane Leslie Conly

In ***The Rudest Alien on Earth*** (2002), Molly Harkin, ten, knows that work on a dairy farm is never done. When her parents, Louis and Kay, started the farm near Glover, cousins, aunts, and uncles helped with the milking, haying, and butchering hogs. No one wants to do farmwork now: "It was hard, didn't pay well, and there was no chance for promotion." Molly's brother works for UPS in Burlington. "Only rich people are buying dairy farms these days." Molly thinks Vermont is beautiful: "The bright green of the field, the dark woods, the pale-blue sky seemed to converge on the white shapes of the house and barn, as if their presence pulled land and sky together." She rides the school bus with her neighbor, Jack Molloy, the smartest boy in class, who teases Molly. One day, when her old dog, Sarge, is waiting for her and Jack to get off the bus, a Border collie is there, too. She is Oluu, an alien from another galaxy, who is capable of changing form. Molly is shocked when the dog speaks to her. When Oluu eats up all the nesting eggs, and Louis tries to shoot her, she turns herself into a bird. During the school day, Oluu listens at the classroom window. Oluu transmits messages to the Wise Ones on her galaxy; they warn her against forming an attachment to any human. When Oluu appears as a pony, Jack is jealous of Molly's good fortune; nothing good ever seems to happen to him. When Jack overhears Molly talking to the pony in the barn—and hears the pony respond—he realizes Oluu is a "shape shifter," visiting from another planet. He borrows Oluu for a ride and tries to converse with her but finds her rude and opinionated. While he naps, Oluu communicates on the Internet with other aliens. Against the rules, Oluu grows fond of Molly. After Molly loses her temper, Oluu travels overseas in various guises until Molly begs her over the Internet to come home. Returning to Vermont, Oluu, seeing Jack struck by a truck, turns into a falcon to follow the ambulance. His skull is fractured, but he will recover. Since Oluu wants to stay on earth, Old Suni comes from her galaxy to effect Oluu's transformation into Luna Tresseida, the granddaughter of Mrs. Turner, who lives quietly in Glover and is an alien, too.

Caroline B. Cooney

Family Reunion (1989) finds Shelley Wollcott, fourteen, in her family's summer cottage in Vermont ("Vermont is entirely treed," she observes) with her bratty brother Angus, twelve, and her patient stepmother, Annette. Her father, Charlie, is working in New York. Shelley and Angus fight continually, annoying and worrying Annette. Shelley's father has been married three times: he divorced his first wife, Celeste, whom he met when a teenager; his second wife, mother to his three children, ran off with a dashing French journalist; Annette is his third. Shelley's elder sister, Joanna, is spending the summer in Paris with their mother and stepfather. Even though Shelley is miserable over the divorce and angry with her mother for abandoning her, she has a lively sense of humor and can joke about the comedic aspects of life. Their summer cottage is on a lake. Her room is bare and free of possessions, with a "gleaming wooden floor." She loves Vermont: "After the sun vanishes, the grass goes black, and the trees and lake turn indigo, like blue-stained shadows, but the sky is translucent." She makes friends with attractive, sympathetic DeWitt, who lives on the other side of the lake. She resents her Midwest relatives, Aunt Maggie and Uncle Todd Preffyn, who boast about a perfect life with their two perfect children. Aunt Maggie is always referring to the Wollcotts as a "broken family—New Yorkers" with no "stability." Aunt Maggie plans a family reunion: everyone is coming, including her grandmother from Arizona and Joanna from Paris. Shelley is vaguely disappointed that Joanna is coming: she is mean to Annette, while Shelley appreciates Annette's good qualities. After their arrival in the Midwest town of Barrington, Shelly compares it to Vermont: "In Vermont, trees fought for sky, but in Barrington each tree was far apart." Angus discovers a family secret: Celeste's son, Toby, is their father's son. Shelley is incredulous at her father's betrayal by not telling them about Toby. She meets him in Barrington—a kind, handsome young man who treats her like a grown-up and tells her the truth about her father. After Charlie and Celeste were divorced, she went to school in Chicago; he worked in New York. Celeste married Richard Donnelly and had a son, Toby. Shortly thereafter, Richard died in an automobile accident. Because of his early love for Celeste, Charlie, without telling anyone, supported the family and paid for Toby's education until Celeste finished law school. The gossips in Barrington always assumed Toby was Charlie's son. This revelation about her father's unheralded generosity makes Shelley proud; she loves Toby like a brother or a cousin (DeWitt in Vermont is her real beau). She thinks her father is perfect despite what everyone says about him. She does not pine anymore for "stability"; furthermore, she is no longer angry with her mother or anyone else.

Peter Cooper

In ***The Secret Papers of Julia Templeton*** (1985), Ben Weisman, fifteen, starts a new school in Newcastle, six miles from Pittsford, after his mother, Deborah, a social worker, divorces his father. Dark, handsome, literary, and athletic, Ben develops a sarcastic shell when members of the football team bully him. He observes that Vermonters talk only about the weather. Cindy O'Rourke, also fifteen and a good student, lives with her parents and younger brother over Michael O'Rourke's Fine Foods store. At school, Ben is assigned to collaborate with Cindy on a research topic, the history of Newcastle. Julia Faith Templeton, eighty-two, is the widow of a Newcastle man whose ancestor was one of the original proprietors of land from King George in 1764. The keeper of the town's history, she expects to turn over her strongbox filled with old documents to suitable stewards. Cindy and Ben meet at the library to begin their research; later, Cindy calls on her old friend, Beechmont, the town drunkard, who is knowledgeable about the history of the town and likes Cindy. John Arnold, the town lawyer, is a descendant of the other proprietor of Newcastle. Just before his death, Arnold's father told him Julia possessed certain papers reflecting badly on the Arnold family. Unaware of this history, Cindy suspects the existence of a third proprietor of Newcastle. Ben looks at Cindy with new appreciation: she is both smart and pretty. Cindy and Ben make an appointment to call upon Julia, who is dying as they arrive. She gives Cindy the key to her safe, asks her to care for Old Burgoyne, her cat, and mumbles, "Bible...the preacher...three...seven ...please." They find the strongbox; someone with a brutal, contorted face grabs it and flees. At Julia's funeral, Ben and Cindy again glimpse that person—Nick Tomasi, Arnold's henchman. Inside the strongbox, Arnold finds a statement from Gideon Ivory Templeton that Captain Jack Turner, a member of Rogers's Rangers and husband of an Abenaki, held the royal grant to Newcastle. Arnold realizes his ancestor murdered the rightful owner to the land; he must eliminate Cindy and Ben. He tries, unsuccessfully, to buy Michael O'Rourke's store for an extravagant price; he offers, unsuccessfully, to provide a better-paying job to Deborah Weisman in another town. Even more troubling to Arnold is the idea that Captain Jack Turner has a living descendant. Nick is dispatched to kill the children, but he cannot bring himself to do so; instead, he joins them to help solve the mystery. Beechmont stops drinking and becomes his former, dapper self; Nick also reforms, now that he is engaged in a worthwhile cause. Cindy's little brother, an electronics wizard, tapes the mayor's meeting with Arnold, who has traced the descendants of Captain Jack Turner to the birth in 1925 of a child named Beechmont Turner Walker. Beechmont, meanwhile, does his own research by digging up the skeleton of his ancestor. When someone burns down his cabin, Beechmont escapes and goes into hiding with Nick; the town authorities assume the bones in the cabin are Beechmont's. In the final week of school, Cindy and Ben, now in love, plan to broadcast the message about Arnold's malfeasance at the Newcastle Fair. Cindy's brother assumes control of the sound system and inserts their tape just as the mayor is about to speak. Everybody listens raptly. Nick, a former pilot, flies overhead skywriting, "MAYOR TELL TRUTH," lands his plane, and strides to the stage. He forces the mayor to explain about the royal grant and introduces Beechmont Turner Walker as the rightful heir and Cindy and Ben as the seekers after the truth.

Peter Campbell Copp

The locale for ***Thunder in October*** (1997) is Hildene, Robert Todd Lincoln's mansion in Manchester, where Jonathan Sage, nine, resides with his father, the custodian. One day Jonathan sees a coydog in the yard and fears the animal will threaten the local chipmunks. The coydog ("Mr. Coy") and the chipmunks ("Little Chip" and "Big Flip") engage Jonathan in conversation, telling him that a teenaged gang is coming to Hildene to hunt and asking him to bicycle to the top of the hill to warn the deer. When the teenagers chase Jonathan, Mr. Coy turns into a bird and flies away with him. The teenagers flee, leaving behind a .45-caliber automatic pistol, which Jonathan hands over to Jake, the foreman at his father's office. Jonathan is watching deer through his binoculars when hunters arrive. He cries out to the deer to escape and runs to the Visitor's Center to report these illegal hunters, who follow him. As the sun sets behind Equinox Mountain, Jonathan hurries to the cemetery to hide in the mausoleum, where he finds a monk, Stephen, to whom he confides his ability to speak with animals. The hunters discover Jonathan's hiding place just as Jake arrives and capture him, too. At the last minute, Marvin the Moose storms the mausoleum and scatters the villains.

Robert Cormier

The narrative in ***I Am the Cheese*** (1977) alternates between taped interviews with Adam Farmer and a bicycle trip he took when he was fourteen, from Monument, Massachusetts, to Rutterburg, just across the Connecticut River from New Hampshire, to visit his father in a hospital. In the sessions with Brint, the interrogator, Adam, though agitated and medicated, is aware that the interviewer is trying to elicit information from him. On the seventy-mile ride, he is frightened on one occasion by unpleasant youths;

another time he is anxious because his bicycle is stolen temporarily. To keep up his spirits, he sings "The Farmer in the Dell" over and over again. He tries to call his girlfriend, Amy Hertz, but he has the wrong number. He talks to the interrogator about Amy and about secrets that his parents have kept from him—his two birth certificates with different birth dates and the existence of an "Aunt Martha," when his parents have told him that he has no other relatives. Brint probes more deeply; Adam senses he is his enemy. While on drugs, he continues to reveal his past. He finally remembers that his real name is Paul Delmonte. His father, Anthony Delmonte, was a reporter in a small town in upstate New York who uncovered corruption in the government in Albany. After he testified in Washington, D.C., attempts on his life persuaded the authorities to put the family into a Witness Reestablishment Program. Three years earlier, Adam traveled to Vermont with his family. On the way to Barre, a car intentionally hit them and killed his mother and father. Adam, now seventeen years old, has been a patient at a hospital in Rutterburg since the accident. Brint keeps him on drugs in the hope of eliciting additional information about his father. He sees himself as Adam Farmer, the cheese, standing alone. (In the nursery rhyme, "The Farmer in the Dell," after the farmer takes a wife, their child a nurse, the dog a cat, and the cat a rat, the cheese stands alone.)

The Rag and Bone Shop (2001) is set in Monument, Massachusetts, with initial and final scenes in Highgate, the residence of star interrogator Trent (only his surname is used). Seven-year-old Alicia Bartlett is murdered in Monument; Jason Dorrant, twelve, the last person to see the victim alive, is the prime suspect. The police and a state senator want immediate closure. Trent, ambitious and preternaturally skillful, rides down to Massachusetts in a limousine with Sarah Downes from the district attorney's office in Wickburg. Convinced of Jason's innocence, she briefs Trent on his file. Trent's entire career is based on extracting confessions; he is even more determined when Senator Harold Gibbons promises him certain rewards should he succeed. Trent, whose wife (killed in an automobile accident) saw through him, despises himself. Jason, timid, fairly bright, a loner, and a victim of bullying by his peers, is happiest with younger children like his little sister. Jason enters the interview room persuaded that the police need his help in solving the crime. The actual interrogation is masterful and terrifying: Trent is by turns avuncular, stern, accusatory, conciliatory, threatening, accommodating, and sly. He twists Jason's words, withholds water, and wears him down. Trent finally convinces Jason that his only recourse is to throw himself on Trent's mercy to achieve mitigation: the police are waiting outside the door to try him as an adult and send him to prison for life. Jason confesses. Triumphant, Trent emerges from the room to learn that the real killer—the little girl's brother—is in custody. Trent returns to Vermont in disgrace and is demoted. The effects on Jason are incalculable. He is on medication and in a psychiatrist's care: the experience may have turned him into a killer. (The title comes from William Butler Yeats's poem, "The Circus Animals' Desertion": "I must lie down where all the ladders start,/In the foul rag-and-bone shop of the heart.")

Emily Costello

Ski Share VT (2006) assembles six young people into one condo for a work-and-ski three-month winter program at Killington. Isis Dean, eighteen, from Burke, Vermont, aspires to join the Killington Crew, which would pay her to ride her snowboard. Eliot Searles from Boston has deferred his acceptance at Williams College for a year and keeps a blog with digital photographs of his experiences. Dolce from Brazil has come, not to ski, but to find out whether she loves her boyfriend, Zé, with whom she keeps in touch by email. Frank, handsome and thoughtful, is a recruit in the ROTC, awaiting call-up orders. Chad Gaza is a stern, unsociable nondrinker; Jenny is a spoiled party girl, a drinker, and a suggestive flirt. Eliot includes all the roommates in his blog, until Chad explains that his parents do not know where he is and want him to return to Yale. Jenny takes novice-skier Dolce to the top of the mountain, where she abandons her to ski with a good-looking member of the ski patrol. The U.S. Snowboarding Open is held in Stratton. Both Isis and Jenny compete; both are offered yearlong contracts on the Killington Crew. After searching the Internet, Eliot learns that Chad is on probation from Yale for sexual assault. Faced with this story, Chad confesses he was drunk and does not remember what happened, although he has not taken a drink since. The consensus of the group is that he should leave. Frank, the only one sympathetic to Chad's plight, senses some ambiguity in Chad's story and confides to Chad that he is gay. Perhaps he and Chad will get together one day. Chad leaves; Frank receives his orders. The roommates rearrange their accommodations: Nick from the Killington Crew joins Jenny, who decides to stop drinking; Zé, who has arrived from Brazil, moves in with Dolce; and Isis and Eliot form the remaining couple.

Elizabeth Craft & Sara Fain

Four best friends from high school in Boulder, Colorado, in ***Bass Ackwards and Belly Up*** (2006) are separating to attend college: Harper Waddle to New York University, Kate Foster to Harvard, Sophie Bushel to the University of Colorado, and Becca Winsberg to Middlebury. When Harper confesses that NYU rejected her and she plans to stay home, follow her dream, and write the Great American Novel, two of the others are inspired to follow her lead: Kate dons a backpack and heads for Europe; Sophie goes to Los Angeles to be an actor. The strands of the plot follow each young woman simultaneously; at Christmastime, they compare notes on their various degrees of self-discovery. Becca's two goals at Middlebury are to ski on the team of her idol, former U.S. Olympic Team Coach Jackson Maddix, and to fall in love for the first time since eighth grade, when Jared Burke spurned her for Kate. She starts off on the wrong foot with both Maddix, who treats her with "cold disdain," and star running back Stuart Pendergrass, who laughs at her on the field, or so she perceives. She skis well until, furious with her parents, she has too much to drink one night and sprains her ankle. She shares two classes with Stuart; they study together, become pals, and step out on a first formal date, which is unsuccessful because of her panic at the depth of her affection for him. In New York for Thanksgiving, she meets Jared and foolishly sleeps with him. At Middlebury, Maddix starts her on the giant slalom course, at which she excels; Stuart stops calling. Eventually, he forgives her for sleeping with Jared, and they begin seeing each other again.

E.J. Craine

In ***The Air Mystery of Isle La Motte*** (1930), "sky buddies" and stepbrothers, Jim Alston and Bob Caldwell, both sixteen, visit Bob's aunt, Belle Fenton, at the farm in North Hero where Bob's mother (who married Jim's father) grew up. Jim and Bob have flown from Texas in their seaplane, *Her Highness* (with both floats and wheels for landing), stopping in the southern part of Quebec to offer their services to Sergeant Bradshaw of the Canadian Mounted Police in the ongoing campaign against smuggling. As they fly above Lake Champlain, the boys view Aunt Belle's turkey farm on Isle La Motte, which is united to North Hero by a long bridge; farther on is Grand Isle, also connected by a bridge, and Gull's Rock and Fisher Island. The Fentons are worried: someone is stealing turkeys from Isle La Motte, despite the presence of a watchman, Hezzy Burley; part of their property is swamp, though Corso, a foreign laborer, and his son are trying to make it arable. On the way to check in again with Sergeant Bradshaw, the boys spy suspicious men in the ravine. They land to warn Bradsaw and watch the action from the sky. Just as the police gain on the villains, Aunt Belle's vegetable peddler, Pedro, appears in his caravan (a large covered vehicle) and loads the smugglers into the back. In a daring maneuver, Bob climbs to a high altitude, turns off the engine, descends silently, and lands in front of the truck. They delay Pedro until the Mounties arrive and round up the desperadoes. Returning to the Fentons' farm, they are shocked to see their friend, the mail pilot, parachute from his burning plane. They land, extinguish the flames at the crash site, save the mailbags, and fly the pilot to Albany. Severe rainstorms ravage the countryside;

the lake begins to rise. The farmers in the area are concerned about their livelihood; those who are flooded stay with the Fentons. Despite the dire situation, "the Vermonters were facing their troubles quietly and without a whimper." The crisis makes the boys think of Ethan Allen and his heroism in North Hero (which was named in his honor). The Fentons, facing ruin, share everything with their neighbors. In the early morning, the boys hear someone crying out from the lake; taking to the air, they spot a man, woman, and baby stranded on a roof. They touch down and tow them to shore. They fly to Fisher's Island to rescue Corso and the boy, a prince in disguise who gives them each an emerald in gratitude. Back at Isle La Motte, they find soldiers parachuting from Canadian planes. With their lariats, the boys capture Hezzy and his accomplices and find hundreds of stolen turkeys. (For further references to Ethan Allen's connection with North Hero, see Cornelia Meigs's *At the Sign of the Two Heroes* in this collection.)

Jordan Cray

Riley Tulane, seventeen, aspires to be an actor in ***Shiver*** (1998) and has already spent a summer at drama camp in the Berkshires. There, he formed an Internet chat group with Dudley Firth, Ethan Viner, Wilson Macdougal, Peyton Caliran, and Natalie Smallwood. Believing he has found his soul mate in Natalie, whom he has never met in person, he is thrilled when her mother, Thea Smallwood, who runs an inn in the Green Mountains, invites the group for a weekend before their drama seminar begins in Manhattan. At his first meeting with the two young women, Riley is disappointed to find that Natalie is the short redhead and Peyton is the tall, stunning blonde; he is also distinctly aware of a hostile atmosphere in the air. Mrs. Smallwood, while shopping in the village, is caught in a raging blizzard: the storm blocks the mountain road; the electricity and telephone service shut down. Riley is shocked to find Ethan's apparently dead body in the woodshed; one by one the others vanish. They reappear, including Ethan, to admit they were taking revenge on Riley for falsifying his application to the seminar. When Riley proves they are mistaken, they become friends again until they realize that none of them put the bloody signs in the bedroom. Someone else is in the house. Natalie finds another reservation in her mother's office for "Tripwire"—Alyce Tripo. They find Wilson's dead body: before dying, he wrote "A-N-A-G-R" in the snow. They remember Alyce Tripo: an unpopular, unattractive girl whose application to the seminar was rejected. Riley has a brainstorm: Ethan was trying to write "anagram." He emails someone at Alyce's school and learns her real name is Alyce Ann Tripo—Peyton Caliran. Meanwhile, Natalie has gone off on skis to seek help, with Peyton accompanying her. Shouting for someone to call the police, Riley pursues them, catching up with them just as Peyton is about to shove Natalie over the cliff. The police arrive in time. Riley, realizing how mistaken his first impression was, looks forward to spending time with Natalie in New York.

Craig Crist-Evans

In ***North of Everything*** (2004), a boy's father leaves Florida to return with his family to his farm in Montpelier, where "a hundred acres stretched like skin along the bank of the Winooski." The boy, about fifteen, helps his father with the chores. Soon, his mother has a baby girl, Carolyn. The boy's father loses weight and is diagnosed with cancer. "The willow trees stand like tired ghosts." At school, his friend, Cynthia, comforts and walks with him, holding his hand. Now the boy drives the tractor because his father is dead. "Up here, north of everything" is the refrain of the story.

Anne Eliot Crompton

The members of thirteen-year-old Chris Strong's family on Strong Mountain in ***Deer Country*** (1973) are his father and mother; his grandfather; his sister Lindy, eleven; and his cousin, Trigg, fifteen, a disturbed youth whose drunken father abandoned him. Chris's father, a third-generation farmer, failed at farming and now works at the furniture factory in the village.

Chris's mother watches TV and pays no attention to Chris, who has one aim in life—to shoot a buck. He has seen the one that he wants, a white-tailed animal with a heavy crown of antlers: "His white chest and throat gleamed pink, reflecting sunset like the snow." A large dog emerges from the woods, his muzzle swollen with porcupine quills, which Chris's grandfather removes. The children adopt the homeless dog and name him "Babe." The point of view switches to the deer in the woods—Velvet, a young buck; Doe, his sister; and Big Buck, their father. Starving and exhausted from navigating in deep snow, they hear menacing noises. Back at the Strongs' farm, the children and their grandfather are sugaring when they hear Babe and other dogs barking in the deeryard (a place where deer gather for wintering). Although it is summer and hunting is illegal, Trigg steals a salt-block, ties it to a fence post to attract the deer, and invites Chris to accompany him to shoot the ten-point buck. Chris is uneasy: game wardens levy big fines for hunting out of season. Just as Trigg has a bead on Big Buck, Chris jostles his arm, and the deer flees. Trigg is angry with Chris; Chris's father is furious with Trigg. Chris's friend, Sam Aaron, returns for the summer, bringing with him a Fresh Air Kid, an African-American named Frank. They meet at Beaver Pond with fishing poles. Chris catches a large fish for their supper; Frank, awed by the creature's beauty, throws it back into the water. Chris is aware of the layered differences among them—Chris, a native Vermonter; Sam, a summer person; and Frank, a city boy. In the late fall, "silver dew stood on silver leaves." The point of view shifts for a moment to the deer and returns to Chris and Lindy, who are deer hunting with their grandfather. Chris sees Doe but does not shoot. Velvet appears. Chris aims and then, admiring the animal's beauty, pauses to think of Frank. When Big Buck enters the scene, Chris pulls the trigger; the magnificent creature falls to the ground. For the first time, Chris throws himself into his grandfather's arms; they hug for a long time. This act of killing provides the family its winter food and makes a man of Chris. Velvet escapes into the woods to await hunting season the following year.

The Ice Trail (1980) is based on the life of Daniel Abbott, aged ten at the start of the action in 1703. He dwells outside Penacook (Concord), New Hampshire, with his father, elder sister, Hannah, and little brother, Jamie. One night when his father is away, Abenakis come to the cabin, kill Hannah, scalp Jamie before Daniel's eyes, burn down the cabin, and carry Daniel off to their encampment on Lake Champlain. His life is saved only because Awasos stays the hand of Natanis, Daniel's potential executioner. Five years later, Daniel is still with the Abenakis, alienated because none of the tribe accepts him except his "father," Awasos, and his "brother," Molemsis. The elders do not allow him to hunt alone because they fear he will flee. Daniel's one desire is to return to the world of the white man. One of the Indians brings back a pair of ice skates stolen from a settler's cabin. No one can stand up on them; Daniel does not reveal that he knows how to skate. After a big feast (he shoots a moose for their supper), he escapes on the skates, heading south. An arrow zips past his shoulder. He continues, skirting the bank, although he knows Real Adders (fierce, scalp-hunting Indians) could be hiding behind any bush or tree. A shout from the bank heralds the arrival of Molemsis, who has followed him on snowshoes, not to take him back but to show him the best way south and to bring him a blanket and some food. Molemsis, who loves Daniel, wonders why he is leaving. Daniel tells him about the Abenaki attack and his brother's death. Molemsis counters that Natanis is seeking revenge for the death of his wife; white men burned her alive in her wigwam. Molemsis and Daniel see the cruel Adders breaking up a beaver dam. Daniel's route leads directly by them and follows along a river and into a forest. A wolf pack rushes past him to attack and tear apart a young buck. When the wolves leave, Daniel helps himself to the remains of the carcass. He staggers to a clearing and collapses at a cabin owned by a white woman. He has finished the first lap of his journey home. (Daniel Abbott made it back to Concord, New Hampshire, where he married and raised sixteen or so children.)

Alice Turner Curtis

The eponymous heroine in ***A Little Maid of Ticonderoga*** (1917) is Faith Carew, ten, whose father owns a mill in "the wilderness" between Whiting and Shoreham in the Green Mountains in 1774. Her parents' friend, Mr. Eldridge, brings his daughter, Esther, from Brandon for a visit. Faith finds Esther a spoiled girl who thinks solely of eating sweets; Esther feels superior to Faith because she lives in a real village. One day Faith, frustrated and upset, runs into the woods, where Colonel Ethan Allen, tall and kind, finds and comforts her. The Carews, believing Faith would benefit from a proper school, send her to Ticonderoga to live with her aunt and uncle, Philip and Priscilla Scott, and their three boys. Kashaqua, an Indian friend of the family, accompanies Faith by foot to Shoreham and thence by canoe to Ticonderoga. Faith meets Nathan Beaman, fifteen, a Shoreham boy who comes often to Ticonderoga, and Louise Trent, the shoemaker's lame daughter. At her new school, Faith befriends Catherine and Caroline Young, daughters of an English officer, who invite her to visit Fort Ticonderoga. Just after they enter the fort, the Young girls spitefully abandon Faith in a dark passageway. Luckily, Nathan finds her, takes her out of the fort down the cliff, calls her the bravest girl he has ever met, and bids her keep secret the hidden entrance to the fort. When Faith's father visits, Faith tells him about her new friend, Louise; he warns her to be careful—the shoemaker is an English spy. While the children skate on the lake, soldiers from the fort stamp out their big fire, fearing someone might use it to send messages to shore. Faith overhears Uncle Philip saying that the Americans could seize the fort if only they knew a secret entrance. Faith accompanies Phelps, a Green Mountain Boy, in his canoe to show him the way to approach the fort. Faith's father comes to fetch her home to the Wilderness, where Esther now lives, too. Faith hopes Ethan Allen will expedite taking the fort after she informs him that the British are sending more soldiers there. She takes Esther with her to Lake Dunmore to leave her message in Ethan Allen's cave where Seth Warner promises to deliver it. The girls' fathers form part of the successful expedition to Fort Ticonderoga. Colonel Allen invites Faith to the fort to thank her for her brave deeds, saying, "Faith is the best of names for a little American girl."

A Little Maid of Vermont (1927) dramatizes the story of Anne Sherwood, ten, whose family farm lies just outside Bennington in 1777. Anne has three older brothers, twins David and Luke, fifteen, and Theodore, seventeen. Her father and eldest brother are stationed with the Green Mountain Boys at Fort Ticonderoga; the twins work the farm. Anne takes care of the geese, hens, and turkeys. It is a time of general anxiety. With the men away, Mrs. Sherwood is frightened when an Indian comes to her door. He haltingly explains he is the Iroquois Gray Wolf, bringing presents from his brother, Narvelet, whom she nursed back to health after he was hurt in the forest. David and Luke wonder whether Gray Wolf is a spy for the British. After Anne falls off a sledge, Gray Wolf finds her crouched in a hollow tree and carries her to a cave where a British officer is in hiding. When Gray Wolf escorts her home, he makes her promise not to mention the cave. Everyone in Bennington talks about the threat of General Burgoyne's great army. In June, Burgoyne lands on the shore of Lake Champlain, planning to capture the two fortresses, Ticonderoga and Mount Independence. Anne realizes the cave she has kept secret is a meeting place for Indian scouts and British officers. Donning an Indian costume made by her mother, she returns to the cave, poses as an Indian girl, and steals a letter to Burgoyne with information collected by his scouts. Luke takes the packet that night to Bennington, warning his family not to mention his absence to anyone. Mrs. Sherwood burns Anne's costume. The Americans abandon the garrison at Fort Ticonderoga; Seth Warner retreats to Hubbardton, where both Theodore and Mr. Sherwood are wounded and return home. When Theodore recovers, he rejoins Warner, accompanied by Luke and David, now sixteen. Delia, Patty, and Anne take butter, eggs, and bread to the soldiers in Bennington. Anne wants to do more, but how can a little maid help? Making her way once more to the cave, she is unaware that Theodore is on the same mission. Meanwhile, troops are massing on the Walloomsac River. Theodore and Anne meet in the cave. His leg is so badly injured he cannot walk; she goes alone to Bennington to carry the letter she found from General Friedrich Baum to Burgoyne: "We shall attack the enemy tomorrow." She reaches the Catamount Tavern where she delivers her message to the Committee of Safety. The Americans win the day: the British loss is great; the American, small by comparison. It is a proud day for the Green Mountain Boys. Since no one has heard of the role Anne played in the victory, Theodore arranges a surprise celebration in the town square on September sixth, the birthday of the Marquis de Lafayette, where Theodore tells the townsfolk of her courage.

D

Barbara Dana

Thelma Beldwin, fourteen, is "jotting down" (as her psychiatrist puts it) notes in ***Crazy Eights*** (1978) from her base in the "northern wilderness" of Lake Bomoseen. The first half of the narrative describes Thelma's life in Maplewood, New Jersey, with her pathetic cipher of a father, her empty, useless mother, and her self-absorbed, beautiful sister, Jennifer, who does not love the man she is marrying in three weeks. Thelma's life is a mess: her only ambition is not to grow up to resemble her mother; her only love is James, the dog her mother will not allow in the house. Tension builds as Thelma's father loses his job, her nervous sister vomits frequently, and wedding visitors take over Thelma's room. Sad, angry, and lonely, Thelma puts a flame to a windowsill at the site of Jennifer's upcoming ceremony (the building does not catch fire) and turns herself in to the police. At Thelma's hearing, the judge recommends the North Woods School, a small place "with a sense of family." Ten houses accommodate twelve students each, with two house parents, a man and a woman. The woods are beautiful "with mountains all around." The staff, "which trusts you," seeks "community feeling" and "responsibility for your own actions." Thelma is assigned to Dr. Stone for sessions three times a week. At first she refuses to talk to him. After she meets Larry, the physical education and yoga teacher, who has "a great and knowing smile," she starts meditation classes. Her headaches diminish, but she begins to visualize her dog—dead. At Larry's behest, she continues meditating, moving through "great pain and fear" to "Light. Silence. Peace." A thoughtful reader who "connects deeply" with Joan of Arc and feels *Siddharta* "has a lot to say," Thelma loves *Catch-22* and, although she does not like the movie quite so much as the novel, she thinks actor Alan Arkin is "terrific as usual and especially handsome." Reading Plato's "The Cave" is a revelation to her: the cave is Maplewood, her parents, and their friends; they are not aware of anything outside their little world. They suffer, she realizes, from "limited visibility." She and her manic-depressive roommate, B.B., ride horses together. When she finds B.B. contemplating suicide, Thelma reaches out to help her—the first time Thelma has empathized with another person. Thelma explains to B.B. an insight that she herself is just beginning to understand: it is not that B.B.'s mother does not love her, but that "she loves you the best she can." As Thelma comes to the end of her journal, she feels connected with "things of the universe that were always inside me, but I had covered them up." She loves Dr. Stone for being "respectful and open-minded and curious." She shares her new insights with Larry, with whom she plays Crazy Eights (remembering when she was a little girl happily playing the card game with her father). Larry, with his extraordinary smile, understands when she tells him that "home is being inside the knowledge of her own soul." (In the interest of full disclosure, the author is married to actor Alan Arkin.)

Dorathea Dana

In ***Sugar Bush*** (1947), the Kolochecks come to Vermont at the suggestion of Uncle Stanislaus, a quarry worker. They were farmers in Poland, but their children—Kinga, sixteen; Casimir, fourteen; Stefan, twelve; Elli (also twelve, an orphan niece whom they adopted); and Calvin Coolidge, five—were born in America. They are protégés of Judge Allan's, a neighbor whose sons, Ethan, sixteen, and Billy, twelve, are friends of the newcomers. The Allans' fine old house serves as a community center for friends and neighbors. Stefan and Elli conceive of the idea of restoring the old meetinghouse on the hill. In the evenings, everyone in the village plays baseball in the meadow. Life is good for the Kolochecks, who help the Allans with the sugaring. The weather is perfect: a cold night followed by sun the next day: "The sky was an intense amethyst color, the shadows on the snow an ultramarine, and a soft tone of peach seemed to have crept into the winter gray of the maple woods that covered the high ridges." They stack the sleds with buckets. The maple trees await the tapping, "a friendly army arrayed in gray uniforms, standing at attention, ready for orders." They set the spouts, tap them, hang the buckets, and put on the lids. The next day they gather and boil the sap. The evaporator and storage tanks are ready in the sap house. When the sap bubbles dangerously close to the edge of the pan, Judge Allan scatters in a few drops of cream. The cash for this crop will settle Allan's debts and help pay for the restoration of the meetinghouse. The children boil eggs in the syrup. Finally, the sugaring-off party takes place: everyone gorges on sugar-on-snow with pickles. The second run is called "sugar snow." They make sugar and molasses as well. The Kolochecks cannot afford the big outlay for equipment and a sugarhouse for the following year; the Allans offer to "go shares" with them again. When school is out, the children (except Calvin) work at the inn, as they did the summer before. To raise funds for the meetinghouse project, they will charge an admission fee for a film, *Sugar Bush*, shot during the sugaring off, and serve a light supper. When the children are unable to sell any tickets, the grown-ups wonder how they can attract an audience. The children reveal that they saved two big cartons of snow and stored them at Simpson's Ice Cream Plant. They invite locals, summer people, and inn guests to a real Vermont sugar-on-snow party in the middle of summer, held at the meetinghouse. The girls all wear old-fashioned costumes. Stefan's voice is used in the film. They make enough money to finish work on the meetinghouse, where suppers, graduations, elections, and other events will be held. The town is proud and impressed that an immigrant family initiated and helped execute the project.

Jeff Danziger

In ***The Champlain Monster*** (1981), Eddie, fourteen, admires his sister, Tracy, a year younger, who is an excellent student and plays the violin. One day while ice-fishing from their father's shanty on Lake Champlain, Eddie brings up an object that, though not a fish, looks like a fish scale, dark green and as big as his hand. He and Tracy pull up five similar items over the next few weeks, all with a ridge of torn flesh along one side. They consult Old Pete, an ice-fisherman, who snagged several of these about ten years earlier. He thinks they were torn from a big fish, but he was unable to search for the creature due to the murky waters of Lake Champlain. By measuring distances between the areas where they find the scales, Tracy figures out the fish is over sixty feet long; she believes it to be extremely old and in a state of hibernation. They agree not to tell anyone because they are afraid someone might harm the fish. When spring comes, Eddie fixes up their canoe so they can move farther out on the lake. One rainy day, they see amid the waves and white caps a portion of the monster in a small patch of calm water. At night, when they are in the canoe, the monster rears its head out of the water: they spot its yellow eyes and pointed nose. Although Tracy tells him to stop, Eddie tries to paddle away; the monster, angered, turns over their boat. Unable to find Tracy or the boat, Eddie swims to shore. Everyone is heartbroken about Tracy's disappearance. Eddie is inconsolable. Old Pete urges him to come out in his boat. They motor as far north as the bridge at Rouses Point, where Pete shows Eddie that Tracy is safe and sound, with the dying monster lying by the shore. They find the monster's large egg. After the monster dies, they cover the carcass with grasses and branches and swear each other to secrecy: they will tell no one where the egg is or when it hatches.

D

Nicole Davidson

Karen Henderson, sixteen, in ***Winterkill*** (1991) is fervently opposed to leaving Manhattan for Killington. Her parents want to "get back to nature"; Karen sees herself "stuck in the boonies with a bunch of hicks." She is surprised, on the first day of high school, that Nona Stewart, her brother Brandon, Matt Welch, and Kurt Haller, the four most popular students, seek her out. When sophomore Rosie Geer warns Karen against the quartet, Karen attributes her attitude to jealousy. Matt appropriates her as his girlfriend and gives her a skiing lesson; Karen is pleased, although she is more attracted to Kurt. Brandon, Matt, and Kurt are fiercely competitive; Karen watches them ski in qualifying rounds for the Mogul Challenge on Bear Mountain. Afterward, everyone celebrates at the Wobbly Barn on Access Road. When Matt leaves the party, Karen follows him outside and witnesses his being run over. Karen, frozen with horror, takes to her bed. Both Brandon and Kurt ski the following day. The police question the young people from the party and dismiss the episode as a hit-and-run accident. Karen is certain the driver intended to kill Matt. Someone borrowed her car that night; she is determined to identify the murderer. She reviews the events of the evening in her mind. Nona insisted on driving Karen to the party, which left her car unattended. Both Nona and Brandon disappeared during the party, as did Jerrie Tilden, a ski instructor, Frank Roselli, who borrowed someone's car to deliver pizza, and Rosie, who says she was visiting her boyfriend at Green Mountain College. Kurt takes Karen skiing; when he kisses her, she is chilled to remember Matt's dying words: "Watch out...for Kurt!" Karen learns that the coat Matt took from the party belonged to Kurt's father, Heinz; therefore, the murderer was after Heinz. Karen assembles all interested parties in Wobbly Barn. As she recounts the evidence, she realizes that Matt's final words meant, "protect Kurt"; all the young people are suspects. Kurt finds old clippings of a news story about his father's skiing with a group caught in an avalanche in Switzerland. Brandon and Nona's parents died there. Karen realizes that from the first day of school Brandon and Nona were using her; they needed her car to kill Heinz. Karen receives a note from Jerrie asking to meet her at the top of the mountain. The confrontation with Nona and Brandon takes place there; fortunately, Jerrie has informed Kurt and Heinz, who race to the site. Brandon forces Karen to ski down the Fiddle, the most dangerous trail. She manages to stop at the edge of the cliff, while Brandon hurtles over. She collapses in Kurt's arms.

Robert Davis

In ***Gid Granger*** (1945), Eben Granger enlists in the army in World War II. His great-grandfather did the same when Lincoln called for volunteers in the Civil War, as did his father in World War I. Eben leaves Gideon ("Gid"), sixteen, in charge of Ledge Farm in the town of Bethel Gilead with his widowed mother, Mary, and his sister, Cissie, fifteen, to help. Gid, no longer free to attend school, makes a budget. Their assets consist of a cellar of root vegetables, salt pork, jelly, maple sugar, plus their butter and eggs; expenses are taxes, insurance, dry groceries, kerosene, flour, and feed. His mother will not borrow cash to fix the truck because so many of her friends lost their farms. To assist the war effort, Gid and Cissie join the Green Mountain Guard to raise poultry, grow fruit and berries, and solve livestock and crop problems. Gid signs up for a Brooklyn youngster's help during his summer vacation. When the Grangers' friend, Limpy Kenn, a powerful dwarf, learns that Gid needs cash for his truck, he shows Gid a big black bear hibernating in a cedar swamp. Gid and Limpy each make about sixty dollars from the meat and the pelt. Every night, Gid checks on their elderly neighbor, Fran Bixby, fearing she will burn down her house. Looking up at her trees, untapped for years, he plans a big sugaring this year. With no men around except Limpy, Gid's mother excuses Cissie from school to help. Fran rents Gid her trees in exchange for five cords of wood. When the sap starts to run, after a harrowing week of unsatisfactory weather, eighteen successive days of heroic effort follow—emptying pans, keeping fires drawing, ladling thickening liquid from pan to pan. The result is three hundred shining cans of syrup, alleviating worries about insurance, taxes, food, and doctor's bills. A buyer offers them an excellent price and puts a crisp one hundred-dollar bill in Gid's hand as down payment. He and his mother exchange brief glances: "They were Vermonters, and they didn't show their feelings before a stranger." Gid worries about storekeeper Lincoln Wait, who extends credit to his needy customers; rich, stingy Nathan Farwell plans to foreclose. Immigrants move in as tenants on the old Hubbard Place next door to Fran. At first Gid is annoyed that these foreigners are "settling on good Vermont land, when they weren't wanted." Giving them a ride to their farm, he is grumpy and rude, until he realizes they have traveled untold miles to safety and regrets his uncharitable behavior. Professor and Mrs. Kryshenko, a girl Cissie's age, and two little boys came here because someone told the professor "a man could paint or write in Vermont without his neighbors calling him crazy." When Gid's mother collapses, the doctor orders her to bed. In response, a "saga of back-road farms" unfolds, "as much a part of the Vermont scene as the green hills themselves." Sixteen women, themselves bone-weary, take turns working in the Granger household; their men do the chores. The summer worker, Binks Jenks, is knowledgeable about machinery and fascinated by the possibilities of the millpond, the old dam, and the wasted waterpower. Binks figures out they could install a power saw at the old dam and, while they are about it, clean out and enlarge the pond for a swimming pool for the village children. Wait loses his store, which has been in his family for generations and served as club, news-bureau, loan office, warm spot to stop, and friendly place. "Every furrow has an end," says Mary sadly. Farwell is negotiating with a chain store. Quick-witted Binks overhears one of the potential buyers mention a "gold mine." The boys search the store, find a treasure trove of American antiques stowed there years earlier by Wait's grandfather, auction the items for twenty thousand dollars, and save the store. The dreaded event occurs: Fran's house burns down. She is safe, but Limpy dies saving her parrot. Fran moves in with the Kryschenkos; Gid and Binks devise a way to bring electricity to the village and make their proposal at a town meeting. Eben, home from war, is moving to Abilene to marry but invests some of his army pay in buying Fran's property. While Eben was away, Gid became a man.

Leon W. Dean

Green Mountain Boy: Seth Warner (1941) focuses on the role of Seth Warner in the American Revolution. Born in 1754 in Woodbury, Connecticut, he, his father, Dr. Benjamin Warner, and his mother, Silence, settle on six hundred acres in Bennington in the New Hampshire Grants. Seth marries his childhood sweetheart, Hester Hurd, and has a son. His cousin, Remember Baker, lives in the Grants with his wife and son, as does Remember's cousin, Ethan Allen, and his family. New York calls the New Hampshire titles illegal and assumes the right to grant and resell the land. The Grants men ("large-framed, muscular, with prominent cheekbones") meet at landlord Stephen Fay's Green Mountain Tavern to form Committees of Safety and organize the Green Mountain Boys. Eleven companies are raised, with Ethan as Colonel Commandant and Seth as Captain. The Boys wear motley uniforms, each with a sprig of evergreen in his hat. After they drive out some New York surveyors, an incensed Governor William Tryon offers a reward for the Boys' officers. In 1774 the First Continental Congress meets in Philadelphia. After the Battles of Concord and Lexington, the struggle with New York over land becomes "a mightier struggle for freedom." Ethan Allen and the Boys seize Fort

Ticonderoga. The Continental Congress does not want to break off relations with England, but Ethan and his followers consider themselves already at war. Ethan proposes the Continental Congress make the Boys part of the militia for regular pay. New York, represented by James Duane, is suspicious of the Allens' Onion River Land Company, which owns sixty thousand acres. At an election of officers for the new regiment, Seth receives forty-one votes to Ethan's five. Ethan, frustrated by delays in General Philip Schuyler's invasion of Canada, attacks Montreal with a small band and is captured by the British. Fierce cold, smallpox, and lack of food and provisions cripple the Canadian campaign. Seth proves a great and compassionate leader. The Grants, under Ira Allen, petition for admission into the Union as a new state but are rejected. The president and secretary of the Continental Congress sign the Declaration of Independence. New York releases control of the Boys' regiment; Seth is promoted to lieutenant colonel. When the Congress continues to refuse the Grants' application, Vermont becomes an independent state on January 16, 1777. Before it draws up a constitution, word comes that General Burgoyne is advancing on Vermont with eight thousand men. The Americans retreat from Fort Ticonderoga. After Seth petitions for help, General John Stark of New Hampshire arrives with his militia; Seth's childhood Indian friend, Chob, comes from Massachusetts with a group of his men. The Americans win the Battle of Bennington, in which Seth's brother is killed. In October, the Americans—"the fighting farmers"—defeat Burgoyne at Saratoga. The British release Ethan Allen in May 1778, after three years in captivity. By this time, Vermont is in a sad condition—crops destroyed, resources expended, poverty rife—and is again refused statehood. Seth is lame and sick; his home is sold for taxes (ironically, the Allens buy it). The surrounding states claim their right to subsume Vermont; Ira Allen negotiates with the enemy to keep Vermont a sovereign state. Seth is wounded in a skirmish with some Indians at Lake George, his regiment annihilated. In 1782 America reaches a preliminary peace with England. Seth's health deteriorates, though he is still a man "of rustic dignity and restraint." In 1784, estranged from the Allens, he returns to his birthplace to die.

The hero of ***Stark of the North Country*** (1941) is John Stark, son of Scot Archibald Stark of New Hampshire. Stark, a natural scout and woodsman, grows up in the company of an Indian friend, Christoe. In the early days of the Indian uprising, Indians capture Stark and take him to St. Francis, where he is exchanged and later becomes second lieutenant to Captain Robert Rogers, recruiting woodsmen and bushfighters to join General William Johnson north of Albany. The regular British Army ridicules the New Hampshire men in a song called "Yankee Doodle." Stark rides with Rogers's Rangers to Canada and, after a bloody battle, becomes a captain. Returning to New Hampshire, he marries Elizabeth ("Molly") Page. In 1759, Lord Jeffrey Amherst, newly appointed commander of the armies, asks Stark to raise some recruits and assigns him the task of building an eighty-mile military road from the lakeside opposite Crown Point to Fort Number Four in Charlestown on the Connecticut River. The highway project is a crippling job—the men are ill, hungry, exhausted. Amherst wants additional New Hampshire men for another assault on Canada; Stark delivers them over his new road to Crown Point and returns to Derryfield, where he becomes a figure of consequence in his community. News comes of the Battle of Lexington. With Americans chafing against English laws, Stark realizes they must fight oppression and tyranny. Almost overnight, two thousand New Hampshire men march into Massachusetts, unanimously electing John Stark colonel. John's fifteen-year-old son, Caleb, enlists. The English initially win the Battle of Bunker Hill, but the Americans keep them in siege; the English finally surrender after their troops fall prey to smallpox. The Americans send an expedition to Canada, including Colonel Ethan Allen and the Green Mountain Boys. Stark and his men intend to go north as well, but they are turned back at Trois Rivières; the withdrawal is perilous, with many men sick. Stark's men make it to Chimney Point; General Schuyler pulls them back to Fort Ticonderoga. The Continental Congress declares independence from England. Benedict Arnold meets the English fleet at Valcour Island, losing the engagement but rescuing most of his ships. Robert Rogers joins the British side and raises the Queen's Rangers; Stark's brother, William, also accepts a commission in the English army, believing the Americans can never win. Stark, feeling dishonored that the Congress is promoting men over his head, resigns and returns home. The English have important plans for the summer of 1777, centered on the genius of General Burgoyne. He guarantees immunity to any person in the New Hampshire Grants (now the independent state of Vermont) who will side with England. General St. Clair abandons Fort Ticonderoga. Vermont rallies, raising private money, and begs New Hampshire for help in stopping the English invasion. Stark agrees to fight, but only if New Hampshire men serve as an independent army. He meets Seth Warner with the Green Mountain Boys in Manchester. As he goes into battle at Bennington, General Stark proclaims, "Tonight the American flag floats over the hill or Molly Stark sleeps a widow!" The Americans are victorious. General Burgoyne writes: "The Hampshire Grants in particular, a country unpeopled and almost unknown in the last war, now abounds in the most active and rebellious race of the continent, and hangs like a gathering storm upon my left." Burgoyne capitulates at Saratoga; Stark fires the victory salute—thirteen for the states "and one more for young Vermont." Stark testifies before the Congress about the dismal situation of homes destroyed and families impoverished while their men were away fighting. At eighty-one, he is unable to attend a memorial to the Battle of Bennington but sends a letter emphasizing that soldiers who are "undisciplined freemen are superior to veteran slaves." He ends, "Live free, or die—death is not the worst of evils."

Old Wolf: The Story of Israel Putnam (1942) focuses on Israel Putnam's feats in the French and Indian Wars. He quickly rises in rank, meets Robert Rogers, the "bluff and bold" leader of Rogers's Rangers, and becomes a scout. In September 1755, Sir William Henry erects Fort William Henry at the head of Lake George. The exploits of Putnam and Rogers in the battles at Fort Carillon (renamed Fort Ticonderoga) and Fort St. Frédéric (renamed Crown Point) form the narrative's main sections related to the New Hampshire Grants. When the French capture Putnam and take him to Canada, he meets another prisoner, Captain Peter Schuyler, who provides clothes and housing to Putnam and introduces him to captive Jemima Sartwell (Howe). After a prisoner exchange, Putnam escorts Jemima and her children back to Fort Edward. As a Revolutionary War general, Putnam leads engagements in Massachusetts (at the Battle of Bunker Hill he said, "Don't one of you shoot until you see the whites of their eyes"), New York, and Pennsylvania. Toward the end, the narrative refers to the seizures of Fort Ticonderoga and Crown Point by Ethan Allen and the Green Mountain Boys.

I Become a Ranger (1945) is narrated by David Ferris, seventeen, on his way to join his father at his pitch (an early settler's encampment) on the Connecticut River in the New Hampshire Grants. Indians capture David; Ranger John Ash rescues him. At Fort Dummer, David finds the Ferris cabin burned with no trace of his parents or his sixteen-year-old sister, Mary. Convinced that Indians murdered them, he accompanies Ash, now his mentor, to Fort Edward to join Robert Rogers ("six feet tall, cockily confident, a superb, robust figure of a man") and the Rangers, a desire to kill Indians smoldering in his heart. The Rangers share this sentiment. They are bitterly aware of the massacre at Fort William Henry, where, after Colonel George Monro surrendered to General Montcalm, the Indians butchered soldiers, desecrated graves, and scalped corpses (including Rogers's own brother). In 1759, the Rangers go into action on Lake Champlain and are ordered to take Crown Point (Fort Frédéric). Captain John Stark is sent to construct a road through the New Hampshire Grants to Fort Number Four on the Connecticut River.

Abenakis capture Captain Kennedy, on a mission under a white flag, and take him to St. Francis, in Canada. In retribution, Rogers's Rangers head north, struggling on snowshoes under terrible conditions, frostbitten, weary, starving, and fighting skirmishes with their foe along the way. As they leave Missisquoi Bay, a large band of Indians burns their whaleboats and steals their food. (Because this mishap means they will have to retreat from St. Francis by way of the Connecticut River, Rogers sends a message to General Amherst requesting supplies be sent to Coos Intervales, about sixty miles north of Fort Number Four.) After an arduous, dispiriting march of twenty-two days from Crown Point, the Rangers enter the village of St. Francis—and see rows of shriveled scalps dangling from door-jambs. Even though their orders are to spare women and children, the Rangers cut them down as they are fleeing and set fire to the houses. (David later looks back with shame at the rage and hatred he felt during the slaughter.) A huge brave emerges from a house with David's sister, Mary. In hand-to-hand combat, David slays the Indian while his comrades, knowing the boy's story, watch the fight. Mary is well; their parents are captives in Montreal. At the end of the day, two hundred Indian warriors and twenty women and children lie dead. Informed by prisoners that three hundred French soldiers and Indians are a few miles behind them, the Rangers make an arduous march toward Lake Memphremagog through unfamiliar territory. For a better chance at survival, Rogers divides the Rangers into smaller parties. David, Ash, and members of their party are captured briefly but escape, meet Rogers on the Passumpsic River, and with great difficulty make their way to the Connecticut River, having had nothing to eat but boiled moccasins for days. When the Rangers arrive at the mouth of the Ammonoosuc, their provisions are not there. The men are too weak to proceed to Fort Number Four. Rogers chooses four men (David among them) to make a raft and float down the river. They lose the raft in the falls and with superhuman strength fell trees to build another. On arrival, they learn General James Wolfe captured Quebec but died on the battlefield. Ash, David, and Mary return to their farm, where they rebuild the house. In spring, the two men return to Crown Point and the Rangers. With the French besieging Quebec, Rogers takes three hundred marauders, including Ash, now a lieutenant, and David, an ensign, to Canada to create some diversion. The French try to negotiate a settlement with General Sir Jeffrey Amherst; the British army under Canadian General Sir Frederick Haldimand takes possession of the city. David finds his father and mother in Crown Point and returns with them and his sister to Fort Dummer. His father foresees oppression from England and war with England. (This novel is dedicated to Merritt Parmelee Allen, whose novels are included in this collection. For another version of Robert Rogers's attack on St. Francis and retreat to the Connecticut River, see Kenneth Roberts's adult novel, *Northwest Passage*. For the Abenaki perspective on the English attack on St. Francis, see Marge Bruchac's *Malian's Song* in this collection.)

Because Asa Barnum, seventeen, has grown up with boats in ***Guns over Champlain*** (1946), Lieutenant Carter Wayne requests his help as guide on the lake in 1813. The Barnums' farm is in Ferrisburgh; Asa has a charming younger sister, Nancy, and a beautiful elder sister, Lois. Asa is by nature reticent, "as is the way with us Vermonters." Lieutenant Thomas Macdonough keeps his boats in Shelburne Bay for the winter. The war with the British is not popular with some Americans. Gabriel Salter has "doubtful allegiance" to the cause and is suspected of smuggling goods to Canada. Lois appears to be in love with his nephew, King. At Diamond Island, Asa and Carter surprise some smugglers, but King escapes. Sheriff Needham stops Asa on his way to Vergennes; Tory Weasel Moran kills Asa's horse. Little Joe, an Indian friend of the family, materializes; Asa sends Joe to tell Asa's father about the horse. The sheriff laconically informs Asa how to escape from his jail, and Asa is soon on his way in Little Joe's canoe to Burlington to join the navy. He looks for Carter at the University of Vermont

(Ira Allen provided the impetus for the founding of UVM in 1791). They join the crew of *Growler*; Macdonough's flagship, *President*, is in for repairs. Their ship, commanded by Lieutenant Sidney Smith, passes Isle La Motte bound for the Richelieu River, engages the enemy, and becomes trapped. The British capture the crew and take it to Montreal. With the aid of British uniforms stolen by Carter, he and Asa escape in a gig and elude their pursuers. They camp out, change clothes, catch a rabbit, and cook it on an Indian's fire. Michael Hagedon, a government agent working with Moran, changes his allegiance and drives Carter and Asa in his wagon to Burlington. Carter introduces Asa to the first president of UVM, Reverend Daniel Clarke Sanders (who served from 1800-1814). British ships attack Burlington and burn barracks and government stores at Swanton. Carter and Asa head for the latter's home to check on King and console Lois, who has admitted to herself that she does not love King. Little Joe guards the homestead. Carter and Asa rejoin the fleet aboard *President*. American General Wade Hampton's force of four thousand men assembles on Cumberland Head. The fleet draws into Chazy, New York, opposite Isle La Motte, then heads for Otter Creek, where it will winter. The crew runs logs into the creek alongside the vessels to serve as buffers against the ice. After Asa saves a man from drowning, Macdonough, "tall, spare, with becoming dignity," visits him in the hospital. "There's sound stuff in you Green Mountain Boys," Macdonough says. "I hope so, sir. My grandfather fought at Bennington," responds Asa. Carter and Asa, now a midshipman, are stationed at Vergennes, where Macdonough awaits the spring campaign. A new flagship, *Saratoga*, is launched. General Alexander Macomb in Burlington asks the governor to call out the militia; the government takes over the university for barracks. Little Joe reports to Asa that Moran is at the Barnum farm demanding three thousand dollars from Asa's father or Moran will burn down his house. The girls, clad in the same English uniforms, flee. Macdonough sends Asa and Carter with ten men; Hagedon kills Moran with a pitchfork. Two weeks later, Macdonough leads the vanguard of the fleet north and casts anchor off Plattsburgh. The summer passes. The battle, when it comes, is fierce and deadly. One by one their guns are disabled, but Macdonough has so moored his ship that he can swing her about and bring to bear fresh guns upon the enemy. Captain Daniel Pring surrenders. The four British commanding officers give up their swords; Macdonough gallantly returns them. Asa spends the winter working on the farm; Carter, badly wounded, visits to recuperate, and he and Lois become engaged. King steals the Barnums' sailboat and vanishes.

In ***Pirate Lair*** (1947), Darius Kent, seventeen, lives in Cornwall in 1803 with his parents, Thomas and Mattie, and his brother, Thaddeus, eleven. His family is on hostile terms with neighbor Oscar Brodt (a former Hessian soldier), because of the mysterious circumstances under which Brodt took over the Tellier farm after Indians attacked and killed the family. Darius, whose personal feud is with the Brodt son, Arnold, finds a birchbark document from Mr. Tellier confirming that Brodt led the Indian raid. The Kents send Darius to his aunt and uncle in New Hampshire to safeguard the document incriminating the Brodts. On the train, Darius meets Mr. Ferguson, who tells him that friends of his in Boston raised a young boy whom Indians had captured and ransomed. In Portsmouth, a person who is looking for the Brodt evidence hits Darius over the head and dumps him on a ship sailing for Philadelphia. With no money to return to Cornwall, Darius is impressed onto *Philadelphia*, heading for Tripoli. On the frigate, Darius meets the man Ferguson described—Jonathan Arms, whose adoptive father is a ship owner in Boston. The main part of the narrative concerns the fighting off Tripoli: Edward Preble commands their squadron; one of the midshipmen is Thomas Macdonough, hero of the Battle of Plattsburgh. After two years, Darius and Jonathan return to the United States, first to Beacon Hill to the Arms family and then to Cornwall by horseback. Jonathan, who has told Celia, his sweetheart, that he will not marry her until he knows his real identity, turns out to be

D

Curtis Tellier, one of the boys taken by Indians twenty-five years earlier. The Brodts leave; Jonathan and Celia will be the Kents' neighbors. (The title refers to the Barbary Coast of Tripolitania—Tunisia, Algeria, and Morocco—where pirates raided merchant ships, and governments paid tribute for immunity from the pirates. When the Unites States refused to pay, it entered into hostilities known as the Tripolitan War, 1801-1805. The Marine Hymn alludes to "the shores of Tripoli.")

Red Man's Trail (1948) finds Kenn Atwood, sixteen, lazing about the family's summer cottage in Ferrisburgh. His father, a lawyer in Hartford, Connecticut, wheelchair bound after an accident, hires Thayer ("Tud") Andrews, seventeen, to take Kenn fishing and boating. They head up the Little Otter. Tud is a serious collector of Indian artifacts. While they are fishing, Major Derrick Moare swoops by in his motor boat and cuts Kenn's line. Also a collector of relics, Moare is piqued that Tud prefers working with Professor Malcolm Dixon at the University of Vermont. Kenn and Tud visit Dixon and his attractive assistant, Miss Dane, and view the Wigwam, where their treasures are locked. Out on the water they see the Snyders, "water gypsies" in the business of smuggling and selling antique Indian items. Moare appears again, accompanied by his pretty young cousin, Laudine. On an expedition, Dixon, Tud, and Kenn find an uninvestigated cave. Kenn, the smallest of the three, crawls through an aperture and, despite rattlesnakes, removes a quiver and arrows, which turn out to be quite valuable. They pass the spot where Zadock Steele escaped from his Indian captors in 1780. Laudine, a pleasant young woman, develops a special affinity for Dixon. She explains that Moare's behavior stems from injured pride at being court-martialed while protecting someone else. When Dixon is injured and hospitalized, they devise a plan to scare off the Snyders. The conflict with the Snyders is resolved after Moare, who is actually a doctor, cures little Ernie Snyder, dying of blood poisoning. Tud and Kenn return to the cave, where they find a skeleton. All works out well: Laudine and Dixon become engaged; Moare rehabilitates Mr. Atwood's legs and opens a practice in Ferrisburgh; and Kenn goes to university with Tud. (Zadock Steele appears in Leon W. Dean's *Royalton Raid* below.)

Border Bullets (1953), the sequel to *Red Man's Trail*, entangles University of Vermont freshman Kenn and his friend, Tud, in a dangerous adventure. In Ferrisburgh for the summer, they are exploring an intriguing cellar hole when a fierce man, with an even fiercer Great Dane, Major, ejects them from the property. At Wheeler's Store in the Hollow, a few miles from the lake, they learn the unfriendly man is Earl Crater, who has leased the property for a large sum for six weeks. When someone shoots Major outside the store, Tud and Kenn carry the wounded dog in Tud's car back to Crater, who locks Kenn in a closet. Crater's nephew, a one-armed boy named Hugh, releases Kenn, but not before Kenn glimpsed a map showing places marked with names like "Old Landing" and "Old Tavern." Tud and Kenn, who befriend Hugh, are uncertain about Crater's intentions, but, after Crater's map is stolen, they surmise that someone else is their enemy. A story in the *Burlington Daily News* exposes a plot to smuggle Chinese aliens over the border from Canada. Soon they are in a deadly fight with the smugglers, led by a man known as Duke. Duke's men capture them, but they manage to seize Duke's cruiser to rescue some of the Chinese before they come under fire. They reach the house where they find Major dead, with Crater's knife in his neck. When the enemy attacks the house, Crater apparently hangs a Chinese person from the window frame to discourage further aggression. Bob, a cohort of Duke's, recaptures Kenn and Tud and takes them to the bowels of the former Red Tavern. Crater tries to turn Bob against Duke by offering to decode the map for him. Tud and Kenn, who were appalled by the shooting of Major and the hanging of the alien, learn that Crater is with the U.S. Government Service, his task to overthrow the attempt by the Russians to smuggle Chinese Communists into the United States. He shot Major to throw the enemy off the scent and feigned the hanging. Crater, Kenn, and Tud take out Kenn's father's boat and ram Duke's cruiser, sending it to the bottom of the lake.

In ***Royalton Raid*** (1949), the Smart family home is in Tunbridge, not far from the little farming settlement of Royalton. One day in 1780, Amos Smart, worried about his vanished hogs, sends his sons, Gideon, seventeen, and Cyrus, thirteen, with a bag of salt to look for them. In the woods, a band of four Indians appears, spears one of the hogs, and binds the boys' wrists. The Indians take the boys to their camp, where a blue-eyed white man in Indian dress holds a position of respect. Three men, Lieutenant Richard Houghton, a Frenchman named La Motte, and Chief Graylock, are in charge of about three hundred Indians and their captives. Gideon tries to escape, but they bring him back and take the prisoners to Royalton. The Indians burn houses, plunder barns, slaughter animals, and kill and scalp humans. The white man helps Gideon escape, but he is recaptured. Hannah Handy (variously spelled "Hendy," "Hendee," and "Handee" in other versions of her story) crosses the river with her little girl to confront Lieutenant Houghton, informing him that his child captives are too small and weak to reach Canada. She leaves with eight or nine children, among whom Gideon manages to infiltrate Cyrus. When Graylock is poised to kill Gideon, the white man prevents his doing so. It begins to snow. The captives are led by towropes, their backs packed with plunder, their heads bowed. The Indians burn houses and take captives in Randolph and Brookfield; one of them is Zadock Steele, who is about Gideon's age. Gideon and Zadock carry a massive iron kettle, hung between them with their leashes secured in the handle. Conditions are harsh and terrible. The prisoners calculate that the militia must be aware of their whereabouts; they also assume that the militia will not attack for fear of inciting the Indians to murder their captives. The Indians feed them only enough to enable them to continue marching. As they approach Lake Champlain, the sight of the huge expanse of water framed with forests awes Gideon. The white man introduces himself as Ahiel Watson, a British missionary married to Graylock's sister, Singing Wind. Watson sympathizes with the Indians' perspective: they have seen their people slain, their lands taken. Graylock, a boy in St. Francis when Robert Rogers and his Rangers attacked, received a head wound his sister believes causes his erratic behavior. At a moment when he could have escaped, Gideon saves Watson's life instead. At the English garrison on Isle aux Noix, Watson finds that Graylock has abducted Singing Wind. Following the Indian custom of using captives to replace their losses, an Indian woman adopts Gideon. Given their choice, the captives elect to go to the British prison. Cold, hungry, and diseased, they are put in a dungeon where Watson is the acting chaplain. Prisoners die, primarily of scurvy. A year has passed since the burning of Royalton. The prisoners try to defend their rights against a sadistic captain of the guard. After they are tortured, they begin to dig a tunnel. About twenty-five men, exhausted, starving, and weak, take part in the breakout. At the lake, they build a raft. They have been away for almost two years. They join forces with Watson to find Graylock and his sister. Gideon is the first to attack Graylock before Watson kills him. After many hardships, the prisoners arrive at the fort in Pittsford. When Gideon finally reaches Tunbridge, his father takes one look at him and says, "It took ye quite a spell to salt them hogs."

After their parents die, seventeen-year-old Ezra Button in ***The White Ox*** (1953) and his elder brother, Jed, settle in a secluded spot on Lake Champlain just across from Split Rock Mountain. The brothers develop a sterling reputation as the "Lake Hawks," known for their daring work against enemy activity on the lake. On one occasion they stole money from a British paymaster and hid it in a tree close to their cabin. Kyle Tucker, a local Tory, is responsible for Jed's arrest and detention in Canada. The action begins when Captain Ebenezer Allen, Ethan's brother, informs Ezra he is trying to apprehend the "dastardly Tory," Tucker. Ezra, keeping watch from his cabin, sees the British cattle boat *Reindeer* pass, unaware that Tucker is aboard. Ezra sees a white ox crash through the boat's barrier and swim ashore, followed by two armed men in a canoe. The white ox, which Jed names "Angel," makes its way to his property. Ezra enlists in the Green Mountain Boys, serving under Allen. After the defeat of General John Burgoyne at Bennington in 1777, Allen's orders are to recapture Fort Ticonderoga. Ezra learns that Jed is to be charged as a spy. Allen proposes using Ezra's hidden money to bribe Tucker into obtaining Jed's release. Ezra is sent to capture a Tory to interrogate and, by coincidence, detains Tucker driving a herd of cattle. Allen threatens to hang Tucker if he does not persuade the British to release Jed; Tucker tries to escape, but Angel, the white ox, chases him into the upper reaches of the Hudson River. Allen's men seize several boats laden with supplies for Burgoyne (who has just lost at Saratoga) before the British take Ezra prisoner and put him aboard *Reindeer*, heading for Fort Ticonderoga. Ezra jumps overboard and swims in the freezing water to the Vermont shore, where he binds and gags a sentry and takes his greatcoat. Making his way with difficulty along the coast, Ezra comes upon Old Pete, a starving Indian scout, whose face is torn by a bullet. While Ezra attends to the old man's wounds, two British officers arrive to inform him of a proposed exchange between his brother and Tucker, if Ezra can deliver the money. Heading for the Rangers' camp at Pawlet, Ezra sees smoke rising from Fort Ticonderoga and Mount Independence. In camp, Allen shelters a Negro woman, Dinah Mattis, and her child, whom he provides with a written document granting their freedom. At his cabin, Ezra finds Angel and the money, still hidden in the basswood tree, which Tucker had failed to find. Now a lieutenant, Ezra travels to Ile aux Noix, a British fortification, to free Jed. Tucker kills the colonel arranging the exchange; Jed is charged with murder. At the trial, Old Pete testifies for the defense, swearing he saw Tucker shoot the colonel; a British witness corroborates his testimony. In the courtroom, Tucker runs amok, attacks Ezra with a knife, and escapes. Jed and Ezra head home to find that Tucker has torched their house. Angel kills Tucker, and the brothers set about rebuilding their cabin.

Franklin W. Dixon

In ***Track of the Zombie*** (1982), the Hardy boys—amateur detectives Joe, seventeen, and his elder brother, Frank—are always eager to accept a new case. Their famous father, Fenton Hardy, is away. Rolf Allen (descended from Ethan Allen) comes all the way from Hunter's Hollow, twenty miles from Burlington, to the Hardys' home in Bayport (a fictional city on Barnet Bay, somewhere in New York) to seek their help. Rolf, who is studying acting with his friend, Lonnie Mindo, tells the Hardys that someone set fire to his parents' woods to force them to move. According to legend in Hunter's Hollow, a Hessian soldier escaped from the Battle of Bennington, disappeared, drowned, and turned into a zombie, still wearing his Hessian uniform. Rolf is convinced that the zombie is the arsonist; moreover, Lonnie found an authentic button from a Hessian uniform in the ashes. Simultaneously, John Tariski, head of Big Top Circus, solicits the Hardys' assistance in a case that may be connected. His circus is plagued with mysterious accidents; he suspects sabotage. He is also heading for Burlington the next day and hires several of the Hardys' classmates to watch for suspicious behavior on the part of circus employees. Once in Burlington, Joe and Frank consult Tyrell Tyson, a successful attorney who pledges to assist them wherever possible. The Hardys find a secret room housing a crypt in the cellar of the Allen property. A matchbox cover leads them to the Hessian Hotel, a front for a gang of thieves, whose entrance is through the boarded-up back door. Briefly trapped by the thieves, the brothers escape. On the track of the zombie, they find messages from him wherever they go. The Hardys' detective kits are well equipped with items like pencil flashlights and noise pellets that exude red smoke upon exploding. Good improvisers, they sit in with a band as guitar players, act as volunteer firefighters, and do a stint as circus clowns. When the circus is set up in Burlington, the Hardys infiltrate as reporters, meeting Bones Arkin, who does a zombie act, and Reptilia, the snake charmer. Their list of suspects lengthens. They return to the Allen house where they find Rolf drugged in a coffin and tackle the zombie—Lonnie Mindo. Someone calls Lonnie from the Hessian Hotel to set up a rendezvous in Burlington; the Hardys go in his place. Bones Arkin and Whip McIntyre, the ringmaster, among others, are waiting for Lonnie. Much to the boys' surprise, the head of the whole operation is Tyrell Tyson, the well-respected lawyer. The Hardys summon the police.

Joe and Frank are spending two weeks at a summer cottage on Lake Ketchumenken in ***The Demon's Den*** (1984) when they stumble upon a new case: the disappearance of George Wetley, a boy at the local camp. They introduce themselves to a Vermont State Trooper, who recognizes them as the famous sons of Fenton Hardy. The boys are instantly suspicious of Larry Smith, the camp director, who seems overly eager to put the blame on Apocalypse, a cult living in an abandoned barn at Needlepoint Cove. The cult members assure the Hardys of their innocence in the kidnapping and state their belief that the "Devil" took George. The Hardy's father informs them of another case that may tie in with theirs: the National Institutes of Health is seeking a scientist, Randolph Rhee, possibly exposed to a bacteria strain during a special project on genetic engineering. Jeffrey Peters at the Vermont Biological Research Center knows his whereabouts. The Hardys follow Smith's trail to the Annual Lumberjack Contest, where they spot his accomplice, Pierre Lafoote, and then, acting on information from Peters, pick up Rhee's trail to Canada. Pierre Lafoote is on the same train to Montreal; in the baggage car is a crate containing George's body—still alive. They send him back to Vermont and alert the police. In Canada, they meet their father and a CIA agent; sneak into a lumber camp; confront Rhee, who is the head of the laboratory experimenting with creating super-athletes; are drugged and thrown in a truck; and wake up in Vermont after interception by the CIA. They rest at Lake Ketchumenken for a few days before returning to Bayport.

Marilyn Cram Donahue

Straight Along a Crooked Road (1985) recounts the experiences of the Hamilton family in 1850, when it undertakes a cross-country trip to a new life in California. Midford Falls near Otter Creek is home to Daniel Hamilton, a cooper, his wife, four boys, Luanna, and little Emmie. For Luanna, fourteen, no place in the world is like Vermont, and she has been looking forward to entering Essex Female Academy. The Hamiltons have been rooted for generations in Midford Falls, which is known for its marble quarry and Merino sheep. Luanna cannot credit the fact they are leaving. Her Aunt Prue and Uncle Fisk, who live in Vergennes, buy the cooperage, the house, and the farm; Great Aunt Clara elects to go to California with the family. Luanna, who has no choice, pledges to return at her first opportunity; her best friend, Nancy Addison, gives her a journal to record her experiences. The other two families heading out West with them are the Douglases and the Crawfords. Luanna is attracted to Ian Douglas, sixteen. All through the Vermont winter the Hamiltons prepare for the journey, making soap, tallow candles, and clothes out of butternut-dyed homespun, and buying shoes with wooden-pegged soles from the cobbler. Their two wagons have canvas hoods stretched high over bent-hickory bows. Luanna makes a final tour of familiar and beloved sites—the schoolhouse, the millpond, the covered bridge on Otter Creek, and Snake Mountain, looking out at Lake Champlain. The rest of the narrative describes the arduous journey as Luanna walks in the dust behind the wagon. She learns tricks from her mother like skimming rich cream from the milk and putting it in a churn hanging under the wagon to make butter by nightfall. She keeps notes in her journal. Death and strife accompany them. When they reach the National Road and join a wagon train, Luanna finally believes that there is "life beyond Vermont." They spend the first winter in a small cabin in Illinois. Daniel uses his lathes to make and sell barrels. Among the books her teacher sent with her, Luanna reads "Rip Van Winkle" and "Legend of Sleeping

Hollow." Luanna becomes increasingly fond of Ian. Cholera sweeps through the wagon train, and pioneers die, including one of her brothers. Cheyenne Indians harass them. They pass dead animals and discarded supplies. Some come down with mountain fever. In Salt Lake City, the Hamiltons decide to spend the winter; her mother is not well enough to continue. Luanna has to say goodbye to Ian, but they declare their love and will find each other in San Bernadino the following summer. Luanna learns from Aunt Clara that the journey in life is important, not its end. (The sequel, *The Valley in Between*, 1987, describes Luanna's life as a pioneer in California.)

D

Marion Doren

Nell of Blue Harbor (1990) is Nell Willow, eleven, a member of a Vermont commune called "The Farm," established by Vietnam veterans as a place "to plant things, raise animals, and make their living from the land." One of the original founders is Nell's father, Thomas Ian Philip ("Tip") Willow, a disabled veteran, whose wife, Ilse, is a poet. Tip and Ilse also have a baby, Abigail. When the commune was formed, members turned over their money to The Farm. Tip comes to a parting of the ways with his old friends when he refuses to relinquish his money from the Veteran's Administration for the plate in his head and the brace on his leg. He decides to leave The Farm to seek a world of books, music, and a proper education for Nell, who has never been outside the commune. The Willows drive to Blue Harbor, Maine, where Nell is assigned the care of Abigail and cooking for the family, while Ilse composes poems and Tip writes about Vietnam. When Nell starts school, Ilse resentfully watches the baby. Never having been to school before, Nell finds going by herself difficult. On her route she meets Daniel Rhodes, with whom she can walk part way. When Nell returns from school laden with homework, Ilse immediately turns Abigail over to Nell, who also cooks, cleans, and pasteurizes the milk. Her teacher, Miss Cavendish, gives Nell a journal. "Maine cold is damper than Vermont cold," she records. When friends from The Farm visit, the men offer to roof the shed, but Tip is too proud to accept. Nell writes in her journal about The Farm, where she had many mothers, fathers, sisters, and brothers. Matters deteriorate in Nell's household: she feels the need of a mother to cook and look after the baby. Her new school friends, Mimi and Daniel, each have loving parents and normal, warm homes. At Christmas, Nell makes presents for everyone; she receives nothing. Tip announces he has a lead on his book and goes to Boston; the next day, Ilse leaves for New York to discuss her book deal. Nell is alone in the house with Abigail. A blizzard comes; the oil tank is empty; and the cow freezes to death. Nell tries her best to cope, wondering what her idol, Laura Ingalls Wilder, would do in this emergency. (Nell's favorite book is *The Little House in the Big Woods*.) Finally, when the baby becomes ill and feverish, Nell calls Emma Moore at The Farm, who says she will come immediately (it is an eight-hour drive). Back at The Farm, Nell breathes in "the fresh, crisp Vermont air, so different from the fishy tang of Blue Harbor." Emma, also her teacher, gives her *Heidi* to read. On his return, Tip is incredulous that Ilse left the children alone. Full of resolution for a new way of life, Tip returns to Maine to bring order to their household and then collects Nell and Abigail; Nell thinks The Farm is a safer place for children. They do not know whether or not Ilse will come back.

Eugenie A. Doyle

Stray Voltage (2002) takes place in 1986 in Greensbrook, situated on Route 14 two miles south of Williamstown. In fact, the highway goes right through the Daley dairy farm, between the house and the barn. After his mother leaves, the family of Ian Daley, eleven, consists of his light-hearted brother, Ray, sixteen, and his taciturn father, Warren. Ian's mother's twin sister, Julie, who lives half a mile away on the LeClaire "home place," where she and her sister grew up, comes over each day to make their meals. Warren and the boys do the backbreaking chores, milking, sugaring, and lumbering. Ian thinks his mother is in Barre with her brother, Jack; she is in California, living with her brother, Charlie, and studying to become a vet. Ian wonders why she left. Was it the stray voltage in the barn, a problem with the power that occurred after a terrible ice storm? Was it her silent husband with the callous, dirt-lined hands? Was it the remoteness of the farm and the relentless hard work? "Everyone pretty much kept to themselves on this road unless you asked for help, and then they'd be nice the way Dad was when Mr. Stanley hurt his back and all the men helped do his second cut." Ian performs a long list of chores each day. One of his worst experiences came in the first grade, "when a substitute told him and Sarah Conroy, the only other farm kid in the class, to put their boots outside, they made the whole room smell like a barn." After that, Ian knows that farm people are different. Not many children live on farms anymore. "He knew stuff they didn't. Even when he seemed to know less than they did, like about CDs, clothes, dances, even sports, he'd drawn comfort from his private stash of useful information from home." The only person in his world who makes Ian feel valuable is Mrs. Worth, his sixth-grade teacher. "Know your roots," she tells the children, "and grow from there." "Stand up for what you believe even if you're standing alone." Ian is steeped in Vermont idiom, such as, "Groundhog Day—half your wood and half your hay." Warren's troubles begin to mount: the power problems persist; the cows become sick; Ian is not concentrating at school; the chores fall behind. Ian realizes that, although Vermont looks pretty on the outside, inside, "That's where the trouble is. That's where the news comes from. Coydogs in those pretty woods. Stray voltage underground and climbing all through that pretty barn. And cows hurting, people fighting, losing money, cats disappearing, moms leaving." Ian struggles with the perplexities in his life. He is angry, tearful, and ill with despair but stands up to his father in a moment of crisis. Finally, Ian is able to forgive his mother and sympathize with his father, who, in desperation, tries to burn down his barn.

E

Genevieve T. Eames

In ***Pat Rides the Trail*** (1949), Pat Carey, fourteen, has a happy and trusting relationship with her widowed mother, her little brother, Billy, nine, and Uncle Ben, who is a native Vermonter (Pat notices "Vermonters don't talk much"). She spends four years weeding the garden, berry picking, and babysitting in order to buy at auction a small bay mare named West Wind. She writes to the Green Mountain Horse Association in Rutland to enter her horse in the Hundred-Mile Trail Ride, held twenty-five miles away in Woodstock this year. She plans to use her saddle money for the entry fee, but Uncle Ben offers to give her a new saddle if her mother lets her participate. Pat practices mornings and evenings, venturing a little farther each day. She passes the farm of the Randalls, who own a small herd of Shetland ponies and cut wood and sell maple syrup to sustain themselves through the winters. Mrs. Randall gives Pat a pony for Billy to ride and as company for West Wind. One evening, Pat takes a shortcut through the posted land of Alvina Buckley, who shouts rudely at her. For Pat's fourteenth birthday, her mother gives her a pair of tan jodhpurs (she was resigned to wearing her clean jeans) and a brown tweed coat; her uncle's present is boots, and Billy's, gloves. When Billy falls ill with tonsillitis, Pat fears she will be unable to go to Woodstock, but her mother and uncle agree she is old enough to ride there by herself (Uncle Ben cannot drive her because of wartime gas rationing). Uncle Ben's main counsel is for her to stay the course: "Been plowin' stony fields all my life and I've learned not to let go the plow handles every time I see a rock." The road to Woodstock is marked with Green Mountain Bridle Trail signs. When Pat arrives, everyone looks more senior and more experienced than she, knows one another, and owns seasoned horses, but she makes friends with Roxy Ferris, who won the lightweight division the year before. Roxy is not riding this time, but she gives Pat some good advice; better still, she attends Green Mountain Academy, where Pat is headed the following year. The first day of the ride is rainy and slippery; Alvina Buckley, looking grim, is competing. The second day is fine and dry; West Wind is in good form. A murmur spreads among the onlookers about Pat's progress: it is probable she will win. On the third day, the route is hilly and hard. When West Wind's hooves go though a rotten board on a bridge, she is lamed and falls to her knees; Pat, too, is hurt. Pat throws away her weights and carefully leads her horse on foot, thus disqualifying herself. When she meets the timekeeper, she reports she is out of the competition. Meanwhile, Alvina Buckley is busy gossiping that Pat cheated by dismounting and leading her horse. The timekeeper quickly clears up the misunderstanding. At the awards ceremony, Pat wins the coveted Best Junior Horseman Trophy, for showing "true concern for her horse and exercising good judgment both in riding and caring for her mount." In addition to the trophy, the other contestants band together to give her a stunning new bridle, "for courage and fine sportsmanship."

William Pritchard Eaton

Members of the Beaver Patrol in Massachusetts in ***Boy Scouts on the Green Mountain Trail*** (1929) undertake a scout trip to Vermont with their scout master, Abe Bruce. Meeting another troop in Pittsfield, they plan to start at Blackington near Williamstown, Massachusetts, hike into Vermont for two days, and come down to Bennington, where a truck will meet them. The boys, cooperative, disciplined, and sportsmanlike, are excited to be on the Long Trail, which winds three hundred miles almost to Canada. The route is marked with round white disks nailed to trees. The first night, camping out, Mr. Bruce tells them stories about famous mountain climbers. Next day, they bury or burn all their refuse, douse the fire, and scatter the embers. They reach the plain around Haystack Mountain and, northward, glimpse Bald Mountain. That afternoon, they find Hell Hollow Camp, where the door is locked, but four adult hikers appear with the key. They spend a jolly evening swapping tales. For the second and final day, some boys elect to make the long trip over Glastenbury Mountain to Bennington, while others go by Bald Mountain. The first route is between eighteen to twenty miles and a steady climb. "From every side they looked off upon a wilderness of peaks and hollows, like a vast, tossing ocean." From the top they view Bennington and Rutland valleys and northwestward to the Equinox range. They meet the other campers, who have a fire going. Some of the boys need to bathe their feet in cold water. Mr. Bruce concedes the hike was overlong, but, when some of the smaller boys lagged behind, the elder ones wordlessly relieved them of their burdens. Once home, the scouts plan another trip to the Green Mountains—an entire week in August. The plan is to start at Pleiad Lake, hike north over Bread Loaf and other mountains to Camel's Hump, and then to Mount Mansfield, the highest mountain in Vermont, coming down into Smugglers' Notch at the end of the trip; Mr. Bruce hires a car to meet them at Stowe. As they approach Bread Loaf, the boys are amazed at the forest: "the size of the trees, and the richness of the moss and ferns, and the dark mystery of the woods." The boys climb to four thousand feet, over Mount Abraham, Lincoln Peak, Nancy Hanks Peak, Mount Ellen, and the next night sleep on top of Camel's Hump. A storm rises; a rain of hail stings their faces. The summit is white with frost. They climb Bolton Mountain to attain Mount Mansfield and treat Mr. Bruce to dinner at Summit House. They are on top of the world (four thousand three hundred and ninety-three feet)—the White Mountains far to the east; the Adirondacks far to the west over the "glittering silver" of Lake Champlain. They walk to Stowe, where the truck meets them. Invigorated, sunburned, and muscled, they would gladly start all over again.

Amy Ehrlich

Where It Stops, Nobody Knows (1988) is divided into four parts, taking place in Montpelier, Vermont; Logan, Utah; Venice, California; and Brooklyn, New York—the four cities where Nina Lewis, thirteen, lives in succession with her mother, Joyce. In the fall, the sun makes the State Capitol's golden dome in Montpelier sparkle. Joyce finds an apartment near Vermont College. Nina enrolls at the Main Street Middle School, the fourteenth school she has entered in her short life. Smart and resourceful, she is accustomed to being the new student in school, one of many skills she has honed in her nomadic life. Joyce and she travel in a van with her dog and often sleep in the vehicle. She sometimes wishes that they were more like conventional families but imagines that Joyce keeps moving because she is looking for something. Nina knows only that Joyce was thirty-five at the time of Nina's birth and never married. Nina is in the eighth grade ("Eighth grade girls can be cold") and finally makes a friend on the basketball team. She also meets a boy, Sam Gordon, whom she likes very much. Joyce becomes more and more unpredictable and lays down increasingly draconian laws curtailing Nina's activities. Nina finds out Joyce has been lying about where she is on the nights she says she is working. Joyce takes Nina shopping in Burlington but will not allow her to travel to Newport for an away game. Suddenly, Nina announces they are moving again. "Why?" pleads Nina, "I really like it here...I think I'm going to make the honor roll." And she has met Sam, her first real friend. When the other young people find out, no one says anything except Sam, who asks her to write to him. The episodes in Utah and California follow the same pattern, except someone comes to the door asking for "Georgia Halloran." By the time they are headed back East, Nina knows they are on the run. Joyce dyes her and Nina's hair blonde and forbids Nina's going to school. One day, Nina comes back from the park with her dog to find her mother gone and three strangers to greet her. She learns the incredible, terrible truth: Joyce is not her mother but a nurse who kidnapped her when she was a baby in the hospital. Nina's real parents are Joe and Cynthia Healy; she has a younger sister, Elizabeth. Nina, in shock, thinks first of Joyce: she wants to visit her in prison (Nina is sentenced to twenty years), but the authorities will not allow it. Nina moves to Virginia Beach and slowly adjusts to her new life as Nina Healy. Her parents do not want to talk about the past. Finally, hoping Nina will put her former life behind her, the Healys allow her to visit Joyce in prison. The meeting is difficult at first; Joyce begs forgiveness. Nina is composed enough—generous enough—to assure Joyce she has nothing to forgive: "You were my mother...We had an exciting life." And then Nina leaves.

Phoebe Erickson

In *Double or Nothing* (1958), Jeff Gates, twelve, his sister, Ellen, eleven, and their parents are new to Vermont. The children desperately want a dog. One day they glimpse a black dog, which has probably been abandoned. When they follow him into the barn, they find two black dogs—twins. They name them "Double" and "Nothing." Meanwhile, their father plans to buy them a boxer. They show their father one of the dogs, asking if they can keep him. The father agrees, so long as it does not belong to anyone and does not run deer. Jeff and Ellen are with the dogs in the forest when they see the dog warden; plunging into the woods, they lose their way. The sun goes down, and the mountains darken. Jeff sends Double home to alert their parents. Double leads the search party back to the children. After this stellar performance, their parents want to keep both dogs. The children still worry that someone will claim their pets. Jeff and Ellen notice that, in the village, summer people seem to make more of a fuss over the twin dogs than "Vermonters [who] would have walked right by." The dogs appear so much at home in their house that the family believes they must have lived there with the former owner, Old Prescott. When a stranger claims them, demanding payment, the dogs chase him up a tree; nevertheless, their mother gives the man some money because he cared for the dogs briefly after Old Prescott died.

Erik E. Esckilsen

The Onion River Mall in ***The Last Mall Rat*** (2003) is located in Shunpike Falls, a socially fractured community: the southern part is the Airport Neighborhood, where the less fortunate people find themselves; the more advantaged live in Laurel Heights. The high school is filled with tough, hopeless young people who cannot find even part-time employment after school; the private preparatory school's graduates attend elite Queensbury College. Mitch Grant, fifteen, lives with his hard-working mother, Sally, close to the airport; his father, Reg, is no longer part of the family. He was a successful real estate executive until he lost his job protesting the building of the mall. Reg had dreams for a Shunpike Commons, a tasteful, coherent central spot to draw the community together. Now the mall, "a glorified warehouse," sprawls along Route 4. Reg, a housepainter, lives in a trailer in another town and cannot help his family financially; Sally works at a printing plant in Quarry. Mitch is not old enough for a legal job; at the mall, employers give him money under the table for insulting customers who are rude to employees or do not buy anything. His mentor in these repellent techniques is The Chair, the best salesman at the mall. Mitch's tired mother, cooking supper with a glass of wine handy on the counter, hears that Mitch's best friend, Jimmy Biggins, beat up and killed an old man; Mitch concedes the existence of gangs in Shunpike but knows that Jimmy, whose parents abuse him, is not guilty. Mitch enlists Page Anderson, whose father also left home, and Marcus Walker, an African-American, in his mall activities, rationalizing that this plan for making money is another form of civil disobedience against people who are discourteous. More and more salespeople demand the "attitude adjustment" services of the Mall Mafia, as they are now known (they wear masks). Mitch begins to feel uncomfortable about what they are doing—what he started. Wanting to call off the activity, Mitch is a bit afraid of Jimmy, who has joined them. A meeting of the Parent-Teachers' Association looks into the Onion River Mall affair. The local newspaper, the *Beacon*, incriminates Jimmy in the mall activity and implies he is armed and dangerous. Jimmy disappears. After Mitch, Page, and Marcus agree to avoid the mall, Mitch arrives home to find both his parents, who demand to know whether he is involved in the "terrorism" at the mall. While in hiding, Jimmy has become something of a hero at the high school. Reg forms a local group to end the crisis at the mall and restore civility to the town. Mitch explains to his father his role in the affair. In turn, Reg tells Mitch about a thoughtless, cruel prank that he perpetrated when he was about Mitch's age. Reg counsels Mitch to turn himself in. Reg, Mitch, Page, and Marcus go the Shunpike Falls Police Department, where the officer listens carefully and mandates community service for their role in the customer-harassment scheme. Mitch tries to negotiate a settlement for Jimmy, who independently turns himself in. Reg is offered a good new job some distance away, where he arranges a group home and a job for Jimmy. For the first time, Mitch is on good terms with his father.

Casey LaPlante, seventeen, in ***The Outside Groove*** (2006) is at the top of her senior high school class in Fliverton in Granite County and the star cross-country runner. She has been accepted at a top private college where she wants to study environmental science and save the planet. At home, however, she feels invisible and unsuccessful because her father, Big Daddy, a former short-track car racer, and her mother, Carol, focus all their attention on her brother, Wade ("the Blade") LaPlante, twenty, a gifted racecar driver. Casey refers to Wade privately as the "man-child" because he still lives at home and behaves promiscuously with the local girls. Casey has a crush on Fletcher Corwin, Wade's pit-crew chief. Wade's goal is to race on "the Circuit" team, a goal Fliverton exalts. Casey astounds her family by buying a stockcar (she has been earning money babysitting) to race in Road Warriors, the starter division; Wade is in Thundermakers. She seeks advice from Uncle Harvey, Big Daddy's former crew chief, who is mysteriously alienated from the family. Uncle Harvey works on her car. Uncle Harvey's advice is: "Don't be shy about cornering on the outside groove." She is confused by the noisy, vibrating, dangerous scene at the racetrack but uses her head and her knowledge of physics and geometry: racing is not just traveling the shortest distance around the track. She does not finish the whole twenty-five laps; no one in the pits except Fletcher speaks to her. Although her schoolmates shun her the following Monday, Fletcher asks her to the prom. Uncle Harvey thinks her racing in her own county is too stressful and takes her to another track in Byam in Corkum County for an "enduro" (a race that tests endurance). "Take what the race gives you. Patience," is Uncle Harvey's advice this time. Three exotically dressed girls, calling themselves The Sharks, befriend Casey; they know all about engines (and the quirks of the other drivers) and sign up as her pit crew. Her mother finds out Casey is meeting Uncle Harvey but will not explain Harvey's estrangement from the family. The Sharks make "Go Casey Go" shirts. After she wins the race, Casey attends the dance in a dress lent to her by the Sharks. She overhears someone say that Wade made Fletcher take her to the dance. When it is time for her to race locally, the Sharks are there. Casey ("The Lady") LaPlante wins. Because Wade wins his division, they receive their trophies together. At a victory party later, Vin Coates, racing reporter with the *Granite County Record*, interviews Casey, not Wade. In the next race, the other drivers decide to prevent her from finishing the course. She watches Wade and is mesmerized by his skill. She wins another race at Demon's Run, where the fans vote for her to race in the Thundermaker division—against her brother—on the Fourth of July. Her father is furious: that is the day Wade will be scouted for the Circuit. Big Daddy also knows about Uncle Harvey's helping her. Uncle Harvey finally tells her the secret: he was in love with her mother, Carol Beech, who chose to marry Big Daddy. Harvey stayed on as his crew chief; the Circuit scouts were recruiting Big Daddy, but after he lost the race, he—and everyone else—blamed Harvey. Uncle Harvey makes her a Thundermaker car; Big Daddy says he will not pay for her college education if she races. She enters and, in the final seconds, she and Wade are in a dead heat. She lifts her foot from the accelerator; Wade wins. He shoves the victory flag into her car for the victory lap. From the winner's podium, Wade thanks his family; Big Daddy and Uncle Harvey make up; and Casey learns there is "more to racing than just driving around in circles." (The racetrack is modeled on the Thunder Road International Speedbowl in Barre, Vermont.)

F

Caroline S. Fairless

Hambone (1980) is eight-year-old Jeremy's pet hog. Jeremy, his brother, Alec, fourteen, and his sister, Stoner, sixteen, help out on their father's farm near Bristol. The defining moment in Jeremy's life was their mother's leaving home when he was six. She writes to him, but he will not open the letters. Before his mother left, Ramona came to help with the cooking and cleaning; afterward, Ramona stayed on. Jeremy notices when he goes to the store that the summer people "look different, stiff like toy soldiers. Their pants are clean and their shirts are new." When Alec and Stoner hoe the garden, Jeremy sits with Alec's Winchester across his knees. His assignment is to shoot the groundhogs, but he cannot force himself to do it. In fact, he cries when he thinks of all the cows, chickens, and pigs they raise for slaughter. The day comes when Hambone is to be killed. His father orders Jeremy to attend. Stoner gently explains to Jeremy why Hambone has to die. She suggests making a memorial to his pet, explaining that the word means to celebrate, commemorate, and honor something. Jeremy digs a big hole and puts in all the items Hambone liked—manure, slop, a wine bottle from which he once drank, and the red ribbon he won at the fair. Jeremy plants a tomato seedling on the memorial and starts to cry. The Hambone plant grows into the biggest and strongest tomato plant for many miles around. A huge storm blows up, toppling trees. Jeremy goes outside to protect the Hambone memorial plant during the storm. His father finds him huddled on the gravesite: the water running down his father's face is not rain. The *Valley Voice* publishes a story about Hambone and the one hundred and thirty-seven tomatoes that his plant bore in the first weeks after the storm.

Clavin Fisher

In ***A Spy at Ticonderoga*** (1975), fourteen-year-old David Holcomb, whose mother died when he was young, is filled with anger and sorrow because the British killed his father at Concord in April 1775. He moves to Simsbury, Connecticut, where his uncle, Noah Phelps, treats him like a son. When the Connecticut Committee of Safety approves and funds its role in the expedition to Fort Ticonderoga, Captain Edward Mott enlists Noah's participation. David is eager to help, too. Noah, uneasy about David's youth, agrees to his joining the expedition if he can elicit information from the Tory spy held at Newgate Prison in East Granby, Connecticut. David succeeds; Noah does not give him a musket but assigns him to chop wood, build cooking fires, and fetch wood. The group sets off for Salisbury, where they pick up ten more militiamen, including Ethan Allen's brother, Levi, and a young Indian horse handler, John Tantaquidgeon, who teaches David to mimic the high-pitched call of the Great Horned Owl. Crossing into Massachusetts, they are joined by Colonel John Easton and his militia. The little army enters the New Hampshire Grants and heads for the Catamount Tavern in Bennington, where Colonel Ethan Allen, "tall, strong, and purposeful," is waiting with some of his Green Mountain Boys. While foraging for food, David and John meet Colonel Benedict Arnold, who, like Ethan Allen, expects to head the expedition. When the leaders discuss the need for intelligence about troop strengths in the fort, Noah volunteers to enter the fort as a Tory; David goes along as his son. Noah tells the sentry he wants a barber's shave before visiting his sister in Shoreham. David befriends a young British soldier, Peter Kennett, who allows him to do some sketching from the battlements. While David is drawing a map of the inside of the giant, star-shaped fort, equipped with one hundred and eighty cannon, he is arrested and locked up. Noah must leave him because the attack is scheduled for the next day. Captain Delaplace puts David in the custody of Peter, who finds him a bunk in the barracks. During the night, David stealthily pours water over the cartridge pouches of the British soldiers. The British muskets fail to fire; the Americans are successful. By using their owl call, John locates and releases David. Colonel Allen sends the British flag to the Continental Congress and, for his courage and ingenuity, offers David any reward he might name. David requests that Peter be released to his charge; Peter comes home with them to Connecticut.

Dorothy Canfield Fisher

The eponymous heroine in ***Understood Betsy*** (1917) is nine-year-old Elizabeth Ann, who enjoys a sheltered life with Great-aunt Harriet and her daughter, Aunt Frances, in the Midwest. Elizabeth Ann is thin, pale, nervous, and spoiled. She never lifts a finger around the house, because "the girl" does the housework. When Aunt Harriet develops tuberculosis and must seek a warmer climate, Aunt Frances reluctantly sends Elizabeth Ann to her relatives in Hillsboro—"reluctantly" because Aunt Frances has always found them "queer" people who do not speak in "clear statements of fact," the way she does. A friend escorts the little girl to New York, where she takes the train from Albany to Hillsboro. Her Great-uncle Henry Putney meets her, addresses her as "Betsy," and, without asking how she "stood the trip," hands her the reins to the wagon so that he can attend to some figuring on a piece of paper. Remembering the way to turn the horses left or right is the first independent thinking Betsy has ever done. Instead of making a fuss over Betsy, Aunt Abigail, plump as a pudding, and Cousin Ann, wise and calm, give her a kitten to care for. Betsy is amazed that she is expected to dress herself and make her own breakfast. The first morning she learns to churn butter. Aunt Abigail tells her about the Putney family's coming up from Connecticut on horseback in 1763. Betsy is fascinated that real people were living in this same house at the time of the Declaration of Independence. The first afternoon, they send her off to school by herself: what a difference from Aunt Frances's accompanying her and lingering for a long time. That evening, with very off-hand (or so it seems to her) instructions, she makes applesauce and sets the table. After supper the family members busy themselves with their special occupations and suggest that Betsy read aloud to them. At school, Betsy is quite shocked that the children are all in one room with one teacher. No one is assigned to a particular "grade": she reads at one level, does sums at another, and often helps some of the younger children with their reading. When the superintendent comes to school, Betsy feels humiliated because she does not answer some of his questions correctly. Cousin Ann seems unsympathetic, saying she guessed "Hemlock Mountain would still be standing" even if Betsy misspelled a few words. Betsy has to think hard about that statement, but soon Cousin Ann is hurrying Betsy outside to wax her maple syrup in the snow. When the mother of little Molly, one of the children Betsy reads with at school, has to go to the hospital, Cousin Ann invites Molly to stay with the Putneys. Betsy loves having a little sister, but she is terrified one day on a walk when Molly falls into a pit. Rejecting the instinct to cry and run home, Molly tries to think what Cousin Ann (whom she greatly esteems) would do: she finds a branch with stumps of limbs resembling a ladder and pushes it down the hole to enable Molly to climb out. Elias Brewster, a poor boy at school, lives with a drunken stepfather and has neither proper clothes nor enough food. The adults hope to interest Mr. Pond in adopting Elias. Betsy thinks up the idea of making clothes for Elias so that Mr. Pond will find the little boy more acceptable. Betsy infers from Cousin Ann's comments that they do not need credit for this task if they are doing it for the right reason. Betsy celebrates her tenth birthday at the Necronsett Valley Fair in Woodford. Because the Putneys are unable to go, Betsy and Molly travel with the Wendells next door; the Wendells discover they must leave the fair early and ask the Vaughns to take home the girls. When Betsy and Molly arrive at the Vaughns' booth, they are nowhere to be found. It is up to Betsy to find a way home. She assesses the situation the way she believes Cousin Ann would. Molly cannot walk eight miles: the train costs fifteen cents each; they have only a dime between them. She goes from booth to booth offering to wash dishes for twenty cents. Finally, at the doughnut counter, a girl who wants to dance with her beau leaves Betsy in charge. She washes dishes and sells goods, too, leaving the change on a shelf for the proprietor. The two girls take the cars to Hillsboro and have started the two-mile walk to the farm when Uncle Henry meets them with the light buggy. All the Putneys are very proud of their Betsy—and show it. In the "rich October splendor," Aunt Frances writes that she will pick up Betsy. Anguished, Betsy knows she must be loyal to Aunt Frances and not show her true feelings nor do anything to hurt her. At it turns out, Aunt Frances and Betsy are each trying not to injure the other: Aunt Frances is to be married; Betsy wants to stay at the Putneys' farm. Events evolve into a state that Betsy recognizes as "Happiness." (For more stories about Hillsboro, see Dorothy Canfield Fisher's collection of adult short stories, *Hillsboro People*.)

Eight of the ten stories in ***Something Old, Something New*** (1949) are set in Vermont. **"Why the Apple Tree Grew in the Pine Woods"** takes place during the American Revolution. A patriot son, living in Arlington with a Loyalist family, joins General Schuyler's regiment. Whenever the young man lets his sister know that he can visit, she meets him in the woods with food. An apple core he throws on the ground grows into a tree, which represents the new country, America. Separate and independent, it sprouted from the soil upon which two countries, England and America, waged war. The narrator finds a moral in the story: "and" (two countries) is always better than "or" (one country). In "**How I Rode the Moose into Kennettown, Mass.**," Jebediah Chillingworth is known for his exaggerated tales. One of them is about a sailor (himself) who kills a bull moose. The narrator, then a little boy, laughs with everybody else in the village over this story. Years later he discovers the story was true and hurries to Jebediah's deathbed to apologize for not believing him. The look ("You didn't believe me all these years?") in the dying man's eyes fills the narrator with lifelong remorse. Later, the narrator's granddaughter finds out the story was false but has not the heart to tell her elderly relative. In "**Indian Witch-Cure**," set in 1762, Hanna Sherwin, sixteen, does all the work in her motherless family; Ann Mary, nineteen, is the "beauty." When Ann Mary falls into a "decline" (she has nothing to do), Hanna takes her on a perilous journey across the mountains to Heath Falls, on the Connecticut River, where dwells an Indian healer, Necronsett. His prescription for Ann Mary is for her to stay alone in a little hut and cultivate a garden of herbs. The outdoor exercise soon puts a bloom in her cheeks, and she sleeps and eats well. She meets and falls in love with the local minister's cousin, Captain Winthrop. When Hanna visits, young Winthrop teaches her to read and write, and she returns to Hillsboro to teach, marry, and have children. Hanna treats all the young women who go into a decline, and the town, in gratitude, names the river after the Indian healer. Winthrop becomes a general under Washington, and Ann Mary becomes a great lady, comely and still illiterate. In "**Why Aunt Hannah Took Bigger Stitches**," old Lemuel Hager, who mowed the grass in the orchard at the narrator's house, tells her that Miss Hannah taught him to read. When she discovered that he was very nearsighted, she gave him her magnifying glass. She said it mattered not to her: she would simply take bigger stitches. Today, every time he reads the evening paper, he thinks of her. In "**Of War and Peace**," a mother with a household of squabbling children almost breaks down because she is so worried about the war. She tells them that all wars have the same cause: "One side wants to do things one way, and the other wants the opposite." When the elder children come home from school, she urges them to talk to the younger ones about ways to solve wars—through institutions like governments, constitutions, rules, and courts. The oldest boy explains to the others about the purposes of the League of Nations. In "**Soldier of the Revolution**," all the Revolutionary War veterans of the town of Sunmore have died. Andrew Bostwick and Will Hunter remember an old man living in the hills; he is brought down, deaf, bent, and carrying a gun, to be honored in the Fourth of July celebration. Someone notices that his gun belonged to a Hessian soldier. The audience is hushed, until one of the boys stands up and makes an impassioned speech: after seventy-five years, he says, it is time to stop taking sides. "**Ann Story: Yankee Pioneer**" presents the life of a famous Vermont heroine. Ann Story's husband, Amos, goes from Connecticut up to Salisbury with his fourteen-year-old son to build a house for the family. While chopping trees for the log cabin, a giant tree falls on Amos and kills him. After the son sees to his father's burial, he walks one hundred and fifty miles back to Connecticut. The young widow, thirty-three, with her three sons (Solomon, Ephraim, and Samuel) and her two daughters (Susanna and Hannah), embark for the wilderness to carry out Amos's plan. In late 1775, Ann and her children move into the log cabin her husband built. She is a model mother and homemaker; she is also a citizen and a patriot. She wants her children to own their own land and not be forced into "semi-feudal subservience to rich folks." She becomes an aid and advisor to the Green Mountain Boys: "Give me a place among you, and see if I am the first to desert my post." When Indians come to the area, she takes the children by boat to hide in the reeds of Otter Creek; they watch while the Indians burn down their home. They rebuild. She and the children collect information to pass to the Boys. They dig a passageway into the bank and make a cave where they hide every night. One day they rescue a pregnant white woman, a captive left behind by the Indians; Ann delivers the woman's baby. Many Vermont Loyalists are on their way to Canada to inform on Vermont settlers. One such traveling Tory wakes the baby, who cries. A Story son alerts the Boys, who capture the whole lot of Loyalists. Self-respect and self-control keep the Boys from killing the Tory fugitives, whom they turn in at Fort Ticonderoga. **"Something Old, Something New"** begins in Vermont around 1850, when the man of the family decides to move out West where he can find "strong fertile soil" to cultivate. He precedes the family, which follows by stage coach and canal boat. The mother hates the trip and complains about everything. They arrive in a place with tall green grass in big natural clearings. "It made the thin sparse green of the stony Vermont upland pasture on the home farm look threadbare." Their father builds them a log cabin with glass windowpanes. The mother, "white-cheeked and bleak," sobs continuously and finally dies, leaving the fifteen-year-old daughter to bring up the children and care for her father.

Paul Fleischman

The four interlinked stories in ***Coming-and-Going Men*** (1985) are about traveling men—a silhouette cutter, a seller of ballads, a painter, a peddler—passing through New Canaan in 1800. In **"The Shade Cutter,"** Cyrus Snype, once famous as a cutter of silhouettes, surveys the village and sees "a church, sharp-spired and white as a bride." Satan overtook him; he drank too much and ruined his reputation by snipping caricatures of two prominent people who took offense. Now, with manacles in his pocket, he is on the track of Satan, seeing signs of his corruption everywhere. He will recognize the Devil, who, they say, casts no shadow. Snype stops at the Plowshare, where many patrons pay him to have their profiles taken. Mr. Grindstaff, the tanner, hires Snype, in exchange for a new pair of boots, to find him an honest wife. Snype sees sinful people all day but, supping at the Plowshare, spies Bethany Beale, the landlord's daughter, whose face lacks "the slightest trace of corruption." He wishes to cut Bethany's profile, but she refuses, suspecting that Snype himself is Satan and would steal her soul. When her mother tells Bethany that Snype is heading for the tannery to cut the profile of Oliver Botts, the man she loves, she seizes the manacles and keys from Snype's room and hurries to the tannery. There, while Grindstaff proposes to her, she claps the handcuffs on Snype and yanks off one of his boots—he does not have a cloven hoof like Satan. Another look at Bethany tells Snype she is not virtuous. He grabs his pack and continues on the track of Satan. In **"Enemies of the Eye,"** Joram serves as apprentice to Mr. Cobb, chandler and soap maker, whose past is obscure. He has a speech impediment and a southern accent but claims to be a native Vermonter. Above all, Mr. Cobb hates crows. He hands his rifle to Joram and sends him forth to shoot crows for twelve cents a carcass; Joram's mother needs the money. Out in the field, he shoots at a crow but kills a lamb by mistake. Unfortunately, the lamb belongs to Rodney Pickett, the most litigious citizen in New Canaan. Joram buries the lamb and tells no one. He continues to kill crows but is anxious about concealing his crime from Mr. Cobb. One day Joram meets Mr. Hamby, a seller of ballads and broadsides. He sings for Joram a song about a soapmaker in Georgia who blinded his sweetheart with lye for flirting with another man. He was not hanged for his crime but suffered "a hole bored in his tongue with a hot awl" and was banished from Savannah. Joram is horrified: can this man be his master? He challenges Mr. Cobb, who remembers "no miscreant act." Joram confesses to Mr. Pickett and pays him his crow-hunting proceeds. Before he leaves his apprenticeship, he throws out some kernels of corn for the crows. In **"Slaves of Sham,"** Simeon Fyfe paints signs, gilds frames, silvers mirrors, and executes panoramas and portraits with his son, Patrick. Fyfe teaches Patrick to see the world as it is. Though he considers George Washington a myth (Fyfe fought briefly at Germantown, where the British beat the Americans), he now makes his living from the panorama, "Prospects of the Glorious Life and Deeds of General Washington," which they will show in New Canaan on the Fourth of July. Mr. Pickett is rude to them as they enter town. They take a room at Mrs. Meese's house in exchange for a sea scene, during the execution of which Mrs. Meese's blonde and exquisite daughter, Delia, reared on romantic novels, enters. Coincidentally, Isaiah Clapshaw rides into town, carrying in his wagon a waxwork of General Washington. Someone rips the canvas of Fyfe's panorama. Patrick, assuming it was Pickett, cuts his horse's harness. Mrs. Pickett, thinking the culprit was Clapshaw, hangs his waxwork from the ceiling of his wagon. A horrendous fight ensues between the two showmen. Fyfe decides to give up illusion. Patrick dreams of Delia and himself, a prince, in love in Persia. Jonathan Wardwell, a peddler of dyes and essences in "**Country Pay**," trades goods for a room in New Canaan, but Mrs. Beale ejects him. He passes on to a big house where Ida, the young daughter of deceased Nathaniel Tewkes, tells him that her fate is to kill herself with a poker in three days—the date her mother died. He tries to sell her a Bible in exchange for her poker. It is All Soul's Eve—Jonathan's birthday. Ida begs him to spend the night, because only he will be able to speak to the ghosts of her parents. He waits for hours on the bridge, but no one comes. His firm has built its reputation on the motto, "Give the people what they need." He reassures Ida that her parents told him she was adopted; hence, her time is a long way off. The next morning, when he opens his trunk, she has substituted her poker for his Bible.

Genevieve Fox

Susan of the Green Mountains (1937) begins in a small log cabin at the Eldredge pitch (an early settler's encampment) on Otter Creek in 1773. The family consists of Susan, fourteen; her brother, Nathan, seventeen; her mother and father; little Faith; and baby Joseph. Susan has no time to be lonely or homesick for Connecticut while she scours the pewter dishes, cards and spins flax into thread, turns the spit, brews dye, washes clothes, makes soap, and pounds corn into grain. Pioneer life is rugged and hard. When their father's ax slips, cutting his leg open, Nathan and Susan do his work, too, clearing the paths, feeding the animals, and bringing in the logs. Colonel West and other Yorkers arrive while her father and Nathan are away; quick-witted Susan mimics an owl call, giving the impression she is signaling to the Green Mountain Boys. The Lathrop family arrives from Connecticut; Susan is delighted to see her friend Jonathan, sixteen. The Eldredges are hosts for a clearing bee for the Lathrops. While her father and Nathan are on a trading expedition for pigs and sheep, Jonathan hastens to the cabin. His mother is sick with lung fever; his father has gone to fetch the doctor in Crown Point. Susan's mother hurries away at once with the baby, leaving Susan and Faith alone. When Colonel West and his followers return to remove the roof of the cabin, the two girls escape on horseback; Susan leaves Faith with a neighbor, Joe Barnes, and rides through the night to summon Colonel Ethan Allen. He and some of the Boys give Colonel West the beech seal (a whipping with green beech strips) and then, guns drawn, force the Yorkers to put back the roof and ready for planting the cornfield, which they destroyed. Allen, who wants the Yorkers to experience what it means to clear the land and build a cabin, is proud of Susan's courage and initiative. The summer of 1774 is peaceful: the women and girls spin and quilt, and the men join forces to cut hay or burn brush. They hold a corn husking, making a merry gathering out of the task and providing plenty to eat and drink. The Continental Congress declares that King George cannot take the colonists' natural rights from them. The pioneers now have the leisure to plant flowers: two years of loneliness, discouragement, and backbreaking work have paid dividends. News comes of the fighting at Lexington and Concord. Some of the settlers on Otter Creek claim that the dispute will not reach them, but others are realistic enough to know that they, too, are involved in the cause. When Colonel Allen sends out a call for recruits, Jonathan joins the Green Mountain Boys. Before he leaves he confides to Susan that they are going to seize Fort Ticonderoga. On the way to deliver a pie to Joe Barnes, Susan overhears a conversation between Colonel West and Bill Bassett, to whom the Colonel gives a letter. Joe is not in his cabin; she borrows his rifle and dons his cap and deerskin jacket. Disguised and hiding behind a tree, she points the rifle through the branches to intercept the letter intended to warn the commandant of the garrison about the impending attack. The night's wait seems long to the families, but the attack takes place without a drop of blood spilled. For her bravery and important service, Ethan Allen sends Susan, by Jonathan, an honorary captain's commission in his company. Susan and Jonathan decide to marry when the war is over. They cannot imagine that, in the years ahead, they will live in a frame house and drive a carriage over a real road.

Border Girl (1939) features the same kind of courageous, responsible young woman as the one in *Susan of the Green Mountains*. In 1812, Deborah Owens, fourteen, lives in Covington, below the Canadian border, with her parents, her grandfather, and her younger siblings, Joe and Polly. Deborah's grandfather fought in the Battle of Bennington; her father, John, is an officer in the Covington militia. Peter Allen, sixteen, and his family live close at hand; Peter's father, Mose, is a Tory. The Owens family attends Training Day for the local militia. Deborah's grandfather, disgusted with the sloppiness of the drilling, wonders what they would do if there were another war. John, who is convinced they will fight the British, takes down his musket, scours out, oils, and loads it, and leans it against the door. When news comes of the threat of Indians, some families leave; others are evacuated to the Tuttles' big barn. The smuggling of embargoed goods to and from Canada is a serious offense; the customs officer will shoot anyone caught in the act. By leading John out on a wintry night to track some alleged smugglers, Mose creates a diversion to allow the real smugglers to take an alternate route. John, incensed, bars the entire Allen family from his home—including Peter. John joins the militia stationed at Derby Line, leaving Deborah and Joe to shovel a path to the barn every morning to milk the cows—until Joe falls ill. While Deborah is shoveling alone, Peter appears, clears the walk, and cleans and skins two rabbits for the Owens's dinner. Next morning, he milks the cows and feeds and waters the stock before the family is awake. He continues to perform these services, at great personal sacrifice, without giving Deborah a chance to thank him. John returns from the border. Neighbor is pitted against neighbor over the smuggling issue. Animals, including their mare, Dolly, disappear. John believes that smugglers like Mose are taking revenge on members of the militia. Deborah leaves Peter a note in the post office they used when they were children. The men organize an anti-smuggling committee. The British fire on Burlington and destroy the barracks nearby. While picking blackberries, Deborah discovers the smugglers' secret road thronged with cattle. After she shows the customs officer the road, he breaks up the smugglers' ring. Hailed as a heroine, Deborah is sad that the Allens and Tuttles are forced to leave. She and Peter, who love each other, say goodbye. The British advance on Plattsburgh from Montreal under Governor-General Sir George Prevost, who offers protection to anyone in Vermont who will refrain from hostilities. John fights with the Covington militia. Lieutenant Thomas Macdonough, only thirty-one, is the brilliant commander of the sea battle. When the guns of *Saratoga* are destroyed, he orders her turned around to fight with the guns on the other side. The British fleet retreats; General Provost surrenders. John returns home safely; Peter enlists for the rest of the war and goes to Lake Erie. After the war, he returns to Covington to marry Deborah.

Frances Frost

Windy Foot at the County Fair (1947) introduces Toby Clark, the protagonist of a four-novel series (the others are *Sleigh Bells for Windy Foot*, *Maple Sugar for Windy Foot*, and *Fireworks for Windy Foot*). Toby, twelve, lives on a farm in Webster near Otter Creek with his parents, Jim and Mary; his sister, Betsy, nine; and brother, John, six. Toby, who wants to be an artist, is an uncommonly kind and thoughtful elder brother. For his birthday, his parents give him Windy Foot, a dappled-gray pony with a black mane; the other horses on the farm are Serena, upon whom everyone learns to ride; Jake, the family driving horse; and Tillie and Tossie, the Belgian farm team, which draws the maple sledge. Cliff, the hired man, is a beloved member of the family. Toby trains Windy Foot all summer until the pony is "hardened and swift and sure" for the race at the county fair. At the fairgrounds, a bully, Lem Strout, challenges Toby. A bystander intervenes in the ensuing fight. Introducing himself as Billy Blue, the groom at the Burnham stable, he offers Toby a stall to keep Windy Foot safe, warning Toby that Lem, also in the race, might try to hurt his pony. Billy also gives Toby a boxing tip—to pivot before he swings, just like a horse turning a corner in a race. At the Burnham stable Toby meets Letitia ("Tish") and her father, Jerry. Tish's face is "haunting and beautiful," Toby thinks. Her mother died when she was a baby; Jerry and Billy raised her. Toby feels guilty about having the Burnhams board Windy Foot when Toby wants to beat her and her horse, Jigs, in the pony race. Tish cannot believe his attitude: "Racing is fun, like playing a game—not a matter of life and death!" Tish meets the family and charms Betsy and Johnny. They watch Toby's father, "handsome, tall, and sunburned," talking quietly to his team in the stoneboat-pulling contest. He wins fifty dollars, which will help buy a new blade for the corn cutter. Toby also meets Tish's friend, Jimmy Slater, fifteen. When Toby finds Lem making threatening gestures at Windy Foot, he is calm and ready to fight; he knocks Lem to the ground. Tish wins a doll for Betsy in a shooting gallery. Toby's father invites the Burnhams and Jimmy Slater to spend Christmas with the Clarks. Billy braids Windy Foot's mane for the pony race. During the race, Lem tries to crowd Toby out and crashes against a fence. Toby and Windy Foot win; Tish and Jimmy are wonderful sports, expressing their happiness for him.

Sleigh Bells for Windy Foot (1948) begins just as Christmas is coming; everyone is making lists and preparations. Tish and Jerry Burnham are expected. Toby works hard scaling down the old sleigh to fit Windy Foot. The sleigh looks beautiful, the body painted vermilion with black runners. When Betsy and Toby snowshoe out to pick partridge berries, they see a fox. Everyone piles in the truck to buy turkeys at the general store. "The sun was slipping down behind the black pines on the western ridge and the sky was beginning to turn the cold apple green of a winter sunset." On the property they see a hungry bear from Canada, which has eaten a pig and clawed a colt. Toby goes outside to do the chores, taking his father's Winchester rifle. When the bear rears up at the stable door, Toby lets him have two shots right in the chest. The family again travels by truck to admire the village tree and sing Christmas carols. The Burnhams arrive. Toby's mother asks the motherless Tish to call her "Aunt Mary." Georgette has her bull calf, which Betsy's parents give to her; in honor of Christmas, Betsy names her new pet "Kris." They exchange gifts before Christmas dinner. In the woods they detect a white buck with six-point antlers "like delicate branches against the green boughs." After dinner, Toby takes Tish in the refurbished sleigh to the village. While they are in the drugstore, Chuck Harris climbs into the sleigh and whips Windy Foot, who runs away. Toby recovers his horse and expresses to the livery man his shock that Chuck behaved in that fashion. The livery man reminds a chastened Toby that he drives to school every day and never offers anyone a ride; furthermore, the village children are jealous that he shot the bear. As the day ends, Tish and Toby take one more run on their skis. Tish falls into a ravine and breaks her leg. With the help of Windy Foot, Toby rescues her and calls the doctor. Tish will stay for New Year's Eve weekend after all.

In ***Maple Sugar for Windy Foot*** (1950), the Clark family is sugaring. As they work, Jim explains the way the Indians discovered maple syrup. When a tree was cut randomly, causing the sap ("sweet water") to drip out, they deduced how to boil it down into syrup. Jim gives each of his children a maple tree. At a sugaring-off party for children in the village, Toby whittles paddles for the guests to use in winding up curls of syrup. After three more sap runs during the rest of March—about six hundred and fifty gallons of syrup—Toby, his father, and Cliff clean the buckets, pans, and tanks. Toby does a charcoal sketch of Cliff "in the fog of the sugarhouse." Cliff's weathered face was "rapt and filled with dignity...There was a deep humbleness in Cliff's face too, and Toby completes the drawing with awe and tenderness." With unceasing rain and rising rivers, they fear a flood. Toby takes Windy Foot and the buggy to school to carry the children to high ground. The horse bravely swims across the river. That night, Toby is asleep when he hears the emergency family whistle: everyone assembles, including the dogs and cats. The dam at the quarry bursts: "The whole valley is coming down." Mary and the younger children hurry up the hill to the sugarhouse. Toby, waist-deep in water, helps take the horses out of the barn. One horse disappears downstream. Windy swims, keeping his head and Toby's above water; Cliff is struggling with Betsy's calf; Jim hangs onto a cow. The Davidsons whirl by in their house; the Clarks' house miraculously stands. Toby weeps. The valley is "shattered and littered." They do not know how many cows they have lost out of a herd of forty. Their house is ruined inside: all Toby's drawings are destroyed, though he knows they are not nearly so important as his parents' work over all those years. With his father, he views the barn "with its dead cattle, its destroyed hay and grain" and the "river-battered acres of what had once been a beautiful farm." Cliff and the calf make it home. First Toby rides Windy to the three (out of ten) homes still standing to make lists of the families' needs and then ten miles to Mr. Riggs's store to buy food and supplies. Tish and Jimmy Slater come to them for Easter, bringing a ham, eggs, and some animals for the Clarks to start over. They also bring Toby a new horse, Golden Hind II (called "Two"). Acknowledging that he has grown too long-legged for Windy, Toby, with great sentiment, gives Windy to his brother and sister. Tish appreciates her brother's generosity. (For three adult versions of Vermont floods and their consequences, see Chris Bohjalian's novel, *The Buffalo Soldier*, Howard Frank Mosher's novella, *Where the Rivers Flow North*, and Dana Yeaton's play, *Mad River Rising*.)

In ***Fireworks for Windy Foot*** (1956), the Clarks are recovering from the flood and planning to buy more cows that summer. Since the disaster, Toby feels he is "deep-down friends" with his father. Excited about the Fourth of July ceremonies, they invite the Burnhams for a visit. Windy Foot and Johnny, dressed as Yankee Doodle, will lead the parade. Toby is part of the "Washington Crossing the Delaware" float. When Toby complains to his father that Pietro Di Marco, "who isn't even an American," is chosen to play General Washington, his father looks grave and asks Toby how he defines an American. An American is someone who was born here, answers Toby. His father decrees that, unless Toby learns what an American is, he will not be allowed to ride in the parade. In the village for the band concert, "The valley lay brilliant green and gold under the slant of light, and Crooked River [an Indian name for Otter Creek] twisted down the valley like living silver." Chuck Harris, the bully who drove Windy Foot around the square the previous year, challenges Toby to a fight. At that moment, Dick Norton and other friends of Toby's walk up, and Chuck backs off. When Toby asks about Pietro, Dick says he is admirable—he mastered English quickly, earned the highest marks, gave the graduation speech, and bats the ball hard. After some sober thinking, Toby tells his father that he realizes all Americans were foreigners once. His father responds that part of being a good citizen means being tolerant of one's neighbors. When Betsy does not return from berrying, Cliff and Toby search for her. A handsome young man appears, carrying Betsy, who has a broken arm and a sprained ankle. It is Pietro, who stays for supper. Toby discovers that Pietro is "sincere, kind, and thoughtful." His father works at the quarry in order to feed his five children. Pietro wants to go to the Massachusetts Institute of Technology to become a naval architect. In the village, after Chuck tries to harass Windy Foot with a whip, the inevitable fight takes place. Remembering Billy Blue's advice about pivoting, Toby beats Chuck easily. The Clarks attend the naturalization ceremony for the Di Marcos, which brings tears to

Toby's eyes. Tish spends the weekend. The parade is grand; Johnny and Windy Foot are the prime attraction. Pietro and his sister, Maria, stay after the parade for lunch and swimming. The big surprise of the afternoon is the arrival of Jerry, who brings Toby a sulky with which to train his horse, Two. Toby feels full of emotion that night, surrounded by his friends, Tish and Pietro, and his family.

G

Nancy Garden

In ***Mystery of the Night Raiders*** (1987), Brian Larrabee, thirteen, is on the train reading his favorite book, *The Collected Sherlock Holmes*, as it pulls into White River Junction. Every summer, he visits his grandparents on their farm in Grove Hill just south of the station. His grandfather is faced with a mystery that threatens his livelihood: his cows are sick, and four have died, with no explanation. The milk co-op no longer accepts his milk. Brian, who tries to reason like Holmes, wonders if someone is poisoning the herd. His grandfather cannot think of a single enemy, except George Knowles, now deceased, whom he fired. Brian meets two contemporaries, Edward ("Numbles") Crane, Jr., and Darcy Dixie Vernon, who are eager to help solve the mystery. Numbles suggests conducting library research on poisons that leave no trace. Brian suspects curare; perhaps someone planted the vines where the cows would eat them. Numbles interviews a worker at the milk co-op; Darcy collects specimens in the pasture; Brian examines all the cows. Another cow dies. Brian finds two small wounds on the cow's neck, which Darcy thinks resemble fang marks. Brian's grandfather asks the children to help him clear bats from the barn, which hang upside-down from the rafters "like black gloves out to dry." The last one, huge with the wing span of a large hawk, eludes them. Numbles wonders if it is a vampire bat, which bites cows and spreads disease. They return to the library to study vampires, but the examples shown in the reference books are smaller than the species in the barn. Brian, rereading "The Adventures of the Sussex Vampire," is convinced they are dealing with a real vampire. Darcy complains that someone next door to her family is making a terrible racket at night. In the cemetery, fresh dirt surrounds the Knowles family graves. Brian, looking into Darcy's neighbors' house, glimpses a fanged woman and a boy sleeping in earthen coffins. Knowing that vampires vanish if they are exposed to the dawn, the three children disguise themselves as vampires and engage the Knowles family in conversation until sunup, when the vampires melt away. The three young people separate for school but pledge to act as monster hunters in the future.

The Case of the Stolen Scarab (2004) is set at Candlestone Inn in Bennet (based on Landgrove/Londonderry) where Nikki Taylor Michaelson, twelve, and her brother, Travis, eleven, have recently come with their mothers, life partners, who adopted the two children when they were babies. Louise, a computer programmer, and Mindy, a tax accountant, are leading a new life as innkeepers. The inn is named after a monolith on the property, a natural phenomenon that intrigues local residents. Almost immediately, two exciting events occur. First, the sheriff reports that thieves in Boston stole a scarab worth half a million dollars, leaving behind a map marked with a route to Bennet. Next, an unknown hiker collapses on the doorstep and awakens suffering from amnesia. In his backpack is a turquoise scarab; the sheriff returns it to the Boston police, who declare it a replica. The sheriff exhorts Nikki and Travis to scrutinize the inn guests. Nikki and Travis keep a list of clues and suspects. The first guests are Mr. and Mrs. Cobb and their son, Herbert, a self-proclaimed "gifted" child who notices some carving on the boulder that may be "ogham" or ancient Celtic writing. Hattie Fletch, an amateur geologist from Boston, arrives, followed by Peter Jordan, also from Boston. Out searching for clues, the children leave their bicycles by the side of the road, follow drops of blood leading to a dark stain and a small piece of blue material, and find a stray dog with the same fabric in her back teeth. When they return to the road, their bicycles are gone. After the arrival of Professor Zorich from Harvard, a Miss Dalrymple, the Tansys and their baby, and the Woodwards, the inn is full. The hiker, released from the hospital, takes a room at Charley and Don's Fox and Hare Restaurant in exchange for doing chores. The dog growls at the Cobbs, but when the hiker comes over, she greets him joyfully. Hugging her, he dredges up his name, Michael Fogarty, and his dog's, Bess. Nikki, devising a trap to catch the criminal, asks Charley and Don to cater a meal at the inn. The centerpiece on the table is the fake scarab, mounted attractively. Upon seeing it, Mr. Cobb confesses: he used to be an art thief, went to prison, married and had Herbert, and found himself in need of money for Herbert's education. Mrs. Tansy, a fence, arranged to meet Mr. Cobb in Bennet to receive the scarab. The Cobbs will stand trial; the professor, impressed by Herbert's knowledge of antiquity, will pay for his education. The sheriff presents Nikki and Travis with deputy sheriff badges.

Dale Blackwell Gasque

In ***Pony Trouble*** (1998), Amy, who lives in Vermont, is an equestrienne; Rebecca, who lives in Maryland, is a gymnast. Rebecca visits Amy in Vermont. In Amy's eyes, Rebecca is a show-off who wears fancy new breeches and boots. To compensate for her beginner status, Rebecca blames her horse and calls him "stupid." The girls quarrel all the time. They take their ponies to the pond for a picnic lunch. When Amy rides her pony, Lightning, into the beaver pond, his legs stick in the mud. She keeps her head and leads him out of the pond, grateful that he has not injured himself. She knows she was showing off. When the girls realize their parents are constantly comparing them, they laugh and agree to help each other instead of competing: Amy will show Rebecca how to swing onto Lightning, if Rebecca will show Amy the way to do cartwheels.

Gail M. Gauthier

Thérèse ("Tessy") LeClerc, the eleven-year-old heroine of ***The Hero of Ticonderoga*** (2001), is indifferent as a student, dissatisfied with her lot in life, and endowed with a lovely sense of humor. She is slightly ashamed of her French-Canadian parents, who run a dairy farm in Cornwall, and is not certain whether her father is literate; her elder brother, Marcel, is in ninth grade. She is forced to go to Catholic school on Saturday mornings. She is not a member of the popular set in her sixth grade and pines to have parents like Deborah Churchill's, whose father dons a suit every day and whose mother wears earrings even around the house. When Tessy's strict and inflexible teacher, Mrs. Ford, goes on compassionate leave, the substitute is, shockingly, a man, and, even more shockingly, uninterested in the rigid schedule that Mrs. Ford had ordained for the children. He has democratic leanings and a poetic sensibility. When the children tell him about the assignment for oral reports on Vermont, with the battle for Fort Ticonderoga as the coveted topic, he suggests they draw straws; Tessy wins. She begins her assignment assuming she will find nothing of interest about Ethan Allen, but she becomes engrossed in her reading and soon, through her own curiosity, engages the attention of the other children. She piques their interest in the guerilla activities of the Green Mountain Boys: one of her classmates makes the comparison to the Vietnam War. Each week they urge her to tell them more about her hero; she gives one section of her report at the site of Fort Ticonderoga itself, which the children visit on a field trip, taking the ferry from Shoreham. At first, she cares solely about her grade; then her reading absorbs her in the struggle for land in the New Hampshire Grants and the social discrepancies between the poor farmers and the rich Yorkers—"the gods of the hills are not the gods of the valley," as Allen says. In her report, she follows Allen in captivity to England and his return to New York; she speaks about Vermont's becoming a Republic. When Deborah Churchill visits the LeClerc farm, a neighbor's fierce dog chases the girls. Mr.

G

Churchill stands uselessly by while Roland LeClerc kills the savage animal with a shovel. When Mrs. Ford returns, she denigrates Tessy's report on Ethan Allen; Tessy's father sits on her bed that night, reads aloud the final ringing passages of her paper, and congratulates her on her good, thorough, and enthusiastic work.

In ***Saving the Planet & Stuff*** (2003), Michael Peter ("Mike") Racine, III, sixteen, unhappy to lose his summer job, jumps at the chance to go to East Branbury (based on Middlebury) to work at the environmental magazine owned by his grandparents' great friends, Walt and Nora Blake. Mike, self-absorbed and sarcastic at first, is surprised to find that the Blakes actually "live their values." They dwell in a solar house and promote precycling ("If you don't buy it, you won't have to recycle it"). They conserve energy, eat no meat, and stack his room with paper, plastic bags, and panty hose, which they do not want to take to the landfill and for which they seek useful purposes. They used to live in the commune on the hill but are now in town so they can bicycle to work. They began *The Earth's Wife* thirty years earlier. Today, the magazine staff includes Nora, publisher; Todd Mylnarski, managing editor; Roberta Ferguson, art director; Maureen Bogda, associate editor; Annette, receptionist; and Amber, Roberta's seventeen-year-old daughter, who answers the telephone during Annette's lunch break. Walt, with no specific job, attends staff meetings. Nora assigns Mike to sorting emails to the editor; later, he will learn ways to respond. At meetings, the staff discusses issues ranging from composting toilets to wind farms to eco-recreation to what date Earth Day should be celebrated. Mike picks up tensions among the members. Todd is clearly changing the direction of the magazine (he often uses the term "eco-style"). Mike notes that Todd refuses to accept telephone calls from Doug Sinclair, the author of an article on Perkins-Simmons, a distributor of possibly contaminated insulation allegedly causing health problems. Mike has never had a real date; Amber reluctantly goes with him to the fair. She is terrified of becoming involved with a local person (Mike points out he is not a local person and only wants one date) because her mother married too young and is stuck in East Branbury. Mike, concerned about the Sinclair affair, searches Perkins-Simmons on the Internet to find out if the term "fungus" has ever been associated with the company's products. This young man, previously uninterested, is suddenly excited about doing research. With an adult job also comes disillusionment. Todd is having an affair with Maureen, is planning to fire Roberta, and wants to take over and change the magazine. Nora, a denouncer of golf as ecologically unacceptable (too much wasted water), is taking golf lessons; Walt is sneaking off to eat hamburgers. Perkins-Simmons, the largest distributor of the questionable insulation, discharges Doug Sinclair. Mike finally bypasses Todd to inform Nora, who calls *The New York Times*, which exposes the healthscandal and provides good coverage for *The Earth's Wife*, as well. Mike comes of age—and learns to turn off the lights when he leaves a room.

Corinne Gerson

In ***My Grandfather the Spy*** (1990), Danny Turner, thirteen, whose mother is an aspiring actress seeking auditions in New York, is spending the summer doing odd jobs at an inn in Paradise, north of Burlington. Marcus and Eva Warren, whose children are Barney, seven, Ellen, five, and Jack, four, tried their hand at farming but, unable to prosper, turned their beautiful old house and outbuildings into a country inn, Heavenly Acres. On the train to Vermont, Danny meets a friendly old man, who introduces himself as Harold Hawkins. At the inn, Danny immediately idolizes Marcus, who treats him like a man, and follows Marcus around, helping to fix up two extra bedrooms in the house and to add two cottages. Every so often, Danny notices a white flash in the bushes. The first guests arrive—Mr. and Mrs. Tuttle and their daughter, Carla, thirteen, who abandoned her summer camp in Vermont after one week. Just as Danny has begun to feel special in the Warren family, Carla's parents propose leaving her with the Warrens as a "summer intern" to look after the younger children and help with the kitchen chores. The "flash in the bushes" is Harold. Danny wonders if he is a spy. Because Harold used to be a farmer as well as a skilled plumber, carpenter, and painter, Marcus and Eva hire him and install him in the little bedroom in the back of the barn. The family adores him and calls him "Gramp." Many more guests arrive. Danny is a bit jealous of Carla's popularity with the Warren family, although he concedes she loves the children and enthusiastically joins in. When he hears that she called him a "wet blanket," he decides to run away, even though he has a sore throat and swollen glands. Hours later, Carla, astride the horse, Glossy, finds him collapsed on the highway and brings him home, promising not to tell anyone he ran away. The doctor diagnoses mumps and, because the younger children have not had the disease, the Warrens move him into Gramp's room. Gramp unlocks his special box and describes his experiences in World War II, showing Danny photographs of his comrades. When Marcus calls away Gramp to cope with a crisis, Danny notices a large stack of hundred-dollar bills in the box. Is Gramp on the run? Danny and Carla have a chance to talk: she reveals that, though rich, she is lonely because her parents are often away. The Warrens mobilize for the county fair. Carla suggests she and Danny nominate Gramp for the fair's Grandfather of the Year award. Danny writes an essay about him for the competition. Some days later, a strange-looking couple named Bromley dines at the inn; during dinner Mrs. Bromley snaps a picture of Gramp. The Bromleys turn out to be judges for the award, which Gramp wins. A buyer offers Marcus a great deal of money for Heavenly Acres. When Marcus and Eva confess that they cannot make the inn pay, Gramp offers them his life savings. While Marcus and Eva are considering this option, the sheriff brings over a copy of *People* magazine, featuring Gramp and disclosing his identity. He is Peter Marikian, who disappeared from a senior citizen group home in Brooklyn. Marcus and Eva accept Gramp's offer just as his son and daughter storm in, wondering where on earth he has been. He quietly explains that, after they persuaded him to give up his farm and move to New York, they had no time for him. Now he is actively engaged with a real family. When they say goodbye, Danny and Carla agree to write to each other.

Beth B. Gilchrist

In ***Kit, Pat, and a Few Boys*** (1921) "Kit" is Katherine Embury, sixteen, a cool, confident, and affluent New Yorker. She finds herself alone in a house full of servants when her mother is called to Bermuda to take care of an ailing sister, her father is on assignment in Alaska, and her brother, Don, is working on a ranch in Wyoming. As her mother departs, she instructs Kit to visit her Aunt Marcia Brunt. When Kit arrives at Aunt Marcia's house, she finds it closed up; Patricia Ward, a neighbor with whom Kit used to play years earlier, invites her to stay with them. The Ward family—mother and father; college-aged sons, Phil and Fred; younger brother, Nick; and younger sister, Marian—is on its way to camp in central Vermont. Pat and her mother judge from Kit's clothes and demeanor that she would not adjust easily to their primitive life "in the wilds of Vermont" and, hiding their disappointment, stay home with her. Kit quickly appreciates their sacrifice and asks to accompany them to Birch Lake near Mooseback Mountain. She soon adapts to sleeping on boughs, eating from wooden plates, and swimming before breakfast. Though their clothes are rough, the Wards' manners are impeccable and their dinner conversation is intelligent and international in scope. They always bring a box of books. Marian is rereading *Little Women*; Pat settles down with *Lorna Doone*; and Kit picks out *Pride and Prejudice*. Despite her privileged background and vacations in Palm Beach, Kit has never experienced the enthusiasm the Ward family displays, from reading to cooking to mountain climbing. The boys are impressed by her good sportsmanship. They climb to the Jade Bowl, a deep, circular pool with a waterfall; the slate from the quarry gives it the dark green color. When she helps Pat make—and serves—shortcakes with berries for supper, she feels, for the first time, a sense of belonging. After watching a village woman make piecrust, Kit bakes four rhubarb pies for dinner. She contributes to life at camp and is "shaken out of her indifference." One day Mrs. Ward and the girls hike to Loon Lake. Kit confides to Pat that she has never felt so alive. The whole group goes berry picking. Mr. Ward proposes a climb up Mooseback. The trail is steep and zigzagging, but the view at the top is worth the climb. When they return to camp, Kit finds a letter from her brother summoning her to New York. He needs an operation for an old football injury. Kit manages the crisis and, in the midst of it, becomes close to her brother again. Boxes of good Vermont products—trout, blueberries—arrive from the Wards. Kit and Don's parents arrive from their various posts; the family is both reunited and enlightened about what has been missing from their lives.

Shannon Gilligan

In ***The Search for Champ*** (1983), a story in the "Choose Your Own Adventure" series, you, the reader, are visiting your grandparents on Lake Champlain with your sister, Mag. Your mission this summer is to look for and photograph Champ, the purported Lake Champlain monster. Your first decision is whether to search at Shelburne Point or at Grand Isle. Paddling your canoe, you are magically rescued from several storms. One of your choices is to stay with your canoe or abandon it when a storm comes up; another is whether or not to enter a haunted house. You succeed in seeing Champ, and some of his friends, several times, and you recover valuable emeralds from the haunted house, which you turn over to the police.

Helen Girvan

In the midst of wartime, the doctor of widow Mary Meredith in ***Felicity Way*** (1942) orders her to the country to rest. She takes a leave of absence from her city job to travel with her two children, Dale, eighteen, and Donald, ten, to Maple Hill near Barre. Mary has inherited Chimneys from her Aunt Felicity Adams, who made a small fortune in Felicity Balm, an aromatic salve derived from her garden herbs. The doctor hopes, for the sake of Mary's health, that she will continue Aunt Felicity's work. Jenny Wright, the housekeeper at Chimneys, runs the household. Warren Webster, Aunt Felicity's lawyer, greets them at the station and introduces them to Michael, his young houseguest who is an evacuee from London. No one knows the whereabouts of the formula for Felicity Balm. Jenny gives Mary and Dale the keys to various desks and cupboards and to Dale a box containing a gold filigree pomander ball, with wishes from Aunt Felicity that the gift will bring her "happiness as well as endeavor." Gregory Hall, a red-haired young man Dale knew as a child, is in Maple Hill for a summer job before going to college. Mysterious events occur: they catch glimpses of a woman in a sleek black car with New York license plate "333"; some of the blue herb jars disappear; someone digs up a plot of rosemary from the garden. Mary finds a note saying the formula is stuffed behind a framed photo, but it has vanished. Dale is shocked when Mary accuses Warren of the theft and he storms out; Jenny reveals that Mary and Warren were once engaged. Another London evacuee, Margaret Locke, Aunt Felicity's goddaughter, arrives. Suspects mount: Will Clarkson runs a small patent medicine factory; Kate Moore is an imperious neighbor; Silas Beade, an elderly local man, loiters on the premises; Mr. Cromwell, the rector, is in possession of the two blue jars. Mary and Dale, more and more eager to stay at Chimneys, cannot afford to do so unless they find the recipe for the balm. The woman from New York, Natalie Dunn, is a cosmetics representative who wants to buy Chimneys. Warren and Mary resolve their romantic tiff; Dale solves the mystery. The thief is jealous Kate Moore, who does not want Mary to stay at Chimneys to marry Warren. Engraved on the golden pomander is the image of rue, the herb also known as "grace o' Sundays." In her work, Aunt Felicity added grace to this rugged climate where people are hardworking and thrifty. Dale, filled with "energy, determination, grace," will study horticulture and chemistry at the University of Vermont and marry Greg.

Christopher Golden

Laws of Nature (2001), the sequel to *Prowlers,* takes place after Molly Hatcher, eighteen, and Jack Dwyer, nineteen, eliminated Owen Tanzer, a member of an ancient race of monsters, when he murdered their best friend, Artie. Their ally in the affair, Bill Cantrell, is, though benign, the same species as the Prowlers and can change his guise at will. When Molly and Jack read about two mutilation murders in central Vermont, they head up Interstate 89 for Buckton in the Green Mountains to investigate. Artie's ghost, which can communicate with Jack from Ghostlands, confirms that some Prowlers have sought sanctuary in Buckton and are killing residents who, they believe, know the whereabouts of a journal revealing Prowler history and secrets. Alan Vance, deputy sheriff in Buckton, aspires to Sheriff John Tackett's job, loves Tina Lemoine, and is deeply worried about the local murders. The Prowlers, having searched everywhere for their book, break into the library, kill the librarian, and capture his daughter just as Molly and Jack figure out where the monsters are heading. When the police arrive, they naturally assume that Molly and Jack are the murderers and take them to the local jail. Molly and Jack suspect Sheriff Tackett might be the Alpha, head of the Prowlers, but he turns out to be human. To prove to the sheriff that they are telling the truth, Jack asks Bill to demonstrate his change of form. The real Alpha is Henri Lemoine, father of Tina (also a Prowler), who wrote the journal. A crowd of Prowlers collects outside the jail, forcing Tackett, Bill, Jack, and Molly (who is going to Yale in the fall but is handy with firearms) to shoot their way out. While killing the Alpha, Bill is severely wounded; the journal is cradled in dead Tina's arms. Tackett, who does not want police or media attention, asks them to leave town. As they drive away, Jack sees no more ghosts; the victims' souls have finally left Bruckton.

Nancy Price Graff

Riley Griffin, the twelve-year-old protagonist in ***A Long Way Home*** (2001), feels sad and resentful. His father and baby sister died in a car accident; he and Kate, his mother, leave their happy home in New York in 1980 to live in Sharon, where he knows no one. "The town is pretty tightly closed against strangers," his mother concedes. They move into his grandfather's old house on the village green. It is late summer, "when the fragrance of ripening apples and moldering flowers fills the air like an overpowering perfume." Kate reconnects with her old high school friend, Sam Mitchell, who lives in a cabin in the woods. Most of the townspeople shun him because he was dishonorably discharged from the army for refusing to fight in Vietnam. He assists Kate in rehabilitating her ramshackle house; Riley grumpily helps with chores. A loner at school, Riley befriends Mary St. Francis and her seven-year old sister, Claire. They live in a trailer; her father, a war hero, drinks. Riley likes American history and his teacher, Mr. Aja, with whom he and Mary play chess; he is pleased when his mother gives him a pair of ancient binoculars used by his great-great-great-grandfather, Silas Griffin, at Gettysburg. Every year, Sam delivers free cords of wood to Mary's trailer; this year he asks Riley to stack it. Although Riley cannot help but like Sam for his kindness and his skills, Riley is angry and incredulous that Sam would not fight in Vietnam. Sam explains to Riley that no one could ever tell him why they were fighting; he also acknowledges that his actions changed his life—and his expectations—forever. As time passes, Riley grudgingly admits that winter in Sharon is beautiful; he and his mother help Sam with his sugaring. Riley works on a research project for Mr. Aja, trying to identify Silas Griffin's regiment. In the spring Sam invites Riley to visit the Gettysburg battlefield and museum. Riley is inspired and thrilled by the site and exhibits, but when he learns that Silas Griffin was on the Confederate side, he feels upset and betrayed and blames Sam. The guide at the museum describes the courage it took for the Confederates to step out in one long line against the Union soldiers bombarding them from two directions. Riley cannot understand why they would do something so "stupid." The guide asserts that they were brave men trying to protect their land and their way of life. "But they lost!" cries

Riley, struggling not to weep. "Win or lose," says the guide, "it sometimes takes tremendous courage to stand up for your principles." On Memorial Day, everyone follows the parade to the cemetery—everyone save Sam. Each student is given a miniature American flag. When Riley and his mother come home, Sam is waiting for them. Riley takes the flag out of his pocket and hands it to Sam. "Here," he says, "this is for you."

G

In ***Taking Wing*** (2005), August ("Gus") Amsler, III, thirteen years old, spends the summer of 1942 with his grandparents in Miller's Run (based on North Pomfret): his mother is resting in a tuberculosis sanatorium; his father is in Texas learning to fly for the Air Corps. The Amsler farm is "set in a bowl, with the farmhouse and big red barn perched halfway up one side and a pond...sunk in the center of the bowl. All around were fields and, beyond them, woods that encircled the pond and the farmhouse like a Christmas wreath." When his grandfather inadvertently kills a mother duck with his mower, Gus assumes responsibility for hatching the eggs. Warning that his project is unlikely to succeed, his grandparents find an incubator and help him set it up. "Hope is the thing with feathers," quotes his grandmother. Gus marks the seven remaining eggs with an "x" on one side and a "y" on the other (breaking one in the process), so that he can turn them frequently, and waters them to keep them damp. The drake discovers the missing nest and flies away. In addition to caring for the eggs, Gus helps his grandmother with her Victory Garden, which President Roosevelt asks each family to maintain, and after dark he and his grandfather, a Civil Air Patrol spotter, sit outside and listen for German airplanes. One day, when Gus surprises a girl in the barn, she drops and breaks an egg with a nearly formed duckling inside. She is Louise Lavictoire, whose French-Canadian father is struggling with a neighboring farm. Gus is surprised to hear his grandparents criticize French-Canadians: they "marry their cousins and uncles and half-sisters," are "thieves and beggars," and "water down God-fearing Yankee stock." (Gus does not know about the shameful Vermont eugenics project, which, in the author's words, was a "despicable program of rejecting foreigners and nonwhites in the twenties and thirties.") After Gus and his grandfather build a brooder, Gus hurries over to Louise's farm to invite her to watch the eggs hatch. He sees how poor her family is. The Lavictoire yard is strewn with wreckage; there are five dirty little children and a sixth on the way. René Lavictoire is illiterate and lame from rickets. The process of the duck hatching fascinates Louise and Gus; he likes Louise's spirit and wit, although he worries about her health. He pores over copies of *Life* magazine for ways to keep her from getting rickets. His grandfather gives Gus a shooting lesson with a deer rifle. Shortly thereafter, a raccoon kills one of the ducks: his grandfather orders Gus to shoot the raccoon. Gus is busy and interested but aches for and worries about his parents. The ducklings are growing up and consider Gus their mother. He drives the wagon to help René and the children with the haying. He earns money from picking bugs off the potato plants but not enough to buy Louise some vitamins, so he helps himself to twenty-nine cents from his grandmother's hiding place. As a result, his grandmother, assuming Louise stole her money, refuses to allow her in the house. Gus confesses. The ducks—mallards—are beautiful, and Gus and Louise finally urge them into the pond. The ducks do not seem to need him any more, but he still needs his parents. When school begins, Gus attends with Louise. She tells him that everyone is expecting her father to fail; no one will help him. At harvest time, the school recesses so that the children can work in the fields. One night Gus finds René at the pond with a dead duck in his hand—food for his children's table. Gus, overcome with distress, points his gun right at the man's heart to force him to drop the duck. After René leaves, Gus cries and cries—for René's obligation to feed his family and for his father's obligation to kill the enemy to protect his loved ones. Gus knows he and his parents have changed irretrievably during this separation. The remaining ducks fly south: he wonders how they can find their way "in the pitch-black darkness of a Vermont night." It has been the best summer of his life, although he is sad that Louise is leaving. Ostracized and desperate, the Lavictoire family is returning to Canada. He and Louise exchange gifts. "She was the sun that had warmed the grass and turned it into hay and brightened this rundown place...she was the sliver of moon that had sparkled on the roof of this old farmhouse and made it look just like its neighbors during the quiet Vermont summer nights." He is going to miss her very much. (The first two lines of Emily Dickinson's poem #254 are, "Hope is the thing with feathers/That perches in the soul." The last two lines are, "Yet never, in extremity/It asked a crumb of me.")

H

Jessie Haas

In ***Keeping Barney*** (1982), Sarah Miles, eleven, moves to Vermont with her father, George, and her mother, Helen. George left his college teaching job to write full-time; their small, former farm belonged to Helen's father. Sarah single-mindedly yearns for a horse (*The Black Stallion* and Marguerite Henry's book about Justin Morgan are her favorite books). She sees a newspaper advertisement seeking winter boarding for Barney, a half-Morgan gelding, hay and expenses provided, while his owner, Missy O'Brien, is at college. Sarah's father wonders whether she can be responsible for a horse, when she forgets to feed her dog, Star; her mother, who once owned a horse, thinks the arrangement will develop responsibility. One of Sarah's two best friends, Albert Jones, works on his father's dairy farm and takes care of two horses, Hercules (Herky) and Ginger; Jill, her other friend, loves to ride but cannot afford a horse because her parents are supporting eight children. Barney settles into the Miles's barn and immediately exhibits his moods, stubbornness, and tricks. He will proceed nicely along the road, while Sarah enjoys "the vision of a flaming autumn woodland, framed between two scimitar ears," and then suddenly dodge into the brush, where a branch sweeps her out of the saddle. Her mother assures her the horse is "canny" and accustomed to having his own way. One day, riding with Albert, she pulls on only one rein and is thrown to the ground on her back. The doctor at the hospital diagnoses a concussion and commands a one-week rest. Sarah harbors a dream that Missy will fall in love at college and let her keep Barney, but Missy writes that she will be home for Thanksgiving week and will collect Barney. Missy is furious when she sees the sores on Barney's mouth: Sarah feels she is a failure for not being able to handle the horse. Missy offers to give her some pointers. Soon Sarah is controlling Barney more lightly: she is paying attention. Before the snow comes, the last day of hunting season, she and Albert ride over Woodfield Mountain. (Albert has already gotten a deer for the Jones family's meat for the winter; Sarah often feels self-indulgent when she remembers that Albert has to feed cows and calves and help with the milking.) They notice a young buck—and then hear a gunshot. Barney leaps and circles: he was hit in the chest. The vet pronounces it "a glancing tear—the bullet didn't lodge"; after he sews up the laceration, he gives Sarah elaborate instructions for caring for Barney. She must wash and dress the wound, give him bran mashes and warm water, and keep exercising him in order for the muscles to heal properly. She works hard, taking scrupulous care of Barney. Each night, Albert brings down one of his horses as company for Barney. Jill, Albert, and her mother and father combine resources to buy a baby goat as a playmate for Barney. Winter passes, and soon Sarah must give back the horse. As they take a final ride up Woodfield Mountain, Albert asks Sarah if she would help condition Herky during the summer. At the end of the summer, her parents will be able to afford to buy her a horse. Missy offers to give her dressage training as well.

A Horse Like Barney (1993), the sequel to *Keeping Barney*, finds Sarah, now twelve, home for the summer while her father writes and her mother tutors math. When her mother has finished working, and before she starts teaching in the fall, she will help Sarah pick out a horse. Missy, home from college and cleaning motel rooms for the summer, offers to drive Sarah around to look at horses for sale. Sarah keeps this activity a secret from her parents. Sarah exercises Albert's horse, Herky, while Albert helps his father bring in the hay. The first horse Sarah and Missy look at is Beau, "tall, lean, elegant," which she loves. The next horse is Roy: Missy is enthusiastic about him, but Sarah, though impressed, admits she is a bit frightened of him. The third horse, Thunder, is a darling, friendly horse—"just like Barney," Sarah thinks—but Missy says that at twenty he is too old. Sarah fears that Thunder may be sold at auction and butchered. Sarah's friend, Jill, takes care of her younger siblings and looks unhappy. Sarah senses that Jill, too, wants a horse but cannot have one. When Sarah is exercising Barney one day, she offers to let Jill ride him while Sarah wheels Jill's bicycle. It is a cool, beautiful day, and she sees a salamander, "bright as a crayon on the brown trail." Sarah tells Albert about Beau, Roy, and Thunder; Albert does not think she should buy Thunder just because she fears he will be slaughtered. When her mother finishes her tutoring, Sarah confesses that she has already started looking at horses and has found the one she wants. Her mother is disappointed and angry: since Sarah started on her own, she says, Sarah can finish on her own and make the final decision herself. Sarah's father reveals that her mother tutored all summer in order to make enough money to buy Sarah a good horse. Sarah takes her mother to see Roy and Thunder: Sarah recognizes the former as the challenging, energetic horse of her future; the latter is the pleasant, friendly horse of her past, just like Barney. She spends the morning on the telephone trying to find a home for Thunder. Simultaneously, her mother buys Thunder—for herself. Sarah will own Roy; she arranges with Missy for Jill to exercise Barney in exchange for riding lessons.

In ***Working Trot*** (1983), James MacLeish, eighteen, is a recent graduate of Phillips Exeter Academy; his classmates are going to college. His parents are bemused by his desire to ride horses for a career. He works for his father's cousin, Tom, and his wife, Marion, who own MacLeish Farm. His second cousin, Gloria, a photographer, is there, and Jennifer Bascomb, training to become an Olympic jumper, who is "taciturn and quarrelsome and unexpectedly nice." Tom and Marion's specialty is taking on spoiled horses and hiring young riders to retrain them: Ginseng, for example, is a show hunter whose mouth has been cut up with a wire snaffle; Lady Peregrine is a runaway. Ghazal, a white stallion, is James's special project in dressage; Tom assigns him a book on the training of horse and rider. James begins with no stirrups and no reins. He tries to unlearn ten years of riding to do what Tom wants, but he does not succeed. He is so sore he can hardly climb the stairs at night. It is all a terrible mistake: "He is angry with Tom, and, unfortunately, hates Ghazal." Then he sees one of Gloria's photographs of the stallion and appreciates his magnitude. When he rides the next day, he suddenly understands everything Tom has been teaching him. "There was elasticity and exchange, in place of the former grim struggle." Tom allows James to use reins and begin dressage; Tom is tough but appreciative. Life at MacLeish Farm is "peaceful, hardworking, monastic." Finally, feeling the need to mix with other people, he invites Gloria to go out for a couple of beers and dancing. He asks himself again whether he wants to concentrate on horses and give up the outside world. He sees a distinction between Jennifer, on the one hand, who is interested in competition, and himself, on the other, who is fascinated by the work. He continues to train with Ghazal—all repetition, "perfection, beauty, harmony," feeling one with the horse. He is at ease in the show world, with the horses, the people, and the atmosphere. At home, he relaxes by rereading *Wuthering Heights*. He spends an evening wrapped up in a blanket with Gloria, who has a cold, and doses her with tea and brandy. They become slightly tipsy; James considers his attraction to Gloria proper—she is, after all, his second cousin. His parents visit to inquire about his plans; his father is dogmatic in his insistence on college. Tom wants

James to buy and train a Morgan. James decides to buy the Morgan, Robbie, and stay at MacLeish Farm. "He sees himself rooted in the Vermont hills, making the native conditions his tools as he schooled Vermont horses to perfection and brought them to the world's attention as mounts for the serious rider." James is where he wants to be. Tom selects five spoiled horses for training in the coming summer. James and Gloria each ride in a schooling event. In the ring, James receives his instructions for the test: "Enter at A, working trot sitting."

The Sixth Sense (1988) is a collection of nine short stories, eight of which are set in Vermont, with alternating points of view—Kris (who reappears in *Skipping School*), James MacLeish (the protagonist in *Working Trot*), and Phillip Johnson (the protagonist in *Skipping School*). **"The Wake"** evokes the unusual relationship between Kris, fifteen, and her Great-aunt Mil, who is over eighty. Kris does her house and yard work twice a week. One day Kris finds Aunt Mil sitting silently in her chair with her old cat, Puttins, dead in her lap. Kris calls her mother. Robert, the other cat, enters the room to inspect the corpse and comfort Aunt Mil. Kris is alternately argumentative and furious with her father; he, in turn, resents her spending so much time with Aunt Mil. Kris is interested in animal behavior and in the relationship between human and animal. She spends the night with Aunt Mil; they hold a wake for Puttins. Aunt Mil observes that one cannot practice for death. In **"Horse Man,"** James MacLeish is at a horse show in which he is not competing because his horse, Ghazal, is lame. His cousin, Gloria, is taking photographs. The beauty of rider Norah Craig stuns James. Her horse belongs to Silver Thimble Farm; she is working with Gary Kunstler, the well-known trainer. Gary, watching James handle the horse of one of his students, asks him to exercise his upper-level horse, Avatar, a national champion. The delirious experience—the opportunity to ride such an animal—is a great gift for James. **"Extended Family"** takes place the summer after Puttins's death. Kris appreciates her rational conversations with Aunt Mil and still argues constantly with her father, who is a high school teacher on vacation. She and he contest every issue; for example, surgical sterilization for pets. He is against the practice, calling it "pedomorphy," or selective breeding for domestic animals; they never grow up but are dominated by humans. Kris wants Aunt Mil to adopt a new kitten. Kris spies an unknown cat in her driveway; at the same moment, a boy comes looking for his cat, Thea. He is Phillip Johnson, recently moved in next door. Kris confides to Aunt Mil her hatred for her father. Aunt Mil points out that he is jealous of her spending so much time away. Kris persuades Aunt Mil to adopt a new pet, but not before Aunt Mil talks to her seriously about her penchant for stubbornness and persistence in her fights with her father. The title story, **"The Sixth Sense,"** returns to James on a rainy day when he is bored. He takes Robbie out riding and dreams of Avatar and his "power, balance, and educated response." He looks for John Stark's military road to Fort Crown Point. His poncho streaming with rain, he muses about why people ride horseback, since they do not use the animal for work or war. Why do people keep breeding Morgans? Is it just a game? He believes riding to be more "essential" than that. He broods about the discipline of dressage, in which horse and rider are one. As the going becomes more slippery and dangerous, James regrets risking the legs of this good young horse. Robbie almost falls and becomes agitated. He is bleeding, his lip bashed on a rock. James hurts his knee. He is lost. He wonders if Robbie knows the way—if he has that mysterious "sixth sense" James has read about. Robbie finds a trail, moving with "power and spring," and unhesitatingly leads James back to the place where Robbie was born. From there, James can find his way to MacLeish Farm. In **"Thea,"** Phillip hears Kris's voice outside talking to Aunt Mil. Kris says her brother, Greg, is crazy about Phillip's sister, Carrie. Phillip wants to befriend Kris and Aunt Mil. His parents have recently moved here from a farm in the Midwest because his father is ill. Phillip finds the housing development distasteful, "conventional, man-produced, ugly." Phillip feels angry and rebellious. When a dog chases Thea,

Kris helps Phillip find her. His mother cries because a raccoon kills their chickens, which she brought here as "a way of still being country people, even in these surroundings." In "**The Bottom Line,**" James's former roommate, now a sophomore in college, visits to ski; it rains. Kip castigates James for dropping out: "You're not really going to spend the rest of your life here?" After Kip leaves to visit a Dartmouth friend, James takes out his horse, Ghazal. As they trot, James wonders why he is living this way. His friend, Kip, will make money and move upward; James is doing what he wants to do now—not planning his future. "I don't do this for the money. I do it because I want to." In "**The Greyhound**," Phillip works for a veterinary clinic. Sharon, an employee, is training to hold down the show greyhounds when they are put to death because they can no longer run fast. Phillip finds "the casual disposal of the ones who proved less fit…dishonorable." Dr. Rossi injects five dogs. Phillip, sick and horrified, rebels and takes the last one home with him. He realizes he has made a mistake: she will need shots, good food, runs, and spaying. He leads her through the woods, knowing he cannot keep her. Kris offers to take the dog, though her father has decreed, "no pets." (A widespread save-the-greyhound movement now flourishes in Vermont.) In "**Winning**," Kris must tell her father about the greyhound. Aunt Mil finds the dog beautiful and suggests naming her Diana; she is proud of Phillip for saving the dog's life. Aunt Mil tells Kris she is bequeathing her house to her. Kris's father refuses to allow her to keep the dog; she responds that, if the dog goes, she goes. She wins her point by bullying her father, an unsatisfactory outcome; she would prefer to win by convincing him of her argument. Depressed, she takes Diana outside. Phillip comes along, pretending not to notice she is deflated, and suggests they take Diana to the athletic field to teach her how to play.

Skipping School (1992), a sequel to three of the stories in *The Sixth Sense*, pursues the life of Phillip Johnson, fifteen, who moves to Vermont after his father, stricken with cancer followed by emphysema, gives up his farm in the Midwest. The Johnsons live in a development house with vinyl clapboards; his father stares at the television set all day. Phillip makes little effort to fit into his new school and has only one friend, Kris, with whom he sits on the bus. After school, he works at a veterinarian's clinic with a team—Dr. Franklin, Dr. Rossi, and Sharon—that struggles daily and personally with the tragedies of, for example, pet owners forced to put down their pets, or greyhound managers, who euthanize their animals when the dogs can no longer race. When someone brings in a box of kittens to be destroyed, Phillip takes them to an abandoned house and begins skipping school to feed and play with them. His sister, Carrie, comes home for the weekend, bringing Derek Hansen, who is also studying to become a nurse. Phillip detests Derek, whom he finds narcissistic and cruel. Phillip does not write his former friends because he has nothing to say: "His old self had melted away like a snowflake on a hot truck hood." On weekends, he looks forward to seeing Kris. Sometimes he visits her and her Great-aunt Mil, who seems to like him. He holds Kris's hand on the bus and marvels at its warmth. He barely goes to class. The guidance counselor asks if he is having suicidal thoughts. When Derek breaks Carrie's heart, their mother hurries to her side, leaving Phillip to take care of their father, who has little to say and encourages him to go out. Aunt Mil calls on his father, telling him, in her warm, direct way, to stop thinking about himself and find a house that needs a little work. At the clinic, Dr. Rossi puts her best friend's beloved old Labrador to sleep. Phillip is in the room. The two women, in tears, hug each other, drawing Phillip into their embrace. Phillip hikes to the kittens' hiding place, builds a fire, warms their milk, and weeps "harshly." His father's attitude has subtly changed: he is now "resigned, and angry, and sad, and full of humor." Phillip brings the kittens home and explains about hiding them in the woods, skipping school, the guidance counselor—everything. His mother gently asks him why he did not just bring the kittens home.

Beware the Mare (1993) introduces Lilian ("Lily") Gifford, ten, in the first of a quartet of stories (the others are *A Blue for Beware*, *Beware and Stogie*, and *Be Well, Beware*). Lily lives in southern Vermont with her mother, Barbie; grandmother, Gracie; and grandfather, Linwood Griffin, a livestock dealer. Lily has learned to ride on a pony, but now her grandfather has traded a steer for a bay mare. The mare seems perfect, but her grandfather is worried: why is she named "Beware"? Her grandmother asks him to check the horse's background. In the meantime, her grandfather makes gestures at Beware to incite her to kick, bite, or fidget, but she stands still, confused but trying to be good. He can find nothing in her behavior of which to beware. Lily is not allowed to pat her yet, but she can look at her and talk softly to her. When her grandfather saddles Beware, she does not bolt; when he bridles her, she lowers her head and reaches out for the bit. Lily is trying not to fall in love with her. Her grandfather looses Beware in the pasture with the other horses for three days to find out whether she will "go wild." Finally Lily is allowed to ride her: she is to take care of the horse all by herself. It is blackfly season, and the horses need rubbing with bug repellent. One day, out in the pasture, Beware steps toward Lily in a menacing way. Lily is frightened, but she reaches out her hands and scratches the horse's belly, just what Beware wanted. Her grandfather discovers that her name started out as an alliterative joke, "Better beware the mare..."

A Blue for Beware (1995) explores the world of the junior horse show. Lily and her friend, Mandy Firestone, enter a number of events with their horses, Beware and Shane. Shane, a braided chestnut, looks like a magazine illustration of a show horse, Lily thinks. In Junior Equitation, Mandy's horse runs away with her, but she takes a prize anyway; no ribbon for Beware. In Junior Pleasure, Lily receives a green ribbon; the judge smiles and tells her to relax, but she finds the ring crowded and confusing. After Shane does badly in the Junior Trail Course, Mandy cries; Lily begins to think horse shows are "stupid." All the children receive purple ribbons in Costume. In Jumping, Lily and Beware are not awarded first place, but Lily does not care: she knows their jumping was "beautiful." Mandy, with some coaching from Lily's grandfather, receives a blue ribbon in Barrel Racing. Beware has been so good all day that Lily aches for her to have a blue ribbon, too. In the Flag Race, Lily gets her wish—and the judge expresses a friendly interest in her riding future. In the last event, Breakaway, the two girls ride as partners (this was Lily's mother's idea), trying to go through the judges' commands while each holds one end of a piece of crepe paper. They win a yellow ribbon; better yet, they are still best friends.

In the fall, when Lily gets off the school bus in ***Be Well, Beware*** (1996), "The leaves look like a bowl of Cornflakes before you put the milk in." Beware does not come when she calls. The mare cannot walk. Lily and her grandmother manage to coax her into the barn. The vet, Dr. Short, diagnoses colic and tells Lily not to walk her. Beware is no better the next day. The second vet, Dr. Brand, agrees with the diagnosis and puts a tube in Beware's nose to insert water into her stomach. She thinks Lily should walk her horse several times a day. Lily stays home from school. The next day, Beware has drunk no water and produced no manure because her bowel is blocked. When Dr. Brand comes again, she thinks Beware may need expensive surgery: if something is not done, Beware will die. Finally, Dr. Brand gives Beware an intravenous solution. The treatment works. Beware regains her health, but she almost died. For Lily, "Nothing will ever seem quite the same."

A fierce and frightening wind in ***Beware and Stogie*** (1998) sends trees crashing down and shuts off the electricity. In the morning, Beware is still there; the two big work horses, the horses Lily's grandfather bought for resale, and Stogie, the wild, impossible-to-catch black Morgan, have run off, as have the cow and calf. Her grandfather sends Lily on Beware to find the cow and calf; if she sees the horses, she is to dismount right away and walk home. She, her mother, and her grandfather cross the meadow together. Lily and Beware head through the swamp, find the cow and calf, and herd them home. Lily hears her grandfather telephoning the sheriff to give him permission to shoot Stogie if he causes any harm.

H

Poor grandfather: he had such high hopes for showing Stogie in Tunbridge. He knows Stogie is "useless," but he loves him because he is "beautiful." Lily goes out again on Beware, up the wood road to look for Stogie. She finds him trapped: he cannot move his head because the haw strap of his halter is twisted around a strong branch. With no time to go for her grandfather, she is the only one who can help. Trying to stay calm, she frees him, standing in front of him to do so. He could hurt her if he wanted. She gets the halter back on him and stops him from drinking too much water. She is in control, far beyond her years. Beware runs home. Lily manages to wrap Stogie's rope around a tree and waits for her grandfather. Her mother and grandfather ride up. On foot, her grandfather is able to approach Stogie, even to put a hand on his neck and rub. With Beware beside him, Stogie walks home obediently—after he has isolated himself for two whole years. Maybe her grandfather can ride Stogie after all: "Anything could happen."

In ***Uncle Daney's Way*** (1994), twelve-year-old Cole Tatro's home is a trailer on a farm near Hogback Mountain. When his mother's Uncle Daney, injured in a logging accident and confined to a wheelchair, moves in with them, the Tatros fix up a stall with electricity and plumbing in their barn. Uncle Daney brings his big skidding horse, Nip. Cole helps Uncle Daney harness Nip to clear some pastureland. After Nip "skins" juniper trees out of the ground, Uncle Daney sprinkles chaff on the torn earth. Cole is seeking a way for Uncle Daney to buy hay for Nip. Cole's father works in the paper mill, and Cole does not want him to feel responsible; his father also needs money for a tractor and a truck to start his own business. Cole and his father open a skidding trail for Nip to bring lumber down for sale. Cole and some neighbors devise a cart and platform so that Nip can graze farther afield and Uncle Daney can visit some of his friends around town. Cole ponders ways to raise money: he picks and sells berries and continues to bring down logs with Nip. When the family hears about a Farm Horse Contest with prize money at the fair, Uncle Daney enters Nip in the single-horse Log Skid. Uncle Daney in his chair will drive Nip, accomplishing the hitching himself and using a crowbar to reach the whippletree (also called "whiffletree," the pivotal horizontal crossbar to which the traces of a draft animal are attached). Because Uncle Daney moves so slowly in the chair, the authorities will allow Cole to push him. At the moment of competition, Uncle Daney claims that he is ill: in fact, he has been planning all along for Cole to compete. Nip performs by verbal commands without reins. Cole feels wonderful: "For just a moment he knew exactly who he was and what he looked like, where he fitted in the world." Cole and Nip win second prize. Ray West, the first-prize winner, wants to contribute to Nip's hay fund; the Allards offer Uncle Daney and Cole a job to train their horses the way Uncle Daney trained Nip. When the Allards propose a fee, Uncle Daney demurs, but Cole steps in: "You can pay us in hay, if that would be all right."

The year is 1884 in ***Westminster West*** (1997), and memories of the Civil War are vivid. Colonel David Gorham and his wife, Jane, run a farm in Westminster West with the help of their hard-working sons, Henry and Ed, and their daughter, Sue, sixteen, who is sturdy, reliable, and conscientious. Sue has a Morgan, "Bright." Their other daughter, fifteen-year-old Clare, is delicate and unable to do chores and looks forward to a second vacation trip with Aunt Emma Campbell, an affluent relative. Sue, jealous of her sister's good fortune, comes upon an old diary of her father's hidden in the attic. She learns from entries dated July 18, 1865, that her father came home with what would today be labeled "post-traumatic stress disorder." He broke into uncontrollable sobs, had terrifying nightmares, relived battles, yearned to be with his comrades on their way out West, and could not bring himself to speak to his fiancée, Jane, who had waited for him for four years. To Sue, these are unimaginable secrets about her parents. The neighbors are talking about a "maniac" who is burning down barns. "Barns told of thrifty forebears and well-tended land, mellow soil, saving ways," but someone is destroying them. Sue's best friend, Minnie Butler, works as a hired girl for the Campbells on their farm north of Rockingham. Just before Clare leaves on her holiday, Sue falls ill. For days she lies in bed and cannot move. Her mother pampers her as she has always catered to Clare, carrying trays and plumping pillows, and hires Minnie to help. Minnie instantly understands that the cause of Jane's anxiety about and overindulgence of Clare (and now Sue) is nursing her beloved dying cousin during the Civil War. Clare returns with a new set of affected mannerisms and reverts to her old, indolent ways, letting her mother do all the work. Sue resolves she will not leave her bed until Clare does her share; the maniac sets fire to the Gorhams' barn and shatters this resolution. Everyone runs downstairs. Sue whistles for Bright and rides him bareback around the countryside mobilizing the neighbors. Instead of joining the others, Clare takes to her bed. In her exhaustion that night, Jane acknowledges her misjudgment in allowing Clare to have her way. After fighting the fire, Sue compares the experience to the aftermath of a battle and has a glimmer of insight into her father's emotions. She remembers Bright shied at some bushes: was the arsonist hiding there, watching? They search the area and find one distinctive boot print. The owner of the boot is Johnny Coombs, who earlier suffered from a fever that damaged his mind. The sheriff arrests him and takes him to the county jail in Newfane. The fire that ejects Sue from her sick bed returns Clare to hers.

In ***Unbroken*** (1999), set in 1910, thirteen-year-old Harriet ("Harry") Gibson's mother dies in a collision between a Model T and her horse-drawn carriage. Dr. Vesper, a devoted family friend, tells Harry that her mother, aware of her bad heart, had made plans to send Harry to West Barrett to stay with her Aunt Sarah Gibson Hall in the house where Harry's father was born and raised. Harry is incredulous: how could her mother want her to live with Aunt Sarah, who clearly hates them? Harry arrives with her colt, Kid, to find Aunt Sarah cold and inhospitable; Uncle Clayton is cowed and uncommunicative. Worse still, Aunt Sarah does not want Harry to continue at the Academy in Barrett. Aunt Sarah is punishing Harry because her mother became pregnant and ruined Aunt Sarah's brother's life. Harry determines to train her colt, her only transportation to school. She is so far from town that no one comes to visit. Lonely and sad, she befriends a rooster, although Aunt Sarah warned her not to make a pet of the animals. When Aunt Sarah orders browbeaten Clayton to kill Harry's pet, she grabs the rooster and runs off. On the road, she meets Uncle Clayton's one-armed brother, Uncle Truman, who lives on the hill, too, in the house where Harry was born. He takes the rooster to his house, lends Harry his dog, and persuades her to go back to Aunt Sarah's. Harry knows she has an ally. Next day, when Uncle Truman comes to dinner, Harry observes that the adults' conversation showed "everything was work here. Everything was food and firewood and racing the summer to get both put away in time." Her mother chose not to live this life. Dr. Vesper takes Harry to Barrett to stay with her friend, Lucretia Mitchell, and sit for her Academy exams. Mrs. Mitchell arranges to keep Harry's horse on the days she is in school. Uncle Truman tells Harry about her mother and also about Aunt Sarah, whose parents died of consumption when she was fourteen, leaving her to raise four siblings, including Harry's father, Walter. Walter had already contracted tuberculosis when he fell in love with Harry's mother, but she chose to marry him anyway. Uncle Truman explains that Aunt Sarah needed more "scope": she never had a chance to go to college. Harry helps the old people with the haying: "sweat, chaff, headache, and the sorrow emptying out of my body. In the hay field, I felt like a figure in a landscape painting, not like a person. It helped." John Gale, whose automobile was involved in her mother's accident, pays Sarah's tuition at the Academy for three years. When Harry tells Uncle Truman she is ashamed of being illegitimate, he reassures her: she was born prematurely when her mother fell in the barn and did not want anyone to know. Setting out to train her colt, Harry is impatient and brusque. She pushes him until he gallops away, dragging her behind him; she suffers excruciating rope burn on her hands. Aunt Sarah drives her to the hospital in the wagon.

When a Model T passes, Aunt Sarah gets out to hold the horse. The experience "panics" and "disintegrates" Harry. Now that she is hurt and cannot ride, Aunt Sarah arranges for her to stay with the Mitchells in town during the week; Harry's heart yearns "strangely" for the old woman and the two old men on the hill. She loves these old people, "weakness and strength mixed together, and whatever they did, they did it out of love."

The star of ***Runaway Radish*** (2001) is a wise pony named Radish. He loves to teach children to ride. Judy is impatient with him at first, but they go on longer rides and soon are winning ribbons in horse shows. Radish teaches her to be patient. In the winter, he rests. One spring Judy cries when she realizes she has grown too big for Radish. Her parents give her a horse named Horton. Judy tells Radish she will always love him best, cries, kisses him, and escorts him to meet Nina, who is so small she is a bit frightened of Radish. He teaches her to be brave. They go on longer rides and soon they, too, are winning ribbons in horse shows. When Nina is unhappy, she always feels better after she spends time with Radish. Nina's parents realize she is too big for Radish and buy her a horse named Count. Radish is lonely. He escapes from the pasture one day to follow Nina and Count. As he runs by, friends and neighbors recognize him and call the state police. He is lost for awhile, but then he smells apples and finds Judy's driveway. She does not live there any more, but Nina and Count ride up; soon Judy arrives by car. Judy and Nina wish Radish could have a home where he would never be too little. They find him a place at a riding camp, where the director needs another pony. Radish is a good teacher. Meg, the smallest student, rides him the first summer and the next. They win prizes. When Meg grows too big, Radish teaches Kevin, Sophie, Robin, and many others. By the time Judy's daughter, Rachel, is ready to learn, the camp is full of boys and girls Radish has taught to ride.

In ***Will You, Won't You?*** (2001), Madeleine ("Mad") Parker, thirteen, lives in Burlington but spends the summer with her grandmother in Barrett near Montpelier. Her mother, an attorney, works for the Justice Department in Washington, D.C.; her father, Lewis Grandcourt, a member of an important lumbering family, is known as "L.G." for "Long Gone." Mad was miserable her last year in middle school, where she made herself invisible. Noticing that Mad is shy and insecure, her grandmother, a charismatic Democratic state senator and powerful chairman of the finance committee, suggests that Mad join the Scottish Country Dance group to learn "social distance." Mad, who wishes she had inherited her grandmother's courage, sustains herself throughout the summer by emailing her mother and her best friend. Morag McAe is the formidable dance instructor; the men wear kilts. Mad is relieved to find Gordie McIver, her old kindergarten friend, in the group; his grandfather, Senator McIver, admires Senator Parker, though he belongs to another political party. Mad has brought her horse, Cloud, but cannot ride him very far because he is afraid of cows. Senator McIver lends his cow, Elvirah, to help Cloud adapt. Shy and awkward at first, Mad begins to master the dance steps, relating the process to learning to ride a horse. As she watches the steps of the dancing, she finds them beautiful, "like cables on an Aran sweater, like calligraphy." Her grandmother and Mad help Senator McIver and Gordie with the haying. "The hay filled the air with its green perfume." The key political issue of the day is Act 88, a bill to ban clear cutting that her grandmother supported; her vote angered many loggers who fear losing their jobs (they all work for Grandcourt Lumber). At the meeting, Mad summons the presence of mind to speak against clear cutting. Mad's mother and her new beau, Bob, visit; Mad learns that her father died while saving a little girl in a hurricane in Honduras. Somehow, this news comforts her. Her grandmother, who has been threatening to retire at seventy, is motivated to stay in politics. The best sixsome of Morag's dancers is chosen to perform at a big rally. When Mad's grandmother develops a painful blister, Mad confidently takes her place while her mother and Bob watch with amazement and pride from the grandstand. (The novel is dedicated to, and the grandmother's character based on, former State Senator Cheryl P. Rivers, who represented Windsor County in Vermont for eleven years. The title is from "Will you, won't you, will you, won't you, will you join the dance?" from Lewis Carroll's *Alice's Adventures in Wonderland*.)

Ever since the death of his dog, Chad Holloway, fourteen, in ***Shaper*** (2002) carries his sorrow around like a heavy stone, punishing everyone in his family: his grandfather, Jeep; his father, Gib, and his mother; his sister, Julia, fifteen; and his little brother, Sky. Grim-faced, sorry for himself, and shrugging coldly whenever addressed, he cannot forgive the accident. His dog, Shep, chased after Julia; a car mortally injured the dog, and Jeep was forced to euthanize him. Jeep gave Chad a new dog, Queenie, which he ignores. David Burton, divorced, and his daughter, Louise, fifteen, move into the house next to the Holloways. David, an expert from Burlington in a new science of training animals, is writing a book, *Behave!*, and asks Chad to be his research assistant. Chad agrees, essentially because he finds Louise the most beautiful girl he has ever seen. David's training, called "shaping," molds an animal's behavior by clicking (using a small cricket toy). Shaping is "conditional or positive reinforcement": each click means a treat, or, "do the right thing, get something good." As Queenie enters into the training, Chad discovers that she is malleable: she is smart and begins to make warm and loving eye contact with him. Disappointingly, whenever Chad comes to work, Louise leaves the house. She spends time at the Holloways' house taking care of Sky (who asks her to read him *Farmer Boy*) and chatting with Julia, who becomes her friend. Chad overhears Louise tell Julia that she and her father are "manipulative." Chad realizes that David purposely shaped Queenie to make Chad appreciate her; he is awakened to the "giving and withholding in his own family, like choosing partners in a dance." Once he understands the dynamic, he invites Louise to go on walks. Julia suffers her own private hell trying to train her horse, Tiger. She pulls and shouts at him and cannot control him. David offers to recondition the horse. Julia makes progress: instead of watching for the wrong moves her horse is making, she looks for the right ones. Chad acknowledges he has been trying to make himself feel bad. Although he has not spoken to Jeep since Shep's death, he knows Jeep has always been a friend to the family: difficult as it was, Jeep had to shoot Shep. At the fair, where everyone goes to watch Julia ride, Chad makes peace with Jeep. They start playing baseball together on Thursday evenings and taking their dogs to the fairgrounds for training. David and Louise come to one of the baseball games. Afterward, Chad and Louise take a stroll, their arms around each other. When she returns to New York, she leaves him her email address.

Randi Hacker

Bright, amusing, and intuitive, Angelina Rossini, the sixteen-year-old narrator of ***Life as I Knew It*** (2006), has unconventional parents: her Italian father, Andrea, and her British mother, Nicola, are old enough to be her grandparents. In fact, her father's daughter by his first wife has a son Angelina's age. Andrea, dashing, exuberant, and demonstrative, loves to sing the songs of Andrew Lloyd Webber (changing the words from *Evita* to "Don't cry for me, Angelina"). In the town of Blodgett near Burlington, many residents are former hippies and play dual roles; for example, Kevin Murphy is a master plumber and adjunct professor of political science at Green Mountain Community College. Angelina grew up with Jacques Henri Tatro, a handsome French-Canadian of Abenaki descent, whom she calls "Jax" (the day she learned to read she sounded out his first name that way). As children, they used to act out scenes from *Little House on the Prairie*. His family is related to everyone in town; Angelina, an only child, feels at home in the Tatros' big house filled with huge logger sons. She has fallen in love with Jax: her great sorrow is that, while Jax has always loved her as his best friend, he is gay (she paraphrases Rhett Butler by commenting, "that is my misfortune"). His father and brothers, adherents of the "Take Back Vermont" philosophy, choose not to acknowledge his sexual orientation. One day, Andrea collapses on the bathroom floor; the EMT/school custodian takes him to the hospital. Nicola accompanies him, while Angelina spends the night with her mother's lesbian friend, Liz, attractive, wise, and comforting. Andrea, who has had a stroke, is paralyzed on his right side and aphasic. From the hospital in Burlington he is moved to rehabilitation, then to a convalescent facility in Winooski. Angelina has always had a better relationship with her father than her mother; perhaps, she thinks, she cannot understand her mother for who she is because Angelina has been more interested in herself. Her father does not improve, but he comes home: this is the end of life as she knew it. She is shocked by how small, old, and white-haired he looks; she is loath to touch him. His new tennis shoes on his useless feet make her sad. Everything is paradoxical with him at home—easier and harder at the same time. One day, he holds her face with his good left hand and makes her look deeply into his eyes: she sees her father in there. From that moment, she empathizes with the situation in which he finds himself. She helps him use the bathroom. She makes dinner, while her father assists her by making left-handed universal signs such as "a little" and "stop." He can only repeat the sound "ho," but with different inflections; she begins to understand his language. The night of the winter concert (the youngsters are singing a medley of Andrew Lloyd Webber songs), Nicola and Angelina bring Andrea in his wheelchair. Room is made for him at the front of the auditorium; everyone is moved by his presence; the director dedicates the concert to him. During the last verse of "Don't cry for me, Argentina," Andrea suddenly starts singing with the soloist. The crowd is hushed with amazement. Andrea never says another word and dies a few days later of a massive heart attack. The memorial service is jammed. Angelina welcomes the crowd and speaks briefly and lovingly about her father. She and her mother are beginning to know and to comfort each other.

Sue Halpern

The narrative of ***Introducing...Sasha Abramowitz*** (2005) is in the form of a memoir by Sasha Marie Curie Abramowitz, eleven, who aspires to be a writer or, perhaps, a pastry chef. Sasha is precocious and amusing. Her style tends to the scholarly, with occasional footnotes and parenthetical phrases highlighting recent vocabulary words introduced by her teacher, Mrs. Blank. Sasha's two professor parents (Barney teaches English; Marcia's field is neuroscience) head a dormitory at Krieger College (based in some respects on Middlebury College). Perhaps because her parents are intellectuals, Sasha is very well read, referring to a range of titles from *Harriet the Spy*, the *Harry Potter* series, the Narnia books, and *Ramona*, to *Mr. Popper's Penguins* and *The Secret Garden*. The family used to have a house, but, now that her elder brother, Danny, is enrolled in a special, expensive school in the Berkshires, her parents accept college housing in exchange for being responsible for boarders. Sasha reveals, through snatches of dialogue from her sessions with a psychiatrist, her ambivalence about Danny, whose suffering from Tourette's Syndrome distresses and embarrasses her. One day at their former house, which had a small pool, Danny was overcome by a bacteria phobia and traumatized their babysitter, Jenny Flum, who resigned her job. Barney and Marcia are now looking for a new babysitter. Sasha's best friend, Carla, proposes they form a detective agency, named Drew Hardy after the well-known teenaged detectives, Nancy Drew and the Hardy Boys (Carla understands about "name recognition"). Sasha tacks up some notices around campus and receives a perplexed call from a student baseball player, Andrew Hardy, twenty-four, who wonders why she has appropriated his name. Before long, Andrew is Sasha's babysitter, a happy coincidence since Barney is a fanatic baseball fan. Andrew, an amateur magician, performs at Pinky Summers's birthday party. Sasha is cross when Andrew chooses her friend, Carla, as his assistant. Sasha's class is excited because Mrs. Blank and her husband are adopting a Guatemalan baby; Andrew is also adopted, Sasha learns. Despite the fact that

Andrew's team never wins, Sasha and her father, ever optimistic, attend all his games. At one, Andrew is hit in the face with a baseball and taken to the hospital. His doctor is concerned because his blood does not clot. Sasha, who has researched Marie Curie and Eleanor Roosevelt, suggests Andrew might have aplastic anemia. The doctor is dumbfounded—and grateful for the correct diagnosis. While Mrs. Blank is on maternity leave, Jennie Flum becomes the substitute teacher. Sasha is thrilled to see her again, although less so when Andrew convalesces at their house; he and Jennie seem very taken with each other. Every other weekend Sasha's parents visit Danny; sometimes she accompanies them. In the summer, they bring Danny home. Jennie, who once hoped to be an actress, inspires the class to put on *Cheaper by the Dozen*, with Sasha as Lillian Gilbreth and James Schroder as the senior Frank Gilbreth. Sasha worries about James's taking the role since he never speaks in class. When she asks him why, he explains cryptically that he has had no practice. When James tries to help by telling her about baseball player Jim Eisenreich's struggle with Tourette's Syndrome, Sasha is furious. Later, she is ashamed when she learns that his parents are deaf and unable to come to the play. As a special surprise, Jenny, who learned sign language as an intern at the National Theater of the Deaf, invites the Schroders to the play and signs to them from the wings. At the cast party, someone notices that Andrew and Danny are missing; everyone leaves to search for them. Sasha feels like Miss Havisham, jilted before her wedding in *Great Expectations*. Andrew suffered a relapse during the play; Danny saved his life by getting him to the hospital, where the doctors performed a splenectomy. Sasha understands why her parents love Danny so much that they would do anything for him; she also deeply appreciates her new friend, James.

Earl Hamner

In ***Lassie: A Christmas Story*** (1997), eight-year-old Timmy Martin's mother, Ruth, is a veterinarian in Hudson's Falls; Grandpa Martin lives above her clinic. While Timmy and his collie, Lassie, pick out a Christmas tree with Grandpa Martin, Ruth leaves some hay for the deer on her way to work. The road is slick and icy, and, when a mountain lion darts across her path, Ruth swerves, toppling herself and her truck into a snow-filled ravine. After a confrontation with the mountain lion, Lassie leads rescuers to Ruth before it is too late. Timmy believes God was watching out for them on this Christmas Eve.

William W. Harvey

In ***Lige Golden: The Man Who Twinkled*** (1924), Elijah ("Lige") is a young blacksmith working in East Burdon in 1879 and dwelling in a lonesome cottage. His story is based on the diary entries of an unnamed youth, the childhood chum of Nathan Wilson, later editor of the *Lynnville* (Vt.) *Times*. Lige, who radiates warmth, optimism, and physical well being, intrigues the two boys. Lige antagonized both Dr. Rush and Reverend Hardiman when he saved the life of Charlie Whiting, who fell into the river while running on logs and almost went over the dam. The doctor lost face when, after he pronounced Charlie dead, Lige revived him by breathing into the boys' lungs. The minister lost face when, after he proclaimed it was "God's will" that Charlie was in heaven, Lige brought him back to life. The boys meet Lige when they are fishing and he shares his trout with them. His eyes twinkle when he talks, and he always enjoys a joke on himself. He is friendly with everyone in the village, especially people who are down on their luck, like Maggie Gillis. Her husband abandoned her with a baby, and she now goes out to do housework and takes in washing. Lige helps her son, who has been a cripple for eighteen years, to learn to walk and teaches him to read. As the boys spend more time with Lige and listen to his ideas on life, the narrator's father urges him to write down what Lige tells him; maybe he will be as good a writer as Robinson Crusoe. Lige, who does not attend church but walks in the mountains, sees goodness in all men. Some turn out to be "tall straight oaks," some "scrubs." To Lige, real faith is "expecting *good* instead of *evil*." More and more boys follow this simple, natural, truthful spirit, inciting gossip that he is corrupting the minds of the youth. Many of the meetings with Lige and the village boys evoke allusions to Christ and his disciples. When the narrator and Nate ask Lige why he came to this sleepy little village, he responds, "on account of a lost relative," and shows them a picture of a beautiful girl. Deacon Withers has a jolly, party-loving daughter, Mary Madeline, seventeen. When villagers hear that Mary spent a night at Lige's cottage and then left town, they set his house ablaze. The boys find Lige, who assures them they have great futures and bids them goodbye. Several weeks later, Governor Fairbain arrives in East Burdon with his sister-in-law, Miss Sarah Wilkins, and Mary Madeline Withers, dressed in white for her marriage to the governor's son, Richard. Mary tells the boys that Lige went to the gold fields with Benjamin Atwood, nephew of the governor, after bringing her and Richard together. In 1921, Lucretia Atwood, Benjamin's widow, publishes a letter testifying that Lige went to prison in California to shield his friend, Benjamin. The boys receive a letter from Lige, saying that he is alive, his father is Dean Withers, and Mary is his half-sister. He cannot give them his address, because he is an escaped convict, but he still loves life, his eyes are still twinkling, and he is neither saint nor hero.

Sheila Hayes

In ***The Tinker's Daughter*** (1995), Holly Gerard, thirteen, deplores her life in East Branbury, where she and her mother were both born. She does not know who her father was; she desperately wishes that she had a normal mother instead of Paisley, who runs a cluttered shop full of junk and used clothes. They live in an apartment behind Paisley's Place, where tourists sometimes "wander down from Manchester." Holly is further aggrieved because her best friend, Linda Wells, has left town, and Holly feels abandoned and alone. The first day of junior high school, Holly's locker-mate is Maddison ("Maddy") Brown, who has recently moved to town to experience a regular teenaged life after a hectic career as a television actress. Holly is charmed by the idea of being best friends with a real star. She learns about Maddy from the Kirby twins, whose parents run the local store: "Gossip is the number-one industry in town." The next day, another new girl, Camilla Moss, enters school; she and her mother, Ernestine, move into Linda's former house. The Kirby twins spread the word that Camilla's father is in prison; everyone at school shuns her. Meanwhile, Holly's new friendship is not blossoming: Maddy seems to think everything in Vermont is "tacky." When Camilla's mother buys some used furniture from Paisley, Holly and Camilla meet; then Holly and Paisley visit Camilla and Ernestine, who are ostracized by other residents. At a meeting of the planning board to hear Ernestine's application to sell goods from her house, everyone speaks against the idea. In Ernestine's defense, Paisley says she was born in this "Eden," where some people are "narrow-minded bigots," but the "Vermont soul" has not vanished. "Vermont is a wonderful state," she says, and, if East Branbury rejects Ernestine and Camilla, they will find a better town in which to live. The meeting adjourns before taking a decision. Holly overhears Maddy tell her father that she only picked Holly as a friend because he wanted a role model to show her the world "through Vermont eyes." Camilla, who has made friends with some of the other girls, interests them in borrowing Paisley's vintage dresses to wear to the Halloween dance and invites Paisley to be a chaperone. At the next town meeting, the chair announces that the Moss application is denied unless a "guarantor" backs the endeavor. Paisley arises once more to announce that she and Ernestine will act as partners, working out of Paisley Place. Holly seconds the motion, saying she believes Ernestine and Camilla will be an asset to the community. Paisley helps Holly with her flapper costume, and, best of all, a boy she likes asks her to dance. Holly still has much to learn, however; when she exults that everyone accepts them "in spite of" who they are, Camilla explodes over that insulting premise: "I want people to like me...because of who I am."

James Hayford

The star of ***Gridley Firing*** (1987) is a skunk whose name, "Gridley," originated with Paul, the elder brother of eleven-year-old Martin Patch. In Woolville, the old woolen mill is now a skiwear factory. Their father, Merle, the fifth generation in his family to own Mapleshade, fears he will lose the farm to William Prince Banner, a rich man who wants to build condominiums, ski resorts, golf courses, riding paths, and ski trails on Merle's land. Paul, who is considered a radical and a pacifist by the community because he opposes the Vietnam War, is honest, thoughtful, and incompatible with Merle. To bring in more income, Ruby, Martin's mother, does housework for three elderly ladies in the village. Martin first meets the skunk when Gridley rescues him by spraying one of Banner's police dogs. Slipping under a fence, Martin and Gridley go on reconnaissance to Banner's estate, where his employees live in a trailer camp. They overhear Banner saying he will force Merle to sell Mapleshade: he owns the mortgage; Merle is in default. Equally worrisome, Banner plans to hire an exterminator from Burlington to rid his property of skunks. After Merle has an inconclusive meeting with Alton Briggs, the president of the bank and a close friend of Banner's, Martin tries talking to Mr. Briggs. Martin is no more successful with Mr. Briggs than his father was, but he uncovers important intelligence: his piano teacher, Phoebe Winslow, serves on the bank's board. She explains to Martin and Gridley about foreclosure (selling property to satisfy a lender's claims) and their need for a lawyer. Martin looks around his family's land and thinks, "Everything about the farm is good." That night a masked mob comes to their house shouting, "Skunk lovers." The hoodlums bring gasoline with the intention of burning out the Patches. Gridley, his wife, and their friends spray the crowd. Paul and his father make up; Phoebe lends Merle ten thousand dollars to pay off the interest on his farm. (The title is from "You may fire when you are ready, Gridley," spoken at the Battle of Manila Bay in 1898 by Montpelier native and hero of the Spanish-American War, Admiral George Dewey, 1837-1917.)

Wilma Pitchford Hays

In this account of the Ann Story drama, ***Trouble at Otter Creek*** (1978), the point of view is Samuel's, Solomon Story's nine-year-old brother. With their father, Amos, dead, their mother is determined to carry out his dream of settling in the New Hampshire Grants. Ann's brother, George, is scornful of the idea of a lone woman settler. Carrying baby Hannah, she and the other children, Solomon, Ephraim, Samuel, and Susanna, walk to their "wilderness home." Solomon leads the oxen and the cow. Once at the cabin, Solomon shows them the hidden trap door to the root cellar at the back of the house in the woods. They all work very hard. Solomon and Ann cut wood for the winter. Samuel weeds and hoes the garden and the corn. Solomon teaches him and Ephraim everything he learned from their father. While fishing, Samuel meets a Yorker surveyor, Dan McKay, who tells Samuel that someone is making a claim on the Story land. Ann sends a letter to Ethan Allen, who arrives with his brother, Levi, his cousin, Seth Warner, and some of the Green Mountain Boys. Allen tells the Storys of plans to make Vermont an independent state and about the impending revolution. When Yorkers arrive, the Green Mountain Boys escape through the root cellar and come around to the front door, where they disarm and arrest the Yorkers. Ann and the children look for a cave where they can hide, if necessary. She fashions shelves to store emergency supplies, blankets, a spade and hatchet, and kettles. One day, when a band of Mohawks comes, the family escapes into the woods, drives the animals away, and watches while the Indians burn down the cabin. Ann's first thought is to rebuild. The fireplace still stands, and the cow and calves are unhurt. Ann assigns tasks to all the children, even little Hannah, who gathers chips of bark to make a pile of kindling. Uncle George was wrong when he said that no woman could be a settler. "A woman with children like mine can," says Ann. When the children grow older, the family spends winters in Rutland so they can attend school. (The author's great-great-great grandfather, Peter Demo, lived before the American Revolution in the territory that became Vermont.)

Marguerite Henry

In ***Justin Morgan Had a Horse*** (1954), Justin Morgan, a teacher, travels in 1791 from Randolph to Springfield, Massachusetts, accompanied by his pupil, Joel Goss, eleven, to collect a debt owed him by farmer Abner Beane. Since Beane cannot pay cash, he gives Justin a big colt, Ebenezer, and includes Little Bub in the trade. Joel falls in love with strong Little Bub and vows some day to own him. Meanwhile, Joel's parents apprentice him for seven years to Mr. Davis, the owner of the sawmill near White River Junction. He works all day, goes to Morgan's school at night, and then trains Little Bub. Ezra Fisk hires Little Bub, now known as "Morgan's horse," to clear his land along the White River. Morgan's horse earns a reputation as an animal that can run as well as pull. Justin receives a condescending invitation from a New Yorker to pit his "workhorse" against some "celebrated racers." The event, which takes place in Brookfield on October 15, 1796, becomes another contest between Vermont and New York. Morgan's horse wins and is much sought after; as an itinerant singing teacher, Justin uses the horse to travel to central Vermont schools. In Woodstock, Justin falls ill and dies; Robert Evans, who worked for Fisk, buys Justin Morgan (the horse's new name) to work his land. Many people bring their mares for breeding. When Evans loses his farm, Justin Morgan is up for sale. Joel, whose apprentice days are almost over, lacks sufficient money to bid on him and does not know who buys the horse. Mr. Chase takes on Joel as a partner and promises to build him a barn for colts if he ever finds Justin Morgan. When the War of 1812 begins, Joel joins the Vermont militia, working for a shoeing-smith sergeant. Since Governor Chittenden cannot bring himself to order the Vermont militia to Plattsburgh, the soldiers volunteer to go. The Americans hinder the British advance by felling trees across the roads and destroying bridges until the British retreat. Joel helps with the wounded men and horses. After the war, Joel continues to live in Randolph. One wintry day, he comes upon six horses hitched to a freight wagon—one is Justin Morgan. Joel buys his beloved horse from the drunken, sadistic owner and brings the horse back to health with steaming mashes of oats, linseed tea, ground corn, and a great deal of love. When Joel hears that President Monroe is coming to Burlington, he sets his heart on the president's riding his horse in the parade. Joel, mounted on Justin Morgan, approaches the grandstand to introduce his horse. President Monroe rides Justin Morgan in the parade and speaks to the crowd about the Green Mountain Boys, who defended American liberty. He expresses his pride in Justin Morgan, "a little workhorse that cleared the fields and did what was asked of him." The audience realizes that the horse is "just like us...American!"

Alison Cragin Herzig

In ***Shadows on the Pond*** (1985), Jill Matthews, fourteen, spends summers with her parents in "the most beautiful barn in Vermont." This year, her father stays in New York with her sister Kate; Jill fears her parents are thinking about a divorce. Jill's best friend, Ptarmigan ("Migan") Todd, lives in Jerusalem Corners all year round. Migan's Aunt Karen is engaged to marry Jim ("Trapper Jeep") McCullough, a large, rough, frightening man. Jill and Migan hurry off to visit the beaver pond and their secret island. "The brown and gray and gold of the stream bed shimmered through the clear water." Reaching the dam, they are alarmed to see Carly, former owner of the Todds' property, who lives in a trailer and, some say, is a drunkard and arsonist. Trapper Jeep claims he has a permit to trap beavers in the dam: the girls pledge to stop him. They find and carefully spring his traps, marking them on a map. Only one trap has a dead beaver in it. Ryan Jameson, who is a baseball star and scholarship student at Jill's school in New York, is visiting Mr. and Mrs. Marks, owners of the general store and friends of his mother's from her Peace Corps service. With Ryans's help, Jill and Migan cut down trees to obstruct the logging road. Ryan often brings along tiny Naomi Marks, whose company he enjoys. They hide when Carly comes. Migan falls from a barn rafter and has to stay in bed. Jill lends her *The Black Stallion*, which captivates her. Alone with Ryan, Jill feels aware of his body. When he holds her hand, she can scarcely breathe. They steal out at night to confiscate some traps; Jeep has caught two more beavers. They notice Carly on the logging road, crouching on the ground, weeping. On the way home, Ryan and Jill kiss, a delicate act of young passion. Later, Ryan, Jill, and Naomi are playing by the creek when a deranged Carly dynamites the beaver dam, which gives way. Jill almost drowns trying to save Naomi; Ryan rescues them both. Trapper Jeep lied about having a permit to trap beavers; Aunt Karen breaks off their engagement. (The author wrote to me that for fifteen years she owned one hundred and twenty-three acres of field, stream, and sugar maples near Bristol in the Northeast Kingdom. Her children spent every summer vacation there: "The years in Vermont were our Camelot.")

Karen Hesse

Phoenix Rising (1994) evokes the horrifying consequences of a nuclear accident at a plant in Cookshire in southern Vermont. A dead zone exists from Vermont to the Atlantic; miraculously, because of the direction of the wind, North Haversham and other towns north of Cookshire were pronounced safe when, after ten terrifying days during which the residents wore surgical masks, workmen capped the leak. Nyle Sumner, thirteen, helps her grandmother run a sheep farm and attends Leland and Gray Union High School in nearby Townshend. Her mother is dead; her father abandoned the family years earlier. Nyle is sensitive and loving. When she goes outside at night, "The wind finally herded the clouds off. Stars appeared, brilliant, sharp-edged, scattered like hard white seeds across the black sky." Nyle's best school friend is Muncie, a dwarf, who is strong, brave, and loyal. In the aftermath of the accident, relatives and friends accommodate refugees. Nyle's grandmother takes in a widow, Miriam Trent, and her fifteen-year-old son, Ezra, who was profoundly irradiated; his father, who headed the nuclear plant, is dead. The Trents move into the big downstairs bedroom, keeping the curtains tightly drawn; Ezra is dying. After Nyle finishes her daily chores, she sits with Ezra, singing and reading to him. Slowly he begins to speak and, finally, to walk; she finds him fascinating. She describes to him the tasks of farming and keeping sheep; she lets him drive the truck. He says he feels like the phoenix: "It burns up, then rises from its ashes." As they spend time together, she believes she is in love him. Before he dies of leukemia, he writes her a moving letter about what she has meant to him.

A Time of Angels (1995), set during the last year of World War I, begins in Boston's West End, where Hannah Gold, fourteen, an artist, lives with her devoted Aunt Rose, a seamstress; her aunt's insensitive companion, Vashti, a nurse; and her two little sisters, Libbie and Evie. The war separates the girls from their parents: her mother is trapped in Russia; her father is fighting somewhere in western Europe. To help out, Hannah hawks newspapers at North Station before school. One day a train almost hits Hannah; a girl with violet eyes pushes her to safety and disappears. Hannah's best friend is Harry Weitz. After Harry's father dies of influenza, Vashti instructs the children to stay indoors. Soon, almost everyone is sick or dead: Aunt Rose dies, and the little girls are very ill. Vashti orders Hannah to travel to Albany to stay with friends. The girl with the violet eyes, whom Hannah considers her guardian angel, escorts her to North Station and puts her instead on a Red Cross hospital train to Vermont. Hannah awakes in a hospital in Brattleboro ("a pretty, tiny town"), unable to speak. A kind, elderly man, Klaus Gerhard, "a German, who is against the war," takes her along the Putney Road and up Black Mountain Road to recuperate at his farm. His property faces West River Mountain. "In the field to the front of the house, cornstalks huddled in groups like soldiers in rustling khaki." Klaus turned his field over to another family to farm because the town "would not do business with Germans." At first, she does not tell him that she cannot eat ham and lard and finally confides she is Jewish. He cooks her nutritious meals and offers her sensible advice. She rides to Brattleboro with Klaus, where a girl calls him a "dirty German." Klaus tells Hannah that President Lincoln addressed Klaus's battalion on the eve of a Civil War battle. Wounded in the fray, Klaus crawled into a cave where a Confederate solider was hiding. The latter dug the bullet out of his leg. When they emerged, a Union officer shot and killed the rebel. Hannah volunteers at the Red Cross to sew and knit for the soldiers. She is eager to return home and works to earn her train fare. She receives no response to her letters to Harry and Vashti because the postman, observing Klaus's happiness with Hannah, has never mailed them. Her guardian angel puts her back on the train to North Station. Arriving in time for the Armistice, she hastens to the Weitzs' house where she finds that Vashti, Harry, and her sisters are alive.

Witness (2001) describes the arrival and infiltration of the Ku Klux Klan in a rural Vermont town in 1924. The Klan slowly makes its presence felt in the community. Someone sets fire to a cross on the hill across the valley. Percelle Johnson, the town constable, worries about two hundred additional Negroes who have moved to town to build the dam. Fitzgerald Flitt is the town doctor. Ira Hirsch is a Jewish shoemaker from New York; he and his six-year-old daughter, Esther, live with Sara Chickering, a farmer. When the Klan threatens Sara, Ira offers to move, but Sara is not afraid. Rita Weaver is a restaurant owner and bootlegger. Leonora Sutter is a twelve-year-old black student who is unhappy because none of the white children plays with her. One day, seeing Esther standing on the railroad tracks, Leonora runs as fast as she can to pluck Esther from in front of the oncoming train. Merlin Van Tornhout is a racist eighteen-year-old in the school. Johnny Reeves is a clergyman and a racist. Reynard Alexander, the newspaper editor, considers himself neutral, though he notes the Klan does good only among white Protestants. He begins to worry about the way the Klan is burrowing into the community. He receives threatening letters from "ordinary, sensible, hardheaded Vermonters," who are duped by the Klan. Harvey Pettibone, who owns a shop with his wife, Viola, becomes a practicing Klansman. The terror builds. The Klan threatens to kill the Sutters and the Hirsches; Ira is shot. Merlin disappears because he cannot bring himself to follow the Klan's orders to poison the Sutters' well, especially after he witnessed Leonora's heroism. The Klan brands and humiliates Johnny Reeves, who commits suicide. Finally, the secretary of state of Vermont rejects the application by the Klan to conduct business there.

Kimberly Heuston

The Shakeress (2002) begins in 1828 in Portsmouth, New Hampshire, where the Hull children, Naomi, thirteen, her elder brother, Ben, and younger siblings, Eli and Glory, stay with their Aunt Thankful after their parents and baby brother die in a fire. Aunt Thankful, mean-spirited and unkind, plans to send Naomi to work in a mill in Manchester. Naomi and Ben agree that, rather than separate, the four children should seek refuge at the Shaker Community in Canterbury, New Hampshire. During the next four years, the young Hulls learn the Shaker ways; each masters a trade. Naomi, assigned to an herbalist, becomes expert at the skill of healing. When she decides to leave, Ben, who takes Shaker wares to market, finds her a place with Olive Farr, a bedridden invalid in Vermont. By the time they arrive in St. Johnsbury, Mormon missionaries have miraculously cured the woman. Ben's friends, the Snows, urge Naomi to stay with them and establish a medical practice in the community. Going to church the first Sunday, they pass the Brick House (just down the road from the Athenaeum) owned by Judge Paddock, founder of St. Johnsbury. His cousins are the wealthy Fairbanks brothers, Erastus and Thaddeus, manufacturers of stoves and scales (Thaddeus established St. Johnsbury Academy). Naomi earns a modest income selling Sister Naomi's Good Wholesome Medicinal Remedies and Vegetable Nostrums at the Fairbanks store.

At church, Naomi meets handsome young Joseph Fairbanks. After a Fourth of July picnic, Joseph invites Naomi to a party at the Brick House. The two Mormon missionaries who cured Olive Farr visit the Snows to extol Joseph Smith. God and his Son appeared to Smith, they say, to reveal to him the existence of secret records in the form of golden tablets, which he translated as the Book of Mormon (the "Golden Book"). Naomi sees Joseph regularly. Together, they listen to a debate at Pearson Academy; Joseph favors objective fact over subjective feeling. When she asks about his belief in God, he replies that God has never spoken to him. The Mormon missionaries, after helping with the haying, speak to a crowd in the Snows' barn. When Naomi hears about the possibility of finding "a more abundant life," she realizes that she must follow this goal. Much as she loves Joseph, who asks her to marry him, she knows that his life in St. Johnsbury cannot be hers. Baptized a Mormon, she heads with a group to Kirtland, Ohio, where other Mormons gather. She leaves Joseph behind, but she finds her relationship with God. (Joseph Smith, 1805-1844, was born in Sharon, Vermont, and founded the Church of Jesus Christ of Latter-day Saints. A granite monument to his memory stands in Sharon, Vermont.)

Hadley Higginson

The "Keeker" of the title in ***Keeker and the Sneaky Pony*** (2006) is Catherine Corey Keegan Dana, aged nine, who has five dogs, two cats, a goat, and a parakeet but yearns for a pony. Her parents buy her a lovely (if occasionally sneaky) Shetland pony named Plum. They help Keeker put on the saddle and bridle for her first ride on Plum, warning her not to go too far. When Keeker and Plum reach the woods, Keeker knows she should turn around and head for home, but her pony is frisky and eager to continue. Once in the woods, Plum, snorting and rearing, slides Keeker onto the trail and dances deeper into the woods. Keeker crossly follows and finds the pony in the midst of a blackberry bramble. Plum runs off, but Keeker steals up on her with a stick to scratch Plum's back, which she loves. Now friends, they amicably ride home. Plum is glad she has a girl rider; she can train her easily. (The epilogue lists some facts about ponies; for example, ponies are not short horses or baby horses but a separate breed.)

In ***Keeker and the Horse Show Show-Off*** (2006), Keeker takes riding lessons. She and Plum love to jump over anything they can find. Keeker decides they should compete in the 4-H horse show and plans what she might say if they win a ribbon. Plum thinks horse shows are for show-offs. In the next stall at the show is a pretty dapple-gray pony, Lulu's Li'l Windsong, with a conceited little owner, Tifni, who is an experienced horse-show competitor. In the jumping contest, however, Tifni turns in her saddle to smile at the judges and misses the last jump altogether. Keeker is surprised when she and Plum win the event; Plum is not surprised at all.

It is mud season in ***Keeker and the Sugar Shack*** (2006). Keeker, now ten, and Plum are bored because they cannot go riding. Keeker puts stockings on her head, pretending to have long braids like Laura Ingalls Wilder. Finally the sun comes out, and she and her mother take their horses on a ride. Someone has bought Crabapple Hill Farm. Keeker imagines a witch lives there. The next day, she and Plum investigate. They cross the fields of Mr. Doolan's dairy farm, make friends with Clancy, his dog, and see smoke issuing from a shack. Then Keeker spies an old lady, cackling and carrying a kettle. Now Keeker is sure she is a witch. Inside the house, she finds her mother eating pancakes with Mavis Yardbottom pouring maple syrup over them.

In ***Keeker and the Springtime Surprise*** (2007), Keeker discovers "Peep," a cedar waxwing, and takes her home. When a mother groundhog makes a home for her babies in Plum's pasture, Plum tries to protect the little family from Mr. Dana, who considers groundhogs pests. Because Mrs. Dana's horse, Pansy, is about to have a foal, neither of Keeker's parents is interested in baby groundhogs. In order to win back her parents' attention, Keeker decides to put on a play. Consulting her parents' library, she chooses Don Quixote because he rode a horse.

Her parents continue to concentrate on Pansy. Plum noses the groundhog family members out of their hole and hurries them to the barn. There they find Pansy and her brand-new, wobbly foal, Rosie. The Danas move the groundhogs to the field behind the barn. As a special treat, Keeker and her parents spend the night in the barn, with Plum in her stall keeping watch over Rosie.

Beth Hilgartner

Colors in the Dreamweaver's Loom (1989) begins in Burlington, where eighteen-year-old Alexandra ("Zan") Scarsdale sadly leaves Vermont, after the death of her Pulitzer Prize-winning novelist father, Alistair Scarsdale, to enter Harvard College. She pulls off Interstate 89 to stretch her legs in the woods, falls, rolls down a slope, and collides with a tree, hitting her head. The next thing she knows, strangers are helping her: twins Karivet, a Prophet, and Iobeh, a Heartmender, who speak no English; in fact, Iobeh communicates only in sign language. Reaching a cluster of stone houses with thatched roofs, they introduce her to an old woman, Eikoheh, the Dream Weaver. Zan, initially frightened of this dream world, moves in to cook, care for the goats, weave, and absorb the language, history, and culture of the Orathi. A warring tribe, the Venathi, wants to seize the Orathi land and change their old forest-living ways. The Orathi believe that Zan is a Wanderer, sent to champion their cause. She and the twins embark, with an elder as guide, to walk to the City, where the Lord lives in splendor. Zan develops spirit-gifts, including the capability to decipher others' thoughts. She testifies to the Lord that she sees no crowding in the City and thus no need to appropriate Orathi lands. The Lord proclaims the Orathi can either leave the lands peaceably or be plunged into war. Zan diplomatically proposes traveling to Windsmeet to consult the gods and request a decree from them. Joined now by Vihena, a Swordswoman, Ychass, a Shapeshifter, and Remarr, a Minstrel, Zan begins the perilous journey through the desert. They face many challenges, including a sandstorm and unfriendly tribes, and finally confront the Trickster, who allots them many arduous tasks. Moving at night to evade pursuers, they reach the god Weaver, who is in charge of the Loom of Fate. Fulfilling the Trickster's commands, they return. She grants their wishes in cruel and perverse ways; for example, she gives Iobeh the ability to speak with a hideous croak for a voice. She rewards Zan by ripping her out of the Loom and flinging her into the void. Arriving at Logan Airport, Zan discovers she has been away five months.

The Feast of the Trickster (1991), the sequel, begins with the Weaver's realization that the Orathi world is in danger of unraveling unless Zan comes back into the Loom. He is also concerned about troublesome Trickster. The Weaver and the other gods send Zan's five companions into the void on a quest for Zan. The Five are Iobeh, the Heartmender; Karivet, the Prophet; Remarr, the Minstrel; Vihena, the Swordswoman; and Ychass, the Shapeshifter. In white robes and veils, they arrive in Plainfield, to be met by three surprised teenagers working at a stable. Angel, Mark, and Brice assume the visitors are aliens from another planet. When the Five explain their quest, the youngsters agree to help by providing more appropriate clothing and locating Zan through the telephone book. They enlist Brigid Chandler from Barre, one of the riders at the stable, in the cause. She offers the Five the use of her parents' house, introducing them as friends from Greece. Meanwhile, Zan is in Cambridge having a breakdown: she thinks a cult abducted her and experiences terrifying dreams. Her psychiatrist, Dr. Isaac Marchbanks, consigns her to the college infirmary. Trickster is torn from the Loom and flung into the void. She, too, lands in Vermont but is soon on her way to Boston, where she disguises herself as a biker in black leather with a spiky punk hairdo. Ychass senses the Trickster's presence. Zan explains to Isaac about the cult, her missing memory, and her dreams about gods and shapeshifters. Trickster traces Zan to the infirmary and works her wiles on Isaac. Zan slips out of the hospital, thinking Isaac is associated with the cult; Isaac and Trickster, who calls herself Antekkereh, travel to Barre to find her. Trickster, who is falling in love with Isaac, persuades him that Zan's recollections are not delusions. The gods assemble all the characters in the other world and give them a choice about their futures. The three youngsters are free to return to their proper sphere. Trickster, drained of her power, becomes a mortal and chooses to stay with Isaac; Zan decides to stay in the other world. Zan gives her name, Social Security number, and driver's license to Trickster and keeps Trickster's name.

Ralph Nading Hill

Jacob Seaworthy in ***The Voyages of Brian Seaworthy*** (1971) is the owner of a shipyard in Long Point, three miles from Burlington; his fleet consists of two side-wheeling steamboats, *Republic* and *Bennington,* and a much smaller tug, *Gloria*. When his son, Brian, is fifteen in 1872, the widowed Seaworthy dies, leaving Brian in the care of the housekeeper, Mrs. Mayberry. Shortly thereafter, Brian's Uncle Rueul, whom he has never met, arrives to act as conservator of the company until Brian comes of age. Brian goes out on the lake that summer with his friend, Barney Barnaby, whose father is captain on *Bennington*. Then the two boys begin their training in the boiler room of *Republic* under Captain Bullard, a harsh taskmaster. As the only firemen on the boat, they are exhausted after going to Plattsburgh and back, because the coal is full of slag that will not burn. Jib Wiley, another member of the crew, is jealous of Brian and calls him "junior" in front of the others. After Jib tightens the nut on the blower valve to make it explode, Brian and Barney are fired. They find jobs with Barney's father on *Bennington*, which runs from Whitehall to St. Jean, Quebec, and back. Chief Barnaby is a good teacher, who says Brian will absorb information "like salt pork does milk gravy." After another accident at Port Kent, near the hotel at Cliff Haven, the boys again lose their jobs and again suspect foul play. They are reassigned to *Gloria*, carrying a ship's part for recasting in New York. They pass a new shipyard that is building the steamboat *Defiance*. They return on the People's Line's finest boat, *St. John*. Aboard, Jennie, the captain's daughter, introduces them to her father, who knew Brian's father and invites them to dinner. Brian goes back to school but does some boating on the weekends, as well as hunting and fishing. *Defiance* is launched. Brian is aboard *Republic* when she races *Defiance*—and it looks as though Captain Bullard loses on purpose. He and Jib are disclosed as crooks; Uncle Rueul (whose real name is Jacob Dugan) is a swindler as well. His partner, the real Uncle Rueul, finally appears. The authorities do not have enough evidence to prosecute Bullard, who ships on with *Defiance*. They all put up for the winter, when the lake freezes, but later, when *Republic* and *Defiance* both venture out in a storm, *Defiance* sinks. Now sixteen, Brian will soon take over the company.

H

Clara Whitehill Hunt

The Barstowes live in an apartment in New York City in ***The Little House in Green Valley*** (1932). Because their father, Edward, is ill and the rent is high, Roger, eight, and Gail, seven, cannot attend movie matinees and are contented to stay home and reread their favorite books—*Heidi, Nils*, *Uncle Remus*, and *Dr. Doolittle*. The family's fortunes change for the better when Aunt Abigail leaves Edward her little white cottage in Green Valley and enough money to travel there every summer. Edward's great-grandfather owned a farm in Vermont, where Edward spent many summers as a boy. The family takes the train to Green Valley and falls in love with the house and the village customs. A neighbor sells vegetables picked by the customer fresh from the garden. The butcher's truck makes house calls. The postmistress lives next door and has a room full of old toys and children's magazines. They hike to the top of the hill for a picnic, stopping at Mrs. Hill's to pick up Fred, who is Roger's age. Mrs. Hill contributes a large slice of cake, while Fred fills a pail with raspberries. Gail is gratified to observe that her mother is always prepared for contingencies, like the mother in *Swiss Family Robinson*. John Seldon, a remote cousin, lives at the former Barstowe farm and invites the family to visit the old homestead. Roger and Gail investigate everything—the big barn, the ancient carriage, the swinging oak. They gather warm eggs and watch the mowing machine, pulled by two glossy black horses. Back in Green Valley, they play games on the many sets of stairs. In the evenings, their father reads to them from *Two Years before the Mast*. They follow the brook to its source. Everything in the country is enjoyable, even washday, and completely different from city life. They pass a fine summer and look forward to many more.

Lee Pennock Huntington

Brothers in Arms (1976) presents a series of chronological vignettes illuminating the agonizing choices faced by families during the American Revolution. The Pennock family came to America in 1714 and settled in Connecticut. In 1768, their son, James, his wife, Thankful, and their ten children move to Strafford, an "untouched wilderness" in the New Hampshire Grants. Bringing what they need to start a new life, they clear trees to till the soil. The family becomes an important part of the community, holding high positions. Seven years later, bitter feelings arise over whether Strafford belongs to the New Hampshire Grants or to New York State. It seems obvious to Aaron, one of the elder Pennock sons, that New York owns the land; in the west the Green Mountain Boys are running Yorkers off settlers' property. People take sides as patriots or Tories. The British and the Americans fight at Lexington and Concord; Ethan Allen seizes Fort Ticonderoga. In 1776, the message of the Declaration of Independence stirs new thoughts in Heman, one of the younger Pennock sons. In 1777, the new state is named Vermont. News comes that Burgoyne's army is advancing from Canada by way of Lake Champlain. The close, prosperous Pennock family calls a meeting. All the brothers refuse to take an oath of allegiance to the revolutionary government, except Heman, who leaves home to stay with his sister, Anne, and her patriot husband, Daniel West. The elder sons join the Queen's Rangers, along with about six hundred other Loyalists from Vermont, New Hampshire, and New York. The British regulars are scornful of the "provincials." The soldiers are fearful of the Indians, who have recently murdered and scalped Loyalist Jane McCrae. At Bennington for the first time the Americans under John Stark meet the Loyalist forces—some of which are friends and relatives. Burgoyne's defeated army and the Queen's Rangers press on to Saratoga. A fearsome battle is fought, the Americans win conclusively, and three Pennocks are killed. Two of the brothers, shocked and angry, emigrate to Canada; three return to Strafford. The town had confiscated and sold the property of James and Thankful to help pay for the rebel cause. The sons buy back their land and work hard to make the farm profitable. In October 1780, the Indians raid Royalton, burning houses and killing or abducting residents. Heman heads to Royalton with the militia; his Tory brothers ask to join the rescue effort. Thankful dies in 1793. After James's death, their children erect a fine marker in the cemetery.

Johanna Hurwitz

In ***Yellow Blue Jay*** (1986), Jay Koota, eight, is not enthusiastic about spending two summer weeks in southern Vermont. His parents rent a big house and invite the Ross family from Ohio to stay with them. Stacey Ross, seven, is the age of Jay's sister, Ellen; their son, Mickey, is twelve. Meeting Jay's worst expectations, Mickey calls him a "yellow blue jay" because Jay does not want to sleep in the upper bunk. When Mickey hikes up Haystack Mountain (the ski lift operator offers a free ride down), Jay refuses to go, visualizing scary images of mountaineers with ropes and bottled oxygen. Instead, he retreats into the woods to build tiny houses with twigs and bits of moss. The two families swim at Snake Lake. Jay, terrified by the name, cannot swim and is ashamed of the flab that hangs over his swimsuit; Mickey is tall, slim, and flat-stomached. Mickey offers to teach Jay to float and, when he is frightened, again calls him a "yellow blue jay." The adults tire of cooking; Jay offers the children's services. It is his idea to serve shish kabob using Mrs. Ross's knitting needles as skewers. The adults are impressed. When a bat flies into the living room, it is Jay who rescues the bat by capturing it in a pail and covering it with newspaper. Another couple from Ohio arrives for lunch, bringing Roger, Mickey's best friend. Roger teases Jay, treating him like a baby. Mickey goes off with Roger, leaving Jay so miserable that he angrily destroys his miniature houses. Later the girls come into the house crying because their elves' cottages are gone. Jay decides to rebuild them secretly. Mickey offers to help and apologizes for going off with Roger. Mickey says, regardless of Jay's age, he thinks of him as a friend. They shake hands. The families visit Bennington to look at some Grandma Moses paintings. Jay accomplishes much in this vacation in Vermont and looks forward to fourth grade.

A Llama in the Family (1994) concerns the Fine family in Wilmington. Adam is ten; April is about to be five. Their father owns a tile and carpet company; their mother, announcing a surprise, invests in a white llama named Ethan Allen to start a business called "Fine Llama Treks." Adam is greatly disappointed the "surprise" is not a mountain bike for him but soon becomes attached to the llama. Ethan Allen is well behaved and usually quiet, though sometimes he hums. His first trick is to come when Adam blows a whistle. Adam does some research about llamas in the school library before bringing Ethan Allen to show the children at school. After his mother puts an advertisement in the paper, customers begin to call. When school is out, Adam helps on a trek with older people (and is sorry for spilling cold blueberry soup on one of the clients). The picnic spot is at Lake Whitingham; he is impressed by the extent of his mother's knowledge about the woods. When it becomes apparent that it will take a long time for his mother to recoup the investment in the llama, Adam ponders ways to raise money. The local paper lists notices from people wishing to swap items. He finds in the attic an old braided rug, which his father helps him mend. A little research at the local flea shop persuades him that the rug is worth something. He cannot believe his eyes when he sees the following announcement in the paper: "Will swap llama for crazy quilt." He telephones the advertiser to say he already has one llama and would give another llama an excellent home. After considerable bargaining with the flea market dealer, Adam swaps his braided rug for a crazy quilt and accompanies his father to pick up the new llama. This one is brown; Adam names him Ira Allen. Having two llamas will help his mother's business and is much more important than his bicycle. His father is so affected by Adam's generosity that he buys him a mountain bike after all—the new refrigerator can wait.

In ***A Llama in the Library*** (1999), the sequel to *A Llama in the Family*, fifth-grader Adam finds that the first Friday in September is sex-education day. Living on farms, the children know about animal reproduction, but Adam and his best friend, Justin, find the material on the video unsettling. When his parents announce they are expecting another baby, Adam is astounded. According to Adam's father, the White House, a big inn in Wilmington, is haunted. To investigate, Adam and Justin sneak into the hotel and speak to a friendly chambermaid, who tells them that several people have reported suspicious incidents. Adam and Justin head for the library, where Mrs. Walsh recommends Joseph A. Citro's *Green Mountain Ghosts, Ghouls, and Unsolved Mysteries.* The chapter on the White House explains that the ghostly owner, whose name was Brown, visits only people named Brown. The boys immediately think of the beautiful new fifth grader, Alana Brown. The following Saturday, Adam takes Alana to the White House. The owner, Mr. Grinwold, is interested in Alana's name and shows them a secret staircase. It is raining quite hard when they emerge. Adam worries about Alana's riding her bicycle: she is not wearing a helmet. When he reads next day that a young bicyclist was killed in an automobile accident that night, he is stricken with sorrow and guilt. At school on Monday, he learns the dead girl was not Alana. Mrs. Walsh invites his mother's two llamas to take part in the grand opening of the renovated library after the holidays (Adam's family celebrates Hanukkah, Justin's family celebrates Christmas, and Alana's family celebrates both). On a bad day in mud season, schools are closed, traffic is paralyzed, and Alana is visiting when Adam's mother goes into labor. Alana calmly turns up the television set to muffle any unusual noises from Adam's little sister and asks Adam to boil water. The baby is named Alana in honor of her help in the delivery. For the library party, everyone dresses in costume. The *Brattleboro Reformer* publishes Adam's picture with one of the llamas and the governor of the state.

H

In ***Faraway Summer*** (1998), the first in a trilogy (the others are *Dear Emma* and *The Unsigned Valentine*), Hadassah ("Dossi"), twelve, and Ruthi Rabinowitz, eighteen, are orphans living in one room of a tenement in New York City in 1910. Ruthi, who works at the Triangle Shirtwaist Factory, applies to the Fresh Air Fund for a two-week country vacation for Dossi. On her way to Jericho, Dossi alights from the train at Essex Junction, where the Meade family meets her. In addition to the parents, the family consists of two boys, Edward, nineteen, and Timothy, sixteen, and two girls, Emma, fourteen, and Nell, nine. When they serve pork at supper, Dossi explains Jews cannot eat pork. Mrs. Meade observes that very few Jews live in Vermont. Nell is friendly toward Dossi; Emma is not: "It is almost as if there were one of those Vermont stone walls separating us." Emma tries to adjust to Dossi's not being a Christian. Dossi has brought a library book, *Anne of Green Gables*, which Emma carelessly leaves out in the rain and then rudely orders Dossi not to tell Emma's mother. Meanwhile, Ruthi writes that she is going to marry Meyer Reisman; they will have a real home again. One night, Dossi is awakened by smoke and alerts the household to a fire in neighbor Tucker's barn. As they work with buckets of water, Dossi thinks of Ruthi's factory, where the windows are nailed down. Dossi realizes that, although the Meades have a big house, land, and plenty of food, they are not immune to worries about dangers such as bad weather, sickness, and fire. Emma suggests they pick blackberries to sell at the general store to raise money to replace Dossi's book. Dossi learns that the granite stone for the new library in New York City comes from local quarries in Dorset. She and Emma are friends by the end of Dossi's worthwhile vacation.

Dear Emma (2002), the second in the trilogy, consists of letters from Dossi, who is in New York City, to Emma, in Jericho. Dossi misses her Vermont family very much. Some of Emma's news, about topics such as heavy snow, black bears, or Emma's brother's wedding, is integrated into Dossi's responses. Dossi often comments upon books she is reading—*Little Women*, *Freckles*, *A Girl of the Limberlost*, and *The Casting Away of Mrs. Lecks and Mrs. Aleshine*. After Dossi's sister, Ruthi, marries Meyer, the two sisters move into his apartment, with a small bed for Dossi in a corner of the living room. The arrangement is not ideal; Meyer is often impatient with Dossi for reading instead of helping Ruthi. Ruthi leaves her job at the Triangle Shirtwaist Factory and is soon pregnant. A diphtheria epidemic sweeps Lower Manhattan; Meyer is fearful for Ruthi. The terrible tragedy of the fire at the factory overwhelms everyone; Ruthi's best friend is one of the dead women. When Dossi writes to Emma about the fire, she alludes to the Tuckers' fire in Vermont the previous summer. Ruthi has a little girl, Sarah Rose. The Meades invite Dossi back for another summer visit to Vermont, and Ruthi urges her to go. Dossi looks forward to eating pancakes with maple syrup, milking cows, and, most of all, being with the Meade family.

The Unsigned Valentine (2006), the third in the trilogy, focuses, through entries in her journal, on Emma's aspirations. Her friend Dossi, to whom she continues to write, wants to become a doctor; Emma, now sixteen, wants to marry, live on a farm, raise a family, and, eventually, develop the town library as an expression of her special passion for books. Her brother, Edward, marries Libby Greene. Emma is attracted to his friend, Cole Berry, who is tall, blue-eyed, and handsome. Hoping to run into him, she goes to a pie social, where she meets a visitor, Grace Coolidge, who lives in Massachusetts with her state senator husband, Calvin. Emma confides in Mrs. Coolidge that she feels tongue-tied at parties; Mrs. Coolidge assures her that reticence is a good quality: when she does have something to say, people will listen. After the well runs dry at Emma's house, a dowser finds a water source, and Eddie and Cole help dig the well. As winter approaches, both Libby and Emma's mother are pregnant. Emma will have to stay home from school to help. At the pond where young people meet in the afternoons, Cole skates with Emma for a while until Josie Wheeler, whose father owns the mill where Cole works, lures him away. Emma loves to read: Alcott and Stowe are her favorite authors. Dossi sends her *Romeo and Juliet*, whose plot Emma finds "absurd"—not like real life at all. When Cole brings some cider to the house, her father announces, much to Emma's embarrassment and distress, that she is too young to be courting and forbids them to see each other. Miserable, Emma informs Dossi that Shakepeare's tragedy has turned into the story of her life. Emma joins the church choir to be close to Cole, although they are not allowed to communicate. She receives an unsigned valentine, which she is certain came from him. Her brother, Tim, now eighteen, takes some of the neighbors' children to school in his wagon. When a fierce rain causes flooding, Tim needs Emma to help fetch them. On the way, Tim stops to assist some neighbors, and Emma goes on alone. No one is at school. She must find Nell. Remembering stories of other floods, she unhitches Dandy, in case he has to swim, and is inching on foot across the bridge when it collapses. She is catapulted into the rushing river amid debris, logs, and furniture, and is struggling to stay afloat when Cole rescues her in a canoe and paddles her to Edward and Libby's house. Despite the savagery of the storm, no human lives were lost; Dandy is safe. The *Jericho Reporter* gives a full report of the flood of April 1912; a piece in the *Burlington Free Press* simultaneously reports on the sinking of the *Titanic*. Grateful to Cole for saving Emma's life, her parents agree to their marrying in two years if they are still so inclined. As the saying goes, "You have to have a summer and a winter together before you know each other." Now Cole is a regular guest at Sunday dinner; Emma quotes to Dossi the title of the latest Shakespeare play she sent, "All's well that ends well."

J

Edgar N. Jackson

Green Mountain Hero (1961) dramatizes the life of early settlers on Otter Creek. The Storys—Amos, Ann, and their children, Solomon, Ephraim, Samuel, Susanna, and Hannah—live in Salisbury, Connecticut, in 1774. After their barn burns down (the arsonist may be Amos's Tory enemy, Zeke Jenny), Amos decides to move the family to Vermont. He and his eldest son, Solomon, thirteen, will find a lot and build a house, with the family to follow. Amos is an experienced woodsman, having served with the British in the French and Indian Wars. Camping out all the way, they stop in Pownal, then Bennington, where Amos discusses the long-standing feud between New York and the New Hampshire Grants and the formation of a local militia known as the Green Mountain Boys. Amos, who is strong, proficient, and brave, warns Solomon of three main dangers in the north woods: wolves, big cats (catamounts), and Indians, who are angry with settlers for taking their land. In Rutland, Amos swaps his horse for a canoe, powder, shot, a saw, a tub of bear grease, and a big kettle. The trader tricks him out of paddles, but Amos fells a tree with an ax and carves two paddles with his knife. He shoots a buck and shows Solomon how to dress the meat. They stop in Pittsford and learn that John Everts has chartered three towns: Salisbury, Middlebury, and New Haven. In Salisbury, Amos finds a plateau near Otter Creek with a spring close by and trees the right size for his log cabin. Amos demonstrates the way to build a woodshed of logs to serve as their shelter while they build their dwelling. They make holes for the smoke and fill chinks between the logs with gray clay from the creek's cliffs. Seven miles up the Indian hunting trail live the Smauleys, who come to the roof raising. The cabin is sixteen by twenty-four feet, with two rooms downstairs and a loft. Amos kills a bear and uses the skin for a rug, the steaks for meat, and the fat for soap and butter. In Rutland, the same horse trader confronts Amos with a bullwhip. Calmly wresting the whip out of the man's hands, Amos says to Solomon, "Never pick a fight, but neither should you let anyone take your rights away." They cut and split wood for the woodshed, burning the branches to make wood ash for the soil; the fireplace ashes are for making soap. They cut down a big oak, struck by lightning, where bees have stored honey. In January 1775, when the heavy snow comes, they fashion furniture. In sugaring season, they make maple sugar because they have no containers for syrup. In spring, they plant corn, pumpkins, melons, squash, and cucumbers in between the stumps, Indian-style. As Amos cuts down a big maple, a huge branch falls on and kills him. Solomon, at fourteen, is the head of the family. After the Smauleys help to bury Amos, Solomon walks back to Connecticut to fetch his family. By the time he reaches Bennington, Ethan Allen has taken Fort Ticonderoga. Ann and her family, with Solomon as "guide and guard," head north toward Salisbury; they meet many settlers leaving because the British and the Indians are seeking revenge for Allen's action. The Green Mountain Boys warn the Storys that Zeke Jenny, their Tory enemy, and his Indian followers are raiding, burning, and taking captives along Lake Champlain. Ann volunteers to serve the Boys by providing shelter, food, and intelligence: "Give me a place among you, and see if I am the first to desert my post." Ann and Solomon dig a cave in a cliff on the creek where they can all hide with their canoe and store emergency food and supplies. They train the children to make a quick, noiseless retreat, each carrying an assigned pack. One night the Indians come while the Storys are in the cave and burn down their cabin; fortunately the woodshed is untouched. The family begins to rebuild at once; again the Smauleys help to raise the roof. Solomon heads to Rutland to reequip their cabin. The Boys bring kegs of powder to stow temporarily in the cave. In early 1776 Ann finds lying in the trail an abandoned woman captive. Ann helps deliver her baby and gives her and her child a home. After the Declaration of Independence is signed in 1776, many Tories, among them Zeke, head for Canada to enlist in the king's army. The Storys spend nights in the cave. As Zeke is passing, he hears the baby cry and forces Ann at gunpoint out of the cave. One of the children carries a message to the Boys, who capture and imprison about one hundred Tories. The settlers begin to return. The Storys pile their cabin high with harvest. After Solomon teaches Ephraim all he knows about hunting, farming, and woodcraft, he enlists in the militia. The Americans win the Battle of Bennington; the army recruits men for Saratoga.

Jacqueline Jackson

After Elizabeth ("Libby") Fletcher's father dies in Illinois in 1903 in ***The Taste of Spruce Gum*** (1966), Libby, eleven, and her mother, Mildred, move to Vermont where, in what Libby considers an act of base betrayal, her mother marries Uncle Charles Fletcher, thirty-five, her father's younger brother. The elder brother, Uncle Henry, runs the business part of Fletcher Brothers Lumber Company in Rutland, while Uncle Charles manages the lumber camp on Shrewsbury Mountain, twenty miles away. Uncle Henry and Aunt Charlotte, who live in Grandmother Fletcher's house, have four children. Hattie, Libby's age, is a bossy show-off. Libby is thin, weak, and almost bald from a long bout with typhoid. Overhearing her grandmother's remark that lumberjacks are drunkards, Libby dreads what lies ahead. On the way up the mountain, her mother gathers some spruce gum, whose taste Libby finds sharp and tart but curiously good. Much to Libby's surprise, the setting is beautiful: "The ground fell away and a great valley was spread below. The quilted mountain flanks and the patchwork field beyond were suffused with sunset. Rosy smoke curled from a tiny city, a pink sliver of water lay in the distance, and on the horizon the uneven line of a mountain range shimmered. The sun rested on its highest peak like a red ball." Libby is angry and resentful: how could Uncle Charles bring her to this alien place? She hates him.

She does not understand his sense of humor. He shows them the place where the men—French-Canadians and Italians—are felling trees. She is fascinated and repelled: soon, she thinks, there will be no forest. She looks down the mountain where "rough logs lay like scattered sulphur matches." Uncle Charles tells them about the year 1816, when it snowed all summer. Libby cannot help comparing her father to Uncle Charles: her father was "like a smooth, polished chest, while Uncle Charles was just a splintery, resiny old board." While carpenters build their new house, the family stays at Jewel Vincent's boarding house, where the men eat their meals. Jewel's husband is a drunk who beats her. When Libby asks Jewel if there are other children in camp, she says the Moranvilles live in one of the shanties, with a boy, Albert, Libby's age; Mary, seven; Wilbur, five; and baby Dan. Libby, trembling with rage and self-pity, confides her unhappiness to Jewel, who retorts that her mother has "spunk": "what can't be cured must be endured." Libby's mother is in charge of camp supplies and keeping the accounts. The men are paid in scrip, which Uncle Henry cashes in Rutland. When her mother is summoned to the Moranvilles to deliver another baby, Libby entertains Mary, Wilbur, and Dan. The new baby is named Mildred, after Libby's mother. Uncle Charles is rather dismissive of the "twilldos," the uneducated workers who will do anything—chop, clear brush, lay a road, or nail a shanty. When the schoolteacher quits, Mildred takes on the task. Libby loves school and learning about the history of Vermont. Albert is a troublemaker, refusing to do lessons. Although he is as tall as Mildred, she beats him into submission. That night, he penitently offers to fill their wood box. In the evenings, Mildred and Libby read. The latter's favorites are *Tanglewood Tales*, *Rip Van Winkle*, *The Wide, Wide World*, and *Robinson Crusoe*. Libby is heartbroken because Uncle Charles never speaks to her. When the Rutland family comes for Thanksgiving, her cousin Hattie lures her into the woods, a destination forbidden by Uncle Charles. He banishes Libby to her room; she hates him. At Christmastime, he carves her a present with a little note saying, "With love from Uncle Charles." Before she can thank him, he and her mother have a terrible fight: Mildred charges that his brother, Henry, is cheating him. That night their house burns down, and they move into one of the shanties. Uncle Charles and Mildred are overly polite to each other. He urges her to take Libby down to Rutland while they rebuild. Having hurt each other badly, Charles and Mildred are both miserable. Jewel announces to Charles that she is divorcing Vincent. While Charles is taking Jewel to Rutland, Vincent gives liquor to some of the lumberjacks. Mildred and Libby make supper for the men. Suddenly, Uncle Henry arrives with terrible news. In an accident on the snowy train track, Jewel was killed and Charles was seriously injured and in the hospital. Mildred takes Uncle Henry's horse (without asking him) and rides to Rutland. Without offering to help Libby, Uncle Henry gets a ride to Rutland on a sawdust wagon, leaving Libby and Lonzo, the spastic hired man, to do all the work and feed the lumberjacks. Libby puts Mrs. Moranville in charge of the kitchen, Libby and Lonzo find and hide Vincent's whiskey to keep as evidence, and then Libby hides away on a lumber wagon heading down the mountain. She is determined to see Uncle Charles, to tell him she loves him, and to call him "Papa." She forces her way into his room where they hug and kiss "with a sob of pain and joy." He is aghast that Uncle Henry left her alone in camp. When the nurse insists she cannot stay, Uncle Charles retorts that she certainly can: "She is my daughter." (In Louisa May Alcott's *Little Women*, Jo March's favorite novel is Susan Warner's *The Wide, Wide World*.)

Caroline E. Jacobs

The three Shaw girls in ***The S.W.F. Club*** (1912) are Pauline Almy, fifteen (named after her Uncle Paul Almy Shaw), Hilary, thirteen, and Patience, ten, who live in Winton near Vergennes. When their father, Phil, declared his intention twenty years earlier to remain a small-town minister, he and his affluent Manhattanite brother, Paul, parted ways. After Hilary suffers from exhaustion and has to leave school, Dr.

Brice prescribes a change of scene. Pauline, knowing her parents cannot afford such a luxury, writes to Uncle Paul, without her parents' permission or knowledge, to request his financial support for a trip for Hilary. Uncle Paul responds that he believes home is the best place for Hilary and proposes to send Pauline twenty-five dollars a month to allow for "simple healthful diversions" within a ten-mile radius. Pauline creates the S.W.F. (Seeing Winton First) Club. She and her sisters invite friends such as Dr. Brice's children, Tom and Josie, to join; grownups like their parents and housekeeper are honorary members. At the S.W.F. Club's first meeting, Tom proposes a sightseeing tour on "Folly," the hotel's old stagecoach. Pauline writes Uncle Paul engaging reports about their adventures; pleased, he sends a little mare, Bedelia, and a light, two-wheeled carriage to take Hilary on excursions. Hilary chooses to go on a picnic and pick cherries at her godparents' farm, The Maples. Absorbed in their simple, homely pleasures, the young people devise a motto: "It's a habit to be happy." They discover that "developing home resources" is a sound philosophy. Phil Shaw takes them on a fishing party; Dr. Brice's excursion is on the old sail ferry to the New York side of the lake. Patience, the youngest child, points out that the club has selfishly forgotten to invite Sextoness Jane to be an honorary member; the lonely old woman is touched and pleased by the invitation. The crowning excitement of the summer is Uncle Paul's surprise visit; he and his younger brother quickly reconcile. When it is Jane's turn to plan a trip, she escorts them by night to the shore, where they watch the long line of canal boats towed down the lake, the red lanterns glowing at the end of each boat. The familiar sight is magical and special. Pauline's expedition, the final one before autumn, is to Fort Edward (which played a role in the French and Indian Wars and the American Revolution) in New York. Inside the "old, gray walls," they feel the presence of the past, the "long-ago days of storm and stress"; in her father's words, they have developed "the hearing ear and the seeing eye" (Proverbs 20:12).

J

Allen Johnson, Jr.

Betsy and John Flint own a Christmas tree farm in ***The Christmas Tree Express*** (1993) near Bear Mountain in 1937. Their ten-year-old son, T.J., small, skinny, and nearsighted, gives a talk at school about a hero—his grandfather, Joe Tanner, chief engineer for the Green Mountain Railroad. Afterward, twin bullies, Ned and Rufe O'Conner, pick a fight with T.J., as they do every day. Sally Fisk, brandishing a big pine branch, intervenes. Her parents, Amos and Jane, who breed and train huskies, explain to the children that the twins misbehave because their mother is dead, and their father drinks. When Sally and T.J. climb up Bear Mountain to watch the beavers at the pond, they come across a wounded Alaskan malamute. T.J. names him "Silver" and takes him home to nurse; if no one claims Silver, T.J. can keep him. The next time the bullies threaten T.J., Silver growls menacingly. Amos can tell Silver has been a sled dog because he knows the commands: "mush on" means "go," "ho" means "stop." Harnessing Silver to a sled on wheels, Sally and T.J. take him out for a drive. They find and rescue the twins, who have fallen over a cliff. Tim O'Conner, their father, is so grateful he swears never to take another drink and to resume working at the garage. The four children become friends. Sally often goes to T.J.'s house to discuss books; their favorites are *Treasure Island*, *Penrod*, and *Wind in the Willows*. Tim and the twins offer to help with the Christmas tree harvest; later, the O'Connors will have Christmas dinner with the Flints and the Fisks. December tenth is Harvest Day. They cut trees, two thousand in all, take them on trailers to the station, and load them on flatcars to be hauled to Twin Forks, where local ministers have purchased them for distribution. The children are at the station to welcome the train, which rushes by without stopping. The rich railroad owner, Mr. Broon, traveling in his private car, canceled the pick-up, thinking it was just another lumber load. No more trains are scheduled until after Christmas. Someone remembers Joe Tanner's old, retired engine. They receive permission from Mr. Broon in Rutland. Mrs. Flint makes a big banner. The whole town turns out to welcome the little engine as it pulls up. The crop is saved; the trees are delivered. With a part of the profits, the two sets of parents buy T.J. and Sally a two-person, varnished dog sled.

K

Bernard & Jonathan Katz

Black Woman (1973) begins in 1746 in Deerfield, Massachusetts, where a slave, Lucy Terry, sixteen, lives with her master and mistress, Ebenezer and Abigail Wells. Abigail teaches Lucy to read (Anne Bradstreet's poem, "Prologue," is a favorite) and to recognize that she is as smart as anyone, black or white, male or female. Black men serve in the militia; one of these soldiers is Abijah Prince, forty. Despite their age difference, Lucy and Abijah fall in love; ten years pass before Abijah, freed by his master, can purchase Lucy's freedom. In 1756, Lucy and Abijah marry; Abijah acquires land in Guilford in the New Hampshire territory and in Sunderland. Abijah cannot believe his eyes when he sees his name, that of a former slave, on a charter from the king. In 1770, the whole family, with four sons and two daughters, moves to its new home. By 1777, two sons, Caesar and Festus, are serving in the militia. In 1784, the Yorkers' last stand against the Vermont troops takes place at Packer's Corners, adjacent to the Prince farm. John Noyes, an ambitious and calculating man, covets the Prince farm. He tries to intimidate them into selling by loosing their cattle and burning their hay. In 1785, the Vermont Legislature and the Governor's Council meet in Norwich to solve disputes over contested land titles. Lucy, fearful of what Noyes can do to them, attends with her daughter, Durexa. Governor Thomas Chittenden and Lieutenant Governor Paul Spooner officiate; councilmen present are Peter Ollcott, Thomas Murdock, Benjamin Emmons, Moses Robinson, Ira Allen, and John Throop. Lucy describes their plight in the "use and possession" of their Guilford farm. Ira Allen immediately objects to her presence: why not take her case to her local selectmen? Lucy responds that her selectmen are in league with John Noyes, her harasser. After the governor grants her a hearing, she recounts their troubles, with the additional hardship of being a black family. The spectators are astounded to hear a black woman speak so articulately. Ira Allen again challenges her, prompted by John Noyes. Lucy calls on two Guilford legislators to affirm her statements; the council finds in her favor. Isaac Tichenor, a renowned lawyer, offers his services if she should ever need them. After her former mistress sends Lucy some poetry by Phillis Wheatley, a black writer, Lucy considers higher education for her youngest son, Abijah. She travels in 1793 to a new college in Williamstown, Massachusetts. Joseph Skinner, a politician and trustee, arranges for her to meet the trustees, one of whom is Theodore Sedgwick, who has antislavery tendencies. Petitioning for the admission of her son, she cites founder Ephraim Williams's will, which provides for the admission of students without mention of race or color. She also cites the Declaration of Independence. The Reverend Doctor Stephen West quotes scripture to prove that Lucy is overstepping the bounds. Lucy facilely quotes scripture back at him, ending, as she looks at her handsome son, "He is our brother and our flesh." West snaps back, "Do you call a nigger my brother?" The trustees reject her petition. Old Moni, ninety-five, one of Ephraim Williams's slaves, comes forward crying, "Shame!" In 1794, Lucy's husband dies. Noyes renews his efforts to seize the Prince farm in Guilford; a dispute also arises concerning the title to the Prince farm in Sunderland. When Eli Bronson takes Lucy to court, she travels to Bennington to consult with Isaac Tichenor. In the Windsor courthouse, Judge Samuel Chase presides; Stephen Row Bradley and Royall Tyler (a famous actor and playwright) represent Bronson. When Tichenor announces that Lucy will argue her own case, Bradley and Tyler vigorously object, but the judge allows it.

At the end of the trial, Tyler sums up with theatrical flair; Lucy speaks simply and directly to the jurors. After her title is validated, the judge congratulates her on "a better argument than I have ever heard from a lawyer in Vermont." (Lucy Terry Prince, a slave brought from Africa, lived from 1730 to 1821. The fifth stanza of the Bradstreet poem that inspires Lucy begins, "I am obnoxious to each carping tongue/Who says my hand a needle better fits." Phillis Wheatley, 1753-1784, was the first African-American woman to be published in America.)

Bobbi Katz

In ***Snow Bunny*** (1976), Debbie Moss, eleven, her parents, and her brother, Danny, seven, move to Vermont during Christmas vacation after their father takes a job at a lumber mill in Warner in southern Vermont. Debbie's new school uses the ski slopes at Round Tree for its winter gym; as a beginner, she is moved from the sixth-grade ski class and put with the first- and second-graders—the same class Danny is in. She resents being called a "snow bunny" by the instructor. She cannot seem to make friends: she hates Vermont. When Frank Duval, a friend of Debbie's father, needs someone to walk his dog because his wife has broken her leg, Debbie volunteers. Because she does not want to accept payment, Frank Duval suggests a trade: private ski lessons in return for dog walking. A former ski instructor at Glen Rush Ski Area, he starts her on short, light skis. He tells her to forget all she learned about snowplowing and to keep her legs parallel as she turns. Frank takes her halfway up the hill on the T-bar lift. "Twist-glide," says Frank. Debbie "strings the turns together like beads on a string." Soon she feels like a real skier—she belongs. They leave the bunny slope and take a chair lift to the novice trails. They ski down the hill, past "the lullaby" of Roaring Brook. The next day, Frank starts her on four-foot skis. Debbie tells her parents that skiing is the greatest feeling in the world. Now, although she misses her friends, "Vermont is home." The next day, skiing with Frank, she buys Danny a Glen Rush Ski Area patch for his jacket and, when Frank suggests inviting her brother to ski with them, she agrees. Frank gives Debbie his daughter's old skis. At school, Valerie Rose, the best skier at school, offers to ski with Debbie: Val checks her speed; Debbie increases hers. They are friends.

Carolyn Keene

In ***Close Encounters*** (2006), Nancy Drew and her two best girlfriends, Bess Marvin and Bess's cousin, George Fayne, travel to Vermont to visit George's mother's friend, Winnie Arnold, who runs a gourmet café in Brody's Junction near Burlington. Winnie has arranged for the girls to stay at Sarah Conway's Under Mountain Inn. Tourists have flocked to town to witness an invasion of aliens; representatives of the media—and the FBI—are also present. The evening of their arrival a sighting occurs: revolving spheres of light descend on a meadow not far away. Nancy and her friends are immediately skeptical, though they concede the perpetrators are very clever. They meet Nathan Blackman, a science fiction writer; Ethan Brody, the mayor; Captain Rupert Greene, a state trooper; and Isabel Sanchez, a producer at *REELTV*, who wants her crew to record the girls' reactions to the UFOs. Nancy agrees to the arrangement as the only way to gain access to the meadow, now proclaimed a police scene. Winnie confides that she believes someone is deliberately sabotaging her restaurant. It would be natural to suspect Ellie Dorian, currently the owner of the Antique Attic, who is Winnie's estranged partner in the restaurant business. On their way to the meadow, the girls stop at Aldwin Nichols's farm for maple syrup. He claims aliens have abducted his dog; shortly thereafter, he, too, disappears. The evidence at the scene is convincing—a charred area of flattened grass and a scattering of small metal shards. When Bess disappears, Nancy interrogates Nathan, who lives on the Nichols property. He demonstrates that the alleged UFOs are, in fact, remote-control model planes, altered to look like spaceships. Arranging to meet him later, Nancy hurries to the inn to bring George up to date—but George has vanished. Nancy finds information in George's computer to persuade her that Isabel is part of the hoax to swell her program's ratings. Nancy sees Under Hill, a rental property advertised at Ellie's store but, before she can go there, someone hits her over the head. She wakes up in a cold, damp room with fellow prisoners Bess and George, whose head is bleeding. Prying open the door of their prison, they find Nathan looking for them. Nancy asks him to take the girls to the hospital and to alert Captain Greene. After Nancy frees Aldwin and his dog, who are locked in the shed, she enters the house, where she finds sufficient evidence to explain the deception and overhears Isabel, her cameraman, Frankie Lee, and Mayor Brody talking. (The mayor is an accomplice to the plot in order to expand tourism.) Bess, meanwhile, has sneaked up behind them with her camcorder. Nancy accuses the three of the crime and elicits a confession. The girls become heroes in Brody's Junction; Ellie and Winnie are business partners once more. In retrospect, Nancy prefers ordinary human crime to the paranormal.

Garret Keizer

The young people in ***God of Beer*** (2002), who live in Salmon Falls, which is off Interstate 91 in Ira County in northeastern Vermont, have little to keep them occupied during the bleak winters. Kyle Nelson, an eighteen-year-old "townie" whose divorced parents work in the local plastics mill, has two best friends—Christopher ("Quaker") Oats, a brilliant student with a full scholarship to Swarthmore College in the fall, and Dinah LaValley, a towering, beautiful basketball star. Kyle, who has always treated Dinah like a sister, is barely aware that he loves her. The social studies teacher presents a thematic unit on "protest movements of the twentieth century." The teacher quotes Gandhi as saying that if God came to India he would need to come as bread and asks Kyle in what guise God would come to Willoughby High. "Beer," says Kyle, without considering his answer. Quaker follows up on the idea. "If beer is our culture," he says to Kyle, "we can change that." Quaker (whose hippie parents are Quakers), Kyle, and Dinah decide on a Beer Rebellion as their protest movement and outline for their teacher the proposal: using civil disobedience, their objectives are to lower the drinking age, raise the drinker's awareness, and destroy the nondrinker's stigma. They take a name and an acronym—Students Undermining a Drunk Society (SUDS). They research alcohol-related issues, receive favorable publicity from other schools, pick up and redeem bottles along the highway, and stage a "live disobedience" party at which some guests are given sodas, in unmarked cans, and a very few receive beer. (Quaker, who does not drink, agrees to drink a beer if he draws one in the lottery.) They decide not to tell their parents and not to call the police until the protest party is underway. After the party, Dinah drives her friend Condor home because he is drunk. In a grotesque automobile accident, Dinah is killed and Condor, badly injured. David Logan, Kyle's woodsman friend, is older than he but still trying to graduate from high school. Distraught by Dinah 's death, David destroys much of the inventory in the local liquor store. David is arrested and, as he tells Kyle, is smart enough to know that his lawyer will try to prove he was too dumb to know any better. At the trial, Quaker enters the courtroom, identifies himself, and, as a statement in David's defense, breaks two bottles of beer on the floor in front of the judge. Quaker and David carry out their community service working at the liquor store; the owner hires David permanently. Most of his friends attend college; Kyle signs on at Northeast Plastics, the mill where his parents work. He knows who he is—"he drinks with the preps and hunts with the chucks"—and he loves Ira County.

Clarence Budington Kelland

Mark Tidd (1913) is the first in a series of three novels (the others are *Mark Tidd in Business* and *Mark Tidd's Citadel*) about Mark Tidd, sixteen, an overweight stutterer and brilliant problem-solver who often draws his schemes from the many books he reads; a favorite is *Tom Sawyer*. Mark's father, Jeffrey, is a patient, kind inventor who is happiest reading Edward Gibbon's *The History of the Decline and Fall of the Roman Empire*; in fact, Mark's full name is Marcus Aurelius

Fortunatus Tidd. Libby Tidd is a wonderful cook and loving caretaker for her husband, who is working on a turbine engine and is fearful someone will steal his idea before he patents it. Mark forms a secret society with his friends, James Briggs ("Tallow") Martin, James ("Plunk") Smalley, and Binney Jenks. They find a cave on an island to serve as a secret meeting place, hide emergency items there, and devise various passwords and signals. Uncle Ike Bond, the bus driver, warns Mark that a stranger is asking questions about an inventor working on a turbine engine. When the boys hurry home, they find a man talking to the unsuspecting Jeffrey; Mark removes the drawings of the turbine before his father can take the man into his shop. The boys elect Uncle Ike a member of their club. When they return to their island cave, they find Sammy, half-Indian, half-French, a huge childlike man who has recently escaped from the poor farm. They vote to make Sammy their ward and lug food to him all winter. At Whiteley's power plant, Jeffrey tests his engine with steam: it works beautifully—one hundred and two horsepower—and is reversible. The boys overhear the stranger, Henry C. Batten from Pittsburgh, consulting with the engineer, Bill Willis. Jeffrey heads to Detroit to apply for a patent; in his absence, someone steals the turbine. The boys, out in Binney's father's horse and rig, recognize the two conspirators at a house. Peeking through a window, they see the turbine, much too heavy for them to lift. Mark and Tallow take Tallow's boat to fetch Sammy and return to the Willis landing. Their strategy is to divert the men with strange noises while Sammy hauls the turbine into the boat. Just then, Zadock Biggs, a tin peddler, drives up and advises them to return to Wicksville to seek adult help. Sammy manages to drag the turbine into the boat, and they head for the island, where they camp out despite the prospect of poison ivy and rattlesnakes. The next day, Willis and Batten discover them on the island. Holding the men off with their slingshots, they send Zadock with Mark's knife to Uncle Ike to signal their distress. The villains find the cave, but the engine is gone, and so is Mark. Uncle Ike, Zadock, and the authorities arrive to arrest the men. Mark emerges from hiding with the engine: he had fashioned wooden sled runners to move the cumbersome item. Meanwhile, in Wicksville, Hamilton Carver, an attorney for the International Engineering Company in Pittsburgh, is trying to persuade Jeffrey to sign over the rights to the engine for five hundred dollars. Mark and the others return in time to explain everything. Mark's parents are very proud of him. Zadock tells them not to do anything about the patent until they hear from him. His schoolmate, millionaire William Abbott, underwrites the Tidd Turbine and makes Jeffrey a rich man; he pays for college for the four boys and protects Sammy from the poor farm.

In ***Mark Tidd in Business*** (1915), Plunk's father, who runs Smalley's Bazar (sic) in Wicksville, is badly hurt in an automobile accident and has to travel to Detroit for medical treatment, accompanied by his wife. Aunt Millie takes care of Plunk, but, with no one to run the store, the Smalleys will soon be bankrupt. Mark proposes that he, Plunk, Tallow, and Binney take charge. The two biggest challenges are that the store is too crowded to find anything, and that Jehoshaphat P. Skip is opening a local branch of the Gigantic Five-and-Ten-Cent Store across the street. Mark holds a grand auction at Smalley's to help clear out the inventory; he plants their old friend, Uncle Ike Bond, in the audience to raise the bidding. The affair proceeds admirably until Skip demands to see Mark's auction permit; the sheriff closes down the auction. Mark's next scheme is a voting contest: with each dime purchase a customer can vote for the handsomest man in Wicksville. The idea catches fire; people buy votes for the contest and rid the store of clutter accumulated for years. Then Skip announces that he owns a chattel mortgage (using movable personal property rather than real estate as security) on Smalley's; the note for five hundred dollars is due in six weeks. Skip continues to try to put Smalley's out of business by informing the wholesale houses in Detroit that the store is bankrupt. Taking a train to Detroit, Mark persuades the wholesalers to provide a new line of credit. Then Mark consults Lawyer Sturgis, who finds that Skip does not have a lease but rents his store by the month from Smalley. Sturgis, acting as Smalley's agent, orders Skip to buy his lease for two hundred dollars or leave the premises. Meanwhile, trade falls off because Wicksville cannot generate enough customers to accommodate two similar stores. The boys' old friend Zadock Biggs has an idea for an "opportunity." In Sunfield, a village twenty-five miles away, the proprietor of the five-and-ten-cent store is heading West and wants to sell his stock. Mark figures out he can take an option on the stock. As part of the plan, Zadock tells Skip about the sale. Mark outwits Skip by optioning the stock for nine hundred dollars and inveigling Skip to buy it back for twelve. Now that Mark has enough money to pay off Smalley's mortgage, he advertises a "foreclosure" for a certain date and time. There, he exposes to the customers the dirty tricks that Skip played to put Smalley out of business. As for the beauty contest, Jupiter Peabody, a mule, wins. The Smalleys return home to congratulate Mark for his persistence and devotion.

In ***Mark Tidd's Citadel*** (1916), the four friends meet at an old summer hotel on Lake Ravona (Lake Raponda) to spend a fishing holiday. The hotel is closed, but Jim Ames, the owner, agrees to rent the premises in exchange for fish and throws in some bedding, dishes, and cooking equipment. The boys find a Japanese boy, Motu, sleeping in the hotel with his dog. When Japanese men come looking for Motu, the boys pledge to help him without asking for explanation. Motu says only that he is expecting "The One Who Will Come." Mark sets a trap for one of the men with bait cans and a string; when the man clatters down the stairs, Tallow laughs silently, like Natty Bumppo in *The Leatherstocking Tales*. While Mark is formulating a scheme to protect Motu, Tallow spends his time absorbed in David Balfour's adventures in *Kidnapped*. Mark creates a citadel "for defensive purposes" on the small island across a bridge from the hotel. Motu risks his safety by saving Binney from drowning and dragging him across Mark's drawbridge. Mark has stocked the citadel with three days' supplies. They still do not know Motu's identity, but they are committed to protecting him. When the Japanese men approach in a boat, the boys fend them off with slingshots and pike poles. Scanning a newspaper, they read that the Japanese minister to the United States has taken a summer cottage in Fullerton, just twenty-five miles away. Mark writes a letter informing him of Motu's whereabouts; Tallow swims to land to hand the missive to a passerby. The siege continues. The boys are running out of drinking water when a large automobile pulls up, discharging a Japanese gentleman in a frock coat who, glimpsing Motu, falls on his knees before him. Motu is a prince, the nephew of the emperor of Japan. Motu extols the bravery of his four American friends, who helped him not because they knew his identity but because it was their duty. The purpose of Motu's enemies was to provoke President Wilson into war with Japan; Motu came to America to make peace between that country and his own. The villains are banished from Japan. The boys return to Wicksville where, in time, they receive four Samurai swords from Motu, a letter of thanks from the emperor, and a communication from President Wilson celebrating their "true, wise, and brave" actions.

Shirley W. Kelley

Little Settlers of Vermont (1963) follows the Davis family, the first settlers of Montpelier, from their home in Massachusetts to the wild and unsettled northern part of Vermont. The Davis children consist of two older boys away at school, Thomas, fourteen, and Jacob, seventeen; Rebecca, sixteen; Hannah, twelve; Polly, eight; and baby Lucy, four. Before they begin their journey on May 24, 1786, their father, Colonel Jacob Davis, describes the struggle for territory between the New Hampshire Grants and the Yorkers, the war and the role of Ethan Allen and the Green Mountain Boys, and the founding of Vermont. They pack their possessions, including feather beds, on a large sled drawn by oxen and driven by the hired man; the girls climb into the horse-drawn sleigh with their parents. They move slowly, stopping at night with friends, and arrive at Fort Dummer, where they meet a tall, straight, slender woman with snow-white hair—Jemima Sartwell (Howe), the "fair captive." She tells her story of being captured by Indians with her children and sold for ransom in Canada. As the Davises pass through Brattleboro and Westminster, their father shows them the grave of William French, who died in the Westminster Massacre fighting for the settlers' rights to their land. They pass through Rockingham, Bellows Falls, and Weathersfield, stopping at inns. On the way to the Stevens Inn in Hartland, they view Windsor where, their father says, leaders came from all over the state to adopt their own constitution and form an independent Republic. Their father explains that Vermont does not belong to the Union, but it has its own Governor Chittenden. From then on, they will see no more inns. When the snow starts, they find shelter with the Handees. Mrs. Handee recounts the story of the Royalton Raid, the burning and pillaging by Indians, and her successful attempt to rescue about fourteen little boys, including her own Michael, captured by Indians. In Royalton, the Davis family boards with the Parkhursts; Mr. Parkhurst praises Seth Warner's heroic actions at the Battles of Hubbardton and Bennington. They move on to Brookfield. The family stays there while Jacob, with the hired man and Cousin Parley Davis, head to Montpelier, leading a horse loaded with cooking utensils, food, and implements, to start surveying and planting, almost exactly a year after they started—May 3, 1787. The whole family moves to the new cabin, thirty-two feet long and sixteen feet wide, with wooden floors, a chimney, and a cellar for vegetables. The epilogue states that in the spring of 1791, Colonel Davis is chosen to represent Montpelier in the state legislature. Many town meetings are held in Parley Davis's house in Montpelier. All the girls marry. Polly and her husband head for Ohio. (Historical accounts give 1781 as the date Colonel Jacob Davis founded Montpelier. For a detailed account of Jemima Sartwell's captivity, see Marguerite Allis's adult novel, *Not Without Peril*.)

K

Louise Andrews Kent

In ***He Went with Champlain*** (1959), French explorer Samuel de Champlain invites Thomas ("Tom") Godfrey Lee, a twelve-year-old orphan whose mother was a cousin of Champlain's, to sail to Canada with him in 1604 on his quest for a northwest passage to the Pacific. Tom, a servant to Champlain, then an adopted son, and finally his friend, lives for much of the next twenty-five years with Indians and learns their languages in northern Quebec and the Great Lakes region. Tom is with Champlain when, passing Trois Rivières, the St. Lawrence River broadens into a beautiful lake. Champlain marks it on his chart as "Lake of the Iroquois," although Tom thinks he should call it "Lake Champlain." They sail past a rounded cape the Indians call "Ticonderoga." At one point, Tom saves the lives of a young Indian woman, Moon Rises, and her son, Small Arrow, who escape to the Green Mountains, which they call "Vermont." Tom respects Champlain for his courage, courtesy, and sense of justice. Tom, spending a great deal of time with the Hurons, admires many of their qualities but witnesses terrible cruelties. Captured by Onienta, Tom is on the brink of dreadful torture when Onienta's mother, Moon Rises, saves him and takes him, feverish and hallucinatory, to her longhouse. When he recovers, Indians carry him by canoe down Lake Champlain, passing *Le Lion Couchant* (Camel's Hump) to the east, to the St. Lawrence River, and back to Canada. He is at his master's bedside when Champlain dies; no one knows what happened to Thomas Godfrey Lee.

M.E. Kerr

The chapters in ***The Son of Someone Famous*** (1974) alternate between sixteen-year-old Brenda Belle Blossom's notes for a novel and sixteen-year-old Adam Blessing's journal. Adam's father is a celebrity, always on the go, addressing the United Nations, meeting with high government officials, or traveling abroad. Adam does not use his father's surname but that of his grandfather, Charlie Blessing, with whom he is staying in Storm in Burlington County. The Choate School recently expelled him; Adam has no other home. He quotes Frost in his journal: "Home is the place where, when you have to go there, they have to take you in." Charlie, calm, kind, and poised to deal with a crisis, is a former veterinarian; a younger doctor, Ted Cutler, has taken over his practice. As a result, Charlie drinks. Dr. Cutler's daughter, Christine, is one of the most popular girls at the high school. Brenda Belle, who lives with her mother and her Aunt Faith, becomes an ally of Adam's at school because they consider themselves "nonentities." They invent a campaign called "Nothing Power," sending flattering notes to people who never receive any attention. Billie Kay Case, Adam's ex-stepmother and a former well-known actress, invites herself to Storm for Christmas. At a New Year's Eve party, the guests actually realize that Billie Kay is a celebrity. Adam admires Christine and, when he hears that she has broken up with Ty Hardin, calls to wish her a happy New Year. When Adam's father summons him to California for his wedding to Electra Lindgren, Adam misses the Valentine's Day costume dance; he planned to go as the Shropshire Lad, from his favorite A. E. Housman poem. Adam becomes depressed and his grades decline. Brenda Belle uncovers a secret tragedy: Dr. Cutler was driving the car that killed Adam's mother, Annabell. When Adam goes out with Christine, they pretend to her father that she is seeing another boy. After Adam's father postpones his marriage, Electra arrives in Storm and tries to kill herself. Adam takes her to the hospital and begs Brenda Belle to go in his place to the masked ball as Sir Walter Raleigh. Malicious people spread the rumor that Electra spent the night with Adam; the school expels him. Meanwhile, Charlie Blossom and Billie Kay Case start a business together. Adam's father invites him to travel with him during the summer. Adam now accepts two truths: his father is an extraordinary man and advantages flow from being the son of someone famous. His father's stature is part of who Adam is "but not the biggest part." As for Brenda, still not one of the elite, she is seeing Milton Merensky, who is teaching her birdcalls. She learns that one can never tell about people, "even when you think you know everything there is to know about them." (One of the most famous stanzas of "The Shropshire Lad" is, "Loveliest of trees, the cherry now/Is hung with bloom along the bough,/And stands about the woodland ride/Wearing white for Eastertide.")

Liza Ketchum

Fire in the Heart (1989) is the middle novel in a trilogy: the first, *West Against the Wind*, describes Abigail Parker's trip to California by wagon train in 1850 and is referred to but not included in this collection; the third is *Twelve Days in August*. In *Fire in the Heart*, Molly O'Connor, fourteen, lives on Rock River Road in Griswold with her father, an architect, her stepmother, Blair, a photographer, and her brother Todd, sixteen. No one speaks of her mother, Ashley, who died in an automobile accident ten years earlier. What are they hiding? After she reads a letter to her father, which was lying open on the front seat of his car, Molly embarks on a quest to decipher the family secret. The letter is from Ramon Roderiguez, a student intern in Nevada City, California, asking for instructions about the disposition of some letters of Ashley's he has found. Molly's best friend, Kai Stewart, a glamorous summer person, arrives from Boston. Molly sees Kai flirting with Todd and talking self-absorbedly about her summer theater work. Molly resents the fact that Kai thinks Vermont is not good enough for her. Molly has a summer job mowing lawns. Her father takes an assignment in New Hampshire for the summer; his absence gives Molly a chance to check his files. First, she writes to Ramon; then she visits her grandmother, now eighty and vague, to look in her photo albums. Someone has removed the pictures of Ashley. An old daguerreotype holds in its case a slip of paper saying, "Receiving my deed, near the Yuba River, California, 1853." Her grandmother suggests Molly call upon her eccentric Cousin Sadie Hall, who now has the photographs from the album. Cousin Sadie gives the images to Molly, along with an envelope full of newspaper clippings. She observes that Molly is like her mother, "stubborn and proud and brave," and that it is time she acted on her own. A 1978 issue of *The Daily Gazette* in California reports the death of Paul Leone and Ashley O'Connor, whose automobile plunged into a ravine. Molly is filled with anger and anguish. She receives a letter from Ramon: the name of her ancestor who received the deed was Abigail Parker. A letter from Abigail to her sister describes burying a gold nugget. Molly telephones Ramon with this news and falls in love with his voice. When Molly tells Todd, Blair, and her father what she knows, Blair offers to accompany her to California, where Ramon puts them up at his mother's. Molly gets in touch with *The Daily Gazette* reporter, who assures her that Paul Leone, who died in the accident, was a surveyor, "an old coot, a confirmed bachelor," and not her mother's lover. Molly and Ramon, who feel as though they have known each other all their lives, stop at the accident site and build a cairn. Following Abigail's detailed instructions, they dig and find a metal box containing a copy of Abigail's diary about her trip across the country and a bag of gold. Ramon and Molly exchange delicious kisses. On the journey, Molly discovers how much she loves her stepmother, Blair; Molly's solving the mystery brings the family together.

In ***Twelve Days in August*** (1993), the third in the trilogy, Todd, sixteen, is at the heart of the drama. During the times Kai is in Vermont, she is Todd's girlfriend. A junior trying out for varsity soccer, Todd hopes to play in the front line as one of the wings with Randy Tovitch, a senior and the varsity team's lead scorer, as striker. Todd's friend, Craig Duffey, is the only African-American trying out. Twelve days remain until the first game. Two new students show up at the field—Rita Beekman and her twin brother, Alex. When Randy, a bully and marijuana smoker, sees what a gifted soccer player Alex is, he fears for his position and starts making homophobic remarks about Alex. Randy stops passing to Alex and threatens Todd that, if he does not support him, Randy will tell people Todd is also gay, provoking Todd into a fight with Randy. Uncle Gordon arrives for a visit, and, as usual, Todd feels some constraint on the part of his parents toward his uncle. Uncle Gordon lends Todd his BMW to take Kai on a date. When Randy challenges Todd again on the highway, Todd loses his head, recklessly chases Randy in the BMW, and ends up driving into a field and terrifying Kai. Todd tells Uncle Gordon about the event. Randy intimidates most of the backfield into calling Alex a "fag." Craig is disgusted with this hate campaign and disappointed that Todd remains neutral and does not defend Alex. At practice, Randy harasses Alex and refuses to pass to him. Rita feels let down that Todd is too cowardly to stand up for her brother. When she heads for Randy's house, he follows her. From a hiding place, they watch Randy's father abusing a horse. Randy comes home and exhibits another side of his character as he cleans and soothes the horse. Todd is torn and distraught over what to do. Uncle Gordon telephones, giving Todd a chance to talk over his problems. Uncle Gordon reveals to Todd that he is gay—his business partner is his lover. Now Todd understands his father's hostile behavior. "Do the right thing," counsels Uncle Gordon. In the game, Todd has a chance to pass to Alex but hesitates; the next time, he passes to Alex, and they score. Uncle Gordon is at the game: afterward, Todd throws himself into his uncle's arms.

The point of view in ***Where the Great Hawk Flies*** (2005) alternates between Daniel Tucker, thirteen, and Hiram Coombs, eleven. They are both survivors of the Royalton Raid of 1780, when redcoats and Indians burned Royalton, Randolph, and Tunbridge, and killed or captured inhabitants along the White River. Daniel's Pequot mother, a respected doctor, hid him in a cave; the Indians terrorized Hiram, who witnessed his uncle's capture and suffers psychotic episodes in which he hears the noises of the raid in his head. In 1782, Daniel is still in Griswold near the White River with his mother, Lila Kate; English father, Caleb; and precocious sister, Rhoda, seven. Hiram's family moved from Connecticut back to Griswold to build and run a store. Hiram comes upon Daniel fishing for trout and calls him a "dirty Injun." Later he steals Daniel's trout and lies to his mother about it. His mother, who is pregnant, is even more prejudiced than her son: she would not dream of using an Indian as a midwife. Daniel's Indian grandfather, a medicine man, is visiting the family. Hiram's Uncle Abner, unhinged by his experience, escapes from Canada and his Indian captors. Daniel's grandfather begins to build his wigwam with Rhoda's help. Daniel receives some birthday presents from his family—a wampum belt, a pouch, and a knife. Hiram steals the pouch to prove to his Uncle Abner that Indians are living next door. Someone tears down Daniel's grandfather's wigwam; the neighbors "warn" Abner out of town. Daniel learns from their grandfather about his belief in a creator; Rhoda inherits their grandfather's skills. The cooper, Mr. Sykes, who is part Abenaki ("although we are all American now"), offers Daniel an apprenticeship; Daniel finds barrel-making appealing as a trade. Hiram's mother goes into labor and is tended by Mrs. Durkee; when the delivery takes too long, Hiram's father sends for Lila Kate. Their grandfather understands about the "demon" that lives in Hiram's head—the noises of the hoof beats in the valley and the women crying for help. When Lila Kate leaves for the Coombs's house, their grandfather sings, dances, and drums. The mother and twin babies survive. Daniel finds his grandfather lying exhausted in the field, choosing to die outside to prevent the family from burning his wigwam as custom requires. Before he dies, he tells Daniel, "whatever happens, always follow the path." Daniel's mother shows her grief by cutting off her hair and covering her face with soot. Daniel goes to Mr. Sykes to make the coffin. He and Rhoda are friends with Hiram now. The noises disappear from Hiram's head. They bury their grandfather wrapped in his wolf skin, with corn kernels for food on the journey, his deerskin shoulder bag, and his war club. The Coombs's girl twin is named Lila Kate after the doctor. In 1844, the two men, Daniel and Hiram, still remain in Griswold, tending the graves. (The story is based on the lives of Margery and Joseph Griswold, the author's great-great-great-great-great-grandparents.)

Natalie Kinsey-Warnock

When Ariel, ten, in ***Canada Geese Quilt*** (1989) hears that her parents are expecting a baby, she goes outside to be by herself for a while. She is not sure whether she is jealous or confused; her grandmother appreciates her feelings. A maker of wonderful quilts, her grandmother suggests they make one together for the baby and asks her to design the new quilt. Ariel draws three Canada geese flying over "a stand of cattails and an apple tree just in bloom. The shape of Miles Hill rose behind the tree." As time goes on, Ariel plants the garden for her mother and works on the wagon while her father tosses up the hay. When her grandmother collapses with a stroke, she is so pale and still that Ariel hardly recognizes her. At first Ariel cannot bring herself to enter her grandmother's room. Then she visits her, taking along the quilt. Before the stroke, her grandmother had appliquéd the design, added a cloth border, and started the quilting. Now it is up to Ariel to finish it, chatting with her grandmother as she does so. The family credits Ariel with bringing her grandmother back to life. Standing outside, Ariel looks at the geese flying south, understanding the wisdom her grandmother has imparted to her. She accepts the fact that her grandmother will not always be with them. When Ariel's baby brother is born, her grandmother wraps him in a quilt showing the night sky, which she made for Ariel before starting the baby's new quilt.

In ***The Night the Bells Rang*** (1991), Mason, eleven, lives on a farm in northern Vermont near the Black River in 1918. He is suffering through a terrible winter: not only is it fiercely cold, but Aden Cutler, a burly teenager at school, is terrorizing Mason. He hates going to school but does not dare tell his parents, Sterling and Geneva. Instead, he angrily takes out his frustrations on his little brother, Ira, five. His father guesses why Mason has lost his mittens and explains that Aden's father, George, was a drunkard who beat his children and his animals. Sterling invites Mason to come to the barn to watch the birth of Chelsea's foal, Jubal. Aden's bullying worsens. Miss MacKnight, the schoolteacher, tells the children about 1816, the Year of No Summer, when people left Vermont in droves. The cold increases the arduousness of the chores. Mason continues to treat his brother badly. When Sterling's birthday approaches, Mason draws him a picture but drops it by mistake over the bridge railing onto the ice. Aden appears and, to Mason's surprise, crawls out over the dangerous, cracking ice to retrieve the picture. Afterward, Aden stops bullying Mason. When sugaring starts, Mason and his father are in the woods every day for three weeks; his mother is expert at boiling and evaporating the sap. Mason returns to school to learn that Aden has enlisted in the army. Mason feels sad that he never thanked Aden for saving his picture; he is confused as to how he feels about himself. Spring comes, the trees leaf out, and Mason and his mother plant the garden, do the chores, and engage in other activities like berrying, swimming in the pond, and fishing on the upper stretches of the Black River. His father takes Mason to collect apples: some will be stored in hemlock sawdust in the cellar; others will be made into cider. Mason wants to stop the earth "from spinning so fast into winter." His father looks sad: is he thinking about the dying of the fall leaves or the soldiers? They make thirty gallons of cider, "sweet and tart at the same time." Word comes that Aden was killed in the Argonne Forest. Mason is heartbroken, wishing he had thanked Aden properly, and resolves to be a better brother. The family prepares for winter. When the war is finally over, everyone brings bells to the church. Mason finds Mrs. Cutler in the crowd and tells her he is very sorry Aden is dead. Tomorrow, he will go over and split her wood. When Mason's turn comes to pull the church bell, he rings it for Aden.

As Long as There Are Mountains (1997) is the story of Iris Huldah Anderson, thirteen, whose great-great-grandfather came over from Scotland and developed the farm in Gilead (now Brighton) in northern Vermont. She lives with her father, Hazen; mother, Edith; brother, Lucien, twenty, a college student who wants to be a writer; and little brother, Ferris. Life at the farm is hard, and money is scarce. (The neighbors tell a familiar joke. A farmer wins a million dollars. What will he do with it? "I guess I'll just keep farming until it is all gone.") Iris feeds twenty-six cows in the mornings and worries at school that she smells of the barn. Edith urges Iris to start acting like a young lady and dress up to go to the wedding of her cousin, Aletta. Iris hates her imperious Aunt Lurline but likes her Uncle Sturgis, who gave up farming to work in the furniture factory. Iris profoundly misses her grandfather, who was killed a year earlier when a tractor rolled over on him. The tension between her father and her brother stems from Lucien's dislike of farming; all she wants to do is to work on the farm. "In the fall, the grasses and trees almost pulsed with color, and the raspy sawing locusts filled our ears." One night the barn catches fire. In agonized shock, Iris and her mother watch as Hazen and Lucien try to rescue the animals. Almost overcome by smoke and flames, they manage to save the horse and a few of the cows; Lucien has to shoot through the barn windows to kill the rest of the cows before the fire reaches them. Iris's twin baby calves perish. Iris finds her cousin Draper's knife in the orchard but tells no one. Traumatized by the effects of the fire, Iris returns to school and is unfriendly to a new student, Alice Mitchell, who is obviously poor and sits alone at lunchtime. Draper confesses to Iris that he was in the barn with two friends whose smoking caused the fire. Hazen, determined to start over, cuts down trees for a new barn; Lucien helps by limbing the branches. Hazen returns to the site alone, where a tree he is cutting kicks backward and pins him to the ground. After Lucien and Iris free and maneuver him home, Edith drives him twenty-five miles to the hospital in Hardwick. While he is in the hospital, where doctors amputate his leg, Uncle Sturgis organizes the neighbors. First, a dozen trucks arrive with enough timber to erect a frame by nightfall. A caravan of cars follows with women bringing pots, pans, and covered dishes. Iris has never seen a barn raising. Uncle Sturgis shows her how to drill and chisel out a mortise hole for a row of beams. At haying time, Edith drives the tractor, while Lucien and Iris load the wagon. Hazen comes home with an artificial limb (Ferris, who has read *Treasure Island* with Iris, wonders if it is a wooden leg). Angry and demoralized, Hazen decides to sell the farm, move to White River Junction, and work in the furniture factory. Iris hopes Lucien will manage the farm, but he needs another kind of life. Lucien says she will not miss the farm, but he is wrong: "As long as I live and even after, as long as there are mountains, and rivers, and stars in the sky, I'll miss this farm with all my heart." They hold an auction; buyers remove the equipment and animals. Meanwhile, Iris learns that Alice Mitchell and her family of nine live in a house made of bales of hay. She plans a house raising for the Mitchells, using the lumber her father cut for the barn. When neighbors arrive at the site, the Mitchells have fled. Edith explains to Iris that some people cannot bear to accept charity. Draper runs away and, when found, confesses his tragic secret. Iris says goodbye to the farm. At the last minute, Uncle Sturgis announces that he is leaving the furniture factory to buy back the cows and equipment sold at auction to run the farm with Hazen.

Shelby, the heroine of ***Sweet Memories Still*** (1997), lives with her parents on a farm in northern Vermont. She is so shy that she does not participate at school for fear she will look foolish. She loves to draw, but when her father brings home an announcement for an art contest, sponsored by Cabot Creamery, she does not have the self-confidence to enter. Just a day before her birthday, her mother is summoned to East Craftsbury to care for Shelby's grandmother. Shelby is sulky and ungracious when asked to accompany her mother. Her grandmother has a new cat, Rutherford, who simply showed up one day. To make up for missing her party, her grandmother gives Shelby a camera—an old, boxy one that belonged to her mother. Shelby feels even more angry and resentful. When her grandmother displays her photograph album, Shelby expects to be bored, but the stories her grandmother relates about the black-and-white images interest her. Her grandmother tells about meeting her future husband: she was at a party reading *Wuthering Heights* when he asked her to dance. Her grandmother feels well enough to take them to church, where she sings a solo. Expatiating on the sermon's text about hiding one's light under a bushel (from the Gospel According to St. Matthew), her grandmother advises Shelby to overcome her shyness and enter the contest. Shelby reacts petulantly, retorting that it is easy for her grandmother to say, when she is so brave and strong. Her grandmother confides that, when young, she was always afraid and let other people make decisions for her; in fact, they persuaded her not to go to college. The family returns from church to find that her grandmother's house has burned to the ground—her furniture, her quilts, her irreplaceable photographs, and Rutherford, all gone. Her grandmother moves to their farm. From memory, Shelby draws her grandmother's photographs and puts them in an album. The final one depicts her grandmother in cap and gown, holding a diploma. The church congregation builds her grandmother a new house; Rutherford is safe. Shelby's mother wants grandmother to stay with them, but she cannot. She will stop by her new house only briefly before going on to college. For the contest, Shelby creates a scene showing her grandfather loading milk cans onto the back of his 1942 truck to take to the creamery. She is indifferent about winning. She fixes a picnic for her grandmother and herself to eat that night on the hill behind the barn, while they talk about life and plan their futures.

In the Language of Loons (1998) depicts Arlis Rowell, twelve, who comes to the Northeast Kingdom in 1969 to stay on his grandparents' farm by Lake Willoughby, where his father grew up. "The old barn came into view, weathered to the color of twilight." Arlis's lawyer father, Carl, is too busy to take care of Arlis now that his mother, Abbie, is experiencing a difficult pregnancy. At school, Jackson Chase torments Arlis, who lacks self-confidence. Arlis's grandfather, Simon, gave up farming: thirty years earlier, twenty farms were in the area; now there are five. On a fishing trip with Arlis, Simon mentions his brother, Walter, who died young, but he does not pursue the subject. When they glimpse a loon on the water, Simon tells Arlis about their habits, as well as about stars, birds, and the woods. Simon sends Arlis back to their fishing site to untangle some snagged line; Arlis disappears for the appropriate amount of time and lazily pretends he has done so. Next time, they find a dead loon entangled in the line. Arlis confesses his culpability; Simon, in turn, tells Arlis about his brother's drowning death and Simon's feelings of guilt. Simon proposes that Arlis start training for long-distance running; Simon was on the track team at his high school. On Wheeler Mountain, Arlis hurts his leg and gives up, knowing his grandfather will be disappointed in him. That night, his grandmother calls him to the television to watch the Americans land on the moon. Arlis realizes he has not been making an effort. He trains by himself in the early mornings. Simon, pleased, teaches him to drive. The birds migrate; the loons are the last ones to leave. His father collects him in time for school, where Arlis goes out for track; his nemesis, Jackson, is on the team. When Arlis beats him, Jackson, furious, redoubles his training. At a meet, Arlis is disappointed to come in seventh. He remembers Simon's advice: "Run for yourself. Enjoy it." When he finally wins a race, his father does not even care: he hates his father. They drive to his grandparents' farm, but, by the time they arrive, Simon is dead. Jackson calls Arlis to say he is sorry. When his father is away singing in a church pageant, Arlis's mother starts to bleed. All the ambulances are busy; Arlis calmly and confidently drives her to the hospital, where her baby is born safely. (For an adult story about a boy and a loon, see Mark Helprin's "A Vermont Tale.")

Lily May Randall, twelve, is a year younger than her sister, Emily, in ***If Wishes Were Horses*** (2000), set on a farm in Barton in the middle of the Depression in 1932. In addition to the two girls, the Randall family is made up of Wesley, their father; Edna, their mother; and their grandmother. It is clear to Lily that everyone in the family prefers Emily; she finds Emily spoiled and hateful. One of Lily's main complaints is that her father will not let her near his horses and will not buy her one. She broods over this injustice while rereading *Black Beauty*. When Great-aunt Nell, grandmother's sister, visits from India, where she is a missionary, Lily plans to court Aunt Nell to make her love Lily more than Emily. When Emily goes to the station with their father to meet Aunt Nell, Lily's heart is poisoned with jealousy and hate. Plunged into self-pity and vengeance, she discovers when she meets Aunt Nell that she is wonderful. When their horse goes lame, Aunt Nell harnesses and drives home Duncan Babcock's bull. She buys a poor old horse that Babcock is sending to the slaughter yard. She borrows Babcock's automobile to drive Lily to the circus in Lyndonville, where they watch a girl rider on a diving horse. At the quarry one day, Lily pushes Emily into the water; the next day Emily has come down with poliomyelitis; Lily is certain she is responsible. Dr. Horace Pembroke says Emily's only hope is the Drinker apparatus (later known as the iron lung), which requires electricity. Wesley, impoverished, his cows killed by lightning, his farm mortgaged, has the iron lung installed. With Emily encased in it, the device helps her breathe; its presence, its hissing sound, takes over the house. Aunt Nell gives her money to the Randalls; she cannot buy Babcock's horse for Lily. "Everything will have to be about Emily," she explains. "Everything's always been about Emily," responds Lily, feeling mean and selfish. She decides to steal the horse and keep him at the old quarry. Going at night to Babcock's house, she overhears men's voices: they are loading whiskey into his car. At home, Lily entertains Emily by reading aloud some of their favorite books—*Little Women* (she skips the part about Beth's death), *My Antonia*, *The Wind in the Willows*. When Babcock discovers the horse (Lily's father calls him "Worthless") is missing, Aunt Nell argues for Lily's keeping him and threatens Babcock that she will tell the sheriff about his bootlegging. Worthless makes Lily forget her family's sadness and hopelessness from time to time, but she knows Emily is wasting away. At the quarry with Worthless, Lily dives from the diving rock into the water to try to contract polio as a punishment. Worthless follows her. They dive together five times; she renames him "Pegasus." After overhearing her father say he has sold his beloved horse and may lose the farm, Lily writes to the circus owner, knowing his response will break her heart. Ben Jarvis from the Drummond and Gary Circus buys Pegasus for five hundred dollars, which Lily turns over to her father for Emily. As Lily continues to read to Emily—*A Passage to India*, *A Tale of Two Cities*, *Jane Eyre*—the two girls grow close and talk comfortably to each other. Lily feels she could never be so brave in the iron lung as Emily. One night Emily asks Lily to help her die: Lily, appalled, tearfully refuses but confides her guilt and fears to Aunt Nell, who disabuses her of any connection between the quarry water and Emily's illness. Emily dies that night; Lily will never know whether Aunt Nell played a role in her death. Grief-stricken, Lily realizes that her wish—to grow up and move as far away from Emily as possible—has come true. Like her great-grandfather, who talked about "ghost pains" in the leg he lost at Gettysburg, Lily will feel ghost pains for Emily and Pegasus for the rest of her life.

A Doctor Like Papa (2002), set in the Northeast Kingdom in 1918, explores the lives of the McKenzie family: Reece, the father; Edith, the mother; Margaret, eleven; her brother, Colin; and Edith's brother, Uncle Owen, whom Edith raised when their parents died. They all love Uncle Owen and worry when he goes to war in France. Margaret wants to be a doctor like her father, even though her mother does not approve. For Decoration Day, asked by her teacher to pick an historical character to describe, Margaret chooses Elizabeth Blackwell, the first woman doctor of medicine in the modern era. In her speech, she acknowledges her mother's influence on her life, saying she wants to be brave and strong like her. Her mother allows her to go on rounds with her father. She helps him set bones and deliver babies (all the female infants in the area are named "Edith" after her mother). As payment, her father receives chickens, potatoes, bread, and maple syrup. Word comes that Uncle Owen is missing in action; then they hear that he is alive, has lost an arm, and is coming home. Almost unrecognizable, he sits, silent and sad. The influenza epidemic spreads through northern Vermont. Many die. On his rounds, when Reece sees a chimney with no smoke, he knows the inhabitants are dead and passes on to the next farm. Terrified of infecting the children, Reece puts Margaret and Colin on the horse, Bess, and sends them to Aunt Clarissa on Dexter Mountain. Hot and thirsty, they stop for a drink of water at a farm, where it looks as though everyone is dead. While they are giving water to a dying dog, Colin sees a face at the window. Margaret tries to imagine what her father would do. Leaving Colin and the dog in the barn, she enters the house to find a little girl and a very sick woman. She sets a kettle of water to boil to fill the house with steam. She wrings a chicken's neck and makes soup. She gives the woman a few sips of soup and reassures her about her daughter, Edith, before the woman dies. Margaret, Colin, Edith, and the dog (whom she names "Grace") sleep together in the barn. Her father finds and brings them home. Clyde, another orphan staying with them, befriends and brings fresh life to Uncle Owen, who helps the family start a new apple orchard. Margaret goes to medical college and returns to the Northeast Kingdom to marry, have a baby (Edith), and practice medicine.

Ruby Sawyer, ten, in ***Lumber Camp Library*** (2002) stays in a lumber camp in northern Vermont in 1922 with her large family: her mother, Mary; her father, Random; and ten brothers and sisters. Ruby admires everything about her father, who calls her "his little jewel." A lumberjack, he does hard, dangerous work better than anyone: he makes riding logs look easy. He teaches her to use an ax and a peavey (an implement consisting of a wooden shaft with a metal point and a hinged hook near the end, used to handle logs) and to drive horses. Showing her the spiked boots of a dead logger hanging in a tree, he says that, according to tradition, the gray jay is the spirit of a dead person. Her mother insists that she attend school; her father lets her ride Bess the three miles to town. When she comes home, she teaches the younger children, noticing that her father listens, too. Her mother has twin boys; Random buys her a piano for which he has been saving for ten years. When her father dies in a logjam, Ruby misses him so much she cannot breathe. They must leave the camp. Her mother sells the horses. Jim Reilly brings twenty-five dollars the lumberjacks collected for the family and cries when he says Random died saving his life. Before they leave, Ruby hangs her father's spiked boots in a tree. In town, her mother takes in laundry; Marvin works at the blacksmith's shop; Albert sweeps out the store. They are closer to the school; the older children can attend. Ruby wants to be as good a teacher as Miss Farnham. When her mother is offered a job as cook at the lumber camp, Ruby drops out of school to care for the younger children. Her mother sells the piano. Ruby, desperate for books, tries to sell raspberry pies but is unsuccessful. As she passes a big, white, beautiful house, a blind woman smells her pies and calls out to her. Ruby does not charge Aurora Graham for the pie; that evening, a box of books arrives for her: *Little Women*, *Anne of Green Gables*, *Tom Sawyer*, *The Call of the Wild*, *The Secret Garden*, *Alice's Adventures in Wonderland*. Ruby goes to Mrs. Graham's house to thank her and stays to read aloud to her from *Jane Eyre*. They invite Mrs. Graham for supper and are soon good friends. Jim Reilly stops by frequently to do chores and asks Ruby to teach him to read and write. He begins coming Sunday afternoons. The younger children adore him. He gets Marvin a job as blacksmith at the camp and buys back Bess for Ruby. Jim shows Ruby a ring he plans to give to her mother when he proposes. Ruby must stop him: no one can take her father's place. When her mother becomes ill, Ruby rides to the camp to leave Jim a note, steals the ring, and throws it over the mountainside. Mrs. Graham invites the whole family to live with her—they need a large house, and she needs them to take care of her. Jim asks Ruby if she has seen the ring. No, she lies, heartlessly telling Jim that her mother would never remarry. Jim stops coming by; Mary's health deteriorates; Ruby feels guilty and is cross with the children. After a gray jay finds the ring, Ruby confesses her perfidy to Jim; he and Mary marry. Mrs. Graham bequeaths them her house. Ruby teaches for fifty years; she builds a cottage she names "Lumber Camp Library."

K

Doris Kirkpatrick

Honey in the Rock (1979) begins in the depths of the Depression in 1936. Sixteen-year-old Linny Storrs, an orphan, lives with her grandparents, Newt and Kit Storrs, in Sadawga Springs on the old homestead where her grandmother's ancestors, Nathan and Abigail Chase, came up from Connecticut, pulling their possessions on a hand sled and siding with Ethan Allen against the Yorkers. As her grandmother says: "Us Chases may not have set the world on fire, but we always stood up straight and took what come." At the bottom of Chase Hill is the house of Uncle Truman, his son, Jared, and daughter-in-law, Mart. Aunt Gloria and Uncle Ned are in Boston. Linny's best friend at high school is Jan Brokowski, who suffers discrimination as a "Polack." The Power Company wants to buy all the land on the Deerfield River: Jan decides to work for the company; Linny thinks the town should resist bringing power to the area. At the town meeting, the townsfolk learn about "eminent domain," the right of the government to take away their property for cash settlements. The women in the audience fantasize about electric lights and washing and milking machines. Aunt Gloria wants Linny to come to Boston to prepare for a good college and meet some "nice" people, "instead of those Polacks and farmhands." Linny could never leave her grandparents and Sadawga Springs—it is home. Workers for the dam pour into town, throwing up shacks along the river. A log-cabin tavern springs up. "Well," says one old timer, "What of it? Vermont was cleared on Jamaica rum." The company imports blacks from the Kimberly mines in South Africa to help build the dam. Men are injured; a doctor and his wife establish a small hospital. A chain store operating on a cash basis buys Mr. Butterfield's store, which has been in his family for four generations; Linny's grandfather can no longer trade his eggs and butter for salt, flour, and kerosene. The company moves the coffins in the old cemetery to make way for construction. Uncle Truman sells out, and Jared and Mart move to Jacksonville. Linny and her grandparents face hard times; Uncle Ned wants them to come to Boston. Taxes are due; Jan helps Jared cut trees to sell as timber. When Jan says power will attract more summer people, Linny says: "Sure, summer people who run around to auctions, buying up antiques, and who let their orchards go to seed." Her grandfather snorts, "Summer folks!" Jared exclaims, "What they done to that house! They opened up the fireplaces and paneled the front room with knotted pine and they've put in a bathroom with a chemical toilet." A hurricane sweeps through New England, leaving eight hundred people dead in its wake. Every able-bodied person sets to work: the men fill sandbags; the women cook and help out in the hospital. Everyone in the community, including Power Company people and summer people, pulls together; the dam does not overflow. After her grandfather breaks his leg and her grandmother has a slight stroke, it is time for them to leave the farm and join their children in Boston. Linny enrolls in nursing school; she will come back to Sadawga Springs to marry Jan. (The title is from a song based on Psalm 81:16: "He should have fed them also with the finest of the wheat: and with honey out of the rock should I have satisfied thee.")

Sheila Solomon Klass

Next Stop: Nowhere (1995) describes Beth Converse, fourteen, whose mother remarries, travels to Europe on her honeymoon, and sends Beth to stay with her father, Pete, in Allenville. This village, decides Beth, a humorous, sarcastic, and sophisticated New Yorker, is "deadsville." She is angry with her father for leaving his teaching position to take up pottery, furious with her mother for being shallow, selfish—and pregnant, and painfully homesick for her first real boyfriend, Josef, a Russian immigrant, sixteen, an outsider, reader, and loner, just like Beth. Beth tells her father that she hates this town, where his family has lived for generations. He assumes she will attend the Ethan Allen High School and lays out rules for an indefinite stay: she cannot believe this is her fate. As her mother used to say, her father "was solid Vermont granite, and nothing could budge him." She yearns for Josef and the sweet kisses they exchanged. On a desultory walk, Beth visits the cemetery where the Converse plot lies. There she meets Harold Peabody, who was her grandfather's closest friend. Suddenly, Josef arrives in town. He has one day to say goodbye before he and his mother emigrate to Israel. Beth and Josef clean up Pete's pottery store and sell some of his work. Initially annoyed and then grateful, Pete treats her and Joseph to a meal at the Allenville Inn, the first time she has had dinner with a boy. When Beth and Pete put Josef on the train, daughter and father are finally friends and allies.

Norma Klein

Bizou (1983) is about Eliane (her nickname, Bizou, means "little kiss" in French), whose mother, Tranquility, an African-American model, married a white French photographer who was killed in Vietnam. Eliane, who attends a bilingual school in Paris, has never been to America and knows nothing about her mother's family. On the plane to New York, Eliane chats with a young man across the aisle while her mother sleeps. He is Nicholas Berend, who was visiting France before entering medical school. Once in New York, he offers to show Tranquility and Eliane the city. Several men on the street make racist remarks; the next day, Tranquility disappears, leaving a note saying she needs some time to herself. Nick, at a loss to know how to help this vulnerable teenager, takes her to Vermont to consult with his former girlfriend, Tara, who attends his medical school. Together, they sympathetically question Eliane about the names of any Americans Tranquility may have mentioned. Eliane recalls that a friend from Paris, Peter Haynes, is stationed with his State Department father in Washington, D.C. With little time left before returning to school, Nick drives Eliane to the Haynes residence. The rest of the narrative follows Eliane's search for her mother's family. In Pittsburgh, she meets four people: a woman who raised an illegitimate child of Tranquility's; the child himself, her half-brother, Duff; her grandfather, Neal Roberts; and, eventually, her remorseful mother. Eliane, her horizon significantly broader, returns to Paris with her mother.

Nancy H. Kleinbaum

Welton Academy in ***Dead Poets Society*** (1989) is an exclusive boys' preparatory school "nestled in the remote hills of Vermont." One hundred years old and three hundred boys strong, the school encourages "tradition, discipline, honor, and excellence." John Keating, a Welton alumnus, is the new junior class English teacher. A Rhodes scholar and former star athlete, he is unconventional and challenging. He urges the boys to "seize the day," to shun conformity, to stand on their desks to look at the world from a different angle, to write original poetry, and to notice that "the powerful play [of life] goes on, and you may contribute a verse." They learn from an old yearbook that he was once a member of a club called the "Dead Poets Society," in which he met illicitly with his friends in an old cave to read poetry aloud and, like Thoreau, "suck the marrow out of life." Antipathies between fathers and students are immediately apparent: Todd, for example, feels that his father loves only his older brother, a superior Welton graduate; Neil's father plans a career for him that Neil fears and abhors. The drama teacher chooses Neil, to his joy, to play Puck in *A Midsummer's Night Dream*, a joint performance by Welton and its sister school, Henley Hall. Mr. Keating exhorts his students to find out "what is unique or different" about themselves. When Neil's father forbids him to act in the play, Mr. Keating pleads with Neil to tell his father what his real aspirations are. Instead, Neil disobeys his father and performs brilliantly. His furious father withdraws him from the school, pledging to send him to military and then medical school. The distraught sixteen-year-old, donning his Puck crown of flowers, responds to his obdurate father by killing himself. The headmaster, Dean Nolan, forces the boys to sign a statement confirming Mr. Keating's responsibility in the affair and discharges him. When Mr. Keating comes to the classroom to collect his personal belongings, Nolan is in charge. One by one, the boys, heartbroken and ashamed, climb upon their desks to pay final tribute to their beloved teacher whom they have sacrificed.

Gordon Korman

Chasing the Falconers (2005), the first of a six-novel series, *On the Run*, starts after John and Louise Falconer, writer and scientist, are sentenced to a life term in a Florida federal prison for passing classified information to an enemy state. Their children, Aiden, fifteen, and Meg, eleven, are put in Sunnyvale Farm, a juvenile detention center in Nebraska. When Aiden inadvertently overturns a lantern in the barn, the facility burns down, and the Falconers escape. Meg is quick-witted and precocious; Aiden is cautious and strategic. Agent Frank Lindenauer of the CIA recruited John and Louise into government service but disappeared after the trial: he holds the key to clearing them. Aiden remembers that in the pretty, white summer cottage his family rented in Colchester nine years earlier, a picture of "Uncle Frank" is stowed with some of his childhood treasures. Meanwhile, FBI Agent Emmanuel Harris learns of the fire at Sunnyvale Farm and the escape of a number of prisoners, including the Falconers. Aiden and Meg walk for a long way, steal some mountain bikes, and make it to the train station. They run into Miguel Reyes, a tough youth detained in Sunnyvale Farm for manslaughter, who helps them into a freight car heading east. At one stop, police surround the train and trap them. Aiden recalls the way his father's serial detective hero, Mac Mulvey, escapes from a locked freezer—through an emergency hatch in the ceiling. They run frantically to an abandoned house spotted by Miguel, where they change their appearances with hair cuts and dye. Miguel steals a car, but after many miles they run out of gas and have no money. Aiden thinks of another Mac Mulvey trick—siphoning gas from another vehicle. Agent Harris is still on their trail. The three young people finally reach New Jersey, where Miguel's family rejects him, so he continues on with the Falconers to Colchester. Police trace them to their motel, but they climb out the bathroom window and slide down a rain-slick cliff onto the shore of Lake Champlain. Alerted by the Vermont police, Agent Harris flies to Ethan Allen Air Base in upstate New York and heads by ferry to Colchester. The three youngsters find the unlocked summer cottage—and the photograph of Frank with their parents. Suddenly, an assassin materializes who shoots Miguel in the shoulder. Aiden and Meg escape, after calling an ambulance for Miguel. Agent Harris, who arrives too late, begins to wonder if the wrong people are in prison. Aiden notices that in the photograph of Frank and their parents, the mounted life preserver says, "Red Jacket Beach Motor Lodge, Malletts Bay, Vermont." Mallets Bay is near Colchester. They are not running away from justice: they are running toward it.

The sequel, ***The Fugitive Factor*** (2005), continues the story at the Red Jacket Beach Motor Lodge in Malletts Bay, where Aiden and Meg seek Uncle Frank's nine-year-old guest registration. When the clerk refuses their request, Meg creates a diversion with the fire alarm while Aiden searches the computer. Uncle Frank is not listed, but his friend, Jane McIntosh, is, as well as her address in Boston. As the fire engines arrive, Aiden and Meg escape in an all-terrain vehicle. Driving east cross-country to avoid roadblocks, they run out of gas. A truck driver takes them to the medical center in St. Johnsbury. Meanwhile in Colchester, Agent Harris, increasingly convinced of the Falconers' innocence, consults with the Colchester police department. Eager to find the children before they are injured, he does not know about the man, whom they call Hairless Joe, who tried to kill them in Colchester. Aiden and Meg escape from St. Johnsbury in the back of an ambulance and take a bus to Boston. They find Jane, who betrays them, but they manage to elude the police, find Frank's motor vehicle records, and locate an address for him in Venice Beach, California. As they head out West, Harris wonders who is trying to kill the youngsters. If it is not the FBI or Juvenile Corrections or the police, who can it be? (The third title in the series is *Now You See Them, Now You Don't*.)

L

West Lathrop

Black River Captive (1946), set in 1757 during the French and Indian Wars, recounts the dramatic experiences of Jethro, fourteen, who, after the death of his adopted grandfather, leaves New Hampshire in search of his father. After his mother's capture by Indians and death ten years earlier, his only souvenir is a knife he made from her family sword. He heads south on a raft with his dog, Tray, stopping at Truesdale's forthouse, where he meets a member of Rogers's Rangers. Despite warnings that Indians are taking and selling young men in Canada, Jethro sets out. Susup, an Indian, captures him and his dog and seizes his precious knife; Pi'el, a runner sent to help Susup, joins them. By canoe, they head south on the Connecticut River and west on the Black River. Jethro is overwhelmed by the despair of captives who come to believe they will never escape. Jethro, witnessing a mortal battle between Pi'el and Flatnose, whose cruelty among settlers is renowned, leaps into the struggle to save Pi'el's life. Jethro and Tray then escape and are recaptured. Exhausted from paddling and marching, Jethro is brought to a village where he is greeted with such hatred that he realizes Pi'el has told no one that Jethro saved his life. Susup houses him in the lodge of a hideous old woman, Mali, with Tray tethered outside. When Tray trots into Mali's lodge, Jethro knows someone in the village has untied him. Another white captive—a girl with golden hair—is in the camp but remembers no English. In the woods, fetching water for

Mali, Jethro meets Ranger Captain Enos Marrett, whom the settlers believed was killed at St. Francis. Jethro manages to retrieve his knife while fixing Mali's roof. The next night, Marrett gives him supplies and sends him and Tray to Fort Number Four to alert the Rangers to an Indian attack nine days hence; Marrett does not escape himself because, as a captive, he can provide intelligence to the settlers. Jethro knows someone is tracking him and hides in a hollow tree stump; his pursuer is Pi'el, who grants his freedom because of the debt between them. Finally Susup catches up with Jethro, who bests the Indian in a fight and leaves him tied up with food and water within reach. When Jethro reaches Fort Number Four, the Rangers welcome him and ask his name. He replies that he hopes someone there has the answer. Captain Allen looks with amazement at the engraving on Jethro's knife: he is Jethro's long-lost father.

Lois Lenski

Abby Peck, twelve, in ***Deer Valley Girl*** (1968) adores all animals, including a stray dog, Hobo, even though she senses in her heart he may be a deer killer. Abby's father, Amos, works in his brother's sawmill in northern Deer Valley. In addition to Abby and her mother, Serena, the family consists of Greg, fourteen; Ken, ten; Susan, nine; and Bunny, the youngest. Their independent grandmother, Sara, resides close at hand. The farm belonged to Amos's great-grandfather, Abner. For generations, the Peck family has feuded with the Otis family over ownership of the northern border of the Peck property. The children from both families carry on the hostility. The Otis children feed the deer, coaxing them into the village to excite the dogs. At a town meeting, Cal Otis proposes a road over Cedar Mountain; Amos opposes the idea, but it passes. Amos tells Serena he suspects Cal of intending to steal the Peck timber. When Hobo escapes from the barn and kills a deer, someone shoots him. Abby, heartbroken, wants to know who did it. One day Myrtie Otis comes to Serena for advice, the first time an Otis has been in a Peck house (although neither woman is by blood an Otis or a Peck). Myrtie believes Amos cut off their water supply and wonders whether the two women can solve the problem themselves. Unfortunately, Sara perpetuates the feud by telling the children never to speak to an Otis. The village celebrates the annual Old Home Day with floats, games, contests, and contra dancing. Myrtie and Serena, now friends, learn that a rusty pipe caused the water problem. Out in the woods, Abby finds that someone has changed the boundary line. Seeing a great white buck with dogs chasing it, she throws stones at them. The sound of a car motor betrays some deer jackers on the new road over Cedar Mountain. Shouting at them, she runs to alert the game warden, but he cannot catch them. Deer hunting season starts; Abby hates the fact that all Vermont boys hunt. Each day Amos and Greg come back empty-handed. At Thanksgiving, Serena invites all the neighbors, including the Otises, for dinner. Cal and Amos hire a lawyer, who determines from the records that the boundaries are wrong: each family owns half of the wood lot. Ironically, Serena raised the money to pay the lawyer by going out to take care of an old woman—the Otis children's grandmother. The former enemies shake hands. Abby's father acknowledges that it was he who shot Abby's dog, Hobo.

Janet Lind

Raymo is six in ***The Bird at Bear Mountain*** (1988) when his father moves to a new job on Rudy Kane's farm with his mother; his brother, Charlie; and a baby sister, Rose Emily. Raymo spies a white bird and chases it to the neighboring farm of old Lester Flood, who takes Raymo out to his barn. There they spot the bird again. Raymo enters first grade. The teacher asks the children to describe their summers: one went to Canada; another to the Atlantic Ocean. When Raymo tells about seeing the bird, everyone laughs and makes fun of him in the yard. That afternoon, Lester sees the bird again. The next day, Raymo tells his parents he is too sick to go to school. Lester teaches him to use a camera. They wait for the bird to appear. When Raymo sees the bird, he clicks the button, and Lester has the film developed. Raymo brings the photograph to school, where the teacher tacks it on the blackboard. On Saturday, two of the boys from his class bicycle up to the farm to see his bird. When the days turn cool, the bird flies toward Bear Mountain. Raymo often visits Lester at milking time; they sit and talk about their white bird.

Anne Lindbergh

In ***Osprey Island*** (1974), Margaret lives in France with her children, Amy and Charles, nine and eleven; Margaret's sister, Caroline, stays in Vermont with her daughter, Lizzie, also nine. The cousins can only see each other during the summers, when "the Vermont air smells of meadows." Lizzie loves maple trees: "the buds made a warm pink glow and you knew that soon there would be leaves. Then came the leaves: soft, pale green ones that opened out like floppy parasols by summertime." One summer, before Amy and Charles are leaving Vermont, they read aloud three words on the back of a picture—CARMAR-OGALI-RETNE. Instantly, the three children and Lizzie's dog, Molly, are transported to a lovely island. Charles, who is interested in birds, calls it "Osprey Island" after the nesting ospreys—big, dark on top, white underneath, with heads like eagles. When the children pronounce the words in reverse, they return with no elapsed time to Vermont. They pledge that each Sunday, at an assigned time, they will meet at Osprey Island. The next Sunday they arrive, bringing food and other supplies. Problems arise at home when Lizzie's mother wonders what happened to the cherry pie in her freezer, and Amy wakes up with poison ivy in Paris in the middle of winter. The following Sunday, it is drizzling in Vermont and gray in Paris but hot and sunny on their island. Lizzie has trouble remembering the mantra for leaving and arrives home so late that her parents fear she has drowned in the lake. When Charles contracts measles, Amy travels alone the following Sunday to meet Lizzie. They encounter some visitors who are suspicious because the girls have no boat. They speak the magic words and, because they are holding hands, both arrive in Paris. By now, the parents know the children are up to something. The next Sunday, the children decide to spend a night on the island; it rains hard, and they are miserable. Back in Vermont, Lizzie comes down with Charles's measles. On the next visit, Lizzie takes her mother to the island by mistake. The ospreys' three eggs hatch into little fluff balls. They all return to Paris and reveal their secret lives to their parents. Margaret and Caroline recall that when they were little they were taken to this same island in Maine. The syllables of the magic words written on the back of the picture are anagrams of their names. The parents prohibit any more magic trips but promise that next summer they will visit Aunt Sophronia in Maine and take a boat to Osprey Island.

Because twelve-year-old Owen Noonan's parents in ***Travel Far, Pay No Fare*** (1992) are divorced (his father left home years earlier), he feels responsible for his mother, Nan-Ellen, who is a writer. They spend summers in the Northeast Kingdom because his deceased Aunt Lyle's husband, Uncle Jack, lives there with his daughter, Parsley, nine. When Owen's mother announces that she and Uncle Jack plan to marry, Owen is outraged: he does not want to leave his school, nor have a new father and sister, nor move permanently to Vermont, where there is not even decent television reception. Parsley feels the same way about the impending marriage; in fact, she has filled the house with stray cats, hoping to drive away her fiercely allergic stepmother-to-be. Owen also discovers that Parsley, an avid reader, is physically able to enter the books she reads with the aid of a magic bookmark she received during the Vermont Summer Reading Marathon (she brought home all the cats in the books she read). Owen's first inkling of her prowess comes when he is swimming, and Parsley is sitting on a rock, reading. In the blink of an eye, she is gone. He starts reading her book and, suddenly, he is at the Mad Tea Party. The Mad Hatter is there, of course, and Alice—and Parsley. They carry on a wild conversation filled with riddles. The bookmark constitutes an escape hatch, so the traveler can return home at a predetermined place in the story. Subsequently,

Parsley takes him into *Little Women*, where Parsley adopts the canary, Pip, before he starves, and into *The Yearling*, where they contrive to save Flag, the deer, before the Baxters shoot him. The magic bookmark works for magazine articles as well, enabling the two to enter a scene in Iceland just before the volcano Krakatoa overflows. Meanwhile, Nan-Ellen and Jack begin to argue over their parenting differences. Owen and Parsley are guiltily pleased that they have brought conflict into the family, but, by the time the wedding takes place, they are close friends through their many adventures together and are reconciled to the new configuration of the family. Owen has some book reports due for his new school, but, since he has been a character in many of the books, he will have no trouble writing about them.

Frederick Lipp

That Cat Is Not For Sale (1998) is set in a general store where Henry has lived for twelve years, sleeping on the counter in an old-fashioned shopping basket. All the customers love Henry and count on seeing him each day. The store has every item they can possibly want or need, but Henry is not for sale: he is a fixture. At night, he sleeps soundly in the cellar after a long day of stretching, purring, and being scratched under his chin; in the morning, the old cat is ready for another day. (The inspiration for the story is Henry, the cat in F.H. Gillingham & Sons' general store in Woodstock, Vermont.)

Bill Littlefield

Almost every summer, the family in ***The Circus in the Woods*** (2001) spends two weeks at a lodge in northern Vermont. This particular summer, Molly is thirteen; her sister, Kip, is ten. "We always came in August. It was always beautiful." If they pick blueberries on the hill behind the lodge, a card in the menu that night will read, "Blueberries picked by Molly and Kip." In Vermont one is always allowed to eat whatever one wants. Molly's family is close. Her father loves to recite poems by W. B. Yeats. Snow, a large, welcoming woman, conducts a day camp in her playhouse. The children plan scavenger hunts and make puppets; Snow reads to them from *Stuart Little*. As Molly grows older, she helps Snow with the activities. One day, bored with camp, Molly wanders off into the woods and, lured by some distinctive calliope music, comes upon a dancer in a pink tutu. The only person with whom she wants to share this experience is Snow. One night she hears the music again and follows it through the woods. This time the dancer, Toni, speaks to her and escorts her to the circus, which is not set up under one big top but twists through the woods. They reach a tent with aerial artists swinging from the ceiling. Male acrobats form a pyramid; one, Jimmy the Monkey, speaks to them. A fortuneteller, Nell, tending a pot on a fire in front of a wooden trailer, makes Molly visualize and smell fire at the lodge—not literal fire, but a message that "what you count on can be gone in minutes." Walking back to the lodge, Molly notices that "the stars always seemed closer and brighter in Vermont." When Molly has an opportunity to tell Snow about the circus in the woods, she already knows about it. Now that Molly is growing up, Snow says, she may forget she ever went to the circus; Molly is certain she will not. Molly, Snow says, is at the point where she wants "adventures and surprises in the dark" as well as the safety of her parents' protection. Stung by a bee, her father has an allergic reaction so violent that for weeks he is in a coma in the hospital. His family moves into the Lodge. Molly walks past the blueberry bushes where Toni is waiting for her. Bruno is the ringmaster; an arcade sparkles. The circus people exist simultaneously in their fantasy lives and their real lives. Toni is actually the sister of the dishwasher at the Lodge and can neither walk nor talk. At the Lodge, Molly finds a copy of *Huckleberry Finn* to reread. When she visits her comatose father in the little hospital, which looks as though it were "designed to fit into the postcard images of Vermont," the nurse caring for her father is Nell from the circus. Sitting by her father's bed, Molly reads to him from Mark Twain and from his favorite Yeats poem. When she comes to the last line of the poem, her father awakes and quotes it. The family does not return to the Lodge, but, after a year of college and a failed summer job, Molly visits Snow's playhouse to talk to her and Nell about the passage of time. (The first two lines of the W.B. Yeats poem, "The Song of the Wandering Aengus," are, "I went to the hazel wood,/Because a fire was in my head..." The last two lines are, "The silver apples of the moon,/The golden apples of the sun." The author wrote to me that the lodge is based on Highland Lodge in Greensboro, where he, his wife, and his daughters have spent time. His novel is for sale at the front desk, "where it sits on a shelf beside some of Wallace Stegner's books.")

Norris Lloyd

William S. ("Billy") Adams, Jr., ten, is in New York City in ***Billy Hunts the Unicorn*** (1964) with his pregnant French mother and his American father, who is a United Nations officer currently working on the problem of impending civil war in the Congo. Having spent four summers as a child at camp in Vermont, Billy's father accepts with alacrity the offer of a friend's farm in Prospect for the summer. Billy does not want to leave his friends in New York. When his father learns that he must lead an emergency mission to the Congo, he asks his brother, Charley, a medical student in Boston, to join the family in his stead. Before he leaves, his father reminds Billy of a game—hunting the unicorn—they played when he was little and suggests that Vermont might be a good place to play it. Billy is bored in Prospect. On the farm next door, the Brown family has only girls; Bee, the oldest, is his age. All the children go to the swimming hole on the West Branch of the White River. Billy, showing off his Australian crawl, is embarrassed when Bee, in her flailing, unconventional style, beats him. Bee wants Billy to teach her French, although she does not have much free time because the Browns are busy weeding and canning. Billy's mother offers to tutor Bee, whose name in French, she says, would be Mademoiselle Béatrice Brun. Billy spends more and more time helping at the Brown farm and grows to like Bee very much. All the children rake the windrows into big piles for Mr. Brown to toss into the hay wagon. Bee and Billy bring home a wounded crow, which they call in French, "Oiseau"; Uncle Charley sets the bird's wing and prepares a bed for it. When Bee breaks her arm jumping from the haymow door, Charley takes her to the Randolph medical center. Billy's father is delayed again in the Congo and suggests Charley drive the family back to New York. Billy does not want to leave and "cannot bear that his father was going to miss [being in] Vermont." Charley carves Billy a "snickersnee" (the word means "knife," but Charley says it is a cane), which Billy takes into the hayfield to look for apples on the old tree. In the tree is Ralph, a summer boy whom Billy has seen in the village. His father finally obtains leave to come; Billy knows of no way to express to his father how much he loves Vermont. His father asks if he caught any unicorns. "No," Billy says, "but I caught a bird, a bee, and a boy."

Elizabeth Low

Even at fifteen, Suzanne ("Zan") Hopewell in ***High Harvest*** (1948) has a strong sense of self: she is responsible, fair, energetic, intelligent, and loving. What Zan loves best is the settlement of mountain farms where she and her nine-year-old brother, Rob, live with their grandmother and their uncle, Mat Holden, the village blacksmith, veterinarian, and plumber. Zan's oldest friend, Will, Lawyer Leatherby's son, has been down-country at college. Mr. Thatcher owns two neglected, scraggly horses, which Mat buys at auction; at last the Holdens have their own team. A shadow is hanging over the valley: the United States Government has sent several agents to offer each farmer four thousand dollars for his property. The government wants to rid the ninety thousand-acre valley of its "old homestead feeling" and set up prefabricated houses. Zan overhears Agent Andrews wooing the support of Mr. Haskins, a wealthy resident, by telling him that the water system is inadequate and the farmers' way of cutting their corn, out of the "dark ages." Zan, a problem-solver, does not subscribe to the "what can't be cured must be endured" approach. At a square dance, she notices the "slow grace," the "smooth gliding," and the cooperation of the dancers. Why not persuade the farmers to cooperate by sharing equipment and manpower? Everyone but Olin Crosby, who wants to sell to the government, participates in Zan's plan and, working together, fills five silos around the countryside. Mr. Haskins, watching, is impressed. Zan visits the town hermit, Zeddio, taking him freshly baked bread and pies. Mr. Thatcher has warned Zeddio to remove the sheep he keeps in the pasture or he will sell them. Because Zeddio is sick, Zan, knowing the acoustics on the mountain, encourages Zeddio to call them. They come at the sound of his voice. The next day he is dead, but Susan does not mourn because, according to Zeddio, death is "going back into the stream of life." Zeddio bequeaths Zan his one hundred acres and his shack, on which fifty dollars in taxes are due. Zan plans to tap his sugar maples and persuades Mat to sign a three-year contract with a company for the equipment. Zan, Mat, and her brave little brother struggle for weeks but they fail: the sap boils down to nothing. Next Zan sends a soil sample to the Department of Agriculture, which recommends potatoes. Rob works like a man in the fields with them; when Rob falls ill, Will helps. He quits his job at the sawmill because Thatcher is cutting down the trees before selling his property to the government. They have never worked so hard in their lives: the plants are beautiful; the rain is plentiful; but, after all their labors, the downcountry market is swamped with potatoes. Discouraged, they store the potatoes in the cellar for spring sale. Sadly, they agree they will have to sell the horses, Beauty and Big Ben. For the first time in her life, Zan feels "trapped and beaten." She has found and read her grandfather's diary and understands his struggle. Without the horses, they will not be able to work the land. At the county fair, she meets Mr. Renfrew, a kindly horse trainer, who wants to rent the horses, will pay ten dollars a month for them, and offers to paint the wagon. When she sees Will, he looks at her with an expression she has not seen on anyone else's face—"a man's look, gentle and considering." Another winter passes; Zan is seventeen and in her last term at school. Her grandmother gives her *The Story of an African Farm*. At town meeting, the residents discuss the government proposal. During a rainstorm, Zan sees five-year-old Sophy Thatcher on a covered bridge and leaps onto the structure just as it rips from its mooring; the surging water carries them downstream. The first person to notice Zan waving her red sweater is Lawyer Leatherby. He alerts several people, including Will, who attaches a long rope to his boat and rows out to rescue Zan and Sophy. The men assembled on the bank pull them to safety. The flood causes much damage. After Olin's farm is under water, and his neighbors herd his drowning animals to safety, he changes his mind about selling. Thatcher, too, after his daughter's brush with death, becomes a different person. The Holdens' fortunes change. Mr. Haskins pays to install a brand new water system for the village; the price of potatoes rises; Mr. Renfrew brings the horses back—along with a bay Morgan foal that Beauty has adopted. Zan, who feels sorry for Mr. Andrews because his project failed, invites him to their sugaring party and speaks seriously to him about replacing his resettlement idea with a government plan to invest in drainage, fertilizer, reforestation, and electrification. Mat and her grandmother can afford to send Zan to college. She is not sure she wants to go, but Will encourages her to attend agricultural college while he is majoring in forestry. When they are through school, he wants to marry her, build a house, and raise a family here in Vermont.

Rose Lucia

Peter and Polly in Spring (1915) introduces Peter Howe, five, and his sister, Polly, eight, and their activities throughout four seasons. The children lead an idyllic life in East St. Johnsbury. Their house is white with green shutters. Their father is a shopkeeper and postmaster; their mother, a homemaker. Their grandmother lives not far away. They can walk anywhere in the village by themselves and know everyone: the blacksmith, Farmer Brown, and the Story Lady, who tells them wonderful tales. Their father and mother are never too busy to explain ideas or words to the children or help them complete difficult tasks. In spring, their father shows them how to tap the trees. They watch the sap run through the spout and drop into the pail. Their mother boils the sap in a large iron kettle for many hours to evaporate the water and thicken the sap into syrup. They see the first bluebirds and a robin redbreast. The mother bird makes a nest and lays several blue eggs. Searching for mayflowers, Polly finds hepaticas, her favorite. The apple blossoms come out. The children plant a vegetable garden. On Decoration Day, they put flowers and flags on the soldiers' graves. The children are assigned chores—bringing in the wood, washing dishes, and going for the cows. When they picnic, they are careful to pick up their papers. Polly figures out a way to go summer sliding: the hill extends to the edge of the roof at the back of the barn. They slide on the shingles, which they pretend are made of glass. They play "rich man, poor man" with daisy petals and make a daisy chain. Polly can tell whether Peter likes butter by putting a buttercup under his chin.

Peter and Polly in Summer (1912) continues the chronicle of the children's daily lives. They pretend to run a store and play with their dog, Wag-Wag. They visit the Story Lady. When she begins, "Once upon a time," they know it is not a true story. Picking wild strawberries, Polly always throws the first one over her shoulder for good luck. They watch a woodchuck, which their father says is not everyone's favorite animal because he digs tunnels in the fields. The children build a playhouse by laying out a floor plan of stones. Their father takes them and John, an older boy, to see Farmer Brown's sheep. Brown spreads salt on the ground so the children can watch the sheep eat it. He explains that the sheep are sheared once a year for their wool. He sells the fleece by the pound to the mill for weaving into cloth. John takes the children horseback riding and shows them some turtle eggs. Peter's friend, Tim, who lives on a farm, has a collie, which drives sheep, and a goat, which pulls a cart. Their father flies kites with the children. In summer, men cut the large field of grass. The raking machine makes rows of hay, which men pile with pitchforks into haycocks. A wagon carries the hay to the barn. Their cat, Blacky, has four kittens.

In ***Peter and Polly in Autumn*** (1918), Blacky catches a fish, which Mother cooks for the cat to eat. Peter goes fishing, too. He finds that when he falls asleep, the fish are more apt to bite. The children ask the blacksmith about the boiling spring because they want to cook an egg in it. He explains that the bubbling spring never gets hot. They can tell fall is coming because the goldenrod and black-eyed Susans are out. Father needs their help with apple picking so their mother can make jelly. Peter rides with the blacksmith to Large Village for a haircut. Their mother makes the children tents out of clotheshorses and blankets. They set up a lemonade stand. They put on a circus with Blacky's kittens and Tim's collie. Polly goes to the village school during the week, but on weekends she runs a school in the barn for Peter, Tim, and the cats and dogs. They go to the fairgrounds in Large Village for Fair Week. They buy balloons and ride the merry-go-round. They gather beechnuts in the woods, but the squirrels eat most of them. Their father uses rotten leaves as compost in his garden. At school, Polly learns about the geography of East St. Johnsbury and about cutting ice on the Moose River in winter. The teacher gives her students a "keepsake box" for saving any items that pertain to the geography lesson. On Halloween, Peter has his birthday party with leapfrog and hide-and-seek. After the first snowflakes come, people begin preparations for winter. The next week is Thanksgiving.

Peter and Polly in Winter (1914) begins just before Thanksgiving. The birds fly south. Peter and Polly make a stone wall into a post office and fill the holes with nuts for the squirrels. When the leaves fall, their father pays them for each full wagon of leaves and burns them. The ice begins to thicken on the river. Their father buys the children skates and shows them how to shove off, first with one foot and then the other. He lets them try to skate by themselves. They are excited when the first snow falls, and they are covered with snow on a visit to their grandmother. The Story Lady tells them that snowflakes are water fairies. The children help their grandmother prepare dinner. Polly rolls out some dough, fills it with mincemeat, and bakes it. Peter, Polly, and Tim mold a snowman. As Christmas approaches, they select a tree for their father to cut down. Sweet-smelling evergreen boughs deck the house. Their mother readies a Give-away Box, which the children fill with games, dolls, candy, and popped corn to make other children happy. The tree is beautiful. Their grandmother gives the children a pony named Brownie. When a heavy storm comes, men dig out the road, and the children build an igloo from one of the big snow piles. They drive with their father in a low sled to Large Village. He allows the children to ride on the runners, although he forbids their "catching rides" with other drivers. They stop at Farmer Brown's to find some brown eggs and feed the horses. Their father ties some bones, with meat and fat attached, on small branches for the birds; he hangs up baskets of grass seed and cracked corn as well. In his workshop, he puts together a sled for the children; their mother also shows them how to slide down the hill on a dishpan. Their father takes them out in the woods for a winter picnic, cooking their supper over a fire. The last event is a sixtieth birthday dinner for their grandmother, with the Story Lady as a guest and favors in the cake. The children go to bed and dream of spring.

Janet Lunn

The Hollow Tree (1997) shows the Loyalist side of the American Revolution in 1775. Thirteen-year-old Phoebe Olcutt's mother is dead; her father, a Dartmouth professor, takes care of her. The Robinson family—her uncle; her Aunt Rachel; her cousins, Gideon, seventeen, and Anne, fifteen—live across the Connecticut River in Orland Village. Phoebe and her cousins use a hollow tree for a letterbox. Phoebe, who has no political affiliation, is close to Gideon, who supports the British; Phoebe's father is a patriot. When her father is killed at the Battle of Bunker Hill, Phoebe moves in with the Robinsons. Two years pass. A Committee of Public Safety forms in Orland Village to drive Tory sympathizers from their homes; Phoebe is horrified by the cruelty of men to their fellows. Checking her former home in Hanover, she finds Gideon, now a British soldier but dressed in mufti. He gives Polly a letter for Polly Grantham, his sweetheart. Later that night, Gideon is caught and hanged as a spy. In the hollow tree, Gideon has left a note: "If discovered, get this message to the Mohawk Elias Brant in Hanover." All Mohawks have joined the British side at the instruction of Thayendenaga (also known as Joseph Brant). The message seeks protection for three Loyalist families. Because Phoebe is a neutral, she decides to deliver the message to General Powell at Fort Ticonderoga, fifty miles away through dense wilderness and over high mountains. She can catch trout and cook it with the aid of her knife and tinderbox. Her Tory friend, Mohawk Peter Sauk, one of her father's Dartmouth students, appears to lead her to the campsite where he has left his mother and sister. He warns Phoebe the route is dangerous and lends her some of his sister's clothes. Phoebe skirts the towns to reach Lake Champlain where she finds a canoe. Before she can appropriate it, a tall boy stops her. James ("Jem") Morrissay, a Tory, suspects she is a rebel spy. He escorts her to a band of twenty-three Loyalist refugees, including Aunt Rachel and Anne, on their way to Fort St. John in Canada. Since General Powell is now there, Phoebe joins them. Anne tells the group that Phoebe is a spy, a daughter of a patriot, and responsible for Gideon's death. The group marches northward, frightened, heartsick, cold, hungry, and unhappy. Phoebe is attracted to Jem but thinks he is interested in her flirtatious cousin. Three armed rebels stumble into their camp and make off with a cow and a blanket. Later, two British soldiers, probably deserters and also armed, steal some food. The refugees fear the Indians, who only a month earlier scalped and murdered Loyalist Jane McRae. One of the carts breaks down. A child contracts measles; soon others catch the disease. They come upon a young man in fringed deerskin on his way to Bellows Falls to visit his mother; thinking he is a spy, they tether his arms and legs. Anne proposes they hang him. Phoebe, indifferent to the young man's politics, frees him with her knife and runs off, fearing for her own safety. Jem, furious, pursues her. She speaks frankly and emotionally: she does not care who wins a war that provokes such terrible deeds on both sides. She and Jem part after he tells her he loves her. Three weeks later she reaches Fort St. John and collapses. When she awakes, she asks for General Powell. Susan Sherwood, Loyalist Justus Sherwood's wife, offers to play intermediary. Justus, once a Green Mountain Boy, has changed his way of thinking. General Powell is pleased with Phoebe's gallant service and provides her with a note of commendation to show at the next refugee camp. Jem is overjoyed to find Phoebe again and covers her face with kisses. He has joined the British army but wants her to marry him when he returns. (In 1784, after the Revolution ends, Loyalists are given land in Canada by royal decree. Phoebe stays with the Morsissays, and, after years in prison, Jem comes home.)

M

Gregory Maguire

Seven Spiders Spinning (1994), the first of a set of seven novels, introduces members of the fifth grade at the Josiah Fawcett Elementary School in Hamlet near Montpelier. The series takes place during one school year. Miss Germaine Earth is the beloved teacher, who considers her children "precious" and "unique." The boys' club is the Copycats, with Chief Sammy Grubb and members Moshe Cohn, Forest Eugene Mopp, Mike Saint Michael, Stan Tomaki, and Hector Yellow. The girls' club is the Tattletales, with Empress Thekla Mustard and acolytes Nina Bueno, Carly Garfunkel, Lois Kennedy the Third, Anna Maria Mastroangelo, Fawn Peters, and Sharday Wren. Pearl Hotchkiss, "smart, brave, and kind," does not believe in clubs. Salim Bannerjee is new to the class: his parents recently moved from Bombay to Vermont to work at a computer company across the river. On the interstate, a truck carrying a crate of seven frozen Ice Age Siberian baby tarantulas crashes: the crate breaks open, the spiders escape, and the driver is taken to intensive care in Montpelier. Pearl, who has not heard about the accident, comes upon the spiders and brings one to school in a plastic bag. The students are reading *Matilda*; another classroom favorite is *Charlotte's Web*. While seeking the first spider, the second spider is accidentally skewered on the point of Anna Maria's sharp pencil. The children, highly competitive, prepare for the Halloween Pageant of Horrors. The Tattletales settle on a skit called "The Haunting of Miss Earth," featuring ghosts of her former students who return because they cannot bear to parted from her. The Copycats plan a spider skit, using a Spider Fun Factory toy manufacturer. The third spider drops unseen onto Sharday's egg salad sandwich and is removed by the janitor's portable trash masher. The fourth spider, climbing inside a pumpkin, is smashed when someone drops it. The three remaining spiders become angry and bloodthirsty. Thekla inadvertently slams the door on the fifth spider. The truck driver regains consciousness and calls reporter Meg Snoople, who will tape her spider-story show in Hamlet. The children decide to combine their skits. The sixth spider is whacked during a dunking-for-apples contest at the Halloween party. Miss Earth is bitten throwing herself into the path of the seventh tarantula (Hubda), which is still at large. The authorities take the remains of the sixth spider to Harvard to create an antidote, for which they need a selection of local sweets. The children donate their trick-or-treat collection toward the medicine. Miss Earth recovers: the children worked together to save her life. They do not need an award: Miss Earth is their prize.

Six Haunted Hairdos (1997), second in the series, begins in November. Miss Earth lives with her mother, Sybilla Earth, who runs the Baked Goods and Auto Repair shop. At school, the children discuss ghosts: the boys believe in them; the girls do not. Thekla thinks up a way to prove how inferior the boys are. She spreads a rumor that six hairdressers on a fall tour of Vermont drowned in the old quarry pool when their minivan went out of control. The girls dress up in exaggerated wigs, call themselves Six Haunted Hairdos, and lure the boys to Hardscrabble Hill, even though Sammy warns that workers are dynamiting for the last time before winter sets in. A rainstorm adds to the effect of the girls' deception; the boys are certain the girls are ghosts. Seeing an elephant ghost, Salim fears it is Baby Tusker, whose death he believes he caused by feeding her peanuts in the Bombay Zoo. Pearl, who has joined the boys (she has a crush on Sammy) and also sees the ghosts, has read *Harriet the Spy* and plans her own investigation. She researches the story about the minivan accident at the library (the librarian is Mr. Dewey) and finds that no such accident ever occurred. The next day, Thekla, to discredit the boys, claims she saw nothing. Back on Hardscrabble Hill, they see a herd of woolly mammoth ghosts. They consult Grandma Earth, who guesses the dynamiting awakened the ghosts, which are always searching for something—perhaps a lost baby. Miss Earth confirms that "only love can heal a haunting." The children must lure Baby Tusker to Vermont. Meanwhile, Pearl has dressed the mastodons in haunted hairdos, hoping to terrify the Tattletales. Baby Tusker appears, but the mastodons do not accept her as their lost baby. The two clubs must cooperate on this project. Miss Earth and Grandma Earth arrive with a sack of chocolate doughnuts. Miss Earth tells the children that she was in love once, but her lover died, and now she is in love with her students. When the ghost of Jeremiah the Mouse menaces Baby Tusker, the herd embraces the baby elephant. Salim climbs to the top of the hill to watch the herd, linked together, disappear.

Five Alien Elves (1998), the third in the series, starts on Christmas Eve when a UFO from Fixipuddle crashes on the Fingerpies' farm. Not knowing where they have landed, the five crewmembers discern in their scan-o-matic a picture of Santa Claus and his elves. Believing he is an evil dictator, they pledge to transform themselves into elves in order to save this planet. In Miss Earth's classroom, the children have a Christmas party at which Hamlet Mayor Timothy Grass dresses as Santa Claus. While he is strolling home, clad in his costume, the alien elves capture and carry him back to their starship. Lois, walking her dog, Reebok, overhears Miss Earth and Grandma Earth discussing Mayor Grass's disappearance and calls an emergency meeting of the Tattletales. The Tattletales join forces with the Copycats to rescue Mayor Grass; Sammy hopes the kidnapper is Bigfoot, which he yearns to see. The alien elves, who have captured Reebok and programmed him to speak English, send him to find a way to liberate the Mayor's elf slaves; two of the aliens reconnoiter around the schoolyard just as Miss Earth's students arrive, her "little grape-pickers in the vineyards of truth." Reebok reports to the children that the elves believe the school is the Fortress of Fear, where Santa tortures toys. The children transform their classroom into a toy workshop and build a huge snowman to resemble Bigfoot. Sammy reads the *Wizard of Oz* while he is waiting for the alien elves to arrive. The elves struggle with and overcome the snowman; the children thank them for delivering them from Bigfoot. The aliens, returning to Fixipuddle, want to take Mayor Grass with them, but Miss Earth, reinforcing the notion that truth is the best policy, recounts the real story of Christmas. They all part as friends.

The fourth in the Hamlet Chronicle Series, ***Four Stupid Cupids*** (2000) opens as Miss Earth's class prepares for Valentine's Day. She asks Fawn, whose mother is a hairdresser, to describe the holiday to Salim. To ensure that every child receives a card, Miss Earth proposes drawing straws. Thekla and Sammy draw each other, though they are archenemies. Memories of love make Miss Earth feel faint: Rocco Tortoni, her beloved fiancé, was run over by a float at the Macy's Thanksgiving Day Parade. To celebrate the holiday, Fawn's Aunt Sophia sends from Athens a red brick amphora painted with four cupids. When Miss Earth arrives home emotionally exhausted, Grandma Earth comments that her daughter is not her usual blend of "Shirley Temple, Florence Nightingale, Mary Poppins, and Pollyanna" (see Eleanor Hodgson Porter in this collection). Grandma Earth favors a match between Miss Earth and Mayor Grass; the Tattletales also take up the cause of finding Miss Earth a gentleman friend and focus on handsome television anchorman, Chad Hunkley. Fawn brings the amphora to show-and-tell. When the vase breaks, four cupids (about the size of gerbils, but winged) emerge from the wreckage. The twins, Milos and Naxos, the baby, Kos, and the baby-sitter, Rhoda, have been in the vase for twenty-three hundred years. Each has a pair of arrows to make two people fall in love. Pearl sends an anonymous card to Sammy, who mistakenly thinks it is from Thekla, currently reading *A Midsummer's Night's Dream*. The Tattletales pin a picture of Chad Hunkley on the board behind Miss Earth's head. The first cupid takes aim, pierces Miss Earth, but misses Chad and hits the class mascot, Kermit the frog. They fall in love. The second arrow hits Miss Earth and a life-sized balloon of Cap'n Trueheart. They fall in love. The boys eliminate the balloon; the girls hold a planning session. The issue at hand: how can they succeed in their romantic plans for Miss Earth and in shipping the cupids to Greece? Fawn suggests Rhoda practice her archery with sharpened pencils; meanwhile, they glue the vase back together. Just as Rhoda shoots her arrow, Jasper Stripe, the janitor, enters the line of fire; he and Miss Earth fall in love. It remains for the baby cupid to bring together Mayor Grass and Miss Earth. Unfortunately, he hits Chad Hunkley's television image instead. Miss Earth falls in love with the television set. The cupids begin to ail. The whole class must work together. Remembering their experience with reporter Meg Snoople, they ask Mayor Grass to call her. Sammy plays cupid by giving the mayor an anonymous card, which the mayor hopes is from Miss Earth. Meg comes to town: "I am reporting live from Hamlet [where the] folks in Vermont may be simple, but they are not simple-minded."

The Spring Egg Hunt is coming up in ***Three Rotten Eggs*** (2002), and so is a lightning storm. A new student, Thaddeus ("Thud") Nero Tweed, arrives just as the storm strikes. He is older than the other children, provocative, and rude. Miss Earth explains that this year the Egg Hunt will benefit the fire engine fund. Thekla suggests that the boys compete against the girls. Miss Earth often hums the songs of famous country star Petunia Whiner. The children hope she is in love with Mayor Grass. Meanwhile, a motorcyclist crashes nearby and spills a briefcase full of eggs. Trooper Hiram Crawdad is immediately on the scene and reports to the laboratory owners about the broken eggs. A professor is dispatched to Vermont to scoop up any vestige of DNA. Lois and Salim come upon three of the scientists' eggs behind Mrs. Clumpett's store. When Lois and Salim show the fertilized eggs to Miss Earth, she locates a suitable mother hen for them. Miss Earth sends Moshe to Mr. Dewey at the town library to research the care and protection of poultry. Lois, Salim, and Thud skip school to visit the eggs. When the first one hatches, it looks like a little dragon and breathes a tiny flame. By chance, the children glimpse an article from *The Boston Globe* reporting the disappearance of genetically altered chickens with snips of DNA from rare Galápagos lizards. The other egg hatches twins. The children assign them the generic name, Flameburper, but give them personal names, too—Amos, Beatrice, and Seymour. The chicks are happily ensconced at the Hen Hotel behind the store. When Trooper Crawdad comes to Miss Earth's classroom to ask about the eggs, Thud lies, but Lois and Salim tell the truth. Meanwhile, the class realizes that its emphasis on competition in every activity is counterproductive; together they must find a way to raise money for the fire engine fund. Their amazement knows no bounds when Thud reveals that his mother is Petunia Whiner. She is hiding in Hamlet because her husband is in prison for embezzlement. She agrees to sing at a benefit; the children can use the Congregational/Unitarian Church because Forest's mother is the minister. They ask Ernie Latucci, WAAK, the Voice of Vermont, to advertise the concert. The professor is still on the track of the chicks; the mother hen fights him off. Many locals play in the concert, with the children singing in the chorus. When the professor starts to chase the cloned chicks, they escape onto the stage where Miss Earth's students carry them to safety. Seymour dies, Amos escapes into the woods, and Beatrice boards at Old Man Fingerpie's farm.

The sixth installment in the series, ***A Couple of April Fools*** (2004), begins just before April Fool's Day. Miss Earth seems distracted. The children wonder if she is engaged to Mayor Grass. With the annual Science Fair approaching, the class assignment is to consider the animal kingdom, tame and wild. The mutant chick living at Fingerpie Farm is off limits for this project. Sammy proposes that they cooperate with the girls. The Tattletales visit the last of the Flameburpers. On her way home, Thekla overhears a conversation between Miss Earth and Mayor Grass, which sounds as though they are quarreling. As an April Fool's trick, the girls persuade Sammy that a missing-link monster is abroad in Foggy Hollow. Thud appears in a gorilla suit. The girls spread the word about the monster. Miss Earth intercepts a note from Thud meant for Sammy, walks up to Foggy Hollow, and disappears. The children unite to help find Miss Earth. The next day Grandma Earth and Trooper Crawdad interrogate the children. Thekla raises suspicions about Mayor Grass. When the children visit Beatrice, she has surrounded herself with a large cocoon and emerges looking like a lizard. Troopers, volunteer fire fighters, and neighbors search for Miss Earth. Thud confesses to Grandma Earth that he wrote the note the police found. Mrs. Fingerpie reports that some animal has tried to break into the hen yard. The children release Beatrice and follow her into the woods but find nothing. Sammy has a "eureka moment" in the middle of the night and returns to the scene with a flashlight. Amos, the missing chick, has transmogrified into a crocodile. The searchers overlooked him because he was submerged in the stream. Of the two cocoons, which is Miss Earth? The children are reminded of the story, "The Lady, or the Tiger?" Miss Earth is rescued and taken to the hospital. Her students' work at the Science Fair is exemplary.

One Final Firecracker (2005), the seventh and final in the series, is a gala reunion of creatures from previous books and a celebration of four important events—graduation from grammar school, the Sinister Sisters Circus, Miss Earth's wedding, and the Fourth of July. At the last meeting of their class, Miss Earth finishes reading *The Incredible Journey*. That is the day they learn that Hubda, the seventh and remaining Siberian snow spider (*Seven Spiders Spinning*), is still at large. Beatrice the Flameburper lives at the Fingerpies' farm, while her brother, Amos, snuggles in his cocoon (*Three Rotten Eggs*). The volunteer fire squad is called out when Amos sets fire to the second cocoon, but by the time the truck arrives at the site he has hatched and vanished. A TV helicopter carrying Meg Snoople and Chad Hunkley (*Four Stupid Cupids*) lands nearby. Thud's mother, Petunia Whiner, is scheduled to sing at Miss Earth's wedding. At Fawn's house, Aunt Sophia has arrived with Rhoda, one of the cupids, which has one arrow left. Sammy is interested in odd and unique creatures (*A Couple of April Fools*), perhaps because his favorite book as a child was *Where the Wild Things Are*. He suspects Amos is looking for his sister, Beatrice. The children go to the circus, where Salim volunteers to be shot from a cannon; he returns, riding on Baby Tusker (*Six Haunted Hairdos*). The space ship carrying the Fixipuddles lands (*Five Alien Elves*). They liberate Beatrice and disguise themselves as human guests for the wedding, a gala celebration with much singing and dancing. Everyone is there, including Hubda hidden in the bride's bouquet. Sammy and Thekla take on the task of hiding Amos, metamorphosed into a full-fledged dragon, from the guests. The Tattletales and Copycats join forces at the Fourth of July parade the next day to resolve some final issues concerning the disposition of the various creatures that have gathered in Hamlet and to find out the identity of the woman in the dark glasses, who calls herself Suzy Denim. Suzy Denim ("pseudonym") is actually Stephanie Queen, revered romance novelist and the third Sinister Sister. The children bid goodbye to all their friends.

Ann M. Martin

In ***Baby-Sitters' Winter Vacation*** (1989), five eighth-graders and two sixth-graders from Connecticut's Stoneybrook Middle School travel by bus to Hooksett Crossing for Winter Carnival at Leicester Lodge. There are seven members of the Baby-Sitters' Club. Kristy Thomas is team captain for Winter Carnival and member of a large family. Claudia Kishi is a Japanese-American artist and champion skier. Stacey McGill is a diabetic whose parents are divorcing. Dawn Schafer's mother is going out with Mary Anne Spier's father. Mary Anne is interested in the history of the Vermont town where they are staying. Mallory Pike is an aspiring writer. Jessi Ramsey is an African-American ballet dancer. The hosts at Leicester Lodge sponsor five events for Winter Carnival: ice skating, a snowball fight, a snow-sculpture contest, and downhill and cross-country skiing competitions. Participation in these activities affords the girls extra school credit. The week brings tensions and spats, competitiveness and misunderstandings, but difficulties, including a heavy storm, are overcome; the winter vacation is a success.

Melissa Mather

In ***One Summer in Between*** (1967), Harriet Brown, nineteen, a Negro student at Jacob's Ladder Teachers College in South Carolina, is taking a sociology course on "Pressures of Emotional Prejudices on Environment." The class members are required to spend a summer in the North researching a new culture and keeping journal notes. Harriet finds a job helping Kate and Tom Daley on their dairy farm in East Barnstead, between Windsor and Woodstock, and caring for the youngest of the Daley brood: Maureen, eleven; Robert, nine; Richard, seven; Mary, five; Timmy, three; and baby John Anthony. Harriet, who has lived in the segregated South her whole life, realizes when Kate shakes her hand that no white person has ever touched her on purpose. Harriet wears a uniform and eats alone in the kitchen. She is surprised by the remoteness of the farm. For additional income, Tom Daley restores summer cottages for "suntanners." Harriet marvels at how hard the family works, hurrying to keep up with haying, weeding, painting, picking, and preserving. "In Vermont, work is pleasure." Harriet is proud and prickly: she feels superior to white people and wants them to leave her alone. She meets no overt racism until the hairdresser refuses to serve her; rather, she deems Vermonters "neutral," perhaps because so few Negroes live there. She joins the choir, finding that the singers hold back instead of projecting their voices. Maureen, the Daleys' oldest child, perceives that Harriet is on guard with white people, distrusting their motives. Harriet resists Kate's civilized, sympathetic overtures and lies to her, embellishing a story about her father's lynching. After a while, she is so engrossed in her work in the garden and kitchen that she forgets to take her days off. She is amazed at the staggering amount of toil that went into the stone walls. She finds that Vermonters respect themselves. She begins to care about the family's problems. Daley friends from Virginia visit, and Harriet tolerates their stereotypical behavior. The Daleys host a huge picnic, and friends arrive bringing food (to ease the burden of the hostess and to avoid feeling beholden to anyone, she is told). When the conversation turns to issues like "busing," she believes they feign interest in "the plight of the Negro" but do not want to sacrifice their own children. By the end of her stay, Harriet lets down her defenses and tells Kate about her mother's death in childbirth (a white doctor would not come to the house). The whole family climbs to the top of the mountain for a spectacular view. Looking at the Daleys' faces, Harriet no longer sees white skin.

Cornelia Meigs

In ***At the Sign of the Two Heroes*** (1920), three seventeen-year-old friends, Howard Beckman, Andrew Lloyd, and Christopher Robeson, are camping out for the summer at Two Heroes Island on Lake Champlain. Their fathers, who grew up here, arranged for Caleb Bucksall's wife to supply them with eggs and milk. Although the Bucksalls are friendly, other residents are not, except for an old Alsatian immigrant, Pierre Lebeau. Pierre seems unhappy but reveals only that, in the days of Ethan Allen and the Green Mountain Boys, the old house on Seven Bays Hill was a tavern named The Two Heroes in honor of Ethan Allen and his brother,

Ira. He suggests they spend several nights there. They borrow a boat from Caleb to explore the Isle of the Four Winds. When a gale comes up, they go ashore and take shelter in a cabin. Hiding in a shed when five men enter, they notice that one is Pierre's grandson, Jean. The shed is a storehouse for stolen goods—silk, fur, and ivory. The leader, a cruel bully named Job Herron, catches sight of the boys, who flee. They now understand that Pierre is worried about his grandson; fearful as they are of Herron, they cannot help liking Jean. Trying to decide what to do, the boys, all of whose great-great-grandfathers fought with the Green Mountain Boys, have three options: take on the smugglers themselves; report the matter to the authorities, or gather more proof. After consulting with Deputy Sheriff Willetts, they drive him in his car to the hideout. They see the smugglers shoving off. The boys and Willetts follow by boat, but the smugglers portage across a narrow neck of land and escape to the other side of North Hero. The boys consult with Pierre, who does not want his grandson to go to prison; Jean's only involvement is sailing the boats and carrying the goods. When a tempest blows up, the smugglers' boats drift away, trapping them with their contraband on the Isle of Four Winds. Mrs. Durfee, Herron's cousin and housekeeper, tries to stop the boys, but Andrew borrows Herron's horse to ride to Four Corners, the local meeting place. None of the assembled men believes his tale. Since Willetts will not accompany him, Andrew seeks Sheriff Thompson on North Hero. As he rides, Andrew plucks a sprig of evergreen for his cap. On the bridge, Andrew meets Jean, who has left Herron's employ and is fleeing to Canada. The sheriff and his posse capture the miscreants. As a reward, the town gives to the boys Ethan Allen's silver cup, which they display on the mantelpiece at the old tavern; Andrew places his sprig of evergreen beside the cup. (In 1779, the Republic of Vermont granted to Ethan Allen and associates a parcel of land named "Two Heroes" in honor of Ethan and Ira. In 1788, the Two Heroes was divided into two separate Townships known as North Hero and South Hero. From James P. Millard, *Lake Passages*, 2007.)

The Covered Bridge (1936), set in 1785, finds Connie Anderson, nine, staying in Boston with her aunt and uncle because her sea captain father and her mother are away on a voyage. Now that her aunt and uncle are planning a trip of their own, their cook, Sarah Macomber, proposes Connie visit her in Hebron Village, where she owns a mountain farm. Connie's uncle is concerned that it is "rough new country, just beginning to be settled"; her aunt worries about the bitter cold. Connie notes that her aunt and uncle intend to be kind; Sarah knows how to be kind. Sarah and Connie take the coach to Vermont, where she meets Cousin Cephas, a selectman, who gives her a sheepdog puppy. Connie has never had to fend for herself; now Sarah is depending on her. The first night, when she is tucked in her bed under many covers, she looks out at "the still, empty beauty of the great hill and long slopes, all softly clear in the moonlight." Next day, Sarah and Connie walk up the hill to watch Sarah's grandson, Peter, spread salt on the surface of a flat rock where the cattle come to lick. Peter, twelve, owns four calves. She and Peter go to school with ten other children, six of whom were given by the village into Mrs. Guyer's charge and use her surname. Much work remains before winter, such as hanging up strings of onions and corn to dry, boiling down apple butter, and pickling eggs. Peter is cutting winter fuel. Sam Breen has an overabundance of corn, hay, pumpkins, and apples, but no trees to cut; Peter trades him loads of wood. One day Ethan Allen, traveling around the state to discuss issues for the next election, visits the school. Jonathan Ennis, the schoolteacher, says Allen has "given Vermont everything he has." Allen sits in front of the fire with the children, telling tales of Vermont when it was a settlement: "No person has come to live here who did not love the land." When a storm threatens, Peter takes a load of wood by oxen-pulled wagon to Breen's farm, accompanied by Sarah and Connie. Breen asks for cash for his goods, instead of waiting for Peter to cut more wood. Sarah answers quietly that she has no money. That night, Peter goes off to sell one of his calves. He runs into Ethan Allen, organizing a barn raising for impoverished widow Jenny McGowan, whose son, Dick, has left without completing the work. Everyone comes, bringing food, implements, loads of wood, and sacks of grain. After Peter sells his calf, he gives half the proceeds to Dick McGowan, whom he persuades to return to his mother. After a landslide occurs, Peter hurries up the hill to help Breen. Connie asks why he does so; because Breen is their neighbor, explains Sarah. Breen's shed collapses, and the terror-stricken sheep and lambs rush out into the rainstorm. The Guyer children help drive them into the big cattle barn near the house. The animals are all saved, the lambs rubbed dry and wrapped in straw. Connie learns to cook and bake; Peter's animals flourish. "What makes spring so exciting," Connie observes, "is seeing, all of a sudden, what winter has accomplished." They give a birthday party for the Guyer children. While they are enjoying the giant birthday cake, a furious rain starts. So much rain falls that Hebron Brook threatens to overflow the covered bridge. Peter, hefting an ax, runs out into the middle, knocks out some of the boards to make space for the water to sweep through, and saves the bridge. When the sun comes out the next day, they climb the hill to search for hepaticas. "What a pity it is that all the people in the world don't know how beautiful it is just here," says Connie. The schoolhouse blows down in the storm, but Cousin Cephas proposes Sarah's big kitchen as a substitute, since most of the children are already on the hill. Connie's father, home from his voyage, comes to fetch her. She is sad to leave, but "You could always think about coming back to a farm. That was the last beautiful thing to think about, that the valley and the mountains and the long slope of the hill would always be there, would always be the same."

The Call of the Mountain (1940) recounts the travails of Nathan Lindsay, nineteen in the 1820s, who was orphaned at nine and informally adopted by Captain Jonathan Bemis, widower, kind man, excellent farmer, and helpful advisor to his neighbors near Brandon, where "weather is like another member of the family." Jonathan also provided a home to Eliza Thomas, a spinster relative. His grandfather set his pitch (an early settler's encampment) in Forest Dale in the early days of the Vermont settlement, calling it Rolling Willows Farm. Jonathan also acquired the Armitage Farm, "Height of Land," on the mountain above Forest Dale. "There are many wide prospects on this wide earth, but not many of just that nobleness of proportion, just that variation and harmony of line and contour which mark the Champlain Valley." Jonathan sends Nathan to Middlebury College. After his death, Jonathan's will settles an annuity on Eliza, provides a cash bequest to his younger brother, Hamilton, a lawyer, and leaves the two farms to Nathan. Hamilton, outraged that "the charity boy" should inherit his land, implies that Nathan was responsible for Jonathan's death. Nathan makes a momentous decision: he signs a paper giving up his inheritance. He believes it is right that Hamilton should have Rolling Willows Farm, but he keeps his legal claim to Height of Land. On his way up the mountain, Nathan stops to visit his friend, Tom Davenport, a blacksmith and inventor (whose early struggles form a subplot of the narrative), and Jonathan's lawyer, Asa Lamb, to tell him he plans to rehabilitate the farm at Height of Land and reclear the land. He lures back Canute, the Armitages' dog, clears ground for pasture, and cuts logs for sale. He is caught up in a "fury of overwork," hearing that Hamilton is suing to break Jonathan's will. In the village, some people subtly shun Nathan: Hamilton spreads word that Nathan influenced Jonathan to change his will. Nathan helps Simon Harding cut ice; in return, Simon assists him in bringing down his logs. In March, the last item on the town meeting agenda is the "indigent poor" who are to be "boarded out." Nathan, shocked that Miss Eliza and her young niece, Joan, have "come on the town," announces he will take them both without pay. Hamilton challenges Nathan's fitness to make such an offer. Rufus Goss, well-respected citizen and Tom Davenport's father-in-law, speaks on Nathan's behalf. Nathan prepares his modest cabin and gathers spruce for the women's beds. Following the boar that went wild after the Armitages' departure, he finds their stack of huge oak logs. He wonders how to skid them out. Hamilton and the county sheriff summon Nathan to court to establish the circumstances of Jonathan's death. Joan corroborates Nathan's testimony: she was next door baking bread and saw Nathan working in the barn, looking in the house, and running for the doctor. When Hamilton, outraged, rides out in the midst of a storm, Nathan follows and saves his life. In the aftermath of the storm, Nathan realizes the conditions necessary to slide out the logs—a thaw and a freeze. Joan hurries to the village for men with hooks and poles. Their arrival is evidence they stand by him: it is a race against time. Meanwhile, Hamilton is recuperating at Nathan's house. Asa draws up a legal document for Hamilton to sign, receiving Rolling Willows from Nathan and withdrawing the charge made against him. As Hamilton lies sick in his house, Nathan talks with him and learns about his resentments and disappointments. They slowly understand and forgive each other. Spring comes and planting time. "The space of the vegetable garden was smoothly penciled with the light grooves of rake and hoe." Nathan sets aside some money from the logging profits to send Joan to school in Middlebury. Nathan knows Joan is too young to think of marrying; he is content to wait. (Nathan's friend, Thomas Davenport, an American blacksmith and inventor of the first electrical motor, was born in Williamstown, Vermont, in 1802, moved to Brandon, and died in Salisbury, Vermont, in 1851.)

In ***Wild Geese Flying*** (1957), the Milton family—the scientist father; the mother; Dick, twelve; Roddy, ten; Anne, eight; and Bella, six—has traveled the world. Now that their father is in Latin America, the family moves into the Champlain Valley house of Mrs. Milton's deceased father, Roger Devons. The house is perfect, but the residents of Jefferson Village are inexplicably unfriendly. One October day in the woods, Dick watches an exhausted, sweating buck run by, pursued by a golden collie. The owner of the dog hurries up to Dick, worried because it is against the law for dogs to chase deer. Dick sprints after and catches the dog. Commander Gerald ("Jerry") Stewart has just returned from service overseas. He seems interested in Dick and the house: Dick confides their troubles to him. Jerry says that villagers are neither quick to accept strangers nor unjust. "We" must seek the source of the problem, he says, and suggests that Dick and his mother consult with Andrew Styles, Roger Devons's lawyer. Dick's mother sends Dick to the Ushers' farm for eggs; Mrs. Usher rudely refuses to sell to him. Just then a bull breaks loose. Sam Usher, fifteen, shouts at Dick to shut the gate; the boys become friends. Rob Dale is surly to Dick at school, telling him his family has no right to the house. While Dick and Anne are in the attic looking through boxes, Martha Jenkins, their grandparents' former laundress, arrives to hang up the laundry of neighbor Mamie Towner, just as Martha did in their grandparents' day. Mrs. Towner storms over to instruct Martha to remove the wet clothes. Mrs. Milton and Dick consult Andrew, who reports that four years earlier an unnamed friend of Roger Devons's asked him to invest a large amount of money. When the friend returned, Devons had just died and no receipt was found. The villagers believe that the friend is entitled to the house. Andrew will not reveal his name, but Dick later finds a receipt for fifteen thousand dollars from his grandfather to Jerry. The Ushers are the Miltons' tenants and have not paid their rent for four months. At Christmastime, the Miltons make presents for the Usher family and struggle up the hill in a snowstorm. Mrs. Milton tells Sara Usher not to worry about the rent: she invites them to be her guests "until things go well with you again." When Mrs. Towner hears from Joe Usher of Mrs. Milton's generosity, she offers to stay with the little girls so that Mrs. Milton can take the boys to the midnight church service. The family befriends little Nadine Wilmer, who stays with her aunt during the week to go to school in the village. One rainy night, the frightened aunt realizes that Nadine has disappeared. Mrs. Milton takes Dick, Roddy, and Rob Dale to find her. The storm flings the boys off the bridge, but Dick manages to clamber out of Stony Brook with

Nadine, and Rob saves Roddy. Later, climbing on the hill, Dick finds where the blue heron lives and visits him frequently. One day he stops Rob Dale from shooting the great bird to sell to a taxidermist but does not report him to the game warden because the Milton family owes Rob a debt. At the school festival, the Miltons are accepted into the community for braving the storm and saving Nadine. By now, Dick is certain Mrs. Usher knows the answer to their worries. After Dick rescues little Betsey Usher from a fall into a well, Mrs. Usher reveals her secret. Roger Devons left some legal papers with her just before he died, but she never told anyone because she thought they were an order to leave the farm. What he actually left were the bonds he had invested for Jerry—now worth twenty thousand dollars.

Jane Claypool Miner

Four sixteen-year-olds in ***A Winter Love Story*** (1993) persuade their parents to allow them to spend the week spanning Christmas and New Year's Eve at Mount Paradise, a ski resort near Mount Snow. Each of the close friends has a different motivation for the trip. Beautiful Lauren Anderson wants to forget breaking up with her sweetheart. Flirtatious Cee Cee Davis looks forward to meeting new men. Competent African-American Tonya Jackson is interested in perfecting her skiing. Anxious Jessica Mitchell is eager to forget for a few days the impending diagnosis of a brain tumor. By the end of the holiday, Lauren acknowledges her shyness. Cee Cee breaks her ankle and meets an attractive intern. Tonya falls in love with an African-American member of the ski patrol and potential Olympic medalist. Jessica forms a meaningful relationship with a young musician and learns that her scan was negative.

George Mendoza

"The Devil's Pocket" (1968) follows two brothers, Marty and Bruce, who are forbidden by their parents to go near the old abandoned quarry where, it is said, several men were trapped in a cave-in and never seen again. "It's the devil's pocket—don't ever throw a penny in it!" warns their father. One day they approach the edge where Marty pulls a dull old penny out of his pocket, throws it in, and climbs down the side of the quarry. Bruce nervously follows him. At the bottom, the large hole is full of echoes. Marty picks up a shiny new penny. Bruce whispers he had "better not take it." "The echoes grew and swelled: BETTER NOT TAKE IT! BETTER NOT TAKE IT!" The boys hurry home. That night they put the penny on the night table; in the morning, it is gone.

Anne Molloy

Decatur ("Decky") Jones, a conscientious, sympathetic, motherless ten-year-old in ***Decky's Secret*** (1944), used to help his father with his delivery business. Now his father, just out of the navy, is working long hours at the mill making army blankets in Valley Falls. Art, his father's shipmate, works the mill's nightshift and sleeps on the couch in their living room during the day. The three are together at suppertime, though, when Decky's father makes good meals—creamed codfish on mashed potatoes or beef and vegetable stew—and ensures that Decky is in bed on time. Decky goes by himself to the hotel for a haircut from Mr. Jasper. Checking first whether Decky has had the mumps, the barber suggests he visit hotel room thirty-four, where Rez Pandora, nine, is quarantined. She is the oldest of five children found abandoned in the deserted Crabtree House on Burnt Mountain. Mr. Bennett, Overseer of the Poor, put the four younger ones in the Home for Children in nearby Johnson City; he has shown an interest in adopting Rez. Decky visits Rez regularly until she is released, when he tells her his secret. Every day, for the last three years, Decky has waved to Engineer Fred McCoy on the mid-afternoon train. Fred always tosses him a package containing a trinket like a bright nickel whistle. When Decky asks his father how he can help with the war effort, his father repairs a bicycle-built-for-two stored in the garage so that Decky and Rez can run errands for the grocer and druggist and collect ration stamps for them. The children are pleased with the responsibility, but their new schedule will prevent them from greeting Fred. Rez suggests Decky write an explanation of his absence to him in care of the railroad. Rez worries constantly about the four younger children; Decky, fearing Rez might run away, writes to Mrs. Bennett about her husband's interest in adopting Rez. Art takes Decky and Rez to a carnival. Afterwards, Rez disappears. Mrs. Bennett comes the instant she receives Decky's letter, but he in the meantime has taken a train to Johnson City to look for Rez. He finds her, her siblings, and Mr. and Mrs. Bennett, who decide to adopt all the children. Townspeople donate toys and clothing. At the instigation of Fred, the engineer, Mr. Irwin Land, the head of the railroad company, invites Decky to come to Boston with a friend, at the railroad's expense, to christen a new streamlined engine renamed "Commodore Decatur."The head citizen of Valley Falls sees Decky and his father off at the train station and gives Decky a gold watch for bringing this honor to the town and continuing his father's delivery business. In Boston, Fred lets him sit in an engine and put his hand on the throttle. Fred discovers that sharing his father with the mill does not mean he has lost him: "They were better friends than ever." (For an anecdote about Stephen Decatur, American naval officer known for his skirmishes against the Barbary pirates in the Tripolitan war, see George R. Muller's *The Hero of Champlain* below.)

M

R.A. Montgomery

In ***The Island of Time*** (1991), a story in the "Choose Your Own Adventure" series, you, the reader, are staying alone in your parents' house on Lake Champlain while they are on a business trip. You decide to visit Providence Island, taking the inflatable Zodiac, and invite your friend, Tom, to come along with you and your dog, Melvin. You are faced with a number of interrelated decisions with important, often dangerous, consequences. When you are caught in a storm and the disabled boat is heading for a dangerous spot in the lake, should you swim for shore or stay with the craft? When you go off course and come to a nineteenth century steamer, *Ticonderoga*, should you take a job aboard the time-warp ship or make your way to shore? When you become separated from Tom, should you try to find him or stay to search a cave? Among your adventures, you come upon some Indians chanting and carrying out a bizarre ceremony; a man armed with a revolver chases you; and you discover that your parents' accountant is an embezzler.

George R. Muller

Hero of Champlain (1961) describes the two-year build up and the confrontation between the American and British fleets at Plattsburgh Bay in 1814. Seventeen-year-old Gideon Mead, who lives in Burlington, is eager to join the navy, but his father, Dexter, and sister, Deborah, sixteen, are opposed. Trapped in a fierce fight with Caleb Klump, his father's drunken stableman, Gideon is rescued by Captain Thomas Macdonough, twenty-nine, who, with Stephen Decatur, is famous for having blown up their ship, *Philadelphia*, when captured by Barbary pirates at Tripoli. Gideon and his cousin, Aze, join the navy to serve under Macdonough, who, anticipating a fight with the British on Lake Champlain, is investigating the navy's capacity. The American fleet consists of six sloops and two gunboats without guns. Macdonough faces twin problems of obtaining more resources and combating traitors like Klump, who are smuggling goods and cattle to the British in Canada. The first winter the fleet puts up at Basin Harbor in Vergennes. Gideon, a warranted midshipman, acts as clerk to Macdonough, now commodore. Macdonough orders Gideon to accompany Eleazer Williams, head of the Secret Corps of Observation, to assess activity at the British shipyard in Fort Isle aux Noix. Dressed as Indians, they count more than forty bateaux (long, light, flat-bottomed boats with sharply pointed bow and stern). At Plattsburgh, Macdonough commissions more sloops. The second year, the squadron winters on Otter Creek. George Smithson deserts to join Klump in his anti-American activities, attempting at one point to set fire to the galleys. The Adam and Noah Brown shipbuilding concern arrives from New York to build six new gunboats. The biggest, *Saratoga*, will be the flagship. They purchase a steamboat, make her over for sail, and name her *Ticonderoga*. Macdonough says, "winning this war will make the United States a true union of states." He fears that, when Napoleon falls, the British will use all of their troops and frigates in Montreal against the United States. "The future of our country may depend on the lake fleet." The Brown company is building ships below Vergennes Falls. Gideon requisitions armaments and supplies and recruits men. In thirty-five working days, Brown launches *Saratoga*, but she is still in need of outfitting, guns, and crew. Macdonough, worrying that General Sir George Prevost will use the present British fleet to bottle up and sink the American fleet, sends Gideon to Windmill Point to scout enemy movements. He sees the British flotilla—a brig, a ketch, and eight more galleys. The Americans set up a strong defense at the mouth of the Otter River. Captain Daniel Pring sails his ships to the Otter, where an American barrage holds them off until *Saratoga* (with too few guns to fight) and some sloops appear on the lake, and the British withdraw. At Fort Isle aux Noix, the enemy lays the keel for a thirty-two-gun frigate. Which fleet will hold the final balance of power? The shipbuilding race continues; the costs are astronomical. Gideon and his men discover Klump rafting masts to the British and overtake and kill him. Gideon is now serving on *Saratoga*. The secretary of war sends four thousand Plattsburgh troops to the West, leaving General Alexander Macomb with fifteen hundred effectives (men ready for combat) to face fifteen thousand British veterans. Meanwhile, the British sack Washington and burn the White House. Gideon again accompanies Eleazer to Canada to determine the number of British guns and their timetable. Disguised, they board HMS *Confiance* and count thirty-seven ports for guns and a furnace for heating shot. Apprehended, they dive overboard and escape. One hard-pressed American officer uses released army prisoners as gunners. Governor Thomas Chittenden refuses to call up the Vermont militia; patriots rush to Plattsburgh's defense under General Samuel Strong, Mayor of Vergennes. Macdonough inspects his fleet, checking the anchoring devices that allow a ship to turn to fire her guns in every direction. The final moment is at hand. The battle is fierce and bloody, with great loss of life. The spanker boom is hit and smashes Macdonough to the deck, but he survives. The battle looks hopeless, until Macdonough orders *Saratoga* turned around, exhibiting a fresh broadside. Aze says, "This is the proudest day our country ever saw." The next instant a sixteen-pound ball takes off his head. Not a single enemy vessel's ensign remains; Prevost's army retreats. The Americans have won. (In reading about Lake Champlain, it is counterintuitive and therefore helpful to know that "up the lake" is toward its source or south, while "down the lake" is toward its outlet or north.)

Rita Murphy

Night Flying (2000) introduces a household of three generations of Hansen women who can fly like birds. Georgia Louisa Hansen (almost sixteen), her mother, Maeve, her two aunts, Eve (a painter) and Suki (a seamstress), and her grandmother live in Hawthorne in an old, rambling Victorian house with a widow's walk. "To the north there is nothing but open meadow and hills down to the Missisquoi River." Georgia's grandmother banished a third daughter, Carmen, years earlier for a reason unknown to Georgia. Her grandmother runs the family with an iron hand and ironclad rules, of which the cardinal ones are "no meat, no men." None of them works because Grandfather Cooney left them a fortune from a single invention. Aside from her best friend, Alice, whose half-Abenaki and half-Irish mother is a midwife, Georgia has no friends at school, and no one knows about the flying. Georgia is waiting for something to happen in her life: she thinks of the town of Hawthorne as "nowhere, Vermont." The angry outcast, Carmen, returns to talk with her mother and ignores Georgia. Hurt by Carmen's attitude, Georgia flies solo, even though her grandmother has ordained that she wait until her sixteenth-birthday initiation. Georgia, listening through a crack in the barn floor, learns that Carmen is her mother. Carmen has returned to Vermont because her mother is leaving the barn and some acreage to Georgia. Georgia, helping Aunt Suki make her initiation dress, wonders if she should confess to her grandmother that she has already taken a solo flight. Mr. Gowen, who helps her grandmother around the place and has always been kind to and interested in Georgia, offers to board a horse in the Hansen barn—the realization of Georgia's dream. During the initiation ceremony, her grandmother asks Georgia if she has ever flown alone. Georgia stalwartly confesses, breaking the barricade of lies that has separated the family members over the years. When Carmen was eighteen she fell in love with Sam Gowen, Mr. Gowen's grandson. After a few nights in the sugar shack with Sam, Carmen became pregnant. Georgia's grandmother forbade Carmen to see Sam again. Carmen delivered Georgia, left her in Maeve's care, and fled with Sam to California. Sam died in an automobile accident the following year. Everyone speaks the truth this night, including Maeve, who reveals that her mother prohibited her from flying for sixteen years and treated her like a slave. Maeve flies with Georgia on her initiation flight. Now Georgia has a new, happy relationship with Maeve, her grandfather, and her horse.

N

John Ney

In ***Ox Goes North*** (1973), fifteen-year-old Franklin Spencer Olmstead, called "Ox" because of his height and weight, lives a privileged life in Palm Beach but feels "lousy" sometimes because his socialite, selfish parents are always traveling. This summer they send him against his will to exclusive Camp Downing in Dexter. He likes the landscape but not the adults, judging from the insincere behavior of the camp owner, "Skipper." Ox bunks with two boys, Steve Lattimore, witty and easygoing, and Tommy Campbell, distracted and depressed. One cabin is devoted entirely to the wealthy and exuberant Connolly youngsters from Boston and their bodyguards. Ox, who is not enthusiastic about organized exercise, is forced to do calisthenics, swimming, horseback riding, and as many other sports as can be squeezed into the day. After Ox and Steve meet Tommy's horrible grandparents, the Shreckers, who live thirty miles away in Taddington, the boys convince Tommy to tell them his problems. His grandparents are trying to drive him mad so they can appropriate his vast trust fund. Steve's mother and his charming, gentle sister, Anne, visit camp to take them to dinner at the Dexter County Club. Unfortunately, Tommy confides to the camp psychiatrist that he has befriended Ox and Steve; the next morning Tommy and his belongings are gone. Ox and Steve borrow two horses and head for Taddington, where they meet Dacoolah Tompkins, a former actress, who passionately hates the Shreckers. Thirty years ago Taddington was made up of native Vermonters; outsiders started arriving and ceding control of the town to the Shreckers. Ox and Steve go to Boston to confront Tommy's psychiatrist, who refuses to believe their story. They plan to seize one of the Connolly children from Camp Downing to make it look as though the Shreckers have kidnapped him. Before they can act, Dacoolah blows up the Shreckers' house with them—and her—inside. All the relatives and key townspeople gather in Taddington to prevent Tommy's telling the truth, but he perseveres. An aunt becomes his guardian; the boys are welcomed back to Camp Downing.

O

Helen Fuller Orton

Andy Draper, twelve, and his sister Joan, ten, in ***Mystery in the Old Cave*** (1950) usually spend just the summers in Vermont; this year their parents keep the rented house for the entire year and enter the children in the local school. Andy and Joan enjoy picking hickory nuts and trudging up the hill to see the sugarhouse. In contrast, Phil Ramsay, also twelve, whose mother died recently, lives with his stern, unpleasant Uncle

John, who forces Phil to work in the yard until he can hardly walk. Andy and Joan notice a stranger near the sugarhouse. Thomas Lane, the grocer who hires Phil as delivery boy, gives him specific directions to an old cave, where, twenty years earlier, thieves hid items stolen from town residents. Phil and Andy, taking flashlights and a spade, find the cave. Uncle John forces Phil to turn over the money he earns at the store and puts him on a diet of bread and water when he returns late. Phil tells Mr. Lane he is running away from home. He spends the first night in the cave, where he meets the stranger, Joe Williams, who is also looking for the treasure. After Joe leaves, Andy and his father arrive at the cave to persuade Phil to stay. Phil discovers a handkerchief filled with stolen jewels. Andy's parents invite Phil to live with them and require Uncle John to sign a paper releasing Phil to them. The townsfolk recover their lost possessions. Phil is the happiest boy in Vermont.

Margaret Otto

In ***Mr. Kipling's Elephant*** (1961), Tim Evans, ten, and his sister, Kate, fourteen, live with their parents on a dairy farm near Naulakha, where Rudyard Kipling is staying in 1895 with his American wife. The children both love *The Jungle Book*; Tim is especially interested in the elephants. Taking his sled to the train station in Brattleboro to fetch a Christmas package from their grandmother, Tim finds in the snow a glove and a notebook, which, according to the baggage master, belong to Rudyard Kipling. Kate and Tim walk over to Naulakha to find Mr. Kipling playing snow golf with Mr. Day, a clergyman. Mr. Kipling, delighted with the discovery, invites them in for a lost-and-found tea. He shows them animal figures given to him by his friend, Joel Chandler Harris; the children are familiar with the Uncle Remus stories. Mr. Kipling is so impressed by Tim's detective work that he sets him a new challenge—to find Jumbo, his elephant. The two rules are that Tim may not touch or move anything because Jumbo is in plain sight, and Tim may ask two questions before he begins his search the next afternoon. No, the elephant is not in the house. No, it is no bigger than a five-year-old calf. Howard, the coachman, drives the children home. Unfortunately, the next day Tim comes down with chicken pox: he will have to stay home from school for three weeks and miss the Christmas party at Naulakha. The days go by slowly. He hears whispering from time to time and knows secrets are abroad in the house. On Christmas Day, Tim's father escorts him to the dining room where the whole room is decorated; the family, Matt, the hired man, and the pets are arrayed as members of the Kipling household. His mother is wearing a sign saying, "I am Mrs. Kipling"; his father is dressed as Mr. Kipling. Overwhelmed and pleased, Tim recites the Kipling poem he has memorized, the words of Kala Nag ("Black Snake"), the work elephant. Kate tells a story about Tim's visiting Mr. Kipling, starting in true Kipling mode, "Once O Best Beloved..." During the party, the Kiplings deliver a large tree decorated by the children in Tim's class with animals from *The Jungle Book*. When Tim is well, he sets out to look for Jumbo. He walks across the pasture, seeing many wild animals, such as foxes, raccoons, and possums, and then he sees Jumbo—a large rock exactly like an elephant lying with his head and body slightly curved. Mr. Kipling helps Tim climb upon Jumbo's back and celebrates the end of the elephant hunt by giving Tim the rock. Mr. Kipling orders men to dig out the rock using block and tackle and drag it, with heavy chains and a pair of oxen, to the Evans farm. (The poem Tim recites from *The Jungle Book* begins, "I will remember what I was. I am sick of rope and chain.")

Janice Ovecka

Cave of Falling Water (1992) consists of three linked stories about three thirteen-year-old girls—Wonkake ("Woni"), an Abenaki; Martha Anne ("Mattie") Hardwicke, a Colonial; and Stacy Adams, a modern girl—who share a secret and a place. In the first story, set in the days before settlers came to Vermont, members of an Abenaki tribe are dying and their food supply is dwindling. Woni's best friend, Falling Water, was a victim of a smallpox epidemic. Hawk, seventeen, a hunter who was Falling Water's intended husband, shows Woni a cave he discovered. They call it Cave of Falling Water as a memorial to her. With instruments chiseled from rock, Woni carves figures on the cave's wall and places an earthenware jug full of corn kernels on a ledge. In the second story, Mattie lives in a log cabin in the New Hampshire Grants, or "Vermont," as the French call it. In her wanderings, she comes upon the cave with Woni's drawings and plants a handful of the Indian corn kernels. Settlers found Gardner's Mill. The Hardwickes spend winters in the town, where Mattie's father assists the blacksmith. Before she leaves the cabin, Mattie refills the clay pot with corn and leaves a note for the next person who discovers the cave. In town, Mattie meets a contemporary, Tom Gardner, son of the mill owner. In the third story, Stacy Adams and her parents move to Gardner's Mill, where Stacy resents her new life and hates their "antique farmhouse." Exploring the woods, she finds the cave and Mattie's note. She tells no one about the cave but plants the corn from the clay pot. Kathy Gardner, the librarian, introduces Stacy to her daughter, Jill, who is in her class at school. At the library, Stacy sees a quilt commemorating the marriage of Mattie Hardwicke to Tom Gardner. Tom and Mattie's original house, built in 1774, is now a museum. Stacy learns that Mattie kept a journal, which mentions the cave; Stacey reveals that she has discovered its location. A state archeologist from the University of Vermont, and Rich Dupree, representing the Abenaki nation, pronounce the cave one of the best finds in Vermont. They take away models of the drawings for exhibition in order to discourage tourists from tramping through the area.

Captive of Pittsford Ridge (1994) is set in Pittsford and Hubbardton in early July 1777. Josiah Freeman, fourteen, lives with Anna, his mother, and his grandfather, a veteran of the French and Indian Wars; his father, Matthew, is fighting with the Green Mountain Boys. Passing neighbors warn them that raiders are on the march, led by Tory Captain Justus Sherwood. They stow their few possessions in their hidey-hole (hideaway) and drive the goats into the woods. When the raiders arrive, grandfather pretends he is loyal to the British. In Hubbardton, Matthew is serving with Captain Johnson under Colonel Seth Warner. The British, who have retaken Fort Ticonderoga, are on the Americans' trail. Josiah and his mother can hear the sounds of battle; Josiah climbs the ridge to scout out the action. The order is given for the Americans to retreat south to Manchester; Captain Johnson is wounded. As Josiah watches, a drummer boy in German uniform staggers up to Josiah and collapses. Josiah helps Hans Klein home, where his mother welcomes the boy despite his being an enemy. The two boys become friends. As Josiah escorts Hans back to his own troops, British soldiers capture Josiah and lodge him with their American prisoners, among whom Josiah finds his father's friend, Captain Johnson. The Germans take Josiah to General von Riedesel, who says Hans claims Josiah is a rebel spy. Hans changes his allegiance and helps Josiah escape. Now Josiah's responsibility is to rebuild and protect his family house and to keep the farm going until his father returns. (The Battle of Hubbardton, a rearguard action, delayed the British and Germans long enough for the Americans to retreat from Fort Ticonderoga and regroup for the Battle of Bennington later that summer. Many Germans escaped from the army and stayed in America. For a story of a Hessian deserter, see Frances Sanger's *The Wooden Mug* in this collection.)

P

Marion Page

The nickname, "Dirty Mary," is a corruption of Deirdre Marie, the first names of the fourteen-year-old heroine in ***Dirty Mary No More*** (1999). Given to her by the little boy she looks after, the pejorative name circulates through the town of Canterbury where Deirdre lives in a trailer camp with her mother, Noreen, a waitress at Tuggle's Café. Deirdre, whose father disappeared years earlier, feels she is "empty" and "missing" something. She often misbehaves in harmless ways, as though she cannot control herself. Friendless at school and taunted by bully Tipper McLam, she meets Emile Fournier, half-Abenaki, half-French-Canadian. Emile's mother is dead, and he stays with his grandmother (Memère) and truck driver father in a fine house in town. Because she finds Emile appealing, she checks out a library book about Abenaki culture to understand his pride in his heritage. Deirdre notices that her pretty mother seems sad and lonely. When Deirdre glimpses Emile's handsome father, Jack, and his fine, ladylike grandmother, she makes a plan. She urges her tired mother to church the following Sunday, where they meet the Fournier family. As luck would have it, Noreen's car will not start, Jack offers to fix it, and soon a romance between Jack and Noreen is progressing nicely. Deirdre yearns to be respectable, to live in a real house, and to free herself from her Dirty Mary persona. The Fourniers invite Noreen and Deirdre to a formal lunch, at which everyone is uncomfortable. Emile shoots his first deer with a bow and arrow, leaves the carcass in front of Deirdre's trailer, and spends a night alone with his ancestors' spirits as part of an Abenaki ritual. When he is suspended from school for missing a few days, Deirdre enlists some of her classmates in a protest march. Carrying banners bearing the legend, "Set Emile Free," some students follow her out of the school. The principal praises her leadership and respect for social justice but cautions her to develop more self-control. Noreen breaks up with Jack, explaining to a heartbroken Deirdre that they do not fit into the Fourniers' way of life. Without thinking through the consequences, Deirdre runs away by bus and is rescued by Mrs. Fournier and Noreen. As recompense for Mrs. Fournier's assistance, Deirdre works at her house after school and on weekends; Emile has a job bagging groceries. Noreen and Deirdre, who had contemplated moving on, decide to stay.

Many young men from Groton enlist in the army in 1861 at the start of ***The Printer's Devil*** (2002). Jacob McRae, his wife, and daughters hear frightful news from their neighbors, the Scotts: one of their sons, Willie, Third Vermont Regiment, fell asleep at his post and faces the firing squad. Much to everyone's relief, he is reprieved. Deliverance ("Livy") McRae, fifteen, who sat through the night with Willie's mother, is flooded with joy: Willie is her special friend. As she walks wearily home from the Scotts' house, an older man driving a mule-drawn wagon with a young lad in the back offers her a ride. The former, Tyler Maldren, and the latter, Jeremiah ("Jem") Harvey, are setting up a printing business and plan to publish a newspaper in Groton. The closest newspaper, *The Caledonian Record*, is in St. Johnsbury, a much bigger town. After hearing that federal marshals have rounded up a group of runaway slaves not far away, Livy stumbles upon a contraband (an escaped slave) about six years old named Solomon and hides him in the sugarhouse. When she returns with food, he is gone. Livy learns in the village that Tyler and Jem are at Peter Paul's infamous store where counterfeiter Bristol Bill hid out in 1849. Livy believes the printers are holding Solomon captive. When the printers do not issue a newspaper, the townspeople suspect they are Confederate spies. Livy, hoping to raise money for her tuition at Peacham Academy, submits local-interest stories to the printers. Tyler persists in asking Livy about the whereabouts of the tunnel under Peter Paul's house. The first issue of *The Groton Journal* finally appears, entirely and anonymously written by Livy. She wonders if she is inadvertently aiding the enemy. Willie Scott is badly injured at the Battle at Lee's Mill and dies of his wounds. Livy, tending her nephew when he runs off, follows him to Mr. Wheatley's, who locks them in his basement. Seeking a way out, Livy finds the trapdoor to the tunnel and a chest filled with printed bills. Tyler and Jem follow her there; Jem identifies himself as an officer in the Confederate Army working with Tyler to steal the money. They have Solomon with them. They tie up Livy and take the chest. When she frees herself, she raises the alarm, even though she is in love with Jem. Tyler is caught, the chest in his possession. That night,

Jem, who is hiding in the sugarhouse, asks Livy to take care of Solomon (who stowed away in his wagon) and provides a letter to protect the boy from the Fugitive Slave Law. Perhaps, after the war, they will meet again. Jem vanishes into the night, and Livy takes Solomon into her house. She plans to sew him some shirts, teach him to read and write, and wait for the war to end. (President Lincoln pardoned William Scott at the request of Vermont Senator Lucius Chittenden.)

Katherine Paterson

In "**No Room in the Inn**," a Christmas story in the collection, ***A Midnight Clear*** (1995), eighteen-year-old Ben lives with his parents in their old farmhouse—now a bed-and-breakfast—about forty miles from Burlington. He feigns disappointment when his parents travel over the holiday but looks forward to relaxing by the fire and watching videos. He drops them off at the airport and, after a difficult, snowy drive, stops by Gracie's restaurant, where he finds her watching television, concerned about the plight of Armenian earthquake victims with no shelter from the weather. A stranger enters for a cup of coffee; later, the same man comes to Ben's house. Fearful of driving in the storm, he seeks protection in Ben's garage. Nervous about harboring an unknown person on the property, Ben reluctantly agrees. Then a little boy knocks, wanting to use the bathroom, followed by a little girl. A woman with a baby asks Ben to warm a baby bottle. Frightened and annoyed, Ben refuses to allow the family to spend the night. As the man is driving away, Ben has a change of heart. He welcomes the family into his house. He will call Gracie: she will help. In "**Poor Little Innocent Lamb**," Isaiah Washington is the sixty-year-old hired hand on a farm near Bethel. The owner, Old Lettie, spends her time poring over her accounts. When her grandniece, Travis, comes to stay in the huge white frame house, the bitter old woman pays no attention to her. Isaiah puts Travis in a tiny room near the stove, takes her to town to buy clothes, and enrolls her in school. When the ewe has twins and cannot care for both, Isaiah, without telling Old Lettie, brings one lamb into the house for Travis to cosset. Travis calls the lamb "Orphan Annie." On Christmas Eve, before Isaiah leaves for church in Bethel with his family, he cooks a nice supper; Travis sets the table festively. While Isaiah is trying to persuade Old Lettie to come downstairs, Orphan Annie seizes the tablecloth in her sharp teeth and pulls its contents to the floor, breaking all the dishes. Old Lettie is furious and pledges to have the lamb slaughtered. Travis decides to run away with her pet. Isaiah persuades her to come instead to Bethel, where Orphan Annie stars in the Christmas pageant. The whole congregation returns to Old Lettie's house to put on the play in her honor. When Isaiah lays the Baby Jesus (his nephew) in her lap, the old woman begins to weep. (While these two stories contain actual Vermont references, the author wrote to Grace Worcester Greene that "in my brain" several other stories—notably "Watchman, Tell Us of the Night," in which the protagonist loses his grandfather's farm and property at auction—are also set in Vermont.)

The eponymous heroine in ***Lyddie*** (1991) is at thirteen the eldest child of Mattie Worthen, whose husband left the family four years earlier to escape the poor farm. His ventures failed because of the loss of demand in England for potash and the collapse of the wool market. Charles is ten; Rachel and Agnes are six and four. The year is 1843. Mattie takes the two little girls to her relatives in Poultney, leaving Lyddie and Charles to cope on the farm near Barrett (modeled on Barre). They firmly believe their father will return. In May, when "the cheek of the hill wore a three-day growth of green," Mattie rents out the pasture, fields, sugar bush, and animals to repay some of her debts, apprentices Lyddie to Mr. Cutler at the tavern, and sends Charles to work at Bakers Mill. Luke Stevens, the son of Quaker neighbors, drives them to town. As a servant girl, Lyddie works long, hard hours, up before dawn to start the fire. The wool from the Cutlers' sheep is sent to Lowell, Massachusetts, to the water-powered mill: "All the wealth that had once been Vermont's seemed to be trickling south or west." When she takes off a few days to visit her old home, she finds a well-spoken fugitive slave, hidden there by abolitionist Reverend Stevens. Lyddie gives the man some money for his escape. After she returns to work, Mrs. Cutler fires her. Lyddie decides that working at a cotton mill is the only way to pay off the family debts and walks to Lowell, where she boards with Mrs. Bedlow, along with other girls at the Concord Corporation. Her assignment is the weaving room in a giant, six-story brick building. Diana Goss, at the neighboring loom, trains Lyddie; Diana is a representative of the Female Labor Reform Association and considered radical and untrustworthy by Lyddie's housemates. In the evenings, one of the boarders reads aloud from *Oliver Twist*, opening up a new, thrilling world for Lyddie, an uneducated mountain girl, and providing a welcome escape from the appalling noise and grueling, dangerous work at the mill. As two years pass, Lyddie becomes proficient at weaving, with concomitant pay increases; her life consists of working and eating automatically and falling into bed. Exhausted, she has an accident—a shuttle strikes her temple. Diana calls Dr. Craven, a handsome young man with whom Lyddie has seen Diana out walking. Luke, on a mission for the Underground Railroad, brings Lyddie a check for fifty dollars from Ezekial Freeman, the former slave whom she helped escape. She gratefully deposits this money with her other savings to pay off the Worthen debts. Shortly thereafter, Uncle Judah arrives with Rachel, now eight (Agnes has died); he sent their mother to the asylum in Brattleboro and is selling the farm. Lyddie begs Mrs. Bedlow to keep Rachel for a fortnight against the rules of the corporation. In the weaving room, the overseer, Mr. Marsden, touches Lyddie inappropriately; when he tries to hug her, she stomps hard with her boot on his foot. She falls ill with a fever, and little Rachel nurses her back to health. Rachel begins working as a "doffer," replacing empty spools with full ones, and starts coughing at night. Charles arrives with the news that the Phinneys have taken him on as a full apprentice at the mill and as a son of the house; further, they want to adopt Rachel. Charles also brings a letter from Luke, who asks Lyddie to marry him and live at the old Worthen farm, which his father has bought. She views this proposal as another kind of slavery and does not respond. At a meeting called to sign a petition for a ten-hour workday, Lyddie finds Diana ill and preoccupied: she is pregnant by a married man and must leave the mill. Shortly thereafter, Lyddie's mother dies. Lyddie befriends Brigid, the newcomer at the next loom, and teaches her to read. Fall comes: "Not the raucous patchwork of the Green Mountains, but the sedate brocade of a Massachusetts city." When Lyddie comes upon Mr. Marsden making improper advances to an unwilling Brigid, Lyddie turns a bucket of water over his head and carries Brigid away. Lyddie is fired for "moral turpitude" (she purchases a dictionary to find out the word means "wickedness") and returns to Vermont. Seeing Luke at her old "squat and homely" farm, she tells him that she is heading West to Oberlin College; as she looks keenly into his face, she knows she will return to him and the farm. (For adult stories about way stations on the Underground Railroad, see Rowland E. Robinson's *Out of Bondage*.)

Jip, His Story (1996), the sequel to *Lyddie*, begins in Barrett in 1855. Eight years earlier, Jip was tumbled off a wagon on West Hill Road and, after living in a succession of foster homes, was placed at the poor farm. Run by Mr. and Mrs. Lyman, the farm has seven residents—four old, two "simple-minded," and Jip, who is about eleven. Jip often wonders why no one came back for him. Is he a gypsy, as people claim? The poor farm, though, is home, and he loves the rocky pastures and the "distant hills, the green deeply pockmarked with the gray…of the granite quarry." Lyman orders Jip to build a cage for a "lunatic," Putnam Nelson, who comes to the poor farm (Lyman figures he may as well reap his board instead of the asylum). Jip is gentle and sweet-tempered with Put, as he calls him. Jip, in fact, takes care of all the humans and animals on the farm. He is accustomed to hard work—milking, plowing, seeding, cultivating, picking, and reaping. Jip is kind to Sheldon, the younger feeble-minded inmate, and makes him feel he is helping Jip. Widow Wilkens and her three chil-

P

dren arrive; her oldest child, Lucy, is about Jip's age. Jip is soon aware of a stranger nosing about, representing a man who is seeking a lost child. Lyman, ever acquisitive, decides he needs more ready cash and sends Sheldon to work at Avery's quarry. Jip is chilled at the idea and begs Sheldon to listen carefully on the job and follow directions. The poor unfortunate is soon killed in an accident. Mrs. Wilkens, eager for Lucy to attend school, insists that Jip accompany her. Since the law requires children to go to school three months of the year, Lyman is forced to acquiesce. The teacher is Lyddie, back from Oberlin; her sweetheart is still Luke, abolitionist and Quaker. Lyddie reads aloud to the children from her favorite book, *Oliver Twist*. After Put has one of his spells, Lyman keeps Jip, the only person who can tame him, at home. Lyddie insists that Lyman allow Jip to return to school, gives Jip a copy of *Uncle Tom's Cabin*, and gravely tells him to let her or Luke know if he needs anything. Shortly thereafter, Jip sees a blonde man in the village whose face looks exactly like his in the mirror; next to him is the stranger who has been asking questions. Jip flees in the wagon to Luke's farm, where Luke explains Jip's background. His mother was a slave of mixed blood who came to Vermont with her little boy by Underground Railroad. Discovering the driver of her wagon was a slave trader, she stealthily lowered her child to the ground as the wagon turned on a sharp curve; she chose to abandon him rather than return him to slavery. The man Jip saw in the village is his white father. Luke says Jip must leave at once for the Northfield train to Canada. Jip agrees to go if he can take Put. Jip assumes a brave face for Put: "We'll never be caught—we're Green Mountain Boys." On the way to Lyddie's house, slave traders kill Put and jail the heartbroken Jip. Lyddie demands a hearing in a court of law. She will swear that Jip is her son, conceived when she was a factory girl in Lowell. Luke will swear he is Jip's father and will beg Lyddie to marry him. Jip is touched but unwilling to allow them to make this sacrifice. He escapes from jail and heads for Montreal, the home of Reverend Ezekial Freeman and his wife, who become Jip's foster parents. When the war starts, Jip joins a Negro regiment.

The ***Preacher's Boy*** (1999) of the title is Robert ("Robbie) Burns Hewlett, ten, whose father is the minister at the Congregational Church in Leonardstown. The three other children in the family are his fifteen-year-old sister, Beth, who is working on becoming a young lady; Letty, who is five; and his twelve-year-old brother, Elliot, who is "simple-minded." Robbie fights furiously with the older Weston boys when they make fun of Elliot. It is the end of the century—1899. Being a minister's son, with the attendant high moral expectations, is hard on an imaginative, high-spirited boy with a "prodigious vocabulary." The secret hiding place for Robbie and his best friend, Willie Beaner, is a deserted cabin in the woods, which belonged to a Civil War veteran who headed out West. Leonardstown is granite quarry territory; the Italian stonecutters go to the Catholic Church in Tyler ten miles away. The members of Robbie's father's congregation do not consider his father sufficiently evangelical; in fact, Robbie has seen his father reading works of naturalist Charles Darwin. After a visiting preacher whips the congregation into a froth about the apocalypse as the year 1900 dawns, Robbie decides, since the world is coming to an end, to enjoy himself; furthermore, he does not believe in God. Willie is horrified to hear that Robbie is an "apeist" (Robbie accepts as correct this term for "atheist," since it fits in nicely with the theory of evolution). Robbie dreams of motorcars—he actually sees one in Leonardstown—and wonders where he can find money to buy a bicycle. When Elliot strays from the Fourth of July parade, everyone looks for him. Robbie's father finds him wandering in the cemetery, carries him home, and falls weeping into his wife's arms. Robbie is seized with jealousy that his father worships this simple boy. In the swimming hole the next day, Robbie is so infuriated with the Weston boys' jibes about Elliot that he holds one of them under water and then, frightened by his passion, runs away to the cabin. To his astonishment, he finds squatters there—a filthy, drunken man, Zeb Finch, and his tattered, equally dirty, daughter, Violet, about Robbie's age. Robbie devises a scheme to raise money for his bicycle: he will write a ransom note claiming that the Finches kidnapped him. Before he can do more than write "help" in raspberry juice on a piece of birchbark, Zeb, overcome by a crazy spell, breaks into the local drugstore. When he hits Violet, Robbie intervenes, and Zeb strikes him on the head with a bottle. Violet calls for assistance, and a passer-by, Mr. Weston, carries Robbie home where his wound becomes infected; he lies ill and feverish for five days. Elliot sits by Robbie's bed, holding a cool cloth to his head and singing softly to him. The police find Robbie's note, arrest Zeb for kidnapping, and take him to jail in Tyler. Robbie's father is called to testify. Robbie staggers off on foot for Tyler. A motorcar pulls up (with Elliot hiding in the back), whose owner drives the boys to the courthouse where Robbie tells his father the whole story. The miracle of being saved by the motorcar restores Robbie's faith in God. During Zeb's parole, Robbie's father finds him a job at the Leonardstown Hotel; Violet goes to school with Robbie and Willie. She forms an attachment to Elliot and often comes over to play paper dolls with him and Letty. When Zeb's parole is up, he and Violet disappear. (This novel is dedicated to Robert Luther Duffus and "his memories of his Vermont boyhood." For an adult story about a boy's growing up in 1898 in Waterbury, Vermont, see Duffus's *That Was Alderbury*.)

Josh Wilkinson, eleven, is angry in ***The Field of Dogs*** (2001) because he was forced to move to Vermont with his mother and stepfather, Greg, who buys him a pair of boots so he can be "a real Vermonter." Manch, Josh's dog, runs off. When Josh catches up with him, he finds him in a field full of dogs laughing and talking in English. Josh is fascinated that the dogs and he share the same problem: they are menaced by a gang of dog bullies, which defines the fight as one between flatlander and native mutts; Josh is experiencing a similar conflict with Wes Rockett, the bully at his school. Wes and his taunting friends order Josh to attend an initiation ceremony and tie his hands. The gang of bullying dogs, led by a silver Weimaraner, appears and, while the boys are momentarily stunned, Josh runs away. Manch runs to the house to tell Josh that one of his dog friends has been hurt. Josh manages to drag the wounded animal back to the house; Greg drives Josh and the animal to the veterinarian, who has to put down the dog. Josh steals Greg's gun and sets out to take revenge on the silver dog. When the dogs charge, Josh shoots wildly at them; Manch throws himself into the mêlée and is badly wounded. Josh runs for help to the nearest house, which happens to belong to Wes. The owners of the Weimaraner refuse to have him destroyed. Again, Greg and Josh, with Wes, are at the vet's, this time with Manch; the vet says the dog will survive. As a result of this ordeal, Josh makes friends with Wes and also with Greg, who speaks sternly about Josh's taking the gun but is, at the same time, understanding and fair. Josh hopes soon to call his stepfather "Dad."

Circumstances force Angel Morgan, eleven, to grow up rapidly in ***The Same Stuff as Stars*** (2002). She and her brother, Bernie, seven, suffered a miserable youth with their father in prison for theft and their mother, Verna, behaving unreliably. One day, Verna removes them from their apartment in Burlington. She takes them to visit their father, Wayne; then she abandons them at their great-grandmother's farm near Barre. Erma Morgan is old and poor, with no proper food in the refrigerator, a house in bad condition, a junk-filled yard, and a broken-down trailer and sugar shack. One night in the yard Angel meets a man with a telescope; she guesses he lives in the trailer. Gentle and kind, he teaches her about the planets and tells Angel she is made of the same stuff as the stars. Angel keeps secret her friendship with the man Erma refers to as "Santy Claus." Angel assumes command of the household, walking two miles to the store and back. A tiny building next to the store houses the Elizabeth Fletcher Irwin Memorial Library; the founder's daughter, Miss Liza, is a delightful old lady who welcomes Angel and Bernie and gives them books to meet their needs. Angel and Bernie travel by bus to school in Chesterville. Angel makes the arrangements, concealing the fact that their mother does not live with them. Soon, her classmates know she is the daughter of Wayne Morgan, the robber of Cumberland Farms in Barre a few years earlier: "Vermont was a small state." Angel looks for her star man, but he has disappeared. Her father, out on parole, comes for her, but she will not leave her grandmother. Erma has maintained the fiction that her son, Ray, died in Vietnam; in truth, he came home a "zombie," almost unable to cope, and has been living in Erma's trailer. Now Ray, Angel's "star man," is a patient at the Barre hospital. She visits him before he dies. To comfort her, Miss Liza reads her Robert Frost's "Take Something Like a Star." Mrs. Morris from Family Services investigates their home situation; Angel assures her she and Bernie are doing fine and suggests Mrs. Morris corroborate that assessment with Miss Liza. One day Bernie does not return from school. The authorities tell Angel that Verna picked him up. Bernie telephones Angel from the hospital: he and Verna were in an automobile accident. Bernie wants to come home to Angel; Verna is remorseful and badly hurt. Angel serenely and responsibly takes charge of Bernie and Erma. (The last stanza of the Frost poem is: "So when at times the mob is swayed/To carry praise or blame too far,/We may take something like a star/To stay our minds on and be staid.")

Bread and Roses, Too (2006) begins in Lawrence, Massachusetts, in 1912, when thousands of foreign mill workers explode into the streets to demand a living wage. Organizers like Joseph J. Ettor, representing the Industrial Workers of the World (whose motto is "solidarity"), provide leadership and funding from other IWW members to help the strikers. Two young people tell the story from alternating perspectives. Rosa Serutti, eleven, is still in school; her father died in a mill fire and her mother and older sister work in the mill. Motherless, illiterate Jake Beale, thirteen, works in the mill; he lives sometimes with an abusive, alcoholic father and often on the street. The children are swept up in the heroism of the workers and their leaders and the callousness and cruelty of the government-summoned militia. Rosa's mother and her women friends raise their participation to a feverish pitch. A young woman, Annie Lopizzo, is shot; Joe Ettor and Arturo Giovannitti are arrested for inciting violence. When the women strikers need a meaningful sign to mark the arrival of Bill Haywood, who is coming from the West with famous woman organizer Elizabeth Gurley Flynn, they turn to Rosa. They need bread, but they yearn for something spiritual as well, explains Rosa's mother. Rosa carefully letters the poster for them: "WE WANT BREAD AND ROSES, TOO." The Lawrence Strikers' Children's Committee sends the children to safety, some to New York, some to Vermont. When Jake finds his father dead from an overdose of whiskey, he stows away on the train to Vermont. Improvising, Rosa pretends to the authorities that he is her brother, Salvatore Serutti. A huge crowd greets the children in Barre and carries them to the Old Socialist Labor Hall, where Rosa and "Sal" are assigned to Mr. and Mrs. Gerbati. Mrs. Gerbati welcomes them warmly. When she offers some of her dead son's clothes to Sal, Mr. Gerbati is still too grief-stricken to allow him to wear them. The children are to attend school in Barre the next day, but Sal confesses to Rosa that he can neither read nor write. Mrs. Gerbati persuades her husband to take Sal with him to work: he manages a granite-cutting business and is a former gravestone artist. Sal shovels granite chips into a pail to dump near the creek and tries to figure out how to run away before his impersonation is discovered. One night, when he is in the office stealing some money, Mr. Gerbati apprehends him. Instead of taking Sal to the police, Mr. Gerbati asks one of his workers to show Sal the monument in the square of Robert Burns, sculpted by Mr. Gerbati's teacher, who was killed by an anarchist. Then in the cemetery Sal views Mr. Gerbati's masterpiece, the gravestone of his son. Sal tells Mr. Gerbati the truth about his identity and his father's death. Meanwhile, Rosa's mother and sister are in jail in Lawrence. The whole world turns against the brutality of the Lawrence police and the Massachusetts militia: Billy Wood, the mill owner, surrenders on March 14, 1912, and twenty-five thousand workers return to the mills. Sal also tells Rosa everything before she returns to Lawrence, her suitcase packed with clothing Mrs. Gerbati has made for her family. The Gerbatis want Sal to stay with them in Barre. (In an epilogue, the author comments in more detail on the historical figures in the narrative and notes that the black granite for the Vietnam Veterans Memorial in Washington, D.C. was sent to Barre for engraving and polishing. For an adult novel about Italian granite workers in Barre, see Mari Tomasi's *Like Lesser Gods*.)

Leigh Peck

They Were Made of Rawhide (1954) narrates the amazing feat of fourteen-year-old Jed McBride, who rides his mustang, Poco, a buckskin stallion of Arabian blood, sixty miles a day for thirty-five consecutive days to win the endurance race from Galveston to Rutland in 1886. Sixty men and mounts enter the contest in Texas; Jed arrives first in Vermont to win five thousand dollars. His technique is to hold Poco at a slow lope for half an hour and then slow him to a walk for ten minutes. After many adventures with fire and flood, Jed crosses the state line into Vermont and is met by a reception committee, including a local veterinarian and the editor of the *Rutland Herald*. Because Jed is a week ahead of the next contestant, he has time to visit his father in a hospital in Boston and make plans to take him home by train, with Poco in a boxcar. Jed loves Vermont—the rocky hills covered with trees, the stone walls standing without mortar, the farmhouses connected to a series of outbuildings. Hundreds of horse-lovers come to Rutland for the ceremony. With his winnings, Jed can afford to buy a horse ranch in Texas.

Robert Newton Peck

In ***A Day No Pigs Would Die*** (1972), Rob Peck, twelve, lives on a five-acre hillside farm outside Learning near Rutland with his father, Haven, his mother, and his Aunt Carrie. It is the Depression era of Calvin Coolidge, just before the Crash. Rob and his family live by the Book of Shaker: they grow their own food, make their own clothes, consider good manners paramount, and are decent and hardworking. Haven slaughters pigs for Clay Sander. They have an aging ox, Solomon; a cow, Daisy; chickens; and a cat, Miss Sarah. Rob's father speaks infrequently but pithily: "A good neighbor can stand without hitching." Rob is in the field one day when he sees Apron, neighbor Tanner's Holstein, choking while giving birth. Rob wrenches the cow's goiter from her mouth, and Apron delivers two fine twin calves, Bob and Bib. As a reward for Rob's heroic action, Tanner presents him with a pig, "Pinky," which becomes his intimate friend. Mr. Tanner wants to show Bob and Bib, with Rob's help, at the Rutland Fair, where Rob will also show Pinky. Pinky wins a blue ribbon; however, she is barren and has to be slaughtered. Knowing his son's heart is breaking, Haven asks Rob to help him slaughter his pet. It is the only time Rob sees his father wipe away a tear. That night, Haven tells Rob he is dying. Rob, as the man of the house, will care for his mother, his aunt, and the farm. Rob takes charge of the funeral and welcomes many more people than he expected. No pigs will die that day because Haven, the butcher, is being laid to rest.

A Part of the Sky (1997), a sequel to *A Day No Pigs Would Die*, begins two weeks after Haven's funeral. Rob has grown up quickly. Ben and Bess Tanner are his stalwart neighbors. Becky Lee Tate is the girl he likes in his class, but, now that he is the man of the family with many chores to do, he cannot always make it to school. When he goes out with the ox, Solomon, to do the plowing on dewy meadow grass, the twenty-year-old animal falls to the ground and expires. Rob borrows Tanner's pair of oxen to pull the carcass into the woods before his mother and aunt can view poor old Solomon, but they insist on taking turns digging the grave. His mother says a few Shaker words over the body, ending, "The resting of death becomes a part of the land, as clouds are a part of the sky." When it is time to breed Tanner's stallion, Rob misses school to help his neighbor and to earn a dollar. Haskell Gamp brings his mare too early; the stallion breaks his ropes and bites Tanner deeply in the shoulder.

Rob does not mind his manners with Gamp, who is slightly the worse for wear with drink. When Rob goes to the Learning Bank to make the monthly mortgage payment, the president is—Haskell Gamp. He coldly warns Rob it is unlikely a thirteen-year-old will be able to make the payments, including the taxes, on the farm. All the farmers are facing the same desperate fate of foreclosure. When Daisy, the cow, dries up, Rob confers with Tanner, who is healing slowly—"You can't kill a Vermonter. We just wear out like a pair of pants."—and tells him he will have to sell Daisy to Clay Sander for dog meat. His mother and aunt are solid in their support of Rob. "You ladies," he says, "are Vermont granite." "Yoke us," smiles his mother, "and we'll pull." Rob gets a job at Ferguson's Feed and Seed to make a few extra dollars. With no rain and the corn crop dying, Rob, his mother, and his aunt spend the day lugging buckets of water from the creek. Ferguson has to let him go from the store. Rob cannot make the bank payments; it is clear that the bank will foreclose. Ferguson offers him and his family the three rooms above the store in return for Rob's help. Many neighbors assist them in the move. Mr. Ferguson comforts Rob by telling him that "home is where you're cozy close to kinfolks. It isn't land, or timber, or fancy furniture. You Pecks are people, not trees."

Millie's Boy (1973), set in Cornwall in 1898, is about sixteen-year-old, redheaded Titmouse ("Tit") Smith. The bullet that kills Tit's alcoholic prostitute mother, Millie, enters Tit's stomach. Sheriff Gus Tobin finds Tit and saves his life; Tit suspects that Gus once loved his mother. While Tit is recuperating at Gus's house, he sees an application for him to the County Farm; under "mother's name" is written, "Millicent Sabbathday." Tit determines to travel to Ticonderoga to look for his father. When he returns to Cornwall, he will order a tombstone of Vermont marble bearing his mother's real name. Tit walks the eight miles to Shoreham, chased by coydogs and bleeding from his bullet wound. Fern Bodeen rescues and takes him in her wagon on the ice across Lake Champlain to Ticonderoga, where he meets Fern's niece, Amy Hallow, also sixteen, who hopes to go to Middlebury College to be a doctor. He tells Fern his story: "Oh, you're Millie's boy," says Fern. She finds him a job at the Ticonderoga Pulp and Paper Company, where he will haul spruce for George Washington Ostrander, whom the employees of Ti Pulp consider an awesome figure because Indians killed his wife and daughter. Seventeen years earlier Ostrander courted Millie, daughter of John Sabbathday. Tit and Amy, attracted to each other, are soon exchanging kisses, though Fern keeps a stern eye on them. Tit knows Fern did not kill his mother, though she was in Cornwall the night of Millie's death and had a motive. Her sister, Emma, married Hank Hallow and had Amy. When Hank ran off with Millie, Emma tried to follow and froze to death. Tit finally meets Ostrander, who regularly beats his dog, Turk, to train him to be a killer. When Ostrander takes off his hat, Tit (who keeps his on) sees his bright red hair. Tit has no need for a father or a surname to be a whole person; he has found Fern and Amy and is the man of the family. When Ostrander tries to force himself on Amy, Tit engages him in a mortal struggle. Just as Tit feels he has lost to Ostrander, Turk attacks and kills him. Gus is moving to Ticonderoga to run a horse ranch and wants Tit for a partner.

In ***Rabbits and Redcoats*** (1976), Chapter Harrow, sixteen, and his friend, Interest Wheelock, seventeen, sneak away from their homes in Shoreham to join Ethan Allen's assault on Fort Ticonderoga in 1775. Chapter, who is carrying a rabbit gun, aspires to be a journalist like Samuel Adams in Boston, not a farmer like his father. When the boys arrive, Ethan Allen and Benedict Arnold are arguing about who will lead the troops. The boys creep toward the loading boats and are soon rowing across the lake. Landing on the sand, they meet Colonel Allen, who recognizes them and orders them to keep to the rear. Chapter looks up at Fort Ti, which the French built in 1755 and General Amherst later took back from General Montcalm. The boys run into the fort, expecting to be killed at any moment. Chapter captures but does not shoot a redcoat, knowing his parents would be very angry if he were to kill him. They talk to General Arnold, who is looking forward to meeting General Burgoyne's troops. Chapter sees his friend, Peter Geer, also sixteen, who was impressed into the British army and is among the captured British soldiers. Having had a surfeit of fighting, the three boys swim for shore. Two years later, Chapter and Interest attend Peter's wedding to Molly Painter, a girl they both know and like.

Hang for Treason (1976) revisits the seizure of Fort Ticonderoga in a more serious vein. The Bookers live south of Shoreham on Lake Champlain in 1775. Able, seventeen, is a patriot; his father, Noah, born in England and the victim of a massacre in 1745 in which Indians burned to death his parents and sisters, is a Tory. Some of Able's friends join the Green Mountain Boys and talk about "independence"; Noah hopes they all "hang for treason." To trade some animals, Noah and Able walk across the ice to Fort Ticonderoga where they find men building a scaffold. Able's friend, Jake Cotter (whose parents raised Noah after the massacre) is hanged for sedition—stealing a cannon. The Bookers take his body home to his parents. One night, Able sneaks out of the house with Luke Shelby to join the Green Mountain Boys. At the initiation, in which their arms are cut with a knife, they meet Ethan Allen and Seth Warner, who imply that the Boys could have saved Jake's life but knew his death would produce massive numbers of volunteers for the cause. Luther Peacham, a schoolmaster from Harvard, stays with the Bookers on his way to a post at Fort Ticonderoga. Able notices a scar on his arm identical to his own. Noah speaks disparagingly of the Allen brothers, whom he considers self-interested "land grabbers" with their ownership of the Onion River Land Company. Able is in love with Mary Comfort, whose father died in a dispute with the Allens over a land deal. When his sweetheart sees the mark on Able's arm, she gives him an ultimatum—choosing between her and Ethan Allen. One night Able is out on horseback near the lake when he hears the sound of muskets and sees Luther, wounded, trying to row ashore. Able's father removes the bullet from Luther's stomach. Luther manages to pass a plan of Fort Ticonderoga to Able; Able carries the map to Ethan Allen, whom he finds quarreling with Benedict Arnold. Able and Luke are in the first boat to the fort. After the fort is taken, Able looks across the lake to see the Booker barn ablaze. He and Luke quickly row back to confront five men admiring the fire. The boys kill four of them before the fifth shoots Luke in the face. Luther appears in time to save Able's life. Able's horribly burned father, mother, and sisters are dead. Able marries Mary and, when he joins the army, wants to serve under Benedict Arnold.

In ***Justice Lion*** (1981), widower Jess Bolt, a "downhiller" and lawyer in the small town of Liberty, roughly in the center of Addison County, aspires to become a county prosecutor. Justice Lion is an "uproader" on Kipp's Mountain; King George deeded the property to his forebear, Kipp Lion, in 1731. "People in town tend to look down their noses at mountain men." Justice supports his family by running a still, though it is the Prohibition period of 1923. A federal agent arrests him for moonshining (distilling and selling liquor illegally). Almost simultaneously, the current district attorney, promoted to judge, appoints Jess district attorney. Jess accepts the job because he is in debt and needs the money, but this decision puts him in the untenable position of prosecuting his old friend, Justice. Years earlier, Jess defended Justice's son, Drury, on a homicide charge. Complicating matters further, Jess's fifteen-year-old son, Muncie, is the best friend of Justice's son, Hem, and is in love with his daughter, Blessing. The Bolts' beloved housekeeper, Patience Bly, a mother figure to Muncie, supplies sugar to the Lions' still. In the courtroom, Muncie is desperately torn between his loyalty to his father and to the Lions. The town, too, is divided but has suffered many difficulties together: "Vermont barns were akin to Vermont farmers, strong in the beam, built to face up to winter." The young lawyer appointed to defend Justice is brave and bright, but the jury finds Justice guilty. The judge sentences the

P

proud old mountain man to a year in the penitentiary. Infuriated at the result, Hem drives recklessly past the Bolts' house, overturns his wagon, and is killed. Muncie cradles Hem's head in his arms; later, the two families are reunited when Muncie marries Blessing.

The central figure in ***Kirk's Law*** (1981) is Collin Richardson Pepper, fifteen, who lives in Greenwich, Connecticut. An expensive preparatory school recently expelled him. His parents tried sending him to a psychiatrist, but Collin remains angry, short-tempered, arrogant, and lazy. Unwilling to tolerate Collin's behavior any longer, his father drives him to northern Vermont to leave him with his old friend Sabbath ("Wishbone") Kirk. His father tells Collin that he is going to "law school"—Kirk's law—until "you start liking yourself." Collin hates his father. Kirk, an old man whose dog is named Tool, throws some pine boughs on the floor for Collin's bed. The first day they go hunting with Kirk's sixteen gauge shotgun and have an angry encounter over a rabbit with an adjoining landowner, Louis Broom. The next day Kirk and Collin chop wood. When Collin is sarcastic, Kirk observes that when Vermonters say something, they mean it. Collin actually does a hard day's work. After it snows, they go out to kill a deer. It is not hunting season, but they need food. "Up here, Kirk was his own justice." After the deer falls, Tool holds its legs while Kirk cuts its throat with a knife. Kirk, who has twisted his leg, instructs Collin in skinning the dear. The smell makes Collin sick; the job takes all morning. Collin helps Kirk home and returns for the deer meat; Louis has taken it. That night, Collin, armed with gun and knife, follows the dragging trail. Deciding that cutting down the deer would make too much noise, he steals two chickens. Kirk complains that his stomach hurts excruciatingly. Collin, who spent his childhood studying medical books with his surgeon grandfather, examines Kirk and thinks his appendix may be about to burst. When he asks how far it is to a doctor, Kirk tells him he cannot stand the pain and to "get it out." Kirk finds some carbolic acid and sterilizes the knife, spoons, needle, thread, and clothespins. He gives Kirk as much brandy as he can swallow and makes the incision. The appendix is healthy, but Collin drains infected pus from a huge abscess. While Kirk is resting, Collin walks to Miss Biddy's for provisions. Coydogs come after him on the way home, but he makes it to Kirk's cabin. When his parents drop by for a visit, Collin does not mention what he has been through. He does not have to boast: the doing was enough. After his parents leave, Kirk calls him "Collie," the first nickname he has ever had. Kirk and Collin now love and respect each other.

Soup (1974), the first of a series of sixteen stories (two are easy readers), introduces a devilishly clever boy, Luther Wesley Vinson, nine. Soup, as he is known, is Rob Peck's best friend in Miss Kelly's third grade in Learning near Rutland; he has a genius for getting Rob into trouble. Rob lives with his parents and Aunt Carrie. Norma Jean Bissell is the girl Rob loves; Janice Riker is the class bully and prime athlete; Miss Boland is the county nurse and football coach. In each of the stories, Rob and Soup have to be home in time for chores. One day Soup and Rob are "whipping" apples and break a stained glass window in the church. Mrs. Stetson, a stern Baptist, storms up to them; when she tries whipping an apple, she, too, breaks a window. Soup and Rob play a torture game with Janice, tying each other to a tree; Aunt Carrie, a good sport, offers herself as a victim, but for an uncomfortably long time Rob is unable to loosen her bonds. Soup shows Rob how to hollow out an acorn to make a pipe, using cornsilk for tobacco, and teaches Rob that parents are not meant to see or know everything. In need of money to go to a picture show, they add a stone to the tinfoil they are selling to Mr. Diskin at the junkyard. He knows about their trick but gives them two dimes anyway; his generosity makes them feel mean. Soup rolls Rob down Dugan's hill in an old apple barrel; the barrel smashes into Mrs. Biscardi's chicken coop and breaks a number of eggs. Soup is naughty but not a bully, like Eddy Tacker. Eddy torments Rob, who finally fights him. Afterward, Rob's mother buys them ice cream.

In ***Soup & Me*** (1975), Soup persuades Rob to go for a swim in Putt's Pond, even though in May the water is extremely cold. While they are in the water, Janice tosses their clothes in the pond. Stealing some dresses from the Baptist Church charity basket, they reach home. Norma Jean asks Rob to the Spring Dance. Miss Boland brings a Victrola to school so the children can practice. Unfortunately, Norma Jean comes down with chicken pox; Rob finds himself dancing with Janice. After Janice collides with Soup and Rob during her soapbox race, Soup swears revenge. At the dump, he builds a torpedo out of a hot water tank taped to wheels. Unable to steer, the boys miss Janice's car and plow into Mrs. Stetson's vegetable garden. Soup inveigles Rob to let him cut his hair so they can buy bubble gum with Rob's quarter for the barber. They dress up as a pirate and a ghost for the Halloween Party. Soup steals a huge pumpkin from Mr. Sutter's plot, which he pushes in a wheelbarrow to the Baptist Church. The pumpkin eludes them and crashes into a barrel of water, drenching everyone. They are assigned to the clean-up detail. Out in the woods, they catch a Tom turkey. The year before, Ally Tidwell's family ate baloney for Thanksgiving; the boys take the bird to the Tidwells for their holiday meal. At Christmastime, because they have no money to buy Miss Kelly a present, they leave her a note saying they will ring a bell for her at five in the afternoon. Once atop the courthouse steeple, Soup kicks over the ladder by mistake. They are stuck, frozen, and forgotten. Miss Kelly finds them, stands the ladder up, and enables them to descend. Once they are safe, she gives them each a hug and kiss.

Soup for President (1978) begins in the fall of the 1936 national election in which Alf Landon contends with President Roosevelt; Learning is a heavily Republican town. Miss Kelly thinks it would be educational for the class to hold its own election. The fourteen boys, the Apes, nominate Soup; the fourteen girls, the Amazons, choose Norma Jean. Soup borrows a ladder from his Uncle Charlie and persuades Rob, his campaign manager, to paint Soup's name in red on the side of Cyrus McGinley's barn. Norma Jean sends Rob a note: if he votes for her, she will be his girlfriend. McGinley arrives to complain about his barn; he is so deaf he cannot understand Soup's quick explanatory patter. Miss Kelly gently urges the boys to remove the paint. When Rob confesses to Miss Kelly that he loves Norma Jean, she recommends his composing a poem or singing her a song. Soup again borrows the ladder, and the boys rapidly cross the Tinker pasture, chased by a huge billy goat. While they are tangled up in the ladder and the goat's horns, Janice lassos them with an old truck tire to force them to vote for Norma Jean. As they are extricating themselves, they talk about how much they love and admire Miss Kelly. After the votes are counted and Soup wins, he gives Norma Jean a sportsmanlike bow. Rob ponders the results: the number of boys and girls is exactly even. Eureka! He runs over to Norma Jean's house, where she admits she voted for Soup because he is more of a leader than she and, moreover, she wanted Rob's candidate to win. He sings to her under her window.

In ***Soup's Drum*** (1980), Rob and Soup attend a party at Norma Jean's, where they meet her cousin, Juliet Rapture, recently moved to Learning. Soup falls instantly in love. Rob's favorite book is *Ivanhoe*, which Miss Kelly recommended to him. Bringing news that a world-famous French horn player is coming to Vermont, Miss Boland starts a school band to march in the Fourth of July parade. After placing an ad in the paper, she hears from a number of musicians, including a fiddler who plays at square dances in Brandon. Because Soup and Rob need instruments, Soup looks in the Grange where the band uniforms are stored. He spies a huge drum called a "Big Boy" and two wool-headed drumsticks. Carrying the heavy drum will require two people. When not enough musicians sign up, Miss Boland offers as incentive an outstanding display of fireworks. Soup carves his initials, "L.W.V.," and Juliet's, "J.R.," on a tree. Unfortunately, Janice Riker assumes she is the object of Soup's affection. Meanwhile, the band members, especially the senior citizens, squabble about the order of the parade; the Home Guard claims it always marches first. The Super-Sweet Fireworks truck arrives. In the middle of the night, Soup rousts Rob from his bed to rearrange the big letters on the sign held up by wires in center field: I LOVE A SUPER-SWEET FOURTH OF JULY. On the big day, the fire engine leads the way. The band, badly out of step, stumbles onto the field. Everything happens at once. When the letters are ignited, they spell out, SOUP LOVES JULIET.

P

Miss Boland's brainstorm in ***Soup on Wheels*** (1981) is to revive the Children's Costume Contest under a new name, Vermont Mardy Grah (sic), and to invite everyone in town to participate. Norma Jean invites Rob to carry her books, which he considers a hopeful sign until the next day, when a new boy, Beverly Bean, starts flirting with Norma Jean. Rob provokes a fight between Eddy and Beverly, in which Beverly neatly dispatches Eddy. The children are assigned the task of distributing pamphlets about the costume parade to all residents of Learning. Soup, figuring they could save time if everyone were outside in the street, tricks Rob into setting off the fire alarm; the results afford ample opportunity to hand out their publicity. They go fishing while Soup seeks inspiration for their costumes. Deciding they should double up and go as Mrs. McGee's mule, they head for the dump where they collect the necessary items. During another midnight excursion, they pass Miss Boland's house and overhear her and Horace Jubert's plans to dress as a mule. Soup decides the key to winning is their entrance rather than their costume. He proposes that they roller-skate down Main Street hill. Unfortunately, they are unable to stop and collide rather violently with Miss Boland and Mr. Jubert. The latter couple receives third prize; Norma Jean and Beverly, as Raggedy Ann and Andy, win second; and Janice is an easy first as a gorilla.

Soup and Rob aspire to be cowboys in ***Soup in the Saddle*** (1983). They borrow a saddle from McGinley's barn and, in a neighboring pasture, pick out a big black horse to ride. The owner, Mr. Carlotta, makes them dismount from Thunderbolt, a former racehorse whose competitive spirit is spurred by ingesting applejack. In Miss Kelly's class the next day, Miss Boland reports that the school board has proclaimed the following Wednesday "Miss Kelly Day" to celebrate her thirty years' service and has invited Vermont's favorite cowboy, Hoot Holler, as special guest. On their way to collect some applejack, Soup and Rob stop to visit Miss Boland, who is depressed that the school board has chosen Dr. Elsa Pinkerton Uppit to speak at the celebration. Uppit, the "sworn enemy of Vermont's one-room schools," aims to effect Miss Kelly's dismissal. Soup formulates a prank, with Miss Boland as co-conspirator. The boys will ask Reed Wilson to donate some paint—pink and a sickly shade of green. Miss Boland will check certain information with Doc Witherspoon. They list other items they need. The boys trick Janice into painting Miss Boland's car pink. In the middle of the night, Soup prints signs saying "Pox," which Rob tacks on trees. On the day of the celebration, Miss Boland, wearing a flamingo-pink wig, is the image of Dr. Uppit. She is too nervous to write her speech, so Soup obliges. Word comes that Dr. Uppit is half an hour ahead of schedule. Soup and Rob drag the applejack, saddle, and blanket to Mr. Carlotta's pasture. After giving Thunderbolt a jolt of hard cider, they mount up and take off at a rapid clip. After painting little green spots on their faces, they stop Dr. Uppit's car to warn her of an epidemic in Learning. Deciding to ride Thunderbolt in the parade, they find themselves in the lead. Miss Boland gives an impassioned speech; Miss Kelly guesses her identity but does not give her away. As punishment, Mr. Carlotta makes the boys clean out his horse stalls.

In ***Soup's Goat*** (1984), Soup's cousin, Sexton Dilly, is visiting for two weeks. Sexton, who goes to a religious school in Burlington, does not want to play any of the games they suggest; he prefers to swear, charging a penny for each performance. At school, Miss Boland makes her customary arrival, this time with a little white goat to publicize Pet Week. She plans a goat-cart race for some of the children. The five winners of the draw are Ally, Janice, Eddy, Soup, and Rob. The children hurry to Arno Fletcher's Billy-the-Kid Goat Farm to pick out their pets. The goats Rob and Soup choose are twins, Nesbit and Orbit, one mean, one nice. Even more exciting news is relayed: Dr. Frank Sumatra, a leading authority on goats and a world explorer, is coming to Learning to preside over Goat Day. Miss Boland lugs her tuba to school to teach the children Dr. Sumatra's favorite song, "A Tropical Moon and You." Since Rob and Soup are forced to entertain Sexton, they take him to the goat farm where they pick up the valuable information that Orbit and Nesbit, once circus performers, escaped from a burning tent while the band played, "A Tropical Moon and You." Janice has finished her goat cart by the time Rob and Soup head for the dump. Soup's plan is to build one cart for the twins to pull because they behave better in tandem. Soup and Rob sneak out at night to practice the song. Sexton threatens to blackmail them, so they include him in the plan. The race begins. When Orbit and Nesbit hear the song, they run so fast that Sexton begins to swear. He sounds so much like a duck (goats are afraid of ducks) that the twins run even faster. Soup and Rob win the race and, in the process, befriend Sexton.

It is December in ***Soup on Ice*** (1985) and intensely cold; Soup and Rob reluctantly go to school, wrapped by their mothers in many layers of clothing. They are thinking about Christmas presents: both of them fervently want an Official Buck Jones Daisy Repeater BB Gun. Miss Boland bursts into the classroom with special news about Christmas festivities. This year, lights will hang from branches of the giant spruce on the village green, every boy and girl will receive a present, and Santa Claus will come to town. Everyone cheers except Ally Tidwell, who does not believe in Santa Claus because his father left home, and his mother is poor. Soup and Rob are shoveling sidewalks when some mean children throw snowballs at Ally and his mother. Thinking Soup and Rob are the malefactors, Stanley ("Slosh") Dubinsky, owner of the pool parlor, chases them, shouting his usual obscenities. In his Christmas composition, Rob wishes for an improved life for the Tidwells. Softhearted Miss Kelly welcomes the badly spelled and illegible essay. When the boys hear that Joe Sutter, the perennial Santa Claus, has broken a leg, they consult Miss Boland about substitutes. They narrow down their choice to—Slosh. Miss Boland delegates them to recruit him. After much cursing, he agrees. Soup, as always, has a plan, which involves, as always, sneaking out of their houses at night. They need Sutter's red Santa suit, as well as a sleigh and a number of articles whose purpose is known only to Soup. As always, Soup obtains Rob's cooperation by telling him how impressed Norma Jean will be by their scheme—whatever it is. On Christmas Eve, the tree lights are turned on (although no one can make them twinkle); everyone is waiting. Soup has fashioned a sail on the sleigh made from a pole-framed horse blanket, so the boys and Slosh can arrive at the ceremony in style. They sail down the hill and onto a treacherous sledding path. Unable to steer, they hit the tree head on and blow out every light. After a wild explosion, the lights start to twinkle. It is a joyful time, and Slosh, who buys a BB gun for Ally, bids everyone call him Uncle Stanley.

As usual, Janice is after Soup and Rob in ***Soup on Fire*** (1987), this time armed with a rope, so they hide behind Horace Jubert's candy store. When she corners them, they climb to the top of the water tower. They remove their apparel to take a quick dip, giving Janice the opportunity to run off with their clothes. When they descend, Sheriff Dillon Blood is waiting at the bottom to point out the rotten and dangerous supports. At the movies the next Saturday, they watch their hero, Fearless Ferguson, in *Cliffhanger*. Listening to the radio at Soup's house, they hear that the Hollywood Heartburn Talent Show, sponsored by Bathsheba Bubble Bath, is coming to Learning to scout movie talent and bringing Fearless. Mrs. Stetson has more news for Miss Kelly's classroom. The same weekend, Bishop Zion Zeal, revivalist, is featuring the Golden Prophets of Eternal Glory choir. Every child must learn to sing, "Rescued from the Burning Flames." All parents hope their children catch the eye of the talent scouts. Soup, of course, has an idea; Rob, of course, demurs, only to be told that this is the way to Norma Jean's heart. Soup proposes they attract attention not as actors but as stuntmen. They find an old garbage wagon at Wilber Wynfield's Wagon Repair Shop. On a midnight excursion, they steal some hay from Janice's parents and fill the wagon. They borrow two large dogs from Soup's mother's cousin. On the appointed day, all the film-star aspirants are there. Hollywood Heartburn arrives, informing the crowd that Fearless is too bashful to emerge from the car. Just as Soup and Rob hitch up the dogs to the wagon, Janice tosses a lighted match into the hay. Fearless quickly sits up. The three of them race down the hill, their wagon on fire. The dogs break away; the wagon is headed for the water tower. They hit a corner of a rotten tower leg, and the giant tank tips and falls to combine effectively with a large receptacle filled with a mountain of bubble bath.

Soup's Uncle (1988) is Vi Burdock, a member of the Hardboilers, one of the largest motorcycle clubs in Vermont, which plans a Beer Belly Blowout in Learning. Soup and Rob climb to the top of a barn roof to watch the cyclists ride into town. Janice removes the ladder. While hiding in the barn, belonging to Micah Tightknicker, they find many jars of colorless liquid. Soup is formulating a plan, which is always bad news for Rob. Uncle Vi takes them for a ride on his bike and then to Swill's Hole, an unsavory tavern belonging to Swill McEnroe. Members of The Leatherettes, a woman's motorcycle club, are there; Uncle Vi falls in love with Tacky Lugwench. Soup hustles Rob to the dump, where he is looking for shoes—or, more precisely, shoe soles. They realize Uncle Vi is seeking bootlegged liquor (it is Prohibition), and the jars in Micah's barn are filled with whiskey. Soup wakes Rob in the middle of the night to prevent Uncle Vi from stealing the jars. Soup has glued many soles to his own shoes to make his legs long enough to drive Uncle Vi's motorcycle. The two boys take a shortcut through the woods and arrive in time to dump the liquor onto the ground and fill the jars with water. They now understand why Micah is so rich; they are performing a community service. They believe no one will ever know they have been there, but Janice throws a cherry bomb at them. Soup notes that the alcohol is running downhill toward Janice and her cherry bombs. The ensuing explosion catapults her into the pigpen. The day of the Beer Belly Blowout arrives. Swill beats up Uncle Vi, accusing him of watering the liquor. Uncle Vi renounces drinking as well as the day's event. Soup and Rob enter the ramp-jump contest disguised as Uncle Vi, riding his motorcycle: Rob sits on Soup's back and steers, with a long duster coat covering them. Landing on the refreshment table, they win; they give the prize money to Uncle Vi to buy a ring for his fiancée, Tacky.

For a change, Miss Boland has bad news for the children of Miss Kelly's class in ***Soup's Hoop*** (1990): Shorty Smith, Learning's basketball center, has sprained his ankle. How can their team beat Pratt Falls? Just as Soup and Rob tack up Soup's hoop as a basketball basket, the Braunschweiger twins, Boris and Lavoris, janitor and plumber respectively, drive up. They are comparatively short, but with them is an excessively tall man, Piffle Shootensinker, who is from Pretzelstein. He cannot make a basket unless inspired by music played by a spitzentootle on the truck radio. Thus Soup's plan is born. He and Rob descend into Soup's cellar to extract the keyboard from an instrument called a "melodeon." Next they head for the Braunschweigers' shop for various pieces of cleaning and plumbing equipment. Soup creates a contraption from a large hot-water tank, consisting of punched holes stuffed with lengths of garden hose ending in rubber cups wired to the keyboard levers of the melodeon. The whole apparatus is connected to a vacuum cleaner plugged into an outlet by extension cords. They will cart it to the locker room to assist Piffle win the game. Soup would also like to procure a sheepdog to assuage Piffle's homesickness for his dog, Adolph. To that end, Soup manufactures a molasses trap, a box filled with wool, into which they lure Janice with a "free candy" sign. The day of the game dawns—the Pratt Falls Wombats versus the Learning Groundhogs. Soup and Rob disguise themselves as Boris and Lavoris, wearing white coveralls with bits of molasses and fuzzy wool for hair, and are admitted free to the game. The Groundhogs are losing until Soup plays the machine while Rob sings a song they composed. This performance inspires Piffle to make a basket. The score is even. Janice arrives covered with molasses-stuck wool, looking enough like Adolph for Piffle to hook his shot just as the gun goes off. Unfortunately, at that moment the ticket taker turns off the lights for Miss Boland's show of sparklers. When the lights go on, there is the ball, stuck in the hoop. Learning wins. Lightning strikes; the spitzentootle shoots into the stadium with Rob, Soup, and Janice aboard. They—and the Drano flame heating the water—crash into a large box belonging to the Dixie Fireworks Company. Everyone thinks the ensuing explosion is part of Miss Boland's display.

Trapped by Janice in a snowy alley in ***Soup in Love*** (1992), Soup and Rob are rescued by Joe Spazzatura, owner of Joe's Diner and Diesel Fuel Shop, who has the largest heart in Learning but, due to the Depression, the fewest customers. Joe happens to be in the alley because his new refrigerator has just arrived; Soup asks if he may keep the big crate. Miss Boland makes her usual enthusiastic entrance to describe her plans for Valentine's Day: everyone is to make a red heart—any size—to hang around town. Norma Jean invites Rob and Soup to meet a newly arrived family: the big brother is Ox Heartburn; his twin sisters are Quickie and Trickie. Soup immediately falls in love with both girls. Ox, conveniently, is taken with Janice. Soup, of course, develops a scheme for Valentine's Day and drags Rob to the dump to collect items. Soup has already figured out where the giant candy canes from last year's Valentine's Day are stored. Rob quickly grasps the plan: Soup will set the big box filled with the valentines on the two candy-cane toboggans. They will push and then steer the sled down Duggan's Hill. It is clear, the minute they start sliding, that they will crash. Thousands of valentines float into the air. The railroad car holding Joe's diner moves with them, hitting a paint factory; red paint frosts the surrounding snow and roofs. Soup wins first prize; Joe has a new and more propitious location.

Soup Ahoy (1994) presents Soup and Rob with the opportunity to meet their favorite radio-program hero, Sinker O. Sailer, whose Rutland-based station offers a personal visit from Sinker to the school that mails in the most box tops from the advertiser's breakfast cereal. Soup and Rob discover that Mr. Jubert feeds the cereal to his pet goat and will trade box tops in exchange for their feeding the goat until the cereal is used up. Soup and Rob win the contest; Miss Boland plans an elaborate picnic for Sinker near Wet Lake, where rumor has it a treasure—a black pearl—is buried. Soup has an idea, always hair-raising news for Rob, and hurries to the dump to fashion a diving suit for Rob, who dives and finds a large black ball on the bottom of the lake. Soup ingeniously creates a boat out of spare parts to convey Sinker to the picnic. The radio-station vehicle arrives with Sinker, who does not look as they had imagined. In fact, when they haul him aboard their boat, he confesses he is neither sailor nor swimmer. He also concedes the black pearl is his lost bowling ball. As they bring him to the celebratory picnic, the broadcast begins. The reporter covers the attack by pirates (Janice and Eddy in a rowboat), Rob and Soup's exciting plummet down Suicide Flume (they forgot a steering wheel), and their stunning entrance into the picnic. Sinker impresses everyone so much that the studio renews his contract.

In ***Soup 1776*** (1995), Miss Kelly's class is studying the American Revolution. For the next Fourth of July, Miss Boland plans a reenactment of the battle held at Learning in 1776. Some dispute whether the founder, patriot Disability Learning, or the redcoats won the battle. While feeding a carrot to Insanity Wacko's mule, Crazy Horse, Soup thinks of an even better idea: he and

Rob will write the script for the pageant, seeking the help of old Mr. Wacko, whose father fought in the American Revolution. Mr. Wacko tells Soup and Rob the villagers changed the name of the founder, Ability Learning, because he proved too cautious a leader. Miss Boland throws herself into planning for the pageant, which she calls "Battle Victory Day." She rehearses the Learning Colonial Marching Fife and Drum Corps at the Grange Hall and posts sign-up sheets for residents to choose parts as patriots or redcoats. The boys spend time in the Learning Free Library researching their pageant script. Miss Boland's brother, Buttercup, a professional wrestler, will play Disability Learning; his long-time enemy, Sharpton Dullard, will take the role of British Colonel Doughboy-Pillsbury. Mr. Wacko will play Sitting Duck, chief of the Wahooligans, with Miss Boland as his squaw, and Buttercup's ladylove, Freebee Cookysheet, as his daughter, Wet Blanket. Dr. P.H. (for "Pan Handle") Dee, who wrote the class's history book, comes to Learning for the celebration. Soup and Rob make sure he does not stay long, suspecting he will not approve of the liberties they have taken with the historical facts. Soup wants to kidnap him, but Rob tells the whole story to Dr. Dee, who takes the next train out of town. The cast members arrive in costume and extemporize. Soup and Rob ride into the fray on Crazy Horse. Soup mistakenly tosses an improvised, lit pipe into the mouth of the cannon, which fires, recoils, and demolishes the statue of Disability Learning. Mr. Wacko offers to rebuild the statue and, in so doing, regains the respect of the community.

The heroine of ***Trig*** (1977) and its sequels, *Trig Sees Red*, *Trig Goes Ape*, and *Trig or Treat,* is Elizabeth Trigman, an eight-year-old, bespectacled tomboy who lives in Clodsburg. Her greatest wish is to play Cops and Robbers with Tyrone ("Bud") Griffin and Samuel ("Skip") Warner. When her Uncle Fred from Burlington brings her a Melvin Purvis official Junior G-Man machine gun, she changes her name to "Trig." With her new toy gun, which makes an appalling sound when the trigger is pulled, she forms a gang with Bud and Skip. The boys squeeze off a burst at Trig's Aunt Alice. The loud, stuttering noise flings Aunt Alice out of the hammock, which the children consider a spectacular outcome. (Melvin Purvis, 1903-1960, joined the FBI in 1927 and captured more public enemies than any other FBI agent in history.)

In ***Trig Sees Red*** (1978), Trig and her cohorts, Bud and Skip, learn that Pop Copperskittle, Clodsburg's only policeman, has lost his job after directing traffic at Six Corners for over fifty years. He remembers the occasion of Trig's birth and that of her mother's. Mayor Swagg installs a traffic light; unfortunately, when he pulls the switch, he blows out the electricity all over Clodsburg. Seeking revenge for Pop's dismissal, Trig dreams up a plan. The following Tuesday is Swagg Day—the day that Iscariot Swagg fired off the town cannon to warn the settlement of the arrival of the British. Mayor Swagg, an enthusiastic bowler, receives in the mail a bright red bowling ball, which he stows in the trunk of his car. On Swagg Day, the mayor prepares to shoot off the cannon. He pours in a generous amount of powder. While his attention is elsewhere, the children steal the bowling ball, drop it into the mouth of the cannon, and adjust its aim. When lit and fired, the ball destroys the new traffic light; Pop regains his old job.

In ***Trig Goes Ape*** (1980), Trig, with her Junior G-man gun, is still leader of the trio with Skip and Bud. The children are excited because Buck Fargo's Wild Ape & Monkey Show is coming to Clodsburg. As everyone knows, the main attraction is Gloria the Gorilla. They head for Mr. Goucher's pasture to shoot off the gun in the direction of his mule, Evelyn. Aroused by the noise, Evelyn gallops toward them, seizes the gun in her jaws, and runs off. The mayor arrives at the ballpark to oversee the construction of a chicken-wire enclosure to contain the visiting animals. The day Buck Fargo's train is due, Miss Millerton brings a picnic lunch to school and excuses the children for the afternoon. The Jessups' chickens are loose because their fencing was used for the apes and monkeys. Trig overhears someone say that mules are afraid of chickens. When the three children herd hundreds of chickens into Mr. Goucher's pasture, Evelyn drops the gun and flees, the chickens right on her tail. The Clodsburg Trombone Assembly marches out, resplendent in uniform, followed by Gloria the Gorilla, who is sleepy and uninteresting. Then Evelyn the mule enters the arena followed by hundreds of chickens. When Gloria jumps on Evelyn's back, the mule begins to buck. The monkeys escape. With the scene out of control, Trig squeezes the trigger on her gun. After the alarming noise, everything is quiet.

Halloween is approaching in ***Trig or Treat*** (1982), and in celebration the First Baptist Church plans a Book of Judges Pageant. The three starring roles are awarded to Skip (Samson), Bud (Gideon), and Trig (Delilah). At rehearsals, Trig worries about not being sufficiently beautiful for the part, although she looks forward to cutting off Skip's curls. At the dump, Trig and Skip collect empty bottles for recycling at the general store in order to buy a vial of perfume. For a costume, she borrows an outfit from Countess Harem's Exotic Appearance Parlor. Still, she is not satisfied that she has done enough. Bud shows her a Jean Harlow platinum blonde wig in the window of Countess Harem's shop. Trig invites Countess Harem to the pageant in exchange for the loan of the wig. The pageant is a chaotic disaster, but the audience thinks it is hilarious. When the spotlight finds Trig, she is lying on pillows, arrayed in her costume, drenched in perfume, bewigged, and wearing a large pair of sunglasses.

Elizabeth Stuart Phelps

The eponymous twelve-year-old heroine in ***Gypsy Breynton*** (1866), christened Jemima, is known as "Gypsy." She and her elder brother, Thomas ("Tom"), sixteen, and younger brother, Winthrop ("Winnie"), five, live with their mother and father, a publisher and bookseller, in Yorkbury near Ripton. The period is the Civil War (Mrs. Breynton mentions "the poor freedmen who are coming into our armies"). Near their house is Kleiner Berg (in Vermont, there are "plenty of mountains"). Gypsy is kind-hearted, truthful, generous, demonstrative, and imaginative; however, her parents often fault her for not thinking before she acts; she is ever remorseful after a misdeed and vows to improve. Her antics are frequently a trial to her pretty young teacher, Miss Melville, whom she adores; after chiding her, Miss Melville always whispers "one or two little loving words of encouragement." Their father keeps a boat at Kleiner Berg Basin, a small body of water; Tom, "as a Vermont boy," thinks that the trout brooks in the mountains are preferable for fishing. Gypsy loves reading—her favorites are the Little Prudy books. One day, when Gypsy and her friend, Sarah Rowe, are playing in the apple tree, Gypsy jumps down and accidentally breaks her father's beloved garden statue. Aghast, she hurries to inform him of her carelessness; he, like her mother, is firm but understanding and appreciates her willingness to confess. On her way home, she is startled to hear a groan issuing from one of the mill workers' tenements. She finds an old lady, Grandmother Littlejohn, with a broken ankle, who claims she has had no supper. Softhearted Gypsy tells her mother, who is well known for making the rounds of the tenements with her basket filled with blancmange, jellies, biscuit, and dried beef. Mrs. Breynton gently explains to Gypsy the way she and her neighbors coordinate their efforts to assist the needy. One evening, Gypsy forgets her turn to carry a meal to Mrs. Littlejohn; she hastens to the old woman's bedside to apologize. The next day, Gypsy's mother sends her with a magazine to the bedside of Peace Maythorne, a sixteen-year-old crippled in a mill accident. Gypsy is charmed and inspired by Peace's serenity of spirit; they become great friends. The highpoint of the summer is a camping trip to Ripton, led by Guy Hallam, a lawyer friend (and Miss Melville's fiancé), and Tom, with Gypsy and Sarah as eager acolytes. They pass through pine forests, "dense and still, where the wind was hoarse." Far above are the "sentinel trees, called by Vermonters the Procession of Pines." Guy and Tom go fishing, instructing the girls to stay in camp. Wandering off, the girls return to find the camp deserted. They wait, frightened, until they hear a sound of "quick panting breath." Gypsy seizes Tom's gun; Sarah jostles her arm and the weapon discharges. She hears a human cry—her brother's. Horrified, she rushes toward the approaching figure and collapses into Tom's arms. He is unhurt, but they are both shaken by the close call. At home, her parents, though stern, express faith that Gypsy will learn by experience and, as always, comfort her with their love and support. (In Ralph Waldo Emerson's poem, *The Adirondacks*, he writes, "Or in the evening twilight's latest red,/Beholding the procession of the pines.")

Georgiana Philips

Having a beautiful, divorced, thirty-two-year-old mother, Caroline, is a great trial to Rosalind Henry, nine, and her little brother, Charlie, in ***Summer of Good Hope*** (1939). They pray Caroline will remarry while she is still young enough to have another baby. Many men are attracted to her, but she does not reciprocate. When Caroline takes the children to a summer colony at a lake near Brandon, the children are pleased that Weldon Harris, a commercial artist, comes to visit. Weldon is very handsome, they think, and a most suitable candidate. Rosalind loves words, rereads *Little Women* and other Alcott books, and plans to be a writer. Unexpectedly, their father, Ned, a remarried reporter, arrives to stay at the inn but take his meals at their cottage. Rosalind often falls asleep listening to the grownups' conversations. She tries to follow the slick, sophisticated exchanges, full of allusions she does not understand; she is accustomed to hearing her socialist mother talk about the poor and unemployment. Rosalind hears Caroline call Weldon's friends "crisp and brittle" and claim Weldon is not serious about social issues. Weldon returns to New York. A new man appears on their dock—Luce Delaney, fired from the Harvard faculty, Rosalind learns, for having leftist tendencies. Encouraged by this news, Rosalind swims out to the float to meet Luce and practice her new vocabulary words. That night while in bed Rosalind is startled to overhear her father say that he regrets not wanting children when he was first married and would remarry Caroline if she would have him back. Rosalind, dazzled by Luce's charm and good looks, falls down the float stairs and has to stay in bed for several days. She contentedly rereads her favorite books, *Black Beauty* and *Alice's Adventures in Wonderland*. Luce talks to her in a grownup way. She knows Luce is interested in Caroline but hears him say he would not want children because of his way of life as a communist. Luce realizes that Caroline is seeing him on the rebound and really loves Weldon. When Weldon returns, the children are delighted: he says he would be pleased to have a baby with their mother.

Ethel Calvert Phillips

In ***Calico*** (1937), Farmer Drake, who lives at Rocky Farm half way up Old Moody Mountain near the hamlet of Little Turkey, purchases a black-and-white spotted pony from a ranch out West. Frisky and adventurous, Calico runs away to the Hatfields' house. Roxy Hatfield, eight, is enchanted with Calico, who performs several tricks for her, standing on his hind legs and turning around in circles. Mr. Hatfield's great friend, Mr. Pope, asks if his son, Oliver, may stay with them indefinitely while Mr. Pope is in Europe. The Hatfields rent Calico and a little green cart to entertain the children. Oliver, a pale boy from New York City, grows as brown and healthy as a country boy. He drives the cart carefully. One day when everyone is away, Roxy invites the Peters children to go for a ride in the cart. They venture too far because she cannot turn the cart around. When they finally reach home, Calico is lame. Her parents are cross with Roxy, who understands her misdeed. At Christmastime, everyone from Little Turkey is invited to the Hatfields' house. The children decorate the Christmas tree with gingerbread animals. After the Peters children contract mumps and are quarantined, Oliver loads the presents and the tree on the sled, which Calico pulls to the sick children's house. Sap is rising in the maple trees; Roxy explains the sugaring process to Oliver. When it rains hard, water rises in the cellar. The brook sweeps the bridge away. The electricity goes down, as do the telephone wires. Since the Hatfields' house is on the highest ground, Captain Daggett rows the Pooles to them in his boat. But who can rescue the Peters family? "Calico and I," says Oliver. He and Calico fetch the members one by one. Oliver is so attached to Calico that he writes to his father in England, asking him to buy the pony. The circus comes to town. Calico's original circus trainer recognizes him. The Hatfields allow Calico to march in the parade with his old partner, Fanny the monkey, on his back. Calico performs in the center of the ring. Mr. Pope cables his permission for Mr. Hatfield to purchase Calico for Oliver and Roxy.

Roberta Piper

Little Red (1963) is about Nan Coburn, eight, who intensely wants a pony. With the county fair a week away, her grandfather offers to buy her a pony if she receives one hundred and ten percent on her arithmetic. Fortunately, her teacher, Miss Dunbar, agrees to add ten percent for "neatness" to her score. Nan chooses Little Red, two years old and not fully broken; her grandfather persuades the owner to throw in a used saddle, bridle, and halter. On their first ride, Little Red, frightened by two pigeons flying into his face, bucks Nan into the mud. She swears never to ride him again. Her father and grandfather make her remount. Her intermittent best friend in third grade, Jean Ross, is not interested in Nan's pony, saying that she herself has won a gold cup. Each time Nan rides Little Red, she feels less frightened. Jean comes over to try riding Little Red. When she falls off, she blames Nan and screams at her. Rebecca, a classmate who lives out in the country, passes by at that moment and offers to hold Little Red. It seems Jean lied about having won a horse show. In winter, Little Red does not exercise sufficiently and breaks a few windowpanes in the barn. Nan worries about her grandfather, who may have pneumonia. He has "always been there. He was a part of her life." When her father, a dairy farmer, comes down with a cold, too, Nan helps with many of the harder chores. Spring comes. Little Red is frisky, but grandfather shows Nan how to flick a leather quirt (a rawhide whip or lash). Her father asks her to check the cover on the pasture spring. When she becomes frustrated with Little Red, she overuses the whip; the pony kicks her, teaching her an important lesson. One day she rides Little Red up to Brookford, where Rebecca lives. Her parents are poor: her father had an accident in the hayloft and now uses a wheelchair. Nan learns that Jean and Rebecca are very different as friends. "Playing with Rebecca was like picking violets." Bob Connor teaches Nan how to jump her pony. When she attempts too high a jump, she realizes she is responsible for what might happen to herself and her pony. School starts; Nan comes down with mumps. While ambulatory, she entertains herself by cleaning a pony cart in the carriage house. When well, she takes Jean for a ride. On the way, Nan picks up Rebecca, who is walking home with a bag of groceries. Jean makes fun of Rebecca's second-hand dress. Rebecca retorts she is not ashamed of being poor; perhaps she would not have to wear used clothes if Jean's father had paid his bill for the wood her father cut before he was hurt. Jean is shocked and shamed into apologizing. Nan is growing in her understanding of people, but she is also growing in size: she is too big to ride Little Red. She cries because everything is changing. Her parents and grandfather have already thought through the problem: they propose buying her Plum, a Morgan mare, and selling Little Red to Bob Connor for his brother; Nan can visit her pony whenever she wants. She takes Little Red on one more ride to Rebecca's. There she thinks of lending Little Red to Rebecca, who is small enough to ride him. Rebecca is the one who deserves the pony.

Dorothy Pitkin

The Grass Was That High (1959) introduces Clarissa ("Kit") Harris, sixteen, who comes from Greenwich, Connecticut, with her parents, Lance and Jan, to spend summer vacation in Seaver Hill near Pomfret at a tenant house on the Clay family dairy farm. Lance, a college professor, is exhausted and depressed. Kit misses her sailboat on the Long Island Sound and finds nothing to do in Seaver Hill. Once Kit meets the Clay family—

parents John and Elva; Jettson, seventeen; Lorry, ten; and Chad, eight—she embraces their farm life. Jettson shows her the way down a cliff to a ledge with a cave bearing an Indian legend on its wall. They look out over the property, owned by the Clays except for a disputed forty acres where the widow Maddox, her older son, Aurelius, and some younger children dwell. Jettson confides to Kit that he wants to be an aviator, not a farmer. Sparkle, the cow, gives birth to a bull calf, which Kit names "Hilltop." When she learns that Jettson's father plans to destroy the calf, she buys him—half for cash, half for chores. Jettson teaches her how to take care of Hilltop. She works as she has never worked before; the summer is slipping away. Jettson announces that Hilltop is good enough to show at the Buxton Parish Show. If he wins a ribbon, his value will be assured; he will not be slaughtered. Kit is suffused with love for the Jettson family and their way of life: she knows now that she wants to be a farmer. Her friend, Alison ("Allie") Wainwright, arrives for a visit. On a picnic, they glimpse the Maddox children, Aurelius and his sister. Kit learns of the long-standing grudge between the Maddoxes and the Clays. Allie, who does not understand Kit's new interests, calls the Clays "narrow, ignorant country people." Still, Allie flirts with Jettson, making Kit jealous. Allie coquettishly arrays herself for the square dance; she and Jettson spend the whole evening together. Kit is so hurt that she calls him "a hayseed" and "a hillbilly" and flounces out of the hall. When she checks the barn, Hilltop is not in his stall. Despite a raging storm, Kit looks for him and finds that, frightened by a bobcat, he has fallen onto the ledge. She climbs down to comfort him. Jettson kills the bobcat and helps Kit haul the calf by rope up the hill. Then he stalks away, stony-faced. She later learns that Aurelius let the calf out, but Jettson and Aurelius had a fight and resolved the feud. She is ashamed of hurting Jettson: it was a "stupid mistake." She spends the night before the fair in Hilltop's stall. Jettson joins her there. He enrolls at the University of Vermont's agricultural school. Kit and Hilltop win the trophy. Afterward, Jettson tells Kit he wants to buy Hilltop, even though she offers to give him the animal. Her parents decide to spend the following summer at the Clay place.

In the sequel, ***Wiser than Winter*** (1960), Kit returns to Seaver Hill two years later to spend the winter with the Clay family and attend the local high school while her parents are abroad. She is still attracted to Jettson, now at the University of Vermont. Kit befriends Miklos ("Mike") Kovacsky, a displaced person and orphan from Hungary (the narrative is set after the revolution of 1956), who lives with the local minister and works for the Clays. Jettson is brusque and unpleasant with Mike, who is unhappy and unpopular at school; Kit, also an outsider, must choose between being "popular" with influential students like Serena Applegate or siding with Mike. Some of the town residents are prejudiced against Mike, who, Mr. Applegate says, is "a 'Hunky' taking a job that could be held by an American," and toward his friend, Aurelius, whom some consider inferior because he is from "up back." Kit notices a change in Jettson, who proudly tells her he killed a buck; she still believes herself in love with him and continues to aspire to own a farm. At school, the English teacher, Mrs. McCracken, stages the annual Christmas pageant, *The Miracle*. She casts Kit as Mary and tall, handsome Mike as Melchior, one of the Magi. Mike, because he is homesick and lonely, perversely acts superior and misses rehearsals. Mike and Aurelius, drawn together by their loner status, build a cabin from an abandoned woodchopper's hut, where Mike, a budding naturalist, keeps his drawings, including a portrait of Kit, whom he loves. In order to persuade Mike to practice for the play, Kit asks him to the school dance, even though she wants to invite Jettson. After the play, Jettson tells her that he is going to the Air Force Academy and asks her to marry him when they are older. Mike sees them together and stalks angrily away; Kit feels she has betrayed Mike and realizes how much he means to her. When Elva goes into labor, John takes her to the hospital, leaving Kit with the two younger boys. She would never have been able to handle the household and the animals in a sudden, fierce storm if Mike had not immediately come to help. At last he and Kit kiss and express the way they feel about each other. Now he is at ease and accepted by people at school, even by Mr. Applegate, who approves his application to the Young Citizens of Vermont Foundation for a scholarship to Middlebury College. Jettson leaves for the Air Force Academy in Colorado Springs. Kit realizes that, at her young age, she does not have to choose between these two fine young men.

Eliza F. Pollard

The protagonist in ***Liberty or Death*** (1909) is Dick ("Wild Dick") Boscowen, seventeen, son of Roger ("the Ranger") Boscowen of the Marshlands, an old comrade of Seth Warner's and one of the first settlers in the New Hampshire Grants. Ethan Allen comes from Bennington to Seth's log hut, White Farm, in the mountains, with news that Yorker sheriffs plan to evict another early settler, John Brakenridge (spelled Breakenridge elsewhere). Charles Langlade, whose wife was killed in the Indian Wars, also lives in the Marsh Settlement. Seth courts Charles's sister, Susan, and they marry. Dick's parents grant him permission to join the Green Mountain Boys; his childhood Indian friend, Jim, accompanies him. After the Green Mountain Boys punish the sheriff's men with the "beech seal" (a whipping with green beech strips), Governor William Tryon outlaws them with a price on their heads. John Munro, a Yorker from Albany, approaches Remember Baker's house to do him harm. Remember's daughter, Mary, escapes to White Farm to bring help (and falls in love with Dick). Captain Ethan Allen leads one section of the Green Mountain Boys; Dick is attached to the other group, headed by Seth Warner. The redcoats are on the road to Concord in 1775; Ethan Allen takes Dick first to Boston, where they meet figures like patriot Samuel Adams, and then to a session to plan the surprise capture of Fort Ticonderoga. Dick is also at Bunker Hill with General Israel Putnam, where he saves the life of Colonel John Stark's son. The Green Mountain Boys choose as their leader Seth Warner, whom they esteem as prudent, well educated, and Christian; some find Ethan impetuous and irreverent. Ethan undertakes an expedition to Montreal with five hundred men. Dick escapes, wounded, but the British capture Ethan and some of his men and take them to England. Seth Warner, Charles Langlade, and Dick all join in the seizure of Quebec under General Richard Montgomery. Every man pins a white paper to his cap inscribed, "liberty or death." Charles is killed; Jim saves Dick's life. The Army of the North retreats from Canada, many sick and without adequate clothes or provisions. Congress accepts the Declaration of Independence on July 4, 1776. Dick's father receives a command in New Hampshire; Dick will serve as a ranger under Colonel Stark. The story ends with the Battle of Bennington, after which the patriots, "husbandmen not warriors," go home to their farms. (The author changes several historical facts to suit her story; for example, Seth Warner married Hester Hurd; it was Remember Baker's son, Ozi, who went for help.)

Eleanor H. Porter

The title character in ***Pollyanna*** (1913) is Pollyanna Whittier, eleven, a brave, charming orphan who goes to Beldingsville to live with her autocratic Aunt Polly Harrington. Though only forty, Aunt Polly is a cross old maid living alone in her large, ancient house. Her helpers are Nancy, a hired girl; Tom, the gardener; and Tom's son, Tim. Aunt Polly never forgave her sister, Jennie, for marrying a poverty-stricken minister instead of the rich man in town whom her parents favored. Now that Jennie and her husband are dead, Aunt Polly deems it inconvenient to care for their young daughter, puts Pollyanna in a stifling, bare attic room, and forbids her to speak of her father. After her mother's death, Pollyanna and her father lived on whatever came in the missionary barrels administered by the Ladies' Aid. Her father taught her the "just being glad" game, whose objective is to find at least one good aspect in every situation. Aunt Polly initiates a series of reading, cooking, and sewing lessons, but Pollyanna still has time to make friends. One of these is John Pendleton, a morose gentleman whom she meets in the village. She brings home a stray kitten and dog and tries

P

to introduce Jimmy Bean, a homeless orphan, into the household; Aunt Polly puts her foot down at the last. Wherever Pollyanna goes, she plays the glad game. One day in the Pendleton Woods, she finds John on the ground, his leg broken. He gives her the keys to his house and bids her summon Dr. Thomas Chilton. When Mr. Pendleton is home again, she brings him some calf's foot jelly; they become friends. Much to Pollyanna's delight, Nancy confides (mistakenly) to her that years earlier Mr. Pendleton and Aunt Polly were in love. Mr. Pendleton invites Pollyanna to live with him and be his little girl; she says she cannot leave Aunt Polly and suggests they all live together. Mr. Pendleton explains that it was Aunt Polly's sister, Jenny—Pollyanna's mother—whom he loved. Pollyanna proposes that he adopt Jimmy, which he does. Pollyanna is struck by an automobile and taken, unconscious, to Aunt Polly's. Since Aunt Polly does not want to see Dr. Chilton (it was he she loved, not Mr. Pendleton), she sends for another doctor. He asserts Pollyanna will never walk again; a specialist confirms this diagnosis. One after another, the villagers visit Aunt Polly to tell her how important the dear little girl is to them. Aunt Polly starts playing the glad game. When Pollyanna is able to sit up, she knits garments for poor children. Dr. Chilton tells Mr. Pendleton he believes Pollyanna can be cured; however, because of the dissolution of his love affair with Aunt Polly long ago, she will not see him. Jimmy overhears this conversation and hurries to tell Aunt Polly what Dr. Chilton said about Pollyanna. Aunt Polly summons Dr. Chilton, and they revive their old love. They are married at Pollyanna's bedside; after spending almost a year in a sanatorium in Boston, Pollyanna is able to walk again. (The word "Pollyanna" has come to mean "foolishly or blindly optimistic," but these epithets do not do justice to the little girl's resolute, generous, and loving nature.)

In ***Pollyanna Grows Up*** (1916), Aunt Polly and Uncle Tom Chilton have an opportunity to live in Germany for a year and look for a boarding school for Pollyanna, almost thirteen. Delia Wetherby, a nurse who fell under Pollyanna's spell at Dr. Ames's sanatorium, proposes that she spend the year in Boston with Delia's sister, Ruth Carew, thirty-three, who, inconsolable and bitter, hides in her Commonwealth Avenue house. Her husband is dead; John Kent spirited away her beloved nephew, Jamie, eight years ago, after the death of Jamie's mother, who was Ruth's sister, Doris. From the start, Ruth resists Polly's bewitching ways; she swears to her sister that she will send Pollyanna away the minute she starts "preaching." Ruth, finally affected by Polly's open heart, adopts Jamie, a poor, wheelchair-bound boy whom Pollyanna has met in the park. He is not "her" Jamie, but Ruth wants to give him a home and her love. Pollyanna rejoins Aunt Polly and Uncle Tom Chilton only briefly in Beldingsville before the Chiltons, fearing the residents' outpouring of devotion will go to Pollyanna's head, take her to Germany for six years. When she returns to Vermont at age twenty, Uncle Tom is dead, and Aunt Polly is in financial difficulties. Jimmy Bean, now Jimmy Pendleton, has grown to be a tall, good-looking fellow, who is nervous about seeing Pollyanna again after all these years: he does not yet realize he is in love with her. Because of her bereavement and her problems, Aunt Polly has reverted to her old "sour, hard" ways. Pollyanna, determined to raise some money to help Aunt Polly, is delighted when Ruth seeks a boarding establishment in Vermont. She arrives with her secretary, Sadie Dean, and Jamie, now on crutches and officially adopted by Ruth. Pollyanna, the Pendletons, and the Carews see a great deal of each other and spend two weeks camping at a mountain lake about forty miles from Beldingsville. A series of romantic misunderstandings occurs. Jimmy, thinking Pollyanna loves Jamie, heroically stands aside. Ruth, who falls in love with John Pendleton, thinks he loves Pollyanna (not knowing it was Pollyanna's mother he once loved). Sadie loves Jamie but believes he loves Pollyanna. Polly loves Jimmy, but when she is informed mistakenly that John loves her, she decides that her duty is to him. Once the misconceptions are clarified, Jimmy and Pollyanna declare their love, only to find that Aunt Polly will not allow her niece to marry a man whose background is a mystery.

Jimmy does not know his parentage; his father left him a "packet" to be opened when he reached the age of thirty. Jimmy believes circumstances justify opening the sealed document right away. He is Ruth's nephew, Jamie Kent. Although Jimmy tells Aunt Polly and Ruth Carew, his real aunt, the news, he magnanimously insists upon keeping the secret from Jamie Carew.

R

Gerald Raftery

When Aunt Martha Arnold leaves for Europe in ***City Dog*** (1953), she ships her collie, Champion Roderick ("Rod") Dhu of Glenartney, to her great-nephew, Ted Carver, sixteen, in Vermont. Beautifully trained and eager to please, Rod is uncertain of his new role. Ted's father, mother, Uncle Bill, and little twin brothers are pleasant enough, but Rod is made to sleep outside. When he sees the woolly animals in the pasture, his instincts tell him he should be herding them. Out walking, Ted often urges Rod to run ahead without an order or to bark noisily at an errant cow, both actions against Rod's training. Ted complains that Rod will herd but not chase; his father explains the difference between instinct and training. Mr. Carver says Rod is "the smartest city dog I ever saw." Overeager, Ted pushes Rod too hard, and a woodchuck gives the dog a bad scratch. Rod does not know what is expected of him. When they pass some friends of Ted's with a mean-looking mastiff, Rod disdainfully avoids the dog. Ted, misreading Rod's behavior, thinks he is afraid of the other dog; when the mastiff runs into the sheep pasture, Rod imperiously challenges him. Uncle Bill sets off after a large raccoon that has eaten some of Ted's pet turtles; Rod chases and corners the animal so that Uncle Bill can shoot it. When the twins wander away, Ted lets Rod sniff one of their tiny sweaters. Rod finds the twins amongst the sheep in a ravine. Ted is hugely disappointed when Aunt Martha announces she is sending her trainer to fetch Rod. They spend their last days together at hunting camp. After a bear steals a ram, the hunters follow Rod on the bear's scent until it is almost dark. Mr. Carver shoots the bear, then trips and falls. Rod, knowing the animal is not dead, leaps at the bear, which lunges at Mr. Carver. Ted shoots as the dog attacks; the bear mauls Rod and advances. Ted calmly shoots again. Rod is badly hurt but alive. Ted hurries ahead for the jeep and drives back right through the sheep pasture fence, while Uncle Bill calls the vet. When Aunt Martha's handler arrives to take Rod away, he says his scars will prevent Rod from being a show dog. The Carvers are joyful that Rod will stay with them to become a country dog.

In ***Slaver's Gold*** (1967), Pete Durning, sixteen, is spending his New Jersey school holidays in southern Vermont, near Roaring Brook and Batten Kill River, working at the dairy of Mr. and Mrs. Foster. Their son, Jeff, is just out of the army; Clyde is also sixteen; Suzanne, bright and ingenious, is fourteen. The Foster grandparents are settled in a cottage close at hand. On the hill above the farm is the century-old mansion built by Grandfather Foster's grandfather, Daniel C. Foster, a master mariner who turned against the slave trade, designated his house a way station on the Underground Railroad, and became a captain in the First Vermont Brigade in the Civil War. Their curiosity piqued by a coded message Grandfather Foster shows them, the young people organize a picnic at the big house. They find the same arcane words carved on the banister posts—twelve sets of words, each with five letters. When Pete returns to school in New Jersey, he researches codes and ciphers at the library and returns to the farm in time for haying. Suzanne and Pete, searching the barn for relevant documents, find a note from "D.C.F." saying that he buried his "ill-gotten gold" in the "Middle Passage" where he stored the "Underground Freight." They must find where he hid the fugitive slaves. Suzanne does her own research at the local library, looking at coin catalogues. With a rented mine detector, they head back to the house. They find an old brass blunderbuss containing a piece of paper saying, "When digging for the treasure don't discount the logs." They pore over old maps, photographs, and geological surveys and search the cellar holes of former neighbors' habitations. Suzanne submits a story about Daniel C. Foster, including the cipher, to her history teacher, who publishes the essay. In response, a college professor informs Suzanne that the key words in the cipher are "slaver's gold." One of his students, skiing in the area, translates the code for them: "At bottom cellar step take bearing thirty feet north and dig." They hasten to the big house only to find the front door wide open. Intruders—perhaps skiers—have found and removed the gold. Their spirits flag. Back at school, Pete hears from Suzanne that the old house burned down. The next time Pete visits, they dig out the jack posts (structural supports). Suzanne, compass in hand, figures out that the intruders could not have found the treasure: their compass would have registered incorrectly because the jack post by the cellar steps is metal. They measure again and find a secret room. Digging, they uncover logs stopped up with plugs. Scores of valuable coins pour from the unplugged logs. Now the family will be able to afford a new tractor for Mr. Foster and a college education for Clyde. (The appendix explains the monoalphabetic cipher, or cryptogram, whose key is the rearrangement of the letters of the alphabet. These different letters are substituted for the letters in the message to create a secret communication.)

Jonathan Rand

In ***Virtual Vampires of Vermont*** (2004), Mike Sherman and Hayley Winthrop, high school classmates in Stowe, try out his new computer game, "Return of the Vampire." His computer has eccentrically been turning itself off and on. When he clicks on "Play," something pulls them through the screen into a world featuring the castle on the game-box cover's illustration. Mike and Hayley run into the woods; a boy vampire their age follows to assure them he is harmless. Named Ivan, he explains they are in the Land of Virtuality. He is a benign vampire, but a malfunction in the machine has created malicious mutated vampires. Ivan needs Mike's computer expertise as well as his and Hayley's help collecting garlic, which protects against vampires. The town of Transylvania has been almost destroyed by giant worms. Mike and Hayley realize the giant worms are computer viruses affecting the system. Mike and Hayley must enter the workings of the computer before Virtuality runs out of energy. Ivan warns them that vampire bats, deranged cats, and robotic wolves roam the castle; they ward off these threats with cloves of garlic. The dungeon's floor is covered with what Ivan warns is a dangerous liquid. While they are analyzing how to reach the virtual door to the machine, Hayley slips and falls. Mike rescues her and discovers the substance is a harmless soft drink. Once inside the computer, he realizes how small Hayley and he are in relation to the electrical components. They wipe clean the wires and buttons. Unfortunately, a giant worm is lurking in the computer. When Mike reconnects a green wire, the giant worm vanishes. The computer shuts down; he must find the power button to restart it. Their candles are burning dangerously low. They climb over the hard drive and around some microchips. Because they are so tiny, the button seems huge, but, combining their strength, they are able to turn on the computer. They can actually feel the power coursing through the machine and fear electrical shock. Mike faints and wakes up in his room. He and Hayley, who is there, too, decide to play the game. When they read the instructions on the screen, their names are incorporated into them. Mike's father comes in; Mike asks how a computer could work without being plugged in. His father explains that he installed a battery pack in this computer in case of power failure, but when he spilled some soda on it, he purchased a new machine and passed the old one on to Mike.

Marilynne K. Roach

In **"The Ghost in the Shed"** (1977), a peddler comes to a remote farmhouse in the Green Mountains where someone murders, robs, and buries him under the shed. The farm changes hands several times. The dead man's spirit is troubled, obsessed with letting someone know where it is. The ghost begins leaving the door to the shed open. The family members close the door. The ghost opens it. The farmer keeps fixing and locking it. The ghost continues to open it. The farmer nails it shut with a six-inch spike and, when that fails, shoves a heavy chest against it. The farmer has a nervous breakdown. He orders the family to use the front door. The ghost bangs around in the shed and finally collapses the walls and roof into splinters. The family digs through the rubble to find a skeleton and the remains of a peddler's pack. A broken watchcase is inscribed, "Samuel Pym." They rebury his bones in the cemetery with a simple stone bearing his name. After that, the shed door remains closed.

Gertrude Robinson

In ***Father and the Mountains*** (1950), the father of the title is Elder David Rowson, a Methodist minister; the mountains are Washington (New Hampshire), Equinox (Vermont), and Greylock (Massachusetts). Rowson, his wife, and his two daughters, Susie, thirteen, and Louise, sixteen, are based in Jefferson, New Hampshire, when he is called by the Troy Conference, which extends from eastern New York into Manchester, Vermont. The girls are excited by the move, although sad that their mother will stay behind for a few weeks with baby Eddie, who has the measles. Lucinda Perkins, head of the church board of trustees, meets Elder Rowson and the girls at the Manchester train station. The church arranges a three-year scholarship for Louise at Green Mountain Academy in Poultney, run by Dr. Dunton, the principal, and catering to three hundred students. Susie will study at home with a tutor, Belle Reye, daughter of the Episcopalian rector. Susie and Belle do some history and read the novels of Sir Walter Scott. Their mother finally joins the family without the baby, who succumbed to the disease. When the county fair comes to town, Mr. Perkins confesses to Rowson that he owns one of the racers, a fine Morgan. The following year, the church provides a scholarship for Susie. Eager to earn money to enter a prize competition offered by a religious publisher, Louise and Susie try unsuccessfully to sell copies of Marian Hartland's *Story of the Bible*. Louise, now a senior at the Academy, has a beau, Ted Burnham, and tutors three local high school girls preparing to enter the Academy. When Louise delivers the valedictory address, her father looks "proud"; her mother looks "sad," according to Susie. Louise, who is going to college, is engaged to Ted, who will enter Syracuse University. When the girls leave home, the Rowsons move to Pittsford, Massachusetts. After her graduation, Louise teaches at a small Ohio college; Susie, after finishing at Syracuse University, comes back to teach at the Academy.

K.S. Rodriguez

Major Meltdown (1999) depicts a weekend at a ski chalet on Steep Mountain, where four inseparable high school friends spend Presidents' Day weekend. The sixteen-year-olds, Dawson Leery, Pacey Witter, Josephine ("Joey") Potter, and Jen Lindley, take advantage of the offer of the Lindleys' family cabin to ski and snowboard. From Dawson's perspective, the point of the weekend is to recapture Joey's affections. Jen is also a former girlfriend of Dawson's. Joey has told Dawson they are too young to be anything more than best friends. The young people try to make each other jealous—Joey trifles with young men on the slopes; Dawson feigns a rekindling of his feelings for Jen—but in the end they realize that friendships are more important than flirtations.

David Roth

Fourteen-year-old Joey Carr's life in Cambridge, Massachusetts, in ***A World for Joey Carr*** (1981) is in disarray: his mother died when he was young; his indifferent father entertains a string of girlfriends. Betty, the latest, is leaving him. When the apartment manager tells Joey he cannot keep his dog, a stray Doberman called Butch, Joey sets out to hitchhike to Carverville in the Northeast Kingdom, where his grandparents, Charles and Martha Webster, live by a small lake. Joey has just crossed into New Hampshire when he encounters a woman slumped in a car. He asks if he can be of help. Hannah Adams, who is dying of cancer, offers him a ride to Carverville. On the way, they stop at a commune, Abaddon Woods, in the White Mountains, where Joey learns Hannah is a witch and he meets an appealing girl. Joey finds Hannah interesting and sympathetic; her quest is to seek a cure for her illness. Wild dogs attack Joey and Hannah; Butch sacrifices his life to kill the dogs and save his friends. Joey and Hannah cross the border into Hollington in a thunderstorm and head for Carverville, high in the hills of Vermont. Joey is "amazed at the different shades of green, where one color now revealed itself as a hundred colors." When Hannah's car breaks down, she abandons it and her possessions, setting them on fire. As they part company, she gives Joey a medal for the "goodness in him that isn't pretense." Joey walks through Carverville, looking for Lake Magogaway. The house is smaller than he remembers; his grandfather is old and confused. Martha says he may stay for a week and then must return with his father. Joey has a fine time playing checkers with his grandfather. When his father fetches him, Joey promises to return the following summer to paint the house. Headed south on Interstate 89, Joey and his father pick up a hitchhiker, Annie, who reminds him of the girl in Abaddon Woods. Annie says his medal is a talisman to lead him to love. Betty comes back to the family: Joey's father asks each of them for a second chance.

S

Frances Sanger

Set in 1777, ***The Silver Teapot*** (1948) looks at events from the perspective of a Bennington family named Drew—Prudence and Trueman; their children, Jane Louise, twelve, and Abraham, fourteen; and Trueman's father. Their grandfather, a hero in the French and Indian Wars, has not been in his right mind since Indians captured his wife, Lucy. After the hostilities ended, Swiss Colonel Henry Bouquet demanded the return of all white captives, but Lucy was not among them. Under the delusion that Lucy is in England visiting her father, their grandfather wears a miniature portrait of her around his neck and dotes on Jane, who reminds him of Lucy and will inherit her silver teapot. Ticonderoga falls to the British, Seth Warner retreats to Hubbardton, and rumors fly that Burgoyne has plans to loose Indians upon the settlers. Borrowing Lucy's portrait one day, Jane goes to the woods to sketch a likeness. An apparently friendly Indian, Musinigon, offers her a basket of berries; he is a member of the Delaware tribe that captured Lucy. When Jane departs, she leaves behind the portrait by mistake. Later, the family notices that the silver teapot has been stolen. Jane feels sad about the loss and guilty about her carelessness. From time to time, Jane and Abraham think they glimpse a light in the cabin that their grandfather built for Lucy. They wonder if Musinigon is a scout for the British. Searching the cabin, they find the silver teapot buried under the hearth. Jane cleans and puts it by their grandfather's bed; once more it disappears. Everyone is talking about Jane McRae; Indians scalped and murdered her as she was on her way to marry a British officer at Burgoyne's camp. Abraham packs and readies the farm wagon for their escape should the Indians come. Many fugitives stop to request food and shelter. Trueman departs with the militia for Bennington; their grandfather insists upon accompanying him. Men march past, soldiers in shabby uniforms, farmers in long blue frocks and homespun trousers. The green flag of the Green Mountain Boys flies alongside the red, white, and blue flag of General Stark. Seth Warner's regiment arrives. The long wait is difficult for the family, but news comes at last that the Americans have won. Abraham makes many trips to the battlefield to collect the wounded. Trueman and his father are safe. Musinigon brings back Lucy, who recognized the portrait that the Delaware showed to her. The family is reunited; Lucy's silver teapot is safe under the hearth where their grandfather reburied it.

The Wooden Mug (1950), a sequel, follows the adventures of Jane and Abraham in 1778. On their way to deliver milk to Goody Bacon, they discover a man who has fallen over a cliff—Karl Bauer, a wounded Hessian deserter. They promise not to tell anyone. Each day Jane carries dried apples and bread to Karl. Trueman gives their grandmother, Lucy, a carved wooden mug. When it disappears from its place, Lucy wonders whether Jane, who is acting strangely, is bewitched. The mug reappears and vanishes several times. Musinigon gives Jane some red calico as a token of his esteem. When he finds her giving food to Karl, Musinigon offers to nurse the Hessian until his wound heals. Captain Noah Bacon comes on a mission from General Washington to recruit additional men. He says that many Hessian mercenaries have no heart for the fight and have deserted. Noah wants Trueman to return with him to assist Washington; Trueman would gladly leave if he could find a Hessian to help on the farm in his absence. When Jane proudly brings Karl home, Noah tells him that the American Congress is giving fifty acres to Hessians who refuse to fight. Even better, now that the French have joined the revolutionaries, Karl will be able to arrange passage for his daughter on a French boat. The wooden mug has been disappearing and reappearing because Karl kindly carved three exactly alike to make a set.

Susan Fromberg Schaeffer

In *The Dragons of North Chittendon* (1986), Arthur, the son of the first chief dragon of the Dark Lands, finds an abandoned baby, Patrick Witherspoon, in a field in North Chittendon and brings him back to Dark Lands. Against the advice of his mother, Arthur gives the baby dragon's milk, which causes Patrick to breathe fire. When Arthur's mother braves a moonlit night to deliver the baby home, the parson of North Chittendon shoots at and wounds her; Arthur helps her fly home. Arthur does all the housework until she is well. As Patrick grows up, he and Arthur dream about each other and share thoughts and concerns: each is disappointed in his respective world. Flying over the Dark Lands, Arthur sees the pure white wings of Regina, the Queen of the Dragons. Arthur knows that the Moon intends to destroy the dragons; the dragons are waiting for Regina to marry and lead them against the Moon. In North Chittendon, eleven little boys go into the woods and are sealed by snow into the deer-yard; Patrick communicates mentally with Arthur, who flies there with Felix, his bat companion. When Arthur's wings ice over, he uses his flamethrowers to clear a path through the snow. The grateful townsfolk gather to hear Arthur greet them in English and return their children. Tiandra, head of the Council of Elders, summons Arthur to speak with his deceased father in the Portal. His imposing father urges Arthur to play a role with Regina in the conflict between the Moon and the dragons. Regina accepts Arthur's proposal and explains her lineage. Her tribe of white dragons is descended from the Moon's dragons, before a dispute arose between the Sun God and the Moon. The angels on the dark side of the Moon are known as Fiends. The Moon threatens to send an overwhelming flood. Arthur presents to the Grand Council of Tribes a dual plan to use the power of the white dragons' singing to hypnotize the humans, while the dragons' flamethrowers dry up the seas. Patrick, whose dreams reveal Arthur's plan, flies with Mother Dragon. Arthur drops a boulder into a volcano, creating a vast explosion. Angry, the Moon glows redder and hotter. Patrick peeks out from atop Mother Dragon's back to see white dragons ringing the entire earth. As the Fiends charge, Arthur receives Patrick's signal about the Dark Angels' poisonous claws and attacks their Commander. The dragons defeat the Fiends. Patrick and Arthur continue to communicate through dreams and meet from time to time. They lament the enmity, misunderstanding, and fear that exist between humans and dragons. Arthur proposes mixing dragon's milk with human milk to forge a bond between the two kinds of creatures. When dragon babies become ill from the mixture, Patrick sends his son, Daniel, now a doctor, to treat the mysterious plague. After that experience, humans no longer shoot down dragons.

Tor Seidler

In ***Terpin*** (1982), Judge Terpin Taft returns to Vermont after leaving home thirty years earlier at seventeen. The elderly train conductor, George, recognizes and congratulates him on his distinguished career. Terpin remembers the last time when, after visiting an aunt downstate, he rode that train into North Haven near Quechee Lake. A man sat in the same car, depressed about his recently deceased wife. In an attempt to console him, Terpin made up a story about his own parents' drowning in a canoeing accident. As Terpin left the train, the man slipped an ancient Greek coin into his pocket. At home, Terpin found his mother bickering with his aunt and uncle over a game of Canasta, as she did every afternoon. His father was a businessman involved in Chamber of Commerce activities. Hearing that the disconsolate man jumped to his death from the train at the North Trestle, Terpin was horrified and guilt-stricken that his well-intentioned falsehood contributed to the man's suicide. That night, as Terpin studied the coin with the image of Socrates engraved upon it, Socrates appeared to him to remind Terpin of a line from his history paper about Socrates: "Your life should express what you truly believe." Before disappearing, Socrates extracted a promise from Terpin to embody that tenet. From then on, Terpin was compelled to tell the truth, even if it hurt the recipients' feelings. He alienated his girlfriend, Melanie Minor, by realistically assessing her class report. He left the football team, because he did not like the sport, to spend his time cross-country skiing. He told the Chamber of Commerce members, who were engaged in a development project called "Heavenly Havens," that it was wrong to cut down birches. Although everyone was angry with him, his heart felt "clean and alive." He was not invited to any Christmas parties; his teacher humiliated him in class for not competing in an essay contest. When his father threatened to send him to military academy, Terpin left home; George allowed him to ride the train for free. Today, North Haven is honoring Terpin, the chief justice of the Supreme Court, by renaming the town for him. He changes hats and coats with a reporter who bears a striking resemblance to him and, leaving his double to listen to the congratulatory speeches, goes skiing to look for that "secret slope that looked like the glowing white beard of Socrates." (The author wrote to me that "I still think of Vermont as my childhood—though Vermont isn't mentioned by name in this novel, I certainly had it in mind for the setting—and make a point of skiing there at least once a winter.")

Alison and Trevor Tuttle in ***Brothers Below Zero*** (2002) have two diametrically opposite sons: John Henry, eleven, is handsome, athletic, and talented at school; Tim, twelve, is nearsighted, awkward at sports, and a mediocre student. The family lives in Williston; Trevor works at the University of Vermont Medical Center. Tim's great-aunt, Winifred V. Tuttle, lives on the hilltop above them. Tim enjoys a special relationship with Aunt Winnie, who spends her days painting the view from her window and encourages Tim to paint, too. When she gives him some paints and brushes, Tim fixes up a space in an unused room at the top of his house; John Henry is working for their neighbor, earning a fine sum of money. Trevor sends out the boys to dig postholes for the split-rail fence. John Henry finishes his easily; Tim struggles and becomes overheated. As always on Trevor's birthday, Aunt Winnie presents him with one of her paintings, *Summer View*. He and Alison are surprised and proud to learn that Tim is the artist of this admirable work. They exclaim with pleasure and hang the painting in the living room. John Henry seethes with jealousy, wondering how he can sabotage Tim's new accomplishment. When Aunt Winnie dies of a heart attack, Tim does not attend the funeral or talk about her, though he misses her "dreadfully," and does not visit her house, though his father gives him the key. He tries and fails to paint her likeness. He misses her more than ever. At Christmastime, John Henry spends his earnings on presents. Feeling guilty and discouraged because he has no money, Tim paints a portrait of his parents and one of John Henry punting a football. On Christmas Eve a blizzard engulfs the landscape. John Henry steals downstairs to look at Tim's gifts. He is so enraged by the beautiful portrait of their parents that he paints warts on their father's nose and a mustache on their mother's upper lip. Upon opening Tim's present, his parents are outraged and disappointed. Tim is shocked and incredulous and runs upstairs sobbing. How could his brother be so cruel? How could his parents believe he would do this? He disappears. His parents rush out to look for him. John Henry, who is home alone, opens Tim's vibrant painting of him and is overwhelmed with self-hatred. He leaves a note for his parents and sets out on snowshoes to look for his brother. Coming upon Tim lying semiconscious in the snow, John Henry tries to drag Tim up the hill but is not strong enough. He puts his parka on Tim and lies next to him, giving him frequent bear hugs to try to keep him warm. The Tuttles, finding John Henry's note, report the boys' disappearance to the police, who take the Tuttles up in a helicopter to search. With a spotlight, they are able to locate the boys because Tim, before collapsing, scuffed out with his boots in the snow a huge outline of Aunt Winnie's smiling face. Trevor, albeit a scientist, now accepts the notion that humans live on after death. Both boys are taken to the hospital but are home by New Year's Eve. Tim walks to the cemetery, followed by John Henry. Tim stands by Aunt Winnie's grave; John Henry holds back to "give him some privacy." Then John Henry approaches Tim to ask him for a painting lesson; Tim agrees in exchange for his brother's teaching him to hit a curve ball.

Barbara Seuling

Robert Dorfman, eight, snake proctor in his third grade room in ***Robert and the Great Escape*** (2003), is devoted to Sally, the class pet snake. For President's Day weekend, Robert's best friend, Paul Felcher, invites him to his parents' rented ski cabin in Vermont. The last afternoon before vacation starts, Mrs. Bernthal, their teacher, reads *Shiloh* to them. At Big Bear Mountain, Paul's father rents skis for the boys and gives them walkie-talkies. They meet Robin Josh, who lives at the resort. The next day they try snowboarding with Robin, who can execute "ollies" (jumps or hops) and ride the "halfpipes" (U-shaped bowl). When they return to school, Sally, the snake, is gone from her glass cage. They find a note: Sally has been kidnapped. When they descend to the nice, warm basement to consult the custodian, Robert feels like Dorothy and her friends entering the great hall of the wizard. Sally is there, comfortable in a shoebox. Because the window in their classroom was broken, the custodian feared Sally would be cold. The children rejoice that Sally is safe. Mrs. Bernthal reads them Kipling's story about a snake, "Rikki-Tikki-Tavi."

Marlene Fanta Shyer

Max Murphy, eleven, the narrator in ***Blood in the Snow*** (1975), is a lonely, sensitive boy living in Paragon. His mother has returned to college; his best friend is Bernice, the crossing guard at school. His father, who works for the Vermont Marble Company, is disappointed that Max does not stand up to Crow Hintz, a large, intimidating bully. When his father gives Max his grandfather's Browning Double Automatic and takes him out for target practice, Max cannot hit anything. "What kind of a boy are you, Max?" asks his father. Greedy to acquire Max's gun, Crow gives him his lunchbox (he destroyed Max's) and offers him anything in his parents' attic in exchange for the gun. When Max spies a flute, he agrees to a trade, with the provision that Crow promise not to shoot any animals or birds. Bernice gives flute lessons to Max, who derives great pleasure from playing the instrument. In the woods one day, practicing with Bernice, he comes upon a fox with his leg caught in a trap. Neither of them can spring the metal teeth. A vulture flies overhead. Max runs to the trailer of Mr. Janka, owner the trap. Mrs. Janka explains that her husband needs the money from selling the pelt. Max hurries to school to raise money to pay Mr. Janka for the fox before the animal expires; soon his Save the Fox Fund lunchbox is overflowing with cash from children and teachers. Crow seizes the lunchbox from Max and runs away. Max asks Bernice to sell his flute and hurries back to check on the fox. In the woods Crow shoots a rabbit: he has used the

Save the Fox Fund to buy shells. Max brings food and water to the dying fox, which looks beseechingly at him; four vultures now hover overhead. When it rains, Max shelters the fox with his coat. Hearing Crow's scream, Max finds Crow's boot clamped in a trap and releases him. Bernice informs the boys that the flute is platinum and valuable. Max trades the flute back to Crow for the gun, because he understands the fox wants Max to put him out of his misery. His father comes upon Max just as he shoots the fox. His father is angry at first, then proud: what Max did took "courage" and "compassion."

S

Marilyn Singer

If only her mother, Lydia, in ***California Demon*** (1992) would teach her daughter, Rosamunde ("Rosie) Rivera, fourteen, some magic charms, Rosie could cast a love spell on Johnny Haines, the handsomest boy in her class. Lydia, whose husband left her, runs a magic shop called "Quicker than the Eye." Experimenting, Rosie opens the wrong bottle by mistake, releasing a malicious imp into the store. The imp, impersonating a clerk, waits on Adam Pauling, who is buying Christmas presents for his children, Danny, twelve, and Laura, ten, who live in California with Adam's estranged wife, Ginny. The scenes alternate between Vermont and California. Danny and Laura are angry with their mother because she has invited her new beau, Biff, for eggnog on Christmas Day. The children go to the beach to open their father's present, a bag labeled "White Magic;" out of the bag come snowflakes—and the imp, "crazy hair, electric blue eyes, and large teeth." Back in Vermont, Lydia, anxious about what the imp might do, dusts off her book of spells, takes up the Craft again, and locates the imp by making a chart of "unnatural occurrences" around the country. She and Rosie note several freak snowstorms in California. Lydia gives Rosie magic lessons, especially in scrying (predicting the future by means of a crystal ball). As her apprenticeship continues, Rosie becomes more graceful and flirtatious and starts going out with Johnnie. He asks what she is reading; she responds, Shirley Jackson's *We Have Always Lived in the Castle*. He asks what he should read; she recommends *The Changeover*, by Margaret Mahy. Lydia finds the sales slip from Adam Pauling, who lives about forty-five miles away in Pendleton. In California, the imp, Mr. Ed, pretends he is the children's slave; they use him to break up the romance between their mother and Biff. Laura begins to question the imp's reliability; Danny assures her he is in charge. In fact, Danny is drunk with power, exhorting Mr. Ed to cause more and more havoc. Watching the news in Vermont, Lydia and Rosie note the mayhem caused at a movie studio in California; in the audience is a boy with P-A-U-L-I-N-G stitched across his back. They instantly make the connection and call Adam. Both Laura and Danny are upset that the imp is out of control. Just as they tell their mother about the genie, Mr. Ed makes Ginny vanish. Once Adam hears his children are under the sway of a malevolent imp, he flies to California with Lydia and Rosie. Meanwhile, Mr. Ed torments the children by taking them to Spitzer's Camp in the mountains. Before they leave, Laura scrawls their destination in soap on her bathroom mirror. Adam, Lydia, and Rosie arrive at Spitzer's Camp for the final confrontation. Mr. Ed tumbles Adam's car over the cliff. Lydia, trying to stuff Mr. Ed back in his bottle, summons the Queen of Genies, who succeeds in capturing him. Ginny reappears, and she and Adam agree to talk over their marital status. Back in Vermont, Rosie learns that Johnnie was only paying attention to her to solicit help with his English paper. When Lydia advertises some "unstable" artifacts for sale, Tony LeSalle, a magician, comes to collect them. He brings his son, Armand, who is also learning the Craft, is good-looking, and lives not far away.

Jan Slepian

Lionel ("Linny") Erda, twelve, and Hilary Brier, eleven, in ***Back to Before*** (1993) are cousins who used to live in Brooklyn and who share a bond: each lacks a parent. Since his mother's death, Linny has felt her "ghost" in his head. He cannot recover from the guilt of going skateboarding on the afternoon she asked him to stay home and died while he was gone. Since her father's leaving home, Hilary has blamed her mother for his departure. She clings to the idea that he wants Hilary to live with him. Linny, "calm, contained, cool," has been visiting Hilary and his Aunt Helen in Colchester for a year. In that time, Hilary and he have found that the town has changed from a quiet spot to "one big outdoor shopping mall." Aunt Helen and Hilary live in a delightfully decorated barn: "It is like going to Oz," as Hilary once said. Linny senses a romantic tension between Aunt Helen and her neighbor, Taylor Dilt. Rain and floods come, cooping up the children inside. When the weather clears, Linny gives Hilary a ride on his bicycle toward Stockville. Up ahead, the sheriff is prohibiting traffic from continuing on the flood-eroded road. As Linny keeps pedaling, he and Hilary are magically swept back into the past in their old Brooklyn neighborhood. Linny's mother is still alive; Hilary's father is still at their former house, but he is living with another woman. Reliving their past—seeing people whose futures they already know—is traumatic. Hilary meets Taylor, who does not recognize her because he has not yet moved to Colchester. She cannot call her mother to reassure her, because they are in different time frames. Linny has a chance to bid his mother a fond farewell; Hilary accepts the fact that her father's departure was not her mother's fault. The two are once more on Linny's bicycle when wind and rain whip up—and Linny awakes in the Colchester hospital with a broken arm. Hilary, who suffered a concussion, remembers nothing about their travel into the past.

Virginia Smiley

Still reeling from her broken engagement to surgeon Justin Caldwell at Bennington General Hospital, Kiley McBride in ***Sugar Bush Nurse*** (1981) takes a private-duty nurse's position at Sugar Bush Acres, a private estate in St. Johnsbury. The patient is wheelchair-bound Victoria Grayson, who has not walked since the death of her husband, Donald, in an automobile accident. Victoria lives in a Vermont-marble mansion with her two sons, Larry and Gregg, who manage a large maple sugar concern and train race horses. Kiley, twenty-one, is attracted to both men, the former serious and responsible, the latter, a playboy and charmer. Kiley is convinced that Victoria is unable to walk because she holds Greg responsible for her husband's death. Kiley realizes she is in love with Gregg but, believing he is engaged to someone else, decides to return to Bennington to accept a job in Justin's new private practice. Victoria's sister-in-law, Aunt Maggie, brings news that hidden in the house is a letter from Donald explaining the accident. Only after Donald's letter is found, confirming that Donald committed suicide by tampering with the brakes on his car, can Gregg, exonerated, admit his love for Kiley.

S

Gilbert Smith

Benjamin ("Ben") White, eighteen, meets Ethan Allen in ***The Green Mountain Boys Ride*** (1932) when Allen brings his horse for shoeing to Ben's father, Lemuel, a blacksmith in Bennington in 1775. Lemuel's daughter, Sarah, is married to James Breakenridge; his tomboy daughter, Phoebe, is fifteen. Colonel Ethan Allen, a price on his head, invites Ben to ride to Albany with him, where, in the central tavern, Allen ostentatiously takes a drink before leaving. Royal governors like James Duane wish to dispossess the settlers. In Bennington, the Green Mountain Boys vote unanimously to defend their lands from Yorkers. Ben's brother, Dick, works as a peddler to earn his way to Dartmouth. Stopping at the house of Yorker John Munro, he falls in love with his daughter, Julia. She warns Dick that Sheriff Ten Eyck is sending a great number of men to serve Duane's writ of ejection on Breakenridge. Dick passes the word to Seth Warner and Remember Baker in Arlington. A month later Munro and an armed posse capture Remember Baker to collect the reward; his son rides to Bennington to alert the Green Mountain Boys. Ethan procures certified copies of documents issued by Governor Wentworth that substantiate settlers' claims. Ben accompanies Allen to Albany to the hearing, where the judge refuses the evidence. Yorkers try to bribe Allen to persuade the settlers to acknowledge Yorkers' rights, saying, "Might makes right." Allen responds, "Might may make right in the courts of Albany, but the gods of the hills are not the gods of the valley." In Bennington the settlers agree that if one is threatened with eviction, others will rally to his cause. Ben, a new constable, rides with the Green Mountain Boys, patrolling the borders. Allen, Warner, Ben, and his friend, Ira, stop with friends in Bridport. As British soldiers from Crown Point enter the front door, Ben and Ira go out the window to help Allen and Warner escape. In Westminster, residents take a stand to abolish the court, which is increasing their heavy taxes. The sheriff engages a force of men from Brattleboro; the Green Mountain Boys bring a band from Rockingham to support the patriots and occupy the courthouse. Among the guards at the door are Ben and his cousin, William French. Judge Chandler promises to keep the peace. In contravention of his orders, the sheriff and his men fire on the courthouse. William is killed, Ben and Dan Houghton are wounded, and Dan dies later. They were unarmed, except for cudgels. The funeral for William is the largest ever held in the Grants; the settlers, not in uniform, render him military honors. They want revenge, but Captain Bellows from New Hampshire urges calm, reminding them that the Green Mountain Boys' credo is to act only in self-defense. Allen enlists men, including Ben, for the seizure of Fort Ticonderoga. Benedict Arnold arrives, expecting to lead the expedition. Meeting vociferous opposition, he volunteers as "a simple solider"; finally, he and Allen agree to march in together. Allen captures the fort "in the name of God Almighty [or, "the Great Jehovah"] and the Continental Congress." The Congress recognizes the Green Mountain Boys as part of the American army from a new state named Vermont. Seth Warner is chosen commander instead of Allen, with Samuel Safford as major. Allen leads an invading force to Canada where his independent action fails; the British capture Allen, take him with his remaining men to England, and threaten them with execution. Ben accompanies Warner to Canada, where the winter is harsh and many men succumb to smallpox. England sends General John Burgoyne thirteen thousand fresh troops; the Americans have no levies to raise more men. Their retreat from Canada is disheartening. After General Arthur St. Clair evacuates Fort Ticonderoga, Ben is with the men serving as rear-guard to the retreating Americans. They reach Hubbardton, where the Green Mountain Boys protect their bivouac with freshly cut trees and brushwood, the way their fathers defended themselves from the Indians. Colonel Warner's men, depleted by illness, are without reinforcements and overwhelmed. To avoid a rout, Warner shouts to his men to scatter into the woods and meet him in Manchester. Ben carries an urgent appeal for help to the New Hampshire Council, which puts General John Stark in command of a regiment. To raise money, Ira Allen proposes confiscating and selling Tory property. The tide turns at the Battle of Bennington, August 16, 1777, in a military and moral triumph, leading to American success at Saratoga.

Alan D. Sophrin

The Wilsons gratefully accept the loan of a summer cottage in Brighton Township in ***The Newcomer*** (1968) to enable Dan, a history professor in Ohio, to finish writing his book, with the help of his daughter, Sandy, sixteen, whom he hires to type the manuscript. At the general store, Sandy learns from Mr. Brewer, the owner, that Wendy Clark, an attractive girl Sandy's age, must give up school. Brighton Township does not have a high school; Whitehead High School involves an expensive commute of thirty miles each way. Dismayed at this social injustice, Sandy probes further: Mr. Brewer, one of three selectmen, voted for reimbursing student transportation to Whitehead; the other two, Mr. Hill, a prosperous farmer, and Gordon Farrell, whose feed business depends upon Mr. Hill's patronage, voted against. Driving home, Sandy gives Wendy a ride to her farm and meets her mother and her brother, John, who has a dazzling smile. As Sandy and Wendy begin swimming together in their time off, Sandy learns more about their family: their father is dead; they and their mother can barely make a go of dairy farming. Ever since the vote at town meeting, Wendy has not seen her sweetheart, Bill Farrell, who plans to attend college downcountry. Wendy does not want Sandy to become involved, but Sandy is an analyst and a problem solver. First, she visits Mr. Hill at his flourishing farm, Hillside, and hears his perspective on the matter: he did not go to school, he says bitterly, and did not have the opportunities of Mr. Clark (Wendy's father, now deceased), who spent all his time reading instead of farming. Sandy also hears Gordon's point of view. He is a former history teacher who shows her his "museum" of old letters and documents, carefully indexed to make history come alive for students. The collection should be at Whitehead High School, but no one there is interested in using it. Sandy discerns that Mr. Farrell would like to return to teaching, but his expenses are high, and he has lost his self-confidence. Sandy talks to Bill, suggesting that his father would be happier teaching if Bill were to find a job or scholarship to help out financially. Finally, she consults with her father who, uninterested at first, chooses to convince Gordon he still has a gift for teaching. Sandy turns the whole situation around: Gordon votes for reimbursing student transportation; Bill obtains a scholarship; Gordon returns to teaching; and Sandy and John and Wendy and Bill spend the rest of the summer going out together.

Elizabeth George Speare

Sixteen-year-old Miriam Willard, an orphan, lives in 1754 at Fort Number Four in ***Calico Captive*** (1957) with her brother-in-law and sister, Captain James Johnson and Susanna; and their children, Sylvanus, six; Susanna, four; and Polly, three. Miriam is attracted to Phineas Whitney, who is studying for the ministry. The Johnson family's lives are harshly disrupted when a raiding party of eleven Indians captures them and their neighbor, Peter Larabee, after killing his family, and marches them, hungry, wet, and exhausted, across the territory that later becomes Vermont. Miriam viciously hates the Indians. On the way, Susanna, stoical and courageous, gives birth to a little girl they call "Captive." At Otter Creek, the party crosses the deep and swirling river. When Peter loses his grip on Captive, the water carries her off. Miriam manages to grab the baby and cling to a tree until two Indians throw a rope tied to a stone into the river to save her and the baby. After losing consciousness, she comes to, wrapped in a blanket in front of a blazing fire, where her clothes are drying. She feels she has measured up at last to her sister's sterling behavior and appreciates the "dignity" of the Indians, who share equally what food they have. From Otter Creek, they travel on Lake Champlain by canoe to St. Francis. The rest of the tale concerns their experiences in the Indian settlement and in Montreal, where they are sold to French families. Susanna is left behind while James tries to arrange ransom. Finally the British reunite them, send them to England, and later return them to the colonies. Miriam lives for the day she will see Phineas again. (The novel is based on *Narrative of the Captivity of Mrs. Johnson: containing an account of her sufferings during four years with the Indians and French*, published in Walpole, New Hampshire, in 1796.)

David Stahler, Jr.

In ***A Gathering of Shades*** (2005), Timothy John Dunkley and Patrice Boisvert, the parents of Aidan, grew up on adjoining farms in the Northeast Kingdom. Timothy hated farming, considered the Kingdom "a squalid backwater," and moved away after he and Patrice were married. He died in an automobile accident; Patrice and Aidan, sixteen, return to Vermont for what she calls "a chance to start over. A chance for you to learn something about your roots." Unable to talk about Timothy or show any emotion, both Aidan and his mother are in deep mourning. His grandmother, Eloise (everyone calls her Memère), is "frank and intense." She gives Aidan a copy of Homer's *The Odyssey*, a bookmark slipped into the title page of Book XI, "A Gathering of Shades." Aidan's father's brother, Uncle Donny Dunkley, still runs the family farm next door with about one hundred cows and hay and cornfields. Aidan climbs up Harper

Mountain to the cemetery, where he meets Angela Unger, whose family has just moved up from Connecticut "to get back to the earth" and "relive their glory days as hippies." Aidan feels "stranded. This farm was an island." Uncle Donny needs his help part-time on the farm. In the evenings, Aidan reads *The Odyssey*, discovering that one of the main characters, Telémakhos (Telemachus), is a son looking for his father. Aidan, miserable and bored, notices his grandmother walking out every evening and follows her. She stands in front of a birdbath, cuts her finger, and drips blood into the basin. Eight people join her in the clearing; each drinks from the basin. One notices Aidan and beckons to him. Aidan can see, hear, and talk to these dead people, who have not yet "moved on." In *The Odyssey*, he comes to the chapter in which Odysseus summons, with libations mixed with spilled blood, the shade of the blind prophet, Teiresias (Tiresias). Odysseus can speak to his mother but not embrace her. Uncle Donny, whose farm is dilapidated, can barely make the payments on his equipment, which is always breaking down. Aidan works hard with him, mowing the rowen (second growth) and repairing the machinery. Hoping to see his father, Aidan joins Memère on another evening when she meets the shades. The next day, he glimpses far off in the woods an auburn-haired boy, whom he recognizes from family photographs as his father in his childhood shape. When Aidan confides these visions to Memère, she advises him to stop chasing his father's ghost and concentrate on living. Thinking about his ancestors' devotion to working the farm and his father's hatred of it, Aidan returns from a hike with Angela to find his mother kissing Uncle Donny. Aidan, furious, shrieks at them and throws himself into the hunt for his father. Aidan goes to the basin, cuts his finger, and bleeds into the water. All the shades come, but Memère drives them away. Aidan reconciles with Uncle Donny. He had thought he could unlock the secret of his father's past, but perhaps there was none. Aidan finds his mother at his father's grave and comforts her. When his father's shade materializes, Aidan waves goodbye to him.

Laura C. Stevenson

The title of ***Happily After All*** (1990) refers to Rebecca ("Becca") Davidson's habit, as a little girl, of confusing the traditional fairy-tale ending, "happily ever after," with "happily after all." Her mother, Rachel, left home when Becca was two, but Becca was blissfully happy being her father's "little princess" in Santa Barbara and is overwhelmed by his death when she is ten. She is even more dismayed when her father's law partner, Mr. Jarvis, informs her that she is to live in Vermont with Rachel, who grew up there. Becca is angry and incredulous as the facts emerge: when Rachel left her husband, intending to take Becca with her, Becca's father kept Becca, letting her believe that Rachel never sought to see nor write to her. Becca refuses to believe Mr. Jarvis, thinking instead of the wonderful times she and her father spent reading *David Copperfield* and *Oliver Twist* ("books are companions, not just books," he said) and other novels given to her by the Book Fairy (whose identity she never knew). Rachel, dressed in old clothes and boots, meets Becca's plane to take her to a dirty, shabby house near Brattleboro, filled with dogs and cats. Becca is sullen and uncommunicative, although she is inwardly excited that Rachel owns horses. Becca likes Patty Ellrow, who keeps a pony at Rachel's and takes riding lessons with her. Patty, an orphan cared for by her grandparents, shows Becca around their school. Becca meets Bill Lavoie, even more unsociable than she, who has an alcoholic father and lives, after a succession of failures, in a foster home with the Amidens. Becca discovers Bill is the smartest boy in the class and a wonderful artist. Rachel, the Amidens' friend, arranges for Bill to work in her barn every day. Becca helps Rachel with the sugaring—it is hard work, wading through the snow, dumping, pouring—and she misses Santa Barbara. "Vermont was so *different*. Even when it was pretty, it wasn't pretty in the right way." Becca finds Rachel changeable: one minute she is fun; the next, judgmental. Becca plans to suffer through six months in Vermont and then ask Mr. Jarvis to bring her home to Santa Barbara. One evening she struggles to push the team into the barn, falls, and is dragged; Bill is hiding there, a gash on his face. Knowing Bill is in trouble from meeting someone in the woods, Becca lies to Rachel and Mr. Amiden to protect him. Rachel discovers Becca is a rider and offers to buy her a pony of her own. Becca knows it is wrong not to tell Rachel her plans. Mr. Amiden is kind and wonderful with horses but does not understand Bill's artistic aspirations. The police find a cache of stolen goods and believe Bill is involved; Becca knows he is not. Her new pony, Gandalph, is beautiful but listless; his former owner died of leukemia when she was fourteen. Gandalph will go perfectly but will not jump, even over a log lying on the ground. When Bill runs away, Becca feels guilty she did not tell the adults what she knew and fears they will send him to the reformatory in Westminster. When Rachel hears from Mr. Jarvis that Becca is unhappy in Vermont, Rachel's face turns to stone. Setting out on Gandalph to look for Bill, Becca takes refuge in an abandoned cottage where she finds Bill, fearful his father will take him away. Mr. Lavoie returns, drunk and abusive. Becca manages to escape, with Mr. Lavoie in pursuit, flinging herself onto her horse and heading him straight for a fence. Gandalph clears it easily, and they race for help. Mr. Jarvis hastens to Vermont to discuss Becca's future, but Becca adamantly does not want to leave her horse, her dog, her friends, and her mother—who was her Book Fairy all along.

Mary Stolz

In ***A Wonderful, Terrible Time*** (1967), best friends Mady Guthrie and Sue Ellen Forrest are eight-year-old "colored" girls living in a racially mixed neighborhood in New York City early in the Vietnam War. Mady's father was shot dead in Mississippi registering black voters; her mother works as a nurse. Sue Ellen's father drives a taxicab; her mother stays home and often takes care of Mady, who loves to read stories about Winnie-the-Pooh. One day, Mr. Forrest narrowly misses a man who steps directly in front of his cab. The man is so grateful that he offers to send Sue Ellen, and a friend, to summer camp in Vermont. Sue Ellen does not want to go to the country with white strangers but agrees reluctantly at her parents' urging and invites Mady. Sue Ellen notices that Bob Frank, a counselor at Camp Oriole, is also colored. Both girls feel frightened and strange. The camp director, Mr. Schering, lives with his family in an old farmhouse that predates the camp. Mady sees woods of Christmas trees, a herd of cows, and wildflowers everywhere. A lake glitters "like glass beads." Sue Ellen is unhappy and wants to go home; Mady loves Camp Oriole. Sue Ellen, rude to the counselors and cross with the other girls, makes no friends; Mady loves "the smell of grass and pine trees in the hot summer sun." Marcia, one of the counselors, helps her make a terrarium to take home a little bit of this world—moss, berry, wintergreen, fern. The campers in their cabin are staging a play. One girl proposes *The Secret Garden*; another suggests a Winnie-the-Pooh story. Sue Ellen overhears them say that "Sour Sue" should play Eeyore because she is so grouchy; she also hears loyal Mady stand up for her. Sue Ellen is designing a book about "colored people," checked, striped, all different colors, which she has shown to no one but Mady. Bob calls Sue Ellen "prickly"; she yearns to tell him that she feels like an "outsider." When the group chooses the story, "In Which Tigger Comes to the Forest and Has Breakfast," Sue volunteers to play Eeyore because, she says, she is "so grouchy." This tacit apology is accepted as such. Mady thinks about their being the only colored people in their cabin. She knows it would be easier in a number of ways to be white, but she would not want to be anyone else. She wishes, though, that being colored were as "silly and cute" as the floral and rainbow people in Sue Ellen's book. When Mady is back in her apartment, she misses camp, but, after she gives her mother the terrarium and tells her about camp, she is glad to be home. (The term "colored" is employed in the novel to describe African-Americans; the epithet was in use in the period described.)

The predominant presence in ***By the Highway Home*** (1971) is a character that never makes an appearance—Beaufort ("Beau") Reed, a Bronze Star hero killed in Vietnam. His Indiana family—parents Amy and Jim; his siblings, Virginia ("Ginger"), sixteen; Catherine ("Catty"), thirteen; and Alexander ("Lexy"), eight—miss him so overwhelmingly they cannot bring themselves to speak of him. Catty is aware that her parents are worried about something other than Beau's death. Her father, an engineer, loses his job, with no prospect of finding another. Many people in similar circumstances become paupers, he says, making Catty, who has a literary frame of reference, think of *The Prince and the Pauper*. Simultaneously, Catty's Aunt Marian Wendell announces that she plans to marry John Grimmett and leave the family home in Vermont, which Great-uncle Henry Wendell runs as an inn for old people. The obvious solution is for the Reed family to help run the inn. Ginger selfishly does not recognize that the family is in crisis. Catty mourns Beau, thinks about him constantly, and wishes she could share her thoughts about him. For example, he loved animals; in fact, he *was* animals, the way Catherine in *Wuthering Heights* says, "I *am* Heathcliff!" The night before they leave Indiana, much of their house burns. In an uncharacteristically unselfish gesture, Ginger saves Catty's Keeping Box, with Beau's photographs and letters in it. During the drive to Vermont, Ginger does not say a nice word to anyone, exhibiting only her discontent. Catty has an insight: Ginger is extremely intelligent, but she never knows what other people are feeling; Catty decides that if you "think about how somebody else is feeling...you won't have time to be afraid." The inn is built of rosy old bricks. Catty is enchanted with the house—the furniture is reminiscent of *Little Women*. Her bedroom is on the top floor. When she sees deer grazing on the meadow, she almost cries out, "Look, Beau!" Cathy has imagined Uncle Henry as King Lear, "shaking a clenched and sinew fist in the face of age." Short, stout, and kind, Uncle Henry keeps five female and two male boarders. Duncan Charters, a nineteen-year-old college student, does the dishes, cleans, and makes the beds in exchange for board for his grandmother. Duncan is tall, handsome, and blue-eyed. Catty befriends Duncan and, when she comments on what good friends he and Beau would have been, Duncan and Aunt Marian, who is also in the room, urge her to talk about her brother. She reads them some letters from her box. In one, Beau quotes A. E. Housman. In her room, she looks with affection at her books, which have just arrived from Indiana. They are filled with characters that make her weep—the Little Mermaid, Oliver, Little Nell, Charlotte, Beth, and Bambi. She copies into her commonplace book a quotation from Simone Weil: "Do not grieve, or keep me always in your thoughts, but think of me as you would remember a book you loved in childhood." Catty adores Vermont. The morning of the wedding, Duncan glories in Catty's beauty; they exchange a meaningful glance. She loves him. Later, at the reception, he regrets what he revealed in his look; she does not. She is growing up, and, as soon as she takes a tray upstairs to one of the elderly lodgers, she will cut in on Duncan, no matter with whom he is dancing. (The title is from Robert Frost's poem, "Reluctance": "Out through the fields and the woods/And over the walls I have wended; /I have climbed the hills of view/And looked at the world, and descended;/I have come by the highway home,/And lo, it is ended." Beau quotes the last line of a stanza from Housman's *Last Poems*, "For 'round me the men will be lying/That learned me the way to behave,/And showed me my business of dying:/*Oh who would not sleep with the brave?*")

In ***Ferris Wheel*** (1977), Pauline ("Polly") Lewis, nine-going-on-ten, faces her first crisis: her best friend since kindergarten, Kate Willard, has moved to California after her father did not receive tenure at the college in eastern Vermont where Polly's father, George, teaches English. Polly's mother, Anna, is a part-time nurse at the college medical facility. Polly's younger brother, Richard ("Rusty"), is her bête noire: she and Rusty fight constantly. Her grandmother, a slim, chic, former schoolteacher, also lives with them. George keeps pigs and chickens but cannot afford being a farmer fulltime: "feed's too expensive, season's too short, land's too stony." When Polly feels at loose ends or frustrated with

Rusty, she whistles for her buckskin pony, Blondel. While George and a helper are rounding up pigs to send to slaughter, one escapes into the woods: Polly and Rusty applaud his liberation. Moya O'Shea, an artist, moves nearby. Polly meets Moya's daughter, Consuela Christina Machado, whose father, a Mexican doctor, did not accompany them to Vermont. At the church supper, Consuela's flamboyant mother broadcasts that she has come to Vermont for "the bracing honesty of the seasons." Out in the field one day, a herd of crowding cattle surrounds a terrified, weeping Rusty; Polly, riding bareback on Blondel, rescues him. The errant pig finds its way home; George renounces raising pet pigs for slaughter. At the annual fair, Polly does not see Consuela anywhere. Imagining what it would be like to be the new person in town, she rides Blondel to Consuela's house to invite her to go on the ferris wheel with her. Together, they look across the Connecticut River to the New Hampshire hills.

In ***Cider Days*** (1978), the sequel to *Ferris Wheel,* Polly, disappointed that her best friend, Kate, has not responded to her letters, has met no one to take her place. She feels friendly toward Consuela, offering to let her ride Blondel whenever she wants, but Polly finds Consuela remote and silent. Polly's wise grandmother suggests that Consuela is just shy, but Polly senses Consuela is unhappy in Vermont—she is not interested in anything or anyone—and strongly desires to return to Mexico. Polly continues to allow her little brother, Rusty, to annoy her: if only she could control her temper. Consuela's mother, Moya—she wants everyone to call her that—is famous, beautiful, exotic, and unconventional. She buzzes around town on a motorcycle. At school, one of the girls makes a derogatory remark about the color of Consuela's skin. Consuela, poised, responds: "My grandmother is Indian and beautiful and she has manners." This year, instead of wandering around the schoolroom and sitting on the floor, each child has a desk; just like *Tom Sawyer*, Polly observes. Moya consults with the Lewises about Consuela's frame of mind, saying she brought her daughter to Vermont because in Mexico she is treated like a doll, a "frippery." Sometimes Polly's parents and grandmother use words—for example, "forbearance, perspective, empathy"—whose meanings she knows, because she looks up the words, but does not quite understand. When her grandmother asks for her favorite book character, she responds, "Ratty from *The Wind in the Willows*." Polly feels grateful for her family and vows to improve relations with Rusty. They work together readying the garden for winter. When Polly feeds Mocha the pig, she notes he is greedy and unfriendly and not a member of the family like Wilbur in *Charlotte's Web.* The Lewises become better acquainted with Moya and Consuela; it occurs to Polly that Consuela might be quiet and reserved to counterbalance her "exuberant" and "dramatic" mother. To ride with Polly, Consuela picks out a purebred Morgan mare she names Favorita. Moya is painting a portrait of Polly; when Polly does artwork at school, she borrows ideas and techniques from Moya. Admiring Moya's talent and confidence, Polly wants to be an artist, too. Moya gives them a painting of Fafeek, their scarecrow, standing in the moonlight with the three children in their Halloween costumes. When Moya goes to New York at Thanksgiving, Consuela stays with the Lewises. She loves Polly's room, saying it looks just like a Beatrix Potter book. "I *love* Beatrix Potter," says Polly. When she turns down Consuela's bed, she puts a copy of *The Tailor of Gloucester* on the bedside table (selecting the right book for one's guest is one of many touches she has picked up from her grandmother). Relaxed and happy, Consuela concedes she would not stay in Mexico after Christmas even if she could—she would miss being here in Vermont with "all of you."

Three kittens are born in a barn in Vermont in ***Cat Walk*** (1983). The black one has white feet with six toes on each (known as "polydactyl"). Their mother tells the kittens they are wild like the animals on the farm, which have no names and never go into the house. The house animals have names, she explains, because they are pets. The farmer's daughter fancies the black kitten, calls him "Tootsy-Wootsy," dresses him like a doll, and pushes him in a baby carriage. Her family takes him to the vet for his shots and brings him into the house, where he sleeps with the Border collie, Juniper. One day, tired of being dressed in a snowsuit, the black kitten escapes. Cold and hungry, he approaches a house where a dog chases him up a tree. The kitten manages to extricate himself from his woolen outfit, climbs into a truck, and arrives at a garage. Jerry, the owner, calls him "Snowshoes," takes him into his house, and feeds him. The kitten loves Jerry and follows him everywhere. Unfortunately, Jerry has a horrid son, Roddy, who attacks the kitten. Knowing he cannot keep the kitten, now a cat, Jerry takes him to the animal haven run by Mr. and Mrs. Archibald Jaffee. They care for wounded, strayed, or abandoned creatures, large and small, returning the healed wild ones to the woods. The Jaffees study the cat carefully because, according to T.S. Eliot, "the naming of cats is a difficult matter." They settle on Maximus and call him "Max." Max's memories about his past fade. His only happy ones are of Juniper. He learns from the other animals the reasons for their being with the Jaffees; the former racing horse, for example, was sold as a hack. Mrs. Jaffee's daughter, Mrs. Oliver, adopts Max and drives off with him through "the spice-colored hills late in the afternoon." Mr. Oliver is not pleased with the new pet. They can name him "Meow Tse Tung," for all he cares, as long as they keep him out of the house. They call him "Mistletoes." Every day, the children leave the cat alone in the mudroom. Because they spend so little time with him, he feels unwelcome. He escapes from the Olivers and walks and walks. He forgets his name. He tries his best to be adopted. He learns to fight. He meets a fox that was caught in a trap but saved by a kind man; the cat is sure the fox was at the Jaffees' home. He makes his way back to their house and climbs into his old basket. He remembers now: his name is Max. (The epigraph is from *Alice's Adventures in Wonderland*. Alice tells the Cheshire Cat that she hopes to reach *somewhere*; the Cat replies she is "sure to do that...if you only walk long enough.")

Phoebe Stone

In 1960 in ***All the Blue Moons at the Wallace Hotel*** (2000), eleven-year-old Fiona Harper's home is the "great, silvery-gray dilapidated" house bought by her art-dealer father. After his death four years earlier, her mother, a successful sculptor, sold most of their possessions, retreated into a reverie, and now never goes anywhere. Fiona takes care of her little sister, Wallace, seven-and-a-half, who spends much of her time dreaming up alternative names for herself and rereading *The Borrowers Afloat*. Sometimes Wallace chooses to wear two dresses to school, "like Heidi." Their only friend is Kipton ("Kip") Jones, who lives in a trailer with his father, a furnace repair man (whose divorced wife lives in another state), and longs to own a hotel when he grows up. Mourning her father, Fiona is ashamed of the house's reputation for the "incident" and does not want anyone to know they live there. They use few of the rooms now, although Fiona remembers when her parents gave grand parties in the ballroom with a jazz band ("Blue Moon" was her father's favorite song). Sometimes it is so cold in the house it feels as though they are in a country of ice, like the girl in "The Child of Snow." Her best friend, Nell Stamford, takes a ballet class; since Fiona cannot afford to attend, Nell teaches Fiona the steps. She practices before school in the ballroom, where Kip made her a barre (in ballet terminology, a waist-high handrail used in warm-up exercises) out of pipes from the back of his father's truck. Fiona yearns to be a ballerina like her Russian grandmother, who had a dancer's smile, "a smile of joy." Fiona's smile of joy is in her heart. Her short-term wish is to dance in the Christmas recital, "The Dance of the Winter Moon." Just before the audition, Fiona learns that Wallace is missing in a snowstorm. Fiona is terrified because she knows Wallace was despondent about her father and also about losing her school project. Fiona misses the tryout to look for Wallace, joined by Kip. Fiona is frantic: if Wallace is lost, Fiona will never be able to recite Robert Louis Stevenson's poem, "The Swing," to her. They finally find her at Mrs. Braverman's, where Wallace is feeding her parakeet while Mrs. Braverman is in the hospital. Fiona sees a note from Mrs. Braverman about Wallace's name, ending, "It's charming and you wouldn't be Wallace without it." Her mother is waiting in a police car with Officer Wolf McKane, the one who came to the house when an enraged art collector shot and killed Fiona's father. The day after Wallace is found, their mother resumes work in her studio, chiseling a statue of Wallace. Her mother has changed completely—she has a look about her "like a freshly swept room." Fiona thinks again of "The Child of Snow" when she sees "the branches are thick with clear ice, making them look like delicate glass deer antlers." After the storm ruins the dance studio, Nell pronounces the ballroom at the Wallace Hotel (Kip's name for their house) perfect for the recital. If Fiona were to offer the ballroom, she would reveal where they live. In the summer, she comes up here to read. She looks around at her favorite books, "The Child of Snow," *The Railway Children*, *The Yearling*, *Little Women*. She will not give up ballet: she will "practice and practice and practice." She is doing so when Nell and the teacher, Carmen Estrellada, arrive. Miss Estrellada is transfixed by Fiona and creates a solo just for her, the part of the full moon—the blue moon, just like her father's song. The house is beautiful with lights ablaze. As Fiona dances her solo, she says goodbye to her sadness, "letting it go like a flower floating off through the snow." (The author says on page 263 of *Vermont Writers: A State of Mind*, by Yvonne Daley, "The town I created was a fictional mishmash of Poughkeepsie memories and my memories of growing up in Goshen, Vermont. For instance, I transformed the rambling old farmhouse on the mountain in Goshen into the dilapidated mansion where the family lives." She wrote to me that "the house was up on a mountain and my sisters and I went to school in Forest Dale in the valley below. The weather in Goshen was always very different from the weather in the valley. We lived in a completely different world up there.")

Cynthia M. Stowe

Dear Mom, in Ohio for a Year (1992) portrays a betrayed and miserable Cassie Hannely, eleven, "dumped" in the "hick" town of Elton by her widowed mother, who leaves Boston for the school year to finish her degree in Ohio. Cassie's mother's sister, Aunt Emily, a therapist, and Uncle Fred, a mason, both vegetarians, are welcoming, but Cassie is so resentful that she cannot fit graciously into their lives and hates their food. Angry and hurt, she refuses to answer her mother's letters, although she composes scores of sarcastic notes that she discards. She is pleasantly surprised by her teacher, Miss Kalish, who runs a friendly, open sixth-grade classroom at Northwood Elementary (which her mother also attended), where the students are cooperative and attentive. On weekends Cassie is restless and bored on their steep mountain in the woods. At Uncle Fred's suggestion, she walks up to Puffet's Pond, where she meets Ernie Bartos, a fourth-grader. Until she makes friends with Cora Hodges, she feels shy and awkward on the school bus. Every Wednesday, Mr. Gagnon, the driver, stops at old Mrs. Parnelli's house to pick up her shopping list, which he attends to during the day. When Cassie expresses her surprise, Cora tells her that everyone helps the old woman: Cora's father and friends split and stack wood for her. Cassie visits Cora's working farm, with cows, horses, and sheep. Cora's great-great-grandfather built the big, white farmhouse. While helping Aunt Emily prepare for a party, Cassie breaks a valuable plate filled with delicate hors d'oeuvres. Aunt Emily, under stress and cross, explodes with fury: Cassie responds that she hates her and hates living in Vermont. She runs off to Puffet's Pond, where Ernie comforts her. They talk about being friends (he is like the brother she never had) despite the difference in their ages and agree to keep their bond a secret. Her mother calls, upset and worried, and explains that she has not abandoned Cassie but, indeed, is trying to make a better life for her. Aunt Emily apologizes for losing her temper and offers to make some meat dishes. Cassie finally writes her mother an amusing letter. She learns that Ernie, though smart, can barely read. Uncle Fred teaches Cassie and Ernie to play chess. When his birthday comes around, Ernie does not want Cassie at his party. His mother and Aunt Emily persuade her and Cora to drop by. On the cake are twelve candles: he has lied about his age because he has been demoted twice. Cassie tells Ernie she regrets embarrassing him; Aunt Emily is also sorry for "meddling." One Wednesday when they stop at Mrs. Parnelli's house, Mr. Gagnon finds her on the floor. She has fallen and broken her hip. He asks Cassie and a classmate to stay with her while he takes the other children in the bus to call an ambulance. Aunt Emily drives Cassie to the hospital to visit Mrs. Parnelli and is proud of the way Cassie behaves. At school, she exhibits a talent for comic writing. She is also writing fluently and frequently to her mother, looking forward to her coming home—to Vermont.

T

Charles Miner Thompson

In ***Calico Cat*** (1908), Jim Edwards, fifteen, lives with his widower father in Ellmington in Adams County. Mr. Edwards, a speculator in lumber and cattle, is stern, uncompromising, and unable to show his son the affection he genuinely feels. Jim's main friend and supporter is his pretty schoolteacher, Nancy Ware, engaged to marry Fred Farnsworth, a storekeeper and currently a grand juror. Bank director Solomon Peaslee, fifty-three, is proud to be appointed to the grand jury. He and his wife, Sarepty, are well off, but they lead a parsimonious life. The bane of Solomon's existence is a calico cat, which makes terrible noises at night, eats his young chickens, and refuses to leave his property. Visiting the house of his neighbor, Mr. Edwards, he sees neither the father (asleep in his bedroom) nor the son (eating apples in the cellar), but he does notice Jim's shotgun. Outside on the fence is the fiendish cat. Solomon loads a marble into the gun and fires, missing the cat but hitting a passerby who falls but rises and walks away. Horrified, Simon beats a quick retreat. Jim hears the shot and assumes that his father is responsible. The father, awakened from his nap, assumes his son fired the shot. The father is hurt that his son should lie; Jim is outraged that, in trying to protect his father, he is accused of the crime. The victim of the shooting is Pete Lamoury, a French-Canadian who is Mr. Edwards's former, dismissed drover. When Jim is arrested, Solomon is greatly alarmed. Squire Tucker, the Justice of the Peace, and Jack Hibbard, the lawyer for the plaintiff, are in the courtroom. Mr. Edwards asks Jim once more to confess. When he refuses, Mr. Edwards will not post his bond; Jim goes to jail, which is the house of the sheriff, Mr. Calkins, and his wife. Nancy Ware is "hotly indignant" and complains to Fred, who visits the Calkins house and finds Jim having a fine time. After questioning the boy, Fred is sure he is shielding someone. Solomon is so worried about Jim that he buys him an expensive harmonica, an astonishing act for a miser. The Grand Jury of Adams County convenes. Mr. Edwards testifies that he believes his son is the culprit. Beside himself with guilt, Solomon confesses. Astonished, the crowd begins to laugh. Samson Page, the state's attorney, insists upon Pete's appearance in court and demonstrates that Pete was not hurt in the slightest and was, in fact, in the act of stealing Solomon's chickens. Jim is excused and released. Mr. Edwards realizes he has a "truthful and courageous" son whom he has treated unjustly. The father and son acknowledge their mutual affection. Solomon's wife forgives him by splurging on oyster stew. Solomon's "neat and comfortable" house and the "cozy pleasantness of the place" strike him. When the calico cat has kittens, Solomon pours some milk in a bowl for her.

Daniel Pierce Thompson

The Green Mountain Boys (1927) begins on Lake Dunmore near Otter Creek. Green Mountain Boys Captain Charles Warrington, Lieutenant Edward Selden, and three comrades, including Long-legged Pete Jones, are camping and fishing. (The author greatly admires the resolute, intrepid, and cool qualities of the Green Mountain Boys and attributes these qualities to the bracing air of this "Switzerland of America.") Spy Jacob Sherwood leads Albany sheriff Munroe and ten men to capture the Boys. Warned by Neshobee, a messenger from Ann Story, the Boys outwit the Yorkers, toss Munroe in the lake, and sentence Sherwood to forty stripes with a green beech rod before releasing him. The Boys carry their fish and venison to Ann Story and her family on Otter Creek, where, for safety, she and her children spend nights in a cave near the house. At midnight, Charles hears the singing of a woman's familiar voice. The Boys head for the compound seized by British Loyalist Colonel Reed (Reid) and his Highlanders near Otter Creek, where he secured a huge tract of land, drove out the inhabitants, and took possession of their sawmills. Charles and his men peacefully assume command of the fort; Charles accepts Donald McIntosh's surrender and invites him and his men into the house to spend the night. After the fort and property are restored to their rightful owners, Edward volunteers to escort Colonel Reed's daughter, Jessy, and her maid, Zilpah Wampum, to the home of Loyalist Major Philip Skene in Skenesboro. Charles visits Captain James Hendee, who lives on property belonging to Charles on Lake Champlain near Snake Mountain. Hendee fought in the French and Indian Wars and suffered the death of two adored wives and the unaccountable disappearance of his son, Edward. At length, Hendee presumed that Edward was dead; by law of inheritance, Edward's share of the property fell to Hendee's brother's son, Jacob Sherwood. Hendee's daughter, Alma, is the singer Charles heard at Ann Story's and the woman with whom he fell in love while traveling incognito for the Boys. He reveals his identity and explains the plight of the settlers. Her suitor is Sherwood, whom she does not love but whose suit her father encourages because of his inheritance. Also part of the household is a maid, Ruth, and Neshobee, whom Hendee captured and brought up as a trusted servant. While Charles is there, a gentleman of "Herculean cast" calling himself "Smith" (Ethan Allen) arrives, tells them about the Battle of Lexington, pretends to be drunk, and is billeted with Charles in the barn. William Darrow, a minion of Sherwood's, arrives to arrest Allen and Charles, but they escape with Neshobee's and Alma's help. Jessy writes to Alma that she and Edward are in love and that Edward knows neither his birthplace nor his parents but grew up in the household of an English nobleman. At a meeting in Middlebury in May 1775, Allen exhorts his followers to join the expedition to capture the British forts at Ticonderoga and Crown Point; they agree to meet at Castleton. Alma writes to Jessy that she had supper with Charles and Edward at her Aunt Story's house. She records Charles's explanation of their goal—the right to defend their home and their property. No matter whether they are called "patriot" or "rebel," he said to her, their principles are immutable. Alma and Charles become engaged. At Castleton, Colonel Benedict Arnold arrives, expecting to lead the troops. Learning from Charles that the men volunteered to serve under Allen, Arnold offers his services as a common soldier. Allen cries that he and Arnold will proceed "on together, like brothers." They travel the Crown Point Road built by General Amherst in 1759. Noah Phelps (see Clavin Fisher's *A Spy at Ticonderoga* in this collection) reports to Allen about intelligence he gathered at the fort. The Boys seize Ticonderoga and Crown Point, and Edward leads the ladies to safety at Alma's house. Alma, now engaged to Charles even though her father still wants her to marry Sherwood, hears from a traveling tinker that Charles is already married and breaks off her engagement. Two years pass. The tinker writes to Alma regretting that he was inadvertently a party to a deception orchestrated by Sherwood. Charles, now a colonel, wants to declare himself to her father, but she begs him to wait. A letter from Jessy reports that the patriots, led by Edward, have commandeered the Skenes' house and taken them all prisoner; she will travel to Albany under Edward's protection. Jessy's father, a British colonel, sends her to the Hendees, where she confides to Alma that she and Edward are engaged. Pete Jones informs them of General Burgoyne's plans. In Albany, John Sherwood, Jacob's dying father, writes a letter to his brother-in-law, confessing his role in the disappearance of Edward, and summons his lawyer to rewrite his will, bequeathing one thousand pounds each to Captain Hendee and to Alma. Sherwood arrives after his father's death, destroys the letter, and tries to bribe the incorruptible lawyer. He hurries to the Hendees, where Alma summarily dismisses his proposal of marriage. She has told her father everything, including Charles's magnanimity in allowing them to reside on his property. Sherwood is secretly a captain in His Majesty's Loyal Americans in the New Hampshire Grants, taking orders from General Burgoyne. Darrow reports to Sherwood that he has seen a young officer whom he believes to be Edward Hendee. Pete Jones warns the Hendees that, with Burgoyne's army and many Indians on the march, they should head for Rutland, twenty miles distant. As they start in the direction of Castleton, a group of Indians, many of whom are white men in disguise, captures the Hendees. Sherwood, the "base dissembler," appears, bringing a clergyman to marry them on the spot; Alma says she would rather die. Neshobee escapes to seek help. General St. Clair evacuates Fort Ticonderoga, the Americans retreat, with General Frazier (Fraser) and his British Regulars and General Reidesel (Riedesel) and his Brunswick forces in pursuit. Charles is in command of the American rearguard; Edward is now a captain. The Battle of Hubbardton ensues; the Green Mountain Boys are "wet, weary, and war-torn." General St. Clair pledges reinforcements. Neshobee finds Charles, who sends Edward to the rescue, with his company of men, including Pete. When the villains notice Neshobee's absence, they march their prisoners toward Hubbardton. On a hill, less than a mile from the battle, Alma and Jessy watch the "fearful spectacle." Edward's company liberates the Hendee party, which makes its escape while Pete and his comrades hold off the Tories. The Hendees, who have heard that Charles is dead, cross the river to hide at Ann Story's. She now has a trap door in her house leading to Otter Creek and an "innermost recess" in her underground fortress. At Hubbardton, the Germans arrive at the battle; with no reinforcements, the Americans scatter to reform at Bennington. The climax of the novel is the siege of Ann Story's house by Sherwood and his henchmen. They try to batter down the door of the cabin; they set fire to the roof; they begin to dig through the turf. Captain Hendee, the women, and Ann's children are in the stronghold; Ann, with her rifle, stands with the men: "Give me a place among you and see whether I am the first to desert the post of danger." The house on fire, the defenders retreat into the last chamber. One desperate chance remains—the casks of gunpowder. Edward ignites them in the passageway: the explosion kills every villain except Sherwood, who escapes, and Darrow, who, before he dies, reveals that John Sherwood defrauded Hendee out of his inheritance; it was Darrow who kidnapped his son—Edward Selden. Charles, whom they thought slain, dashes up. The Americans win the great Battle of Bennington. The grand finale features a wedding for Alma and Charles, Jessy and Edward, Ruth and Pete, and Zilpah and Neshobee, with two special guests, Ann Story and Ethan Allen.

This modern version of ***The Green Mountain Boys*** (2000) updates the classic historical romance in an abridged edition of less than half the length of the original. The aim of the editors (Carol E. Washington and Ida H. Washington) was "to bring *The Green Mountain Boys* a renewal of life, to give again in these adventures from our history their rightful place in the American literary scene. Our product is not designed to be 'simplifed' reading, but to bring the book sufficiently up to date in language and style for readers of today to enjoy the rich contents within its covers."

Julian F. Thompson

Duncan ("Slam-Dunc") Banigan, seventeen, in ***Discontinued*** (1985) is tall, nice-looking, athletic, and honest. He has learned to get along at his school in Newark, New Jersey, by memorizing what the teacher thinks is important. He has a good relationship with his pretty girlfriend, Terry Bissonette. One day, as he approaches his home, his mother, Ruth, and brother, Brian, climb into a car, which blows up in front of his eyes. He is in a state of shock from the time of the police interrogations until after the funeral, attended by his father, Gerald, who divorced his mother when Duncan was two, and his grandmother, who has no room for him in her small apartment. Duncan's kind neighbor, Dottie Michalis, suggests that she oversee him in her house or his. She and Duncan both assume Brian was a drug dealer. In Brian's papers, Duncan finds a note: "Dudu, check this out: fetish, swillys, boobytune." He deciphers the code easily: "boobytune" is Burlington, and "swillys" is South Willard Street. With Dottie to help perfect his disguise—short haircut, eyeglasses, and a dog—he heads for Burlington and the house of Abraham Fetish on South Willard Street. Under the pretext of completing a high school assignment, Duncan moves into the Friends of Nukismetic Humanism House, directed by Abraham. The members believe in "a fated nuclear encounter for the benefit of humanity." Caitlin Fetish, twenty-five, is Abraham's tall, athletic daughter. Abraham asks Duncan to take meditation courses to change his "aura" and assigns him to the NU-HU store on Lake Champlain, which sells health food, much of which the Friends grow themselves. Duncan wonders why Brian wanted him here. At the house on South Willard Street, the Friends—a kind of cult—share chores. Duncan, reaching Dottie from a public telephone, learns of strange calls to him and break-ins at his house. Caitlin, who likes Duncan because he is clean, smart, and hardworking, starts shooting baskets with him. Working at the warehouse one day, Duncan stumbles into a room filled with bales of marijuana. Shocked by this contamination of the health food operation, Duncan does not want to leave because he is in love with Caitlin. After they make love, he tells her about the warehouse. That night, she, her father, and several others replace the marijuana with bales of herbs like catnip. Duncan persuades himself that NU-HU is not involved in drugs. A new boarder, Mister Carlo, recognizes Duncan as "the kid from New Jersey." Carlo, whose English is imperfect, misunderstood Abraham's instructions and shockingly used gelignite to blow up Brian (and his mother) instead of enlarging a photograph of him as proof that Brian, their agent, was underselling them. Terry calls Duncan on a public telephone and mentions seeing a "Spanish-looking man": Duncan realizes she is talking about Carlo and remembers seeing him at the funeral. Now Duncan knows that Caitlin lied about the marijuana; the world is rotten after all. Carlo reveals to Caitlin what happened in New Jersey. Abraham, on a business trip, worries about Caitlin and heads home. Terry flies to Burlington. Carlo is waiting in Duncan's room to kill him. Duncan is in Abraham's study, going through his documents. When the five converge, Abraham tells Duncan what happened to his brother and mother. Duncan looks at them grimly. Does he want revenge? "Smiling sweetly and sadly," Duncan touches Caitlin's shoulder lightly and takes Terry home to New Jersey.

In ***Simon Pure*** (1987), Simon Storn, fifteen, enrolls in his father's alma mater, Riddle University, three hundred miles from Simon's home in Peacemeal near Plainfield. Simon is intellectually advanced because his mother, Maria, a brain researcher, exposed Simon to poets, scientists, and economists: his Scholastic Aptitude Test scores were in the ninety-ninth to one-hundredth percentile nationally. Socially, however, he is not so advanced: never having had a girlfriend, he considers himself a "sociosexual island...unto himself" (paraphrasing John Donne's *Meditation XVII*, "No man is an island, entire of itself"). The president of the university, Henry ("Gates") Portcullis, is happy to accept his former roommate's son but wonders whether a boy of fifteen can handle the "residential life" at Riddle. The rest of the novel, which is peripheral to Vermont except for Simon's frequent references to it, concerns an attempt by a faction at the university to transform it into a business school and to fire Portcullis. Henry confides to his glamorous resident advisor, Amanda Dollop, that he lives in a little rural town in Vermont where everything is "peaceful" and "simple"; he is not sure he wants to settle there. Portcullis invites Simon for supper with his wife, Betsey, amusing and dismissive of her husband's rank, and his fourteen-year-old daughter, Kate, smart, abrasive, and taunting. She tries to find out who he really is; soon she and Simon are kindred spirits—and in love. Many of the students are involved in commercial ventures. One wants to sell Simon insurance in case of a nuclear attack: Simon points out that Vermont town meetings brought the nuclear freeze idea to national attention. Simon uncovers a plot to overthrow Portcullis and transform the university. Unfortunately, his adversaries feed Simon too many beers: he tells indiscreet stories (one is about "dumb flatlanders who'd moved into Peacemeal and how Solzhenitsyn had told him that Vermont's climate reminded him of home: 'eleffen munts uff vinter and vun munt of mediocre shledding'") and reveals who told him about the plot. One of the conspirators says he thinks he may have "passed through Peacemeal on his way to Stowe." The cabal decides to incriminate Simon's father: "Why would someone live in Peacemeal, Vermont, unless he had something to hide?" The plot is foiled. ("Simon pure" means anything genuine, from a character in *A Bold Stroke for a Wife*, by Susannah Centlivre, 1718.)

The title character in ***Shepherd*** (1993) is Shepherd Catlett, seventeen, a senior in high school, whose self-assessment is that he is a good student (a National Merit finalist), decent looking, not a trouble-maker, and possessed of an "accepting" attitude stemming from growing up on a farm. His father, Darwin, mother, Laura, and uncle, Elbie, are dairy farmers on Highridge Road above the town of Burnside in central Vermont. His best friend is neighbor Tara Garza, with whom he grew up: they have much in common and sit together on the bus. Dwayne and Dwight Delbert, who also live on Highridge Road, frequently miss school. Shep is a reader, making easy allusions to novels like *Silas Marner* and *The Old Man and the Sea*. Listening to popular music one day he hears a spoken phrase on a tape that sounds like, "Savor life," and then, "Save her life." Tara has a weekend job as a waitress to save up to leave Burnside after graduation, even though, as a top student, she could attend any college. Because Shep studied French for three years, his advisor suggests a year of beginning Spanish. In the class he cannot help but notice provocative freshman Mary Sutherland. He is astounded when Mary seductively asks him for help with her Spanish; he quickly agrees. He hears gossip around school that Mary spends time with seniors of ill repute; when she asks him for supper, he accepts. During their tutoring session, Mary teases and flirts with him, but says she is entangled with someone else. At school, he cannot stop thinking about her and, in order to concentrate on his homework, goes outside to sit in the grandstand. There, unnoticed, he witnesses the brutish physical education teacher beating up Dwayne. Shocked, Shep tells Tara, who urges him to go to Mr. Reese, the principal; Shep has given his word to Dwayne not to report the incident. Shep continues obsessing about Mary, even lying to Tara about his relationship with her. When Tara sees him in his mother's car with Mary, Shep feels he "has squandered something valuable." He believes, though, that he loves Mary. Tara tells him that Mary is drinking excessively with the older boys. Shep storms into a boy's house during a drunken party to persuade Mary to leave with him—to "save her." Instead, a boy curses Shep and attacks him. Feeling he has spoiled his life, Shep will not speak to Tara when she calls. As an act of atonement, he cleans the cow manure from his uncle's barn and struggles to come to some sort of "conclusion" about his life. When the school gathers in the gym for the weekly assembly, the armed Delbert family takes over, demanding a fair fight between Dwayne and the teacher who assaulted him. Only after the confrontation does Shep realize the guns were not loaded. Both girls emerge from the stadium to hug him. Shep's mother semi-adopts Mary; Tara decides to move to Burlington; Shep, at the University of Vermont, will be able to tell her every day how much he loves her.

A sophisticated fifteen-year-old when she narrates ***The Trials of Molly Sheldon*** (1995), Molly Sheldon, who lives in Saphouse Junction, is twelve when the events occur. Her father, Ira, a seventh-generation Vermonter, runs the Happy Hunting Ground convenience store and a factory in Spofford to age his "facsimile furniture." He loves turning on his "rustic charm" and treats his customers with verve and showmanship. Her mother, Ellen, a perfectionist, owns a weekly newspaper, *The Evaporator*. One of her weekly columns describes the "tendency some flatlanders have to want the same advantages they'd previously enjoyed in Greenwich, Connecticut, while living the 'simple life' in quaint and rural, inexpensive old Vermont." Molly discovers to her surprise that she can "see pain and cure it." Molly and Eben Wheeler, her favorite male companion, attend school in nearby Honeyfield, an affluent town. Several afternoons a week, Molly works at her father's store under the unpleasant eye of manager Carleton Major. Eben, who is from Jenkins Hollow, is looking for a map of the area to hunt for treasure in the dumps around old home sites. Legend has it that an Old Trader's Cave exists, where Zachariah Pleasant stored his valuable goods. While Molly and Eben follow the map, which Ira created, she tells him a bit about the "pain-and-healing business." Eben finds an intact earthenware crock, which he gives to Ira. Several local women, led by Esther Carp, begin picketing Ira's store, claiming he sells pornographic materials. The following week, chartered buses arrive with demonstrators demanding censorship of Ira's books and videos. The locals, with glamorous Cleo Purloin in the lead, stage a counter-demonstration. Eben intervenes in Molly's life in two ways: he tells Carleton about Molly's healing powers; he tells Molly about Cleo's spending a night at her father's camp above Eben's house. Molly receives a message that Carleton wants to see her: she wakes up in a cave, surrounded by three people in rubber celebrity masks. One of them, she is certain, is Esther; another is Carleton. They hold a trial to determine whether Molly is a witch, asking what initiations she underwent, which demons are her lovers, and who her accomplices are. They know about her cures and her friendship with Eben, "the devil's spawn" (they claim Eben's father abused him). Just as Carleton threatens to search her body for a witch's mark, her parents, Eben, and the two town constables burst into the cave. Esther and her husband built their camp on the mouth of Old Trader's Cave. Molly is not sure what happened between her father and Cleo, but she understands and loves him more than ever.

In ***Ghost Story*** (1997), Anna Larrimore, fourteen, unwillingly moves from New York to Boynton Falls ("this absolutely nowhere village in Vermont") with her parents, who run a country inn. Lonely and friendless, Anna is sufficiently self-aware to know that she is often unpleasant to her parents, whom she finds "boring." They assign her tasks at the inn: she cleans several rooms in the mornings (one is occupied by Mrs. Capilary, whose paintings Anna admires) and acts as hostess in the lobby in the afternoons. Unexpectedly, she gains two friends. One is Caleb Grosscup, a high school boy who runs the dishwasher at the inn. Despite being born without a left hand, he is a talented basketball player who shoots baskets with her in their time off. The other is a ghost, Roxy Cray, who lived from 1804 to 1818 and was a "serving wench" at the inn. Roxy's instructions are to stay in the inn until something unspecified happens, when "forever will begin for me." Roxy tells Anna about the customs at the inn in the olden days and helps her with her housekeeping. More guests arrive. One couple, calling themselves "the Washingtons," turns out to be Jeremy Lump and Lily Laser, "the most famous rock-and-roll duo in the world." Lily recognizes "Mrs. Capilary" as Dotty Knucks, a famous woman athlete and feminist. Another newcomer is Tony DeForest, in his late twenties, a supremely handsome photographer who "just loves Vermont." Asking Anna to show him some photogenic sites, like Boynton Gorge, Tony is enthusiastic about her "virginal" and, at the same time, "sensual" looks and wants to use her as model (suggesting she not tell her parents). She does tell Roxy, who warns Anna against artists. A painter seduced Roxy, giving her something to "make it safe"; she became pregnant and died at the hands of an abortionist. Meanwhile, Anna enjoys playing basketball with Caleb, who urges her to try out for the school team and compliments her on not acting like a "flatlander." She is delighted that Caleb, a "genuine local person," accepts her. Her parents, however, are concerned, especially since they hear her talking to herself (actually to Roxy), and urge her to consult with the Lawrences, psychologists staying at the inn. To placate her parents, Anna meets with them; they spend the entire time telling her they are "authentic space travelers." Anna begins running in the mornings, partly as exercise and partly as an excuse to meet Tony and Magda, a glamorous bubble gum-chewing model, who joins Tony at the inn. Anna enjoys the photographic sessions—one day Tony imitates a Wyeth setting; the next he recreates a Manet scene. Roxy again warns Anna, saying she has found photographs of nudes in Tony's room. One day, when Tony picks up Anna to shoot a calisthenics video on a beautiful site at the gorge, Magda is not in the car. He gives Anna a rich chocolate brownie to eat with her coffee. While she is jogging in place and doing jumping jacks, she begins to feel "spacey"—relaxed yet confident. Tony tells her to take off her clothes, "before she loses her high." Mrs. Capilary, warned by Jeremy and Lily that Tony is a pornographer, arrives in time to witness Anna's pushing Tony off the precipice. In fact, it was Roxy who did so, but Anna cannot explain this to Mrs. Capilary. They agree to report to the police that Tony slipped and fell. Anna never sees Roxy again: her reason for being at the inn was to save Anna from the same fate that befell Roxy. Anna and Caleb start running in the early mornings and shooting baskets every afternoon. He suggests they go to the movies together.

Mary Wolfe Thompson

Virginia ("Ginger") Clyde, sixteen, in ***Green Threshold*** (1954) lives for one purpose only—to care for her brother, the center of her life. When Horace ("Hal") Brandon Clyde was eighteen and she, five, their parents were killed in an automobile accident; since then, Ginger and Hal have lived with their Aunt Barbie. Hal became an architect, fought in the Korean War, was badly wounded, and is now confined to a wheelchair. His apathy and indifference are so acute that Aunt Barbie moves the three of them to Oldchester off Route 7, where they buy a lovely house, "Skyacre," with Hal's G.I. benefits. Hal sketches plans and takes measurements to renovate the house, assisted by next-door neighbor Alec McPherson, a bright young man Ginger's age. Alec takes Ginger to a dance on the green. When Ginger notices that Prue Ballard, the daughter of the real estate agent, is interested in Hal, she cannot suppress her jealousy: she wants to become an architect to be Hal's partner. Once Skyacre is finished, Hal is again restless and bored. When a man offers to buy the house and property, Hal decides to sell at a profit and buy, remodel, and resell houses as a business. Meanwhile, Ginger's school friend, Donna Miller, and her family are living on church land; a neighbor, contesting their rights to the spring, cuts off their water supply. Hal starts work on an old mansion, the House on the Green, and clearly trusts Alec's taste more than Ginger's. Ginger, knowing Hal cares for Prue, intercepts her calls and visits. A buyer for the House on the Green surfaces, requesting special features like a gallery and a conservatory. Hal is independent now, able to hoist himself into a specially equipped car. Just as they find a house to function as their home, Hal's office, and Aunt Barbie's studio, a double catastrophe strikes: the buyer of Skyacre angrily claims that he was defrauded because the house is partially on church land, and the buyer of the House on the Green declares bankruptcy. Alec, whose grandfather was town clerk, proposes they search for the old leases to Skyacre: they are successful both in their own case and in that of the Millers. Ginger, touched by the language in the old documents, pledges that she will never again be jealous, "as long as wood grows and water runs." Prue and Hal become engaged; Ginger realizes that architecture is not for her, but, when she and Alec marry, they will be partners.

Snow Slopes (1957) is a ski resort at Bromley Mountain near Westbury where Arleigh Burd, seventeen, helps her widowed mother, Susan, run Intervale, an inn for tourists and skiers. Arleigh cannot ski because she suffered polio as a child, leaving her with a lame leg. Susan is child-like and improvident; if Arleigh does not find a part-time job after school, she will not be able to attend the University of Vermont. Her father's brother, Uncle Charles, often visits to research the Underground Railroad, hoping to prove that Intervale was one of the way stations. Snow Slopes hires Arleigh for the information desk; she recommends Intervale to Gary Caldwell, a slim, attractive college man looking for a place to stay with his parents. Gary's father, a historian, shares an interest in the Underground Railroad with Uncle Charles, who learns that the Lintons, a Quaker family, once owned Intervale. Another inn guest is Sonia Fisher, a glamorous first-rank skier, who tries to appropriate Gary. The Caldwells become regular guests at Intervale that winter; Sonia manages to stay there as well, disguising her jealousy of Arleigh whom Gary obviously likes. In the attic, Mr. Caldwell finds a note about a "consignment" (of fugitive slaves) dated 1837. In the cellar, Gary and Arleigh discover a report of the antislavery society of Westbury in the false bottom of a desk. Just as the Burds make a dent in their debts, Susan buys an expensive sofa. Arleigh, dismayed, pays the oil bill with her college fund. The next time the Caldwells come, they find an obeah (amulet) in the barn. Sonia continues to compete for Gary's attention. When Sonia is seriously hurt—perhaps paralyzed—in a skiing accident, Arleigh has an epiphany: her only handicap is self-pity. A neighbor, Mr. Adams, begins sugaring on their property, which will produce extra income for the Hurds. The slaves' hiding place turns out to be the sap house. Susan and Uncle Charles announce their engagement, Uncle Charles offers to pay Arleigh's tuition at the University of Vermont, and Gary, at Dartmouth, hopes to continue seeing Arleigh.

Two in the Wilderness (1967) is the first novel of a trilogy (the others are *Wilderness Winter* and *Wilderness Wedding*) about the Aiken family, settlers of the town of Windham. In 1773, Edward Aiken traveled from his home in Londonderry, New Hampshire, to establish a pitch (an early settler's encampment) in Windham in the southern part of the New Hampshire Grants. The following summer, when this story begins, he returns on a twenty-day trip with Tabitha, twelve, Ezekiel, ten, and their dog, Shadrack; they cross the Connecticut River on a raft, paying one partridge as fare. Arriving at his clearing, Edward sends the children to bathe in the pond and wash their clothes. He has brought leather to mend their moccasins. He shoots a deer, their first meat since they left home, and plants corn between the stumps. With logs he cut the previous year, he builds a cabin. The children strain to steady the logs for him and peel long strips of bark from elm trees for the roof. Edward makes a chimney of stone and wattle. The door consists of eight slabs with wooden crosspieces held by wooden pins and two pairs of wooden hinges with a bar inside, so that nothing can open it. After Edward leaves to fetch the rest of the family, Tabitha and Zeke feel the emptiness of his absence. The first day is the hardest, but they slip into a routine. To keep Zeke occupied, Tabitha sends him off to fashion a snare line. She does not allow him to take the gun. She cooks, cleans, mends their clothes, and digs groundnuts for stew, marking off the passing days on Edward's time-log. One night she hears a panther on the roof; a bear chases the dog; they hear a wolf chorus. The wild berries are plentiful. They take their bark buckets to the pond for clay to pack into the chinks between the cabin's logs. Once when Zeke is chopping wood, the hatchet slips and gashes his instep. Tabitha hurries into the meadow to find a puffball (a kind of mushroom that when pressed releases the enclosed spores in puffs of dust). Grabbing a clean shirt and a bucket of water, she washes the wound, squeezes the brown powder on it, and gently bandages it.

T

While Zeke recuperates, Tabitha tends the snares, finding a rabbit and a partridge, and resets the traps. Frightened by being in the woods alone, she or Zeke will carry a gun from now on. The corn prospers, but, when a heavy rain comes, they fear it will beat down the stalks. Many trees fall; part of the roof is damaged. The children fit sheets of bark onto the damaged places. They smell smoke. Lightning has split a pine tree; fire has started deep within it. Tabitha tries to beat out the flames with a broom, while Zeke digs around the tree. They find that a vixen is robbing their snares but, after seeing her cubs, they do not harm the mother. Zeke glimpses a deer in the meadow, shoots—and misses. Two Indians come to the cabin. Tabitha, remembering what her father told her about Indian hospitality, invites them to share their stew by the fire. Tabitha handles herself well throughout the visit but bursts into tears of relief after the Indians leave. They return with deer meat and a hide to salute the children's bravery. As the time approaches for their family's arrival, the children furiously prepare by cleaning, making spruce beds, and stacking wood. More than six weeks have passed; the children can hardly endure the wait. Finally the family comes. Tabitha has supper ready. Edward has settled their claim: they are the first settlers of the Town of Windham. (This book is dedicated to Gerald Raftery, whose work is included in this collection. Edward Aiken, the first homesteader of Windham, Vermont, was the great-great-great-grandfather of David George Aiken, 1892-1984, who served as both governor of Vermont and United States senator.)

Wilderness Winter (1968) starts with the arrival of the rest of the Aiken family—Patience, the mother; twins Jonathan and David; and baby Prudence. Tabitha notices her father's severity in the way he issues instructions. They help make a stable for Daisy, the cow. Edward has brought, among other items, an auger and a corn knife wrapped in the feather bed that Daisy carried. Edward and Patience cut the corn and stand the bundles upright; the children husk it. When the twins do not attend to their work, Edward spanks them. He makes a table, two benches, a couple of stools, and plates, bowls, and spoons out of wood. He roars at Tabitha if she does not hold the adz at the right angle. Patience sends Tabitha and Zeke for a saucer-shaped stone for a lamp; they find, instead, a human footprint. Edward does not believe them. He makes a sleeping loft for the older children and cuts down a hollow buttonwood tree to make a plumping mill for pounding the corn into meal. He shoots a bear; the meat is delicious, though he and Patience are especially interested in the useful fat from the carcass. Edward clears more fields, felling trees and rolling the logs into piles for burning. From the ashes they will make and sell potash. Edward, anticipating winter, works them until they ache. When the snow comes, he makes a sled for the twins and snowshoes for everyone. He shoots a turkey for Thanksgiving and a deer for their winter's supply of meat. They cut and smoke the meat; someone has to watch the fire, even at night. The cabin smells pleasantly of hickory smoke. Tabitha and Zeke think they spot someone in the woods; again, Edward does not believe them. Daisy has a calf. They make lye soap. When the weather is right, Edward bores holes in the sugar maples, whittles spouts, and assembles containers to gather the sap. Shadrack comes back accompanied by a tame black dog. Edward is annoyed that they have neighbors: he has seen smoke about six miles away. Patience, on the other hand, is pleased to have company: she is expecting another baby. Soon they meet Nathan Armstrong, fifteen, and his father, James. The Armstrongs traveled to the Grants on the Connecticut River and brought many possessions by canoe. James offers to carry their potash to market by river. He has oxen and can bring millstones to Edward's milldam. When Patience gives birth to baby Israel, Mrs. Armstrong assists. Her daughter, Jerusha, is Tabitha's age. Edward and James disagree on the construction of the wheel for the dam and its use: Edward, a hard worker though stubborn, does not want to share it with neighbors. After James finds baby Prue lost in the woods, Edward agrees to anything James wants. A surveyor and his young Indian assistant measure out Edward's one hundred acres. Edward and

James work on the mill, the dam, and the mill-race, which will feed water to the mill wheel. James contributes money to be reimbursed after people pay to grind their corn. Edward's dream is a reality—the first gristmill in the town of Windham.

Wilderness Wedding (1970) begins two years later. Zeke notices that Tabitha and Nathan spend a great deal of time together. The Armstrongs' dog has puppies, fathered by Shadrack, and the Aikens take three home. In addition to corn, Edward plants a field of flax for Patience to make linen. When they are fifteen and eighteen, Tabitha and Nathan decide to marry. He travels to Connecticut to fetch the team of young oxen given him by his grandparents. Patience realizes they have been working so hard she has not taught the children to read. Making a small paddle from a slice of wood, she writes the alphabet in charcoal on the wood, covering the letters with a thin piece of cow's horn so they do not smudge (thus, a "hornbook"). Nathan chooses a site on the flat by the Connecticut River and plans sawed-board floors (instead of dirt) and a sawed-board door, made in two sections. At the Aikens' house, they pick the flax plants, spread them to dry, and pull them through a great comb to tear off the seed pods (called "rippling"). Edward reminds Nathan to fix a price on his land with one of the proprietors for his grant. When the cabin is ready, the young people, Tabitha in a new deerskin dress, marry on August 2, 1771. They walk to their new home. Some of the men help build a stable. Gray Cloud, a neighboring Abenaki, warning that the river is rising, invites them to stay at his longhouse (a communal dwelling built of poles and bark). The low shelter has three smoke holes in the roof, a fire under each. While Nathan is away saying goodbye to his dying sister, Hannah, a panther appears at the stable. Tabitha thinks quickly. First, she opens the door and whistles loudly. Then she lights a pine knot as a torch, gathers an armful of firewood, and kindles a fire as close to the stable as she dares. Gray Cloud and a second Indian shoot the panther. Before moving the cabin to higher ground, Nathan and Tabitha consult with Gray Cloud. Log by log, the cabin comes down; the oxen pull each log to the new site. Reverend Julius Roberts, the circuit rider for the area, visits on a horse (Tabitha has never seen one) and looks admiringly at Jerusha. The snow is deep. Nathan and Tabitha string a Christmas tree with cranberries. They visit the Indians to exchange gifts; the women show Tabitha how they wet, dry, and wet again strips of willow to weave into baskets. Nathan makes a checkerboard. They sugar and plant corn "when the leaves on the white oaks are the size of mouse ears." They raise four sheep; pumpkin vines grow everywhere. In May, Patience comes, with little Israel and a calf, to make linen garments and assist at the birth of James Nathaniel Armstrong. Gray Cloud presents an elaborately embroidered deerskin to the baby. Jerusha is engaged to Reverend Roberts. Everyone is happy.

Mary Towne

For the last three summers, the Munsons—Willard and Florence; Wanda, twelve; and Andrew, ten—in ***Wanda the Worrywart*** (1989) have spent a two-week vacation at Potter's Lodge and Family Camp on Lake Heron (based on Averill) in the Northeast Kingdom. This year Phyllis, Wanda's former step-grandmother, who makes a career of staying with other people, preferably relatives, accompanies them. Phyllis constantly complains about the "rustic" nature of the facilities. Possessed of a vivid imagination, Wanda worries about every contingency—whether she will throw up in the car on the way to Vermont (she never has) or whether she will lose herself in the woods (she leaves blazes in magic marker on every rock). The other children her age at camp, Sally, Steve and Angie Hyatt and their cousin, Gus, tease her but are nice—especially Gus, upon whom she has a mild crush. It occurs to Wanda and her father, simultaneously, that marrying off Phyllis to a rich retiree would do everyone a favor. A regular at the camp is Drew Farnsworth, a wealthy man devoted to fishing on Lake Heron. Phyllis begins playing bridge with Drew in the evenings; before long, he invites her to go fishing (for this outing, she chooses a chiffon dress and a picture hat). On the same day, Ray and Nora Wallace, lodge managers, organize a picnic at Great Harriman Lake. As the gang heads there, Wanda peers through borrowed binoculars at Phyllis and Drew in their boat. Coming back from the picnic, she looks again: Drew is there, but Phyllis is not. Wanda is seized with anxiety: has he pushed her overboard for startling the fish? Wanda follows her earlier trail blazes and finds Phyllis stretched out on the ground, messy, bitten, scratched, weepy, and sore of ankle, after a quarrel with Drew. Wanda, naturally, is equipped with an ace bandage for the leg, water from a canteen, and first-aid cream to dab on the bites and scratches. Wanda helps Phyllis limp to the Ledge Trail and agrees, reluctantly, not to tell anyone about her mishap. The events Wanda anticipates sometimes do come to pass, but no one will know. Drew catches—and throws back—a legendary giant fish and, saying Phyllis brings him luck, invites her to play bridge again that night.

In ***Steve the Sure*** (1990), the sequel, the focus is on Steve Hyatt, twelve, an attractive, bright, self-confident youth. A natural leader, Steve is so argumentative and such a know-it-all that he angers and annoys his sister, Angie; his cousin, Gus; Wanda; and other children his age at Potter's Lodge. In a tennis match, for example, he invariably bosses his partner. When he decides to go swimming alone in Great Harriman Lake against the rules, Ray angrily rows out to bring him in. Some of the old-timers put money into a corporation to help preserve the lodge; Steve mistakenly believes the Lodge is having financial difficulties. When a guest thinks she has won at bingo, Steve points out that she misread a number on her card; the other children are furious with him. Finding himself alone, he offers to take Motley, a dog belonging to guests named Kirby, for a walk. Out of sorts, he is rude to Doris, who is in charge of the dining room. Nora criticizes his manners; then, seeing he is unhappy, she gives him a job distributing and collecting lunch-order forms from the cabins. When he continues to be impolite, Nora says he is arrogant and will soon have no friends. He conceives of a way to display other people's strengths and to earn money for the Lodge—a talent show. The children choose their acts: Angie, dance; Gus, harmonica; Wanda, birdcalls; Sally, impersonation; Hugh, magic tricks; Rita, lassoing; and Fred Erskine, a newcomer, a one-man band. Steve modestly says he will work backstage. They rehearse at the boathouse annex. Mrs. Kirby, informed that Motley is a nuisance, asks Steve to train him. The rehearsals are spotty because no one is in charge; Fred proposes outrageous props and sets. In the middle of one rehearsal, Fred's older brother, Todd, barges in to take out a sailboat. Steve mildly suggests that Todd watch the wind on the water. Rebuffed, Steve continues to keep the boat in view and notices that Todd has not put down the centerboard. The boat is soon uncontrollable without a keel. Steve rows out and, in a "conversational way," reminds Todd about the centerboard. He is trying not to show off. Steve brings Motley as his act to the last rehearsal. When Gus tells him to take the dog out, Steve declares he will go, too, and leave them to their "pathetic show." They ask him to fix it, but he reminds them that they are always telling him he is too bossy. They really want his help, however, so he gives them useful, straightforward, diplomatic advice. The talent show goes well, except for Motley's act—the Kirbys distract him by sitting in the front row and applauding loudly. Steve is happy because he and Gus are friends again, and the Lodge is not in need of money for repairs. He learns to keep a less prominent profile, but he still hates being wrong.

Margaret P. Trask

In ***Three for Treasure*** (1962), Melissa ("Lissa") Duffield, nine, and her brother Danny, eleven, fly to Vermont to spend a summer month near Pleasant Valley. On the plane they meet Loretta Plum, a dealer in antiques. Waiting for them at the airport are their grandparents with Martin Hatch, six, whom they consider a pest to be avoided. Martin, who idolizes the two older children, is there because his mother is in the hospital. Their grandmother tells them a story about Aunt Melly, who grew up in the house with her and owned a beautiful doll. One day Aunt Melly pretended the redcoats were coming, slit open her doll, hid her silver tea set inside, and buried the doll in the orchard. Enchanted with the idea of buried treasure, the children write to Aunt Melly in London to ask where the doll is hidden. The first night Danny feels a bit homesick, but, when he hears Martin crying for his mother, he comforts the little boy and forgets his own anxiety. While exploring the next day, Lissa falls into a deep hole created by a waterfall. Danny and Martin manage to shove a tree branch down for her to clasp. Danny instructs Martin to hold on tight to the other end while he runs for their grandfather. When her grandfather pulls her out, Lissa is freezing and frightened, but she deeply appreciates Martin's saving her life. Aunt Melly writes that she made a map and hid it in a hole in an old salad bowl. The children follow the instructions on the map—a certain number of steps from the biggest tree—and dig, but they find nothing. Their grandfather remembers that the biggest tree in the orchard was cut down. They measure again, dig, and find the doll, disintegrated except for her china head, arms, legs—and the tea set. The local paper sends photographers and publishes a fine article, which the children send to Aunt Melly. Mrs. Plum is avid to buy the antique silver, but they refuse to sell. While they are busy at their chores, someone steals the tea set. Certain it is Mrs. Plum, Lissa and Danny run after her car, parked by the roadside, and pluck a box from the front seat. It contains her lunch. Meanwhile, Martin has run away. When recovered, he explains that he took the tea set to the hospital to show his mother.

At the Sign of the Rocking Horse (1964) is set in Dublin Center, where Ann Cassidy ("Cassie") Clifford, eleven, and her best friend, Fergus MacDougall, wonder what they will do all summer. Cassie's great-aunt, Emerald Blomquist, sells antiques in a wing at the far end of the Cliffords' house. Cassie sometimes cleans and dusts the objects. Her father, Adam, is deputy sheriff of the town, as well as game and tree warden, realtor, and selectman. Because Emerald led a glamorous life as the wife of a wealthy man before returning to Vermont a widow, Cassie chooses her as a subject for a writing contest. Fergus's family has a summer boarder, Mr. Fisher, who, appropriately, spends his time fishing. Shortly after Cassie's essay is published, two more people arrive in town. Horace Bagley, a painter, is another boarder for the MacDougalls; Elmore ("Red") Rivers is the town "bad boy," who has been away for two years. Both Mr. Fisher and Mr. Bagley spend a great deal of time in Emerald's shop, admiring her antique clock and the old rocking horse. Cassie is glad the horse is not for sale; it has sentimental value for her as well as a secret compartment. Everyone prepares for the church supper. While they are enjoying the food and the raffles, someone steals Emerald's valuable jewelry. Adam calls the state police; before long, Corporal Phelps and Trooper Wallace arrive. From their tree house, Cassie and Fergus overhear the interrogation of the witnesses. Someone saw a car carrying a man with a woman in a white hat. The children help the police search the grass, where Cassie finds one of Emerald's pearl earrings and is delighted when the police fingerprint her. She and Fergus make up a timeline and a list of suspects: Red Rivers, Mr. Fisher, Mr. Bagley, and Gram Banks, a neighbor who came late to the church supper. From their vantage point, they watch Gram Banks leave her house with a basket over her arm. They follow her to the sugarhouse, where they find her feeding a fawn with a nursing bottle. Cassie and Fergus continue up the hill to the abandoned lodge where they enjoy playing. They are shocked when two passengers fitting the description of the robbers drive up. Just as Cassie and Fergus accuse them of the robbery, her father arrives to greet his potential renters. Cassie hopes they will not harm the baby mice in the bureau drawer. Later, while dusting in the shop, Cassie finds the jewelry behind the old clock. Mr. Bagley enters, acting strangely. Cassie can tell from his expression that he is the thief. Her father comes just in time, followed by the police, who arrest Mr. Bagley. Everyone adjourns to Emerald's for supper. Mr. Tobin, who owns some Shetland ponies, gives one to Cassie because she caught the thief.

V

Jean Van Leeuwen

Merciless Marvin the Magnificent, a city mouse in ***The Great Summer Camp Catastrophe*** (1992), lives happily with his friends, Raymond the Rat and Fats the Fuse, in a dollhouse in the toy department at Macy's. Snacking in the delicatessen one morning before the store opens, they hear voices and hide in a cookie container. Before they know what is happening, store employees have taped up the box, stacked it with others, and shipped the mice to Camp Moose-a-Honk, a boys' camp in northwestern Vermont. The three mice find the country very large and very quiet; they fear predatory animals. Out scouting, Marvin meets Ellsworth Peabody, a field mouse whose family has lived on the meadow for generations. He informs Marvin that there is no bus service to New York City until the end of the summer and suggests they stow away in one of the parents' cars returning to the city after Visitor's Day. The mice stay in a box under Sam's bed and follow him as he engages in various sports—archery, soccer, baseball, and swimming. Raymond finds them a Ping-Pong ball with which to practice baseball. Marvin also acquires a miniature birchbark canoe, made in arts and crafts class, which they take onto the lake with Popsicle sticks for paddles. After a counselor orders the boys to clean up the cabin, the mice's box is thrown away, but they take refuge in Sam's knapsack. They sneak into the kitchen to devour a wheel of Vermont cheddar. They hope to escape in a shopping bag of clothes that Sam gives to his mother to take home, but she makes him keep them. Out in the meadow, they fall into Ellsworth's hole, where he resides with his large family. Subsisting on seeds and nuts, he is satisfied with his life; Marvin, who loves camp, is always searching for more out of life. The mice are carried onto the bus in Sam's knapsack. From the bus station in New York City they catch the subway for Macy's.

Marjorie Vetter

In ***Champlain Summer*** (1959), Kit Turner, fifteen, is excited to be with her older brother, Ken, at their summer cottage, built by her great-grandfather, a Vergennes merchant, on Lake Champlain. She is in awe of her glamorous Great-aunt Charlotte Penfield, who is disdainful of Kit's tomboyish ways. Kit is disappointed that the Lesters have rented a companion cottage and brought their coquettish daughter, Elaine, who will ruin everything. When Kit meets Bates Cunningham, a slim, slightly lame, poetry-quoting young man whose parents have leased a large house, she is intrigued; when she sees him again, she is in love. The hired woman, Martha, sobers Kit by telling her of another class of society in Vermont: the people who lost their jobs when the big woolen mill near Burlington closed and are dependent on ice fishing for a living. One of these fishermen, William Howard, recently drowned, leaving a destitute wife and four young children. Kit visits the library in Vergennes, passing the monument to Commander Macdonough (hero of the Battle of Plattsburgh), to read about Howard's death. Bates asks her to take him on a tour of the countryside. She is knowledgeable about Vermont history and fills in the background on the places they visit. On a picnic to Bristol Gap, she talks to some polite boys who turn out to be the Howards' sons. Kit consults with her friends about ways to raise money for the Howard family. They decide to put on a play, which Bates will write, and hold the performance at his house. Kit suggests a series of tableaux on the history of Vermont. When Bates and Kit visit Crown Point and Fort Ticonderoga, Elaine joins them, making Kit jealous. One weekend, when Kits' parents and Ken are away, a terrific storm blows up. Charlotte is reduced to helplessness; Kit runs around securing the windows and doors. Charlotte falls and hits her head; their car and the neighbor's car are gone. Although she is forbidden to take out the motorboat alone, Kit recognizes the emergency and crosses the lake to the Westport harbor to fetch a doctor. She no longer fears Charlotte. Kit thinks only of Bates, but, when the season's big dance is announced, he asks Elaine. Kit imagines she is heartbroken, but she goes to the dance with her friend, Ray, and has a lovely time. People are generous with props and costumes; their play is a great success. At first, Mrs. Howard tells Kit that she cannot accept their charity, but she changes her mind after Ray explains the gift is intended as a memorial to her husband. Kit knows she has gained self-confidence this summer. (The poem Bates quotes to Kit is Robert Louis Stevenson's "Romance," which begins, "I will make you brooches and toys for your delight/Of bird-song at morning and star-shine at night./I will make a palace fit for you and me,/Of green days in forests and blue days at sea." The poem that Kit quotes in response is Arthur Guiterman's "Vergennes," which starts, "New York says, 'I'm the finest in the nation,/With pretty near eight million population!'/Replies Vergennes, Vermont, 'I do declare!/But I'm the smallest city anywhere!'")

Phillip Viereck

Independence Must Be Won (1964) portrays the grim period in 1777 when the rebels anticipate the arrival of General John Burgoyne's army of fifteen thousand. They are making every effort to ready the new fort, Mount Independence, directly across from Fort Ticonderoga (commanded by General Arthur St. Clair). Mount Independence is shaped like an eight-point star; two thousand people are garrisoned there. Nathan Robinson, thirteen, who lives with his parents in Castleton, carries provisions by oxen to the fort, where he finds his brother, Tim, an army cannoneer, and Abe Graham, a friend from Castleton. Abe introduces Nathan to Whit Dewey, who is visiting his sick father at the fort. Leaving the fort together, Nathan and Whit travel to the Deweys' cabin, where Nathan spends the night with Whit and his sister, Rachael. A constitutional convention is held in Windsor: Vermont becomes an independent republic. Nathan travels the Hubbardton road, leading his horse, Emma, to take his second load to the fort, stopping with the Deweys on the way. With Whit away again to see their father, Rachael is handling all the chores. Following the military road, Nathan arrives at the fort to learn that Whit's father has died. Tim says the situation is dire: the Americans do not have enough men to defend the two forts; the farmers say they are too busy at home to provide reinforcements. Tim also believes it is dangerous, what with Indian raids, for Tim to return home (Whit has left by boat). The redcoats drag a cannon to the top of Sugar Hill; the British fleet prepares for activity. The American cannon crews and the big guns aboard the British galleys pound each other. Tim is ordered to take his cannon crew to Fort Ticonderoga. The next morning, the Americans retreat from the great stone fort built by Montcalm and captured by Ethan Allen. The history of Ticonderoga and the labor invested in building Mount Independence make Nathan weep with humiliation. He watches Tim order his crew to tear up the wooden bridge linking the two forts. General St. Clair heads the American retreat from the fort, leaving Seth Warner in charge of the rearguard action to slow the British advance. Tim is hit. Nathan, with Abe's help, loads Tim onto Emma's back. Tim has suffered a head wound and a broken arm, which they splint. Nathan and Abe, with Tim on Emma, are at the rear of the retreat; Colonel Simon Fraser and General Friedrich Riedesel (dubbed "Red Hazel") are just behind. Nathan and Abe find a surgeon who warns them that Tim will die if he is moved any farther. Abe helps Nathan carry Tim to Whit's cabin before rejoining his regiment. Because Tim's head wound is so severe, and Rachael, too, is sick, the four young people cannot evacuate to Castleton but stay in the cabin without a fire. Even so, six Hessians pull into the clearing, "smart and neat" in their blue jackets. They take Emma, but not the cow, because General Burgoyne has ordered no milk cows slaughtered to feed his troops. Whit and Nathan try to conceal the spot where their side road meets the main road so that Indians will not find them. On the high hill above Castleton, they can hear reports of muskets from Hubbardton. Abe returns to report on the battle: the men from Massachusetts led by Colonel Ebenezer Francis (who is later killed) and Seth Warner's Green Mountain Boys ("who fought like catamounts") confront two thousand enemy troops. St. Clair tries to send reinforcements, but they flee. The enemy overcomes the Americans. Rachael recovers sufficiently to take care of Tim; they fall in love. After five weeks of hiding, the four head for Castleton, where they find Nathan's parents alive. That morning Vermont and New Hampshire troops defeat the Hessians near Bennington. Those who turn out in the thousands for the battle are mostly settlers—farmers. They realize that independence is not a gift: it must be won. (One diagram shows a revolutionary rifle and its equipment; another, the way a cannon is loaded and fired. Mount Independence was built by Thaddeus Kosciusko, 1746-1817, a Polish patriot and engineer.)

W

Amelia Elizabeth Walden

In ***Skymountain*** (1950), Robin Young, eighteen, who has enjoyed every privilege in life, comes to Skymountain (Middlebury College) to train as a champion skier. She is spoiled and conceited and views John Fifer, a local youth, as a "yokel" and a "farmer's son." Before long, she loses all her money (her mother does, that is), falls in her first slalom race, and discovers that her "taciturn Vermonter" has taken the place of her former boyfriend in her heart. She has learned that love and respect are more important than money and social position.

Mildred Walker

Calder Bailey, twelve, is spending the summer in Weldon (based on Grafton) in ***A Piece of the World*** (1972) because of the divorce of her mother, a television personality, and her father, a novelist. Her ancestor, Jonathan Calder, "hewed his land out of the wilderness"; her grandmother, Mardie, sells antiques in the barn next to the family house. Calder wanders into the woods where she finds an imposing boulder. Unbeknownst to Calder, Walt Bolles, a neighbor a few years older than she, is watching as she climbs exultantly onto the rock. Calder is in Mardie's shop one day reading *Wuthering Heights* when geologist Binghampton Cooley happens in to buy a cane. An expert on the rocks in the area, he exhibits a picture of the rock that Calder found earlier. Mardie identifies it as "Serpentine Rock," which Mr. Cooley says is an "erratic boulder," moved by the glacial drift from its original place. Mr. Cooley tells Calder, "Every rock is a piece of the world that was here long before you and will be after you." Mardie, president of the Weldon Development Society, wants to cut a trail to the rock, clear away the trees, and print and sell brochures to entice tourists to the site. The rock is on Walt's Aunt Lil's property up on the Old Town Road; he is living with her while his father is in the veterans' hospital. Aunt Lil is planning to sell the farm—and the wood lot containing the rock—to pay for Walt to go to high school in the larger town of Spencer. Mr. Cooley, a quietly intelligent, sympathetic, and optimistic presence, asks Calder and Walt to show him the rock. Mardie has a sign made for Walt to hammer into a white birch tree. Mardie calls this tourist project her "quest" (Calder thinks of *Idylls of the King*). Mr. Cooley, Walt, and Calder are opposed to the trail; Calder hates the bossy way her grandmother is acting. Mardie further proposes a "rustic ladder" for tourists to climb upon the rock and, perhaps, a stone fireplace for barbecues. Calder persuades Walt to hitchhike with her to visit his father in the hospital. Meanwhile, Mardie is furious because Walt, to express his disapproval of the tourist project, cuts deep blazes in the trees. Calder's mother writes that she is remarrying and coming to pick up Calder, who retreats to her room and comforts herself by rereading *The Wind in the Willows*. John Ward, a developer, decides to buy the rock, split it with dynamite, move it to the village common, and cement it back together. Hordes of people watch the dynamiting. The inside of the rock is dark green. Walt has put his name, and Calder's initials, inside one of the pieces. She is thrilled with his generosity. Mr. Cooley says the rock "has brought the wilderness into the village." Before Calder leaves with her mother and stepfather, she climbs the rock once more.

Ruth Wallace-Brodeur

In ***The Kenton Year*** (1980), nine-year-old Mandy's father, William Clough McPherson, died in an automobile accident. Her mother, Anne, takes Mandy to Kenton, where Anne spent summers on a hill above a lake. They begin to meet local people. Emma Severy welcomes them. She owns the general store, where she is also postmistress, and is married to a selectman. Mandy immediately befriends Shandee, a large, kind man who sells plants from his wonderful garden. While out on the lake fishing, Mandy encounters Carrie Marquand, a girl her age, and her pleasant family. Mandy and her mother also meet Martin Wechsler, who runs a county newspaper, *The Crawford World*. The only person they do not like is Irving Neele, the hardware store owner, who refers to Shandee as "the village simpleton." Mandy enlists Carrie and her older brothers, David and Paul, in playing a prank on Neele by disassembling his trailer and reassembling it on the roof of his barn. Neele is so unpopular that everyone, including his wife, is delighted. After Shandee helps Neele remove the trailer from the roof, Neele is kinder toward him. Mandy chops kindling for Shandee. When the church well runs dry, he teaches Mandy how to use a divining rod to search for water. At the end of the summer, Mandy does not want to return to Boston: "Kenton was home." Anne decides to buy the house and apply for a job with Martin, so they can stay. She arranges a birthday party for Mandy with their closest friends; Shandee brings a perfect blue spruce tree. The only cloud on the horizon is Mandy's schoolmate, Corinne Haskell, who circulates rumors of a romance between Anne and Martin. Martin buys them cross-country skis and encourages Mandy to enter the Crawford County winter carnival races. With newly acquired determination, she qualifies at the race in nearby Whitefield; with newly acquired competitive spirit, she is consumed with the desire to finish in the top ten. She places sixth in the event. Mandy works hard chiseling a wooden sign. On the anniversary of her father's death, she takes her mother to the top of their favorite hill, with the lake on one side, their house on the other, and blueberry fields stretching beyond. The carving spells out, "WILLIAM CLOUGH MCPHERSON HILL."

The Cate family in ***The Godmother Tree*** (1992) moves so often that changing homes becomes a way of life. For Daniel Cate, a farm hand, employment is fragile; he jumps at the chance of a better job cross county in Redfield; his wife, Franny, throws herself into each move with energy and, finally, tears of exhaustion. Laura, ten, is accustomed to leaving friends and making new ones; Ryan, fourteen, resents missing the chance to pitch his first summer-league game; Luther, at sixteen, is leaving school anyway to help his father and dreams only of wildlife. Laura admires Luther, whom she finds sympathetic: she can confide in him and show him her drawings; sometimes he reads to her from his Narnia books. The new house is bigger than any they have lived in; the other hired hand lives in an ell off their house. The new boss, Ralph Turner, wants to promote Daniel to farm manager so Ralph can travel with his wife: Daniel will receive a raise and all the beef and milk his family needs. Swimming in the lake, Laura sees a huge and ancient tree standing alone in the field. She climbs into it before going home to draw it, labeling it, "The Godmother Tree." Thinking of Narnia, she calls this magical land "Loria," derived from her own name. Daniel notices that "mishaps" occur around the place; for example, unexplained smoke in the house and strange smells. One day someone snips pieces from the laundry on the clothesline; then someone switches the vegetables in the garden. Can the new developer in the neighborhood be harassing them? Laura knows Ryan is ashamed of them, but she cannot believe he would commit these petty acts. Luther is distraught at inadvertently mowing the legs off two fawns lying in the grass and drives away in the truck. Laura's mother takes her to Middlebury to see Uncle Ed, Aunt Barbara, and her grandmother. When they return, Luther has recovered. It transpires that Ryan is the troublemaker because he hates Vermont. Daniel announces that Ryan is not going to watch anymore TV; instead, he is going to help Luther outside. Everyone feels better by the time the Addison County Fair comes around. Luther shows his cows; their mother enters her zucchini relish; Laura submits a flower arrangement. Laura spends much of her time at Loria and is ready to face her new school and her new classmates. She knows that "she can find her Godmother Tree anywhere."

W

Mary Ella Waller

A New York charitable organization sends Miffins, a homeless, crippled orphan about thirteen in ***The Little Citizen*** (1902), to live with foster parents in Hurdyville near Barnet. His plight touches the hearts of Jacob and Martha Foss, whose own son died eighteen years earlier when he was about Miffins's age. The Foss farm, The Roost, stands on the slope of Beaver Tail Mountain—barns, vegetable garden, orchard, home pasture for the cows, sugar patch, wood lot, and back pasture for the horses. Miffins befriends another orphan, fifteen-year-old Nance Liscomb, who spends winters in Hurdyville with her father's widow; she wants to teach Miffins some manners and the "rights of free-born Vermonters." Bright and beautiful, Nance is a splendid horsewoman (she aspires to join a circus) and a constant reader of favorite novels like *Little Women*, *David Copperfield*, *The Old Curiosity Shop*, *The Pickwick Papers*, and *Robinson Crusoe*. Miffins responds well to Jacob and Martha's loving care and soon, healthier and happier, learns to use his crutch (his thigh is twisted and his leg shrunken) and is able to help Martha around the house. He and Nance spend time at the wood lot while Nance practices with the horse, Napoleon. Advised by Miffins about transportation, Nance takes the train to New York where, felicitously, she meets handsome young John Anstey, a Yale graduate and friend of her Barnard cousins in Manhattan. Enchanted by her spirit and looks, he accompanies her to the circus where she is sickened by the squalid atmosphere; John then takes Nance home to his mother, who telegraphs the Liscombs that she is safe. After Nance returns to Vermont, John learns he has incipient tuberculosis. His doctor recommends the country; simultaneously, Nance reports to his mother that the Hurdyville district school lacks a teacher. Before long, John is the new schoolmaster and a boarder at The Roost. Soon the schoolchildren worship him, the villagers respect him, and Jacob and Martha treat him like another son. John, who came to the Green Hills to fight for his life, has given "new life to the whole village." Every girl and woman is knitting mufflers and mittens for the residents of the Newsboys' Home in New York. Christmas comes—and a huge storm—but presents arrive from New York, and the celebration is warm and loving. In March they sugar, tapping seven hundred sugar maples. Nance and the dogs are in the woods when they are traumatized by something "tawny yellow," as Nance describes it. The men and boys go out on a "still hunt" (stalking) with guns; Miff stays up at the pines with the rifle John has taught him to use. He is lying on the ground when he sees a mountain lion just a few feet away. He fires and hits it squarely; the others run up to finish off the huge beast—one hundred and eighty-two pounds and seven feet long. With Jacob's example of "honest toil," Miffins is developing into a man. The Barnards send Nance to boarding school in New York, accompanied by John who must see his doctor. Martha and Jacob visit a relative, leaving Muffins alone overnight. When he sets out the next day with Napoleon and the wagon to meet them at the station in Barnet, it is raining hard. He is shocked to realize that the dam is threatening to give way. In order to warn the villagers, he must ride Napoleon. Sitting on the horse's back is excruciatingly painful for him. He reaches the village in time to warn the residents to flee. The water from the freshet reaches the second story of many houses and drowns scores of cows and horses. Martha and Jacob adopt the brave boy and christen him James Anstey Foss. The villagers hail him as a hero—"The Little Citizen"—and take up a collection to send him to college.

In ***A Daughter of the Rich*** (1906), Hazel Clyde, thirteen, has all the material advantages a girl could want—an elegant house in New York City, lavish clothes, a doting father, and a French personal maid. Despite being rich, the motherless child is languid and lonely. After a bout with scarlet fever, in which she loses her hair and her appetite, the family physician, Dr. Heath, recommends the "life-giving Green Hills" for a year's recuperation, where a loving, close family could serve as a tonic. His Yale classmate, Benjamin Blossom, lives on Hunger Mountain near Barton's River. Badly injured in a logging accident, Benjamin recovered but had to mortgage the farm to pay his bills. Mary Blossom explains to the children about their financial difficulties and the great assistance a paying guest's twenty-five dollars a week will provide. When Hazel arrives at the Blossom farmhouse in April of 1897, she finds Rose, seventeen, who hopes to go away to college; March, fifteen, an artist who wants to be an architect; the twins, Buddy and Cherry; baby May; and the hired man and best family friend, Malachi ("Chi") Graham. The younger children immediately welcome Hazel; Rose and March are colder in their greeting. At first they are disconcerted by her wealth and upbringing; after a month, gentle, generous Hazel is initiated into the children's secret society, NBBOO (Nobody's Business But Our Own). Their society names are Molly Stark (Rose); the Marquis de Lafayette (March); Martha Washington (Cherry); and Ethan Allen (Buddy). Hazel chooses Barbara Frietchie (the heroine of the John Greenleaf Whittier poem containing the lines, "'Shoot, if you must, this old gray head/But spare your country's flag,' she said.") Their main order of business is to earn money to alleviate the family's financial pressures. They decide to raise chickens for sale (they plant corn that day) and to pick berries for making preserves. After much urging on Hazel's part, they allow her to lend them the requisite money to invest in glass jars and pounds of sugar for the enterprise. Hazel writes to her favorite cousin, Jack Sherrill, at Harvard, asking him to order some of their goods. He responds to his dear cousin, "rusticating in the Green Mountains," that he will take seventeen dozen of each kind of berry preserve. He organizes a trip to Vermont with some of his friends, including Maude Seaton, rumored to be his fiancée. Rose is humiliated (and ashamed of her fierce pride) when the elegant city friends arrive to find her in a straw bonnet selling pails of blackberries in the road. Later, when the Blossoms provide tea for Jack's friends, Rose is at her most beautiful, dressed in one of her mother's lovely old dresses. Jack begins to think romantically about her. The young people clear one hundred and ten dollars on the jams and two hundred and seventeen dollars on the chicken project, which Chi oversaw. Hazel wants to give her share of the profits to Rose for her college fund, but Rose's pride will not let her accept. They speak frankly about the barrier between them: Hazel weeps while telling Rose she cannot help being rich. They use part of the money to send March to the Academy in Barton's River. A young lawyer, Alan Ford, his mother, and his sister, Ruth, delicate from an injury, move to the mountain and become close friends with the Blossoms. The families share Thanksgiving and Christmas holidays. Hazel gives one of the guests a copy of her favorite novel, *Lorna Doone*. At Christmas, Hazel welcomes her father, her cousin Jack, and Dr. Heath, who wants to check on Ruth. Jack is now in love with Rose, who will not acknowledge her reciprocal feelings. March rides his horse to the Academy each day so that he will not have to pay board. During a terrible snowstorm, while Hazel is in New York visiting her father, March's horse returns without his rider. Chi ventures out into the snow to find him; March is ill for several weeks with chills and fever. March is uncomfortable meeting affluent people; his mother says his father's wealth is in "love and esteem." Now that March is seventeen, Hazel's father offers to send him to college, with an additional two years in Europe. March feels he cannot accept this largesse because he is in love with Hazel. Hazel invites Rose to visit her in New York. At a dance Rose attends with Jack, she overhears gossip about her being a fortune hunter, which makes her so heartsick that she leaves abruptly for Hunger Mountain. When the war starts (it is 1898), Jack and Chi enlist. After Jack is seriously wounded, Chi sends a note to Rose from Jack, "stained with his heart's blood." After his convalescence, Jack and Rose marry. March is hopeful that he and Hazel will marry some day, too.

W

Chad Walsh

Nellie Smith and her parents in ***Nellie and Her Flying Crocodile*** (1956) live in Villville and spend summers in their cottage at Lake Iroquois in Hinesburg. A tentacled flying creature (a "seddalonk") seizes Nellie, carries her off toward the small island in the middle of the lake, and drops her. A flying crocodile (a "bahagohunk") gently catches her with his long tongue and takes her to his nest in a tree on the shore of Lake Champlain, where he plans to keep her as his little girl. She is relieved to see her father, who rescues her in a helicopter, but she misses Hunky, as she calls her new friend. One day, on an outing to pick blueberries, she lies down to rest in a cave and falls asleep. Hunky finds and carries her home to her frantic parents, who gratefully invite him to stay in their boathouse. Mr. Smith spends much of his days fishing from Hunky's back. At the annual Lake Iroquois picnic, Hunky's tribe, citizens of Bahaland, join the fun and elect Hunky their king and Nellie their queen. When Hunky proposes that the Smiths live in a cottage that the bahagohunks will build and suspend between two great trees, they agree. For a few weeks they enjoy the life—fresh fish every day, lots of exercise, no city pressure or noises—but after a while they decide they must return to their other life. Undaunted, Hunky joins them in Villville.

Gertrude Chandler Warner

In ***The Mystery at Snowflake Inn*** (1995), James Alden takes his grandchildren (Henry, fourteen; Jessie, twelve; Violet, ten; and Benny, four, better known as the "boxcar children") to spend Christmas at Snowflake Inn in Bennington with Soo Lee, seven, an adopted Korean girl. Ralph Winston manages Snowflake Inn, built in 1767, with his son, Larry, and niece, Betsy Calvert. The other guests are the Millers, a couple with two sulky children, Hannah and Davey. Ralph shows the children a mysterious nook that is revealed when he presses with his cane against a certain brick to open a hidden door. During the Revolutionary War the owner hid Colonial spies here. Later, the Underground Railroad used the inn as a way station. Inexplicable accidents occur. The children congregate for a sleigh ride only to find someone has taken the horses. After someone stuffs the chimney with rags and an old coat, they almost suffocate. Someone smashes Betsy's windowpane; someone unplugs the refrigerator. The cook leaves in a huff. The children, undeterred in their plan to celebrate Christmas, decorate the rooms with ornaments and shop for and cook the Christmas meal themselves. The children are so well behaved and hardworking that Betsy breaks down and confesses: she wanted to incriminate Larry in order to inherit the inn and sell it to open a restaurant in Philadelphia. Uncle Ralph forgives her.

In ***The Stuffed Bear Mystery*** (2002), James Alden drops off his four Alden grandchildren at Raymond and Peggy Firman's Woolly Farm near the town of Old Mills. "Doc" Firman runs a sheep farm as well as a Toy Hospital; Peggy makes "Peggy Bears," stuffed with their sheep's silky fleece. The children smell sap boiling in the sugarhouse while they are having breakfast, help Doc with the shearing, and work in Peggy's booth at the Teddy Bear Jamboree. When a valuable German bear, "Herr Bear," which Doc is repairing for Miss Withers, disappears, he is worried. Herr Bear is one of twin antique bears; the female is missing from the set. Volunteering to solve the mystery, the children search the Internet for information about three potential suspects at the Jamboree. They learn that Professor Tweedy is an expert on antique bears. Elsa Keppel is the daughter of the maker of Herr Bears, whose enterprise closed in Germany. Hazel Sayer is trying to manufacture a talking bear. The missing-bear mystery is solved when the outwardly suspicious Professor Tweedy turns out to be a judge at the Best Bears Contest, and the apparently questionable Mrs. Keppel only borrowed Herr Bear, which belonged to her brother, to reunite the bear briefly with Fraulein Bear, her childhood toy. In a grand gesture, Miss Withers returns Herr Bear to Mrs. Keppel.

Ida H. Washington

The Sanford family in ***Brave Enough*** (2003) decides to leave New Jersey for the New Hampshire Grants in 1776, when Rob is seven, Elizabeth, five, and Will, a baby. Ben, a comrade of Rob's father, Thomas, in the French and Indian Wars, recommends Pittsford. Once in the village, Thomas temporarily leaves his wife and smaller children there and takes Rob by canoe on Otter Creek to find a clearing and erect a shelter. They plant a garden of corn, squash, beans, and potatoes and return to fetch the rest of the family. Rob's mother brings a rose bush to stand by the door of the finished cabin. Ira Allen stops by to inform Thomas of the Yorkers' attempts to take Grants property. When Indians return to their old campsite near the Sanfords' cabin, Rob's mother insists upon moving to a new spot. In the second clearing are neighbors, the Brittells, with a son, Claudius, about Rob's age. In early spring, the sap runs. With his ax, Thomas cuts where there are old tomahawk scars on the tree trunks. The Indians caught sap in bark troughs and threw in hot stones to make it boil. Thomas pours some syrup into a wooden trough and breaks up the lumps with a wooden hoe ("hoed sugar") to keep it fine for use on cornmeal mush. Between planting and harvest, Thomas goes to Pittsford for supplies. Indians are making trouble along the creek and lakeshore; some families move back to the settlements. In Pittsford, the residents form a Committee of Safety. By the creek, the men build a fort, using William Cox's house as a blockhouse. Several other cabins dot their valley; good neighbors are essential to this pioneer life. Rumors fly about settlers being captured by Indians; the British retake Fort Ticonderoga in 1777. Three years pass; Rob is now ten. Thomas reminds him that the big potato cellar they dug in the riverbank would make a good hiding place. Shortly thereafter, Indians capture the men and boys and torch the cabins. When Rob, hands bound behind him, stumbles and falls to the ground, his captors leave him. Finding his mother, siblings, and other families, he leads them to the potato cellar. He remembers his father's telling him that pioneers should always look ahead. From the ruins of their cabin, he excavates flint and steel, a kettle and dipper, and pieces of charred quilt. He gets a fire going and puts potatoes in the hot coals. No rescuers find them that day or the next. He finds hay in the shed and spreads it on the dirt floor. Heading for help in Pittsford, he walks past destroyed cabins, feeling as though he is the only person still alive in the whole world. He spends a cold night on the ground. Hungry and lame, he presses on. Finally he comes upon Ben, his father's friend, and some soldiers from the fort at Pittsford. Ben takes Rob to the fort, while the soldiers collect the families from their hiding place. Pittsford builds a blockhouse, Fort Vengeance. Three years later Rob's father returns home, full of terrible tales about the march to Canada and prison life. When Thomas and Rob return to their clearing, they find their horses—and the rose bush—alive. (A white marble monument in Weybridge commemorates the town's founding and the disastrous raid. For another story about the Cox family, see Grace Neil Anderson's *In the Shadow of Cox Mountain* in this collection.)

Kenneth B. Webb

From Plymouth Notch to President (1978) is a fictionalized biography of Calvin Coolidge from age eleven to seventeen. In 1883, Calvin lives on a farm in Plymouth Notch with his father, John, a storekeeper and legislator; his ailing mother, Vikki; his grandfather, Galusha; his sister, Abbie, eight; and his Aunt Abigail, who grew up on the farm with her brother, John. His grandfather tells Calvin no life is better than a farmer's: "He's richer every fall than he was the year before." When Galusha dies at the age of sixty-three, Calvin contemplates the change

W

called "death" with sadness but not despair. Calvin's teacher assesses his overall performance: while not at the top of his class, Calvin is "methodical, faithful, honest, and punctual." He likes to read mystery stories such as "The Pit and the Pendulum" and "The Purloined Letter." He is also a player of practical jokes with his best friends, Dell Ward and Clarence Blanchard. When John attends the Windsor County Court in Woodstock, he takes Calvin along. Vikki dies of consumption at the age of thirty-nine. The two children, always close, help each other through their sorrow. Fortunately, their chores keep them busy. John explains that, although God has a master plan they cannot understand, the harder they try, the more wonderful it becomes. Wanting Calvin to be educated beyond the local schoolhouse, John sends him first to the Liberal Institute at Union Hall. When Calvin is ready, he enters Black River Academy in Ludlow where, in 1886, one hundred and twenty-five students were enrolled. The principal, George Sherman, says a good mind is like a good horse: "He'll do equally well on any good road." At first Calvin is homesick in his boarding house, but he knows his father would not want him to "run out on an obligation." His grandmother reminds him that the more education he receives, the more choices he will have; Dell does not need more education because he wants to be a sheep farmer. Back at school, Calvin continues French, starts Latin, and, reluctantly, Greek. By his junior year, he has a new interest in and understanding of his courses. The school's motto is "live and grow forever." (The school closed its doors in 1924.) In 1888, the political contest is between Benjamin Harrison and Grover Cleveland. As staunch Republicans, Calvin and his friends support Harrison. They push a donkey up the stairs into a Democratic teacher's room and leave a note on the black board: "Bray for us poor Democrats." Abbie, who comes to the Academy and is loved by everyone, dies at fifteen. Deeply saddened, Calvin tries to embrace the precept, "Man is the master of circumstance." He and his father attend the dedication of the Battle of Bennington monument. When Calvin shakes President Harrison's hand with an axman's grip, Harrison says, "A real Vermonter—I can feel that." (The epilogue states that Calvin went on to Amherst College, married Grace Goodhue of Burlington, and became a lawyer in Massachusetts, then governor. Elected vice president, he succeeded to the presidency in 1923 after Harding's death and was reelected president in 1924. He attributed his success to "persistence and determination," which, he said, "alone are omnipotent.")

Dorothy West

Dot, the title character in ***Dot and Dash at the Maple Sugar Camp*** (1938), is the six-year-old, sensible, unspoiled only child of Dr. Davidson and his ailing wife. When her mother undergoes an operation in New York, Dot and her black and white fox terrier, Dash, travel to Vermont by train to visit her Aunt Betty and Uncle Jack. They usually live in Mapletown but are at their camp on Bread Loaf Mountain during sugaring season. The first morning, Uncle Jack takes Dot and Dash in a horse-drawn bobsled to the sugarhouse, where Jeff, the hired hand, is boiling sap. Wandering off into the maples, Dot is soon lost, but Dash saves her by blocking her path and barking until her uncle comes running. Later Dash runs away and has a confrontation with a porcupine. When the sugaring is finished, Dot and Aunt Betty set up a stand by the highway to sell maple syrup and maple sugar to tourists. While Dot is in charge, a customer wants to buy a jug. She leaves her station to confirm the price with Aunt Betty; the man drives off with the syrup. Aunt Betty hopes to win first prize at the maple festival in Mapleton. During the wood-chopping contest, Dash escapes. When Dot hurries after him, she spies the thief's car. Waiting for him, Dot and Dash fall asleep in the back seat. The next thing Dot knows, she is miles from Mapleton. The driver, Mr. Elston, shocked to learn they are in his car, drives them safely home. He explains to Aunt Betty and Uncle Jack that he is a buyer for a large food company. He left their farm without paying because he was in a hurry to sample other maple syrup; he was seeking the prime maple syrup—and Aunt Betty's product is the winner. Mrs. Davidson, recovered from her operation, comes with her husband to the farm to pick up Dot and Dash. Dot is sorry to leave but knows she will return again "to spend many happy hours among the magic maples."

Newlin B. Wildes

Martin Crews, sixteen and a junior in boarding school in 1919, is looking for a summer job in ***The Best Summer*** (1965). At the house of his "proper" Bostonian parents, a guest recommends he apply to her friend, Mary Howett, who owns a farm near Pomfret that has been in her family since 1793. He drives with his parents to Howett Farm, where Mary hires him after he fills the wood box without being asked, and returns by train a few days later. Mary's helpers (people do not work *for* her) are her farmer, Jud Holloway, his assistant, Phil Morton, and Emmy Searles, eighteen, in the kitchen. Harriet Copperthwaite, Mary's friend from Boston, is visiting. Jud is hard on Martin and gives him all the dirty chores. Miss Copperthwaite offers to tutor Martin in French some evenings, and Emmy takes him to the baseball diamond near the town hall, where he is invited to play shortstop in a big game with the town of Sharon on the Fourth of July. Martin spends his free time playing with Sally, a half-Morgan mare out of Nyjia, a blind, purebred Arab mare and the joy of Mary's life. After the ball game, which his team wins, Emmy invites him to her house. The Searles family has many children and many extra cows to milk, because they are helping their sick neighbor (he receives his payment for his milk just the same); Martin is impressed with the way everyone in the Searles household works together. At Mary's suggestion, Martin rides Sally every morning before chores. Jud continues to make his life miserable. One night, Jud leaves the mowing machine out in the yard. Nyjia, left loose by Jud, catches her hind leg in the black iron guards of the cutter bar. The summoned veterinarian is disgusted by the accident. Phil tells Martin that Jud lost his farm and then his wife. He boards his four children at his sister's and walks six miles there and six miles back every Sunday. Martin tells Mary that it was he who let out the mare, but Jud will not let him "take that for me. 'Twouldn't do." Mary says they will forget the whole occurrence. "You ain't a bad kid," Jud acknowledges. Mary invites Martin back for the next summer; with the wages, she says, he can buy Sally. Mary will build a little house for Jud, so that he can have his family with him. Martin knows that Mary is an extraordinary woman. When his father asks if he had a "worthwhile summer," Martin responds, "It was the best summer I've ever had. So far." (As a boy, the author worked during the summers on a farm that still exists in North Pomfret, Vermont.)

W

In ***The Horse That Had Everything*** (1966), Richard Jonathan ("Rick") Ballou, fourteen, lives with his widowed father, Kink, a portrait painter, in Parnell Center. Kink is tolerant, amused, and ironic; Rick is shy, introverted, and sensitive. Most of the time, Rick loves Vermont "for its solitude and grandeur," but he is lonely. He has one friend, Suzie, twelve, who lives on a dairy farm. Although he and his father have a donkey, a steer, an old mare, a rooster, some hens, and a cat, Rick wants a horse of his own. Five miles away, Slade Corcoran raises Thoroughbreds at Bellemead Stable. Rick works horses there occasionally because, as the trainer says, "his hands are gentle and firm." Kink takes Rick to look at Corcoran's new colt, beautiful but with an "off hind leg" resulting from a pinched nerve or a muscle tear. Rick visits the colt every day and learns how to massage his leg. When Corcoran decides to put the colt down, Rick begs to take the colt to raise. Corcoran agrees on the condition that Rick never reveal the colt's breeding. The colt arrives, terrified, and the "slim, serious boy with the quiet hands and voice" stays with him through the night. When Kink finds Rick and the colt asleep in the stall, he thinks, "The country is a good place to raise a boy." Suzie and Rick take the colt, whom they call San (for Sans Peur, after one of his parents), to the pond every day, where he swims with them. The vet thinks the leg is improving. In April, the "weather was like a good apple pie, warm in the middle and crisp around the edges," San, a yearling, is in magnificent shape, with no trace of a limp, and exhibits "quiet dignity...poise, confidence, pride." Corcoran wants to take San back to race him, claiming Rick has no bill of sale; however, Kink speaks to two employees of Corcoran's who witnessed his giving Rick the colt. The matter of ownership settled, Rick wonders if it is selfish not to allow San to run as he was bred to do. San spends every night outside Rick's bedroom; Kink asks a carpenter to build a stall next to Rick's room with a tight-fitting swinging door. Corcoran keeps pressing Rick to train the horse and finally urges him to register San with the Jockey Club under his proper name. Rick, now sixteen years old, hays with Suzie's father after chores and starts breaking San to saddle and bridle. Several times he takes out Cissy Parlance from his class at school but realizes it is the newly grown-up Suzie whom he loves. They ride together after haying on Saturdays and on Sundays. When San is three, Rick watches him run one day and makes his decision: Kink hires Able Marvin to train San, which means that Rick will not be with his horse for two months. At the first race, Kink, Rick, and Suzie sit in Corcoran's box. Rick is rapt with amazement and admiration. San is splendid, forty lengths in front of the pack, the crowd on its feet—and then San runs away, with his helpless jockey clinging to his mane, jumps the fence, and heads for the pond. Corcoran offers Rick a fortune for the horse, but Rick turns him down. When Rick and Suzie have their own farm, they will raise Thoroughbreds.

Doug Wilhelm

In ***Scene of the Crime*** (1993), one of the "Choose Your Own Adventure" series, you, the reader, are riding your bike in your hometown of Grantshire when you come upon a sign advertising the proposed Maple Grove Mall. Knowing that Frank Sorrell, the only person on the city council opposing the development, has disappeared, you become suspicious when you witness another councilman, Tom Collins, apparently taking a bribe from a man in a dark car. Determined to solve this mystery, you meet a number of challenges and opportunities. Should you go to the *Grantshire Observer*, or find Sorrell's daughter, Andrea, or round up your friends, Kate, with a talent for technology, and Corky, a quick thinker? The three of you are soon involved in solving a serious case of bribery related to the town's land development that the newspaper editor does not have time to investigate, and the police chief scorns as childish imagination. You must decide whether to follow Strassen's car or go to Andrea's house. You become more entangled in the crime. Should you stay outside the Belleville Transport Company or go inside? Try to escape or stay in the truck? Stake out the parking lot or become reporters? Call Councilman Collins or approach Strassen? Your most thrilling decision is to intercept, photograph, and tape the meeting and the payoff between Strassen and Collins. You succeed, evade the villains, and provide your findings to the newspaper editor. On the front page the next day is your photograph and story; the FBI arrest the conspirators.

In ***The Underground Railroad*** (1996), also one of the "Choose Your Own Adventure" series, you, the reader, are embroiled in a conflict in 1853 between antislavery and property-rights people, not only in your own town of Randolph (then known as Slab City because of the rough-hewn lumber lying beside the sawmills on the river), but in your own family. Your mother, who works for the *Green Mountain Herald*, is an abolitionist; your father, an injured sawyer, believes escaped slaves are property belonging to their owners. Your friend, Zebediah, is a Quaker. You are faced with difficult choices between one nerve-racking course and another. The action begins when an operator on the Underground Railroad, stationmaster Loren Griswold, is arrested for harboring fugitives: the Fugitive Slave Act of 1850 prohibits helping or harboring fugitive slaves. The alternatives available to you extend from the ethical to the expedient. Should you try to help the runaways or care for your friend, who is bleeding to death? Leave the wagon to hide with the slave girl or try to outride the slave hunters? Provide a woman slave with a potentially dangerous knife or find a wrench to take apart the bed to which she is manacled? Run to the house where the men are assembling or help round up the women, as your mother proposes? Try to help the captives on your own or become part of the new Underground Railroad way station? You learn, from one of your experiences, that a slave girl you meet is just like you. You are impressed when the local judge confronts the feuding mill workers by reading to them from the Vermont constitution (1777), the first in the land to outlaw slavery.

Russell Trainor, now thirteen, narrates in ***The Revealers*** (2003) his experience in seventh grade at Parkland (sometimes referred to as "Darkland") Middle School in central Vermont. Russell is miserable, trying to make himself invisible to a cruel bully, Richie Parker. Afraid to go to school, he seeks the advice of Elliot Gekewicz, the least popular boy in school. Elliot suggests they communicate by instant messaging. The two boys notice that a clique of girls led by Bethany De Mere is mistreating Catalina Aarons, a new student from the Philippines. When they approach Catalina, Elliot is delighted that she, too, knows all about dinosaurs. The three new friends decide to investigate scientifically the problem of bullying: they form the Bully Lab. Elliot is tired of being bullied by three "Jock Rots," as he calls them, and, the next time they taunt him, he fights back. They throw him off a bridge onto some rocks, where he hurts his head and breaks a leg. Catalina writes a dignified essay about her heritage, her parents, and their divorce, which she shows to Russell and Elliot. They enlist the aid of Mr. Dallas, network administrator for KidNet, who shows them how to send her letter to the whole seventh grade and who cautions them to use the system responsibly. By mistake, they send the letter to the entire school, including Mrs. Capelli, the principal. The ramifications of their action are immediately apparent: seventh grade girls begin making friends with Catalina, and other children submit their bullying stories. Russell, Elliot, and Catalina decide to publish these stories under the title, *The Darkland Revealer*. Tales pour in about hectoring and intimidation. Members of their class are impressed by their electronic publishing; they are receiving attention and respect. Russell tries to interview Richie about why he is a bully, but, when Russell calls Richie's father "a dad from hell," Richie explodes and breaks Russell's mother's tape recorder. Someone sends an essay to the Website complaining about Bethany's domination of her clique and her cheating in a social studies assignment. Mrs. Capelli summons them to a meeting with Bethany's furious father, a lawyer. Mrs. Capelli decides to revoke student access to the SchoolStream Network. Mr. Dallas, who believes the way to improve conditions is to learn by making mistakes, is upset. It dawns on Russell that Bethany sent the message herself to destroy *The Darkland Revealer*'s purpose by causing it to cease operations. In the two weeks before the principal shuts down the network, Russell, Elliot, and Catalina prepare an exhibit for the Creative Science Fair. "The Bully Lab: An Interactive Scientific Investigation" sets forth their methodology, conclusions, taped interviews, and video reenactments of bullying. The judges are struck with the creativity and impact of the project, discussing with Russell, Elliot, and Catalina their approach and asking good questions about various components of the effort. They congratulate Mrs. Capelli effusively, assuming that she has closed the network only temporarily. As he leaves, Russell thinks he catches one of the judges giving him a wink.

Fifteen-year-old Matt Shaw appears to have every advantage in ***Falling*** (2007). His father, a distinguished surgeon, and his mother, a successful real estate agent, are leading citizens in Rutland and busy after work with "clubs, committees, and fundraisers." Matt's beloved older brother, Neal, nineteen, was an all-state basketball player and his best friend. Now Matt, burdened with a terrible secret, cannot go home after school and, although he is a gifted player, will not play basketball. Neal is a drug addict, and Matt is determined to protect him. Matt's sole companion is his iPod, which comforts him with music while he walks for hours. Katie Henoch, also fifteen and a ninth grader at Rutland Middle School, lives modestly with her mother, an employee at the Price Chopper grocery; her father, a Gulf War veteran, disappeared years earlier. Idly entering a chat room on the Internet, Katie and Matt meet. As they converse, Matt drops sufficient clues (he lives in "Vermont, of all nowhere places") for Katie to recognize his identity. Katie, unlike Matt, is one of a close circle of friends, made up of Tam, Samantha, and Hope, to whom she reports her experience, saying she "connected" to Matt in a "cosmic" way. Matt's sole friend is Kingsley James ("KJ"), who lives next door. KJ loves basketball but is not skillful or big enough to make the team. Everyone at school wonders why Matt has given up basketball; Katie, sensing he has a secret sorrow, believes she can save him. Matt misses "the flow" he felt when he played. When Katie and Matt meet in person, they talk easily to each other; soon, they hold hands, then kiss. With Katie, Matt does not feel "empty and pointless" any more. When he arrives home one day, a police officer is waiting with his parents who, noticing a series of thefts, suspect Matt, not Neal. At school, a woman detective named Casey urges Matt to tell her what is bothering him; everyone has observed the changes in his behavior. Matt and Katie walk up a hill where the leaves looked like "a host of tiny green lights"; the "old wooded mountains" are a "rumpled, high, and shadowy backdrop." He wonders if life has any import; Katie believes they are part of something significant. She shows him her rock collection to illustrate that one can decide what is meaningless or meaningful: "It's a *choice*." Matt feels "the flow" again, thanks to Katie, and shoots a few baskets with KJ. Matt's emotions are still bottled up with his worries about Neal. After Neal steals Matt's iPod, Matt explodes in class and curses a teacher. The police, already aware of the afternoon traffic at his house, come to school to interrogate him. Tam, eager to help by finding out what is wrong with Matt, engages KJ in a basketball game. Dazzled by her, KJ readily tells her that Neal is a heroin dealer. Sadly, while Matt is telling Katie everything, Tam is simultaneously spreading the word through the school. Matt is wild with anger and confronts Katie, telling her he never wants to see her again. Katie is distraught that he thinks she betrayed him, when she believes they were meant for each other. Hurrying to Matt's house to explain, she finds Neal in his apartment at the rear of the house. Miserable and weeping, she collapses on his couch. Murmuring that he has something to make her feel better, Neil coaxes her to take a sniff. When he tries to rape her, she resists him; he hits her hard and knocks her out. When Matt arrives, the brothers struggle brutally; Matt manages to dial 911. Neal, insane with anger and fear, gathers up his paraphernalia and runs. The ambulance arrives—and Detective Casey. Matt pretends he called 911 by mistake, but Katie emerges from the house to say, "Tell the truth or I will." Detective Casey comforts Matt: this is a good outcome for Neal, who will be ordered into treatment and rehabilitation. Katie is taken to the hospital. Matt has a charming exchange with Detective Casey about whether he can win back Katie. She thinks he can, if he is "patient and real." (For several years, the author led a weekly after-school writers' group at Rutland Middle School.)

Charles Morrow Wilson

In 1824 in ***The Great Turkey Drive*** (1964), sixty-seven people, many of them women and children, drive eight thousand turkeys from Fyster through Putney to Boston. Major Amos Grout, hero of the Battle of Plattsburgh, where he lost a leg, lives in Fyster with his wife, Dame Abby, three daughters, and two sons, Jason, sixteen, and Abel, fourteen. They are raising turkeys for the big November drive. Their neighbor, Cynthia Prouty, an orphan living with Asa Bills and his wife, tends her "poults" (young fowl). The boys plant early oats for the turkeys in an enclosed plot and buckwheat for the open hillside. They welcome Cynthia's birds to feed there, too, since success comes from working together or not at all. The schoolmaster, Squire Hunnicutt, presides over a big township meeting to review details of the drive. The participants elect Major Grout grand marshal; he cannot walk, but he can drive a wagon and bring leather to mend boots, as well as flour, shelled corn, and salted pork. They choose Asa Bills, a logger, as drive boss; he nominates Jason as his deputy driver. A key and experienced driver is Merry Hasmer, known as

"The Redhead." When someone expresses concern about the number of women volunteers, Dame Temperance Cunningham points out that, even if all the men signed up, they would still be short of drivers. She will drive a team, help with the cooking, and tend camp. By now, the turkeys have grown from hatchlings to long-necked featherlings; the boys patrol for foxes while the heavy farm work continues. Jason, Hunnicutt, and Bills, carrying light muskets, scout the route for three weeks. The Grouts' pasture, rail-fenced, is the receiving corral for the wagons, teams, and turkeys. Turkeys and humans, a mile-long column, take to the open country. They pass through an oak grove; the turkeys feed on acorns and, later, beechnuts. The first camping supper is abundant, wooden plates heaped with fried ham, buttered biscuits, roast potato dabbed with bacon grease, and white beans boiled with onions. The dessert is "frumenty," pudding made from boiling barley and maple sugar in water. As the drive proceeds, the meals become more frugal. Each night Major Grout gathers the leaders to critique their progress. Because they are not making good enough time, they keep the wagons on the charted route and drive the turkeys a shorter, cross-country route. They circle Terrible Mountain. The Redhead sees a Canadian lynx (catamount) and shoots to warn it away, not to kill it. Abel walks ahead, blazing trails and scouting for wolves; he and Cynthia, who is chosen message-runner, become friends. A covered bridge over a river becomes a turkey trap: the birds settle down in the darkness and go to sleep. The drivers lift them out with implements made from torn clothing and sticks. The weather turns colder: they must reach the ferry at Putney before the river freezes. Food supplies dwindle. Abel and Cynthia notice footprints of Indians, perhaps waiting in ambush to stop the drive. The Redhead mystifies the Indians by driving the turkeys in a different direction. Only six of the eight wagons arrive at the camping site; Indians commandeer two, which a Catholic priest returns. In a snowstorm, the men light a fire to ward off wolves and shoot deer and bear for food. As they near the Connecticut River Valley, they follow a remnant of the old Crown Point Road. Putney has a white church with spire, a red schoolhouse, and a partial square of log houses. Jason makes a favorable deal to carry the turkeys by ferry; in return, the drivers provide the manpower to pull the cable and agree never to mention the terms. Old Nancy, the lead bird, helps guide the birds across New Hampshire and into Massachusetts. Major Grout oversees the warming of a big tub of pinesap to treat about five hundred turkeys in need of foot care. Cynthia, whose mother was raised by Mohawks, supplements the human diet by foraging for wild parsnips ("Indian biscuits"), tubers, wild onions, valley cress, wild ginger, and prickly pear. Squire Hunnicutt and Jason press ahead to Boston to negotiate with Captain Jedovah Queech, the turkey buyer. Jason's final terms are one gold dollar for each bird, plus a bounty of one silver dime for each bird from twenty-five to thirty pounds, and one federal quarter-dollar for each bird above thirty pounds. The weighing of the heaviest birds alone takes ten hours. Driving the turkeys into Boston, Jason and Hunnicutt are arrested on the bridge; the noise of the constable's whistle stampedes the turkeys into the common. Fortunately, Josiah Quincy, president of Harvard College and mayor of Boston, is summoned by Queech and comes to the rescue. He invites Jason to enter Harvard College the next day. The drive nets each Grout more than three hundred dollars.

Crown Point: The Destiny Road (1965) follows the dramatic story of the building of a road from Springfield through Rutland (then Pennycook) to Crown Point in 1759. General Jeffrey Amherst, understanding the importance to the British of a roadway across the Green Mountains, investigates the Connecticut River near Springfield, where he meets two young men, Bren Masoret, sixteen, son of a French-Indian trader, and Val Armistead, a fifteen-year-old orphan, apprentice to Trader Masoret, and Bren's adopted brother. Amherst signs on Bren and Val as his scouts. Bren and Val take Amherst to Retawa, the Deerskin village where Bren was born. The British soldiers arrive in their "regulation reds"; Amherst orders buckskins for them from Trader Masoret. At the trading post, the clerks and the tailors are Indian. Amherst, a kind, forthright, pleasant gentleman, walks out with Bren and Val to assess the lay of the land—which taller peaks to circle, which deep ravines to bridge, and which marshy strips to corduroy (to build a road of logs laid down crosswise). They visit a flint mine: the Iroquois make peaceful implements; the Abenaki, "cold country people" from the upper Connecticut River, make arrowheads and spearheads. Bren and Val travel all the way to Pennycook, carrying only "tantics" (strips of dried venison) and "tassies" (layers of cooked bean meal and thinly sliced dried beef). They stop in another Indian village, where Bren shows Val the way to make dugout and birchbark canoes. The women and girls locate digestible roots. Bren and Val have a fine lunch of meat stew followed by wild sweet plums and crusted rolls filled with wild berries and maple syrup. Continuing their route, they make "mind pictures" of the rivers the road will have to cross and the smooth ground the road can follow. Bren shows Val how to trail him and how to "stealth walk." They cross the Green Mountains and "back-trail" themselves to memorize their route. On their return, Amherst attaches them to a professional surveyor, Lucius Onion, who demonstrates how to measure by eye "an exact one yard footpace." He indicates directions with blaze marks shaped like an arrowhead barely two inches long and with small neat stakes. Bren recommends that, once in the mountains, they select established Indian trails. Ten miles out, soldiers under Quartermaster Pelkey erect a camp for the road-builders. Bren feels they are being watched because the Indians think they are measuring with magic tools; Indians shoot Onion, wearing a rain cape resembling French gear, in the leg. Bren borrows a pony to pull Onion on a litter to a Squaheag villages. French-speakers dressed as Iroquois capture Bren and Val, but they escape, running desperately until eventually they meet a contingent of British soldiers and some Indians, led by Captain John Stark of Rogers's Rangers. He and his men, clad in brown jackets and striped blue breeches, will build the road from the Crown Point end. Amherst, who gives Bren and Val the rank of "leftenant," rides with them back to the road-builders' camp, where they find some of the New Hampshire volunteers—plowmen, hunters, and loggers, led by John Goff. The men fell trees. Oxen arrive, pulling plows to clear and level the road. More volunteers come; a barracks goes up. Because supplies are slow to arrive, Goff hires Indians to hunt deer for the workers. The road progresses. By the end of September, the men finish three bridges, and the race with winter is on. They make culverts from old, hollow hemlocks. As they battle northwest, the Yorker flatlanders—Rangers and militiamen—are moving southeast from Crown Point. An Indian hunting party makes off with two wagons of supplies; two French spies burn some of their buildings. Pelkey sends Bren and Val to investigate the progress from the northwest as the two sides compete to reach Pennycook first. November comes, and the last of the long bridges takes shape. Now the two building teams are within sight and hailing distance of each other. New Hampshire wins the race just as snow begins to fall. One day Bren will have a trading post; Val will have a farm in these mountains where they have worked so hard and made so many friends among the New Hampshire militiamen. Pelkey receives orders for other duty; Bren and Val are in charge of the outpost. In July 1760, Goff and his regiment arrive at Crown Point to embark for the Battle of Montreal. Bren and Val provision the companies of horsemen as they pass on the new road. Amherst brings them golden epaulets and appoints them patrol masters of the Crown Point Road. (The character John Goff, spelled Goffe, appears in Kenneth Andler's *Mission to Fort No. 4* in this collection.)

The Green Mountain Toymakers (1965), set in Springfield in 1845, tells the story of Joel Ellis, the inventor of the Ellis Steam Excavator, a seventeen-year-old orphan and apprentice to his uncle, Jason Dewey, at his machine shop in Thetford. One day, Joel happens to see Matt Bretton struggling to adjust and operate Joel's steam digger and stops to help him. This fortuitous meeting leads to a productive partnership for Joel with Big Tommy Bretton, Bretton's nephew, and Little Tommy Meechum. Big and Little Tommy run a water mill on the Black River where they make "novelty wood." They began by cutting timbers for the railroad, moved to hardwood hubs for wagons, and now specialize in rolling hoops and sticks for children. Joel wants to invent lathes for shaping wood, using steam engines. His partners invite him home for lumber pie (leftovers) where he meets Missy Abby Rawlings, a painter and embroiderer confined to a chair. Bretton and Meechum show Joel a miniature log cabin, with a window of real glass and a carved door that opens, and a toy locomotive. Missy Abby paints the toys. Joel is inspired by the idea of shaping the toys of cedar and ash on lathes. First he makes Missy Abby a wheeled chair by chiseling, grooving, and setting each part, using no nails, screws, or glue. Joel sets off for Boston, hauling hoops and sticks in the wagon, to buy a steam engine for the new partnership with the money he saved from his apprenticeship. While he is gone, the neighbors gather for a Helpful Bee to build a stone house for the new steam engine. The partners begin the stressful process of finishing Christmas orders and making presents for less fortunate children in the village. Pinckney Frost, an itinerant parson gifted in the use of a pole lathe run with a foot pedal, joins the team, which they call Green Mountain Toys Dreamed Up By Green Mountain Children. Joel returns to Boston to meet with Stevens and Whittier, Notions Brokers, who order more hoops and sticks and many sets of new toys. When they ask to meet the firm's painter, Joel explains that she is lame. They recommend Austerlitz, a "bloodless surgeon" in Boston. The partners initiate a toymaking club for young people, helping them to work in their own homes and paying them for their products. Missy Abby and her mother travel to Boston, where the doctor assures them that he can help her walk again; he also orders copies of the wheeled chair and what he calls a "perambulator," a frame on wheels for those trying to walk. The partners enlarge their log shed and institute a guild for young toymakers to train and encourage them to devise new toys; they will pay royalties and seek patents for them. Joel invents the Ellis Ripping Lather for cutting out movable parts for the Ellis Maplewood Dolls and begins work on a catalogue. After a flood washes out part of their wood shop, they rebuild a better one. The schoolmaster and his boys shovel out the debris. This second Christmas, all the guilders present Joel with samples of their new toys to fill his catalogue. Missy Abby can walk; she and Big Tommy plan to marry.

Nancy Hope Wilson

In ***Mountain Pose*** (2001), Ellie Dunklee, twelve, lives with her sculptor father, Warren, in Massachusetts. When Ellie was five, her mother, Helen, died; Ellie barely knows her grandmother, Aurelia Sprague, who, everyone tells her, is unsympathetic. When Aurelia dies at Hart Farm near Brattleboro, Uncle Lyman, her mother's investment banker brother, asks them there to meet Helen's lawyer and best friend, Mary Norris. Aurelia's will bequeaths the farm to Ellie, to be held in trust until her maturity, along with an endowment to pay the taxes and maintain the property (the hired man, Harold Hodgkins, or "Hodge," will stay on), and a provision instructing her to read her ancestors' diaries. Ellie finds the house warm and attractive. Uncle Lyman inherits nothing from his mother but an empty blanket chest. They travel to Vermont a second time to consult with Mary, who gives Ellie the diaries. The diarist, Sarah Evans, her great-great-grandmother, has many elements in common with Ellie: their birthdays are the same day; their mothers both died when they were five. In the cemetery, she finds her gravestone (Sarah Evans Whitcomb, 1870-1954) and talks to Hodge, who refers to her grandmother as "Ellie" (Ellie never knew that was Aurelia's nickname). Mary and Uncle Lyman come to Massachusetts to discuss more details. Ellie wonders if Uncle Lyman is flirting with Mary. Ellie finds an opportunity to ask him about his great-grandmother, Sarah, whom he actually met. He confides to Ellie that Aurelia left him the blanket chest to continue punishing him because he once shut his sister,

Helen, in it. When Ellie contracts the flu, Mary sits with her and translates the coded sections of the diaries, which are written in an early form of shorthand. The dread secret of the family is that Charles Whitcomb physically abused his wife, Sarah, and his daughter, Eunice; after Eunice married and had a child, her husband physically abused her daughter, Aurelia. When Ellie's father does not receive tenure, he, Ellie, and Uncle Lyman go to Hart Farm to bury Aurelia's ashes. Ellie watches her father and Mary embrace and realizes they are in love. Ellie explains a new insight to her father: no one really knew Aurelia, but Hart Farm brings them all—Warren, Ellie, Mary, Lyman, and Helen—together: "We're all connected somehow." They climb the hill to the cemetery with Hodge and his wife, Ivy. Walter finds a perfect new job in Wisconsin and, after he and Mary marry, the new family heads there. They will spend holidays and summers at Hart Farm. (The title is the name of a yoga posture, pressing down with the feet and reaching up with the hands. The author wrote to me that the inspiration for this story was the discovery of diaries belonging to her great-grandmother and great-great-grandmother in the house in Marlboro, Vermont, which has been in the family for generations. When she was growing up, "My ancestors buried on the hill were very alive to me.")

Elizabeth Winthrop

Counting on Grace (2006) is set in 1910 in North Pownal, where the town depends upon the cotton mill for its survival. The law states that no children under fifteen can work in the mill when school is in session, but in fact many do. Grace Forcier, twelve-and-a-half, speaks French at home to her family. Her old grandfather, Pépé, came down from Canada in 1892 and faced resentment from the Irish workers competing for jobs. Her father, Joseph, is too ill from exposure to the dusty air in the mill to work. Her mother, Adeline, and older sister, Delia, both work in the weaving room. Grace wants to work in the mill to help her family. Grace and her best friend, Arthur Trottier, are the best readers in Miss Lesley's class. When French Johnny, the mill supervisor, comes for Arthur (his mother needs him to doff her frames), Arthur tries to escape but is caught and sent to the mill. Grace leaves school, too, to go into training watching Delia doff the bobbins, but Grace feels awkward and slow. Miss Lesley offers to tutor Grace and Arthur on Sundays: it is their secret. All the families are poor; even Father Alain chops wood to make enough money to live. Miss Lesley helps Arthur write a letter to Anna Putnam at the Vermont Chapter of the National Child Labor Committee in Bennington to inform her that underage children are working in the mill. Inspectors come from time to time, but French Johnny always orders the children to hide in the big elevator until the inspectors leave. Grace finds the first few weeks at the mill horrendous and exhausting: she must pay attention every minute. Once, when her mind wanders, her mother cuffs her hard. She is miserable and furious. When Grace's father is able to work again, they tie Pépé to the bed because they cannot afford to pay Madame Bouvier to watch him. One Sunday when Grace is ill and left at home with her grandfather, he disappears. She staggers out to look for him. French Johnny finds and brings her home. A train struck and killed grandfather as he was trying to return to Canada. Now that Pépé is gone, they rent out his bed to occasional boarders. Grace and Arthur continue sessions with Miss Lesley, who wants Grace to take the teachers' certification test to enter the Normal School in Bennington. The children take turns reading *A Red Badge of Courage* and are enthralled by it. Her mother thinks Grace will have no life but the mill. Arthur is hoping an inspector will come in answer to his letter; Grace says no one cares about kids in a "nowhere Vermont town." An inspector does come in the form of Lewis Hine, a photographer, who takes pictures of the children and the conditions in the mill. Arthur is so desperate to escape the mill that he purposely mangles his hand in a machine. When Mr. Hine sends Grace her photograph, her mother tears it up and destroys Grace's notebook, too. The mill orders Arthur to return as a sweeper, or he and his mother will lose their mill housing. Miss Lesley is fired for interference. Fall comes: "The wind is up. Vermont in September gives you warnings." Grace has grown out of her work clothes: Delia lends her a smock; she borrows a pair of her brother's union suits. In the weaving room, loose cloth from her smock catches in a machine, which twists her up against it. French Johnny has to cut off her dress with a knife; everyone sees her sprawled against his arm with the union suit showing. Shocked by the accident and ashamed, Grace decides to run away to North Adams, Massachusetts, where Miss Lesley lives; after all, her mother cannot count on her the way she can on Delia. As Grace swings onto a freight car, mill officials catch her. Her mother comes to fetch her and gives her permission to substitute as teacher at the mill until the owners find a new one. (In *The Red Badge of Courage*, Grace and Arthur's favorite book, the hero's wound is self-inflicted.)

G. Clifton Wisler

Mr. Lincoln's Drummer (1995) chronicles the experiences of William J. ("Willie") Johnston, Jr., who is an eleven-year-old drummer in the Third Vermont Volunteer Regiment Army of the Potomac. Willie is a high-spirited, mischievous boy in St. Johnsbury. His father operates a tailor shop, aided by his mother, who also takes care of the younger children. Willie's father receives a large order for uniforms from Colonel Breed Hyde of the Third Vermont Volunteer Infantry. After the men of the Third depart, many of the women take up sewing. Times are hard for the Johnstons: Willie has to leave school early to help out with odd jobs. The Northern side is faring badly by the time a recruiter comes to St. Johnsbury with this message: "As Ethan Allen and his brave Green Mountain lads stood tall against the British, we must now stand for the Union." When his father signs up, Willie does, too, as a drummer. Assigned to different companies, they are sent to Camp Griffin, Virginia. The musicians in Willie's Company D—fife, drum, and bugle—are called "P.F." for "peach fuzz." The winter of 1862 passes slowly. Sometimes Willie is allowed to visit his father's company. Willie's officers tell him "the drummer is the heart of the company." When they finally move out, he carries a twenty-pound pack and his drum; sailing to Richmond, he sees the ironclad *Monitor* in the harbor. The conditions are miserable—a buggy and muggy landscape, a drenching rain, and mud that bogs down the equipment wagons. Willie is wet through; many men develop fever. Some of the soldiers find hams in a smokehouse; when the owner rides out to complain, the officer laughs at him. The war news is discouraging: the rebels defeat General Ulysses S. Grant at Shiloh in Tennessee; *Merrimac* (a scuttled Union ship that the Confederates raised, covered with iron plates, and used in engagements against the North) scatters the Union fleet. Slaves flock to the Union lines begging protection. Out gathering twigs one day, Willie meets and befriends a young rebel drummer. They begin trading goods regularly—mostly tobacco for blankets. At the Battle of Lee's Mills, Willie beats assembly; the company stands to arms. Later, when he beats recall, eight men are dead. He has "seen the elephant," as the veterans term a man's first time under fire. They press on toward Richmond. Stonewall Jackson has scored some victories in the Shenandoah Valley; rebels are looting stores behind the Union line. The men of the Third Vermont wait and wait, until General George B. McClellan finally decides to probe the enemy defenses. Their mission is to prevent the capture of the division hospital and General Fitz-John Porter's hundreds of wounded soldiers. "Vermonters have iron in their backbones," declares General William B. Franklin. They retreat after the Battle of Savage's Station, abandoning many wounded men. At Malvern Hill, many soldiers discard their possessions and weapons; no one is in proper uniform any longer. Three thousand Union men are killed and nothing accomplished—no glory, no success. Wounded, Willie beats retreat again; the men arrive at Harrison's Landing. Slave women offer to cook, sew, and tend the wounded. Willie, trembling with a chill, is chosen to beat his drum when the division parades before General Franklin, the corps commander, and President

W

Lincoln. Lincoln stops to chat with Willie, the one drummer who did not abandon his drum. After the event, Willie collapses and is taken to Virginia Hospital in Arlington, where General Jacob H. Smith visits him. Willie stays in the hospital until Christmas of 1862, when the Third fights at Fredericksburg, and Willie is assigned as a nurse to a hospital in Baltimore. There, an officer orders Willie cleaned up and taken to Washington, D.C., where he chats briefly with President Lincoln and receives the Congressional Medal of Honor from Secretary of War Edwin M. Stanton. Why me? Willie wonders. Perhaps, someone suggests, because Lincoln's precious son, also named Willie, had just died at the same age. ("To have seen the elephant" is British military slang dating back to the nineteenth century. The goal of the Peninsula Campaign, launched by the Union in the spring of 1862 and commanded by General McClellan, was to capture the capital of the Confederacy, Richmond.)

Maia Wojciechowska

David Earl, son of champion rodeo clown Lee Earl in ***A Kingdom in a Horse*** (1965), travels around the country with his father, who saves riders' lives by distracting the bulls. Now thirteen, David is old enough to realize his ambition of working with his father; when he enters the ring, his father is so fearful for his son's safety that he loses his concentration; a bull gores him. After his recovery, Lee, determined to create a normal life for David, moves to Middlebury, the birthplace of his deceased wife, and becomes a blacksmith. David, furious and disappointed, hates Vermont; most of all, he hates his father. When Lee offers to buy him a horse at auction, David retorts he hates horses. Attracted to a lovely chestnut mare, he is too proud to admit his feelings. Recent widow Sarah Tierney, an old woman from Cornwall, bids for the horse and calls her "Gypsy." Lee helps Sarah with gear and advice. David, filled with self-pity, makes no friends and does badly in school. Miserable and lonely, he bicycles eight miles to Sarah's to take her horse out for a ride at night and cries when he thinks that she might have been his. He often spies on Sarah with Gypsy, both hating and loving the old woman. One day, he meets her in town on her way to Burlington and hurries to her house to spend several hours with Gypsy. He carelessly leaves the stall gate open. The horse eats a bushel of corn and is crippled with colic. David despises himself for not confessing and helping Sarah walk the horse. When Gypsy recovers, Sarah wants to show her at the big Western event in Burlington in the spring. David continues to watch Sarah and her horse secretly, no longer jealous but wistful that the two enjoy such a perfect relationship. He is living a "borrowed life," his loneliness a "physical pain." Taking Gypsy out again one night, he gets her feet wet; the next day Sarah calls Lee, fearing Gypsy has laminitis (a painful disease affecting a horse's feet). David runs away, stopping at Sarah's to confess his transgressions. Understanding that Gypsy was meant to be David's, Sarah persuades him to stay to help her cure her horse. The veterinarian diagnoses a pulled tendon. David confides to Sarah that he aspires to become a veterinarian, running a nursing home for old horses. Sarah loves his plan and wants to implement it on her farm, where she has room for twenty box stalls. Sarah writes her will, leaving her property and money to Lee in trust for David to create "a horse kingdom." Sarah invites Lee to sell his house and move with David into hers. David trains Gypsy for the show and teaches Sarah what she needs to know to ride her. The day of the fair, Sarah is not well enough to go; to his great joy, David rides Gypsy.

Nancy Means Wright

Sixteen-year-old Drusie Valentini, perceptive and humorous, leads an unconventional life in ***Down the Strings*** (1982). Her father, Dominic, heads the family's traveling marionette show. Fey, an artistic young woman from Bennington College, is Dominic's assistant and companion. Her mother, Elizabeth, fled to Europe with Theron, an artist. Her little brother, Punch (his real name is Quigley), is spoiled by candy and other snacks; her grandmother is strict and censorious. When the Valentinis are not on tour, they live in Broken House in "cool, green" Branbury in central Vermont. Punch often puts on a puppet show on the lawn and charges admission to passersby. Their talented father creates shows in which his marionettes take on the personality of members of the audience: "It's supposed to be yourself coming down those strings." Some of the rowdier boys at school persuade Drusie to open her house for a party while her father and Fey are out of town. Hordes of young people turn up, some of whom are already high and all of whom have been drinking. Into this nightmare scene arrives her grandmother, unannounced, before Drusie can clean up the mess. To bring order and discipline to Drusie's life, her grandmother sends her to Saint Catherine's, a boarding school in New Hampshire. At school she makes two friends. One is Nina, who is distraught from causing an automobile accident in which her twin brother was killed. The other is Drusie's English teacher, Miss Fern, who is interested in her writing. Drusie focuses most of her energy on seeing her mother at Christmastime. She stays in Boston with Elizabeth and Theron, who is not happy with her sleeping on the living room sofa. He paints in the mornings, has a Scotch and a sandwich for lunch, and goes for a walk to "perceive" things in the afternoons. Miss Fern and Drusie visit Nina in the hospital. After Christmas, Drusie is reunited in Branbury with her father, who assumes that she and Punch will come to Europe with him and Fey instead of returning to school. With so many choices ahead of her—Paris, high school in Vermont, or boarding school in New Hampshire—Drusie feels like "that forked road in the Frost poem." She comforts herself by rereading *Wuthering Heights*. Her mother leaves Theron and returns to Branbury, telling Drusie she still loves Dominic. Fey describes to Drusie her childhood in a series of foster homes. Drusie, feeling responsible for trying to clean up the mess of the adults' lives, returns to boarding school in New Hampshire. (The poem Drusie quotes is Robert Frost's "The Road Not Taken," which ends, "Two roads diverged in a wood, and I—/I took the one less traveled by,/And that has made all the difference.")

Zoe Elwood, eleven, whose home is in Branbury in ***The Pea Soup Poisonings*** (2006), has one passionate goal: to join her brother Kelby's all-boy club, Northern Spy (named after the apples in their father's orchard). To achieve this end, Zoe must walk the beam in her father's barn and solve a crime. As to the first, Zoe's father drags her off the beam before she is halfway across; as to the second, her friend Alice Fairweather's grandmother, Agnes, has just died from poisoning, and the police suspect the pea soup served by the Misses Gertie and Maud Bagley. Kelby grants her five days to find the murderer; her friend, Spence Riley, who is not a member of the club, signs on as her assistant. Alice calls Zoe to report that two strangers, calling themselves "relatives," have just taken Great-aunt Thelma (deceased Agnes's sister) to the state mental institution in Rockbury. Zoe and Spence search Thelma's house, find a small golden key, and hurry by bus to Rockbury, where they help Thelma escape and take her to the Bagleys' house. Cedric and Chloe Wolfadder, the two strangers, kidnap Spence. Thelma, in disguise, redeems her possessions with the key from her safe deposit box at the Branbury National Bank—a will, a deed to her house, and her birth certificate. She was born on a farm of three hundred and sixty acres in Alburg, which she plans to leave to Alice. Someone is willing to kill for that farm. Zoe makes a photocopy of the deed and hides it at Thelma's house. The Wolfadders discover Zoe and take her to the attic where they have hidden Spence. The children now know the motive: Cedric and Chloe plan to turn Thelma's farm into a game-hunting park. As the kidnappers head to Canada with their captives, Zoe memorizes the license plate, escapes, and is soon following them in a police car. Spence has the evidence—a letter from the Plum Bush Zoo—and the police arrest the Wolfadders. Now Zoe has one day left to find proof the couple poisoned the soup. She hurries to Alice's house, where Alice's mother, Madeline, seems surprised to see her. Searching Agnes's boxes in the basement, Alice and Zoe find a picture of Madeline and Chloe and a container of malathion (insecticide).

Madeline confesses—before midnight—and Zoe successfully walks the beam and receives her detective badge.

Zoe has achieved sergeant's rank in ***The Great Circus Train Robbery*** (2007), the sequel to *The Pea Soup Poisonings*, and aspires to a lieutenancy in the club led by her brother, Chief Detective Zelby. Hopeful that the new neighbor, Juniper Boomer, is a murderer, or at least a spy, she has him under surveillance. Zoe's best friend, Spence, a cellist, prizes his newly acquired antique Lionel train set. When one of the rail cars is stolen, Zoe happily assumes that Juniper is the thief. Spence agrees to help Zoe with her spying if she will assist him in an essay contest on steam trains. At the town library, the children consult with their librarian friend, Ms. Delores, whose niece, Tulip the clown, is arriving with the Great North Country Quirkus Circus. Inspired by Nancy Drew's sleuthing techniques, Zoe persuades Spence to steal into Juniper's house while the latter is away shopping. They find a photograph of a boy in a train engineer's hat and a few suspicious messages on his computer. Accompanied by Ms. Delores, Zoe and Spence volunteer for jobs at the circus: Zoe will zip Tulip into her costume; Spence will help Hackberry, the nervous clown, by pushing him back into the ring whenever he retreats. Zoe and Spence see in the stands a mysterious stranger with a black mustache: could it be Juniper poised to steal another toy train? They learn that Hackberry is separated from his wife and is Juniper's adopted brother. Someone steals Spence's red advertising car and a rail car from the trunk of Hackberry's car. Spence and Zoe make another foray into Juniper's house, where he succumbs to a sedative she puts in his root beer. Spence finds one of his own cars buried in the cellar. Zoe figures out that Spence's train set once belonged to Hackberry—and that something valuable is hidden in one of the cars. A precious ring turns up in the passenger car. For the showdown at the circus, Spence alerts their parents and Ms. Delores informs a policeman friend. Zoe has a new idea about the identity of the baggage car thief: Mrs. Hackberry must have used her husband's trained monkey. Spence, magnanimous, offers to return the train set to Hackberry, who wants Spence to keep it; Hackberry will visit it now and then. His goal in stealing the train cars was to confirm his parentage: he was Willow Boomer's legitimate son by her first husband.

Hildreth Wriston

Downstreet with Edith (1935) provides a portrait of family life in Fletcher Falls in northeastern Vermont when Theodore Roosevelt is president, and home electricity is in the offing. Fletcher Falls has an upstreet, with the green, the post office, the church, and the schoolhouse, and a downstreet, with the mill, the sash-and-blind factory, and the electric-light station. Edith, six, and Frederick, eight, live downstreet. Their father is the postmaster; their grandfather owns the mill. Uncle Henry, Aunt Minnie, and their three children, Timothy, Dorothea, and Marjorie, live just across the river with their grandparents. Edith and Frederick know everyone in town—Jenny, the hired girl; Roxanna, the dressmaker; Mr. Snay, who banks up their house with evergreen boughs in winter; Mr. Stufflebeam, a carpenter who sometimes gives them scraps of wood and this year makes their Christmas sleds. Saturday nights they take baths; they must wear winter underwear after November first. One of their favorite books is *Black Beauty*. Sunday afternoons they visit Uncle Henry's family; some evenings the grown-ups roller-skate at the Odd Fellows' Hall upstreet over the post office. Their Christmas is merry, although they have a slight accident with the sleds, and Frederick comes down with measles. Edith cannot go to school; she watches the men cut ice. Then she has the measles, which is fun because Dr. Phil swings her to the ceiling. The children play soldiers with their mothers' buttons; the electric-light men come and cut holes in the plaster. Then it is perfect sugaring weather. Mr. Brown, one of the rural mail carriers, takes them on his route to Cousin Emmy Holt's, where they watch the sugaring. In another part of the Holts' farmhouse live the Tatros, who are "Canucks." The sap boiler is so big it nearly fills the sugarhouse. The children watch the ice go out on the river and attend the Decoration Day ceremonies. All the soldiers' graves have bright new flags. When Dr. Phil's horse is frightened by the band and drowns in the river, he horsewhips the boy who was supposed to be watching the animal. Edith is terrified of the river because she understood her mother to say it was full of "holes." Her birthday surprise is a ride in Mr. Horner's red automobile. Aunt Minnie, approaching in her horse-drawn carriage from the other direction, holds her frightened horses. When gypsies come to town, the children go to visit them. They are allowed to keep a gypsy dog. When he runs away, Edith forces herself to wade into the river after him and finds no holes after all. Now she will never be frightened again: the river is her friend, and she is glad she lives beside it.

In ***Camping Down at Highgate*** (1939), Emily, nine, and her brother, Theodore, ten, are staying with their parents, grandmother, and sister, Joan, five, at Highgate Springs in the summer of 1905. "Everything is nicer at camp." They sleep in tents, leave the table when they feel like it, and make more noise than at home. Uncle Albert and Aunt Em, with Mark, eleven, and bossy Arabella, thirteen, join them. They notice a boy from the hotel, whose father owns a yacht. Their father rents them a rowboat to take out fishing on Missisquoi Bay. While digging for worms, Emily finds an Indian arrowhead, which reminds her that "real" Indians once lived here; she has met only the Indians who live at a camp close at hand—not in wigwams—and make baskets for sale. The boy from the hotel, Harry Macomber, is a good sport and a fine addition to their group. Playing Indian, they create their own camp, bringing blankets and supplies. Theodore brings another friend, Roger Thayer, who is camping with his widowed mother. In Roger's tent, they listen to a gramophone and play Parcheesi. Theodore wants to change their Indian game into something more meaningful; for example, they could go exploring on behalf of the white settlement, seeking a river large enough for navigation and creating a birchbark map. Uncle Albert takes the gang to Swanton in a rig borrowed from the dairy farmer. On the way, their horse bolts when they meet Harry's father in his motor car. Uncle Albert takes Emily to an arrowhead dealer, but she refuses to sell her talisman. When they are out fishing one day, a storm comes up, and Mr. Macomber rescues them in his motor launch. The days Emily cannot go outside, she happily reads *Boy Captive of Deerfield.* One of the traditions of the summer is to hold a big chowder dinner and invite the other campers. The ladies bring oilcloths, dishes, glasses, and cutlery; the men set up big tables. Someone plays the banjo, and everyone sings. Emily suddenly realizes her talisman is missing. Their mother asks Theodore and Emily to take Joan to the sulfur spring. When they turn their backs for a minute, she disappears. They find her at the Indian camp, contentedly learning to weave baskets, but Emily feels she has failed her mother. When the Macombers invite her parents to a dance at the hotel, Emily's mother again entrusts Joan to her. In the middle of the night, Emily hears a clatter of hoofs: a bull is loose. She rows Joan in a neighbor's boat to the hotel to warn her parents not to come home the regular way. Her mother is proud of the way Emily assumed responsibility for others. At the bonfire and cookout on the last night, Emily finds her talisman. Her father will have it set in silver, so she can wear it around her neck.

Because their father works for the U.S. Customs service, the Halliday children in ***Open Water*** (1942) have been in many parts of the country, but they think Vermont is "the best place yet." Their land is near the Canadian border on a part of Mr. Berlanger's farm that runs down to Lake Champlain. Their Great-aunt Lou, who is "interested in everything," is visiting. Bill, thirteen; Allison, twelve; Judy, nine; and Prentiss ("Punk"), eight, are enthusiastic about financing a boat with their combined allowances. The government plans to put another patrol boat on the lake, either at Alburg or on their shore. The revenue man, Officer Bob Gallagher, comes to assess their boathouse. Mr. Berlanger's son, Arlin, fourteen, tells the children about a rumrunners' cave. If only they had a motor boat, they could patrol the lake. Bill asks Captain Orcutt in the village if he would sell them his old boat, *Nancy Lee*. He agrees, helping them paint and caulk it, and replaces the rotten wood himself. Lou proposes that they devise a budget for the remaining expenses, such as the motor. When they have done so, she gives them the exact amount as birthday presents. Joe Ribieau, the fisherman, installs the motor, and Mr. Berlanger's horses pull the boat into the water. After some supervision by their father, they take the boat out on their own. They find a channel into a creek, where they spot two men fishing, and motor as far as Gander Bay, where they pretend to be members of Rogers's Rangers, hiding their boats before the long trek to St. Francis. They pass the government boat and suddenly see the cave. Allison climbs into the darkness and touches something warm and furry. They keep this discovery a secret. They return to the cave to find a boat moored there. That night, Officer Gallagher says the items currently being smuggled are "wool, furs, jewels, and aliens." It must have been a pelt that Allison touched. The children split up, two in the boat and two on the cliff, using mirrors to signal when any boats approach. Near the cave, they see the same two men fishing. When Judy signals that the two men have entered the cave, Bill realizes he should have told his father long before now. Later, he shows the cave to his father and Gallagher. Their parents allow them to take the boat to camp overnight in the little bay. In the middle of the night, Punk develops a bad stomachache. Bill knows they must go home. Navigating with difficulty in the dark, they run out of gas. Fortunately, Joe, headed for Gander Bay, rescues them. The government sets a trap for the smugglers, and, at a signal, its boats roar into action. The four children and their father follow in *Nancy Lee*. The smugglers try to escape by land, but the government has stationed its men on the road. By morning, Gallagher reports their smugglers are in jail. The children receive a reward of two hundred dollars, which they share with Arlin, who told them about the cave. They are excited about their lives—and "the open water inviting them to more adventures."

In ***Show Lamb*** (1953), Chad Warner, eleven, lives with his little sister, Molly, his father, Joshua, his mother, and his Aunt Abigail on a Merino sheep farm in the Black River Valley in 1850. Joshua's father, a sheep farmer before him, came to the Vermont wilderness to build a new life, while his brothers went out West. Chad's two burning, interrelated desires are to raise a show lamb and to please his father. The children's upbringing is strict: they are not allowed to speak at meals; they attend family prayers and memorize verses of the Bible before church every Sunday. The chores for Joshua and Mac, the flockmaster, are unremitting; a constant worry is the fluctuating price of wool. Chad has many duties, too—the horses, the cow, the pigs. Uncle Ezra and Aunt Betsy and their children live not far away; mischievous Joel is Chad's contemporary. Chad is overjoyed when his father, Joshua, asks him to help with lambing even though he has school the next day. During the night, seventy-nine lambs are born. Chad's task is to make certain each mother cares for her lamb. The ewe with twins refuses to recognize one of them: Chad carries the rejected baby into the house for the women to nurse and give to Molly as a pet (a "cosset"). Chad has had cossets before and now wants to raise, feed, and groom his own lamb to show at the Tunbridge Fair; Joshua does not think Chad is old enough. The neighboring Crawford farm is failing because the owner is "shiftless"; the Crawford children stop coming to school because they have no proper clothes. Joshua offers Crawford a load of hay to tide him over; Crawford leaves the gate open, and the rams escape. Chad remains calm while he and his dog, Shep, herd them back in. Chad picks out what he considers to be the best lamb from Joshua's flock and pretends it is his; he confides this secret to Aunt Abigail, who was raised on the farm and understands. One day, Chad and Joel take their rifles to hunt woodchucks; as they pass the Crawford farm, Abner throws a stone at them. The boys swear revenge. Chad makes an identification disk for his lamb, which he names "Champion," and attaches it with a wire concealed in the woolly neck.

The shearing and dipping process begins: the fleece comes off the back of the sheep like a jacket. One of the Crawford boys shoots Shep in the foot; Joshua is furious. The tense situation between the two families escalates into a feud. While Joshua is away at market, Abner reports a bobcat prowling on their side of the valley. Chad, out tracking the bobcat with Joel, suddenly sees it hovering in a tree above Molly, who is sitting in the grass with her pet lamb. Chad shoots the bobcat with his rifle. Joshua and Mac choose which sheep to take to the fair; one is Champion. On the road, two riders driving a large herd overtake the Warners' little flock. As they pass by, Chad recognizes Crawford and Abner. The next day, Champion is missing. When they arrive at the fair, Joshua grimly seeks out Crawford to ask if he has an extra sheep. Crawford refuses to let him look; the appraiser intervenes. A crowd gathers. Chad explains to the appraiser that his sheep is marked. After the appraiser finds Champion in Crawford's flock, he offers Joshua a great deal of money for his sheep; Joshua says, "Ask the boy. It is his lamb." Joshua steps into the winner's circle three times for his sheep, but when Champion wins and Joshua's name is called again, he tells the crowd, "Chadwick Warner is the owner of that one." On the way home, Chad and his father talk about fleeces, market prices, and mutton: they are partners.

For the Marvin family at ***Hill Farm*** (1956), the famous North Branch flood of eleven years earlier is never far from their thoughts. Dave Marvin, twelve, lives on the family farm near Bald Peak with his father, Henry; his mother; an older brother, Hank, a logger; a sister, Sandra, thirteen; and a little brother, Billy. Dave heard the story of the flood many times from their grandfather. After grandfather's farm was swallowed up, he always blamed the Power Company. Dave is not sure he wants to be a farmer when he grows up. One day, Dave sees Sam Hornby, their neighbor and transporter of their milk, scooping cream from the top of their good Jersey milk and adding water. As Dave drives the cultivator, he can look down at Hornby's place, which was once Dave's grandfather's land. Dave indignantly reports the incident to Henry, who says he will handle the matter. Dave tells his best friend, Jay, but feels uneasy and guilty after doing so. While Dave and Jay are snooping around Hornby's barn looking for evidence, Hornby discovers them and gives Dave a licking with a switch on the backs of his legs. Dave's older brother teaches him to ride his motorcycle. Some say the Power Company is raising the level of the reservoir; Dave has seen the new boards on the sides of the reservoir. Dave decides to lead one of Hornby's cows away and milk it in order to make up for their loss, but the cow escapes. Henry stops using Hornby to truck his milk to market. When Dave overhears people in the country store taunting Hornby, Dave feels ashamed of himself and sorry for the unfortunate man. The whole family sets to work bringing in the hay. Dave drives the tractor up and down the length of the meadow, worrying about the missing cow, and approaches the barn. The fork rises from the truck, grasping a huge pile of hay, and dumps it where they can spread it with pitchforks. Finally, Dave confesses everything to Henry, who sends him to find the cow. She has not been milked in a week; Dave takes responsibility for getting her back in shape. At the reservoir, Dave notices that the water has risen and looks menacing and swollen. His parents are in town when Dave hears on the radio that a flood is coming. He borrows Hank's motorcycle, warns Hornby, and carries Hornby's wife and baby back to the Marvin farm. Meanwhile, Sandra and Billy lead the animals to safety. His parents are still not home. The electricity goes out, and Dave milks all the cows by hand. Hornby loses everything and gives up, deciding to stick to the trucking business. Henry gives him back their milk delivery. Dave, understanding that Hornby is not bad, just unlucky, offers to take care of his three cows and one bull until he can sell them. Dave proposes to Henry that the Marvins buy back grandfather's land from Hornby. Dave loves the land—"the smell of the cows and the smell of the sun on the ferns along the edge of the woods"—

and has never felt so much a part of it. He cannot wait to start cultivating the new land.

Susan's Secret (1957), set in St. Johnsbury in 1857, entangles Susan in a secret drama that she barely understands. Her father, Dan, is a newspaperman on the *Green Mountain Freeman*; her mother takes care of the household and the children—Susan, ten; Daniel, thirteen; and two little girls, Molly and baby Dacia. Susan attends the Academy with her best friend, Melissa Page, and every Sunday goes to church, followed by a visit to Uncle Silas, Aunt May, and their invalid cousin, Edwin, in their big, white house next to the Academy. The grown-ups are upset about the visiting minister's sermon, in which he refers pejoratively to "abolitionists in our midst." Susan, Daniel, and Edwin read to each other from *The Green Mountain Boys*. Unexpected events begin to trouble Susan. She hears a bump over the kitchen, where no room exists. She sees her mother hide a copy of *The Liberator* (an anti-slavery journal published by William Lloyd Garrison from 1831-1865), advertising a meeting of the Anti-Slavery Association, with inexplicable phrases like "the Underground Railroad" and "the Fugitive Slave Law." Her father takes mysterious trips to Randolph. Daniel and Edwin refer to "fugitives" escaping from Seth Graham's farm to Canada. Susan sees her mother at night carrying a tray upstairs. Just before Susan's birthday party, a boy brings a message from Melissa's mother forbidding her daughter to play with Susan. Bullies at school taunt her, saying she is an "abolitionist." She figures out the location of the secret room and realizes her parents are sheltering fugitive slaves. After Daniel, visiting their grandmother in Danville, suffers a serious fall, Susan's parents go to him, leaving Susan in charge of the little girls—and of feeding the fugitives, a couple and a little boy. She reassures her mother: she knows about them and will take care of everyone. In the night, she hears the familiar rap on the door and a voice saying, "they must get away that night." She will have to take the fugitives in the wagon. The Negro father helps harness Nan and Bess and shows Susan the false bottom in the wagon. She suddenly realizes she does not know where to take them; she relaxes the reins, and the horses confidently head for the correct farmhouse fifteen miles away. The house of the Endicotts, who greet them and send word to her father, is one of the way stations on the Underground Railroad. Susan talks with the fugitives and learns about their lives in Virginia. Later, she talks seriously to her parents about the situation. The abolitionists' short-term goal is to change the law about capturing runaways and sending them home; the long-term goal is to change the law in order to abolish slavery throughout the country. Susan grows up during these few days and is relieved that no more secrets exist in the family.

A Yankee Musket (1959) recounts the story of a family's involvement in the events leading up to the Battle of Hubbardton in 1777. Stephen Tuttle, thirteen, lives on Otter Creek with his mother and father, Amos; his brother, Jonas, sixteen; and younger sister and brother, Deborah and Mark. The Tuttles are settlers on the frontier of the New Hampshire Grants with few neighbors. Amos sends Stephen and Jonas to have their grain ground in Castleton, the site of Remington's Tavern, where Ethan Allen assembled the Green Mountain Boys to plan the attack on Fort Ticonderoga two years earlier. In Castleton, Geoffrey Adams, a Tory boy Stephen's age, taunts him. A convention in Windsor declares the Grants the independent state of Vermont. Amos instructs the children not to use the road approaching their house so as not to alert marauding Indians to their presence. Stephen and Jonas cut an alternative bridle trail (where Stephen kills a ten-point buck to provide their meat for the winter) to enable them to reach their neighbors in case of emergency. When Stephen falls from a tree and breaks an arm, his father takes him to Castleton to be treated by Dr. Adams, Geoffrey's Tory father. The situation becomes so serious that Seth Warner and Ira Allen warn the settlers in Otter Creek Valley to seek protection at Fort Ranger in Rutland. Colonel Warner, "majestic and commanding," is raising another militia. Jonas enlists. Amos gives Stephen a musket thrown away by a deserter. After General St. Clair surrenders, the Tuttles watch the soldiers retreating from Fort Ticonderoga, with General Simon Fraser and the British not far behind. The Tuttles pack up to leave, after two years' backbreaking work building their home. Amos counsels Stephen, in case of emergency, to stop and think what is best to do, not what he wants to do. While Stephen is out getting the cow, he hears noises; Indians and British soldiers take his father prisoner and plunder the house. While the Americans are fighting at Hubbardton, Stephen leads the family and the cow over the notch to Rutland. Spending one night on the way, they reach Fort Ranger. A patrol of Hessian dragoons captures Stephen, who is wandering outside the fort, and takes him (but not before he hides his musket) to Castleton and General von Riedesel, who assigns him to help Mr. Remington in the tavern kitchen. Stephen slips away and hides in the Adams's attic, where he finds Geoffrey. Together, they escape in Geoffrey's canoe and become friends as they make it back with great difficulty to Fort Ranger. Colonel Warner, who sends Geoffrey on parole to his father in house detention, pulls together his forces and heads to Bennington to confront General Burgoyne. The Americans enjoy a great victory, but Stephen knows what it feels like to be a loser, too. Warner issues Stephen a pass to recover his musket on the Rutland-Castleton Road and return to his family.

For the third summer, Andy Varden, fourteen, and his family in ***Andy and the Red Canoe*** (1960) are spending the summer at Burleigh on a lake near the Canadian border. Andy's older sister, Sally, is there and his cousin, Bill, fifteen. Andy has his heart set on traveling by canoe to the source of the river; his parents agree to let him go as long as Bill is captain of the expedition. At the end of four or five days, Andy's father will pick them up in his car. The boys provision, pack up, and are on their way, cooking and sleeping out and telephoning Andy's father each afternoon to check in. At the village of Hydeville, they stop at a circus. Andy notices a red-haired boy working in one of the concessions. Later, the boy, Red, comes to their canoe, saying he has run away from his Uncle Willie because the latter is engaged in gambling. That night the boys hear on the radio that the police are seeking William Dugan for picking pockets at the circus. When Andy agrees to take Red with them, Bill grows angry and walks off. Andy and Red paddle on and, when it starts to rain, find shelter in a dilapidated field barn. Andy, now in charge, is nervous and regrets his quarrel with Bill. Was he able to hitchhike home before dark? Andy also feels guilty that he did not tell his father when he spoke to him on the telephone. Uncle Willie finds them, announcing that he has "withdrawn from circulation temporarily until the rustic clientele calmed down." Uncle Willie cooks the boys a wonderful breakfast and turns out to be an experienced paddler; however, Uncle Willie is heading for Canada, and Andy knows fewer and fewer opportunities to telephone home will present themselves. Andy is familiar enough with the map to know the existence of a north-south route close by. Uncomfortable and frightened, he makes a break for it, taking his hatchet but forgetting matches. When it gets dark and starts to rain, he snuggles down in the hollow between two big roots of a tree. Meanwhile, Bill, studying a map, sees why Andy was keen on following the river and wishes he could rejoin him. He spends the night of the storm in a motel and alerts Andy's father who calls the state police. They are looking for Red, too. On their way, the troopers pick up Bill, who has been worried that the two boys might have tipped over and drowned. Andy makes his difficult way down the mountain to the road. A member of the search party finds him and takes him to Nick's Place, the rendezvous designated by the police. Bill is there with Red and Uncle Willie, who is not the thief. The canoe is safe. When Andy looks at the map again, he believes he did reach the source of the river. Later, they will return to check. His parents are impressed by his courage and proud of his resourcefulness.

Z

Paul Zindel

In ***Loch*** (1994), Dr. Sam Perkins, a widowed oceanographer, makes his home in Inverness on Lake Alban in northern Vermont with his son Luke, fifteen, and daughter, Zaidee, ten. Luke has been called "Loch" ever since, at age five, he saw a beast rear out of the water to devour two sheep drinking from a steep slope at the lake's edge. Sam has a well-paying job with Anthony Cavenger, who hunts prehistoric creatures in Lake Alban; Loch likes Cavenger's daughter, Sarah. Erdon, a photographer, is shooting the day's hunt. Sarah takes Erdon on the catamaran; Loch and Zaidee go on Cavenger's yacht, *The Revelation*. Sam oversees the sonar graphic recorders that are searching for plesiosaurs (extinct marine reptiles of the Mesozoic Era). He finds a floating log and a cluster of beavers; then he detects something alive and deep. The trawlers drag their nets. One of the beasts bites Erdon in two as he lies on the catamaran's bow. Loch jumps into a raft and saves Sarah just as the monster crashes down on her boat; it explodes. Cavenger sends for more boats. The team calls the younger creature, "Beast," and the larger one, "Rogue." Sam theorizes that they came from Lake Champlain, following a salmon run on the river to Lake Alban, and were trapped by the salmon grid. Sam leaves his children on the shore, ordering them not to go out in a boat. They disobey and take the bass boat, rationalizing that they will stay in the shallows. Loch brings his scuba-diving gear. When he gets into the water, an undertow sucks him into a cave where he sees a baby plesiosaur, about the size of a seal. He pets and feeds it and starts swimming with it, calling it "Wee Beastie." Jess Sanderson, caretaker of the logging mill, is standing on the pier when two long-necked heads rise from the lake and bite off his legs. Sarah arrives in her father's motor launch to collect Loch and Zaidee. Hoping to move Wee Beastie before the frogmen come, they plan to use raw fish to lure him over the grid and into the safety of Lake Champlain. Cavenger, infuriated with his lack of success at netting the water beasts, gives instructions to his fleet not to capture but to kill them. Loch is convinced the creatures have feelings and intelligence. Sarah takes Loch by motor boat to the logging camp, where something powerful is spilling logs out of the pond. They find a whole family of plesiosaurs. Their idea is to lead the beasts to Sam who, having resigned from his job in disgust, attempts to open the grid. Cavenger's men shoot at Rogue, which is trying to protect his family. Rogue kills Cavenger before the yacht explodes. The herd of leviathans, which makes the sounds of a multitude of cellos, is sucked into the safety of the lake. Wee Beastie wants to stay with his human friends, but they drive him toward the others.

Resources

Bibliography

Appendixes

Indexes

Notes and Additions

BIBLIOGRAPHY, alphabetically by author

This list gives full name of author, title, city of publication, publisher, date of publication, illustrator, setting with quotation marks to indicate fictional places, author's residence, author's dates if deceased, and author's connections to Vermont. (Because of space limitations, only the author's Vermont-related awards and honors are mentioned.) It includes 255 authors of 441 works of fiction set in Vermont. Titles are presented for each author by publication date in ascending order. Titles marked with an (*) asterisk (49 titles or eleven percent) take place only partially in Vermont. Fifty-three percent (136) of the authors lives—or lived—in Vermont full-time or part-time. The abbreviation (YA) stands for young adult fiction for readers from ages 12-18 (164 titles); (CF) signifies children's fiction for ages 7-12 (208 titles); and (E) represents picture books and easy readers (69 titles).

A

Jacob Abbott, (YA)*Marco Paul's Voyages & Travels in Vermont*, from *Marco Paul's Travels in the Pursuit of Knowledge* (Boston: B.B. Mussey, 1843; New York: Harper & Brothers, 1852, illustrated by Carl Emil Doepler & William Roberts; reissued by BiblioBazaar, Charleston, South Carolina, 2006), set in Montpelier.

Abbott (1803-1879), author of the *Rollo Books*, pastor, and founder of schools, lived in Massachusetts and Maine.

Jane Ludlow Drake Abbott, (YA)*Happy House* (New York: Lippincott, 1920), set on North Hero Island.

Abbott (1885-1962) lived in New Jersey.

Katharine Beall Adams, (YA)**Mehitable* (New York: Macmillan, 1920), set in "Cherryville" in 1913.

Adams lived in Maryland.

Louisa May Alcott, (YA)"A Country Christmas," from *Kitty's Class Day and Other Stories* (Boston: A.K. Loring, 1868).

Alcott (1832-1888) lived in Massachusetts.

Merritt Parmelee Allen, (YA)*Raiders' Hoard* (New York: Longman's, 1936), set in St. Albans in 1864.

(YA)*The Green Cockade* (New York: Longman's, 1942, illustrated by Henry Sampson Gillette), set in Bennington in 1774.

(YA)**The Flicker's Feather* (New York: Longman's, 1953, illustrated by Tom O'Sullivan), set on Lake Champlain and Otter Creek in 1758.

Allen (1893-1954) lived in Bristol, Vermont.

Julia Alvarez, (CF)*How Tía Lola Came to Visit / Stay* (New York: Knopf, 2001), set in Middlebury.

(YA)**Finding Miracles* (New York: Knopf, 2004, reissued by Laurel-Leaf Books, 2006), set near Burlington.

Alvarez graduated from Middlebury College in 1971, attended the Bread Loaf Writers' Conference in 1986, and was a professor and is now writer in residence at Middlebury College. She lives in Weybridge, Vermont.

Grace Whitney Neil Anderson, (YA)*In the Shadow of Cox Mountain* (Rutland, Vt.: Academy Books, 1993, illustrated by Grace Brigham), set in Pittsford in 1773.

Anderson (1921-1997) lived in Pittsford, Vermont.

M.T. (Matthew Tobin) Anderson, (CF)*The Game of Sunken Places* (New York: Scholastic, 2004), set in "Gerenford."

Anderson was chair of the faculty of Vermont College's MFA in Writing for Children and Young Adults and lives in Boston, Massachusetts.

Kenneth Andler, (CF)**Mission to Fort No. 4* (Hanover, N.H.: The Regional Center for Educational Training, 1975, illustrated by Max R. Kaufmann), set on the Connecticut River in 1775.

Andler (1904-1994) lived in Newport, New Hampshire.

Jennifer Armstrong, (CF)**Steal Away* (New York: Orchard Books, 1992), Dorothy Canfield Fisher Children's Book Award Master List, 1993-1994, and 2007 choice of the Barre Learning for Life Committee through a grant from the Vermont Humanities Council's Creating Communities of Readers program.

Armstrong lives in Saratoga Springs, New York.

Jim (James Edward) Arnosky, (E)*Nathaniel* (New York: Addison-Wesley, 1978, illustrated by Jim Arnosky), set in northern Vermont.

(E)*Mud Time and More: Nathaniel Stories* (New York: Addison-Wesley, 1979, illustrated by Jim Arnosky), set in northern Vermont.

(CF)*Little Champ* (New York: Putnam, 1995, illustrated by Jim Arnosky), set on an island in Lake Champlain.

Arnosky lives in South Ryegate, Vermont.

Robert Arthur, (YA) "Obstinate Uncle Otis," from *Ghosts and More Ghosts* (New York: Random, 1963), set in "Hillport."
Arthur (1909-1969) lived in Philadelphia, Pennsylvania.

Frank Asch, (CF)*Up River* (New York: Simon & Schuster, 1995, photography by Ted Levin & Steve Lehmer), set on Otter Creek.
Asch lives in Middletown Springs, Vermont.

Robert Paul Ashley, Jr., (YA)*Rebel Raiders: A Story of the St. Albans Raid* (Philadelphia & Toronto: John C. Winston, 1956, illustrated by Floyd James Torbert), set in St. Albans in 1864.
Dr. Ashley (1915-2006) lived in Ripon, Wisconsin.

Kay Avery, (E)*Wee Willow Whistle* (New York: Knopf, 1947, illustrated by Winifred Bromhall).
(CF)*All for a Horse* (New York: Crowell, 1955, illustrated by Aldren Auld Watson), set near "Larson Junction."
(CF)*All for a Friend* (New York: Crowell, 1956, illustrated by Aldren Auld Watson), set near "Larson Junction."
(CF)*All for a Ghost* (New York: Crowell, 1957, illustrated by Aldren Auld Watson), set near "Larson Junction."
(YA)*Goodbye Blue Jeans* (New York: Ives Washburn, Inc, 1963, illustrated by Richard Lewis), set in "Linville."
Avery (1908-2005), who was a schoolteacher in Walden, Vermont, from 1963-1967, was born and lived in Middletown Springs, Vermont.

Mary Azarian, (E)*A Farmer's Alphabet* (New York: Godine, 1981, illustrated by Mary Azarian).
Azarian lives in Calais, Vermont.

B

Katharine Jay Bacon, (CF)*Pip and Emma* (New York: Atheneum, 1986), set in "Doe's Crossing."
(YA)*Shadow and Light* (New York: Macmillan, 1987), Dorothy Canfield Fisher Children's Book Award Master List, 1988-1989, set in "Doe's Crossing."
(YA)*Finn* (New York: Simon & Schuster, 1998).
Bacon lives in Hartland, Vermont.

Arthur Scott Bailey, (CF)*The Tale of Muley Cow* (New York: Grosset & Dunlop, 1921, illustrated by Harry L. Smith, in the "Slumber-Town Tales" series), set in Pleasant Valley.
(CF)*The Tale of Nimble Deer* (New York: Grosset & Dunlop, 1922, illustrated by Harry L. Smith, in the "Sleepy-Time Tales" series), set in Pleasant Valley. *The Tale of Solomon Owl* was reissued by D. N. Goodchild, Philadelphia, in 2007.
Bailey (1877-1949) was born in St. Albans, studied at the University of Vermont, and moved to Montclair, New Jersey. His family came to Vermont in 1798, when Daniel Bailey was among the pioneer founders of Fletcher, Vermont.

Carolyn Sherwin Bailey, (CF) "A Sugar Heart for Bethia," from *Homespun Playdays* (New York: Viking, 1941, illustrated by Grace Paull), set near Barre.
Bailey (1875-1961) lived in New York and Temple, New Hampshire.

Carin Greenberg Baker, (YA)*A Time to Love* (New York: Scholastic, 1994, created by Jennifer Baker), set in "Landon."
(CF)*Pride of the Green Mountains: The story of a trusty Morgan horse and the girl who turns to him for help* (Dyers Ville, Iowa: Ertl Publishing, 1996, illustrated by Sandy Rabinowitz, Treasured Horses Collection, reprinted by Scholastic in 1998 and Gareth Stevens in 1999), set in Morrisville in 1864.
Baker, a television writer, producer, and author of the seven-book Karate Club series, lives in New York.

Jeff Barth, (CF)*A Thanksgiving Story in Vermont—1852* (Charlotte, Vt.: Parable Publishing House, 1989, illustrated by Shelia Mitchinson), set near Stowe.
Barth lives in Middlebury, Vermont.

Hetty Burlingame Beatty (Whitney), (CF) *Bryn* (Boston: Houghton Mifflin, 1965, illustrated by Hetty B. Beatty).
Beatty (1907-1971), a sculptor, illustrator, and writer, lived in Massachusetts and Bermuda.

Jeanne Granger Betancourt, (CF)*The Rainbow Kid* (New York: Avon, 1983), set in Burlington.
(CF)*Turtle Time* (New York: Avon, 1985), set in Burlington.
(CF)*Puppy Love* (New York: Avon, 1986), set in Burlington.
(CF)*Crazy Christmas* (New York: Bantam, 1988), set in Burlington.
(CF)*Valentine Blues* (New York: Bantam, 1990), set in Burlington.
(YA)*More Than Meets the Eye* (New York: Bantam, 1990), set in Rutland.
Betancourt was born in Burlington, Vermont, taught in high schools in Rutland, Bennington, and Burlington from 1961-1965, and lives in New York City and rural Connecticut.

Bibliography

Cynthia Blair (Smith), (YA)*The Candy Cane Caper* (New York: Fawcett, 1987), set in "Ridgewood."
Blair lives on Long Island, New York.

Lenore Blegvad, (CF)*Kitty and Mr. Kipling: Neighbors in Vermont* (New York: Margaret K. McElderry, 2005, illustrated by Erik Blegvad), set in Dummerston in 1896.
The Blegvads live in London, the South of France, and Wardsboro, Vermont.

Larry Bograd, (YA) "Willie and the Christmas Spruces," from *In Short: How to Teach the Young Adult Short Story* (New York: Heineman, 2005, Suzanne I. Barchers, editor).
Bograd lives in Denver, Colorado.

Carole Roberts Bolton, (YA)**The Dark Rosaleen* (New York: Morrow, 1964), set on and near Route 7.
Bolton was born in Pennsylvania, worked in New York City, and lives in Montville, Maine.

Gary Bowen, (CF)*The Mare's Nest* (New York: HarperCollins, 2001, illustrated by Warren G. Kimble), set in Whitingham, Heartwellville, Ira, Thetford, Ewells Mill, Wallace Pond, Albany, Swanton, Hinesburg, East Middlebury, and Rutland in 1846.
Bowen, also an illustrator, lives in Whiting, Vermont.

Bianca Ryley Bradbury, (YA)*Laughter in Our House* (New York: Washburn, 1964), set in "Foxton."
Bradbury (1908-1982) lived in Connecticut.

Ann Brashares, (YA)**Forever in Blue: The Fourth Summer of the Sisterhood* (New York: Delacorte Press, 2007, one of the Traveling Pants series).
Brashares lives in Brooklyn, New York.

Robert Douglas Bright, Sr., (E)*Miss Pattie* (Garden City, N.Y.: Doubleday, 1954, illustrated by Robert Bright).
Bright (1902-1988) lived in Massachusetts and New Mexico.

Winifred Bromhall, (E)*Mrs. Polly's Party* (New York: Knopf, 1949, illustrated by Winifred Bromhall).
Bromhall was born in England, came to the United States in 1924, and lived in Boston and New York City.

Alice Redfield Brown, (YA)*The Secret of the Clan: A Story for Girls* (New York: Macmillan, 1912, illustrated by Sarah K. Smith), set in Montpelier.
Brown (1857-1948), whose pseudonym was Martin Redfield, lived in Hampton Falls, New Hampshire.

Edna Adelaide Brown, (YA)*At the Butterfly House* (Boston: Lothrop, 1918, illustrated by John Goss), set in "Ridgefield."
Brown (1875-1944) lived in Providence, Rhode Island.

Marc (Tolon) Brown, (E)*Buster's Sugartime: Postcards from Buster* (Boston: Little, Brown, 2006, illustrated by Marc Brown, based on the 2005 television show).
Brown lives in Hingham and Martha's Vineyard, Massachusetts.

Joseph Bruchac, III, (E)*Fox Song* (New York: Philomel, 1993, illustrated by Paul Morin), set on the Winooski River.
(YA)**Hidden Roots* (New York: Scholastic, 2004), Dorothy Canfield Fisher Children's Book Award Master List, 2005-2006, set in Arlington in 1954.
Dr. Bruchac, an Abenaki poet, storyteller, and publisher, lives in Greenfield Center, New York.

Marge Bruchac, (CF)**Malian's Song* (Middlebury, Vt.: Vermont Folklife Center, 2006, illustrated by William Maugham), set in 1759.
Dr. Bruchac, sister of Joseph Bruchac, is an Abenaki historian, museum consultant, teacher, and performer who lives in Northampton, Massachusetts.

Bonnie Bryant, (YA)*Snow Ride: The Saddle Club* (New York: Bantam Skylark, 1992). set in Sugarbush.
Bryant, author under the pseudonym B.B. Hiller of novels based on movies such as *Teenage Mutant Ninja Turtles*, lives in New York City.

Louella Bryant, (YA)*The Black Bonnet* (Shelburne, Vt.: New England Press, 1996), set in Burlington in 1858.
Bryant, once a teacher in Jericho, lives in Lincoln, Vermont, and Louisville, Kentucky.

Pearl Sydenstricker Buck, (CF) "The Christmas Secret," from *Once Upon A Christmas* (New York: John Day, 1972, illustrated by Donald Lizzul).
Buck (1892-1973) lived in Chester and Danby, Vermont.

David Budbill, (E)*Christmas Tree Farm* (New York: Macmillan, 1974, illustrated by Donald Carrick).
(CF)*Snowshoe Trek to Otter River* (New York: Dial Press, 1976, illustrated by Lorence J. Bjorklund), Dorothy Canfield Fisher Children's Book Award Master List, 1977-1978, set near Otter River.
(CF)*Bones on Black Spruce Mountain* (New York: Dial Press, 1978), winner of the Dorothy Canfield Fisher Children's Book Award, 1980, set in Judevine. These two novels have been reissued and are available from Bondcliff Books in Littleton, New Hampshire.

Budbill, a poet and playwright, was a guest lecturer at the University of Vermont in 1995 and received the Vermont Arts Council award for lifetime achievement in the arts in 2001. He lives in Wolcott, Vermont.

Cynthia Butler, (CF)*Michael Hendee* (Lyme, N.H.: Regional Center for Educational Training, 1976, illustrated by Allianora Rosse), set in Royalton in 1780.
Butler lives in Boxborough, Massachusetts.

C

Eleanor Frances Cameron, (YA)**To the Green Mountains* (New York: Dutton, 1975), set in 1918.
Cameron (1912-1996) was born in Canada and lived in California.

Flavia A. Camp Canfield, (CF)*The Kidnapped Campers: A Story of Out-of-Doors* (New York: Harcourt, 1908), set in "Melton" and Jericho. Harcourt published the 1921 sequel, *The Kidnapped Campers on the Road*, which is unavailable except from the Library of Congress.
Canfield (1844-1930), a writer and artist and the mother of Dorothy Canfield Fisher, lived in Kansas, Nebraska, Ohio, and Arlington, Vermont.

Carol Hatfield Carrick, (E)*The Highest Balloon on the Common* (New York: Greenwillow, 1977, illustrated by David Carrick).
Carrick lives in Martha's Vineyard, Massachusetts.

Donald F. Carrick, (E)*The Deer in the Pasture* (New York: Greenwillow, 1976, illustrated by Donald Carrick).
Carrick (1929-1989) lived with his wife, Carol, in Martha's Vineyard, Massachusetts, and spent summers in Craftsbury, Vermont.

Margaret F. Carty, (CF)*Christmas in Vermont: Three Stories* (Shelburne, Vt.: New England Press, 1983, illustrated by Marilynn Langley).
Carty lives in Marshfield, Vermont.

Jean Caryl (Korn Kaplan), (CF)*Bones and the Smiling Mackerel* (New York: Funk, 1964, illustrated by Jessica Zemsky), set in "South Hill."
Caryl lives in Scarsdale, New York.

Betty (Elizabeth) Cavanna (Harrison) (YA)*Angel on Skis* (New York: Morrow, 1957, illustrated by Isabel Dawson), Dorothy Canfield Fisher Children's Book Award Master List, 1958-1959, set at Bromley.
Cavanna (1909-2001) lived in New Jersey, Pennsylvania, and France.

Cora Cheney (Partridge), (CF)*The Doll of Lilac Valley* (New York: Knopf, 1959, illustrated by Carol Beech), Dorothy Canfield Fisher Children's Book Award Master List, 1960-1961, set in Townshend.
(CF)*The Mystery of the Disappearing Cars: Two Boys Discover the Secret of Model T Mountain*, with her husband, Ben Partridge (New York: Knopf, 1964, illustrated by Dick Pfahl), set in "Johnson's Junction."
Cheney (1916-1999) lived in West Townshend, Vermont.

Marjorie Chickering, (YA)*Hayseed Summer* (New York: Funk, 1963, illustrated by Ernest Kurt Barth), set in "Hillsboro."
(YA)**Yankee Trader: Ben Tanner—1799* (New York: Funk, 1966), set in St. Johnsbury in 1799.
Chickering was born in Walden, Vermont, worked for a year in St. Johnsbury, and lives in Naples, Florida.

Marilyn Grace Carlson Childs, (CF)*Mandate for a Morgan Horse: Autobiography of a Real Horse* (New York: Carlton Press, 1967, illustrated by William H. Lucas), set in Randolph.
Childs, who graduated from Vermont Junior College in 1942, lives in Tunbridge, Vermont.

Florence Choate & Elizabeth Curtis, (YA)*Linda Takes Over* (New York: Lippincott, 1949, illustrated by Florence Choate & Elizabeth Curtis), set near "Hillsboro."
Choate (1885-1968) and Curtis (1873-1946) lived in New York City and spent summers in Newfane, Vermont.

Eileen Christelow, (E)*The Five-Dog Night* (New York: Clarion, 1993, illustrated by Eileen Christelow).
(E)*The Great Pig Escape* (New York: Clarion, 1994, illustrated by Eileen Christelow), set in Putney.
(E)**The Great Pig Search* (New York: Clarion, 2001, illustrated by Eileen Christelow).
Christelow lives in East Dummerston, Vermont.

Barbara Clayton, (YA)*Halfway Hannah* (New York: Funk, 1964), set in "Alps Junction."
Clayton is the pseudonym of Barbara Littlefield Pluff, who lives in Lynnfield, Massachusetts.

Jessica Clerk, (CF)*Sukey Johnson Builds a House* (New York: McGraw Hill School Division, 2001, illustrated by Selina Alko), set in Rutland.
Clerk, a writer, poet, and artist, lives in Sharon, Connecticut.

Catherine Emma Cate Coblentz, (CF)*The Blue Cat of Castle Town* (New York: Longman's, 1949, illustrated by Janice Holland, reissued by Countryman Press, Woodstock, Vermont, 1983), set in Castleton in 1835.

Coblentz (1897-1951) was born in Hardwick, Vermont, and lived in Washington, D.C.

Carroll Burleigh Colby, (CF) "The Little Egyptian Prince," "Escape from Wolves," "Plague of Worms," "Skeleton in the Pasture," "The Deacon and the Lynx," from *The Weirdest People in the World* (New York: Sterling, 1973).

Colby (1904-1977) lived in Claremont, New Hampshire.

Jane Leslie Conly, (CF)*The Rudest Alien on Earth* (New York: Holt, 2002), set near Glover.

Conly lives in Baltimore, Maryland.

Caroline B. Cooney, (YA)*Family Reunion* (New York: Bantam, 1989), Dorothy Canfield Fisher Children's Book Award Master List, 1990-1991.

Cooney lives in Westbrook, Connecticut, and New York City.

Peter I. Cooper, (YA)*The Secret Papers of Julia Templeton* (Camden, Maine: Down East Books, 1985), set in "Newcastle."

Cooper lives in Rutland, Vermont.

Peter Campbell Copp, (CF)*Thunder in October: The Adventures of Jonathan Sage at Hildene* (Manchester, Vt.: Apple Press, 1997, illustrated by Judy Faircloth Sgantas), set in Manchester.

Copp, who was Resident Caretaker of Robert Todd Lincoln's summer estate in Manchester, Vermont, lives in Dorset, Vermont.

Robert Edmund Cormier, (YA)**I Am the Cheese: A Novel* (New York: Pantheon, 1977), set in "Rutterburg."

(YA)**The Rag and Bone Shop* (New York: Delacorte, 2001), set in Highgate.

Cormier (1925-2000), a Bread Loaf Writers' Conference Fellow in 1968, lived in Leominster, Massachusetts.

Emily Costello, (YA)*Ski Share VT: Expert (Partiers) Only* (New York: Simon Pulse, 2006), set in Killington.

Costello lives in Boston, Massachusetts.

Elizabeth Craft & Sarah Fain, (YA)**Bass Ackwards and Belly Up* (New York: Little, Brown, 2006), set in Middlebury.

Craft and Fain both live in Los Angeles, California.

Edith Janice Craine, (YA)*The Air Mystery of Isle La Motte* (Cleveland, Ohio: World Syndicate Publishing, 1930, the first title in the "Sky Buddies" series), set in Isle La Motte.

Craine was born in 1881.

Jordan Cray, (YA)*Shiver* (New York: Simon & Schuster, 1998, the central novel with *Gemini 7* and *Stalker* in the *Danger.com* trilogy of thrillers for teenagers).

Craig Crist-Evans, (YA)*North of Everything* (Cambridge: Candlewick, 2004), set in Montpelier.

Crist-Evans (1954-2005), a poet and writer, co-developed, directed, and taught at Vermont College's MFA in Writing for Children and Young Adults, and did postgraduate work at Norwich University. He lived in Montpelier, Vermont.

Anne Eliot Crompton, (CF)*Deer Country* (Boston: Little, Brown, 1973, illustrated by Maggie Kaufman Smith), set on "Strong Mountain."

(CF)*The Ice Trail* (New York: Methuen, 1980), set on Lake Champlain in 1703.

Crompton lives in Chesterfield, Massachusetts.

Linda M. Cunningham, (E)*The Copper Angel of Piper's Mill and How She Saved Her Town* (Camden, Maine: Down East, 1989, illustrated by Grace Goldberg), set on the Connecticut River in 1820.

Cunningham lives in Maine.

Alice Turner Curtis, (CF)*A Little Maid of Ticonderoga* (New York: Knopf, 1917, reissued 1955, illustrated by Sandra James), set in "Wilderness" in 1774.

(CF)*A Little Maid of Vermont* (Philadelphia: Penn Publishing, 1927, illustrated by Grace Norcross), set in Bennington in 1777.

Curtis (1860-1958), author of the Little Maid series of children's books, lived in Sullivan, Maine.

D

Barbara Dana (Arkin), (YA)**Crazy Eights* (New York: Harper, 1978), set on Lake Bomoseen.

Dana lives in Chappaqua, New York.

Dorathea Dana (Dankovszky), (CF)*Sugar Bush* (New York: T. Nelson, 1947, illustrated by Dorathea Dankovszky).

Dana (1901-1986) lived in New York and died in Placida, Florida.

Jeff Danziger, (CF)*The Champlain Monster* (Plainfield, Vt.: Lanser Press, 1981, illustrated by Jeff Danziger, reissued by New England Press, Shelburne, Vermont, 1983), set on Lake Champlain.

Danziger lived in Plainfield, Vermont, taught high school English in East Montpelier until 1983, and now lives in New York.

Nicole Davidson, (YA)*Winterkill* (New York: Avon, 1991), set in Killington.

Davidson, a pseudonym of Kathryn Jensen, lives in Baltimore, Maryland.

Robert Davis, (YA)*Gid Granger* (New York: Holiday House, 1945, illustrated by Charles Banks Wilson), set in Bethel Gilead in 1917.

Davis, a fifth-generation Vermont Congregational minister, taught at Middlebury College, Vermont, for about a decade from the mid-1930s to the mid-1940s.

Leon W. Dean, (YA) *Green Mountain Boy: Seth Warner* (New York: Farrar & Rinehart, 1941), set in the New Hampshire Grants in 1754.

(YA)*Stark of the North Country* (New York: J.J. Little & Ives, 1941), set in the New Hampshire Grants in 1759.

(YA)**Old Wolf: Story of Israel Putnam* (New York: Farrar & Rinehart, 1942), set near Lake Champlain.

(YA)*I Become a Ranger: A Novel of the French and Indian War* (New York: Farrar & Rinehart, 1945), set on Lake Champlain in 1759.

(YA)*Guns Over Champlain* (New York: Farrar & Rinehart, 1946), set in Ferrisburgh in 1813.

(YA)**Pirate Lair* (New York: Farrar & Rinehart, 1947, illustrated by Kurt Werth), set in Cornwall in 1803.

(YA)*Red Man's Trail* (New York: Farrar & Rinehart, 1948, illustrated by Kurt Werth), set in Ferrisburgh.

(YA)*Royalton Raid* (New York: Farrar & Rinehart, 1949), set in Tunbridge, Royalton, and on Lake Champlain in 1780.

(YA)*Border Bullets* (New York: Ariel, 1953, illustrated by Joshua Tolford), set in Ferrisburgh.

(YA)*The White Ox: Being a Story of One Ezra Button and the Adventures That Befell Him in the Neighborhood of Lake Champlain in New England* (New York: Ariel, 1953, illustrated by Tom Leamon), set on Lake Champlain in 1777.

Dean (1889-1982), a professor of English at the University of Vermont, lived in Burlington, Vermont.

Franklin W. Dixon, (CF)*Track of the Zombie: Hardy Boys Number 71* (New York: Simon & Schuster, 1982, illustrated by Leslie H. Morrill), set in "Hunter's Hollow."

(CF)**The Demon's Den: Hardy Boys Number 81* (New York: Simon & Schuster, 1984, illustrated by Paul Frame), set at "Lake Ketchumenken." Edward L. Stratemeyer (1862-1930) created the Hardy Boys series in 1927.

Dixon was a pseudonym of many writers, including Canadian Leslie Charlie McFarlane (1902-1977), who wrote the first eleven novels in the series. According to the Beinecke Manuscript Collection at Yale, the author of Number 71 was Vincent Buranelli, Lilo Wuenn, editor; the author of Number 81 is unrecorded.

Marilyn Cram Donahue, (YA)**Straight Along a Crooked Road* (New York: Walker's American History Series for Young People, 1985), set in "Midford Falls" in 1850.

Donahue lives in Highland, California.

Marion Walker Doren, (CF)**Nell of Blue Harbor* (New York: Harcourt, 1990), set at "The Farm."

Doren lives in Mount Pleasant, South Carolina.

Eugenie A. Doyle, (CF)*Stray Voltage* (Asheville, N.C.: Front Street, 2002), set in "Greensbrook" in 1986.

Doyle lives in Bristol, Vermont.

E

Genevieve Torrey Eames, (CF)*Pat Rides the Trail* (New York: Julian Messner, 1949, illustrated by Dan Noonan), set near Woodstock.

Like her heroine, Eames (1894-1991) rode the Woodstock Hundred-Mile Trail Ride. She was born in California, lived in Pennsylvania, New Jersey, New York, and Vermont, and died in Plymouth, Massachusetts.

Walter Pritchard Eaton, (CF)*Boy Scouts on the Green Mountain Trail* (Boston: W.A. Wilde, 1929), set on the Long Trail.

Eaton (1878-1957), who attended the Bread Loaf Writers' Conference in 1946, lived in Massachusetts.

Amy Ehrlich, (YA)**Where It Stops, Nobody Knows* (New York: Dial, 1988, republished as *Joyride*, Candlewick, 2001), winner of the Dorothy Canfield Fisher Children's Book Award, 1990, set in Montpelier.

(E)*Parents in the Pigpen, Pigs in the Tub* (New York: Dial, 1993, illustrated by Steven Kellogg).

Ehrlich, who attended Bennington College, lives in Barnet, Vermont.

Phoebe Erickson (Blair), (CF)*Double or Nothing* (New York: Harper, 1958, illustrated by Phoebe Erickson), winner of the Dorothy Canfield Fisher Children's Book Award in 1960.

Erickson (1907-2006) was born on a farm in Wisconsin, lived in Quechee and Brownsville, Vermont, and died in Concord, New Hampshire.

Erik E. Esckilsen, (YA)*The Last Mall Rat* (Boston: Houghton Mifflin, 2003), set in "Shunpike."

(YA)*The Outside Groove* (Boston: Houghton Mifflin, 2006), set in "Fliverton."

Esckilsen, a former Vermont Humanities Council Reading and Discussion scholar, teaches at Champlain College and lives in Burlington, Vermont.

F

Caroline S. Fairless, (CF)*Hambone* (Plattsburgh, N.Y.: Tundra Books, 1980, illustrated by Wendy Edelson), set near Bristol.

Reverend Fairless, who lived in New Haven and Worcester, Vermont, from 1971 to 1978, lives in Hollywood, Maryland.

Rachi (Rachel K.) Farrow, (E)*Charlie's Dream* (New York: Pantheon, 1978, illustrated by Rachi Farrow).

Farrow lives in Randolph Center, Vermont.

Anne Lindbergh Feydy (*see* Lindbergh)

Clavin Cargill Fisher, (YA)*A Spy at Ticonderoga* (Stockbridge, Mass: Berkshire Traveler Press, 1975, illustrated by Jeanne Johns), set in 1775.

Fisher, born in 1912, lived in Simsbury, Connecticut.

Dorothy (Dorothea Frances) Canfield Fisher, (CF)*Understood Betsy* (New York: Henry Holt, 1917, reissued by Holt, 1999, and reprinted by Kessinger Publishing in 2004), set in "Hillsboro."

(CF)*Something Old, Something New: Stories of People Who Are America* (New York: William R. Scott: 1949).

Fisher (1879-1958) received a doctoral degree from Columbia University, brought the Montessori Method of child rearing to the United States, and presided over the first adult education program in the United States. She served on the Book-of-Month-Club selection committee for twenty-five years, received an honorary doctorate from the University of Vermont, and was the first woman to serve on the Vermont Board of Education. She lived in Arlington, Vermont.

Paul Fleischman, (YA)*Coming-and-Going Men: Four Tales* (New York: Harper, 1985, illustrated by Randy Gaul), set in New Canaan in 1800.

Fleischman, the son of writer Sid Fleischman, has sojourned in Milton, Vermont (about six months in 1977), Nebraska, France, New Mexico, North Carolina, and lives in Aromas, California. His novel, *Seedfolks*, was the Vermont Humanities Council's 2005 selection for Vermont Reads.

Sid (Albert Sidney) Fleischman, (E)*The Hey Hey Man* (Boston: Little, Brown, 1979, illustrated by Nadine Bernard Westcott).

Fleischman, the father of writer Paul Fleischman, lives in Santa Monica, California.

Genevieve May Fox (Fuller), (YA)*Susan of the Green Mountains* (Boston: Little, Brown, 1937, illustrated by Forrest Walker Orr), set in "Northborough" in 1773.

(YA)*Border Girl* (Boston: Little, Brown, 1939), set in "Covington" in 1812.

Fox (1877-1968) lived in Addison County, Vermont, with her husband, Dr. Raymond G. Fuller, a native Vermonter.

Frances Mary Frost, (CF)*Windy Foot at the County Fair* (New York: McGraw, 1947, illustrated by Lee Townsend), set in "Webster."

(CF)*Sleigh Bells for Windy Foot* (New York: McGraw, 1948, illustrated by Lee Townsend), set in "Webster."

(CF)*Maple Sugar for Windy Foot* (New York: McGraw, 1950, illustrated by Lee Townsend), set in "Webster."

(CF)*Fireworks for Windy Foot* (New York: McGraw, 1956, illustrated by Lee Townsend), set in "Webster."

Frost (1905-1959), a poet and novelist, was born in St. Albans, attended Middlebury College, and lived in New York City and St. Albans, Vermont.

G

Nancy Garden, (CF)*Mystery of the Night Raiders: Monster Hunters Case #1* (New York: Farrar, Straus & Giroux, 1987), set in "Grove Hill."

(CF)*The Case of the Stolen Scarab: A Candlestone Inn Mystery* (Ridley Park, Penn.: Two Lives Publications, 2004), set in "Bennet." *The Case of the Vanishing Valuables*, a sequel to the Candlestone Inn Mystery, is due around 2008.

Garden, who for many years has spent weekends and holidays with friends in Landgrove, Vermont, lives in Carlisle, Massachusetts, and Maine.

Dale Blackwell Gasque, (CF)*Pony Trouble* (New York: Hyperion, 1998, illustrated by Stacey Schuett).

Gasque lives in Randolph Center, Vermont.

Patricia Lee Gauch, (E)*Aaron and the Green Mountain Boys* (New York: Coward McGann, 1972, illustrated by Margot Ladd Tomes), set in Bennington in 1777.

Gauch lives in Basking Ridge, New Jersey.

Gail Gauthier, (CF)*The Hero of Ticonderoga* (New York: Putnam, 2001), set in Cornwall.

(YA)*Saving the Planet & Stuff* (New York: Putnam, 2003), set in "East Branbury."

Gauthier grew up in Sudbury, Vermont, went to the Otter Valley Union High School in Brandon, spent a few years in Cornwall, and graduated from the University of Vermont. She lives in Marlborough, Connecticut.

Corinne Gerson, (CF)*My Grandfather the Spy* (New York: Walker, 1990), set in "Paradise."

Gerson lives in New York.

Gail Gibbons, (E)*The Missing Maple Syrup Sap Mystery or How Maple Syrup Is Made* (New York: Warne, 1979, illustrated by Gail Gibbons).

Gibbons lives in Corinth, Vermont.

Beth Bradford Gilchrist, (YA)*Kit, Pat, and a Few Boys* (New York: The Century Co., 1921, illustrated by Charles M. Relyea), set near "Edgeville."

Gilchrist (1879-1957) was born in Peacham, Vermont, and lived in Rutland, Vermont.

Shannon Gilligan, (CF)*The Search for Champ: Choose Your Own Adventure #14* (New York: Bantam, 1983, illustrated by Anthony Kramer), set on Lake Champlain.

Gilligan lives with her writer husband, R. A. Montgomery, in Warren, Vermont.

Helen Masterman Girvan, (YA)*Felicity Way* (New York: Farrar & Rinehart, 1942, illustrated by Gertrude Howe), set in Maple Hill.

Girvan (1891-1990) was born in Minnesota and died in Salisbury, Connecticut.

Christopher Golden, (YA)*Laws of Nature: Prowlers* (New York: Pocket Pulse, 2001), set in "Buckton." This is the second in a series of thrillers for teenagers: *Prowlers* (2001), *Predator and Prey* (2001), and *Wild Things* (2002).

Golden, author of the Buffy the Vampire Slayer series, lives in Massachusetts.

Nancy Price Graff, (CF)*A Long Way Home* (New York: Clarion, 2001), set in Sharon in 1980.

(CF)*Taking Wing* (New York: Clarion, 2005), Dorothy Canfield Fisher Children's Book Award Master List, 2006-2007, set in "Miller's Run" in 1942.

Graff, who graduated from Middlebury College, lives in Montpelier, Vermont.

H

Jessie Haas, (CF)*Keeping Barney* (New York: Greenwillow, 1982), Dorothy Canfield Fisher Children's Book Award Master List, 1983-1984.

(YA)*Working Trot* (New York: Greenwillow, 1983).

(YA)*The Sixth Sense and Other Stories* (New York: Greenwillow, 1988).

(YA)*Skipping School* (New York: Greenwillow, 1992), Dorothy Canfield Fisher Children's Book Award Master List, 1993-1994.

(CF)*Beware the Mare* (New York: Greenwillow, 1993, illustrated by Martha Haas).

(CF)*A Horse Like Barney* (New York: Greenwillow, 1993).

(E)*Mowing* (New York: Greenwillow, 1994, illustrated by Jos. A. Smith).

(CF)*Uncle Daney's Way* (New York: Greenwillow, 1994), Dorothy Canfield Fisher Children's Book Award Master List, 1997-1997, set near Hogback Mountain.

(CF)*A Blue for Beware* (New York: Greenwillow Books, 1995, illustrated by Jos. A. Smith), Dorothy Canfield Fisher Children's Book Award Master List, 1996-1997.

(E)*No Foal Yet* (New York: Greenwillow, 1995, illustrated by Jos. A. Smith).

(CF)*Be Well, Beware* (New York: Greenwillow, 1996, illustrated by Jos. A. Smith), Dorothy Canfield Fisher Children's Book Award Master List, 1997-1998.

(E)*Sugaring* (New York: Greenwillow, 1996, illustrated by Jos. A. Smith).

(YA)*Westminster West* (New York: Greenwillow, 1997), set in Westminster West in 1884.

(CF)*Beware and Stogie* (New York: Greenwillow, 1998, illustrated by Jessie Haas).

(CF)*Unbroken* (New York: Greenwillow, 1999), Dorothy Canfield Fisher Children's Book Award Master List, 2000-2001, set in "Barrett."

(E)*Hurry!* (New York: Greenwillow, 2000, illustrated by Jos. A. Smith).

(YA)*Will You, Won't You?* (New York: Greenwillow, 2001), set in "Barrett."

(CF)*Runaway Radish* (New York: Greenwillow, 2002, illustrated by Margot Apple), Dorothy Canfield Fisher Children's Book Award Master List, 2002-2003.

(YA)*Shaper* (New York: Greenwillow, 2002), set in "Barrett."

Haas lives in Westminster West, Vermont.

Randi (Dawn) Hacker, (YA)*Life as I Knew It* (New York: Simon & Schuster, 2006), set in "Blodgett."

Hacker taught in public schools in northern Vermont and received a master's degree in English as a Second Language from St. Michael's College in Colchester, Vermont. She wrote the original story and the teleplay for the comedy series *Windy Acres*, produced by Kingdom County Productions and Vermont Public Television. She lives in Lawrence, Kansas, and spends summers in Montgomery, Vermont.

Sue Halpern, (CF)*Introducing...Sasha Abramowitz* (New York: Farrar, Straus & Giroux, 2005), set in "Krieger."

Halpern is a scholar in residence at Middlebury College and lives with her husband, writer Bill McKibben, in Ripton, Vermont.

Earl Henry Hamner, Jr. & Don Sipes, (CF)*Lassie: A Christmas Story* (Nashville, Tenn.: T. Nelson, 1997, illustrated by Kevin Burke), set in "Hudson Falls."

Hamner lives in Studio City, California. His son, television writer Scott Hamner, lives in Vermont. Sipes lives in California.

Kathleen McKinley Harris, (E)*The Wonderful Hay Tumble* (New York: Morrow, 1988, illustrated by Dick Gackenbach), set in Mansfield before 1848.

Harris vacationed in Hyde Park, Vermont, as a child and now lives in Charlotte, Vermont.

William Wirt Harvey, (YA)*Lige Golden: The Man Who Twinkled* (Boston: B.J. Brimmer, 1924, illustrated by Thomas Hunt), set in "East Burdon" in 1879.

Harvey, born in 1866, lived in Burke, Vermont.

Sheila Hayes, (YA)*The Tinker's Daughter* (New York: Dutton, 1995), set in "East Branbury."

Hayes lives in Briarcliff Manor, New York.

James Hayford, (CF)*Gridley Firing* (Shelburne, Vt.: New England Press, 1987, illustrated by Mary Azarian), set in "Woolville."

Hayford (1913-1993), a native Vermonter, lived in Orleans, Vermont.

Wilma Pitchford Hays, (CF)*Trouble at Otter Creek* (Middletown, Conn.: Xerox Education Publications Weekly Reader Children's Book Club, 1978, illustrated by Marilyn T. Miller), set on Otter Creek in 1775.

Hays (1907-2006), who participated in a Bread Loaf Writers' Conference, lived in Venice, Florida.

Marguerite Breithaupt Henry, (CF)*Justin Morgan Had a Horse* (Rand McNally, 1954, illustrated by Wesley Dennis), set in Randolph in 1791.

Henry (1902-1997) was born in Wisconsin and died in Rancho Santa Fe, California.

Alison Cragin Herzig, (YA)*Shadows on the Pond* (Boston: Little, Brown, 1985), set in "Jerusalem Corners."

Herzig, who owned property and spent time in Bristol, Vermont, for fifteen years, lives in New York City.

Karen Hesse, (YA)*Phoenix Rising* (New York: Holt, 1994), Dorothy Canfield Fisher Children's Book Award Master List, 1995-1996, set near Townshend.

(YA)*A Time of Angels* (New York: Hyperion, 1995), set in Brattleboro.

(YA)*Witness* (New York: Scholastic, 2001), Dorothy Canfield Fisher Children's Book Award Master List, 2002-2003, Vermont Humanities Council 2003 selection for Vermont Reads, set in southern Vermont in 1924. While not explicitly stated, three other books by Hesse are set in Vermont—*Wish on a Unicorn*, 1991, Williamsville/Newfane; *Sable*, 1994, Williamsville/Newfane; and *Just Juice*, 1998, West Brattleboro.

In 1997-1998, the Vermont State Legislature recognized Karen Hesse on being named the 1998 recipient of the John Newbery Medal for *Out of the Dust*. Hesse lives in Brattleboro, Vermont.

Kimberley Burton Heuston, (YA)**The Shakeress* (Asheville, N.C.: Front Street, 2002), set in St. Johnsbury in 1832.

Heuston, who visited St. Johnsbury often as a child and later received a degree in 2000 from Vermont College's MFA in Writing for Children and Young Adults, lives in Sandy, Utah.

Hadley Higginson, (CF)*Keeker and the Sneaky Pony: The Sneaky Pony Series* (San Francisco: Chronicle Books, 2006, illustrated by Maja Andersen).

(CF)*Keeker and the Horse Show Show-Off: The Sneaky Pony Series* (San Francisco: Chronicle Books, 2006, illustrated by Maja Andersen).

(CF)*Keeker and the Sugar Shack: The Sneaky Pony Series* (San Francisco: Chronicle Books, 2006, illustrated by Maja Andersen).

(CF)*Keeker and the Springtime Surprise: The Sneaky Pony Series* (San Francisco: Chronicle Books, 2007, illustrated by Lisa Perrett). The fifth in the series, *Keeker and the Pony Camp Catastrophe*, is scheduled for the fall of 2007.

Higginson grew up in Brandon, Vermont, went to the University of Vermont, lived in Burlington for almost a decade, and currently lives in Roanoke, Virginia.

Beth Hilgartner, (YA)**Colors in the Dreamweaver's Loom* (Boston: Houghton Mifflin, 1989), set near Burlington.

(YA)* *The Feast of the Trickster* (Boston: Houghton Mifflin, 1991), set in Plainfield.

Hilgartner lived in Barre, Vermont, and now lives in Orford, New Hampshire.

Ralph Nading Hill, (YA)*The Voyages of Brian Seaworthy, an Historical Adventure on Lake Champlain* (Montpelier, Vt.: *Vermont Life* magazine & Vermont Historical Society, 1971), set on Lake Champlain in 1872.

Hill (1917-1987), senior editor of *Vermont Life* from 1951-1987, was born and lived in Burlington, Vermont.

Stephen Huneck, (E)*Sally's Snow Adventure* (New York: Abrams, 2006, illustrated by Stephen Huneck). Also in the series are *Sally Goes to the Beach* (2000), *Sally Goes to the Mountains* (2001), *Sally Goes to the Farm* (2002), and *Sally Goes to the Vet* (2004).

Huneck, creator of the Dog Chapel at Dog Mountain in East St. Johnsbury, lives in St. Johnsbury, Vermont.

Clara Whitehill Hunt, (CF)*The Little House in Green Valley* (Boston: Houghton Mifflin, 1932, illustrated by Emma Lillian Brock), set in "Green Valley."

Hunt (1871-1958) was a librarian in Philadelphia, Pennsylvania, and Newark, New Jersey.

Lee Pennock Huntington, (CF)*Brothers in Arms* (Taftsville, Vt.: Countryman Press, 1976), set in Strafford in 1768.

Huntington lives in Norwich, Vermont.

Johanna Hurwitz, (CF)*Yellow Blue Jay* (New York: Morrow, 1986, illustrated by Donald Carrick, reissued as *Bunk Mates*, Scholastic, 1988), set near Haystack Mountain.

(CF)*A Llama in the Family* (New York: Morrow, 1994, illustrated by Mark Graham), set in Wilmington.

(CF)*Faraway Summer* (New York: Morrow, 1998, illustrated by Mary Azarian), set in Jericho in 1910.

(CF)*A Llama in the Library* (New York: Morrow, 1999, illustrated by Mark Graham), set in Wilmington.

(CF)**Dear Emma* (New York: HarperCollins, 2002, illustrated by Barbara Garrison), set in 1910.

(CF)*The Unsigned Valentine and Other Events in the Life of Emma Meade* (New York: HarperCollins, 2006, illustrated by Mary Azarian), set in Jericho in 1911.

Hurwitz lives in Great Neck, New York, and Wilmington, Vermont.

I

Anne Isaacs, (E)*Pancakes for Supper!* (New York: Scholastic, 2006, illustrated by Marc Teague, based on Helen Bannerman's *The Story of Little Black Sambo*, 1899), set near "Whisker Creek" in the early 1800s.

Isaacs, who was a writer in residence for a month at the Dorset Colony House in Dorset, Vermont, lives near Berkeley, California.

J

Edgar Newman Jackson, (YA)*Green Mountain Hero* (New York: Lantern Press, 1961, illustrated by James O. Jackson, reprinted by New England Press, 1988), set in Salisbury in 1774.

Jackson (1910-1994), a Methodist minister, was born in Cold Springs Harbor, New York, and was a professor at Union Graduate School (later Union Institute & University in Cincinnati, Ohio, one of whose "Academic Centers" is Vermont College in Montpelier). He lived in Chelsea (where this novel was written) and Corinth, Vermont.

Jacqueline Dougan Jackson, (CF)*The Taste of Spruce Gum* (Boston: Little, Brown, 1966, illustrated by Lilian Isabel Obligado), winner of the Dorothy Canfield Fisher Children's Book Award, 1968, set on Shrewsbury Mountain in 1903.

Jackson lives in Springfield, Illinois, and spends summers on Lake Iroquois in Hinesburg, Vermont.

Woody Jackson, (E)*A Cow's Alfalfa-Bet* (Boston: Houghton Mifflin, 2003, illustrated by Woody Jackson).

Jackson, whose paintings of cows adorn Ben & Jerry's ice cream trucks, lives in Middlebury, Vermont.

Caroline Emilia Jacobs, (YA)*The S.W.F. Club* (Cleveland, Ohio: Goldsmith Publishing, 1912), set in "Winton."

Jacobs (1872-1909), whose pseudonym was Emilia Blanchard Elliott, lived in Ohio.

William Jaspersohn, (E)*The Two Brothers* (Middlebury, Vt.: Vermont Folklife Center Family Heritage Series, 2000, illustrated by Michael Anthony Donato), set in central Vermont in the 1880s.

Jaspersohn lives in Johnson, Vermont.

Allen Johnson, Jr., (CF)*The Christmas Tree Express* (Birmingham, Ala.: Seacoast Publishing, 1993, illustrated by Lisbeth Keetle), set in "Masonville" in 1937.

Johnson, who lived in Middlebury for twenty-three years and founded the Vermont State Craft Center, lives in Mercer Island, Washington.

K

Bernard & Jonathan Katz, (YA)*Black Woman: The Fictionalized Biography of Lucy Terry Prince* (New York: Pantheon, 1973), set in Guilford in 1746.

Bernard Katz (1911-2003) was the father of Jonathan Katz, who lives in New York City.

Bobbi Katz, (CF)*Snow Bunny* (Niles, Ill.: Albert Whitman, 1976, illustrated by Michael Norman), set in "Warner."

Katz, a writer and poet, lives in New York.

Carolyn Keene, (CF)*Close Encounters: Nancy Drew (All New) Girl Detective #21*(New York: Simon & Schuster, 2006), set in "Brody's Junction."

"Carolyn Keene" is a collective pseudonym. *See* Dorothy West.

Garret Keizer, (YA)*God of Beer* (New York: HarperCollins, 2002), set in "Ira County."

Keizer, who was a high school English teacher and minister in rural Vermont, lives in Sutton, Vermont.

Clarence Budington Kelland, (YA)*Mark Tidd: His Adventures and Strategies* (New York: Harper, 1913), set in "Wicksville."

(YA)*Mark Tidd in Business* (New York: Harper, 1915), set in "Wicksville."

(YA)*Mark Tidd's Citadel* (New York: Harper, 1916, illustrated by W. W. Clarke), set in "Wicksville." A fourth novel in the series, *Mark Tidd in the Backwoods*, takes the boys to Michigan.

Kelland (1881-1964), who wrote many adult stories about Scattergood Baines, philanthropist and entrepreneur of "Coldriver," Vermont, lived in Detroit, Michigan, and Wilmington, Vermont.

Shirley Whitney Kelley, (CF)*Little Settlers of Vermont: A True Story of the Journey of a Pioneer Family through New England* (Orford, N.H.: Equity Publishing, 1963, illustrated by Kenneth T. Fogg, Jr.), set in Montpelier in 1786.

Kelley (1895-1975) lived in Washington County, Vermont.

Louise Andrews Kent, (YA)**He Went with Champlain* (Boston: Houghton Mifflin, 1959, illustrated by Anthony D'Adamo).

Kent (1886-1969) lived in Maple Corner, Calais, Vermont.

M. E. Kerr, (YA)*The Son of Someone Famous* (New York: Harper, 1974), set in "Storm."

Kerr is the pseudonym of Marijane Agnes Meaker, who attended Vermont Junior College in Montpelier from 1945 to 1946 and lives in East Hampton, New York.

Liza Ketchum, (YA)**Fire in the Heart* (New York: Holiday House, 1989), set in "Griswold."

(YA)*Twelve Days in August* (New York: Holiday House, 1993), set in "Griswold."

(YA)*Where the Great Hawk Flies* (New York: Clarion, 2005), set in "Griswold" in 1784.

Ketchum taught school in Essex, Vermont, participated in the Vermont Council of the Arts Artist in Education program, was an adjunct faculty member at the University of Vermont, and was on the faculty of Vermont College's MFA in Writing for Children and Young Adults. She lives in Watertown, Massachusetts.

Vivian Kill, (E)*Crazy Jane* (Bethel, Vt.: My Little Jessie Press, 2004, illustrated by Janet Hayward Burnham).

Kill, a native Vermonter, grew up on a farm and lives in Strafford, Vermont.

Natalie Kinsey-Warnock, (CF)*Canada Geese Quilt* (New York: Dutton, 1989, illustrated by Leslie W. Bowman), Dorothy Canfield Fisher Children's Book Award Master List, 1990-1991, set in the Northeast Kingdom.

(CF)*The Night the Bells Rang* (New York: Cobblehill, 1991, illustrated by Leslie W. Bowman), set near the Black River in 1918.

(E)**Wilderness Cat* (New York: Cobblehill, 1992, illustrated by Mark Graham), set in the 1700s in Craftsbury.

(E)*When Spring Comes* (New York: Dutton, 1993, illustrated by Stacey Schuett).

(CF)*As Long as There Are Mountains* (New York: Cobblehill, 1997), Dorothy Canfield Fisher Children's Book Award Master List, 1998-1999, set in Gilead. The Vermont Humanities Council's 2006 selection for Vermont Reads, this novel was also the 2006 choice of the Barre Learning for Life Committee through a grant from the Vermont Humanities Council's Creating Communities of Readers program.

(CF)*Sweet Memories Still* (New York: Cobblehill, 1997, illustrated by Laurie Harden), set near Craftsbury.

(CF)*In the Language of Loons* (New York: Cobblehill, 1998), set in the Northeast Kingdom in 1969.

(CF)*If Wishes Were Horses* (New York: Dutton, 2000), set in Barton in 1932.

(E)*A Farm of Her Own* (New York: Dutton, 2001, illustrated by Kathleen Kolb, originally published as *When Emma Remembers*, 1998), set in the Northeast Kingdom.

(E)*From Dawn Till Dusk: A Vermont Farm Year* (Boston: Houghton Mifflin, 2002, illustrated by Mary Azarian), nominated for the Red Clover Award, 2004.

(CF)*A Doctor Like Papa* (New York: HarperCollins, 2002, illustrated by James Bernardin), set in the Northeast Kingdom in 1918.

(CF)*Lumber Camp Library* (New York: HarperCollins, 2002, illustrated by James Bernardin), set in northern Vermont in 1920. This novel was the 2006 choice of the

Milton Literacy Action Team through a grant from the Vermont Humanities Council's Creating Communities of Readers program.

(E)*A Christmas Like Helen's* (Boston: Houghton Mifflin, 2004, illustrated by Mary Azarian), set in the early 1900s.

(E)*Nora's Ark* (New York: HarperCollins, 2005, illustrated by Emily Arnold McCully), nominated for the Red Clover Award, 2007, set in 1927.

Kinsey-Warnock grew up on a dairy farm in the Northeast Kingdom, went to Johnson State College in Vermont, and lives in South Albany, Vermont.

Doris Upton Kirkpatrick, (YA)*Honey in the Rock* (New York: Elsevier, 1979), Dorothy Canfield Fisher Children's Book Award Master List, 1980-1981, set in "Sadawga Springs" in 1936.

Kirkpatrick (1902-1984), a graduate of Middlebury College in 1924 and an Associated Press reporter in Vermont from 1957-1964, was born and later lived in Whitingham, Vermont.

Sheila Solomon Klass, (YA)*Next Stop: Nowhere* (New York: Scholastic, 1995), set in "Allenville."

Klass, mother of pediatrician-writer Perri Elizabeth Klass and writer David Klass, lives in New York City.

Norma Klein, (YA)**Bizou: A Novel* (New York: Viking, 1983), set in southern Vermont.

Klein (1938-1989) lived in Connecticut.

Nancy H. Kleinbaum, (YA)*Dead Poets Society* (New York: Random, 1989, based on Tom Schulman's screenplay), set in "Welton."

Kleinbaum lives in Mt. Kisco, New York.

Gordon Richard Korman, (YA)**Chasing the Falconers: On the Run #1* (New York: Scholastic, 2005), set in Colchester.

(YA)**The Fugitive Factor: On the Run #2* (New York: Scholastic, 2005), set in Mallets Bay and St. Johnsbury.

Korman lives in New York.

L

Willem Lange, (E)*John and Tom* (Middlebury, Vt.: Vermont Folklife Center Family Heritage Series, 2001, illustrated by Bert Dodson).

Lange lives in East Montpelier, Vermont.

West Lathrop, (CF)*Black River Captive* (New York: Random, 1946, illustrated by Dwight Logan), set on the Black River in 1757.

West Lathrop is the pseudonym of Dorothy West Lathrop (1892-1984), who was born in Vermont and died in Fairfield, Connecticut.

Lois Lenski, (CF)*Deer Valley Girl* (New York: Lippincott, 1968, illustrated by Lois Lenski), set in "Deer Valley."

Lenski (1893-1974) lived in Ohio and died in Florida.

Julius Bernard Lester, (E) "The Incredible Adventure of Adalbert the Alligator," from *Ackamarackus: Julius Lester's Sumptuously Silly Fantastically Funny Fables* (New York: Scholastic, 2001, illustrated by Emilie Chollat).

Lester, who was a lay reader for nine years at the synagogue in St. Johnsbury, Vermont, lives in Belchertown, Massachusetts.

Janet Lind, (CF)*The Bird at Bear Mountain* (South Burlington, Vt.: Vermont Migrant Education Project, 1988, illustrated by Kathleen Kolb).

Raised on a grain farm in Iowa, Lind moved to Vermont in 1970 and lived in Calais, Vermont.

Anne Spencer Lindbergh (Feydy Sapieyevski), (CF)**Osprey Island* (Boston: Houghton Mifflin, 1974, illustrated by Maggie Kaufman Smith).

(CF)*Travel Far, Pay No Fare* (New York: HarperCollins, 1992), set in the Northeast Kingdom.

Lindbergh (1940-1993), eldest daughter of aviator/authors Charles A. and Anne Morrow Lindbergh, was born in Thetford, Vermont, was married to Vermont writer Noel Perrin (1927-2004), and lived in Barnet, Vermont.

Reeve Lindbergh, (E)*The Visit* (New York: Dial Books, 2005, illustrated by Wendy Anderson Halperin).

Lindbergh, younger sister of Anne Lindbergh, lives with her husband, writer Nathaniel Tripp, in St. Johnsbury, Vermont.

Frederick Lipp, (CF)*That Cat Is Not For Sale* (Portland, Me.: Sloan Publishing, 1998, illustrated by Britta Bruce), set in Woodstock.

Lipp lives in Portland, Maine.

Bill Littlefield, (YA)*The Circus in the Woods* (Boston: Houghton Mifflin, 2001), set in Greensboro.

Littlefield, host of NPR's "Only a Game," lives in Needham, Massachusetts.

Mary Norris Lloyd, (CF)*Billy Hunts the Unicorn* (New York: Hastings House, 1964, illustrated by her daughter, Robin Lloyd Papish), set in "Prospect."

Lloyd (1908-1993) lived in Winnetka, Illinois, and Rochester, Vermont.

Sara London, (E)*Firehorse Max* (New York: HarperCollins, 1997, illustrated by Ann Arnold), set in Burlington in 1900.

London grew up in Burlington, Vermont, and now lives in Northampton, Massachusetts.

Elizabeth Hammond Low, (YA)*High Harvest* (New York: Harcourt, 1948, illustrated by Douglas W. Gorsline), set near "Mink Mountain."

(E)*Mouse, Mouse, Go Out of My House* (Boston: Little, Brown, 1958, illustrated by Ronni Solbert).

(E)*Snug in the Snow* (Boston: Little, Brown, 1963, illustrated by Ronni Solbert).

Low (1898-1991) lived in Brooklyn, New York, and had a summer home in Vermont.

Rose Lucia, (CF)*Peter and Polly in Spring, in Summer, in Autumn, in Winter* (Montpelier, Vt.: Kellogg-Hubbard Library combined edition, 1983, originally published in four volumes by the American Book Company in New York in 1915, 1912, 1918, 1914), set in East St. Johnsbury.

Lucia (1874-1938) was born in Vergennes, Vermont, lived in Montpelier, and was Supervisor of Rural Schools in Vermont. The bridge across the North Branch of the Winooski River near the Kellogg-Hubbard Library bears a plaque in her memory.

Janet Louise Swoboda Lunn, (YA)*The Hollow Tree* (New York: Knopf, 1997), set in "Orland Village" in 1775.

Lunn lived as a child in Norwich, Vermont, and now lives in Hillier, Ontario, Canada.

M

Gregory Maguire, (CF)*Seven Spiders Spinning* (New York: Clarion, 1994, illustrated by Dirk Zimmer), set in "Hamlet."

(CF)*Six Haunted Hairdos* (New York: Clarion, 1997, illustrated by Elaine Clayton), set in "Hamlet."

(CF)*Five Alien Elves* (New York: Clarion, 1998, illustrated by Elaine Clayton), set in "Hamlet."

(CF)*Four Stupid Cupids* (New York: Clarion, 2000, illustrated by Elaine Clayton), set in "Hamlet."

(CF)*Three Rotten Eggs* (New York: Clarion, 2002, illustrated by Elaine Clayton), set in "Hamlet."

(CF)*A Couple of April Fools* (New York: Clarion, 2004, illustrated by Elaine Clayton), set in "Hamlet."

(CF)*One Final Firecracker* (New York: Clarion, 2005, illustrated by Elaine Clayton), set in "Hamlet."

Maguire, a fellow at the Bread Loaf Writers' Conference in 1978, lives in Concord, Massachusetts, and Strafford, Vermont.

Ann Matthews Martin, (CF)*Baby-Sitters' Winter Vacation: The Baby-Sitters Club Super Special #3* (New York: Scholastic, 1989), set in "Hooksett Crossing."

Martin lives in Hudson Valley, New York.

Melissa Mather (Ambros), (YA)*One Summer in Between* (New York: Harper & Row, 1967), set in "East Barnstead."

Mather lives in Windsor, Vermont.

Michael Rene Medearis & Angela Shelf Medearis, (E)*Daisy and the Doll* (Middlebury, Vt.: Vermont Folklife Center Family Heritage Series, 2000, illustrated by Larry Johnson), set in Grafton in 1891.

The Medearises live in Austin, Texas.

Cornelia Lynde Meigs, (YA)*At the Sign of the Two Heroes* (New York: The Century Co., 1920, illustrated by S. Gordan Smyth, written under the pseudonym, Adair Aldon), set in North Hero and South Hero in 1919.

(CF)*The Covered Bridge* (New York: Macmillan, 1936, illustrated by Marguerite Lofft de Angeli), set in "Hebron" in 1785.

(YA)*Call of the Mountain* (Boston: Little, Brown, 1940, illustrated by James Daugherty), set near Brandon in the 1820s.

(E)*Mother Makes Christmas: A Story Parade Picture Book* (New York: Grosset, 1940, illustrated by Lois Lenski).

(CF)*Wild Geese Flying* (New York: Macmillan, 1957, illustrated by Charles Geer), Dorothy Canfield Fisher Children's Book Award Master List, 1958-1959, set in "Jefferson Village."

Meigs (1884-1973) lived in Havre de Grace, Maryland, and at Green Pastures in Brandon, Vermont. Her mother's father and mother were pioneers from Vermont to Illinois.

George Mendoza, (CF) "The Devil's Pocket," from *The Crack in the Wall and Other Terribly Weird Tales* (New York: Dial Press, 1968, illustrated by Mercer Mayer).

Mendoza lives in New York.

Jane Claypool Miner, (YA)*A Winter Love Story* (New York: Scholastic, 1993), set in "Mount Paradise."

Miner lives in Olivenhain, California.

Anne S. Baker Molloy, (CF)*Decky's Secret* (Boston: Houghton Mifflin, 1944, illustrated by George & Doris Hauman), set in "Valley Falls."

Molloy (1907-1999) lived in Boston, Massachusetts, and Portsmouth, New Hampshire.

R. A. Montgomery, (CF)*The Island of Time: Choose Your Own Adventure #115* (New York: Bantam, 1991, illustrated by Ron Wing), set on Lake Champlain.
Montgomery lives with his wife, writer Shannon Gilligan, in Warren, Vermont.

Will Moses, (E)*Silent Night* (New York: Philomel, 1997, illustrated by Will Moses).
Moses, great-grandson of Anna Mary Robertson ("Grandma") Moses, lives in Eagle Bridge, New York.

Charles George Geoffrey Muller, (YA)*Hero of Champlain* (New York: John Day, 1961), set on Lake Champlain in 1814.
Muller (1897-1987) lived in Michigan and New York.

Rita Murphy, (YA)*Night Flying* (New York: Delacorte, 2000), Dorothy Canfield Fisher Children's Book Award Master List, 2001-2002, set in "Hawthorne."
Murphy lives in Burlington, Vermont.

Liza Ketchum Murrow (*see* Ketchum)

N

John Ney, (YA)*Ox Goes North: More Trouble for the Kid at the Top* (New York: Harper, 1973), set in "Dexter."
Ney lives in Indianatown, Florida.

O

Helen Fuller Orton, (CF)*Mystery in the Old Cave* (New York: Lippincott, 1950, illustrated by Robert Doremus), set in Bennington. In *The Treasure in the Little Trunk* (New York: Lippincott, 1932), which is not included in this collection, nine-year-old Patty Armstrong moves with her family from Vermont to upstate New York in 1832.
Orton (1872-1975) lived on Long Island, New York.

Margaret Glover Otto, (E)*Syrup* (New York: Henry Holt, 1956, illustrated by Polly Jackson), set in "Westville."
(CF)*Mr. Kipling's Elephant* (New York: Knopf, 1961, illustrated by Harold Berson), set in Dummerston in 1895.
Otto (1909-1976) was a frequent visitor to Brattleboro, Vermont, and lived in Westport, Connecticut.

Janice Ovecka, (CF)*Cave of Falling Water* (Shelburne, Vt.: New England Press, 1992, illustrated by David Kanietakeron Fadden), set in "Gardner's Mills."
(CF)*Captive of Pittsford Ridge* (Shelburne, Vt.: New England Press, 1994), set in Pittsford in 1777.
Ovecka lives in Brandon, Vermont.

P

Marion Page, (YA)*Dirty Mary No More* (Los Altos Hills, Calif.: May Davenport, 1999), set in "Canterbury."
(YA)*The Printer's Devil* (Unionville, N.Y.: Royal Fireworks, 2002), set in Groton in 1861.
Page lives in Groton, Vermont.

Katherine Wolmendorf Paterson, (E)*The Smallest Cow in the World* (New York: HarperCollins, 1991, illustrated by Jane Clark Brown, originally published by the Vermont Migrant Education Program in 1988).
(YA)**Lyddie* (New York: Dutton, 1991), Dorothy Canfield Fisher Children's Book Award Master List, 1992-1993, set in "Barrett" in 1843.
(YA)"No Room in the Inn," "Poor Little Innocent Lamb," from *A Midnight Clear: Stories for the Christmas Season* (New York: Dutton, 1995). "No Room in the Inn" was reprinted in the collection, *Home for Christmas: Stories for Young and Old* (Farmington, Penn: Plough Publishing, 2002).
(CF)*Jip, His Story* (New York: Dutton, 1996) Dorothy Canfield Fisher Children's Book Award Master List, 1997-1998, set in "Barrett" in 1855. This novel was the 2005 choice of the Barre Learning for Life Committee through a grant from the Vermont Humanities Council's Creating Communities of Readers program.
(E)*Marvin's Best Christmas Present Ever* (New York: HarperCollins, 1997, illustrated by Jane Clark Brown).
(CF)*Preacher's Boy* (New York: Clarion, 1999), set in "Leonardstown."
(CF)*The Field of Dogs* (New York: HarperCollins, 2001, illustrated by Emily Arnold McCully).
(E)*Marvin One Too Many* (New York: HarperCollins, 2001, illustrated by Jane Clark Brown).
(CF)*The Same Stuff as Stars* (New York: Clarion, 2002), Dorothy Canfield Fisher Children's Book Award Master List, 2003-2004, set near Barre. This novel was the 2004 choice of the Barre Learning for Life Committee through a grant from the Vermont Humanities Council's Creating Communities of Readers program.
(CF)**Bread and Roses, Too* (New York: Clarion, 2006), Dorothy Canfield Fisher Children's Book Award Master List, 2007-2008, set in Barre in 1912.
In 1997-1998, the Vermont State Legislature recognized Katherine Paterson on being named the 1998 recipient of the Hans Christian Andersen Award for Children's Literature. Paterson, who received honorary degrees from Norwich University and St. Michael's College in Vermont, lives in Barre, Vermont.

Tracey Campbell Pearson, (E)*The Storekeeper* (New York: Dial, 1988, illustrated by Tracey Campbell Pearson), set in Jericho.

(E)*Where Does Joe Go?* (New York: Farrar, Straus & Giroux, 1999, illustrated by Tracey Campbell Pearson), set in Jericho.

Pearson lives in Jericho, Vermont.

Leigh Peck, (CF)**They Were Made of Rawhide* (Boston: Houghton Mifflin, 1954, illustrated by Aldren Auld Watson), set in Rutland in 1886.

Peck (1901-1969) lived in Cameron, Texas.

Robert Newton Peck, (YA)*A Day No Pigs Would Die* (New York: Knopf, 1972), set in "Learning" in 1929.

(YA)**Millie's Boy* (New York: Knopf, 1973), set in Cornwall in 1898.

(CF)*Soup* (New York: Knopf, 1974, illustrated by Charles C. Gehm), Dorothy Canfield Fisher Children's Book Award Master List, 1975-1976, set in "Learning."

(CF)*Soup & Me* (New York: Knopf, 1975, illustrated by Charles Lilly), set in "Learning."

(CF)*Rabbits and Redcoats* (New York: Walker, 1976, illustrated by Laura Lydecker), set in Shoreham in 1775.

(YA)*Hang for Treason* (Garden City, N.Y.: Doubleday, 1976), set on Lake Champlain in 1775.

(CF)*Trig* (Boston: Little, Brown, 1977, illustrated by Pamela Johnson), set in "Clodsburg."

(CF)*Trig Sees Red* (Boston: Little, Brown, 1978, illustrated by Pamela Johnson), set in "Clodsburg."

(CF)*Soup for President* (New York: Knopf, 1978, illustrated by Ted Lewin), set in "Learning" in 1936.

(CF)*Soup's Drum* (New York: Knopf, 1980, illustrated by Charles Robinson), set in "Learning."

(CF)*Trig Goes Ape* (Boston: Little, Brown, 1980, illustrated by Pamela Johnson), set in "Clodsburg."

(CF)*Soup on Wheels* (New York: Knopf, 1981, illustrated by Charles Robinson), set in "Learning."

(YA)*Justice Lion* (Boston: Little, Brown, 1981), set in "Liberty" in 1923.

(YA)*Kirk's Law* (Garden City, N.Y.: Doubleday, 1981), set in northern Vermont.

(CF)*Trig or Treat* (Boston: Little, Brown, 1982, illustrated by Pamela Johnson), set in "Clodsburg."

(CF)*Soup in the Saddle* (New York: Knopf, 1983, illustrated by Charles Robinson), set in "Learning."

(CF)*Soup's Goat* (New York: Knopf, 1984, illustrated by Charles Robinson), set in "Learning."

(CF)*Soup on Ice* (New York: Knopf, 1985, illustrated by Charles Robinson), set in "Learning."

(CF)*Soup on Fire* (New York: Delacorte, 1987, illustrated by Charles Robinson), set in "Learning."

(CF)*Soup's Uncle* (New York: Delacorte, 1988, illustrated by Charles Robinson), set in "Learning."

(CF)*Soup's Hoop* (New York: Delacorte, 1990, illustrated by Charles Robinson), set in "Learning."

(E)*Little Soup's Birthday* (New York: Dell, 1991, illustrated by Charles Robinson), set in "Learning."

(CF)*Soup in Love* (New York: Delacorte, 1992, illustrated by Charles Robinson), set in "Learning."

(E)*Little Soup's Bunny* (New York: Dell, 1993, illustrated by Charles Robinson, set in "Learning."

(CF)*Soup Ahoy* (New York: Random, 1994, illustrated by Charles Robinson), set in "Learning."

(CF)*Soup 1776* (New York: Knopf, 1995, illustrated by Charles Robinson), set in "Learning."

(YA)*A Part of the Sky* (New York: Random, 1997), set in "Learning" in 1925.

A native Vermonter, Peck lives in Longwood, Florida.

Elizabeth Stuart Phelps (Ward), (YA)*Gypsy Breynton* (Boston, Mass.: Graves & Young, 1866), set in "Yorkbury."

Phelps (1844-1911), a "Victorian feminist" (as her biographer, Lori Duin Kelly, calls her), lived in Newton Center, Massachusetts.

Georgiana Cushman Philips, (YA)*Summer of Good Hope* (New York: Putnam, 1939, illustrated by Margaret Sommerfield), set in Brandon.

Philips, a native of Irvington, New York, spent her childhood summers in, and later moved to, Vermont.

Ethel Calvert Phillips, (CF)*Calico* (Boston: Houghton Mifflin, 1937, illustrated by Maginel Wright Enright Barney, sister of Frank Lloyd Wright), set at "Little Turkey."

Phillips, who died in 1947, lived in Nutley, New Jersey.

Roberta Bicknell Piper, (CF)*Little Red* (New York: Scribner, 1963, illustrated by Joan Berg).

Piper grew up in Chelsea, Vermont, graduated from the University of Vermont, and lives in Murphysboro, Illinois.

Dorothy Horton Pitkin, (YA)*The Grass Was That High* (New York: Pantheon, 1959, illustrated by Genevieve Vaughan-Jackson), Dorothy Canfield Fisher Children's Book Award Master List, 1960-1961, set in "Seaver Hill" in 1954.

(YA)*Wiser Than Winter* (New York: Pantheon, 1960), set in "Seaver Hill" in 1956.

Pitkin (1899-1972), whose daughter and son-in-law ran a dairy farm in Vermont, lived in Peterborough, New Hampshire.

Eliza Frances Pollard, (YA)*Liberty or Death: A Story of the Green Mountain Boys in the American Revolution* (New York: Dodd, Mead, 1909), set in the New Hampshire Grants in 1775.

Pollard, who lived in England, died in 1911.

Eleanor Emily Hodgson Porter, (CF)*Pollyanna* (Boston: L.C. Page, 1913, reissued by HarperFestival, 2006), set in "Beldingsville."

(YA)**Pollyanna Grows Up* (Boston: L.C. Page, 1915, reissued by Barbour & Company, 1993), set in "Beldingsville."

Porter (1868-1920) was born in Littleton, New Hampshire, and lived in Massachusetts.

Carol Purdy, (E)*Least of All* (New York: Macmillan, 1987, illustrated by Tim Arnold).

Purdy lives near Red Bluff, California.

R

Gerald Bransfield Raftery, (CF)*City Dog* (New York: Morrow, 1953, illustrated by L.D. Cram).

(CF)*Slaver's Gold* (New York: Vanguard, 1967), set near Roaring Branch and Batten Kill River.

Raftery (1905-1986), who was librarian from 1964 at the Martha Canfield Memorial Library in Arlington, lived in Arlington, Vermont.

Jonathan Rand, (CF) *Virtual Vampires of Vermont: American Chillers #13* (Topinabee Island, Mich.: AudioCraft Publishing, 2004), set in Stowe.

Rand lives in the northern part of lower Michigan.

Marilynne Kathleen Roach, (CF) "The Ghost in the Shed," from *Encounters with the Invisible World: Short Stories* (New York: Crowell, 1977, illustrated by Marilynne K. Roach), set in the Green Mountains.

Roach, who was a fellow in 1977 at the Bread Loaf Writers' Conference, lives in Watertown, Massachusetts.

Gertrude Robinson, (CF)*Father and the Mountains* (New York: Oxford University Press, 1950, illustrated by Dorothy Bayley Morse), set in Manchester.

Robinson, born in 1876, lived in Maine.

K. S. Rodriguez, (YA)*Major Meltdown* (New York: Pocket Books, 1999, based on the television show *Dawson's Creek*, created by Kevin Williamson), set on "Steep Mountain."

Rodriguez lives in New York City.

Nan Parson Rossiter, (E)*The Way Home* (New York: Dutton, 1999, illustrated by Nan Parson Rossiter).

(E)*Sugar on Snow* (New York: Dutton, 2002, illustrated by Nan Parson Rossiter).

Rossiter, who with her family visits maple sugar farms in the Montpelier, Vermont, area every spring, lives in New Milford, Connecticut.

David Roth, (YA)**A World for Joey Carr* (New York: Beaufort Book Company, 1981), set in "Carverville."

Roth lives in Bristol, New Hampshire.

Ken (Kenneth) Rush, (Jr.), (E)*What About Emma?* (New York: Orchard Books, 1996, illustrated by Ken Rush).

Rush lives in Danby, Vermont.

S

Frances (Ella Fitz) Sanger, (CF)*The Silver Teapot* (Philadelphia: Westminster Press, 1948, illustrated by Ursula Koering), set in Bennington in 1777.

(CF)*The Wooden Mug* (Philadelphia: Westminster Press, 1950, illustrated by Marian Larer), set in Bennington in 1778.

Sanger was born in Summertown, Tennessee, and lived in Hollywood, California.

Susan Fromberg Schaeffer, (CF)*The Dragons of North Chittendon* (New York: Simon & Schuster 1986, illustrated by Darcy May), set in "North Chittendon."

Schaeffer lives in Chicago, Illinois, and South Newfane, Vermont.

Leda Schubert, (E)*Here Comes Darrell* (Boston: Houghton Mifflin, 2005, illustrated by Mary Azarian).

Schubert, who is on the faculty of Vermont College's MFA in Writing for Children and Young Adults and was the school library media consultant for the Vermont Department of Education, lives in Plainfield, Vermont.

Tor Seidler, (CF)*Terpin* (New York: Farrar, Straus & Giroux, 1982, reissued by Laura Geringer Books, 2002, illustrated by Peter McCarty), set in "North Haven."

(CF)*Brothers Below Zero* (New York: Laura Geringer Books, 2002, illustrated by Peter McCarty), set in Williston.

Born in New Hampshire, Seidler lived with his family in Burlington, Vermont, until he was twelve; he now lives in New York City.

Martina Selway, (E)*Don't Forget to Write* (Nashville, Tenn.: Ideals Children's Books, 1992, illustrated by Martina Selway), set in Manchester.

Selway lives in Surrey, England.

Barbara Seuling, (CF)**Robert and the Great Escape* (Chicago, Ill.: Cricket Books, 2003, illustrated by Paul Brewer), set at "Big Bear Mountain."

Seuling, director of The Manuscript Workshop in Landgrove, divides her time between Landgrove, Vermont, and New York City.

Marlene Fanta Shyer, (CF)*Blood in the Snow* (Boston: Houghton Mifflin, 1975, illustrated by Maggie Kaufman Smith), Dorothy Canfield Fisher Children's Book Award Master List, 1976-1977, set in "Paragon."

Shyer, who spent several summers with her husband and children at The Old Ark, a "bucolic paradise" in Wilmington, Vermont, lives in Larchmont, New York.

Marilyn Singer, (YA)**California Demon* (New York: Hyperion, 1992), set near "Pendleton."

Singer lives in Brooklyn, New York.

Jan (Janice B.) Slepian, (CF)**Back to Before* (New York: Philomel, 1993), set in Colchester.

Slepian lives in Maplewood, New Jersey.

Esphyr Slobodkina, (E)*The Clock* (New York: Abelard, 1956, illustrated by Esphyr Slobodkina).

Slobodkina (1908-2002) lived in Glen Head, New York.

Virginia Kester Smiley, (YA)*Sugar Bush Nurse* (New York: Thomas Bouregy, 1981), set in St. Johnsbury.

Smiley lives in Webster, New York.

Gilbert Smith, (YA)*The Green Mountain Boys Ride* (New York: The Century Co., 1932, illustrated by Frank Dobias), set in Bennington in 1775.

Gilbert Smith is the pseudonym of Mary Gilbert Smith (1878-1951), who lived in Wallingford, Vermont.

Alan David Sophrin, (YA)*The Newcomer* (New York: John Day, 1968), set in Brighton Township.

Sophrin lived in Bennington and now lives in Charleston, Vermont.

Elizabeth George Speare, (YA)**Calico Captive* (Boston: Houghton Mifflin, 1957), Dorothy Canfield Fisher Children's Book Award Master List, 1958-1959, set in 1754.

Speare (1908-1994) lived in Wethersfield, Connecticut.

David Stahler, Jr., (YA) *A Gathering of Shades* (New York: HarperTempest, 2005), set in the Northeast Kingdom.

A fourth-generation Vermonter, Stahler graduated from Middlebury College in 1994, teaches at Lyndon Institute, and lives in Lyndonville, Vermont.

Laura Caroline Stevenson, (CF)*Happily After All* (Boston: Houghton Mifflin, 1990), Dorothy Canfield Fisher Children's Book Award Master List, 1991-1992, set near Brattleboro.

Stevenson teaches at Marlboro College and lives with her writer husband, Franklin D. Reeve, in Wilmington, Vermont.

Mary Slattery Stolz, (CF)**A Wonderful, Terrible Time* (New York, Harper, 1967, illustrated by Louis S. Glanzman), Dorothy Canfield Fisher Children's Book Award Master List, 1968-1969, set at "Camp Oriole."

(YA)*By the Highway Home* (New York: Harper, 1971).

(CF)*Ferris Wheel* (New York: Harper, 1977), set on the Connecticut River.

(CF)*Cider Days* (New York: Harper, 1978), set on the Connecticut River.

(CF)*Cat Walk* (New York: Harper, 1983, illustrated by Erik Blegvad), Dorothy Canfield Fisher Children's Book Award Master List, 1984-1985.

Stolz (1920-2006) lived in Stamford, Connecticut, and Longboat Key, Florida.

Phoebe Stone, (CF)**All the Blue Moons at the Wallace Hotel* (Boston: Little, Brown, 2000), set in 1960.

Stone, daughter of Vermont State Poet Ruth Stone, lives in Middlebury, Vermont.

Cynthia Stowe, (YA)*Dear Mom, in Ohio for a Year* (New York: Scholastic, 1992), set in "Elton."

Stowe lives in Greenfield, Massachusetts.

T

Abigail Thomas, (E)*Lily* (New York: Holt, 1994, illustrated by William Low).

Thomas lives in New York City.

Eliza Thomas, (E)**The Red Blanket* (New York: Scholastic, 2004, illustrated by Joe Cepeda), set in Montpelier.

Thomas lives in Montpelier, Vermont.

Charles Miner Thompson, (YA)*Calico Cat* (Boston: Houghton Mifflin, 1908), set in "Ellmington."

Thompson (1864-1941), a grandson of Judge Daniel Pierce Thompson, was born in Montpelier, Vermont.

Daniel Pierce Thompson, (YA)*The Green Mountain Boys: A Historical Tale of the Early Settlement of Vermont* (New York: Thomas Nelson, 1927, illustrated by Carle Michel Boog, originally published in 1838), set in the New Hampshire Grants.

(YA)*The Green Mountain Boys: A Vermont classic in a new and readable version* (Weybridge, Vt.: Cherry Tree Books, 2000), edited by Ida H. Washington with her daughter, Carol E. Washington, and illustrated by another daughter, Ida W. Smoak. *See* Ida H. Washington.

Judge Thompson (1795-1868), a graduate of Middlebury College, lived in Montpelier, Vermont.

Julian Francis Thompson, (YA)**Discontinued* (New York: Scholastic, 1985), set in Burlington.

(YA)**Simon Pure* (New York: Scholastic, 1987), set in "Peacemeal."

(YA)*Shepherd* (New York: Holt, 1993), set in "Burnside."

(YA)*The Trials of Molly Sheldon* (New York: Holt, 1995), set in "Saphouse Junction."

(YA)*Ghost Story* (New York: Holt, 1997), set in "Boynton Falls."

Thompson lives in West Rupert and Burlington, Vermont.

Mary Wolfe Thompson, (YA)*Green Threshold* (New York: Longmans, 1954), set in "Oldchester."

(YA)*Snow Slopes* (New York: Longman's, 1957, illustrated by Frank Kramer), set in "Westbury."

(CF)*Two in the Wilderness: Before Vermont Had a Name* (New York: David McKay, 1967, illustrated by Tom O'Sullivan), winner of the Dorothy Canfield Fisher Children's Book Award in 1969, set in Windham.

(CF)*Wilderness Winter* (New York: McKay, 1968, illustrated by Ursula Koering), set in Windham.

(CF)*Wilderness Wedding* (New York: McKay, 1970, illustrated by Ursula Koering), set in Windham.

Thompson (1886-1970) lived in North Bennington, Vermont.

Mary Towne, (CF)*Wanda the Worrywart* (New York: Atheneum, 1989), set on "Lake Heron."

(CF)*Steve the Sure* (New York: Atheneum, 1990), set on "Lake Heron."

Mary Towne is a pseudonym of Mary Spelman, who spent summers with her family at Quimby Country Lodge and Cottages in Averill, Vermont, lived in West Redding, Connecticut, and now lives in southern California.

Margaret Pope Trask, (CF)*Three for Treasure* (New York: Crowell, 1962, illustrated by Paul Frame), Dorothy Canfield Fisher Children's Book Award Master List, 1963-1964, set in Pleasant Valley.

(CF)*At the Sign of the Rocking Horse* (New York: Crowell, 1964, illustrated by Harold Berson), set in "Dublin Center."

Trask, who died in 1990, raised Brown Swiss cows with her husband on their farm in Underhill, Vermont.

Nathaniel Tripp, (E)*Snow Comes to the Farm* (Cambridge, Mass.: Candlewick, 2001, illustrated by Kate A. Kiesler), set in northern Vermont.

Tripp lives with his wife, writer Reeve Lindbergh, in St. Johnsbury, Vermont.

Tasha Tudor, (E)*Corgiville Fair* (New York: HarperCollins, 1971, reprinted by Little, Brown, 1998), set "west of New Hampshire and east of Vermont." Others in the series are *The Great Corgiville Kidnapping* (1997) and *Corgiville Christmas* (2003).

Tudor, born in 1915, lives in Marlboro, Vermont.

V

Jean Van Leeuwen, (CF)*The Great Summer Camp Catastrophe* (New York, Dial, 1992, illustrated by Diane de Groat), set at "Camp Moose-a-Honk."

Van Leeuwen lives in Chappaqua, New York.

Kathryn Mademann Vaughan, (E)*Little One—Good Night: A Lullaby from Vermont* (Dorset, Vt.: Chaser Media, 2003, illustrated by Anharad Llewelyn Edson).

Vaughan lives in Dorset, Vermont.

Marjorie Meyn Vetter, (YA)*Champlain Summer* (New York: Funk, 1959), set in Vergennes.

Vetter (1898-1977) was born in New York and spent summers in Vergennes, Vermont.

Phillip Viereck, (YA)*Independence Must Be Won* (New York: John Day, 1964, illustrated by Ellen Viereck), Dorothy Canfield Fisher Children's Book Award Master List, 1965-1966, set at Mount Independence and Castleton in 1777.

Viereck lives with his wife, illustrator Ellen Kingsbury Viereck, in North Bennington, Vermont.

W

Amelia Elizabeth Walden, (YA)*Skymountain* (New York: William Morrow, 1950), set on "Skymountain."
Walden (1909-2004) lived in Westport, Connecticut.

Mildred Walker (Schemm), (CF)*A Piece of the World* (New York: Atheneum, 1972, illustrated by Christine Price), set in "Weldon."
Walker (1905-1998) lived in Grafton, Vermont.

Ruth Wallace-Brodeur, (CF)*The Kenton Year* (New York: Atheneum, 1980), set in "Kenton."
(CF)*The Godmother Tree* (New York: HarperCollins, 1992, originally published by the Vermont Migrant Education Program in 1988), set in "Redfield."
Wallace-Brodeur lives in Montpelier, Vermont.

Mary Ella Waller, (YA)*The Little Citizen* (Boston: Lothrop, 1902, illustrated by H. G. Burgess), set in "Hurdyville."
(YA)*A Daughter of the Rich and Her Friends, The Blossoms of Mt. Hunger* (Boston: Little, Brown, 1906, illustrated by Ellen Bernard Thompson Pyle), set on Hunger Mountain and in "Barton's River" in 1897.
Waller (1855-1938) lived in Bethel, Vermont.

Chad Walsh, (E)*Nellie and Her Flying Crocodile* (New York: Harper, 1956, illustrated by Marc Simont), set on Lake Iroquois.
Walsh (1914-1991), a poet, literary critic, and novelist, lived in Shelburne, Vermont.

Mildred Pitts Walter, (E)*Alec's Primer* (Middlebury, Vt.: Vermont Folklife Center Family Heritage Series, 2004, illustrated by Larry Johnson), set in 1850.
Walter lives in Denver, Colorado.

Gertrude Chandler Warner, (CF)*The Mystery at the Snowflake Inn: Boxcar Children Mystery #3* (Morton Grove, Ill.: Albert Whitman, 1994, illustrated by Charles Tang).
(CF)*The Stuffed Bear Mystery: Boxcar Children Mystery #90* (Morton Grove, Ill.: Albert Whitman, 2002, illustrated by Hodges Soileau). The original *The Boxcar Children*, about four orphans who take up residence in an abandoned boxcar, was published by Rand McNally in 1924; a revised edition was issued by Scott Foresman in 1942 and the series continues.
Warner (1890-1979) lived in Putnam, Connecticut.

Ida Harrison Washington, (YA)*The Green Mountain Boys* (Weybridge, Vt.: Cherry Tree Books, 2000), co-edited by Carol E. Washington. *See* Daniel Pierce Thompson.
(CF)*Brave Enough: The Story of Rob Sanford, Vermont Pioneer Boy* (Weybridge, Vt.: Cherry Tree Books, 2003, illustrated by I.W. Smoak and C.E. Washington), set in Weybridge in 1778.
Washington, whose first postgraduate degree is from Middlebury College, is the author of a biography of Dorothy Canfield Fisher (New England Press, 1982), a past president of the League of Vermont Writers, and a former member of the board of the Vermont Humanities Council. She lives in Weybridge, Vermont.

Nancy Dingman Watson, (E)*Sugar on Snow* (New York: Viking, 1964, illustrated by Aldren Auld Watson), set in Putney. Putney is also the setting for her picture books, *What is One?* (1954), *Whose Birthday Is It?* (1954), and *What Does A Begin With?*" (1956), all illustrated by Aldren Auld Watson.
Watson (1922-2001) and her artist husband, Aldren Auld Watson, brought up their eight children on the family farm in Putney, Vermont.

Kenneth Beals Webb, (YA)*From Plymouth Notch to President: The Farm Boyhood of Calvin Coolidge* (Taftsville, Vt.: Countryman Press, 1978, illustrated by Florence Baker Karpin), set in Plymouth in 1883.
Webb (1902-1984) founded the Farm and Wilderness Camps in Plymouth, Vermont, and the Woodstock Country School, in Woodstock, Vermont.

Rosemary Wells, (E)*Waiting for the Evening Star* (New York: Dial, 1993, illustrated by Susan Jeffers), set in "Barstowe."
Wells lives in Briarcliff Manor, New York.

Dorothy West, (CF)*Dot and Dash at the Maple Sugar Camp* (New York: Cupples & Leon, 1938), set on Bread Loaf Mountain.
West is the pseudonym of Mildred Augustine Wirt Benson (1905-2002), who wrote twenty-three Nancy Drew mysteries under the collective pseudonym, Carolyn Keene. *See* Carolyn Keene. This story was inspired by Benson's grandfather's life in Vermont; she lived in Iowa and Ohio.

Newlin B. Wildes, (YA)*The Best Summer* (Chicago: Rand McNally, 1965, illustrated by Albert Micale), Dorothy Canfield Fisher Children's Book Award Master List, 1966-1967, set in Pomfret in 1919.
(YA)*The Horse That Had Everything* (Chicago: Rand McNally, 1966, illustrated by Albert Micale), Dorothy

Canfield Fisher Children's Book Award Master List, 1967-1968, set in "Parnell Center."

Wildes (1902-1982), an author and film writer, lived in New York and spent summers in and then moved to Pomfret, Vermont.

Doug Wilhelm, (CF) *Scene of the Crime: Choose Your Own Adventure #175* (New York: Bantam, 1993, illustrated by Thomas La Padula), set in "Grantshire."

(CF)*The Underground Railroad: Choose Your Own Adventure* #137 (New York: Bantam, 1996, illustrated by Ron Wing), set in Randolph in 1853.

(CF)*The Revealers* (New York: Farrar, Straus & Giroux, 2003), set in central Vermont.

(YA)*Falling* (New York: Farrar, Straus & Giroux, 2007), set in Rutland.

Wilhelm lives in Rutland Town, Vermont.

Charles Morrow Wilson, (YA)*The Great Turkey Drive* (New York: David McKay, 1964, illustrated by Leonard Vosburgh), set between "Fyster" and Putney in 1824.

(YA)*Crown Point: The Destiny Road* (New York: David McKay, 1965, illustrated by Leonard Vosburgh), set between Springfield and Rutland in 1759.

(YA)*The Green Mountain Toymakers* (New York: Ives Washburn, 1965), set in Springfield in 1845.

Wilson (1905-1977) lived in Putney, Vermont.

Nancy Hope Wilson, (CF)*Mountain Pose* (New York: Farrar, Straus & Giroux, 2001), set near Brattleboro.

Wilson, who grew up in Lexington, Massachusetts, and Marlboro, Vermont, lives in Amherst, Massachusetts.

Elizabeth Winthrop, (YA)*Counting on Grace* (New York: Wendy Lamb Books, 2006), Dorothy Canfield Fisher Children's Book Award Master List, 2007-2008, Vermont Humanities Council 2007 selection for Vermont Reads, set in North Pownal in 1910.

Winthrop, the daughter of Stewart Alsop, lives in northwestern Massachusetts and New York.

Gary Clifton Wisler, (CF)**Mr. Lincoln's Drummer* (New York: Dutton, 1995), set in St. Johnsbury in 1862.

Wisler lives in Plano, Texas.

Maia Teresa Wojciechowska, (CF)*A Kingdom in a Horse* (New York: Harper, 1965), set in Middlebury.

Wojciechowska (1927-2002) lived in New York City.

Nancy Means Wright, (YA)**Down the Strings* (New York: Dutton, 1982, reissued by Author's Guild/Back in Print, 2007), set in "Branbury."

(CF)*The Pea Soup Poisonings* (Boonsboro, Md.: Hilliard & Harris, 2006), set in "Branbury."

(CF)*The Great Circus Train Robbery* (Boonsboro, Md.: Hilliard & Harris, 2007), set in "Branbury."

Wright is a Vermont Humanities Council Reading and Discussion scholar, a 1959 Bread Loaf Writers' Conference scholar, a 1965 graduate of Middlebury, a League of Vermont Writers president from 1978-1980, and a 1995 recipient of a Vermont College MFA. She lives in Cornwall, Vermont.

Hildreth Tyler Wriston, (CF)*Downstreet with Edith* (Garden City, N.Y.: Doubleday, 1935, illustrated by Grace Paull), set in "Fletcher Falls" in the early 1900s.

(CF)*Camping Down at Highgate* (Garden City, N.Y.: Doubleday, 1939, illustrated by Ruth Holbrook), set in Highgate in 1905.

(CF) *Open Water* (Garden City, N.Y.: Doubleday, 1942, illustrated by Dorothy Bayley Morse), set on Lake Champlain.

(CF)*Show Lamb* (New York: Abingdon, 1953, illustrated by Peter Burchard), set in the Black River Valley in 1850.

(CF)*Hill Farm* (New York: Abingdon, 1956, illustrated by Peter Burchard), Dorothy Canfield Fisher Children's Book Award Master List, 1957-1958.

(CF)*Susan's Secret* (New York: Farrar, Straus & Cudahy, 1957, illustrated by Witold Tadeusz J. Mars), Dorothy Canfield Fisher Children's Book Award Master List, 1958-1959, set in Montpelier in the 1850s.

(CF)*A Yankee Musket* (New York: Abingdon Press, 1959, illustrated by Jo Polseno), Dorothy Canfield Fisher Children's Book Award Master List, 1960-1961, set in Otter Creek in 1777.

(YA)*Andy and the Red Canoe* (New York: Farrar, Straus & Cudahy, 1960, illustrated by W. T. Mars), set in "Burleigh."

Wriston (1899-1968) was born and lived in Enosburg Falls, Vermont, and spent summers in Highgate Springs, Vermont.

Z

Paul Zindel, (YA)*Loch: A Novel* (New York: HarperCollins, 1994, illustrated by Wayne McLoughlin), set in "Lake Alban."

Zindel (1936-2003) lived in New York City.

APPENDIX A: Authors and Titles, by age group

YOUNG ADULT FICTION (YA)

Jacob Abbott, *Marco Paul's Voyages & Travels in Vermont*
Jane D. Abbott, *Happy House*
Katharine Adams, *Mehitable*
Louisa May Alcott, "A Country Christmas"
Merritt P. Allen, *Raiders' Hoard, The Flicker's Feather, The Green Cockade*
Julia Alvarez, *Finding Miracles*
Grace Neil Anderson, *In the Shadow of Cox Mountain*
Robert Arthur, "Obstinate Uncle Otis"
Robert P. Ashley, *Rebel Raiders*
Kay Avery, *Goodbye Blue Jeans*
Katharine Jay Bacon, *Finn*, *Shadow and Light*
Carin Greenberg Baker, *A Time to Love*
Jeanne Betancourt, *More Than Meets the Eye*
Cynthia Blair, *The Candy Cane Caper*
Larry Bograd, "Willie and the Christmas Spruces"
Carole Bolton, *The Dark Rosaleen*
Bianca Bradbury, *Laughter in Our House*
Ann Brashares, *Forever in Blue*
Alice Brown, *The Secret of the Clan*
Edna A. Brown, *At the Butterfly House*
Joseph Bruchac, *Hidden Roots*
Bonnie Bryant, *Snow Ride*
Louella Bryant, *The Black Bonnet*
Eleanor Cameron, *To the Green Mountains*
Betty Cavanna, *Angel on Skis*
Marjorie Chickering, *Hayseed Summer, Yankee Trader*
Florence Choate & Elizabeth Curtis, *Linda Takes Over*
Barbara Clayton, *Halfway Hannah*
Caroline B. Cooney, *Family Reunion*
Peter Cooper, *The Secret Papers of Julia Templeton*
Robert Cormier, *I Am the Cheese*, *The Rag and Bone Shop*
Emily Costello, *Ski Share VT*
Elizabeth Craft & Sarah Fain, *Bass Ackwards and Belly Up*
E. J. Craine, *The Air Mystery of Isle La Motte*
Jordan Cray, *Shiver*
Craig Crist-Evans, *North of Everything*
Barbara Dana, *Crazy Eights*
Nicole Davidson, *Winterkill*
Robert Davis, *Gid Granger*
Leon W. Dean, *Border Bullets, Green Mountain Boy, Guns Over Champlain, I Become a Ranger, Old Wolf, Pirate Lair, Red Man's Trail, Royalton Raid, Stark of the North Country, The White Ox*
Marilyn Cram Donahue, *Straight Along a Crooked Road*
Amy Ehrlich, *Where It Stops*, *Nobody Knows*
Erik E. Esckilsen, *The Last Mall Rat, The Outside Groove*
Clavin Fisher, *A Spy at Ticonderoga*
Paul Fleischman, *Coming-and-Going Men*
Genevieve Fox, *Border Girl, Susan of the Green Mountains*
Gail Gauthier, *Saving the Planet & Stuff*
Beth B. Gilchrist, *Kit, Pat, and a Few Boys*
Helen Girvan, *Felicity Way*
Christopher Golden, *Laws of Nature*
Jessie Haas, *Shaper, The Sixth Sense*, *Skipping School*, *Westminster West*, *Will You, Won't You?*, *Working Trot*
Randi Hacker, *Life as I Knew It*
William W. Harvey, *Lige Golden*
Sheila Hayes, *The Tinker's Daughter*
Alison Cragin Herzig, *Shadows on the Pond*
Karen Hesse, *Phoenix Rising*, *A Time of Angels*, *Witness*
Kimberly Heuston, *The Shakeress*
Beth Hilgartner, *Colors in the Dreamweaver's Loom*, *The Feast of the Trickster*
Ralph Nading Hill, *The Voyages of Brian Seaworthy*
Edgar N. Jackson, *Green Mountain Hero*
Caroline E. Jacobs, *The S.W.F. Club*
Barnard & Jonathan Katz, *Black Woman*
Garret Keizer, *God of Beer*
Clarence B. Kelland, *Mark Tidd*, *Mark Tidd in Business*, *Mark Tidd's Citadel*
Louise Andrews Kent, *He Went with Champlain*
M. E. Kerr, *The Son of Someone Famous*
Liza Ketchum, *Fire in the Heart*, *Twelve Days in August*, *Where the Great Hawk Flies*
Doris Kirkpatrick, *Honey in the Rock*
Sheila Solomon Klass, *Next Stop: Nowhere*
Norma Klein, *Bizou*
Nancy H. Kleinbaum, *Dead Poets Society*
Gordon Korman, *Chasing the Falconers*, *The Fugitive Factor*
Bill Littlefield, *The Circus in the Woods*
Elizabeth Low, *High Harvest*
Janet Lunn, *The Hollow Tree*
Melissa Mather, *One Summer in Between*

Cornelia L. Meigs, *At the Sign of the Two Heroes*, *Call of the Mountain*
Jane Claypool Miner, *A Winter Love Story*
Charles G. Muller, *Hero of Champlain*
Rita Murphy, *Night Flying*
John Ney, *Ox Goes North*
Mary Page, *Dirty Mary No More*, *The Printer's Devil*
Katherine Paterson, *Lyddie*, *A Midnight Clear*
Robert Newton Peck, *A Day No Pigs Would Die*, *Hang for Treason*, *Justice Lion*, *Kirk's Law*, *Millie's Boy*, *A Part of the Sky*
Elizabeth Stuart Phelps, *Gypsy Breynton*
Georgiana Philips, *Summer of Good Hope*
Dorothy Pitkin, *The Grass Was That High*, *Wiser Than Winter*
Eliza F. Pollard, *Liberty or Death*
Eleanor H. Porter, *Pollyanna Grows Up*
K. S. Rodriguez, *Major Meltdown*
David Roth, *A World for Joey Carr*
Marilyn Singer, *California Demon*
Virginia Smiley, *Sugar Bush Nurse*
Gilbert Smith, *The Green Mountain Boys Ride*
Alan D. Sophrin, *The Newcomer*
Elizabeth George Speare, *Calico Captive*
David Stahler, Jr., *A Gathering of Shades*
Mary Stolz, *By the Highway Home*
Cynthia M. Stowe, *Dear Mom, in Ohio for a Year*
Charles Miner Thompson, *Calico Cat*
Daniel Pierce Thompson, *The Green Mountain Boys*
Julian F. Thompson, *Discontinued*, *Ghost Story*, *Shepherd*, *Simon Pure*, *The Trials of Molly Sheldon*
Mary Wolfe Thompson, *Green Threshold*, *Snow Slopes*
Marjorie M. Vetter, *Champlain Summer*
Phillip Viereck, *Independence Must Be Won*
Amelia Walden, *Skymountain*
Mary Ella Waller, *A Daughter of the Rich*, *The Little Citizen*
Ida H. & Carol E. Washington, *The Green Mountain Boys*
Kenneth B. Webb, *From Plymouth Notch to President*
Newlin B. Wildes, *The Best Summer*, *The Horse That Had Everything*
Doug Wilhelm, *Falling*
Charles Morrow Wilson, *Crown Point*, *The Great Turkey Drive*, *The Green Mountain Toymakers*
Elizabeth Winthrop, *Counting on Grace*
Nancy Means Wright, *Down the Strings*
Hildreth T. Wriston, *Andy and the Red Canoe*
Paul Zindel, *Loch*

CHILDREN'S FICTION (CF)

Julia Alvarez, *How Tía Lola Came to Visit/Stay*
M. T. Anderson, *The Game of Sunken Places*
Kenneth Andler, *Mission to Fort No. 4*
Jennifer Armstrong, *Steal Away*
Jim Arnosky, *Little Champ*
Frank Asch, *Up River*
Kay Avery, *All for a Friend*, *All for a Ghost*, *All for a Horse*
Katharine Jay Bacon, *Pip and Emma*
Arthur Scott Bailey, *The Tale of Muley Cow*, *The Tale of Nimble Deer*
Carolyn S. Bailey, "A Sugar Heart for Bethia"
Carin Greenberg Baker, *Pride of the Green Mountains*
Jeff Barth, *A Thanksgiving Story in Vermont—1852*
Hetty B. Beatty, *Bryn*
Jeanne Betancourt, *Crazy Christmas*, *Puppy Love*, *The Rainbow Kid*, *Turtle Time*, *Valentine Blues*
Lenore Blegvad, *Kitty and Mr. Kipling*
Gary Bowen, *The Mare's Nest*
Marge Bruchac, *Malian's Song*
Pearl S. Buck, "The Christmas Secret"
David Budbill, *Bones on Black Spruce Mountain*, *Snowshoe Trek to Otter River*
Cynthia Butler, *Michael Hendee*
Flavia Camp Canfield, *The Kidnapped Campers*
Margaret F. Carty, *Christmas in Vermont*
Jean Caryl, *Bones and the Smiling Mackerel*
Cora Cheney, *The Doll of Lilac Valley*, *The Mystery of the Disappearing Cars*
Marilyn C. Childs, *Mandate for a Morgan Horse*
Jessica Clerk, *Sukey Johnson Builds a House*
Catherine C. Coblentz, *The Blue Cat of Castle Town*
Carroll B. Colby, *The Weirdest People in the World*
Jane Leslie Conly, *The Rudest Alien on Earth*
Peter Campbell Copp, *Thunder in October*
Anne Eliot Crompton, *Deer Country*, *The Ice Trail*
Alice Turner Curtis, *A Little Maid of Ticonderoga*, *A Little Maid of Vermont*
Dorathea Dana, *Sugar Bush*
Jeff Danziger, *The Champlain Monster*
Franklin W. Dixon, *The Demon's Den*, *Track of the Zombie*
Marion Doren, *Nell of Blue Harbor*
Eugenie A. Doyle, *Stray Voltage*
Genevieve T. Eames, *Pat Rides the Trail*
Walter Pritchard Eaton, *Boy Scouts on the Green Mountain Trail*

Phoebe Erickson, *Double or Nothing*
Caroline S. Fairless, *Hambone*
Dorothy Canfield Fisher, *Understood Betsy*, *Something Old, Something New*
Frances Frost, *Fireworks for Windy Foot*, *Maple Sugar for Windy Foot*, *Sleigh Bells for Windy Foot*, *Windy Foot at the County Fair*
Nancy Garden, *The Case of the Stolen Scarab*, *Mystery of the Night Raiders*
Dale Blackwell Gasque, *Pony Trouble*
Gail Gauthier, *The Hero of Ticonderoga*
Corinne Gerson, *My Grandfather the Spy*
Shannon Gilligan, *The Search for Champ*
Nancy Price Graff, *A Long Way Home*, *Taking Wing*
Jessie Haas, *Be Well, Beware*, *Beware and Stogie*, *Beware the Mare*, *A Blue for Beware*, *A Horse Like Barney*, *Keeping Barney*, *Uncle Daney's Way*, *Unbroken*, *Runaway Radish*
Sue Halpern, *Introducing...Sasha Abramowitz*
Earl Hamner & Don Snipes, *Lassie: A Christmas Story*
James Hayford, *Gridley Firing*
Wilma Pitchford Hays, *Trouble at Otter Creek*
Marguerite Henry, *Justin Morgan Had a Horse*
Hadley Higginson, *Keeker and the Horse Show Show-Off*, *Keeker and the Sneaky Pony*, *Keeker and the Springtime Surprise*, *Keeker and the Sugar Shack*
Clara Whitehill Hunt, *The Little House in Green Valley*
Lee Pennock Huntington, *Brothers in Arms*
Johanna Hurwitz, *Dear Emma*, *Faraway Summer*, *A Llama in the Family*, *A Llama in the Library*, *The Unsigned Valentine*, *Yellow Blue Jay*
Jacqueline Jackson, *The Taste of Spruce Gum*
Allen Johnson, Jr., *The Christmas Tree Express*
Bobbi Katz, *Snow Bunny*
Carolyn Keene, *Close Encounters*
Shirley W. Kelley, *Little Settlers of Vermont*
Natalie Kinsey-Warnock, *As Long as There Are Mountains*, *Canada Geese Quilt*, *A Doctor Like Papa*, *If Wishes Were Horses*, *In the Language of Loons*, *Lumber Camp Library*, *The Night the Bells Rang*, *Sweet Memories Still*
West Lathrop, *Black River Captive*
Lois Lenski, *Deer Valley Girl*
Janet Lind, *The Bird at Bear Mountain*
Anne Lindbergh, *Osprey Island*, *Travel Far, Pay No Fare*
Frederick Lipp, *That Cat Is Not For Sale*
Norris Lloyd, *Billy Hunts the Unicorn*
Rose Lucia, *Peter and Polly in Autumn*, *in Spring*, *in Summer*, *in Winter*
Gregory Maguire, *A Couple of April Fools*, *Five Alien Elves*, *Four Stupid Cupids*, *One Final Firecracker*, *Seven Spiders Spinning*, *Six Haunted Hairdos*, *Three Rotten Eggs*
Ann M. Martin, *Baby-Sitters' Winter Vacation*
Cornelia L. Meigs, *The Covered Bridge*, *Wild Geese Flying*
George Mendoza, "The Devil's Pocket"
Anne Molloy, *Decky's Secret*
R. A. Montgomery, *The Island of Time*
Helen Fuller Orton, *Mystery in the Old Cave*
Margaret Otto, *Mr. Kipling's Elephant*
Janice Ovecka, *Captive of Pittsford Ridge*, *Cave of Falling Water*
Katherine Paterson, *Bread and Roses, Too*, *The Field of Dogs*, *Jip, His Story*, *Preacher's Boy*, *The Same Stuff as Stars*
Leigh Peck, *They Were Made of Rawhide*
Robert Newton Peck, *Rabbits and Redcoats*, *Soup*, *Soup 1776*, *Soup Ahoy*, *Soup & Me*, *Soup for President*, *Soup in Love*, *Soup in the Saddle*, *Soup on Fire*, *Soup on Ice*, *Soup on Wheels*, *Soup's Drum*, *Soup's Goat*, *Soup's Hoop*, *Soup's Uncle*, *Trig*, *Trig Goes Ape*, *Trig or Treat*, *Trig Sees Red*
Ethel Calvert Phillips, *Calico*
Roberta Piper, *Little Red*
Eleanor H. Porter, *Pollyanna*
Gerald Raftery, *City Dog*, *Slaver's Gold*
Jonathan Rand, *Virtual Vampires of Vermont*
Marilynne K. Roach, "The Ghost in the Shed"
Gertrude Robinson, *Father and the Mountains*
Frances Sanger, *The Silver Teapot*, *The Wooden Mug*
Susan Fromberg Schaeffer, *The Dragons of North Chittendon*
Tor Seidler, *Brothers Below Zero*, *Terpin*
Barbara Seuling, *Robert and the Great Escape*
Marlene Fanta Shyer, *Blood in the Snow*
Jan Slepian, *Back to Before*
Laura C. Stevenson, *Happily After All*
Mary Stolz, *Cat Walk*, *Cider Days*, *Ferris Wheel*, *A Wonderful, Terrible Time*
Phoebe Stone, *All the Blue Moons at the Wallace Hotel*
Mary Wolfe Thompson, *Two in the Wilderness*, *Wilderness Wedding*, *Wilderness Winter*
Mary Towne, *Steve the Sure*, *Wanda the Worrywart*

Margaret P. Trask, *At the Sign of the Rocking Horse*, *Three for Treasure*
Jean Van Leeuwen, *The Great Summer Camp Catastrophe*
Mildred Walker, *A Piece of the World*
Ruth Wallace-Brodeur, *The Godmother Tree*, *The Kenton Year*
Gertrude Chandler Warner, *The Mystery at Snowflake Inn*, *The Stuffed Bear Mystery*
Ida H. Washington, *Brave Enough*
Dorothy West, *Dot and Dash at the Maple Sugar Camp*
Doug Wilhelm, *The Revealers*, *Scene of the Crime*, *The Underground Railroad*
Nancy Hope Wilson, *Mountain Pose*
G. Clifton Wisler, *Mr. Lincoln's Drummer*
Maia Wojciechowska, *A Kingdom in a Horse*
Nancy Means Wright, *The Great Circus Train Robbery*, *The Pea Soup Poisonings*
Hildreth T. Wriston, *Camping Down at Highgate*, *Downstreet with Edith*, *Hill Farm*, *Open Water*, *Show Lamb*, *Susan's Secret*, *A Yankee Musket*

PICTURE BOOKS AND EASY READERS (E)

Jim Arnosky, *Mud Time and More*, *Nathaniel*
Kay Avery, *Wee Willow Whistle*
Mary Azarian, *A Farmer's Alphabet*
Robert Bright, *Miss Pattie*
Winifred Bromhall, *Mrs. Polly's Party*
Marc Brown, *Buster's Sugartime*
Joseph Bruchac, *Fox Song*
David Budbill, *Christmas Tree Farm*
Carol Carrick, *The Highest Balloon on the Common*
Donald Carrick, *The Deer in the Pasture*
Eileen Christelow, *The Great Pig Escape*, *The Great Pig Search*, *The Five-Dog Night*
Linda Cunningham, *The Copper Angel of Piper's Mill*
Amy Ehrlich, *Parents in the Pigpen*
Rachi Farrow, *Charlie's Dream*
Sid Fleischman, *The Hey Hey Man*
Patricia Lee Gauch, *Aaron and the Green Mountain Boys*
Gail Gibbons, *The Missing Maple Syrup Sap Mystery*
Jessie Haas, *Hurry!*, *Mowing*, *No Foal Yet*, *Sugaring*
Kathleen McKinley Harris, *The Wonderful Hay Tumble*
Stephen Huneck, *Sally's Snow Adventure*
Anne Isaacs, *Pancakes for Supper!*
Woody Jackson, *A Cow's Alfalfa-Bet*
William Jaspersohn, *The Two Brothers*
Vivian Kill, *Crazy Jane*
Natalie Kinsey-Warnock, *A Christmas Like Helen's*, *A Farm of Her Own*, *From Dawn Till Dusk*, *Nora's Ark*, *When Spring Comes*, *Wilderness Cat*
Willem Lange, *John and Tom*
Julius Lester, "The Incredible Adventure of Adalbert the Alligator"
Reeve Lindbergh, *The Visit*
Sara London, *Firehorse Max*
Elizabeth Low, *Mouse, Mouse, Snug in the Snow*
Michael & Angela Medearis, *Daisy and the Doll*
Cornelia L. Meigs, *Mother Makes Christmas*
Will Moses, *Silent Night*
Margaret Otto, *Syrup*
Katherine Paterson, *Marvin One Too Many*, *Marvin's Best Christmas Present Ever*, *The Smallest Cow in the World*
Tracey Campbell Pearson, *The Storekeeper*, *Where Does Joe Go?*
Robert Newton Peck, *Little Soup's Birthday*, *Little Soup's Bunny*
Carol Purdy, *Least of All*
Nan Parson Rossiter, *Sugar on Snow*, *The Way Home*
Ken Rush, *What About Emma?*
Leda Schubert, *Here Comes Darrell*
Martina Selway, *Don't Forget to Write*
Esphyr Slobodkina, *The Clock*
Abigail Thomas, *Lily*
Eliza Thomas, *The Red Blanket*
Nathaniel Tripp, *Snow Comes to the Farm*
Tasha Tudor, *Corgiville Fair*
Kathryn Mademann Vaughan, *Little One—Goodnight*
Chad Walsh, *Nellie and Her Flying Crocodile*
Mildred Pitts Walker, *Alec's Primer*
Nancy Dingman Watson, *Sugar on Snow*
Rosemary Wells, *Waiting for the Evening Star*

APPENDIX B: Genres, alphabetically by category

FANTASY/SCIENCE FICTION

M.T. Anderson, *The Game of Sunken Places*
Jim Arnosky, *Little Champ*
Katharine Jay Bacon, *Pip and Emma*
Arthur Scott Bailey, *The Tale of Muley Cow, The Tale of Nimble Deer*
Robert Bright, *Miss Pattie*
Marc Brown, *Buster's Sugartime*
Marilyn C. Childs, *Mandate for a Morgan Horse*
Eileen Christelow, *The Great Pig Escape, The Great Pig Search*
Catherine C. Coblentz, *The Blue Cat of Castle Town*
Jane Leslie Conly, *The Rudest Alien on Earth*
Peter Campbell Copp, *Thunder in October*
Anne Eliot Crompton, *Deer Country*
Jeff Danziger, *The Champlain Monster*
Amy Ehrlich, *Parents in the Pigpen*
Nancy Garden, *Mystery of the Night Raiders*
Shannon Gilligan, *The Search for Champ*
Christopher Golden, *Laws of Nature*
James Hayford, *Gridley Firing*
Beth Hilgartner, *Colors in the Dreamweaver's Loom, The Feast of the Trickster*
Anne Lindbergh, *Osprey Island, Travel Far, Pay No Fare*
Bill Littlefield, *The Circus in the Woods*
R. A. Montgomery, *The Island of Time*
Rita Murphy, *Night Flying*
Katherine Paterson, *The Field of Dogs*
Jonathan Rand, *Virtual Vampires of Vermont*
David Roth, *A World for Joey Carr*
Susan Fromberg Schaeffer, *The Dragons of North Chittendon*
Tor Seidler, *Terpin*
Marilyn Singer, *California Demon*
Jan Slepian, *Back to Before*
Esphyr Slobodkina, *The Clock*
David Stahler, Jr., *A Gathering of Shades*
Mary Stolz, *Cat Walk*
Julian F. Thompson, *Ghost Story*
Tasha Tudor, *Corgiville Fair*
Jean Van Leeuwen, *The Great Summer Camp Catastrophe*
Kathryn Mademann Vaughan, *Little One—Good Night*
Chad Walsh, *Nellie and Her Flying Crocodile*
Paul Zindel, *Loch*

HISTORICAL FICTION

Merritt P. Allen, *The Flicker's Feather, The Green Cockade*
Grace Neil Anderson, *In the Shadow of Cox Mountain*
Kenneth Andler, *Mission to Fort No. 4*
Jennifer Armstrong, *Steal Away*
Robert Ashley, *Rebel Raiders*
Carin Greenberg Baker, *Pride of the Green Mountains*
Jeff Barth, *A Thanksgiving Story in Vermont—1852*
Lenore Blegvad, *Kitty and Mr. Kipling*
Marge Bruchac, *Malian's Song*
Louella Bryant, *The Black Bonnet*
Cynthia Butler, *Michael Hendee*
Marjorie Chickering, *Yankee Trader*
Anne Eliot Crompton, *The Ice Trail*
Linda Cunningham, *The Copper Angel of Piper's Mill*
Alice Turner Curtis, *A Little Maid of Ticonderoga, A Little Maid of Vermont*
Leon W. Dean, *Green Mountain Boy, Guns over Champlain, I Become a Ranger, Old Wolf, Pirate Lair, Royalton Raid, Stark of the North Country, The White Ox*
Marilyn Cram Donahue, *Straight Along a Crooked Road*
Clavin Fisher, *A Spy at Ticonderoga*
Genevieve Fox, *Border Girl, Susan of the Green Mountains*
Nancy Price Graff, *Taking Wing*
Robert Davis, *Gid Granger*
Patricia Lee Gauch, *Aaron and the Green Mountain Boys*
Jessie Haas, *Unbroken, Westminster West*
Wilma Pitchford Hays, *Trouble at Otter Creek*
Marguerite Henry, *Justin Morgan Had a Horse*
Karen Hesse, *A Time of Angels, Witness*
Kimberly Heuston, *The Shakeress*
Ralph Nading Hill, *The Voyages of Brian Seaworthy*
Lee Pennock Huntington, *Brothers in Arms*
Johanna Hurwitz, *Dear Emma, Faraway Summer, The Unsigned Valentine*
Edgar N. Jackson, *Green Mountain Hero*
Jacqueline Jackson, *The Taste of Spruce Gum*
William Jaspersohn, *The Two Brothers*
Bernard & Jonathan Katz, *Black Woman*

Shirley W. Kelley, *The Little Settlers of Vermont*
Louise Andrews Kent, *He Went with Champlain*
Liza Ketchum, *Where the Great Hawk Flies*
Natalie Kinsey-Warnock, *A Christmas Like Helen's*, *A Doctor Like Papa*, *If Wishes Were Horses*, *Lumber Camp Library*, *The Night the Bells Rang*, *Nora's Ark*, *When Spring Comes*, *Wilderness Cat*
Doris Kirkpatrick, *Honey in the Rock*
West Lathrop, *Black River Captive*
Janet Lunn, *The Hollow Tree*
Michael & Angela Medearis, *Daisy and the Doll*
Cornelia L. Meigs, *The Call of the Mountain*, *The Covered Bridge*
George G. Muller, *Hero of Champlain*
Margaret Otto, *Mr. Kipling's Elephant*
Janice Ovecka, *Captive of Pittsford Ridge*, *Cave of Falling Water*
Marion Page, *The Printer's Devil*
Katherine Paterson, *Bread and Roses, Too*, *Jip, His Story*, *Lyddie*, *Preacher's Boy*
Leigh Peck, *They Were Made of Rawhide*
Robert Newton Peck, *A Day No Pigs Would Die*, *Hang for Treason*, *Justice Lion*, *Millie's Boy*, *A Part of the Sky*, *Rabbits and Redcoats*
Eliza Frances Pollard, *Liberty or Death*
Carol Purdy, *Least of All*
Gertrude Robinson, *Father and the Mountains*
Frances Sanger, *The Silver Teapot*, *The Wooden Mug*
Gilbert Smith, *The Green Mountain Boys Ride*
Elizabeth George Speare, *Calico Captive*
Daniel Pierce Thompson, *The Green Mountain Boys*
Mary Wolfe Thompson, *Two in the Wilderness*, *Wilderness Wedding*, *Wilderness Winter*
Phillip Viereck, *Independence Must Be Won*
Mildred Pitts Walter, *Alec's Primer*
Ida H. Washington, *Brave Enough*, *The Green Mountain Boys*
Kenneth B. Webb, *From Plymouth Notch to President*
Doug Wilhelm, *The Underground Railroad*
Charles Morrow Wilson, *Crown Point*, *The Great Turkey Drive*, *The Green Mountain Toymakers*
Elizabeth Winthrop, *Counting on Grace*
G. Clifton Wisler, *Mr. Lincoln's Drummer*
Hildreth T. Wriston, *Camping Down at Highgate*, *Downstreet with Edith*, *Show Lamb*, *Susan's Secret*, *A Yankee Musket*

HUMOROUS FICTION

Julia Alvarez, *How Tía Lola Came to Visit / Stay*
Jim Arnosky, *Nathaniel*, *Mud Time and More*
Winifred Bromhall, *Mrs. Polly's Party*
Jean Caryl, *Bones and the Smiling Mackerel*
Eileen Christelow, *The Five-Dog Night*
Phoebe Erickson, *Double or Nothing*
Rachi Farrow, *Charlie's Dream*
Sid Fleischman, *The Hey Hey Man*
Corinne Gerson, *My Grandfather the Spy*
Kathleen McKinley Harris, *The Wonderful Hay Tumble*
Hadley Higginson, *Keeker and the Horse Show Show-Off*, *Keeker and the Sneaky Pony*, *Keeker and the Springtime Surprise*, *Keeker and the Sugar Shack*
Stephen Huneck, *Sally's Snow Adventure*
Johanna Hurwitz, *A Llama in the Family*, *A Llama in the Library*
Anne Isaacs, *Pancakes for Supper!*
Woody Jackson, *A Cow's Alfalfa-Bet*
Clarence B. Kelland, *Mark Tidd in Business*
Vivian Kill, *Crazy Jane*
Sheila Solomon Klass, *Next Stop: Nowhere*
Frederick Lipp, *That Cat Is Not For Sale*
Sara London, *Firehorse Max*
Elizabeth Low, *Mouse, Mouse*
Gregory Maguire, *A Couple of April Fools*, *Five Alien Elves*, *Four Stupid Cupids*, *One Final Firecracker*, *Seven Spiders Spinning*, *Six Haunted Hairdos*, *Three Rotten Eggs*
John Ney, *Ox Goes North*
Margaret Otto, *Syrup*
Tracey Campbell Pearson, *The Storekeeper*, *Where Does Joe Go?*
Robert Newton Peck, *Little Soup's Birthday*, *Little Soup's Bunny*, *Soup*, *Soup 1776*, *Soup Ahoy*, *Soup & Me*, *Soup for President*, *Soup in Love*, *Soup in the Saddle*, *Soup on Fire*, *Soup on Ice*, *Soup on Wheels*, *Soup's Drum*, *Soup's Goat*, *Soup's Hoop*, *Soup's Uncle*, *Trig*, *Trig Goes Ape*, *Trig or Treat*, *Trig Sees Red*
Martina Selway, *Don't Forget to Write*
Barbara Seuling, *Robert and the Great Escape*
Abigail Thomas, *Lily*
Charles Miner Thompson, *Calico Cat*
Mary Towne, *Wanda the Worrywart*, *Steve the Sure*

MYSTERY/SUSPENSE FICTION

Merritt P. Allen, *Raiders' Hoard*
Gary Bowen, *The Mare's Nest*
Flavia Camp Canfield, *The Kidnapped Campers*
Cora Cheney, *The Mystery of the Disappearing Cars*
Peter Cooper, *The Secret Papers of Julia Templeton*
Robert Cormier, *I am the Cheese*, *The Rag and Bone Shop*
E. J. Craine, *The Air Mystery of Isle La Motte*
Jordan Cray, *Shiver*
Nicole Davidson, *Winterkill*
Leon W. Dean, *Border Bullets*, *Red Man's Trail*
Franklin W. Dixon, *The Demon's Den*, *Track of the Zombie*
Nancy Garden, *The Case of the Stolen Scarab*
Gail Gibbons, *The Missing Maple Syrup Sap Mystery*
Helen Girvan, *Felicity Way*
Carolyn Keene, *Close Encounters*
Clarence B. Kelland, *Mark Tidd*, *Mark Tidd's Citadel*
Gordon Korman, *Chasing the Falconers*, *The Fugitive Factor*
Cornelia L. Meigs, *At the Sign of the Two Heroes*, *Wild Geese Flying*
Helen Fuller Orton, *Mystery in the Old Cave*
Julian F. Thompson, *Discontinued*
Margaret P. Trask, *At the Sign of the Rocking Horse*, *Three for Treasure*
Gertrude Chandler Warner, *The Mystery at Snowflake Inn*, *The Stuffed Bear Mystery*
Doug Wilhelm, *Scene of the Crime*
Nancy Means Wright, *The Great Circus Train Robbery*, *The Pea Soup Poisonings*

REALISTIC FICTION

Jacob Abbott, *Marco Paul's Voyages & Travels in Vermont*
Katharine Adams, *Mehitable*
Julia Alvarez, *Finding Miracles*
Frank Asch, *Up River*
Kay Avery, *All for a Friend*, *All for a Ghost*, *All for a Horse*, *Goodbye Blue Jeans*, *Wee Willow Whistle*
Mary Azarian, *A Farmer's Alphabet*
Katharine Jay Bacon, *Finn*, *Shadow and Light*
Hetty B. Beatty, *Bryn*
Jeanne Betancourt, *Crazy Christmas*, *More Than Meets the Eye*, *Puppy Love*, *The Rainbow Kid*, *Turtle Time*, *Valentine Blues*
Bianca Bradbury, *Laughter in Our House*
Alice Brown, *The Secret of the Clan*
Edna A. Brown, *At the Butterfly House*
Joseph Bruchac, *Fox Song*, *Hidden Roots*
David Budbill, *Bones on Black Spruce Mountain*, *Christmas Tree Farm*
Eleanor Cameron, *To the Green Mountains*
Carol Carrick, *The Highest Balloon on the Common*
Donald Carrick, *The Deer in the Pasture*
Betty Cavanna, *Angel on Skis*
Cora Cheney, *The Doll of Lilac Valley*
Marjorie Chickering, *Hayseed Summer*
Florence Choate & Elizabeth Curtis, *Linda Takes Over*
Barbara Clayton, *Halfway Hannah*
Jessica Clerk, *Sukey Johnson Builds a House*
Caroline B. Cooney, *Family Reunion*
Craig Crist-Evans, *North of Everything*
Barbara Dana, *Crazy Eights*
Dorathea Dana, *Sugar Bush*
Marion Doren, *Nell of Blue Harbor*
Eugenie Doyle, *Stray Voltage*
Genevieve T. Eames, *Pat Rides the Trail*
Walter Pritchard Eaton, *Boy Scouts on the Green Mountain Trail*
Amy Ehrlich, *Where It Stops, Nobody Knows*
Erik E. Esckilsen, *The Last Mall Rat*, *The Outside Groove*
Caroline S. Fairless, *Hambone*
Dorothy Canfield Fisher, *Understood Betsy*
Frances Frost, *Fireworks for Windy Foot*, *Maple Sugar for Windy Foot*, *Sleigh Bells for Windy Foot*, *Windy Foot at the County Fair*
Dale Blackwell Gasque, *Pony Trouble*
Gail Gauthier, *The Hero of Ticonderoga*, *Saving the Planet & Stuff*
Beth B. Gilchrist, *Kit, Pat, and a Few Boys*
Nancy Price Graff, *A Long Way Home*
Jessie Haas, *Be Well, Beware*, *Beware the Mare*, *Beware and Stogie*, *A Blue for Beware*, *A Horse Like Barney*, *Hurry!*, *Keeping Barney*, *Mowing*, *No Foal Yet*, *Runaway Radish*, *Shaper*, *Skipping School*, *Sugaring*, *Uncle Daney's Way*, *Will You, Won't You?*, *Working Trot*
Randi Hacker, *Life as I Knew It*
Sue Halpern, *Introducing…Sasha Abramowitz*
Earl Hamner & Don Snipes, *Lassie: A Christmas Story*
William W. Harvey, *Lige Golden*
Sheila Hayes, *The Tinker's Daughter*
Alison Cragin Herzig, *Shadows on the Pond*
Karen Hesse, *Phoenix Rising*
Clara Whitehill Hunt, *The Little House in Green Valley*
Johanna Hurwitz, *Yellow Blue Jay*

Caroline E. Jacobs, *The S.W.F. Club*
Allen Johnson, Jr., *The Christmas Tree Express*
Bobbi Katz, *Snow Bunny*
Garret Keizer, *God of Beer*
M. E. Kerr, *The Son of Someone Famous*
Liza Ketchum, *Fire in the Heart, Twelve Days in August*
Natalie Kinsey-Warnock, *As Long as There Are Mountains, The Canada Geese Quilt, A Farm of Her Own, From Dawn Till Dusk, In the Language of Loons, Sweet Memories Still*
Norma Klein, *Bizou*
Nancy H. Kleinbaum, *Dead Poets Society*
Willem Lange, *John and Tom*
Lois Lenski, *Deer Valley Girl*
Janet Lind, *The Bird at Bear Mountain*
Reeve Lindbergh, *The Visit*
Norris Lloyd, *Billy Hunts the Unicorn*
Elizabeth Low, *High Harvest, Snug in the Snow*
Rose Lucia, *Peter and Polly in Spring, in Summer, in Autumn, in Winter*
Ann M. Martin, *Baby-Sitters' Winter Vacation*
Melissa Mather, *One Summer in Between*
Cornelia L. Meigs, *Mother Makes Christmas*
Anne Molloy, *Decky's Secret*
Will Moses, *Silent Night*
Marion Page, *Dirty Mary No More*
Katherine Paterson, *Marvin One Too Many, Marvin's Best Christmas Present Ever, The Same Stuff as Stars, The Smallest Cow in the World*
Robert Newton Peck, *Kirk's Law*
Elizabeth Stuart Phelps, *Gypsy Breynton*
Georgiana Philips, *Summer of Good Hope*
Ethel Calvert Phillips, *Calico*
Roberta Piper, *Little Red*
Dorothy Pitkin, *The Grass Was That High, Wiser Than Winter*
Eleanor H. Porter, *Pollyanna, Pollyanna Grows Up*
Gerald Raftery, *City Dog, Slaver's Gold*
Nan Parson Rossiter, *Sugar on Snow, The Way Home*
Ken Rush, *What About Emma?*
Leda Schubert, *Here Comes Darrell*
Tor Seidler, *Brothers Below Zero, Terpin*
Marlene Fanta Shyer, *Blood in the Snow*
Alan D. Sophrin, *The Newcomer*
Laura C. Stevenson, *Happily After All*
Mary Stolz, *By the Highway Home, Cider Days, Ferris Wheel, A Wonderful, Terrible Time*
Phoebe Stone, *All the Blue Moons at the Wallace Hotel*
Cynthia M. Stowe, *Dear Mom, in Ohio for a Year*
Eliza Thomas, *The Red Blanket*
Julian F. Thompson, *Shepherd, Simon Pure, The Trials of Molly Sheldon*
Mary Wolfe Thompson, *Green Threshold, Snow Slopes*
Nathaniel Tripp, *Snow Comes to the Farm*
Marjorie M. Vetter, *Champlain Summer*
Mildred Walker, *A Piece of the World*
Ruth Wallace-Brodeur, *The Godmother Tree, The Kenton Year*
Mary Ella Waller, *A Daughter of the Rich, The Little Citizen*
Nancy Dingman Watson, *Sugar on Snow*
Rosemary Wells, *Waiting for the Evening Star*
Dorothy West, *Dot and Dash at the Maple Sugar Camp*
Newlin B. Wildes, *The Best Summer, The Horse That Had Everything*
Doug Wilhelm, *Falling, The Revealers*
Nancy Pope Wilson, *Mountain Pose*
Maia Wojciechowska, *A Kingdom in a Horse*
Nancy Means Wright, *Down the Strings*
Hildreth Wriston, *Andy and the Red Canoe, Hill Farm, Open Water*

ROMANCE FICTION

Jane D. Abbott, *Happy House*
Carin Greenberg Baker, *A Time to Love*
Cynthia Blair, *The Candy Cane Caper*
Carole Bolton, *The Dark Rosaleen*
Ann Brashares, *Forever in Blue*
Bonnie Bryant, *Snow Ride*
Emily Costello, *Ski Share VT*
Elizabeth Craft & Sarah Fain, *Bass Ackwards and Belly Up*
Jane Claypool Miner, *A Winter Love Story*
K. S. Rodriguez, *Major Meltdown*
Virginia Smiley, *Sugar Bush Nurse*
Amelia Walden, *Skymountain*

SHORT STORIES

Louisa May Alcott, "A Country Christmas"
Robert Arthur, "Obstinate Uncle Otis"
Carolyn S. Bailey, "A Sugar Heart for Bethia"
Larry Bograd, "Willie and the Christmas Spruces"
Pearl S. Buck, "The Christmas Secret"

David Budbill, *Snowshoe Trek to Otter River*
Margaret F. Carty, *Christmas in Vermont*
Carroll B. Colby, "The Deacon and the Lynx," "Escape from Wolves," "The Little Egyptian Prince," "Plague of Worms," "Skeleton in the Pasture"
Dorothy Canfield Fisher, *Something Old, Something New*
Paul Fleischman, *Coming-and-Going Men*
Jessie Haas, *The Sixth Sense and Other Stories*
Julius Lester, "The Incredible Adventure of Adalbert the Alligator"
George Mendoza, "The Devil's Pocket"
Katherine Paterson, *A Midnight Clear*
Marilynne K. Roach, "The Ghost in the Shed"

APPENDIX C: Authors and titles, by publication date

1838

1838 Daniel Pierce Thompson, *The Green Mountain Boys*

1843

1843 Jacob Abbott, *Marco Paul's Voyages & Travels in Vermont*

1866

1866 Elizabeth Stuart Phelps, *Gypsy Breynton*

1868

1868 Louisa May Alcott, "A Country Christmas"

1902

1902 Mary Ella Waller, *The Little Citizen*

1906

1906 Mary Ella Waller, *A Daughter of the Rich*

1908

1908 Flavia Camp Canfield, *The Kidnapped Campers*

1908 Charles Miner Thompson, *Calico Cat*

1909

1909 Eliza Pollard, *Liberty or Death*

1912

1912 Alice Brown, *The Secret of the Clan*

1912 Caroline E. Jacobs, *The S.W.F. Club*

1912 Rose Lucia, *Peter and Polly in Summer*

1913

1913 Clarence B. Kelland, *Mark Tidd*

1913 Eleanor H. Porter, *Pollyanna*

1914

1914 Rose Lucia, *Peter and Polly in Winter*

1915

1915 Clarence B. Kelland, *Mark Tidd in Business*

1915 Rose Lucia, *Peter and Polly in Spring*

1915 Eleanor H. Porter, *Pollyanna Grows Up*

1916

1916 Clarence B. Kelland, *Mark Tidd's Citadel*

1917

1917 Alice Turner Curtis, *A Little Maid of Ticonderoga*

1917 Dorothy Canfield Fisher, *Understood Betsy*

1918

1918 Edna A. Brown, *At the Butterfly House*

1918 Rose Lucia, *Peter and Polly in Fall*

1920

1920 Jane D. Abbott, *Happy House*

1920 Katharine Adams, *Mehitable*

1920 Cornelia L. Meigs, *At the Sign of the Two Heroes*

1921

1921 Arthur Scott Bailey, *The Tale of Muley Cow*

1921 Beth B. Gilchrist, *Kit, Pat, and a Few Boys*

1922

1922 Arthur Scott Bailey, *The Tale of Nimble Deer*

1924

1924 William W. Harvey, *Lige Golden*

1927

1927 Alice Turner Curtis, *A Little Maid of Vermont*

1927 Daniel Pierce Thompson, *The Green Mountain Boys*

1929

1929 Walter Pritchard Eaton, *Boy Scouts on the Green Mountain Trail*

1930

1930 E. J. Craine, *The Air Mystery of Isle La Motte*

1932

1932 Clara Whitehill Hunt, *The Little House in Green Valley*

1932 Gilbert Smith, *The Green Mountain Boys Ride*

1935

1935 Hildreth T. Wriston, *Downstreet with Edith*

1936

1936 Merritt P. Allen, *Raiders' Hoard*

1936 Cornelia L. Meigs, *The Covered Bridge*

1937

1937 Genevieve Fox, *Susan of the Green Mountains*

1937 Ethel Calvert Phillips, *Calico*

1938

1938 Dorothy West, *Dot and Dash at the Maple Sugar Camp*

1939

1939 Genevieve Fox, *Border Girl*

1939 Georgiana Philips, *Summer of Good Hope*

1939 Hildreth T. Wriston, *Camping Down at Highgate*

1940

1940 Cornelia L. Meigs, *Mother Makes Christmas*

1940 Cornelia L. Meigs, *The Call of the Mountain*

1941

1941 Carolyn S. Bailey, "A Sugar Heart for Bethia"

1941 Leon W. Dean, *Green Mountain Boy*

1941 Leon W. Dean, *Stark of the North Country*

1942

1942 Merritt P. Allen, *The Green Cockade*
1942 Leon W. Dean, *Old Wolf*
1942 Helen Girvan, *Felicity Way*
1942 Hildreth T. Wriston, *Open Water*

1944

1944 Anne Molloy, *Decky's Secret*

1945

1945 Leon W. Dean, *I Become a Ranger*
1945 Robert Davis, *Gid Granger*

1946

1946 Leon W. Dean, *Guns over Champlain*
1946 West Lathrop, *Black River Captive*

1947

1947 Kay Avery, *Wee Willow Whistle*
1947 Dorathea Dana, *Sugar Bush*
1947 Leon W. Dean, *Pirate Lair*
1947 Frances Frost, *Windy Foot at the County Fair*

1948

1948 Leon W. Dean, *Red Man's Trail*
1948 Frances Frost, *Sleigh Bells for Windy Foot*
1948 Elizabeth Low, *High Harvest*
1948 Frances Sanger, *The Silver Teapot*

1949

1949 Winifred Bromhall, *Mrs. Polly's Party*
1949 Florence Choate & Elizabeth Curtis, *Linda Takes Over*
1949 Catherine C. Coblentz, *The Blue Cat of Castle Town*
1949 Leon W. Dean, *Royalton Raid*
1949 Genevieve T. Eames, *Pat Rides the Trail*
1949 Dorothy Canfield Fisher, *Something Old, Something New*

1950

1950 Frances Frost, *Maple Sugar for Windy Foot*
1950 Helen Fuller Orton, *Mystery in the Old Cave*
1950 Gertrude Robinson, *Father and the Mountains*
1950 Frances Sanger, *The Wooden Mug*
1950 Elizabeth Walden, *Skymountain*

1953

1953 Merritt P. Allen, *The Flicker's Feather*
1953 Leon W. Dean, *Border Bullets*
1953 Leon W. Dean, *The White Ox*
1953 Gerald Raftery, *City Dog*
1953 Hildreth T. Wriston, *Show Lamb*

1954

1954 Robert Bright, *Miss Pattie*
1954 Marguerite Henry, *Justin Morgan Had a Horse*
1954 Leigh Peck, *They Were Made of Rawhide*
1954 Mary Wolfe Thompson, *Green Threshold*

1955

1955 Kay Avery, *All for a Horse*

1956

1956 Kay Avery, *All for a Friend*
1956 Robert Ashley, *Rebel Raiders*
1956 Frances Frost, *Fireworks for Windy Foot*
1956 Margaret Otto, *Syrup*
1956 Esphyr Slobodkina, *The Clock*
1956 Chad Walsh, *Nellie and Her Flying Crocodile*
1956 Hildreth T. Wriston, *Hill Farm*

1957

1957 Kay Avery, *All for a Ghost*
1957 Betty Cavanna, *Angel on Skis*
1957 Cornelia L. Meigs, *Wild Geese Flying*
1957 Elizabeth George Speare, *Calico Captive*
1957 Mary Wolfe Thompson, *Snow Slopes*
1957 Hildreth T. Wriston, *Susan's Secret*

1958

1958 Phoebe Erickson, *Double or Nothing*
1958 Elizabeth Low, *Mouse, Mouse*

1959

1959 Cora Cheney, *The Doll of Lilac Valley*
1959 Louise Andrews Kent, *He Went with Champlain*
1959 Dorothy Pitkin, *The Grass Was That High*
1959 Marjorie M. Vetter, *Champlain Summer*
1959 Hildreth T. Wriston, *A Yankee Musket*

1960

1960 Dorothy Pitkin, *Wiser Than Winter*
1960 Hildreth T. Wriston, *Andy and the Red Canoe*

1961

1961 Edgar N. Jackson, *Green Mountain Hero*
1961 George G. Muller, *Hero of Champlain*
1961 Margaret Otto, *Mr. Kipling's Elephant*

1962

1962 Marjorie Chickering, *Hayseed Summer*
1962 Margaret P. Trask, *Three for Treasure*

1963

1963 Robert Arthur, "Obstinate Uncle Otis"
1963 Kay Avery, *Goodbye Blue Jeans*
1963 Shirley W. Kelley, *The Little Settlers of Vermont*
1963 Elizabeth Low, *Snug in the Snow*
1963 Roberta Piper, *Little Red*

1964

1964 Carole Bolton, *The Dark Rosaleen*
1964 Bianca Bradbury, *Laughter in Our House*

1964 Jean Caryl, *Bones and the Smiling Mackerel*
1964 Barbara Clayton, *Halfway Hannah*
1964 Cora Cheney, *The Mystery of the Disappearing Cars*
1964 Norris Lloyd, *Billy Hunts the Unicorn*
1964 Margaret P. Trask, *At the Sign of the Rocking Horse*
1964 Phillip Viereck, *Independence Must Be Won*
1964 Nancy Dingman Watson, *Sugar on Snow*
1964 Charles Morrow Wilson, *The Great Turkey Drive*

1965

1965 Hetty B. Beatty, *Bryn*
1965 Newlin B. Wildes, *The Best Summer*
1965 Charles Morrow Wilson, *Crown Point, The Green Mountain Toymakers*
1965 Maia Wojciechowska, *A Kingdom in a Horse*

1966

1966 Marjorie Chickering, *Yankee Trader*
1966 Jacqueline Jackson, *The Taste of Spruce Gum*
1966 Newlin B. Wildes, *The Horse That Had Everything*

1967

1967 Marilyn C. Childs, *Mandate for a Morgan Horse*
1967 Melissa Mather, *One Summer in Between*
1967 Gerald Raftery, *Slaver's Gold*
1967 Mary Stolz, *A Wonderful, Terrible Time*
1967 Mary Wolfe Thompson, *Two in the Wilderness*

1968

1968 Lois Lenksi, *Deer Valley Girl*
1968 George Mendoza, "The Devil's Pocket"
1968 Alan D. Sophrin, *The Newcomer*
1968 Mary Wolfe Thompson, *Wilderness Winter*

1970

1970 Mary Wolfe Thompson, *Wilderness Wedding*

1971

1971 Ralph Nading Hill, *The Voyages of Brian Seaworthy*
1971 Mary Stolz, *By the Highway Home*
1971 Tasha Tudor, *Corgiville Fair*

1972

1972 Pearl S. Buck, "The Christmas Secret"
1972 Patricia Lee Gauch, *Aaron and the Green Mountain Boys*
1972 Robert Newton Peck, *A Day No Pigs Would Die*
1972 Mildred Walker, *A Piece of the World*

1973

1973 Carroll B. Colby, *The Weirdest People in the World*
1973 Anne Eliot Crompton, *Deer Country*
1973 Bernard & Jonathan Katz, *Black Woman*
1973 John Ney, *Ox Goes North*
1973 Robert Newton Peck, *Millie's Boy*

1974

1974 David Budbill, *Christmas Tree Farm*
1974 M. E. Kerr, *The Son of Someone Famous*
1974 Anne Lindbergh, *Osprey Island*
1974 Robert Newton Peck, *Soup*

1975

1975 Kenneth Andler, *Mission to Fort No. 4*
1975 Eleanor Cameron, *To the Green Mountains*
1975 Clavin Fisher, *A Spy at Ticonderoga*
1975 Robert Newton Peck, *Soup & Me*
1975 Marlene Fanta Shyer, *Blood in the Snow*

1976

1976 David Budbill, *Snowshoe Trek to Otter River*
1976 Cynthia Butler, *Michael Hendee*
1976 Donald Carrick, *The Deer in the Pasture*
1976 Lee Pennock Huntington, *Brothers in Arms*
1976 Bobbi Katz, *Snow Bunny*
1976 Robert Newton Peck, *Hang for Treason, Rabbits and Redcoats*

1977

1977 Carol Carrick, *The Highest Balloon on the Common*
1977 Robert Cormier, *I Am the Cheese*
1977 Robert Newton Peck, *Trig*
1977 Marilynne K. Roach, "The Ghost in the Shed"
1977 Mary Stolz, *Ferris Wheel*

1978

1978 Jim Arnosky, *Nathaniel*
1978 David Budbill, *Bones on Black Spruce Mountain*
1978 Barbara Dana, *Crazy Eights*
1978 Rachi Farrow, *Charlie's Dream*
1978 Wilma Pitchford Hays, *Trouble at Otter Creek*
1978 Robert Newton Peck, *Soup for President, Trig Sees Red*
1978 Mary Stolz, *Cider Days*
1978 Kenneth B. Webb, *From Plymouth Notch to President*

1979

1979 Jim Arnosky, *Mud Time and More*
1979 Sid Fleischman, *The Hey Hey Man*
1979 Gail Gibbons, *The Missing Maple Syrup Sap Mystery*
1979 Doris Kirkpatrick, *Honey in the Rock*

1980

1980 Anne Eliot Crompton, *The Ice Trail*
1980 Caroline S. Fairless, *Hambone*
1980 Robert Newton Peck, *Soup's Drum, Trig Goes Ape*
1980 Ruth Wallace-Brodeur, *The Kenton Year*

1981

1981 Mary Azarian, *A Farmer's Alphabet*

1981 Jeff Danziger, *Lake Champlain Monster*

1981 Robert Newton Peck, *Justice Lion, Kirk's Law, Soup on Wheels*

1981 David Roth, *A World for Joey Carr*

1981 Virginia Smiley, *Sugar Bush Nurse*

1982

1982 Franklin W. Dixon, *Track of the Zombie*

1982 Jessie Haas, *Keeping Barney*

1982 Robert Newton Peck, *Trig or Treat*

1982 Tor Seidler, *Terpin*

1982 Nancy Means Wright, *Down the Strings*

1983

1983 Jeanne Betancourt, *The Rainbow Kid*

1983 Margaret F. Carty, *Christmas in Vermont*

1983 Shannon Gilligan, *The Search for Champ*

1983 Jessie Haas, *Working Trot*

1983 Norma Klein, *Bizou*

1983 Robert Newton Peck, *Soup in the Saddle*

1983 Mary Stolz, *Cat Walk*

1984

1984 Carin Greenberg Baker, *A Time to Love*

1984 Franklin W. Dixon, *The Demon's Den*

1984 Robert Newton Peck, *Soup's Goat*

1985

1985 Jeanne Betancourt, *Turtle Time*

1985 Peter Cooper, *The Secret Papers of Julia Templeton*

1985 Marilyn Cram Donahue, *Straight Along a Crooked Road*

1985 Paul Fleischman, *Coming-and-Going Men*

1985 Alison Cragin Herzig, *Shadows on the Pond*

1985 Robert Newton Peck, *Soup on Ice*

1985 Julian F. Thompson, *Discontinued*

1986

1986 Jeanne Betancourt, *Puppy Love*

1986 Johanna Hurwitz, *Yellow Blue Jay*

1986 Susan Fromberg Schaeffer, *The Dragons of North Chittendon*

1987

1987 Katharine Jay Bacon, *Shadow and Light*

1987 Cynthia Blair, *The Candy Cane Caper*

1987 Nancy Garden, *Mystery of the Night Raiders*

1987 James Hayford, *Gridley Firing*

1987 Robert Newton Peck, *Soup on Fire*

1987 Carol Purdy, *Least of All*

1987 Julian F. Thompson, *Simon Pure*

1988

1988 Jeanne Betancourt, *Crazy Christmas*

1988 Amy Ehrlich, *Where It Stops, Nobody Knows*

1988 Jessie Haas, *The Sixth Sense*

1988 Kathleen McKinley Harris, *The Wonderful Hay Tumble*

1988 Janet Lind, *The Bird at Bear Mountain*

1988 Tracey Campbell Pearson, *The Storekeeper*

1988 Robert Newton Peck, *Soup's Uncle*

1989

1989 Jeff Barth, *A Thanksgiving Story in Vermont—1852*

1989 Caroline B. Cooney, *Family Reunion*

1989 Linda Cunningham, *The Copper Angel of Piper's Mill*

1989 Beth Hilgartner, *Colors in the Dreamweaver's Loom*

1989 Nancy H. Kleinbaum, *Dead Poets Society*

1989 Liza Ketchum, *Fire in the Heart*

1989 Natalie Kinsey-Warnock, *The Canada Geese Quilt*

1989 Ann M. Martin, *Baby-Sitters' Winter Vacation*

1989 Mary Towne, *Wanda the Worrywart*

1990

1990 Jeanne Betancourt, *More Than Meets the Eye, Valentine Blues*

1990 Marion Doren, *Nell of Blue Harbor*

1990 Corinne Gerson, *My Grandfather the Spy*

1990 Robert Newton Peck, *Soup's Hoop*

1990 Laura C. Stevenson, *Happily After All*

1990 Mary Towne, *Steve the Sure*

1991

1991 Nicole Davidson, *Winterkill*

1991 Beth Hilgartner, *The Feast of the Trickster*

1991 Natalie Kinsey-Warnock, *The Night the Bells Rang*

1991 R. A. Montgomery, *The Island of Time*

1991 Katherine Paterson, *Lyddie*

1991 Katherine Paterson, *The Smallest Cow in the World*

1991 Robert Newton Peck, *Little Soup's Birthday*

1992

1992 Jennifer Armstrong, *Steal Away*

1992 Bonnie Bryant, *Snow Ride*

1992 Jessie Haas, *Skipping School*

1992 Natalie Kinsey-Warnock, *Wilderness Cat*

1992 Anne Lindbergh, *Travel Far, Pay No Fare*

1992 Janice Ovecka, *Cave of Falling Water*

1992 Robert Newton Peck, *Soup in Love*

1992 Martina Selway, *Don't Forget to Write*

1992 Marilyn Singer, *California Demon*

1992 Cynthia M. Stowe, *Dear Mom, in Ohio for a Year*

1992 Jean Van Leeuwen, *The Great Summer Camp Catastrophe*

1992 Ruth Wallace-Brodeur, *The Godmother Tree*

1993

1993 Grace Neil Anderson, *In the Shadow of Cox Mountain*
1993 Joseph Bruchac, *Fox Song*
1993 Eileen Christelow, *The Five-Dog Night*
1993 Amy Ehrlich, *Parents in the Pigpen*
1993 Jessie Haas, *Beware the Mare*
1993 Allen Johnson, Jr., *The Christmas Tree Express*
1993 Liza Ketchum, *Twelve Days in August*
1993 Natalie Kinsey-Warnock, *When Spring Comes*
1993 Jane Claypool Miner, *A Winter Love Story*
1993 Robert Newton Peck, *Little Soup's Bunny*
1993 Jan Slepian, *Back to Before*
1993 Julian F. Thompson, *Shepherd*
1993 Rosemary Wells, *Waiting for the Evening Star*
1993 Doug Wilhelm, *Scene of the Crime*

1994

1994 Eileen Christelow, *The Great Pig Escape*
1994 Jessie Haas, *Mowing, Uncle Daney's Way*
1994 Karen Hesse, *Phoenix Rising*
1994 Johanna Hurwitz, *A Llama in the Family*
1994 Gregory Maguire, *Seven Spiders Spinning*
1994 Janice Ovecka, *Captive of Pittsford Ridge*
1994 Robert Newton Peck, *Soup Ahoy*
1994 Abigail Thomas, *Lily*
1994 Gertrude Chandler Warner, *The Mystery at Snowflake Inn*
1994 Paul Zindel, *Loch*

1995

1995 Jim Arnosky, *Little Champ*
1995 Frank Asch, *Up River*
1995 Jessie Haas, *A Blue for Beware, No Foal Yet*
1995 Sheila Hayes, *The Tinker's Daughter*
1995 Karen Hesse, *A Time of Angels*
1995 Sheila Solomon Klass, *Next Stop: Nowhere*
1995 Katherine Paterson, *A Midnight Clear*
1995 Robert Newton Peck, *Soup 1776*
1995 Julian F. Thompson, *The Trials of Molly Sheldon*
1995 G. Clifton Wisler, *Mr. Lincoln's Drummer*

1996

1996 Carin Greenberg Baker, *Pride of the Green Mountains*
1996 Louella Bryant, *The Black Bonnet*
1996 Jessie Haas, *Be Well, Beware, Sugaring*
1996 Katherine Paterson, *Jip, His Story*
1996 Ken Rush, *What About Emma?*
1996 Doug Wilhelm, *The Underground Railroad*

1997

1997 Peter Campbell Copp, *Thunder in October*
1997 Jessie Haas, *Westminster West*
1997 Earl Hamner & Don Snipes, *Lassie: A Christmas Story*
1997 Natalie Kinsey-Warnock, *As Long as There Are Mountains, Sweet Memories Still*
1997 Sara London, *Firehorse Max*
1997 Janet Lunn, *The Hollow Tree*
1997 Gregory Maguire, *Six Haunted Hairdos*
1977 Will Moses, *Silent Night*
1997 Katherine Paterson, *Marvin's Best Christmas Present Ever*
1997 Robert Newton Peck, *A Part of the Sky*
1997 Julian F. Thompson, *Ghost Story*
1997 G. Clifton Wisler, *Mr. Lincoln's Drummer*

1998

1998 Katharine Jay Bacon, *Finn*
1998 Jordan Cray, *Shiver*
1998 Dale Blackwell Gasque, *Pony Trouble*
1998 Jessie Haas, *Beware and Stogie*
1998 Johanna Hurwitz, *Faraway Summer*
1998 Natalie Kinsey-Warnock, *In the Language of Loons*
1998 Frederick Lipp, *That Cat Is Not For Sale*
1998 Gregory Maguire, *Five Alien Elves*

1999

1999 Jessie Haas, *Unbroken*
1999 Johanna Hurwitz, *A Llama in the Library*
1999 Marion Page, *Dirty Mary No More*
1999 Katherine Paterson, *Preacher's Boy*
1999 Tracey Campbell Pearson, *Where Does Joe Go?*
1999 K. S. Rodriguez, *Major Meltdown*
1999 Nan Parson Rossiter, *The Way Home*

2000

2000 Jessie Haas, *Hurry!*
2000 William Jaspersohn, *The Two Brothers*
2000 Natalie Kinsey-Warnock, *If Wishes Were Horses*
2000 Gregory Maguire, *Four Stupid Cupids*
2000 Michael & Angela Medearis, *Daisy and the Doll*
2000 Rita Murphy, *Night Flying*
2000 Phoebe Stone, *All the Blue Moons at the Wallace Hotel*
2000 Ida H. Washington, *The Green Mountain Boys*

2001

2001 Julia Alvarez, *How Tía Lola Came to Visit/Stay*
2001 Gary Bowen, *The Mare's Nest*
2001 Eileen Christelow, *The Great Pig Search*
2001 Jessica Clerk, *Sukey Johnson Builds a House*
2001 Robert Cormier, *The Rag and Bone Shop*

2001 Gail Gauthier, *The Hero of Ticonderoga*
2001 Christopher Golden, *Laws of Nature*
2001 Nancy Price Graff, *A Long Way Home*
2001 Jessie Haas, *Runaway Radish*, *Will You, Won't You?*
2001 Karen Hesse, *Witness*
2001 Natalie Kinsey-Warnock, *A Farm of Her Own*
2001 Willem Lange, *John and Tom*
2001 Julius Lester, "The Incredible Adventure of Adalbert the Alligator"
2001 Bill Littlefield, *The Circus in the Woods*
2001 Katherine Paterson, *The Field of Dogs*, *Marvin One Too Many*
2001 Nathaniel Tripp, *Snow Comes to the Farm*
2001 Nancy Pope Wilson, *Mountain Pose*

2002

2002 Jane Leslie Conly, *The Rudest Alien on Earth*
2002 Eugenie A. Doyle, *Stray Voltage*
2002 Jessie Haas, *Shaper*
2002 Kimberly Heuston, *The Shakeress*
2002 Johanna Hurwitz, *Dear Emma*
2002 Garret Keizer, *God of Beer*
2002 Natalie Kinsey-Warnock, *A Doctor Like Papa*, *From Dawn Till Dusk*, *Lumber Camp Library*
2002 Gregory Maguire, *Three Rotten Eggs*
2002 Katherine Paterson, *The Same Stuff as Stars*
2002 Marion Page, *The Printer's Devil*
2002 Nan Parson Rossiter, *Sugar on Snow*
2002 Tor Seidler, *Brothers Below Zero*
2002 Gertrude Chandler Warner, *The Stuffed Bear Mystery*

2003

2003 Erik E. Esckilsen, *The Last Mall Rat*
2003 Gail Gauthier, *Saving the Planet & Stuff*
2003 Woody Jackson, *A Cow's Alfalfa-Bet*
2003 Barbara Seuling, *Robert and the Great Escape*
2003 Kathryn Mademann Vaughan, *Little One—Good Night*
2003 Ida H. Washington, *Brave Enough*
2003 Dough Wilhelm, *The Revealers*

2004

2004 Julia Alvarez, *Finding Miracles*
2004 M.T. Anderson, *The Game of Sunken Places*
2004 Joseph Bruchac, *Hidden Roots*
2004 Craig Crist-Evans, *North of Everything*
2004 Nancy Garden, *The Case of the Stolen Scarab*
2004 Vivian Kill, *Crazy Jane*
2004 Natalie Kinsey-Warnock, *A Christmas Like Helen's*
2004 Gregory Maguire, *A Couple of April Fools*
2004 Jonathan Rand, *Virtual Vampires of Vermont*
2004 Eliza Thomas, *The Red Blanket*
2004 Mildred Pitts Walter, *Alec's Primer*

2005

2005 Lenore Blegvad, *Kitty and Mr. Kipling*
2005 Larry Bograd, "Willie and the Christmas Spruces"
2005 Nancy Price Graff, *Taking Wing*
2005 Sue Halpern, *Introducing...Sasha Abramowitz*
2005 Liza Ketchum, *Where the Great Hawk Flies*
2005 Natalie Kinsey-Warnock, *Nora's Ark*
2005 Gordon Korman, *Chasing the Falconers*, *The Fugitive Factor*
2005 Reeve Lindbergh, *The Visit*
2005 Gregory Maguire, *One Final Firecracker*
2005 Leda Schubert, *Here Comes Darrell*
2005 David Stahler, Jr., *A Gathering of Shades*

2006

2006 Marc Brown, *Buster's Sugartime*
2006 Marge Bruchac, *Malian's Song*
2006 Emily Costello, *Ski Share VT*
2006 Elizabeth Craft & Sarah Fain, *Bass Ackwards and Belly Up*
2006 Erik E. Esckilsen, *The Outside Groove*
2006 Randi Hacker, *Life as I Knew It*
2006 Hadley Higginson, *Keeker and the Horse Show Show-Off*, *Keeker and the Sneaky Pony*, *Keeker and the Sugar Shack*
2006 Stephen Huneck, *Sally's Snow Adventure*
2006 Johanna Hurwitz, *The Unsigned Valentine*
2006 Anne Isaacs, *Pancakes for Supper!*
2006 Carolyn Keene, *Close Encounters*
2006 Katherine Paterson, *Bread and Roses, Too*
2006 Elizabeth Winthrop, *Counting on Grace*
2006 Nancy Means Wright, *The Pea Soup Poisonings*

2007

2007 Ann Brashares, *Forever in Blue*
2007 Hadley Higginson, *Keeker and the Springtime Surprise*
2007 Doug Wilhelm, *Falling*
2007 Nancy Means Wright, *The Great Circus Train Robbery*

APPENDIX D: Authors Living in Vermont, past or present, part-time or full-time

A

Merritt P. Allen, Bristol
Julia Alvarez, Weybridge
Grace Neil Anderson, Pittsford
Jim Arnosky, South Ryegate
Frank Asch, Middletown Springs
Kay Avery, Middletown Springs & Rutland
Mary Azarian, Calais

B

Katharine Jay Bacon, Hartland
Arthur Scott Bailey, St. Albans
Jeff Barth, Middlebury
Jeanne Betancourt, Burlington
Lenore Blegvad, Wardsboro
Gary Bowen, Whiting
Louella Bryant, Jericho & Lincoln
Pearl Buck, Chester & Danby
David Budbill, Wolcott

C

Flavia Camp Canfield, Arlington
Donald & Carol Carrick, Craftsbury
Margaret F. Carty, Marshfield
Cora Cheney, West Townshend
Marjorie Chickering, Walden & St. Johnsbury
Marilyn C. Childs, Tunbridge
Florence Choate, Newfane
Eileen Christelow, East Dummerston
Catherine C. Coblentz, Hardwick
Peter Cooper, Rutland
Peter Campbell Copp, Dorset
Craig Crist-Evans, Montpelier
Elizabeth Curtis, Newfane

D

Jeff Danziger, Plainfield
Robert Davis, Middlebury
Leon W. Dean, Burlington
Eugenie Doyle, Bristol

E

Genevieve T. Eames, near Woodstock
Amy Ehrlich, Barnet
Phoebe Erickson, Woodstock
Erik E. Esckilsen, Burlington

F

Caroline S. Fairless, New Haven & Worcester
Rachi Farrow, Randolph Center
Dorothy Canfield Fisher, Arlington
Paul Fleischman, Milton
Genevieve Fox, Addison County
Frances Frost, St. Albans

G

Dale Gasque, Randolph Center
Gail Gauthier, Sudbury & Cornwall
Gail Gibbons, Corinth
Beth B. Gilchrist, Peacham & Rutland
Shannon Gilligan, Warren
Nancy Price Graff, Montpelier

H

Jessie Haas, Westminster West
Randi Hacker, Montgomery
Sue Halpern, Ripton
Kathleen McKinley Harris, Charlotte
William W. Harvey, Caledonia County
James Hayford, Orleans
Alison Cragin Herzig, Bristol
Karen Hesse, Brattleboro
Kimberly Heuston, St. Johnsbury
Hadley Higginson, Brandon & Burlington
Ralph Nading Hill, Burlington
Stephen Huneck, St. Johnsbury
Lee Pennock Huntington, Norwich
Johanna Hurwitz, Wilmington

J

Edgar N. Jackson, Chelsea & Corinth
Jacqueline Jackson, Lake Iroquois
Woody Jackson, Middlebury
William Jaspersohn, Johnson
Allen Johnson, Jr., Middlebury

K

Garrett Keizer, Sutton
Clarence B. Kelland, Wilmington
Shirley W. Kelley, Washington County
Louise Andrews Kent, Calais
M. E. Kerr, Montpelier
Liza Ketchum, Marlboro
Vivian Kill, Strafford
Natalie Kinsey-Warnock, South Albany
Doris Kirkpatrick, Whitingham

L

Willem Lange, East Montpelier
Dorothy West Lathrop
Janet Lind, Calais
Anne Lindbergh, Barnet
Reeve Lindbergh, St. Johnsbury
Norris Lloyd, Rochester
Sara London, Burlington
Elizabeth Low
Rose Lucia, East St. Johnsbury
Janet Lunn, Norwich

M

Gregory Maguire, Strafford
Melissa Mather, Windsor
Cornelia L. Meigs, Brandon
R. A. Montgomery, Warren
Rita Murphy, Burlington

O

Janice Ovecka, Brandon

P

Marion Page, Groton
Katherine Paterson, Barre
Tracey Campbell Pearson, Jericho
Robert Newton Peck
Georgiana Philips
Roberta Piper, Chelsea

R

Gerald Raftery, Arlington
Ken Rush, Danby

S

Susan Fromberg Schaeffer, South Newfane
Leda Schubert, Plainfield
Tor Seidler, Burlington
Barbara Seuling, Landgrove
Mary Gilbert Smith, Wallingford
Alan D. Sophrin, Bennington & Charleston
David Stahler, Jr., Lyndonville
Laura C. Stevenson, Wilmington
Phoebe Stone, Middlebury

T

Eliza Thomas, Montpelier
Charles Miner Thompson, Montpelier
Daniel Pierce Thompson, Montpelier
Julian F. Thompson, West Rupert & Burlington
Mary Wolfe Thompson, North Bennington
Mary Towne, Averill
Margaret P. Trask, Underhill
Nathaniel Tripp, St. Johnsbury
Tasha Tudor, Marlboro

V

Kathryn Mademann Vaughan, Dorset
Marjorie M. Vetter, Vergennes
Phillip Viereck, North Bennington

W

Mildred Walker, Grafton
Ruth Wallace-Brodeur, Montpelier
Mary Ella Waller, Bethel
Chad Walsh, Shelburne
Ida H. Washington, Weybridge
Nancy Dingman Watson, Putney
Kenneth B. Webb, Plymouth & Woodstock
Newlin B. Wildes, Pomfret
Doug Wilhelm, Rutland Town
Charles Morrow Wilson, Putney
Nancy Hope Wilson, Marlboro
Nancy Means Wright, Cornwall
Hildreth Wriston, Enosburg Falls & Highgate Springs

APPENDIX E: Vermont Children's Book Awards

The Dorothy Canfield Fisher Children's Book Award

The Dorothy Canfield Fisher Children's Book Award program, sponsored by the Vermont Department of Libraries and the Vermont PTA, is designed to acquaint Vermont's fourth-through-eighth-grade students with some of the best children's literature available. Each March, an eight-member committee of librarians, teachers, and parents selects thirty children's books written by American or Canadian authors and published in the previous calendar year. This Master List is sent to all Vermont schools and libraries, which then purchase copies of the books. In April of the next year, children who have participated in the DCF program vote for their favorite book from the list. The winning author is invited to accept the award and speak to an audience of children from the participating schools and libraries at an award ceremony that usually takes place in late spring.

Winners from this collection of the Dorothy Canfield Fisher Children's Book Award:

David Budbill, *Bones on Black Spruce Mountain* (1980)
Amy Ehrlich, *Where It Stops, Nobody Knows* (1990)
Phoebe Erickson, *Double or Nothing* (1960)
Jacqueline Jackson, *The Taste of Spruce Gum* (1968)
Mary Wolfe Thompson, *Two in the Wilderness* (1969)

Nominees from this collection for the Dorothy Canfield Fisher Children's Book Award Master List:

1957-1958
Hildreth T. Wriston, *Hill Farm*
1958-1959
Betty Cavanna, *Angel on Skis*
Cornelia L. Meigs, *Wild Geese Flying*
Elizabeth George Speare, *Calico Captive*
Hildreth T. Wriston, *Susan's Secret*
1959-1960
Phoebe Erickson, *Double or Nothing*
1960-1961
Cora Cheney, *The Doll of Lilac Valley*
Dorothy Pitkin, *The Grass Was That High*
Hildreth T. Wriston, *A Yankee Musket*
1963-1964
Margaret P. Trask, *Three for Treasure*
1965-1966
Phillip Viereck, *Independence Must Be Won*
1966-1967
Newlin B. Wildes, *The Best Summer*
1967-1968
Jacqueline Jackson, *The Taste of Spruce Gum*
Newlin B. Wildes, *The Horse That Had Everything*
1968-1969
Mary Stolz, *A Wonderful, Terrible Time*
Mary Wolfe Thompson, *Two in the Wilderness*
1975-1976
Robert Newton Peck, *Soup*
1976-1977
Marlene Fanta Shyer, *Blood in the Snow*
1977-1978
David Budbill, *Snowshoe Trek to Otter River*
1979-1980
David Budbill, *Bones on Black Spruce Mountain*
1980-1981
Doris Kirkpatrick, *Honey in the Rock*
1983-1984
Jessie Haas, *Keeping Barney*
1984-1985
Mary Stolz, *Cat Walk*
1988-1989
Katharine Jay Bacon, *Shadow and Light*
1989-1990
Amy Ehrlich, *Where It Stops, Nobody Knows*
1990-1991
Caroline B. Cooney, *Family Reunion*
Natalie Kinsey-Warnock, *The Canada Geese Quilt*
1991-1992
Laura C. Stevenson, *Happily After All*
1992-1993
Katherine Paterson, *Lyddie*
1993-1994
Jennifer Armstrong, *Steal Away*
Jessie Haas, *Skipping School*

1995-1996

Jessie Haas, *Uncle Daney's Way*

Karen Hesse, *Phoenix Rising*

1996-1997

Jessie Haas, *A Blue for Beware*

1997-1998

Jessie Haas, *Be Well, Beware*

Katherine Paterson, *Jip, His Story*

1998-1999

Natalie Kinsey-Warnock, *As Long as There Are Mountains*

2000-2001

Jessie Haas, *Unbroken*

2001-2002

Rita Murphy, *Night Flying*

2002-2003

Jessie Haas, *Runaway Radish*

Karen Hesse, *Witness*

2003-2004

Katherine Paterson, *The Same Stuff as Stars*

2005-2006

Joseph Bruchac, *Hidden Roots*

2006-2007

Nancy Price Graff, *Taking Wing*

2007-2008

Katherine Paterson, *Bread and Roses, Too*

Elizabeth Winthrop, *Counting on Grace*

The Red Clover Award

The Red Clover Award, begun in 1996, is Vermont's children's choice picture book award for children in kindergarten through the fourth grade. The award is given annually to one of ten picture books nominated by a committee of teachers, librarians, and sponsors. Children read the books with their teachers and librarians and vote for their favorite in mid-April. The Red Clover Award is cosponsored by the Vermont Center for the Book, the Vermont Department of Libraries, the Vermont Department of Education, and Windham County Reads.

Nominees from this collection for the Red Clover Award

Natalie Kinsey-Warnock, *From Dawn Till Dusk: A Vermont Farm Year*, illustrated by Mary Azarian (2004)

Natalie Kinsey-Warnock, *Nora's Ark*, illustrated by Emily Arnold McCully (2007)

INDEX 1: Real Places, alphabetically

INDEX 2: Titles, alphabetically with Authors

D

F

G

H

I

J

K

L

M

T

U

V

W

Y

INDEX 3: Subjects, alphabetically

INDEX 4:
Illustrators, alphabetically, Living in Vermont

NOTES AND ADDITIONS

Notes and Additions